The Crime, Justice and Society Course Team

Jill Alger

Ann Boomer

Val Byrne

Pat Cooke

Rudi Dallos

Nigel Draper

Mike Fitzgerald

Stuart Hall

Frank Heathcote

Pam Higgins

Joan Higgs

Carol Johns

Liz Joseph

Victor Jupp

Maggie Lawson

Gregor McLennan

John Muncie

Jennie Pawson

Stella Pilsworth

Roger Sapsford

Phil Scraton

Joe Sim

Paul Smith

Hilary Taylor

Eleanor Thompson

This Reader is one part of an Open University integrated teaching system and the selection is therefore related to other material available to students. It is designed to evoke the critical understanding of students. Opinions expressed in it are not necessarily those of the course team or of the University.

Crime and Society

Readings in History and Theory

Compiled by
Mike Fitzgerald, Gregor McLennan
and Jennie Pawson
at the Open University

ROUTLEDGE
London
in association with
THE OPEN UNIVERSITY PRESS

First published in 1981
Reprinted 1985, 1986
by Routledge & Kegan Paul plc

Reprinted 1988, 1990 by Routledge
11 New Fetter Lane, London EC4P 4EE

Printed in Great Britain by
Redwood Press Limited, Melksham, Wiltshire

British Library Cataloguing in Publication Data

Crime and society.
1. Crime and criminals–Great Britain–Addresses
essays, lectures
I. Fitzgerald, Mike   II. McLennan, Gregor
III. Pawson, Jennie
364'.0941   HV6021

ISBN 0-415-02755-1

Contents

Acknowledgments

The Open University and the publishers would like to thank the following for permission to reproduce copyright material. All possible care has been taken to trace ownership of the selections included and to make full acknowledgment for their use.

Reading

1   © Douglas Hay, 1975.
2, 6   Reprinted by permission of Hutchinson General Books Limited, 1980, 1979.
3   © Michael Ignatieff, 1978. Reprinted by permission of Pantheon Books, a Division of Random House, Inc., and of Macmillan, London and Basingstoke.
4   Reprinted by permission of Sweet & Maxwell Ltd, 1968.
5   © R.D. Storch, 1975.
7   Copyright Sage Publications, Inc., Beverly Hills, 1980.
10   Reprinted by permission of Oxford University Press, 1971.
12   Reprinted by permission of Routledge & Kegan Paul Ltd, 1973.
13   © Stanley Cohen, 1981.
14, 15, 16, 17, 18, 19, 20 © The Open University, 1981.

General introduction

Traditionally, criminology has been dominated by the twin concerns of locating the causes of crime in the individual and of
attempting to improve the operational effectiveness of the
criminal justice system. But some of the most recent and valuable studies of crime have sought to move considerably beyond
these narrow concerns, and raise questions not only about
crime and crime control but also about the social and historical
structures within which they are located.

In producing this set of readings and in constructing the
Open University course 'Crime, Justice and Society' (for which
this volume is the Course Reader) we have tried to reflect this
movement. The book therefore has a rather unusual format,
combining theory and history, sociology and psychology.

Part I is a selection from some of the most interesting historical
work on crime and crime control. Apart from the historical
insights which these readings display, the issues they raise -
about law, ideology, policing, delinquency - remain of central
importance today. In Part II, we outline and assess major
sociological and psychological approaches to crime, attempting
to make explicit the theoretical paradigms which underlie and
cut across the different disciplines.

In putting this book together, we recognize that we have
been unable (not least because of the constraints of space) to
cover every aspect of criminology. We decided to focus on
history and theory, with particular reference to Britain. Thus
we have not included cross-cultural and comparative material,
nor have we described and analysed the contemporary criminal
justice system, and the controversies surrounding it. (These
are covered elsewhere in the Open University course.)

Although the book is intended, in the first instance, for
Open University students, we believe that it provides a new
point of departure for introducing criminology.

PART I HISTORY:
Introduction

The first part of the book brings together extracts from recent work in the social history of law and crime. The use of an extended selection of this kind reflects the need to supply the historical dimension to problems of crime and society - a dimension which has often been lacking in criminological analysis. The study of past patterns of crime and control is interesting in its own right, but also enhances consideration of contemporary issues. There are two aspects to the uses of history in this context.

First, by focusing on particular sociohistorical contexts, we are struck by the fact that definitions of law, crime and punishment *change* according to economic and ideological circumstances.

It is often pointed out, for example, how feudal legal relations based on fixed status and residence were adapted to meet the demands of a new social system requiring a 'free' mobile labour force (J. Hall, 'Theft, Law and Society', Bobbs-Merrill, Indianapolis, 1952).

Second, a historical awareness guards against the impression that features of law-breaking, policing or punishment are either entirely new, or, conversely, remain unchanged. Instances of 'hooliganism', 'crime waves' and threats to public order in the historical literature can be placed alongside frequent journalistic panics about moral degeneration today. Similarly, a historical perspective helps to make us aware, for example, that questions of the nature and extent of police powers, far from being only a 'contemporary' issue, have been present as a major topic of debate and disagreement since the formation of the police force itself. The permanently close but shifting relation between 'political' and 'criminal' illegality is itself of central importance to both historians and criminologists.

Our readings deal with the eighteenth and nineteenth centuries, and are limited to British (predominantly English) examples. The idea here is to provide indispensable 'background'

3

material for general issues rather than to illustrate a chrono-
logical or evolutionary sequence. The sections are therefore
organized on a thematic basis.

The first group of readings highlights the relationship
between judicial ideologies and economic development. In
eighteenth-century Britain there was a remarkable increase
in the number of statutes which dealt with offences against
private property, and which carried the death penalty. But
the mechanisms of punishment were dramatically arbitrary.
The dispensation of the law rested as much on the power and
mercy of the judges themselves as on the formal requirements
of the new relations of capitalist ownership. Douglas Hay's
article, taken from the influential collection on the eighteenth
century, 'Albion's Fatal Tree', cogently summarizes and inter-
prets the complex interplay of coercion, ritual and justice in
pre-industrial capitalism. Hay's piece is balanced by the reading from Brewer's and Styles's book 'An Ungovernable People',
which emphasizes the reactions of the popular classes to the
controls of what E.P. Thompson has termed 'patrician society'.
These plebeian responses ranged from cautious deference to
turbulent resistance to the process by which customary economic
and cultural practices were 'criminalized'. Finally in this section, Michael Ignatieff discusses the competing strategies for
prison reform in the late eighteenth century. He definitively
points up the contradictory elements in the reformers' conception of scientific punishment and social discipline.

The second set of readings centres on the formation and
development of the police. In the 1820s, new procedures of
crime control were created, and Michael Weisser has argued
that 'the method devised for dealing with political criminals was
the police' ('Crime and Punishment in Early Modern Europe',
Harvester Press, 1979, p.156). This argument may be right,
but it does not bring out the paradox that, even then - and
certainly today - the police best fulfil this function when their
main concern is seen to be the control of non-political offences.

To view the police as direct participants in 'class struggle'
rather than detectors of the criminal fraternity is often thought
to be itself an 'ideological' interpretation of their function.
Our readings here suggest otherwise; but they also indicate
that there need be no contradiction between the 'civil' and
'political' functions of the police.

In the views of nineteenth-century observers, at least, there
was a direct connection between policing the criminally
'dangerous', and dealing with political opposition to the social
system. The reading from Radzinowicz illustrates the different
strands of thinking about the role of the New Police, while
Storch and Cohen (who deals with a considerably later period)
describe the quasi-political effects of policing working-class
communities. In sharp contrast, the employing class were
inspected rather than policed. The extract from Carson is
appropriate here because it shows the failure of entrepreneurs

to fulfil legal obligations in one central case: the Factory Acts.
However, these failings were regarded as misdemeanours rather
than crimes, and consequently employers were encouraged to
reform, but were not prosecuted.

The image of the teeming industrial city, its hidden 'abysses'
and criminal areas, has fascinated observers for the best part
of two centuries. On the one hand, this imagery expressed a
growing Victorian concern about the apparent and lawless
separation of the 'dangerous' class from 'respectable' and
'industrious' workers. Henry Mayhew was the first and most
impressive recorder of the sunken classes, and our extracts
from 'London Labour and the London Poor' (4 vols, written 1851)
illustrate the widely held notion of specifically criminal areas.
The readings also include a description of particular social
groups which engaged in irregular economies and unrespectable
cultural activities.

Gareth Stedman Jones's account of 'outcast London' centres
on the last quarter of the nineteenth century. The perceptions
and strategies of those seeking the moral reform of the human
'residuum' are analysed by him in terms of several interrelated
social factors: the residential segregation of classes, the
casual labour market, and the return of political class conflict
in the 1880s. Throughout this suggestive piece, the tangible
but uneven relationship of social conditions to poverty, crime
and disorder is apparent.

The final section in this part takes up the isolation of youth
as a particular category of offenders. Mayhew once more
provides a vivid illustration of London street life in his description of child street-sellers, vagrants and delinquents. In
particular we can see how their attempts to maintain a subsistence level of existence were subjected to processes of
criminalization. Pinchbeck's and Hewitt's account of major
legislative landmarks in juvenile justice throughout the nineteenth century highlights the contemporary dilemma of whether
to control the 'problem' of delinquency by punitive or reformative methods. The recent proposal to mete out 'short, sharp
shocks' to criminalized youth can indeed be seen, in its combination of retributive and moralistic motives, as but a further
stage in the logic of this development.

It has not been possible to include articles on the regulation of poverty (the Poor Law, for example) or on the profound
changes in popular leisure which exercised the police for
several decades. Such material is highly relevant to apparently
narrower questions of criminal 'subcultures' and conceptions
of legal and moral discipline. If a historical perspective assists
a sharper analytical perspective on contemporary events, that
is justification enough for a substantial 'history' section in a
Reader of this kind. Finally, we should repeat that while a
theoretical and historical perspective on crime is encouraged
here, our material is restricted to modern British society.

Law and Ideology

1 Property, authority and the criminal law

Douglas Hay

[...] All men of property knew that judges, justices and juries had to be chosen from their own ranks. The jury, the supposed guarantee that an Englishman would be tried by his equals, had a sharp property qualification. The reason, simply put, was that the common Englishman could not be trusted to share in the operation of the law. A panel of the poor would not convict a labourer who stole wood from a lord's park, a sheep from a farmer's fold, or corn from a merchant's yard. As Gisborne pointed out, even as witnesses 'many of the common people... are found to make use of a very blameable latitude in their interpretation of the ninth commandment; and think that they are guilty of no breach of it in deviating, though upon oath, from strict truth, *in favour* of the party accused'.[1] The cottager who appeared in court charged with theft had no illusions about being tried by 'his equals and neighbours', whatever the writers of law books claimed.[2] The twelve men sitting opposite him were employers, overseers of the poor, propertied men. In most cases they were the equals and neighbours of the prosecutor, not the accused, and this was especially true in cases of theft. The point is not that such juries convicted against the evidence, but rather that a more democratic jury might not have convicted at all. In the constitutional struggles of the seventeenth century, 'middling men' of moderate property had wanted the widest possible extension of trial by jury; the Crown had tried to restrict it because juries shielded sedition. There was another small group, however, who had also wanted to control juries. Winstanley and the Diggers repudiated them as protectors of property against the rights of the poor. There were no Diggers in the eighteenth century, but cottagers and labourers were undoubtedly aware that English justice was still the creature of judges and juries.[3]

Eighteenth-century 'justice' was not, however, a nonsense.

Source: D. Hay, P. Linebaugh and E.P. Thompson, 'Albion's Fatal Tree', Allen Lane, 1975, extracts from pp.38-63.

It remained a powerful and evocative word, even if it bore a
much more limited meaning than a twentieth-century (or seventeenth century) egalitarian would give it. In a society radically
divided between rich and poor, the powerful and the powerless,
the occasional victory of a cottager in the courts or the rare
spectacle of a titled villain on the gallows made a sharp impression. Moreover, it would be wrong to suggest that the law had
to be wholly consistent to persuade men of its legitimacy.
'Justice', in the sense of rational, bureaucratic decisions made
in the common interest, is a peculiarly modern conception. It
was gaining ground in the eighteenth century. Most reformers
worked to bring about such law, and of all such schemes
Jeremy Bentham's was the logical conclusion. Yet his plan for
a criminal code that was precise, consistent and wholly enforced
was alien to the thought of most eighteenth-century Englishmen.
They tended to think of justice in personal terms, and were
more struck by understanding of individual cases than by the
delights of abstract schemes. Where authority is embodied in
direct personal relationships, men will often accept power,
even enormous, despotic power, when it comes from the 'good
King', the father of his people, who tempers justice with
mercy. A form of this powerful psychic configuration was one
of the most distinctive aspects of the unreformed criminal law.
Bentham could not understand it, but it was the law's greatest
strength as an ideological system, especially among the poor,
and in the countryside.

The prerogative of mercy ran throughout the administration of
the criminal law, from the lowest to the highest level. At the
top sat the high court judges, and their free use of the royal
pardon became a crucial argument in the arsenal of conservatives
opposing reform. At the lowest jurisdiction, that of the Justice
of the Peace, the same discretion allowed the magistrate to
make decisions that sometimes escaped legal categories altogether.
Although he frequently made obeisance to the rules when con-
victing, [...] he could dispense with them when pardoning, and
the absence of a jury made it even easier for him to do so.
Latitude in the direction of mercy caused some critics to com-
plain that many justices, partly from laziness or carelessness
'but frequently from benevolent views improperly indulged',
judged cases 'partly or entirely by their own unauthorized
ideas of equity'.[4] This element of discretion impressed Weber
when he examined the office of JP. He compared it to Arabic
'khadi justice' - a formalistic administration of law that was
nevertheless based on ethical or practical judgements rather
than on a fixed, 'rational' set of rules. It could combine rigid
tradition with 'a sphere of free discretion and grace of the
ruler'.[5] Thus it allowed the paternalist JP to compose quarrels,
intervene with prosecutors on behalf of culprits, and in the
final instance to dismiss a case entirely. The right of the pardon
was not limited, however, to high court judges and Justices of

the Peace. The mode of prosecution, the manner of trial and the treatment of condemned convicts gave some of the same power to all men of property. 'Irrationality', in the sense used by Weber, and the 'grace of the ruler' which grew from it pervaded the entire administration of the law.

Almost all prosecutions were initiated by private persons, at their discretion, and conducted in accordance with their wishes. Accustomed to organized state police and rigorous state prosecution, French visitors were inclined to marvel at this peculiar English institution. Charles Cottu, a French judge who toured the Northern Circuit in the early nineteenth century, exclaimed,[6]

> The English [that is, state officials] appear to attach no importance to a discovery of the causes which may have induced the prisoner to commit the crime: they scarcely even affix any to the establishment of his guilt. I am ignorant whether this temper of mind arises from their fear of augmenting the already excessive number of public offenders, or whether it proceeds from their natural humanity; it is however an undoubted fact, that they make no effort to obtain proofs of the crime, confiding its punishment entirely to the hatred or resentment of the injured party; careless too, about the conviction of the accused, whether his victim shall yield to feelings of compassion, or give way to indolence.

Cottu did not appear to have heard, or understood, the traditional arguments of English gentlemen against a constabulary and state prosecution: that it could lead to despotism, a political police serving the Crown. He did understand, however, the consequences of private prosecution. The victim of the crime could decide himself upon the severity of the prosecution, either enforcing the letter of the law, or reducing the charge. He could even pardon the offence completely by not going to court. The reformers' objections to this system are well known. Private prosecution was capricious and uncertain, and too often rogues escaped due to the distaste, compassion or fear of their victims. But reformers failed to acknowledge the great power this conferred on the prosecutor to make the law serve his own purposes. In Cottu's words, the accuser became 'the arbitrator of the culprit's fate', and the law became an expression of his will. In short, it was in the hands of the gentleman who went to law to evoke gratitude as well as fear in the maintenance of deference.

In a rural parish with a relatively settled population there were many alternatives to a rigorous prosecution. The accused man could be made to post a bond not to offend again, or be given the choice of leaving the neighbourhood. The threat of prosecution could be held over his head to ensure his future good behaviour. He might also be allowed to escape the law by making compensation for his crime, and the negotiations between Richard Ainsworth and his master Nicholas Blundell in 1709

were repeated in all parts of England, throughout the century.
Ainsworth was caught stealing, begged Blundell repeatedly
not to prosecute, and entered into negotiations to work on one
of his master's houses in return for forgiveness.[7] Other accused
men simply appealed to the merciful feelings of the man who
held them in his power. The wretched thief begging on his
knees for forgiveness is not a literary conceit, but a reality
described in many legal depositions. Critics of the law objected,
however, that many prosecutions were dropped through fear
as well as compassion. Certainly it is true that feeling against
some prosecutors ran so high that they went in fear of their
lives from popular opinion, or felt obliged to defend their
actions in the press. Yet where certainty of enforcement had
to be sacrificed to public opinion, even then graciously
granted mercy could produce gratifying deference. Especially
where the prosecutor was a landed gentleman, acts of mercy
helped create the mental structure of paternalism. The papers
of any large landed proprietor are peppered with appeals for
pardons, and earnest thanks for them - pardons for poachers,
for stealers of holly, for embezzlers of coal. 'I hope his Lordship
will not insist upon your acquainting my Master of it,' wrote
one poacher to a steward, 'as it would be productive of very
great injury to me...we are afraid the crime is so great that it
will not admit of any excuse and therefore all we can say is
that our future good behaviour shall be such that his Lordship
will not repent of his Lenity and goodness in forgiving us.'[8]
The phrases of benevolence constantly recur on the other
side: 'it may so happen that my Good Lord Stafford may be
inclined (as he generally is) to pardon the offenders...'[9] Such
acts were personal ties, not the distant decisions of bureaucracies. They also bridged great vertical distances in the social
order: in this case, between some day labourers caught pilfering, and the Lord Lieutenant of the county. We cannot, of
course, infer gratitude from begging letters, but there is
enough evidence to suggest that much of it was genuine. Many
prosecutors, peers included, made the most of their mercy by
requiring the pardoned man to sign a letter of apology and
gratitude, which was printed in the county newspaper.

The nature of the criminal trial gave enormous discretion to
men of property other than the prosecutor. Because the law
did not allow those accused of felony to employ an attorney to
address the jury, a poor man's defence was often a halting,
confused statement. If he had a clear alibi he was lucky: to
establish innocence in more complicated cases might be very
difficult, even when the judge was sympathetic. Character
witnesses were thus extremely important, and very frequently
used. It was not uncommon for a man accused of sheep-stealing,
a capital offence, to bring a dozen acquaintances to court to
testify to his honesty. If the jury did convict, such favourable
testimony might still induce the judge to pass a lesser sentence,
or recommend a pardon. Yet in character testimony too, the

word of a man of property had the greatest weight. Judges
respected the evidence of employers, respectable farmers and
neighbouring gentlemen, not mere neighbours and friends. A
labourer accused of a serious crime learned again his enormous
dependence on the power of property to help him, or abandon
him, as it chose: 'I am now going to take a dredful tryal and
god nose but my poor Life may Lay at Stake,' William Sheffield
wrote to his masters a month before the assizes,[10]

> therefore I hope Both of you will stand my frend this time
> jest to Come and give me a Careckter for the time that I Lived
> with you and I hope you will do that for me the judg I am
> told will Look Upon that as a great thing in my Behaff... So
> pray my dear mastters Consider my Unhappy state this time
> for gods sake and stand my frend and if plees god it should
> Ever Laye in my power I will neaver think nothing two much
> to make you amends Eaver to Lay my selfe at your feet if I
> can be of haney serviss to you for your passt goodness to me
> in so doing...

If respectable character witnesses did not succeed in convincing
the jury to acquit, their support was the first step in influencing the judge to consider a pardon. A free or conditional pardon
from the king was the hope of almost every capital convict in
the eighteenth century, and many men under lighter sentences
also struggled to obtain it. For the historian it epitomizes the
discretionary element of the law, and the use of mercy in
justifying the social order.

Pardons were very common. Roughly half of those condemned
to death during the eighteenth century did not go to the gallows, but were transported to the colonies or imprisoned. In
many cases the judge made the decision before he left the
assize town, but if he did not intend to recommend mercy, it
was still possible to petition the king, through the Secretary
of State, up to the moment of execution. The grounds for mercy
were ostensibly that the offence was minor, or that the convict
was of good character, or that the crime he had committed was
not common enough in that county to require an exemplary
hanging. The judges also used the pardon when necessary to
meet the requests of local gentry or to propitiate popular feelings
of justice. The bench could ultimately decide whom to recommend for mercy and whom to leave to hang, but they were not
usually willing to antagonize a body of respectable feeling.
Justice Ashurst, asked to endorse a pardon for a horse-
stealer from Cambridge, reported to the king, 'I had whilst
on Circuit received such favourable Accounts of him as induced
me to reprieve him & had those accounts remain'd uncontra-
dicted I should have thought there could be no objection...for
a free Pardon...But I have this day received a letter from some
Gentlemen of the University desiring to retract their former
applications for mercy ...'[11] The judges were well aware that
the gentry of the county were charged with government and
criminal justice between assize times, and hence usually gave

their opinions a serious hearing. The pardon could be used,
however, to show mercy when the death penalty seemed too
severe, and this discretion became part of the explicit justification of the law to the poor. In passing sentence of death on
a prosperous sheep-stealer in 1787, Sir Beaumont Hotham
argued that the law understood the trials of the poor and properly held the rich rogue to stricter account. 'He noted the
difference between a poor wretch in distress committing such
a crime, and a man of seeming reputation; - that the latter,
under the mask of a fair and upright character, was enabled
to make depredations on his neighbours and the public, without
being suspected, therefore was not to be guarded against,
and consequently, in his eye, was much more culpable than the
poor man, who commits such acts from real want.'[12] Since most
death sentences were pronounced for theft, the most recent
historian of the pardon concludes that it moderated the barb-
arity of the criminal law in the interests of humanity. It was
erratic and capricious, but a useful palliative until Parliament
reformed the law in the nineteenth century.[13]

Such an analysis stresses the narrowly legal use of the pardon, but ignores its social significance, the crucial point that
interests us here. As in so many other areas of the law, custom
and procedure allowed wholly extra-judicial considerations
great influence. The pardon allowed the bench to recognize
poverty, when necessary, as an excuse, even though the law
itself did not. But the manner in which a pardon was obtained
made it an important element in eighteenth-century social
relations in three other ways. In the first place, the claims of
class saved far more men who had been left to hang by the
assizes judge than did the claims of humanity. Again and again
in petitions the magic words recur: 'his parents are respectable
persons in Denbighshire'; his father is 'a respectable farmer';
his brother is 'a builder of character and eminence in London'.[14]
There are very few petitions that plead what one in 1787 called
'the common excuse for larceny, poverty and distress'.[15] It
may have been the common excuse, but those requesting pardons knew it held little weight - only two of the hundreds of
petitions that year bothered to mention it. In contrast, the
excuse of respectability was pleaded *in extenso* [...]

The pardon thus served to save a good many respectable
villains. It was all very well to hang Dr Dodd and Lord Ferrers,
but to hang every errant son of the rich who tried his hand at
highway robbery to pay gambling debts would have made too
great a carnage in the better circles. Pardons also favoured
those with connections for another reason: mercy was part of
the currency of patronage. Petitions were most effective from
great men, and the common course was for a plea to be passed
up through increasingly higher levels of the social scale,
between men bound together by the links of patronage and
obligation. The bald language of place-seekers recurs here too;
trading in life and death became part of·the game of interest.

'If anything can be done in consequence of the inclosed letter,'
wrote Lord Viscount Hinchingbrooke, 'I shall be very thankful
for it - as the writer of it is a particular friend of mine in the
county of Huntingdon.'[16] Sir George Yonge forwarded another
application for mercy from 'Sir John Pole, a Neighbour of mine
and a gentleman of Family, and Considerable Property in
Devonshire and Dorsetshire - If there is occasion for it,
Humanity as well as regard to the application from such a
respectable Quarter make me wish to interfere with success.'[17]
Often a long chain of interest and connection had to rattle
before the judges and the king listened [...]

Beyond class favouritism and games of influence, the pardon
had an equally important role to play in the ideology of mercy.
The poor did not see the elaborate ramifications of interest
and connection. Although the convolutions of the patronage
system at the lowest level were known to every man who wished
to become a tidewaiter, the law was set apart, and no gentleman wished to admit too openly that justice itself was but
another part of the system. Moreover, pardon-dealing went on
at the highest levels only, well concealed from the eyes of the
poor. Therefore the royal prerogative of mercy could be
presented as something altogether more mysterious, more sacred
and more absolute in its determinations. Pardons were presented
as acts of grace rather than as favours to interests. At the
lowest levels, within the immediate experience of the poor,
pardons were indeed part of the tissue of paternalism, expressed
in the most personal terms. The great majority of petitions for
mercy were written by gentlemen on behalf of labourers. It
was an important self-justification of the ruling class that once
the poor had been chastised sufficiently to protect property, it
was the duty of a gentleman to protect 'his' people. Thus
William Trumbull of Berkshire struggled to save a youth from
the gallows when he discovered that the boy's father had been
a servant to his own father, the Secretary of State, many years
before.[18] A Norfolk gentleman asked for mercy on the grounds
that 'all this man's family live in the neighbourhood near Norwich and are employed occasionally by me.'[19] And the Duke of
Richmond obtained a pardon for a man who claimed to have
once saved the life of the Duke's father.[20] Men facing imminent
death tried to exploit some improbably remote connections. The
son of Lord Courtenay's former butler appealed to Sir George
Yonge on behalf of another relative, on the grounds that Yonge
had known the butler years before: 'for Sir George it is in
your power to save him from death if Sir George you will be
so kind ...'[21] These were not empty or exaggerated words.
Influence in pardons, though rarely the only factor considered,
was extremely important. A convicted labourer, even in a
rural parish, was likely to know only a few men of property
well enough to ask for their help, and if they were feeling more
vengeful than merciful, death was a pretty sure thing. [...]

Petitions for pardons were occasionally opposed, but usually

by determined prosecutors. Where a prosecutor had second
thoughts or wished to indulge his humanity after exacting
terror and recovering his property, he sometimes was the first
to add his name to a plea for mercy - and thereby gave it
greater weight. Most successful petitions, however, were begun
by other men of respectable position, with good connections,
and their activity on behalf of the condemned could only
enhance their reputations as men of compassion and magnanimity.
To the poor, the intercession of a local gentleman was proof of
his power to approach the throne. He took no blame if the petition failed, for an unanswered plea was attributed to the
determination of the king, who was popularly believed to sign
all death warrants. A successful outcome was attributed to
mercy at the same exalted height - and Blackstone argued
that 'these repeated acts of goodness coming immediately from
his own hand, endear the sovereign to his subjects, and
contribute more than anything to root in their hearts that filial
affection, and personal loyalty, which are the sure establishment of a prince'.[22] And all the chaplains, country gentlemen
and peers who had helped to obtain a pardon shared somewhat
in the reflected glory of the merciful ruler.

The pardon is important because it often put the principal
instrument of legal terror - the gallows - directly in the hands
of those who held power. In this it was simply the clearest
example of the prevailing custom at all levels of criminal justice.
Here was the peculiar genius of the law. It allowed the rulers
of England to make the courts a selective instrument of class
justice, yet simultaneously to proclaim the law's incorruptible
impartiality, and absolute determinacy. Their political and
social power was reinforced daily by bonds of obligation on one
side and condescension on the other, as prosecutors, gentlemen
and peers decided to invoke the law or agreed to show mercy.
Discretion allowed a prosecutor to terrorize the petty thief
and then command his gratitude, or at least the approval of
his neighbourhood as a man of compassion. It allowed the class
that passed one of the bloodiest penal codes in Europe to congratulate itself on its humanity. It encouraged loyalty to the
king and the state:

> And Earthly Power doth then show likest God's
> When mercy seasons justice.

And in the countryside the power of gentlemen and peers to
punish or forgive worked in the same way to maintain the
fabric of obedience, gratitude and deference. The law was
important as gross coercion; it was equally important as ideology. Its majesty, justice and mercy helped to create the spirit
of consent and submission, the 'mind-forged manacles', which
Blake saw binding the English poor. But consent, Archdeacon
Paley's phrase, must be managed 'with delicacy and circumspection'. To understand fully the social functions of the

eighteenth-century criminal law, we must understand how it
embodied those virtues too.

DELICACY AND CIRCUMSPECTION

Deference in eighteenth-century England, although pervasive,
was not complete. The gentry managed to maintain order without anything resembling the political police used by the French,
but it was order that often seemed to rest on precarious foundations. The common Englishman was renowned for his riots, and
also for his dislike of standing armies. Although the ideology
of justice could be used by gentlemen to quiet a mob, and with
success, words sometimes lost their magic. Then the discretion embodied in the law allowed the authorities to use terror
with great flexibility. Examples of this delicate adjustment of
state power are legion, especially in decisions about executions,
the most emotive act in civil government. In 1756 Justice Willes
was holding the Warwick Assizes when food riots broke out in
the county. He announced his intention of trying and execut-
ing immediately all rioters brought before him, adjourning the
court from week to week until order had been restored. Within
days he convicted four,

> And, when I passed Sentence upon Them, I said a good deal
> to show the heinous nature of their crime, and the great folly
> of the attempt... And I ordered the captain and another
> notorious offender to be executed on Wednesday next; and
> told...the others...that I would adjourn 'till Monday s'en
> night, and that then, if the insurrection was quite at end,
> I would apply to his Majesty to pardon them; but if not, I
> would immediately execute the two other persons that were
> convicted.

No one thought it strange to hang some men for crimes committed
by others. The Secretary of State wrote to Willes to congratulate
him, and expressed the hope that other judges would follow his
example in similar cases. 'The King, the Duke, the whole court,
are full of Commendation, & the general voice is, that these
Insolent Rioters could not have fallen into better Hands.'[23]

Gentlemen were very sensitive to opinion in their neighbourhoods, for there might be serious consequences if the show of
force was either not quite impressive enough, or so brutal that
it outraged men and destroyed the mystique of justice. Lord
Hardwicke, when Chief Justice, ordered a Cornish rioter's
body to hang in chains, a refinement of capital punishment
that added infamy to death. He agreed to respite that part of
the sentence, however, when the local gentry informed him
that[24]

> in the present circumstances of affairs it would be more
> advisable not to do it, for tho' his crimes, as your Lordship
> says, demand the most terrifying Example yet there must be
> the greatest regard had for the Peace of our Country, which

we were apprehensive might be again disturbed if that measure was pursued. It is undoubtedly in theory right and
would be extremely necessary in most parts of the Kingdom,
but in this there has been such an unaccountable run in his
favour, that if any of his particular Friends should cut Him
down, which would be a fresh insult upon Authority, The
Rabble would call it the last blow, and the spirit might
revive... We are in hopes that the examples are carried far
enough to work upon the Fears of his friends, without giving
them the opportunity of any new Triumph.

Edmund Burke used the same argument a half-century later in
the case of the Gordon rioters. A week of looting, arson and
unchecked defiance of authority severely shook the foundations
of order. Burke therefore advised the government to limit the
number of executions in spite of the gravity of the offence: 'If
I understand the temper of the publick at this moment, a very
great part of the lower, and some of the middling people of
this city, are in a very critical disposition, and such as ought
to be managed with *firmness and delicacy*.' He continued, 'In
general they rather approve than blame the principles of the
rioters... This keeps their minds in a suspended and anxious
state, which may very easily be exasperated, by an injudicious severity, into desperate resolutions; or by weak measures,
on the part of the Government, it may be encouraged to the
pursuit of courses, which may be of the most dangerous consequences to the public...' His recommendation was for six
executions with maximum publicity, a calculated blend of terror
and mercy under the strict rule of law.[25]

The rulers of eighteenth-century England spent much time
gauging opinion in this way. The facade of power had to be
kept undamaged. The gentry were acutely aware that their
security depended on *belief* - belief in the justice of their rule,
and in its adamantine strength. Hence, punishment at times
had to be waived or mitigated to meet popular ideas of justice,
and to prevent popular outrage from going too far and thereby
realizing its own strength. The aim above all was to avoid
exposing the law and authority either to ridicule or to too
close scrutiny. Contempt of court was therefore punished
severely: the convict who heard the death sentence with no
sign of repentance, and who instead damned the judge, could
hope for no pardon. It was also important for those administering and using the law to be circumspect, discreet - to leave
unsaid anything that might mar the illusion of power. Hence a
gentleman who trifled with the mob or called into question the
ultimate justice of the law was execrated by his fellows as a
knave and a fool. Lord George Gordon did both. The impotence
of England's governors in the face of disorder, and the measure
of their contempt for class traitors, was epitomized by a curious
scene in the House of Commons in June 1780. As Gordon's
supporters raged outside and threatened to break in upon
the Honourable Members, several MPs followed him about the

House with their hands on their swords, vowing to run him
through if the mob broke in. When Gordon continued his wayward career a few years later by publishing a protest of the
convicts of Newgate against capital punishment for theft, he
was committed to prison as a libeller of justice. Most gentlemen
thought him mad.

Discretion was necessary in thousands of small things, too.
It permeated the operations of the law. The decisions that
moved the levers of fear and mercy were decisions of propertied
men, and they made them privately, among themselves. At
the most informal level, before Justices of the Peace - country
gentlemen - the operation of the law was often the result of an
agreement on tactics between the JP and the prosecutor,
especially when the latter was a friend or powerful neighbour.
At the level of prosecution, the gentry particularly were likely
to allow the offender to escape if they were not completely
sure of a conviction: it was better to feign mercy rather than
reveal impotence. Since the legal process was largely a secret
between landowner and magistrate, nothing was easier to
arrange. Where a JP wished to chastise, but found to his
chagrin that the legislature had somehow failed to pass the
right law, he was advised to use others:[26]

> Complaints are made to magistrates, with respect to a thou-
> sand immoral and wicked actions, over which they have no
> jurisdiction whatever. In such cases, *it will be prudence to
> conceal the infirmity of their authority*: but they will fre-
> quently find that [the statute against swearing] has been vio-
> lated by one or both parties. I should then recommend, that
> they should exert their full authority in the punishment of
> *this* offence; and to dismiss the parties, with an admonition
> or a reprimand, where the law has given them no power to
> act.

The opacity of the law also made it possible for the rulers of
England to act in concert in managing hangings, arranging
backstage the precise moment of the emotional climax. This was
crucial not only at times of disorder; it was part of the routine
administration of the law. The Hanoverians themselves sometimes took seriously their legal prerogatives in this respect.
Shortly after he came to the throne, George III agreed to the
routine mitigation of the death sentence to one of transportation in the case of a highway robber. He gave instructions,
however, that[27]

> as his Majesty hopes so to terrify this unhappy Man, on the
> present occasion that he may not hereafter be guilty of the
> like offense; it is the King's intention that *he should not be
> acquainted of his Majesty's having extended his royal mercy
> towards him, 'till he comes to the place of execution*. It will
> be proper therefore, that you give orders to the sheriffs,
> for this purpose, so that he be carried with the others, who
> are to suffer; to the place of execution, and that he be
> informed, then, and not before then, of the reprieve ...

'Circumspection' is a euphemism in such circumstances. The private manipulation of the law by the wealthy and powerful was in truth a ruling-class conspiracy, in the most exact meaning of the word. The king, judges, magistrates and gentry used private, extra-legal dealings among themselves to bend the statute and common law to their own purposes. The legal definition of conspiracy does not require explicit agreement; those party to it need not even all know one another, provided they are working together for the same ends. In this case, the common assumptions of the conspirators lay so deep that they were never questioned, and rarely made explicit.[28]

It is important to recognize this fact, for it raises some important methodological questions for the student of authority and the law. There is a danger, which perhaps this essay has not avoided, of giving the impression that a system of authority is *something*, rather than the actions of living men. The invisible hand of Adam Smith's political economy was metaphor, shorthand for an effect rather than a cause; it was a description of recurrent patterns of useful behaviour forged out of the energy, conflicts and greed of thousands of individuals in a capitalist market. In a somewhat similar way, much of the ideological structure surrounding the criminal law was the product of countless short-term decisions. It was often a question of intuition, and of trial and error. In handling a mob it was useful to appeal to ideals of English justice: but that was a lesson that was slowly learned over many generations, and rarely raised to the level of theory. The necessity of gauging reactions to executions was an immediate problem of public order, not a plot worked out by eighteenth-century experts in public relations for a fee. The difficulty for the historian of the law is twofold. He must make explicit convictions that were often unspoken, for if left unspoken we cannot understand the actions of the men who held them.[29] Yet in describing how convictions and actions moulded the administration of justice, he must never forget that history is made by men, not by the Cunning of Reason or the Cunning of System. The course of history is the result of a complex of human actions - purposive, accidental, sometimes determined - and it cannot be reduced to one transcendent purpose. The cunning of a ruling class is a more substantial concept, however, for such a group of men is agreed on ultimate ends. However much they believed in justice (and they did); however sacred they held property (and they worshipped it); however merciful they were to the poor (and many were); the gentlemen of England knew that their duty was, above all, to rule. On that depended everything. They acted accordingly.

Seen in this light, much of the historical literature on the eighteenth-century ruling class seems misconceived. Their attitudes to the law are often made a test of their moral worth. Romilly and the other reformers usually have received alphas, as the forerunners of the armies of liberal enlightenment and

humanitarianism, and as the 'winners'. But in praising the
reformers we caricature the conservatives. Descriptions of a
ruling class in terms of abstract moral judgement have contradictory results, because they are profoundly unhistorical.
The substantial literature on the county magistrate is another
case in point. Historians have reached divergent conclusions,
although the present consensus seems to be that their rule
was 'in general upright and humane'.[30] Still, pessimists (to
borrow the terms of another moral debate) can find evidence
that many JPs were 'pretty great tyrants', and at least one
optimistic historian has hailed them as the finest governors the
world has ever known. These peculiarly idealist explanations,
which count or weigh the number of good acts against the
number of bad, then judge whether or not to admit the
eighteenth-century ruling class into the heavenly kingdom of
twentieth-century respectability, hinder rather than aid
understanding. Nor does it help to take a relativist moral tack,
and assert that the rulers of England were about as humane
as the society that they lived in, some a bit better, some a bit
worse. Humanity and inhumanity are real dispositions, rooted
in individuals, and more or less general, perhaps, in groups
of men with similar experiences. But conscious dispositions
can be shaped by much deeper social imperatives, justifications
are not always the same as motives, and even the sincerest
convictions and most authentic emotional responses may be
called forth, or subdued, or even at times reversed, by the
patterns of power within a culture or a class. Men were merciful
and merciless in the eighteenth century: the historian's task
is to answer the questions when, and why. It is not something
we can judge in the light of eternity. Rather, we should be
content to know why Lord Montagu was able to please his ladies
by saving a man's life, and why a Midlands cleric was prepared
to use the gallows to help his parishioner find God.

The second question raised by a discussion of the law as
ideology is evidential: how can we prove that it worked? Much
of the evidence cited here comes from the avowed intentions
and observations of the rulers, not the ruled. Perhaps much
of what the gentry interpreted as the deference and gratitude
of the poor was in fact conscious deception. Perhaps the
ordinary Englishman played the role assigned to him, but was
never convinced by the play. The eighteenth century produced
much genteel cant about justice, but it also produced a large
popular literature marked by cynicism and disrespect for the
law. And there were many more forceful demonstrations of
incredulity, including riots at executions, and rogues who
mocked their judges.

Much research remains to be done before we can give confident answers to some of these questions. But two general
points may be made. In the first place, most of the evidence
that we have of loud popular disrespect for the law comes from
London, and London differed in important ways from the rest

of eighteenth-century English society. It had a highly transient
population, and a large body of disorderly and parasitic poor
living on the gathered wealth of commerce, the port and the
disorderly and parasitic rich. In sharp contrast to the provinces,
the men hanged at Tyburn were mostly born in distant places.
They had come to London from the country, and in doing so
left behind the close and persisting personal relationships that
still characterized much of English society. And it was in such
intimate dealings of fear and gratitude that much of the ideology of justice was realized. Some historians have suggested
that 'urban alienation' accounts for London disorder and crime
in the eighteenth century. It may be more correct to say that
the instruments of control there were weaker, in part because
the class relationships that fostered deference were. Resistance
to the law, disrespect for its majesty, scorn for its justice
were greater. Equally, judicial mercy in London was more often
a bureaucratic lottery than a convincing expression of paternalism.

The provinces too erupted in disorder: food riots, militia
riots, excise riots, turnpike riots, gang poaching, endemic
and often violent smuggling. The hegemony of the law was
never complete and unbroken, even in the most deeply rural,
most traditional counties. The fabric of authority was torn
and reknit constantly. The important fact remains, however,
that it was reknit readily. The closer mesh of economic and
social ties in rural society, the public nature of those relationships compared to the complexity and obscurity of much of
metropolitan life, allowed the creation of an ideology that was
much more pervasive than in London. When it was momentarily
challenged in a county riot or by a defiant labourer, no serious
harm resulted; the prevailing code was, in fact, usually
strengthened. An ideology endures not by being wholly enforced
and rigidly defined. Its effectiveness lies first in its very
elasticity, the fact that men are not required to make it a credo,
that it seems to them the product of their own minds and their
own experience. And the law did not enforce uniform obedience,
did not seek total control; indeed, it sacrificed punishment
when necessary to preserve the belief in justice. The courts
dealt in terror, pain and death, but also in moral ideals, control of arbitrary power, mercy for the weak. In doing so they
made it possible to disguise much of the class interest of the
law. The second strength of an ideology is its generality. Provided that its depths are not explored too often or by too many,
it remains a reservoir of belief throughout the society and
flows into the gaps made by individual acts of protest. Therefore, those using it are concerned above all with surface
appearances. Undoubtedly the gentleman accepting an apology
from the man in his power, the thief or the rioter, would have
been gratified to know that the contrition was absolute, from
the soul. But provided that the act of contrition was public
and convincing, that it served to sustain general belief in

the justice of the social order, it sufficed. It became part of
the untested general idea, the ideology which made it possible
to stigmatize dissent as acts of individuals, of rogues and
criminals and madmen.

The hypothesis presented here is that the criminal law,
more than any other social institution, made it possible to
govern eighteenth-century England without a police force and
without a large army. The ideology of the law was crucial in
sustaining the hegemony of the English ruling class. This
argument, if sound, helps us to explain their resistance to
suggestions for drastic legal reform. It also casts some light
on the membership of that ruling class, and the character
of their society.

The long resistance to reform of the criminal law has perplexed
later writers. The conservatives who opposed reform have
been generally criticized, but historians have failed adequately
to explain the growth in numbers of capital statutes and the
simultaneous extension of the pardon. When the criminal law
is seen not simply as a coercive instrument to punish crime,
however, both problems seem largely resolved.

The post-revolution Parliaments passed more and more capital
statutes in order to make *every* kind of theft, malicious damage
or rebellion an act punishable by death. Although most executions took place under Tudor statutes rather than these fresh-
minted ones, the new legislation gave the power to make
terrible examples when necessary. Sometimes the new laws
merely re-created the death penalty for offences which had
been affected by the development of benefit of clergy; more
often they added it to newly defined offences, including some
not foreseen by the lawmakers of Elizabeth's time, such as the
forging of banknotes. But if gentlemen in Parliament were
willing to hang a proportion of offenders every year in order
to stage the moral drama of the gallows, it is extremely doubtful that they ever believed that the capital statutes should be
strictly enforced.[31] The impact of sentencing and hanging
could only be diminished if it became too common: 'It is certain,'
wrote Burke, 'that a great havock among criminals hardens,
rather than subdues, the minds of people inclined to the same
crimes; and therefore fails of answering its purpose as an
example.'[32] Equally important, a return to the severities of the
Tudors and early Stuarts probably would not have been tolerated
by the people. At that period and earlier the gentry and the
great houses usually had small armies of their own with which
local disaffection could be crushed when necessary. But from the
later seventeenth century the importance of managing opinion
had made nuance, discretion and less obvious coercion a necessary part of the art of ruling. If London rioted at Tyburn,
how much worse would disorder be if the executions were four
times as numerous? In the counties, three or six hangings in
each, twice a year, afforded splendid occasion for lessons in

justice and power; but scores of victims would have revolted the people. Although some gentlemen in Parliament did pen bloody new laws in the heat of anger and an uncompromising spirit of revenge, they saw the wisdom of pardons when confronted with long gaol calendars and the spectre of county towns festooned with corpses.

Considerations such as these probably influenced the judges most in determining their general policy over the century. For although it is asserted that after 1750 a constantly declining proportion of death sentences was actually carried out, this is only true in London. In the home counties the proportion of condemned who were executed remained fairly steady over the same period. But the common element in both jurisdictions was the effect of the differing policies on the absolute numbers hanged. In both cases, the number of the condemned who actually died on the gallows was relatively constant over much of the century. The law made enough examples to inculcate fear, but not so many as to harden or repel a populace that had to assent, in some measure at least, to the rule of property.

The second great paradox about the old criminal law, the delay in reform long after a good case had been made that capital statutes allowed theft to increase by making prosecutions uncertain, may also be resolved. Romilly and Eden and the other reformers proposed to replace capital punishment with lesser penalties, and the model which they followed implicitly and sometimes used publicly was that of Beccaria: 'a fixed code of laws, which must be observed to the letter.'[33] But Beccaria's plan made no provision for the needs of government. The conservative gentlemen of England balked not only at the 'unconstitutional' police that such plans required: they instinctively rejected rational plans as pernicious. A complete rationalization of the criminal law would remove those very elements of discretion, such as the pardon, which contributed so much to the maintenance of order and deference. Beccaria's thought, as Venturi has pointed out, was no mere mélange of humanitarianism and reason. His machine-like system of judgement and punishment would work only where differences of power between men did not exist, where the 'perhaps unnecessary right of property' had disappeared. His principal European opponents seized on this fact: his ideas, they claimed, spelt the end of all authority.[34]

In England the opposition was muffled, since the rhetoric of Whiggism denied that arbitrary measures existed and claimed that the criminal law was *already* fixed and determinate. Most of the opponents of reform therefore argued only that it was impossible to create a schedule of crimes and punishments complete enough to do 'justice' to the subtle differences between cases. But there were hints even in England of the deeper fears for authority. In 1817 Christian, always a frank defender of the unreformed law, recalled Livy's description of the fixed laws enacted after the expulsion of the Roman kings:

The King was a man from whom you might obtain by petition,
what was right, and even what was wrong: with him there
was room for favour and for kindness: he had the power of
showing his displeasure, and of granting a pardon; he knew
how to discriminate between a friend and an enemy. The laws
were a thing deaf and inexorable, more favourable and advantageous to the weak than to the powerful: they admitted of
no relaxation or indulgence, if you exceeded their limits.

'He knew how to discriminate between a friend and an enemy'
– no criminal code could do that, in Christian's opinion. And
had not the French Revolution shown that rigid laws could
favour the poor rather than the propertied? With such reforms,
the judge concluded, 'we should all be involved in republican
gloom, melancholy, and sadness'.[35]

Throughout the period we have been considering, the
importance of the law as an instrument of authority and a
breeder of values remained paramount. The English ruling
class entered the eighteenth century with some of its strongest
ideological weapons greatly weakened. The Divine Right of
Kings had been jettisoned in the interests of gentry power,
but the monarchy lost as a consequence much of its potency
as a source of authority, and so too did religion. At the same
time control had flowed away from the executive in the extreme
decentralization of government which characterized the century.
With Stuarts plotting in Europe, Jacobitism suspected everywhere at home, and a lumpily unattractive German prince on
the throne, English justice became a more important focus of
beliefs about the nation and the social order. Perhaps some of
the tension abated after the last Jacobite attempt in 1745,
which may help to account for Blackstone's relatively favourable attitude to reform in mid-century. But within a few decades
renewed assaults on the structure of authority – the riots of
1766 and 1780, Wilkes and the French Revolution – determined
the English ruling class to repel any attacks on the mystery
and majesty of the law.

In doing so they apparently sacrificed some security of
property. Romilly and the rest of the reformers were undoubtedly right that convictions in the courts were uncertain, and
that the occasional terror of the gallows would always be less
effective than sure detection of crime and moderate punishments.
Yet the argument had little weight with the gentry and aristocracy. In the first place they had large numbers of personal
servants to guard their plate and their wives. Their problem
was not attack from without but disloyalty within their houses.
No code of laws or police force would protect them there. Their
own judgement of character and the fair treatment of servants
within the family were the only real guarantees they could
have. Nor did the technicalities of the law bother country
gentlemen when they did come to try pilferers of their woods
and gardens. For as MPs they passed a mass of legislation that
allowed them, as JPs, to convict offenders without the trouble

of legalistic indictments or tender-minded juries. In cases
involving grain, wood, trees, garden produce, fruit, turnips,
dogs, cattle, horses, the hedges of parks and game, summary
proceedings usually yielded a speedy and simple conviction.[36]
The other crime from which the gentry commonly suffered was
sabotage: arson, cattle-maiming, the destruction of trees.
Although all these offences were punished by death, few
offenders were ever caught. Here too gentlemen knew that a
reform of the capital statutes would not increase the certainty
of a conviction. Moreover, sabotage was primarily an attack on
their authority rather than their property. Their greatest
protection against such assaults was acquiescence in their right
to rule: the belief in their neighbourhoods that they were kind
and just landlords and magistrates. In one area alone were
they exposed to the danger of great financial loss from theft.
Their largest possession was land. The only way it could be
taken from them illegally was by forgery – and it is significant
that forgery was punished with unmitigated severity throughout the century, by death.[37]

Lower down the social scale, the property of men in trade
and manufacturing and farming was much less secure. In the
eighteenth century very few of the offences from which such
men suffered were punishable on summary conviction. Instead,
to recover embezzled banknotes or shop-lifted calico or stolen
sheep, it was necessary to go to the expense and trouble of
a full criminal trial. Its outcome was always uncertain: the
technicalities of indictment or the misplaced sympathies of
juries allowed many thieves to escape. After the trial came the
misplaced sympathies of petitioners for pardons. Martin Madan,
anxious to see property secured by a more rigorous execution
of the laws, argued that 'the outside influences of great
supporters' had too great effect on the prerogative of mercy.
The result was that the great indulged their humanity at the
expense of lesser men's property.[38]

There was, therefore, a division of interest among propertied
Englishmen about the purpose of the criminal law. The reformers'
campaign spoke to humanitarians of all classes, men revolted
by the public agonies of the condemned at the gallows. But
their argument that capital punishment should be replaced by
a more certain protection of property appealed mostly to that
great body of 'middling men', almost half the nation, who
earned from £25 to £150 a year at mid-century, and created
more than half of England's wealth.[39] Although they could use
the discretionary elements of the law to a limited degree, their
property was the prey of thieves undeterred by terror. Their
complaints did not impress a tiny but powerful ruling class,
whose immense personal property in land was secure, who
could afford to protect their other goods without public support,
and who in any case were most concerned with the law as an
instrument of authority.

It is in such terms that we must work toward a definition of

the ruling class of eighteenth-century England. Far from being
the property of Marxist or *marxisant* historians, the term is a
leitmotiv in studies of the period.[40] Partly this is due to the
testimony of the sources: gentry and aristocracy claimed the
title with complete assurance. Its historical usage, however,
remains imprecise. Usually it has been defined in terms of
income or status: the rents of the great landed estate, or the
exact meaning contemporaries gave to the word 'gentleman'.
Class, however, is a social relationship, not simply an aggregate of individuals. As a relationship based upon differences
of power and wealth, it must be sought in the life of the
institutions that men create and within which they meet. The
law defined and maintained the bounds of power and wealth,
and when we ask who controlled the criminal law, we see a
familiar constellation: monarchy, aristocracy, gentry and, to
a lesser extent, the great merchants. In numbers they were
no more than 3 per cent of the population. But their discretionary use of the law maintained their rule and moulded social
consciousness. An operational definition of the ruling class -
asking who controlled a critical institution like the law, and
how they manipulated it - is a more useful approach than drawing horizontal lines in Blackstone's list of forty status levels.
For it is necessary to define in detail what it means to rule.

Many historians, confronted with the hegemony of the
eighteenth-century ruling class, have described it in terms
of absolute control and paternal benevolence. Max Beloff
argued that after the Restoration they enjoyed an unparalleled
sense of security which explained 'the leniency with which
isolated disturbances were on the whole treated, when compared with the ferocity shown by the same class towards their
social inferiors in the times of the Tudors and early Stuarts'.[41]
It seems more likely that the relative insecurity of England's
governors, their crucial dependence on the deference of the
governed, compelled them to moderate that ferocity. More
recent writing has stressed the importance of patronage; Harold
Perkin has argued that this was the central bond of eighteenth-
century society. Patronage created vertical chains of loyalty;
it was, in fact, 'the module of which the social structure was
built'. Powerful men bound less powerful ones to them through
paternalism, controlling the income, even the 'life-chances' of
the dependent client or tenant or labourer. Such ties, repeated
endlessly, formed a 'mesh of vertical loyalties'. Social control
in the eighteenth century seems a gentle yoke from this perspective: a spontaneous, uncalculated and peaceful relationship
of gratitude and gifts. The system is ultimately a self-adjusting
one of shared moral values, values which are not contrived
but autonomous. At one point the author concedes that insubordination was 'ruthlessly suppressed'. But mostly social solidarity grew quietly: 'those who lived within its embrace...
[called it] friendship.'[42] Coercion was an exceptional act, to
handle exceptional deviance.

Yet it is difficult to understand how those loyalties endured
when patronage was uneven, interrupted, often capricious.
Many contemporaries testified to the fickleness of wealth: disappointed office-seekers, unemployed labourers or weavers,
paupers dumped over parish boundaries. Riot was a common-
place; so too were hangings. Benevolence, in short, was not
a simple positive act: it contained within it the ever-present
threat of malice. In economic relations a landlord keeping his
rents low was benevolent because he could, with impunity,
raise them. A justice giving charity to a wandering beggar was
benevolent because he could whip him instead. Benevolence,
all patronage, was given meaning by its contingency. It was
the obverse of coercion, terror's conspiracy of silence. When
patronage failed, force could be invoked; but when coercion
inflamed men's minds, at the crucial moment mercy could calm
them.

A ruling class organizes its power in the state. The sanction
of the state is force, but it is force that is legitimized, however imperfectly, and therefore the state deals also in ideologies.
Loyalties do not grow simply in complex societies: they are
twisted, invoked and often consciously created. Eighteenth-
century England was not a free market of patronage relations.
It was a society with a bloody penal code, an astute ruling
class who manipulated it to their advantage, and a people
schooled in the lessons of Justice, Terror and Mercy. The
benevolence of rich men to poor, and all the ramifications of
patronage, were upheld by the sanction of the gallows and the
rhetoric of the death sentence.

Notes
1 Thomas Gisborne, 'An Enquiry into the Duties of Men in
  the Higher and Middle Classes of Society in Great Britain',
  1794, p.284 note b.
2 Blackstone, 'Commentaries', 12th ed., vol.IV, p.350.
3 The class function of juries was also reflected in the fact
  that two important kinds of offences were removed from
  their jurisdiction. In neither game cases nor excise prosecutions could juries of 'middling men' be trusted to convict. They felt the law to be unjust, a denial of the rights
  of property. Hence both offences were punishable on summary conviction by justices and excise commissioners acting
  without a jury. For all other property offences, tradesmen
  and farmers would not decide against the evidence.
4 Gisborne, op. cit., p.28.
5 'From Max Weber', ed. H.H. Gerth and C. Wright Mills,
  1970, pp.216-21. Brougham anticipated Weber in 1828,
  declaring 'there is not a worse-constituted tribunal on the
  face of the earth, not even that of the Turkish Cadi, than
  that at which summary convictions on the Game Laws constantly take place; I mean a bench or a brace of sporting
  justices': see J.L. and Barbara Hammond, 'The Village

Labourer' (1911), 1966, p.188.

6 Cottu, 'The Administration of Criminal Justice in England', 1822, p.37.

7 Nicholas Blundell, 'Blundell's Diary and Letter Book, 1702-28', ed. Margaret Blundell, Liverpool, 1952, pp.109-11.

8 Staffs, RO, D593/L/1/15/10, Worsey to Howard, 15 October 1780.

9 Staffs, RO, D593/M/2/1/8, letter of Thomas Heath, 5 November 1798.

10 William Sheffield to Evans, Hinds and Best, re his trial at Aylesbury, Lent 1787; PRO, HO 47/6. Sheffield's employers found it inconvenient to attend; he was condemned, although Best wrote on his behalf.

11 Report of Justice Ashurst, 10 April 1787, re John Higgins; PRO, HO 47/6.

12 'An Account of the Life, Trial, and Behaviour of William Bagnall' (WSL, Broad-sheets 2).

13 Leon Radzinowicz, 'A History of English Criminal Law ...', 1948, vol.1, pp.116, 137.

14 Justice Perryn's report, 3 December 1787, on John Knott, and letter of the Bishop of Salisbury (n.d.), re Joseph Moreland, PRO, HO 47/6. Moreland's petition is endorsed, 'family and connection respectable'. Cf. Justice Cardil's recommendation of mercy for John Jepson, a highway robber: he was young, and 'I find that his Mother and Relations live very reputably, *which are Considerations that will have their due weight with your Majesty in favour of this unhappy young man*'. (Emphasis in original; PRO, SP 36/111 fos. 46-7.)

15 John Eden on behalf of Smith, PRO, HO 42/12 fo. 157 (1787).

16 Hinchingbrooke to Townshend, 31 October 1787, PRO, HO 42/12.

17 Yonge to Nepean, 24 October 1787, PRO, HO 42/12 fo.130.

18 Brit. Mus. Add. MSS, 32,732 fo. 479 (1753).

19 PRO, HO 42/12 fo. 137.

20 Brit. Mus. Add. MSS, 33,732, Richmond to Newcastle, Strasbourg, 21 October 1753.

21 PRO, HO 32/12 fo. 88 (1787). John Dennis demanded that the Pelhams should help him 'and never be ashamed to hear yourselves named to a free and accepted Mason'. Brit. Mus. Add. MSS, 32,734 fo. 182 (1754).

22 Blackstone, 'Commentaries', vol.IV, p.397. Blackstone explicitly repudiates Beccaria on this crucial question.

23 Brit. Mus. Add. MSS, 32,867 fos. 3-4, 8-11, 94.

24 Brit. Mus. Add. MSS, 35,585 fos. 299-303.

25 Some Thoughts on the Approaching Executions, 'Works', 1812, vol.IX, pp.268-71. My emphasis.

26 Christian, 'Charges delivered to Grand Juries in the Isle of Ely', 1819, p.291 (my emphasis, followed by Christian's).

27 C. Jenkinson to Recorder of London, 22 May 1761; PRO, SP 44/87, fos. 19 and 20 (my emphasis).

28 The legal definition requires that the purpose should be unlawful, not simply 'extra-legal'. But here the law falls into a 'vagueness [which] renders it possible for judges to treat all combinations to effect any purpose which happens to be distasteful to them as indictable crimes, by declaring this purpose to be "unlawful"'. ('Kenny's Outlines of Criminal Law', 19th ed, 1966, p.430). Many eighteenth-century Englishmen would have found private agreements by the powerful to manipulate the law not only distasteful but deceitful and dangerous. But only judges and legislators can make matters of taste also matters of law.

29 Those who describe beliefs that are widely held but seldom expressed are often unrepresentative figures. Nourse was an Anglican cleric who converted to Roman Catholicism and literature, Madan another eccentric clergyman whose call for more hangings was repudiated by the judges. The Evangelicals (More, Gisborne) were often embarrassingly direct in their social prescriptions, Cottu was a foreigner, and Christian was a long-winded, egotistical bore. For these reasons they sometimes raised in argument points that more conventional men thought banal or indiscreet, or did not think consciously of at all.

30 G.E. Mingay, 'English Landed Society in the Eighteenth Century', 1963, p.119.

31 This is Paley's doctrine, embraced by every subsequent conservative apologist. Radzinowicz explicitly rejects it on the grounds that the divergence between the law and its administration was increasing (Radzinowicz, vol.1, p.164, n.59). His argument ignores the probability that Parliament passed many laws in part *because* they knew they would not be rigorously enforced; that is, that they legislated on the basis of their experience.

32 Some Thoughts on the Approaching Executions, 'Works', vol.IX, p.270.

33 Cesare Beccaria, 'On Crimes and Punishments', trans. Henry Paolucci, New York, 1963, ch.4, p.16.

34 Franco Venturi, 'Utopia and Reform in the Enlightenment', Cambridge, 1971, p.101, quoting Beccaria, ch.30. On this statement compare Paolucci on Beccaria, op. cit., p.74, n.39.

35 Christian, 'Charges', pp.278-9.

36 The growth of this body of legislation was remarked by lawyers, who sometimes argued that it threatened trial by jury; its expansion paralleled the growth in capital statutes.

37 'Forgery is also punished capitally, and nobody complains that this punishment is too severe, because when contracts sustain action property can never be secure unless the forging of false ones be restrained.' Adam Smith, 'Lectures on Justice, Police, Revenue and Arms' (1763), ed. Edwin Cannan, 1896, p.150.

38 Martin Madan, 'Thoughts on Executive Justice ...',

1785, pp.55ff.

39 Derived from the estimates of Joseph Massie in 1760, the figures can be trusted only as general estimates (Peter Mathias, The Social Structure in the Eighteenth Century: a Calculation by Joseph Massie, 'Economic History Reviews', 2nd ser., X, 1957, pp.30-45). According to Massie, families with this range of income accounted for 48 per cent of the population and 57 per cent of the total of all families' 'annual income and expenses'. Above them, with incomes of more than £200, were the landed gentry, great merchants and aristocracy. The merchants, 1.6 per cent of the population, accounted for another 8.9 per cent of total income, and the landed classes (1.2 per cent of the population) over 14 per cent.

40 Max Beloff, 'Public Order and Popular Disturbances 1660-1714', 1938, p.154, discussed the 'social thinking' of the Restoration ruling class; David Mathew in 'The Social Structure in Caroline England', Oxford, 1948, p.8, asserted that 'within the general structure the diverse elements were being moulded which would in time form themselves into a ruling class'; W.R. Brock wrote that country life taught 'a code of behaviour and first lessons in public life' to the eighteenth-century ruling class ('New Cambridge Modern History', vol.VII, 1957, p.243); Esther Moir referred to the landowners as 'the backbone of the traditional ruling class' in 'The Justice of the Peace', Harmondsworth, 1969. Latterly a certain embarrassment occasionally has attached to the term. Peter Laslett, in 'The World We Have Lost', 1965, discussed at length why the governors of eighteenth-century England constituted the only class, but avoided joining the evocative words: England had one class, but they were a 'ruling segment'. Harold Perkin, however, with a similar interpretation of the dynamics of society, readmitted the term: 'The Origin of Modern English Society', 1969, p.56.

41 Beloff, op. cit., p.154.

42 Perkin, op. cit., pp.32-49, a sustained historical use of the idea of 'social control' currently orthodox in the sociological literature. The origins of the concept lie at least as far back as Durkheim's 'social conscience', and it has a marked ideological history of its own. Its increasingly common usage in historical writing, often with little critical examination, therefore bears watching. Its assumption of the relative autonomy of normative sanctions seems dubious, particularly in descriptions of the power of the state.

2 Popular attitudes to the law in the eighteenth century

John Brewer and *John Styles*

The question of the relationship between the legal system, authority and state power in seventeenth- and eighteenth-century England is one of quite extraordinary complexity. On the one hand, the courts were powerful regulatory mechanisms, dealing not only with crime but numerous aspects of social and economic life. It is no exaggeration to argue that the long arm of the law was the strongest limb of the body politic. But, on the other hand, law enforcement varied in its intensity and efficiency: some areas were virtually 'lawless zones'; the practice of local courts sometimes deviated considerably from the letter of the law as enacted or interpreted in Westminster; and most legal officials were rank amateurs who were as much concerned with the preservation of local harmony as they were with the (often divisive) business of litigation. In sum, there were considerable institutional constraints on the exercise of authority through the law.

The absence of a class of legal administrators, the tensions between centre and locality and the remarkable variations in law enforcement make it extremely difficult to generalize about either state power or the exercise of authority. Because they both manifested themselves primarily through the law, they were mediated by a complex, varied, almost idiosyncratic process. The disparate ways in which this process or mechanism operated have received relatively little attention from historians. [...] Just how well equipped was the Stuart state to deal with the recalcitrant villager and the enraged grain rioter? How extensive and effective was the authority that opposed the Kingswood colliers' destruction of turnpikes, the Yorkshiremen's counterfeiting operations, the attempts of debtors to obtain their liberty and the efforts of radicals to alter the polity? These questions can be satisfactorily answered only by a careful examination of the relevant statutes and common

Source: J. Brewer and J. Styles (eds), 'An Ungovernable People', Hutchinson, 1980, extracts from pp.12-20.

law, by scrutiny of the structures of authority and officialdom and, most significantly, by the delineation of the judicial process through which action was taken by those in authority. Only by piecing together these different components can we make specific such abstractions as 'state power' and 'the rule of law'. [...]

Seventeenth- and eighteenth-century Englishmen's conceptions of government were intimately bound up with their actual experience of the law. This sense of the political nature of the law (and of the legal nature of politics) was in part a direct consequence of the state's use of the courts as the chief means of exercising authority and enforcing regulations. It was in the courtroom or, at least, in the presence of the justice of the peace and his clerk, that men were most aware of the powers that were wielded over them. Good governance was equated with justice, and the fair dispensation of the law with good government: in this sense 'the rule of law' was no empty phrase.

Indeed, the notion of 'the rule of law' was central to seventeenth- and eighteenth-century Englishmen's understanding of what was both special and laudable about their political system. It was a shibboleth of English politics that English law was the birthright of every citizen who, unlike many of his European counterparts, was subject not to the whim of a capricious individual but to a set of prescriptions that bound *all* members of the polity.[1] Such a characterization of the English 'rule of law' will not, of course, pass muster as an accurate description of the modus operandi of the legal process, but it did serve as an idealization, a potent 'fiction', to use Edmund Morgan's term,[2] which commanded widespread assent from both patricians and plebeians.

The purchase of this ideology of 'the rule of law' had several important consequences. [...] Those in authority were constrained to some extent by their obligation to act in accordance with this ideology. They recognized (and, as Douglas Hay has pointed out, flaunted their recognition.[3]) that they should be bound by the laws which they themselves had a duty to enforce and that they were obliged to follow certain defined procedural rules. Because authority derived its legitimacy from the rule of law, 'the law' was used as a standard by which to judge the just exercise of the authority. Authorities therefore chose to limit themselves in order to acquire greater effectiveness: they traded unmediated power for legitimacy.

This self-imposed restraint had its effect not only on authority and the perceived obligations of a patrician class, but also helped shape the opinions of the humbler members of society who, for whatever reason, came within the purview of the law. It is, of course, notoriously difficult to capture that most elusive of historical quarries, popular attitudes towards the law. We can recover patrician views with relative ease (though there is a distressing tendency to simplify them). Lawyer's books, legal treatises, assize sermons, justices'

diaries, gentlemen's letters and memoirs: they all provide
evidence that is readily to hand. But the *menu peuple* wrote
little and still less has been preserved. Fortunately, some sorts
of conflict [...] often generated evidence that otherwise would
not be available to us. Indeed, it is often *only* when conflict
occurred that evidence of demotic attitudes survives. The
investigations of authority and the depositions of the courts,
recorded precisely because there was a dispute, frequently
illuminate popular beliefs and conduct which might otherwise
be obscured or hidden. Such evidence, however, needs to be
handled with care and sensitivity: those who find themselves
in court or before a magistrate are as likely to say what is
expected of them, or what they think most appropriate in the
circumstances (which, after all, might sometimes be a matter of
life and death to them), as they are to blurt out the truth or
reveal their true feelings. Nevertheless, these conflicts [...]
reveal how widespread was popular knowledge of the law and
the extent to which people made explicit assumptions which,
under 'normal circumstances', they would have been unlikely
or reluctant to express openly or publicly. The Kingswood
colliers' letter to the turnpike commissioners, the pamphlets
objecting to imprisonment for debt or urging popular sovereignty, the depositions and counter-depositions of Yorkshire
coiners: these rich and highly informative materials could have
been generated only in the context of an acrimonious dispute.
Popular views of authority and the law were forged in the
crucible of conflict. Inchoate ideas were given shape and
definition, private grumblings previously confined to the ale-
house or the parlour were shouted in the market-place.
Occasionally men and women were led to redefine their relationship not only with other individuals or groups but towards
the law itself.

What, then, were these attitudes, and how were they affected
by the notion of 'the rule of law'? At first sight the chief
dramatis personae [...] - the seventeenth-century villager
and grain rioter, the incarcerated debtor, the sturdy Kingswood collier, the Yorkshire counterfeiter and the Hanoverian
radical - appear remarkably cavalier in their attitudes towards
the law. Time and again our discussion focuses on a conflict
between, on the one hand, statute law and its conventional
enforcement - the law of those in authority - and, on the
other, the people's own notions of justice or of the legitimacy
of certain illegal acts. It would seem that the law of patrician
society was not the justice of plebeian culture. But it is
important to understand the character of the criticism directed
at the law and its office-holders, and the nature of the disputes between the humble and those in authority. Criticism
of particular pieces of legislation or of the conduct of individual
magistrates and court officers - attacks on specific injustices
and abuses - were rarely generalized into a critique of authority
or the law. On the contrary, magistrates and laws were usually

judged according to their degree of conformity to 'the rule of law'. Popular grievances, often vividly expressed in judicial language, took the form either of complaints about authority's failure to execute the letter of the law, or of attacks on the recalcitrance and moral obtuseness of those who, for whatever reason, refused to fulfil the social and moral purposes for which the law had been created. In sum, grievances were more likely to be expressed in terms of authority's dereliction of duty than as an explicit challenge to authority itself.

The notion that all men were under the law therefore provided the ideological framework for most of these sorts of dispute [...] This is not to take a consensual view of seventeenth- and eighteenth-century English society. Though patricians and plebeians both used the language of 'the rule of law', their understanding of what we have called its social and moral purposes could differ sharply. All men assumed that the law should work *pro bono publico*, but one man's view of the public good was often regarded by another as a flagrant instance of private interest. Different meanings were attached to the well-worn cliché of 'the rule of law'.

Such differences of interpretation and meaning can be seen in the attitudes adopted by those who challenged authority, and go far towards explaining why popular criticism remained within the parameters of legal debate. The opponents of the magistrate or of a particular law seized (and laid special emphasis) upon certain aspects of the tradition of the rule of law which appeared to justify resistance to office-holders or to legitimate participation or intervention in the legal process. They drew particularly on the assumption that, if all men were subject to the law, then those in authority were *accountable* for their actions – accountable both in law and to the law. In the spheres of both politics and the law this precept was highly controversial. Was it to be narrowly construed to mean simply that legal action could be taken against office-holders who abused their trust, or did it imply, as many plebeians clearly thought, that injured parties could take extra-legal action to secure redress? These essays demonstrate the extent of the belief, sustained even by those who did not necessarily have access to the law, that they were entitled to assert their notion of the common good, and to ensure that it was secured and sustained by the law and those who executed it. It was legitimate to show the magistrate how he ought to enforce the assize of bread or to demonstrate the fundamental illegality of imprisonment for debt by a mass breakout from gaol. Such were particular examples of the belief, exploited and generalized by Wilkite radicals, in the strongly asserted right to *participate* in securing justice.

Though it was not altogether clear whether these participatory assumptions were peculiarly English, there were many features of the English judicial system which served to reinforce them. Office-holders, as we have seen, were never a class apart.

Men from all classes, with the notable exception of the labouring poor, contributed to the workings of a citizen judiciary.
Often such service was seen as an imposition, but it was also
a source of pride for the men of small property who enjoyed
the social standing that came with minor parochial office.
Moreover, the absence of a legal post was no necessary barrier
to involvement in the judicial process. The 'hue and cry', the
posse comitatus, the use of the pillory, but, above all, trial
by jury - 'putting oneself on one's country' - all explicitly
required participation in the workings of justice. There were
therefore both ideological and institutional aspects of the
English judicial system which encouraged the assertion of the
popular right to secure the fair and equitable enactment of
justice.

It was also the assumption of those who regarded themselves
as injured parties that this popular right commanded at least
grudging recognition from those in authority. The actions of
aggrieved parties were therefore often highly demonstrative:
they were designed to draw attention to complaints and to
cajole those in power into remedying the situation. They were
neither knee-jerk responses to misfortune nor the temper
tantrums of a restrained or frustrated child; rather, they
were actions deliberately undertaken as part of a *negotiative
process* whose outcome, it was hoped, would satisfy both the
aggrieved party and the authorities.[4]

The pursuit of redress could take either legal or extra-legal
forms, though more often than not the two were combined.
Petitioning and litigation went hand in hand with riots, demonstrations and the anonymous letter. These protests were neither
indiscriminate nor unconstrained. The level of violence or disorder almost invariably corresponded to the lack of responsive-
ness of those in authority. When first aired, a grievance was
more likely to be taken through accepted legal or political chan-
nels; it was only when authorities declined to act that hostilities escalated.

There was an expectation, therefore, that those in authority
knew that protests about specific grievances were intended
to provoke a remedial response, and not to challenge authority
per se. Such an assumption was only possible as long as the
aggrieved had some faith in authority's willingness to be bound
by the law and the ideals it was supposed to embody. Negotiation, of course, was not carried on between equals: those in
authority were far more powerful than those seeking redress,
even if both parties were in some sense bound by overlapping
conceptions of law and justice. Equally, the aggrieved were
playing a very dangerous game in which the odds were heavily
against them: [...] the breakdown of the negotiative process
could have disastrous consequences for those who pursued
redress. But the willingness of those resisting innovation (as
in the case of the Kingswood colliers and the turnpikes),
asserting a traditional right (grain rioters), or challenging a

hallowed but legally dubious procedure (imprisonment for debt) to operate within the parameters of the rule of law is truly remarkable.

In examining the negotiative process we have turned from a discussion of attitudes towards the law to the question of the tactics and stratagems employed by those who had contact with the legal process. There were a number of general features of the English judicial system which made it extremely suscep-tible to exploitation by individuals or groups. First and fore-most, the legal process was of a highly discretionary nature. The amateur officials who manned the courts might be active or indolent; their own predilections affected those offences that were winked at and those that were prosecuted with rigour. Constables and justices acted in a pragmatic, *ad hoc* way. The sentence meted out as punishment, the pardon offered the contrite offender: both were very much the gift - to be granted or withheld - of the appropriate officers of the court. Nearly all prosecutions were brought privately: the decision to prosecute, the choice of the court in which the case was tried,[5] the nature of the charge and the statute under which it was brought were largely in the hands of the party who initiated proceedings. The entire legal fabric, from prosecu-tion to punishment, was shot through with discretion. In con-sequence it was not difficult for office-holders to employ their position for their own private ends (including that of making money from the law), or for citizens to use the law either to legitimate some particular end such as commercial profit or the reformation of manners, or maliciously to prosecute an opponent, enemy or business rival.

This selective, non-bureaucratic operation of the law has recently been emphasized by Douglas Hay in his discussion of the socially discriminatory operation of the eighteenth-century legal process. He shows how a discretionary system, operating in a society where there were gross inequalities of wealth, was highly conducive to manipulation and control by the propertied men who created the substance of the law, overlooked its execution as justices of the peace and were the customary prosecutors in trials for theft. Discretion, Hay argues, facili-tated the use of the courts as a 'selective instrument of class justice'.[6] The patrician elite, able to choose whether to pro-secute, whether to provide character references for the accused and whether to ask that mercy be extended to the guilty, wielded a veritable sword of Damocles over plebeian Englishmen. Discretion meant that the leaders of society had both the opportunity to be kind *and* the capacity to be malicious. Such a powerful weapon was used to evoke either plebeian gratitude or plebeian fear and to cement the sometimes fragile bonds of deference.

The use of the judicial process as a class tool was, of course, one of its most important functions. The substance of the law served to legitimate existing social arrangements and to facilitate

those changes desired by the patrician class of lawmakers.
Seemingly impartial legislation was enforced partially and access
to the law was restricted to those who could afford to pay legal
costs and fees which, in the higher courts of the land, were
substantial. *Pace* the fiction of 'the rule of law', justice was
not necessarily the perquisite of every Englishman. But this
does not mean that we should regard the seventeenth- and
eighteenth-century legal process as simply an instrument of
an elite, or as serving only a class function. The discretion
and voluntaristic nature of the legal system that aided patrician power also enabled others to exploit the law. Indeed, if
this had not been the case, if the courts had not provided a
forum or an arena open, within limits, to many groups whose
purposes cannot be characterized as the exercise of class
justice, then the fiction of the rule of law would not have been
so potent. When seventeenth- and eighteenth-century Englishmen thought of the law, they thought not only of the criminal
law and its preoccupation with theft, but of the common law
in its broadest sense and of the body of regulations and
equitable practice which oiled the social mechanism and mediated
disputes of all kinds, including those that occurred within
as well as between classes. Their apprehension of the law was
a comprehensive one which embraced the juridical and political
aspects of the society and which saw the benefits (inequitably
distributed as they were) of such a system. No doubt this
helped humbler men to reach a grudging accommodation with
the more egregious aspects of the criminal process.
  Even though the plebeian and the underdog were invariably
disadvantaged when they clashed with those in authority or
had recourse to the courts, they knew that they were never
merely the passive victims of a process that they were powerless
to affect. Seventeenth-century villagers, eighteenth-century
debtors, the colliers of Kingswood and the coiners of Halifax,
as well as the metropolitan radicals supporting Wilkes, were all
prepared to make concerted efforts to exploit, alter or evade
the law and to bargain with, bully and bamboozle those in
authority. The ideology of the rule of law was invoked to
justify the prosecution and policing of officials and the public
presentation of grievances; archaic procedures were used to
further radical ends; one authority was played off against
another; actions were brought to test the legality of particular
laws, and extra-legal action was legitimized by appeals to the
principles of justice which the law was supposed to embody.
The room for manoeuvre may have been limited, but it was
exploited to the full.

In examining the workings of authority through the judicial
process, the different attitudes towards the law and the tactics
employed by litigants and those who confronted authority,
these studies emphasize a number of paradoxes. In seventeenth-
and eighteenth-century England the law was a remarkably

potent force. It was the chief means of exercising authority,
the main vehicle of state power, an important way of resolving
disputes and, because of the extraordinarily widespread
acceptance of the notion of the rule of law, a vital means of
legitimizing private initiatives. Yet, for all that, the imprimatur
of the law conferred only limited power on those who were its
beneficiaries. Both the *modus operandi* of the law and the
ideology that lay behind it served to constrain authority and
to limit those who tried to manipulate the legal process. Moreover, though one of the main functions of the law was to
facilitate the (largely local) exercise of authority by a govern-
ing class, that was never its sole function or role. The law was
not the absolute property of patricians, but a limited multiple-
use right available to most Englishmen, apart (a big caveat
this) from the labouring poor. Finally, there were both widely
shared and sharply differing ideas about the nature of the law
in seventeenth- and eighteenth-century England. The fiction
of the rule of law commanded remarkable support and was the
framework within which most conflict occurred. On the other
hand, appeal to this common prescription should not be allowed
to conceal the considerable divergences of opinion about what
the rule of law entailed. Such differences point to the intense
economic, social and political conflicts that underpin legal
activities. [...]

Notes

1 This is what we take to be the ideology of 'the rule of law'.
2 Edmund S. Morgan, 'New York Review of Books', vol.25,
  no.3 (March 1978), pp.13–18.
3 D. Hay, Property, Authority and the Criminal Law, in
  Hay et al., 'Albion's Fatal Tree', pp.32–9.
4 See the important reflections on this subject in E.P.
  Thompson, Eighteenth Century English Society: Class
  Struggle without Class, 'Social History', vol.3, no.2
  (May 1978), pp.133–65, especially pp.150–1.
5 The prosecutor's control over the choice of the court, once
  the decision to take *criminal* proceedings had been made,
  was very limited. Of course, in the case of assaults,
  trespasses, etc., the aggrieved party had the option of a
  remedy in the civil courts.
6 Hay, op. cit., p.48.

3 The ideological origins of the penitentiary

Michael Ignatieff

Howard was one of those rare men whose private compulsions seem to capture the imagination of their class. The attempt to raise a statue in his honor in 1786, as well as the hagiographies and elegies published after his death indicate how deeply his private quest appealed to his contemporaries. [...]

The veneration accorded Howard the man helps to explain the appeal of Howard the disciplinarian. He became the symbol of the philanthropic vocation, canonized by a middle class seeking representations of its best virtues. There is irony in Howard's reputation, since he was lauded by the very gentlemen whose neglect was set out in page after page of 'The State of the Prisons.' Having demonstrated the emptiness of the magistracy's reputation for solicitude, he found his own crusade taken up as a vindication of that reputation. The irony is superficial though, since Howard had no intention of embarrassing his own class. While his censure angered individual magistrates, it did not antagonize them collectively because he cast his campaign in terms of a confrontation with Evil in the abstract, rather than with particular groups of men. Hence, he was able to gain a reputation for disinterested, apolitical philanthropy, which vested his disciplinary ideas with particular authority.

His ideas appealed, above all, to that sector of the middle class in which he himself had his roots, the Nonconformist businessmen, professionals, and small gentry. While Nonconformity was deeply fissured, he had friends in many camps. The Quakers, who were to be the most consistent advocates of prison reform, were much admired by Howard. He was drawn to Quaker asceticism and adopted the dress 'of a plain Friend.' His own brand of piety was strongly reminiscent of the Quaker traditions of silent prayer, 'suffering' introspection, and faith in the illumining power of God's light. Quakers, for their part, were bound to be drawn to the idea of imprisonment as a

Source: 'A Just Measure of Pain', Macmillan, 1978, extracts from pp.57-79.

purgatory, as a forced withdrawal from the distractions of the senses into silent and solitary confrontation with the self. Howard conceived a convict's process of reformation in terms similar to the spiritual awakening of a believer at a Quaker meeting. From out of the silence of an ascetic vigil, the convict and believer alike would begin to hear the inner voice of conscience and feel the transforming power of God's love.

As the most rigorously self-disciplined of all the Nonconformist sects, the Quakers were naturally drawn to the idea of using regimens of discipline to reform the confined. For the Friends, discipline originally meant the rules of thought and action chosen by their sect to mark themselves off as a community from the sinful world: plain dress, 'thee and thou' forms of address; and refusal to pay tithes, swear oaths, or doff hats before authority. By the end of the seventeenth century, the Quakers began to turn from discipline as a collective statement of apartness to discipline as an instrument of control over others. This change corresponded to their own social transformation from a persecuted, inward-looking sect of small craftsmen during the Civil War to a prosperous society of employers and merchants by the mid-eighteenth century.[1] Because of their experience with collective self-discipline, the Friends displayed a particular aptitude for devising institutional regimens for others. John Bellers's sketch for a Colledge of Industry in 1696, the Pennsylvania Quakers' reform of the Walnut Street jail in Philadelphia in 1786, and the Quaker asylum for the insane built at York in 1813 by Samuel Tuke are the most famous examples of this aptitude.[2]

The Quakers were also drawn to Howard's campaign because of their own bitter experience with imprisonment during the persecutions of the 1670s. Despite the increasing integration of the Friends into English society during the eighteenth century, they continued to be sent to prison for refusing to swear oaths, serve in wars, or pay tithes. As the sect with the strictest definition of what was due Caesar, they were in perennial conflict with Caesar's laws. Hence, of all sects, they asked the most searching questions about the right of the state to coerce citizens.

Having denied the right of the magistrate to compel men in matters of conscience, they were also led to deny his right to take human life in punishment. The abolition of the capital penalties in Pennsylvania and the reform of abuses in the Walnut Street jail followed from their doctrinal concern to set strict limits to the use of state force. When Howard set out to harmonize the imperatives of discipline and humanity, Quakers were among the first to enlist in his support.

Howard's closest friend and eventual co-adjutor on the penitentiary commission of 1779 was the Quaker physician John Fothergill.[3] By dint of relentless hard work and good connections with the Nonconformist establishment, Fothergill built up the most successful medical practice of his day, earning an

estimated £10,000 a year taking care of the Wedgwoods,
Gurneys, Darbys, Hanburys, Barclays, and other leading
families in Nonconformist industry and banking. Like Howard,
Fothergill was keenly interested in science. An amateur
botanist himself, he subsidized Joseph Priestley's scientific
research, besides treating him as a patient. Fothergill was
also a mainstay of London philanthropy and a restless promoter
of schemes for the 'improvement' of hygiene in the metropolis.
He wrote short treatises advocating hygienic burial practices
for paupers and the construction of roads through the war-
rens of the city's criminal quarters to open them up to the
beneficial circulation of air and commercial traffic. He was also
the leading spirit behind the establishment of a boarding school
for poor Quaker children at Ackworth in Yorkshire. At the
school, the children's 'active minds' were 'put under a kind
of restraint,' Fothergill proudly asserted, and 'habituated to
silence, attention and due subordination.' Howard, who toured
the school in 1779, found that it accorded exactly with his
conception of discipline.[4]

Fothergill was drawn to prison reform, not simply because he
was a Quaker, but also because he formed part of a group of
medical men who were revolutionizing the practice of institutional hygiene and management in hospitals, dispensaries, and
workhouses. James Lind, the superintendent of Haslar naval
hospital in Portsmouth; William Smith, the physician who
wrote a scathing denunciation of the squalor in the jails of
the London area in 1776; and Thomas Percival, the Manchester
authority on hospital 'police' and urban hygiene, were among
those whose experience in hygiene in hospitals, foundling
hospitals, dispensaries, troop transports, and men-o'-war
provided Howard with the hygienic regimen he sought to introduce into prisons: uniforms, baths, delousing, whitewashing
and liming of walls, regular diet, and medical inspections.[5]
They in turn took up the campaign to publicize these techniques
among magistrates and aldermen. For these medical men, therefore, prison reform was only one element of a general attack
on the hygienic problems of all institutions dealing with the
poor.

These doctors regarded the hygienic reform of institutions
as a moral, no less than a medical crusade. The sicknesses of the
poor were interpreted as the outward sign of their inward want
of discipline, morality, and honor. As John Mason Good,
physician of Cold Bath Fields prison, put it in 1795, 'The poor
are in general but little habituated to cleanliness'; they were
therefore liable to disease, because 'they feel not, from want
of education, the same happy exertion of delicacy, honour and
moral sentiment which everywhere else is to be met with.'[6]
This, of course, is the language of social and moral condemnation veiled as the language of medicine. The same tendency
to slide from medical into moral and class categories is evident
in Daniel Layard's pamphlet on jail fever, which appeared in

1773. Filth and disease were as natural to the poor, he asserted, as cleanliness and health were to the virtuous and industrious. The poor were 'bound in the chains' of addiction to riotous living, sexual indulgence and intemperance.[7] They were susceptible to disease because they were susceptible to vice.

It was particularly easy for eighteenth century doctors to couch the language of class fear and moral opprobrium in the language of medicine. In their structure of assumptions, they drew a much less distinct demarcation between the body and the mind than nineteenth century medicine was to do. Their thought was imbued with the Hartleian materialism then in the ascendant at the medical school in Edinburgh.[8] According to David Hartley, the psyche was no less material than the body. Disturbance of the bodily system produced perceptual distortions and mental anguish, just as psychic disturbance could contribute to the breakdown of physical functioning. Hence, it followed that physical diseases could have 'moral' causes. John Coakley Lettsom, the wealthy London physician and protégé of Fothergill's, for example, had no trouble understanding that mental depression or remorse contributed to the mortality rates in prison, just as he attributed jail fever, not merely to improper hygiene, but also to improper discipline. Habits of intoxication, no less than bed lice, caused prisoners to succumb to typhus. Hartleian categories provided 'scientific' legitimacy, therefore, for 'medical' condemnations of the indiscipline of the poor.

Since disease in institutions had moral as well as physical causes, hygienic rituals were designed to fulfill disciplinary functions. To teach the poor to be clean, it was necessary to teach them to be godly, tractable, and self-disciplined. Hartleian assumptions led the doctors to be confident that once the bodies of the poor were subjected to regulation, their minds would acquire a taste for order.

Driven by this confidence, the Nonconformist doctors of the 1770s sought to transform the hospital from a warehouse for the dying into an institution for the moral reform of the poor through hygienic regimen. At the opening of the Liverpool Infirmary in 1791, Thomas Percival insisted that institutional confinement was the sole way to change the poor. The sick could not be cured in their homes; they had to be given moral therapy in the hygienic asceticism of an institutional quarantine.[9]

Early prison reformers owed much of their conceptual framework to these hospital reformers. Jonas Hanway, for example, was arguing within their categories when he described crime as a disease 'which spreads destruction like a pestilence and immorality as an epidemical disorder which diffuses its morbid qualities.'[10] Like the doctors, he saw crime issuing from the same source as disease, from the squalid, riotous, and undisciplined quarters of the poor. Prisons too were breeding grounds of pestilence and crime alike. In the fetid and riotous wards of Newgate, the 'contagion' of criminal values was passed

from hardened offender to novice, just as typhus spread from
the 'old lags' to the recent arrivals. Like the hospital, the
penitentiary was created to enforce a quarantine both moral
and medical. Behind its walls, the contagion of criminality
would be isolated from the healthy, moral population outside.
Within the prison itself the separate confinement of each
offender in a cell would prevent the bacillus of vice from spreading from the hardened to the uninitiate.

Through the doctors and through his own friendships, Howard was able to draw upon another circle for support: the
Nonconformist scientists and intellectuals of the dissenting
academies and the scientific societies. Two members of the
Manchester Literary and Philosophical Society, Thomas Butter-
worth Bayley and Thomas Percival, were to play leading roles
in the construction of two new prisons in Lancashire, 'built
on Mr. Howard's plan.' Erasmus Darwin, the key figure of the
Lichfield Society, was to write one of his elephantine elegies
in Howard's honor.[11]

The scientific societies provided the meeting ground for
intellectuals and the leading manufacturers of the Midlands
and the North, men like James Watt and Matthew Boulton, pro-
prietors of the Soho Engineering works in Birmingham; Jedediah
Strutt, the Derbyshire cotton factory dynast; Abraham Darby,
founder of the iron and steel dynasty in Coalbrookdale, and
Josiah Wedgwood, the pottery magnate from North Staffordshire.[12] These new industrialists were Quaker or Unitarian
in religion, moderate or radical Whig in politics, scientific in
their enthusiasms, and philanthropic in their avocations. These
magnates financed a host of reform causes – the abolition of
slavery, the construction of hospitals and dispensaries, the
advancement of technical education, and the improvement of
schools for the poor.

They are, however, best known as the fathers of the factory
system and scientific management. Besides introducing
mechanization, extended division of labor, and systematic rout-
ing of the work process, they also devised the new disciplines
of industrial labor: punch clocks, bells, rules, and fines. In
order to reduce turnover and stabilize the labor force in their
early factories, they provided schools, chapels, and homes
for their workers in model villages.[13]

Like the hospital and prison reformers these early industrialists rationalized their new discipline as an attempt to reform
the morals and manners of their workers. In 1815, for example,
the Strutts boasted that before the establishment of their works
in Cromford and Belper, 'the inhabitants were notorious for
vice and immorality.'[14] Regular work and wages, together with
the stabilizing influence of a closely supervised village community, had transformed their behavior. Now, the Strutts said,
'their industry, decorous behavior, attendance on public worship
and general good conduct,' were 'very conspicuous.' Wedgwood,
for his part, claimed that the drunkenness, sloppy workmanship,

idleness, and violence of the potteries had been stamped out in his industrial fiefdom in Etruria. The punch clock, the fines, and his own intense and unremitting supervision had transformed the workers and 'made machines of the men as cannot err.'[15] In that first generation of industrialization, factories could still be justified not simply as technical achievements, but as moral ones as well.[16]

These Nonconformist industrialists, scientists, and doctors were also bound together by politics, most favoring one or another of the proposals for parliamentary reform which germinated in the 1770s. Fothergill, Howard, T.B. Bayley, and G.O. Paul lent their support to Christopher Wyvill's campaign for additions to the county representation in Parliament, retrenchment of expenditure, and reform in the administration of finance.[17] Wedgwood favored the more radical program of Major Cartwright and John Jebb, who advocated annual Parliaments and universal manhood suffrage.

Many figures who are better known as Whig radicals in the 1780s were involved in prison reform. John Jebb wrote a treatise on institutional discipline in 1785, based on his experience as a director of a House of Industry in Suffolk in the 1770s.[18] Other radicals - William Smith, Josiah Dornford, and William Blizard - wrote tracts denouncing the condition of London prisons and the state of the police.[19] The Duke of Richmond, who introduced the first reform bill into the Lords in 1780, was also responsible for directing the construction of the first penitentiary house in England, opened at Horsham in Sussex in 1778.[20]

These men integrated prison reform into a general attack on the administrative and political structure of the ancien régime. They took up Howard's indictment as further proof of the administrative incapacity of the Tory squirearchy. This is not to imply that prison reform became a 'party matter.' The cause enlisted support across the political spectrum. Nevertheless, it was among the Whig Nonconformist reformers that Howard found his most attentive hearing. The success of his crusade therefore was bound up with the whole resurgence of the Whig oppositional tradition.

This resurgence reflects the rise of the Nonconformist petty bourgeoisie into the ranks of the landowning and industrial middle class. The ascent of Howard's own family, from the carpet warehouse to the country estate in one generation, epitomizes the success of a whole segment of Nonconformity. Their struggle, launched in 1769 to repeal the Corporation and Test Acts debarring Dissenters from public office, was their first attempt to win political rights commensurate with their economic power.[21] Howard himself had felt the weight of these acts in 1773 when he found himself required upon taking office as sheriff of Bedford to submit to the humiliation of falsely swearing allegiance to the Thirty-Nine Articles of the Established Church.[22]

The long descent into the American War also helped to revive
Nonconformist political radicalism. Ties of religion, politics,
and commercial interest linked English Nonconformists closely
to the American colonists. To take but one example, Howard's
friend John Fothergill had relatives among the Quakers in
Philadelphia, visited there in the 1750s, and established close
friendships with Benjamin Franklin and Benjamin Rush. When
in London in the 1770s, the Americans joined Fothergill to
discuss politics with other 'Honest Whigs' at fortnightly meetings in the London Tavern.[23] It was in circles such as this that
the political philosophy of the Whigs was revived and recast
in response to the colonial crisis, the struggle over the Test
Acts, and the cause of parliamentary reform. Richard Price,
Joseph Priestley, and James Burgh were the major voices of
this new radicalism. It was to these writers that Rush, Franklin,
and other American revolutionaries turned to justify their
opposition to the British attempt to impose taxes and quarter
standing armies on a people unrepresented in Parliament. From
their writings too came the key principles of the American
constitution, in particular the idea of checks and balances.[24]
In England, the same writers provided Fothergill, Howard,
Bayley, and other Whig reformers with the reasons for supporting the struggle of the colonists.

The actual outbreak of war in 1776 struck men like Fothergill,
Howard, and Price with the force of a personal tragedy. For
a decade they had struggled to mobilize opinion against it and
had tried in vain to devise a compromise that would prevent
a fatal estrangement with their American friends. When the
government persisted in blundering into armed conflict, the
Whig radicals interpreted the war as much more than a political
error. Both Price and Fothergill saw it as nothing less than
divine punishment for a nation that had lost its way morally.
At the outbreak of war, Price wrote:[25]

> In this hour of danger, it would become us to turn our
> thoughts to Heaven. This is what our brethren in the colon-
> ies are doing. From one end of North America to the other
> they are fasting and praying. But what are we doing? -
> shocking thought - we are running wild after pleasure and
> forgetting everything serious and decent in Masquerades -
> we are gambling in gaming houses; trafficking in boroughs;
> perjuring ourselves at elections; and selling ourselves for
> places - which side is providence likely to favour?

In their anguish over their country's fratricidal conflict with
the colonies, they saw writ large the fatal consequence of the
corruption of the political elite. Men who might have opposed
the government's course allowed themselves to be bought off
with offers of place or preferment; others who might have
raised their voices against ministerial folly were too immersed
in pleasure to devote themselves to public issues. The Whig
opposition was in a frame of mind analogous to that of liberal
opponents of the Vietnam War after 1968. The brutalities of

policy abroad seemed to reveal deeper faults in the moral structure of society at home.[26]

The war vindicated the Whig opposition's appeals for political, administrative, and moral reform. It lent credibility to their argument that the imperial blunders of the ministry had occurred because a Parliament seeded with hirelings had lacked the independence to mount an effective opposition. In the strained and disillusioned wartime climate a host of proposals were put forward to restore the power of Parliament, right the balance of the constitution, and root out corruption in government departments. Appearing as it did in 1777, Howard's 'The State of the Prisons' was swept up in the general clamor for reform.

At the center of this ferment was the circle of intellectuals who gathered at Bowood, the estate of the Whig politician Lord Shelburne. Jeremy Bentham, Samuel Romilly, Richard Price, and Joseph Priestley were the leading members of the group. Bowood could be described as the meeting ground of the materialist, scientific strain of Nonconformity represented by Priestley, and the continental Enlightenment, represented by Bentham and Romilly.[27] The relationship between these two traditions is exceedingly complex.

There was much about the *philosophes* that disturbed even those English reformers who admitted their influence. Romilly had family connections with the Rousseauian radicals of Geneva, and he visited most of the leading salons of Paris in the 1780s, paying calls on Diderot, d'Alembert, and Helvetius. He exchanged memoranda on hospitals and criminal law reform with Mirabeau. Until the September Massacres of 1792, Romilly remained a devoted supporter of the French Revolution and wrote two accounts of it for his increasingly apprehensive English audience.[28] His own legal thought owes much to Voltaire, Beccaria, and Montesquieu. Yet Romilly was also the son of a Huguenot watchmaker, and the Huguenot side of his nature was repelled by the atheism and libertinism openly espoused in Paris salons during the 1780s.[29] The same ambivalence is evident in Priestley. As Lord Shelburne's librarian and personal companion, he was required to accompany him on his visits to Paris. Yet he also disapproved of the religious and sexual opinions of the salons and preferred to stay in his hotel rooms as much as possible.[30]

Howard, for his part, called Paris a 'dirty city' and took his ideas instead from good Protestant cities like Amsterdam and Rotterdam.[31] In 'The State of the Prisons', Howard makes little reference to Voltaire, Beccaria, or other key figures involved in the revolution in legal philosophy. In Europe, only the actual institutional practices of places like the Maison de Force seem to have influenced him deeply. In fact, Howard was by his own admission a 'plodder.' He had no taste for French theorizing.[32]

Hence, as Caroline Robbins has argued, the revival of Whig

political ideology in the 1770s probably owed more to a rediscovery of the English radical tradition of the seventeenth
century than to the influence of the European Enlightenment.[33]
Yet the distinction between the English and European traditions must not be overdrawn. References to Montesquieu,
Voltaire, and Beccaria recur in the writings of the Whig ideologues, and though Priestley's materialism drew on English
sources, it was not substantially different from the continental
version articulated by Offray de la Mettrie, Helvetius, or
Cabanis.

English materialism derived largely from the work of David
Hartley and John Locke. Since their doctrine denied the
existence of innate ideas, it offered an immensely influential
'scientific' rebuttal of the idea of original sin, and hence of
the notion that criminals were incorrigible.[34] Materialism enabled
prison reformers to ascribe criminality to incorrect socialization
rather than to innate propensities. As Bentham put it, criminals
were 'froward children, persons of unsound mind,' who lacked
the self-discipline to control their passions according to the
dictates of reason.[35] They were not incorrigible monsters,
merely defective creatures whose infantile desires drove them
to ignore the long-term cost of short-term gratifications.
Crime, therefore, was not sin but improper calculation.

Thus Howard and Bentham both denied criminal incorrigibility,
but from diametrically opposed positions - one accepting the
idea of original sin, the other denying it. One insisted on the
universality of guilt, the other on the universality of reason.
Materialists like Bentham and Priestley asserted that men could
be improved by correctly socializing their instincts for pleasure.
Howard believed men could be changed by awakening their
consciousness of sin.

Howard's thought was cast not in the vernacular of mechanism,
but in an older religious language, closer to Wesley's than to
Hartley's. For him, criminals were not defective machines but
lost souls estranged from God. Nevertheless, during the 1770s
the Hartleian climate of belief in reformist circles did provide
the context necessary for the acceptance of Howard's disciplinary ideas. Materialist psychology, by collapsing the mind-
body distinction, seemed to offer a scientific explanation for
Howard's claim that men's moral behavior could be altered by
disciplining their bodies. Materialist psychology implied that a
regimen applied to the body by the external force of authority
would first become a habit and then gradually be transformed
into a moral preference. Through routinization and repetition,
the regimens of discipline would be internalized as moral
duties.

The materialist conception of reformation also assumed that
such programming could be aided by systematic moral reeduca-
tion directed at the mind. If all ideas, including moral ones,
were derived from external sensation, it followed that people
could be socialized by taking control over their sources of

sensation. The attraction of the 'total institution' then was
that it afforded such a complete measure of control over the
criminal's 'associations.' Materialist optimism of this sort also
pervaded the Whig call for parliamentary and administrative
reform in the 1770s. As James Burgh said, 'An able statesman
can change the manners of the people at pleasure.' Is it not
evident, he asserted, 'that by management the human species
may be moulded into any conceivable shape.'[36]

The factory masters, doctors, and hospital reformers who
took their politics from Burgh and Priestley also spoke of the
human species as machines to be tinkered with and improved.
Josiah Wedgwood boasted that he would 'make machines of men
as cannot err.' Bentham crowed that his Panopticon was a
'machine for grinding rogues honest.' Robert Owen, who was
strongly influenced by the materialism of the 1780s, asserted
that the 'animate mechanisms' of New Lanark had been rendered
as efficient as the 'inanimate mechanisms' under his management.[37]

Some of these disciplinarians, it should be said, saw themselves in terms no less materialistic than they saw their workers.
In 1782, Josiah Wedgwood wrote to cheer up his friend James
Watt, who was tired and depressed from his labors at the Soho
engineering works in Birmingham:[38]

Your mind, my friend, is too active, too powerful for your
body and harasses it beyond its bearing. If this was the
case with any other machine under your direction....you
would soon find out a remedy. For the present permit me to
advise a more ample use of the oil of delegation through your
whole machinery. Seriously, I shall conclude in saying to you
what Dr. Fothergill desired me to say to Brindley, 'Spare
your machine a little or like others under your direction, it
will wear out the sooner by hard and constant usage.'

In the symbolic system that materialist assumptions made possible, managing the self and managing other men became
analogous to the management of machines. Likewise, the reformation of men could be seen, in Bentham's words, as a 'species
of manufacture,' requiring 'its particular capital or stock in
trade,' that is, a technology of its own.[39]

This materialist optimism was an international phenomenon.
In France, it inspired the movement for hospital and asylum
reform during the revolutionary decades. Materialist arguments legitimized the medical profession's struggle to establish
a monopoly over the management of asylums and the discipline
of prisons by casting criminality and insanity as medical
pathologies rooted in the lesions of the brain. P.J.G. Cabanis,
the medical practitioner and ideologist of the revolutionary
period, was particularly influential in spreading the idea that
'criminal habits and aberrations of reason are always accompanied by certain organic peculiarities manifested in the external
form of the body, or in the features of the physiognomy.'[40]
Such arguments were transparent claims to medical hegemony

in the ordering of the deviant. Cabanis was not the first to advance such claims. In 1749, the author of 'Man a Machine,' Offray de la Mettrie, had predicted that there would be a day when guilt and innocence would become matters for medical men alone to decide. As he said, 'It is much to be wish'd that we had none for judges but the most skilful physicians.' This prescient anticipation of the ascendancy that doctors and psychiatrists currently enjoy in the diagnostic stages of the criminal justice process followed naturally from a materialist model of crime that denied individual responsibility.[41]

In France, the most dramatic breakthrough for the medical profession in the field of institutional discipline was the appointment in 1792 of Philippe Pinel as superintendent of the asylum of Bicêtre in Paris. The act that made him famous, striking off the fetters of the insane, is so often regarded only as a humanitarian gesture that its connection to the disciplinary thought of the period has been obscured. As Pinel saw it, chains merely constrained the body. Discipline actually habituated the mind to order. Accordingly, he replaced chains with a disciplinary regimen of surveillance, hard labor, and submission to rules. Pinel's equation of discipline with therapy in turn assumed that madness, like crime, was a loss of self-control, a straying from the path of reason into the entangling thickets of passion. For the mind to regain the path of order, it was necessary first for it to relearn the habits of punctuality, obedience, and diligence.[42]

Pinel's conception of therapy reached England through a translation of his work that appeared in 1806. Like Howard, he found his most receptive and attentive audience among the Quakers. The asylum for the insane founded in 1813 by the York Friends, under the leadership of Samuel Tuke, was the first to replace chaining and blistering of patients with a 'moral regime' supervised by doctors.[43]

In America, the materialist enthusiasm for discipline was articulated chiefly by Benjamin Rush, Philadelphia 'mad doctor,' physician, philanthropist, and politician. Like his friend Fothergill, Rush had imbibed Hartleian views during his student days at Edinburgh medical school.[44] In his 'Enquiry into the Influence of Physical Causes Upon the Moral Faculty' he echoed Cabanis's belief that criminality and insanity were medical pathologies, and he stridently predicted that doctors would soon be able to prescribe cures for crime just as they prescribed 'Peruvian bark for curing the intermittent fever.'[45] Like Cabanis, he maintained that the 'cultivation of the moral faculty' should become the work of the medical profession acting in the name of the state.

In his philanthropic avocations, Rush actually sought to vindicate his disciplinary faith. Along with a number of prominent Philadelphia Quakers, he served on the committee to introduce reformative discipline into the Walnut Street jail. When he visited the prison in 1792 he recorded his satisfaction with the experiment:[46]

> All busy in working at: 1. sawing marble, 2. grinding plaster
> of Paris, 3. weaving, 4. shoemaking, 5. tayloring, 6. turn-
> ing, 7. cutting or chipping logwood.
>   Care of morals: Preaching, reading good books, cleanli-
> ness in dress, rooms etc., bathing, no loud speaking, no
> wine and as little tobacco as possible. No obscene or pro-
> fane conversation. Constant work, familiarity with garden,
> a beautiful one, 1200 heads of cabbages, supplies the jail
> with vegetables, kept by the prisoners....

When the Duc de Rochefoucauld-Liancourt, the French institutional reformer, visited the new prison in 1795, he found
that those condemned for crimes previously punishable by death
were confined in cells 8' by 6' by 9' and were not allowed out
even for exercise. There was a toilet in each cell and a small
penned exercise yard attached so that prisoners remained in
solitude even during recreation. The rest of the prisoners
were confined in dormitories and worked together in workshops
during the day. While the rule of silence was not prescribed,
they were forbidden to 'bawl after one another or to converse
on the causes of their detention or to reproach each other on
any account.' General quiet was necessary, the duke was told,
in order to eliminate the distractions of sense and to prepare
the prisoner 'to be converted, as it were, into a new being.'[47]

The Philadelphia hospital for the insane offered Rush another
opportunity to order men's minds through the regulation of
their bodies. Rush was a consultant at the hospital as well as
the author of a major treatise on insanity. His most notable
contribution to the technology of therapeutic discipline was
'the tranquilizer,' a chair designed to subdue patients suffering from hysteria. They were strapped into the chair, and
their heads were immobilized in a set of wooden blinkers. A
toilet in the seat provided for their evacuations. They were
to remain so confined until they became manageable. For
patients suffering from 'torpid madness,' Rush devised a
'gyrator,' a rotating table. Lethargic or catatonic patients
were strapped down on the table and rotated at high speed to
force blood to the head and to shock the brain, so Rush argued,
into rational activity. Both were discontinued, however, after
patients were injured resisting Rush's benevolent therapies.[48]

While the prison reformers often spoke of deviants as machines
to be tinkered with, they were also able, quite contradictorily,
to think of them, in Hanway's words, as 'free agents, capable
of chosing the good and repenting from evil.'[49] Jeremy Bentham
alternated, with no apparent sense of contradiction, between
referring to criminals as defective mechanisms and calling them
rational creatures entitled to the protection of the community.[50]
Howard insisted not only that criminals were rational, but also
that they were capable of shame. Criminals could be reformed,
in other words, because they had a conscience like everyone

else. As one reformer put it, there was in every person,
criminals included, 'a respect for law which he never violates
by the first offense without a compunction that leaves his mind
open to correction.'[51] The moral law, another reformer wrote,
was 'engraved as it were upon the human mind.'[52]

The reformers had some difficulty finding a place for the idea
of conscience in their associationist assumptions. Materialist
psychology explicitly denied the concept of an innate sense
of right. Duty, Locke had insisted, was not inscribed on the
human heart. It was an obligation learned through the rewards
and punishments that a child received at the hands of authority.
People were rational enough to discern the good, Locke believed,
but if their moral socialization was faulty, there was no inner
voice of conscience to call their ego back from its restless
search for pleasure.[53]

By the 1740s, these unsettling implications had been glossed
over in associationist theory. The third Earl of Shaftesbury
insisted, for example, that people possessed a 'natural moral
sense which enabled them, if not prevented by adverse circumstance or environment to discover the laws of nature and attain
to virtue.'[54] Bishop Butler's sermons in the 1740s took up the
same sunny theme: 'Conscience and self love, if we understand
our true happiness, lead us in the same way. Duty and interest
are perfectly coincident.'[55]

These glosses on the Lockian text spirited the idea of conscience back into associationist moral theory and offered
validation for two distinct and contradictory approaches to
the reformation of the deviant, one through the routinization
of the body, the other through direct appeals to their conscience. In this second conception, the aim of punishment was
to arouse guilt.

The reformers of the 1780s were not the first to discover the
social utility of guilt. In his discussion of corporal punishment
in 'Thoughts on Education,' Locke had argued that tutors
should make sparing use of the rod, lest children lose the
shame of being beaten. 'Shame of doing Amiss and deserving
Punishment,' he said, 'is the only true Restrain belonging
to Virtue.' 'The smart of the rod, if shame accompanies it not,
soon ceases, and is forgotten, and will quickly by use, lose
its terror.'[56] When applied beyond the master-pupil relationship
to the society at large, this idea implied that a social order
ruled by terror could never be as stable as one bound together
by voluntary obligation to the law. As Archbishop Tillotson
was to put it in a sermon that Henry Fielding liked to quote
in the 1750s, 'fear of the Magistrates' power' was but a 'weak
and loose principle of obedience.' It would cease 'whenever
men can rebel with safety and advantage.' Rulers must make
their subjects ashamed to disobey, the archbishop argued.
'Conscience will hold a man fast when all other obligations
break.'[57]

If social order depended on making citizens feel ashamed at

the prospect of punishment, then it was essential that the actual infliction of punishment conserve its moral legitimacy in the eyes of the public. The key problem for social order, therefore, was to represent the suffering of punishment in such a way that those who endured it and those who watched its infliction conserved their moral respect for those who inflicted it. The efficacy of punishment depended on its legitimacy. Hence a paradox: the most painful punishments, those that aroused the greatest guilt, were those that observed the strictest standards of justice and morality. From such punishment there could be no psychological escape into contempt for the punisher, assertions of innocence, or protests against its cruelty. Nothing in the penalty's infliction would divert offenders from contemplating their own guilt. Once convinced of the justice of their sentence and the benevolent intentions of their captors, they could only surrender to the horrors of remorse.

Certainly the reformers of the 1780s were not the first to see that punishment could only arouse guilt if it did not alienate the offender or the public. But they were the first to argue that criminals actually had a capacity for remorse, which could be awakened by carefully legitimated and scientifically inflicted pain. Locke, for example, had been dubious about the reclamation of offenders. He doubted that they had a conscience to work upon. In the 'Second Treatise of Government,' for example, criminals were dismissed as slaves, whose wrongdoings conferred on society the right to exploit them as it saw fit. [58]

Howard, by contrast, had little doubt that he could govern criminals by appealing to their better nature:[59]

The notion that convicts are ungoverneable is certainly erroneous. There is a mode of managing some of the most desperate with ease to yourself and advantage to them. Shew them that you have humanity, and that you aim to make them useful members of society; and let them see and hear the rules and orders of the prison that they may be convinced they are not defrauded in their provisions or clothes, by contractors or gaolers. Such conduct would prevent mutiny in prisons and attempts to escape; which I am fully persuaded are often owing to prisoners being made desperate by the profaneness, inhumanity and ill-usage of their keepers.

If the criminal conscience could be won over by fair treatment, it could also be alienated by abuse. The reformers were insistent that physical punishments like whipping, as well as the squalor of prisons, were eroding respect for law among offenders and the general public at large. Since there does not seem to have been any very noticeable public outcry against prison abuses or physical punishments prior to the reform movement itself, it appears that the reformers took their own heightened sensitivity to physical cruelty as symptomatic of general social feeling.

They warned that 'the capricious severity' of needlessly
frequent executions and bloody public scourgings stigmatized
offenders and 'confirmed them in villainy instead of leading
to a happy alteration in their conduct.'[60] 'Excessive correction,'
as one writer of the 1790s put it, 'counteracts the very intention of the law by drawing from the multitude a greater degree
of compassion for the sufferer than of indignation for the
offense.'[61]

The prison reformers' heightened sensitivity to institutional
abuse and physical cruelty reflected a deep-seated anxiety
about the legitimacy of the legal system in the eyes of the
public, particularly the poor. In the Whig radical advocacy
of parliamentary reform in the 1770s one can detect a similar
anxiety and a desire to use reform to fortify public respect for
law. The Whig political writers liked to dwell, for example,
on the contrast between public order in republican and
monarchical government. Richard Price observed that public
hangings were rare in Massachusetts because the people had
a hand in the making of the laws. In England, where the
citizen's internal obligation was not fortified by democratic
participation, executions were a daily occurrence.[62] Benjamin
Rush echoed this theme in 1787 when he argued that capital
punishments were 'the natural offspring of monarchical governments.' Since kings believe they possess their authority by
divine right, they naturally assume 'the divine power of taking
away human life.' Considering their subjects as their property,
they shed their blood 'with as little emotion as men shed the
blood of sheep or cattle.' Republican governments, he said,
'speak a very different language. They appreciate human life
and increase public and private obligations to preserve it.'[63]

In their effort to devise a firmer basis for social order in an
unequal society, the Whig reformers placed renewed emphasis
on the need for government to conform to the wishes of the
people. None of them, with the exception of Major Cartwright,
could be called democrats, but they all insisted, as Price put
it, that 'civil government...is the creature of the people.'[64]
The propertyless might not be entitled to vote, Burgh said,
but they needed to be convinced that their governors were
seeking the public good and not simply lining their pockets.[65]

The revival of consensual conceptions of authority during
the American War helps to explain the prison reformers' insistence on finding a way to inflict pain without alienating the
offender. But how were they to put such theory into practice?
Howard insisted that 'gentle discipline [was] commonly more
efficacious than severity.'[66] In place of the 'gothic mode of
correction,' he proposed 'the more rational plan' of 'softening
the mind in order to aid its amendment.'[67] As John Brewster,
author of 'On the Prevention of Crimes,' said in a chilling
phrase, 'There are cords of love as well as fetters of iron.'
Undaunted souls who would not bend before the 'passion of
fear' might be won over by 'more tender impressions.'[68] Cords

of love bound minds in guilty remorse; fetters of iron bound only the body, leaving the mind free to fester in anger.

By cords of love, Brewster meant the reformative and utilitarian justifications of punishment that would persuade the offender to accept his sufferings and face his own guilt. It is important to see these new theories of punishment as arguments directed at the prisoner. Reformative theory presented punishment to offenders as being 'in their best interests' while utilitarian theory cast it as an impartial act of social necessity. In rejecting retributive theory, the reformers sought, in effect, to take the anger out of punishment. As it was legitimized to the prisoner, punishment was no longer to be, in Bentham's words, 'an act of wrath or vengeance,' but an act of calculation, disciplined by considerations of the social good and the offenders' needs.[69]

It was the prison chaplain who would bind prisoners with the cords of love. He would persuade offenders to accept their sufferings as an impartial and benevolent condemnation. He would force them to accept their own guilt. It was he who would enclose them in the ideological prison. In the 1790s, prisoners began to hear words such as these from the pulpits of prison chapels:[70]

The laws of our country are not instruments of vengeance but of correction. The punishment inflicted by the magistrate is not to be considered as the resentment of a man subject to various passions, who might mistake or wilfully torture the object of his displeasures, but as a mutual benefit to the offender and that society against which the offence was committed. Harbour not then within your breast any seeds of malice or ill-will against those who have been instrumental in bringing you to punishment.

Yet sermons alone could not convince prisoners to accept the justice of their sufferings. In addition, of course, it was necessary that the discipline of the institution itself give confirmation of the benevolence and impartiality of the legal system. The reformers' task, in other words, was to make punishment self-evidently rational. On this question, Jeremy Bentham proved to be the most influential mind.

His conception of punishment is most graphically illustrated by his discussion of whipping. The severity of a whipping depended on the strength of the person who inflicted it and the degree of indignation that the offender aroused in the crowd. It struck Bentham as unjust and irrational that punishment should vary according to the emotions of those who inflicted it and those who watched. In his view, its severity should depend only on the gravity of the offense. Accordingly, he envisaged a whipping machine, a rotary flail made of canes and whalebone, which could be made to lash the backs of each offender with the same unvarying force to the number of strokes chosen by the operator.[71]

In his conception of pain, therefore, what was rational was

impersonal, and what was impersonal was humane. Punishment
should not be scattered by a monarch's wrathful hand, but
apportioned to each crime as precisely as the market allocated
prices to commodities. Ideally, machines could be used to
inflict the exact price for crime. Punishment would then become
a science, an objective use of pain by the state for the regulation of the egoistic calculus of individuals.

Bentham's idea of a science of pain should be seen in the
context of the widespread belief within the Scottish Enlightenment and the parliamentary reformers of the 1770s that government itself could become a science.[72] Bentham thus was not alone
in believing that men would one day discover the laws govern-
ing finance, administration, and social order. In these theories
of government, punishment occupied pride of place, as the
chief instrument available to a state to canalize the egoistic
pursuits of individuals to lawful ends.[73]

This idea of authority permeated conceptions of philanthropy
in the 1770s. The benevolence of early factory masters and
institutional reformers is often interpreted as an effort to
introduce an idealized version of rural paternalism into an
industrial and institutional context. Yet Wedgwood, Strutt,
or Howard did not use the old language of deference to describe their philanthropy, but chose instead new phrases like
'political humanity' and 'scientific humanity.'[74] They aspired,
as Thomas Bernard of the Society for Bettering the Condition
of the Poor put it in 1798, 'to make the inquiry into all that
concerns the poor and the promotion of their happiness a
science.'[75] In Bernard's mind, this meant replacing indiscriminate almsgiving with a systematic attempt to distinguish between
the deserving and the undeserving poor. In the factory, the
notion of scientific authority implied an attempt to reconcile
the profitable exploitation of labor and the protection of its
moral well-being. In the case of prisons, it meant reconciling
deterrence and rehabilitation, punishment and reform.

But how was a rational authority system to be established in
prisons and factories? How were the imperatives of 'humanity'
and 'terror,' 'profit' and 'benevolence' to be reconciled in
practice? As far as the reformers were concerned, these questions translated into another: how was the supervisory personnel of these institutions to be controlled?

The answer was by an authority of rules. The prison reformers believed that punishment had lost its moral authority among
the poor because those who inflicted it had been allowed unlimited discretion. Prisons had degenerated into squalid nur-
series of crime because magistrates had failed to enforce explicit
rules regarding discipline, hygiene, and hard labor. Corruption, favoritism, and cruelty flowered in prisons because the
keepers' authority was not kept in check by rules and inspections. In place of 'unregulated discretion' the reformers proposed to substitute 'mild government by rule.'[76]

In Howard's mind, the rules were supposed to apply to the

staff no less than to the prisoners. Half of the new rules that
he proposed were directed against trafficking, verbal abuse,
fee taking, or physical acts of cruelty by staff. They also laid
out a sequence of custodial tasks, inspection tours, roll calls,
bed checks, and night patrols. The guards no less than the
inmates were to be routinized by formal regulations.[77]

The reformers' attack on the fee system was particularly
designed to limit custodial discretion. By abolishing fees, the
reformers hoped to convert the keeper from an independent
contractor into a paid subordinate of the state. To ensure his
accountability, the reformers proposed that quarterly inspections by magistrates become mandatory.

This attack on discretion implied that punishment was too
central to the exercise of class rule to be left to private contractors. Instead, the state would now supervise its infliction
directly.

The rules also applied to the prisoners and prescribed a
minute grid of deprivations designed to standardize the institutional day, to add the burden of monotony to the terrors of
solitude, and above all to silence the inmate subculture. That
subculture, no less than the keepers' discretion, had frustrated attempts to inflict a just and unvarying quantum of pain.
The rules were intended to win back the prison from both the
criminals and their keepers. In place of the unwritten, customary, and corrupt division of power between criminals and
custodians, the reformers proposed to subject both to the
disciplines of a formal code enforced from the outside.

Inspection was to be the watchword of the new authority. In
'Panopticon,' the sketch for a penitentiary that he published
in 1791, Bentham placed both prisoner and guard alike under
the constant surveillance of an inspector patrolling in the
central inspection tower. From this vantage point, the inspectors
had a clear view of the prisoners in their cells and the guards
on their rounds. In this way, the custodial staff were kept
'under the same irresistible control' as the prisoners.[78]

Such inspection was to be democratic. Members of the general
public were given free admission to the inspection tower to keep
the inspectors under surveillance. Omnipresent inspection,
of everyone, by everyone, was Bentham's solution to the old
question of who guards the guards.

Rules, therefore, had a double meaning for the reformers.
They were an enumeration of the inmates' deprivations, but
also a charter of their rights. They bound both sides of the
institutional encounter in obedience to an impartial code enforced
from outside. As such they reconciled the interests of the state,
the custodians, and the prisoners alike.

Solitary confinement, likewise, reconciled terror and humanity. The reformers did not doubt that it was an instrument of
suffering. John Brewster dwelt graphically on the anguish that
solitude would induce:[79]

To be abstracted from a world where he has endeavoured to

confound the order of society, to be buried in a solitude
where he has no companion but reflection, no counsellor
but thought, the offender will find the severest punishment
he can receive. The sudden change of scene that he experiences, the window which admits but a few rays of light,
the midnight silence which surround him, all inspire him
with a degree of horror which he never felt before. The impression is greatly heightened by his being obliged to think.
No intoxicating cup benumbs his senses, no tumultuous
revel dissipates his mind. Left alone and feelingly alive to
the strings of remorse, he revolves on his present situation
and connects it with that train of events which has banished
him from society and placed him there.

Solitude, as Jonas Hanway did not hesitate to admit, was the
'most terrible penalty,' short of death, that a society could
inflict. It was also, he insisted, 'the most humane.'[80] No rough
or brutal hands were laid upon the offenders. The state, as
it were, struck off their chains and withdrew, leaving them
alone with their conscience. In the silence of their cells,
superintended by an authority too systematic to be evaded,
too rational to be resisted, prisoners would surrender to the
lash of remorse. 'He who torments mankind,' said Offray de la
Mettrie, 'becomes his own tormentor.'[81]

Such was the theory of the penitentiary as enunciated by the
constituency of Nonconformist doctors, philanthropists, and
magistrates in London and the manufacturing towns who arose
to support Howard's crusades. They took up the idea of the
penitentiary because, as a system of authority and as a machine
for the remaking of men, it reflected some of their deepest
political, psychological and religious assumptions. It promised,
above all, to restore the legitimacy of a legal system that they
feared was jeopardized by the excessive severities and gratuitous abuses of the Bloody Code.

Yet the appeal of the penitentiary reached beyond this
immediate milieu to figures like William Blackstone and to scores
of rural justices who were later to launch the construction of
new prisons. Their support for prison reform cannot be
explained in terms of an intellectual affinity with Howard's
conception of discipline, but in terms of the objective urgency
of reform in the decade of the 1770s. Had Howard's 'State of
the Prisons' been published at any other time, figures outside
the small circle of reforming Dissenters might have been disposed to dismiss it as a worthy but tedious tract. Instead, it
appeared at a moment of acute crisis in the administration of
criminal justice.

References
 1 Elizabeth Isichei, 'Victorian Quakers', 1970, pp.xx-xxi;
   E.D. Bebb, 'Nonconformity and Social and Economic Life,
   1660-1800', 1935, pp.60-70.
 2 John Bellers, 'Proposals for Raising a Colledge of

Industry...', 1696; Samuel Tuke, 'Description of the Retreat, An Institution Near York for Insane Persons of the Society of Friends', 1813; Philadelphia, 'Report' of the Society for Alleviating the Misery of Public Prisons, 1786.

3 Arthur Raistrick, 'Quakers in Science and Industry' (1950), 1968 ed., pp.290-301.

4 J. Howard, 'An Account of the Principal Lazarettos of Europe', 1789, p.133.

5 See also J.C. Lettsom, 'Of the Improvement of Medicine in London on the Basis of Public Good', 2nd ed., 1775; also his 'Hints Respecting the Prison of Newgate', 1794.

6 J.M. Good, 'A Dissertation on the Diseases of Prisons and Poorhouses', 1795, p.27.

7 Daniel Layard, 'Directions to Prevent Jail Distemper', 1772, pp.5-6.

8 Benjamin Rush, 'The Autobiography of Benjamin Rush', ed. by G.W. Corner, 1948, p.94; David Hartley, 'Observations on Man' (1749), 1792 ed.

9 Thomas Percival, 'Medical Ethics', 1803, pp.128-9.

10 Jonas Hanway, 'The Neglect of the Effectual Separation of Prisoners and the Want of Good Order and Religious Economy in our Prisons...', 1784, p.4.

11 William Turner, An Essay on Crimes and Punishments (1784), in 'Memoirs of the Literary and Philosophical Society of Manchester', II, 1785; A.E. Musson and Eric Robinson, 'Science and Technology in the Industrial Revolution', 1969, p.196; Brian Simon, 'Studies in the History of Education', 1960, pp.18-32.

12 Neil McKendrick, Wedgwood and his Friends, 'Horizon' 1, no.5. May 1959, pp.88-96, 128-30; Arthur Raistrick, 'Dynasty of Iron Founders: The Darbys and Coalbrookdale', 1953, p.98; Eric Roll, 'An Early Experiment in Industrial Organization', 1930; S.D. Chapman, 'The Early Factory Masters', 1967, p.196.

13 R.S. Fitton and A.P. Wadsworth, 'The Strutts and the Arkwrights', 1958, pp.97-8; Chapman, 'Factory Masters', p.157; Neil McKendrick, Josiah Wedgwood and Factory Discipline, 'Historical Journal' 4, no.1, 1961, pp.30-55.

14 P.P. 1815, III, p.217.

15 McKendrick, Wedgwood and Factory Discipline, p.34.

16 McKendrick, Wedgwood and His Friends, pp.90-4.

17 J. Aikin, 'A View of the Character and Public Services of the Late John Howard', 1792, p.229; John Fothergill, 'Chain of Friendship; Selected Letters of Dr. John Fothergill of London, 1735-1780', ed. Betsy C. Corner and Christopher C. Booth, 1971, p.492; Christopher Wyvill, 'Political Papers', IV, 1794, pp.236-7; Caroline Robbins, 'The Eighteenth Century Commonwealthman', 1961, p.354.

18 John Jebb, 'Thoughts on the Construction and Polity of Prisons', 1785.

19 Ian Christie, 'Wilkes, Wyvill and Reform', 1962, p.85;
Josiah Dornford, 'Nine Letters...to the Lord Mayor and
Aldermen of London', 1786; William Smith, 'State of the
Gaols in London, Westminster...', 1776; on Smith see
Surrey R.O. QS 2/1/25; William Blizard, 'Desultory Reflections on Police', 1785; see also D.N.B.
20 A.G. Olson, 'The Radical Duke', 1961, pp.52-4; West
Sussex, R.O. QAP/4, 1778.
21 Anthony Lincoln, 'Some Political and Social Ideas of English
Dissent, 1763-1800', 1938, pp.24-5.
22 Aikin, 'View', pp.58-64.
23 Robbins, 'Commonwealthman', p.336.
24 Bernard Bailyn, 'The Ideological Origins of the American
Revolution', 1967, pp.40-1.
25 Quoted in Lincoln, 'Dissent', p.133.
26 Fothergill, 'Chain of Friendship', p.492; also his Considerations Relative to the North American Colonies (1765) and An
English Freeholder's Address to his Countrymen (1779)
in 'Works', ed. J.C. Lettsom, 1803, pp.444-83; Richard
Price, 'Observations on the Nature of Civil Liberty', 1776,
pp.14, 73; Joseph Priestley, 'An Address to the Dissenters
on the Subject of the Difference with America', 1775.
27 John Norris, 'Shelburne and Reform', 1963, p.83; Joseph
Priestley, 'Memoirs: Written by Himself to the Year 1795',
1902 ed., pp.47-54.
28 Samuel Romilly, 'Letters Containing An Account of the
Late Revolution in France', 1792; 'Thoughts on the Probable
Influence of The French Revolution on Great Britain',
1790.
29 Romilly, 'Memoirs of the Life of Sir Samuel Romilly Written
by Himself...', 1840, I, p.227.
30 Priestley, 'Memoirs', p.47.
31 Bodleian Misc. Eng. Mss. e. 399.
32 Aikin, 'View', p.225.
33 Robbins, 'Commonwealthman', p.7; Lincoln, 'Dissent', p.2.
34 Hartley, 'Observations on Man', pp.15-17.
35 Jeremy Bentham, 'Letter to Lord Pelham', 1802, p.5;
'Panopticon', 1791, p.40; Samuel Denne, 'Letter to Sir
Robert Ladbroke...', 1771, pp.58-9.
36 James Burgh, 'Political Disquisitions', III, 1775, pp.176-8.
37 Bentham, 'Letter to Lord Pelham', p.6; Robert Owen, 'A
New View of Society...', 1813, p.95; McKendrick, Wedgwood
and Factory Discipline, p.34.
38 Julia Wedgwood, 'The Personal Life of Josiah Wedgwood',
1915, p.295.
39 Bentham, 'Letter to Lord Pelham', p.6.
40 P.J.G. Cabanis, 'Sketch of the Revolutions of Medical
Science and Views Relating to its Reform', 1806, pp.304-11;
Claude Adrien Helvetius, 'A Treatise on Man', 1777 ed.,
II, pp.440-47; Cabanis, 'Rapports du physique et du moral
de l'homme', 1830 ed., I, p.455.

41 Offray de la Mettrie, 'Man a Machine', 1750 ed., pp.43-4; Harvey Mitchell, Nature, Knowledge and Power: Hospital Reform, Poverty and Medicine in France, 1774-1800, unpublished paper, 1977, University of British Columbia; Michel Foucault et al., 'Les Machines à guérir: aux origines de l'hôpital moderne', 1976; L.S. Greenbaum, Health Care and Hospital Building in France: Reform Proposals of Dupont de Nemours and Condorcet, 'Studies in Voltaire and the Eighteenth Century' 152, no.2, 1976, pp.895-930; Jean-Pierre Peter, Disease and the Sick at the End of the Eighteenth Century, in Robert Forster and Orest Ranum, eds, 'Biology of Man in History', 1975, pp.85-124.
42 Philippe Pinel, 'A Treatise on Insanity', 1806 ed.; M. Foucault, 'Madness and Civilization', 1965.
43 Tuke, 'Description of the Retreat'; Kathleen Jones, 'Lunacy, Law and Conscience', 1955; William Parry-Jones, 'The Trade in Lunacy', 1972.
44 Nathan G. Goodman, 'Benjamin Rush: Physician and Citizen', 1934; Sarah Reidman and C.C. Green, 'Benjamin Rush', 1964.
45 Benjamin Rush, 'An Enquiry into the Influence of Physical Causes Upon the Moral Faculty' (1786), 1839 ed., p.21.
46 Rush, 'Autobiography', p.80; David Rothman, 'The Discovery of the Asylum', 1971, pp.92-3.
47 Duke de La Rochefoucauld-Liancourt, 'A Comparative View of Mild and Sanguinary Laws', 1796, p.20.
48 Goodman, 'Rush', p.267.
49 Hanway, 'Defects of Police', p.xii.
50 Bentham, 'Rationale of Punishment', p.28.
51 G.O. Paul, 'Considerations on the Defects of Prison', 1784, p.50.
52 Turner, Essay on Crimes and Punishments.
53 John Locke, 'An Essay Concerning Human Understanding', ed. Peter H. Nidditch, I, iii, 5-12.
54 Robbins, 'Commonwealthman', p.14.
55 Butler, 'Fifteen Sermons', p.47.
56 J.L. Axtell, ed., 'The Educational Writings of John Locke', 1968, p.177.
57 Quoted in H. Fielding, 'A Proposal', p.77.
58 Locke, 'The Second Treatise of Government (1698)', Laslett ed., 1968, II, 8; VI, 85.
59 Howard, 'Lazarettos', p.222.
60 John Brewster, 'On the Prevention of Crimes', 1792, pp.4-5.
61 Eden, 'Principles', p.13; Romilly, 'Life', II, p.486.
62 Price, 'Observations', p.14.
63 Benjamin Rush, 'An Enquiry into the Effects of Public Punishments and Upon Society', 1787, p.13; also his 'Considerations on the Injustice and Impolicy of Punishing Murder by Death', 1792.
64 Price, 'Observations', p.6; Joseph Priestley, 'Lectures on History and General Policy', 1826 ed., pp.342-4.

65 Burgh, 'Disquisitions', p.216.
66 John Howard, 'The State of the Prisons in England and Wales...', 1777, p.39.
67 Ibid., pp.39-40.
68 Brewster, 'On the Prevention of Crimes', pp.4-5.
69 Jeremy Bentham, 'Rationale of Punishment', 1830, p.21; A.C. Ewing, 'The Morality of Punishment', 1929, p.5; H.L.A. Hart, 'Punishment and Responsibility', 1968, p.10.
70 Brewster, 'Sermons for Prisons', 1790, p.15.
71 Bentham, 'Rationale of Punishment', p.82.
72 Joseph Priestley, 'An Essay on the First Principles of Government', 1768, p.129; 'Lectures on History', p.398; William Godwin, 'Enquiry Concerning Political Justice', ed. K.C. Carter, 1971, p.68.
73 The centrality of punishment as the chief instrument of the state is clearly outlined in Locke, 'Second Treatise', I, 6.
74 Jebb, 'Prisons', p.x; Hutchins, 'Hanway', p.35.
75 Society for Bettering the Condition of the Poor, 'Reports', 1798, p.xii; Eileen Yeo, Social Science and Social Change: a Social History of Social Science and Social Investigation in Britain, 1830-1890, unpublished Ph.D. thesis, University of Sussex, 1972, for discussion of Bernard; David E. Owen, 'English Philanthropy, 1660-1960', 1964, p.97.
76 G.O. Paul, 'An Address to His Majesty's Justices of the Peace...', 1809, p.48.
77 Howard, 'Lazarettos', p.174; Beds. R.O. PE 254/1801; Berks. R.O. QAG/3/1; Lancs. R.O. QGV/2/2/1793; for examples of early penitentiary rules.
78 Bentham, 'Panopticon', p.39.
79 Brewster, 'On the Prevention of Crimes', p.27.
80 Hanway, 'Solitude in Imprisonment', p.141.
81 Mettrie, 'Man a Machine', p.43.

Policing

4   Towards a national standard of police

Leon Radzinowicz

[...] All this deference to local autonomy, to the right of parishes, towns, Quarter Sessions and others to decide for themselves what kind and quantity of police they would have and whether, indeed, they would have any effective police at all, could not disguise the increasingly obvious fact that whenever real emergencies arose the provincial authorities were relying for help upon the central government. In cases of riots, disturbances, lock-outs, often in cases of serious crime, the cry was for the Metropolitan Police or the army. The renewed Chartist threats to public order in 1842 and again in 1848 served to emphasise this dependence. In the same years the figures of commitments for trial reached unprecedented heights: over thirty-one thousand for 1842, over thirty thousand for 1848.

The pressure of popular unrest upon inadequate police was felt again both in county and borough areas. New forces, where they had been established, had not had time to organise themselves, to gain public acceptance or to consolidate their positions before the second wave of Chartism broke over them in 1842. Many, as has been seen, were still very inadequate. In Lancashire, one of the most troubled areas, the force was actually reduced by two hundred men at the beginning of August 1842. Rioting broke out within a few days and the police, in the words of the Chief Constable, found themselves 'completely crippled'.[1] A force of seventeen men in Preston was beaten by the mob who became masters of the town until troops arrived.[2] Even the boroughs where police forces had been imposed by special statute were not exempt from trouble. In Bolton the mob virtually took possession of the town for a whole day before troops could relieve it.[3] In Manchester the rioters, armed with bludgeons and pikes, levied money and food in the suburbs whilst the police, themselves unarmed, were 'dreadfully abused', one killed and others dangerously

Source: 'A History of the English Criminal Law', Stevens, 1968, vol.4, pp.270-302.

injured.[4] In Birmingham a Chartist leader was alleged to have
claimed that a 'raw lobster' (a policeman) had been thrown
into the canal by his bodyguard, and military, pensioners and
special constables were called out.[5] Riots were particularly
severe in the Potteries where the few constables who tried to
keep order were at the mercy of the mobs, who easily retained
the upper hand until the military arrived.[6] Even in rural areas
a police station was demolished, a policeman murdered.[7]

Evidence accumulated that the traditional devices for meeting
such situations were obsolescent. In 1842 information came from
various sources on the difficulty of recruiting special constables to face rioters and their comparative helplessness even
if recruited.[8] Appeals for their support proved more effective
during the last Chartist crisis in 1848, when many enrolled
not only in London but in Manchester, Liverpool and the Potteries and perhaps the most serious of the provincial disturbances, at Ashton-under-Lyne, was put down by the efforts
of a large number of special constables with only a small body
of soldiers.[9] But it was clear that they could not meet the bulk
of emergencies, and the Home Office was most reluctant to see
them armed.[10]

Nor was there any repetition of the suggestion made by the
government in 1839 that armed voluntary associations should
come forward for the protection of property; though a few in
fact did so their value was not very great.[11] The general
official policy was not to put arms into circulation. On the
advice of the Duke of Wellington they were supplied only to
pensioners in Manchester and Birmingham.[12] There was hesitation in allowing them for the regular police, and Sir Charles
Shaw had to write twice to the Home Office even to obtain a
supply of cutlasses to enable his force to face the armed mobs
in Manchester. At the peak of the Rebecca riots in South Wales
in the following year, the Home Office would at first allow only
cutlasses to the detachment of Metropolitan Police sent down
to help, though it later agreed that the magistrates could dis-
tribute firearms on their own responsibility.[13] In 1848 the
necessity of arming the police to meet special emergencies was
admitted not only in the metropolis but in some provincial
boroughs, such as Manchester and Liverpool, but it remained
a very exceptional measure.[14]

The weakening of traditional local devices for dealing with
disorder was not the only thing that urged local authorities
towards the establishment of adequate regular police forces.
The government might not be willing to proceed forthwith
to legislative compulsion, but it increasingly put other pressures upon them to accept the responsibilities for police which
they so vehemently claimed. This was done by withdrawing,
tentatively at first but later absolutely, the alternative resources
upon which they had come to rely. The response to local
demands for the help of the Metropolitan Police and the army
hardened as a matter of deliberate policy.

The decision to allow London police to go to Wales in 1843 was only a temporary reversal of the general policy followed in this respect by the Home Office during the riots of 1842. Sir James Graham, well remembering the events in Birmingham in 1839, was completely opposed to sending the Metropolitan Police to supplement inadequate provincial forces. On a suggestion that a detachment should be despatched to Scotland in August 1842, he wrote to Peel, 'I could not detach at this moment more than 20 men; as a Force they could not be powerful; as an interference on my part with their local arrangements, it would diminish their responsibility for keeping the peace; and if anything went wrong, the London Police would bear the blame.'[15]

Home Office resistance to sending detachments of police from the metropolis to deal with the Rebecca riots in the following year was at first equally strong. The first request for help from the Carmarthenshire magistrates in April received the blunt reply that 'It is the duty of the magistracy either by the adoption of the Rural Police Act or by the swearing in special constables to preserve the tranquility of the County and to put down outrages . . . Sir James Graham is not prepared to supply civil force at the public expense to put down these local disturbances.'[16] Three officers had, however, been despatched to help organise a patrolling force of special constables, though this proved to be of little use.[17] The next demand came from Cardiganshire. Again refusing to comply, the Home Office promised instead that if a rural police were established two officers would be sent to help set it on foot.[18] A little later there was a further request from the Vice-Lieutenant of Carmarthenshire,[19] and the Home Office, abandoning their intransigent attitude, at last sent down a score of policemen. Finally, in October a detachment of fifty was detailed for duty in the disturbed districts of Wales, to co-operate with both the civil and military authorities. Eventually, since this force was obviously far too small to deal effectively with disturbances so formidable, so well organised, and so widespread, and since special constables were not forthcoming,[20] troops had to be called in.

These concessions were made, however, in the expectation that magistrates would regard them as exceptional and would at once proceed to establish police forces in their own counties. That was far from being the attitude of some of them. Even in counties where such measures had been under serious consideration they were abandoned once the London police had provided an increased sense of security, the magistrates going so far as to repudiate any obligation to cover the expense of the detachments out of the county rates.[21] Only under the threat that the military would be withdrawn if a rural police were not established did the Cardiganshire magistrates comply in 1844; those of Radnorshire would go no further than the appointment of three superintendents to supervise parish constables.[22]

Similar tussles took place in England. In Staffordshire the magistrates were warned that 'unless an adequate police force be provided in the Potteries the military must be withdrawn since they cannot be allowed to supply the place of constables.'[23] As a result they decided to adopt the Rural Constabulary Act of 1839 for the area, and followed this up in 1843 by adopting it for the whole county. In the West Riding of Yorkshire, where conditions were equally bad and where the local magistrates had been so rash as to apply for reimbursement of the cost of providing barracks for troops brought in to protect them, the Home Office went to the length of asking the military commander for the North-Eastern District, General Brotherton, to send a report on the state of the police.[24]

> The town of Huddersfield during these disturbances [he replied] was a most conspicuous and deplorable example of the helplessness of such large towns without an adequate police force . . . nowhere did the magistrates betray more alarm and nowhere did they rely so exclusively on the troops for protection, expressing at the same time their total want of confidence in the special constabulary force and consequently bringing the troops at once into contact with the mob without any previous attempt to disperse it by the special constables or the three constables, which three constables, I believe, constitute the total amount of permanent civil force kept up in this extensive and populous town.

He added his own opinion that, whilst it might be economical and convenient for the local magistrates, who were manufacturers, to have troops to protect their property, this was a misuse of the armed forces and not the means most conducive to public safety. Meanwhile, the Home Office had also written to the Lord-Lieutenant, getting the reply that he himself had already pointed out to the magistrates the urgent necessity of adopting the Act of 1839, but that he thought it most improbable that they would do so.[25]

Such a situation brought out the basic weakness of the existing system on both sides. The local magistrates and Watch Committees, having to face the responsibility for the whole expense of such police as they appointed, tended to appoint as few as possible. The Home Office, uneasily aware that the public peace throughout the country was threatened by this attitude, reacted strongly against being blackmailed into providing central protection, by means either of the metropolitan force or the army. Yet, as it made no contribution to the cost of local forces, it had no means of obliging local authorities to provide forces which were either adequate in numbers or efficient in organisation and operation.

The importance both of the financial element and of local resentment of pressure from the centre was very apparent in the attempts made to induce the Durham magistrates to increase the county police force following strikes and unrest in the local

collieries in 1844. In that year some thirty thousand miners
had laid down their picks, and almost every mine in Northumberland and Durham stood idle.[26] The urgency of increasing the
police to deal with such emergencies in future was impressed
upon the magistrates, on the recommendation of the Home Office,
by Lord Londonderry, the Lord-Lieutenant. Since it had just
been agreed that the new collieries and railways in the area
should contribute to the county rate he hoped that the obstacle
of expense would no longer be regarded as insuperable. The
response, however, was disappointing: a motion to increase
the county police at once met violent opposition from Whig
magistrates who 'would not hear of Govt. Recommendation as
any reason to influence their Conduct'. He could only hope
either that the magistrates with agricultural interests would
change their minds when they saw the mining districts paying
their fair share of rates, or that when another miners' strike
broke out, the magistracy, again forced to ask for government
aid, would 'perceive their present folly in not taking advice
and fair and proper precautions against the moment of need.'[27]
The Home Secretary was left with no further weapon to secure
compliance: he could do no more than 'extremely regret' the
situation.

As in other matters, the widespread alarm stirred up by the
Chartist revival in 1848 brought a temporary relaxation of the
veto on sending troops. Russell and Sir George Grey were
more prepared to temporise than Peel and Graham. The state
of society had altered, argued Russell, since 'the time when
every man was ready to arm to go out into the streets for the
purpose of keeping the peace of the town.' When municipal
authorities had done what they could in recruiting special
constables they generally had to apply for military aid as well.[28]
But there were no more detachments of the Metropolitan Police
and exhortations to provide a basic regular force locally, as
a first line of defence, were renewed.

In 1844 a circular had gone to thirty-eight boroughs with
populations of twenty thousand or more which had not provided police in the proportion of one to every thousand inhabitants, warning them of the decision to withdraw altogether the
many small military detachments stationed up and down the
country. This made it unequivocally clear that the army was not
under any circumstances to be used as a substitute for police.
There should be sufficient civil force in all large towns not only
to protect life and property in ordinary circumstances but,
with the aid of special constables, to repress any sudden
disturbance of the peace. It was hoped that the withdrawal
of troops would force upon the boroughs the urgent necessity
of placing their police forces on a better footing. Only fourteen of them did so.

THE CASE FOR COMPULSION

The condition of stalemate was more apparent than real. The
hope had always been that permissive rather than mandatory
legislation, local rather than central control, would eventually
make regular police forces generally acceptable. Taking the
country as a whole, the results were disappointing, but there
were some areas in which the permissive approach succeeded.
In these pioneers were able, like the first Commissioners in
London, to demonstrate the usefulness and possibilities of
county forces on the basis allowed by the Rural Constabulary
Acts, and to secure the increasing support of magistrates and
public. On this success mandatory legislation could be based.
    The most prominent of the county pioneers was J.B.B.
M'Hardy. In his brilliant essay on Victorian England, G.M.
Young observes:[29]

> There are many famous men to whom England owes less than
> she owes to Captain M'Hardy, Chief Constable of Essex. But
> his career, and his achievement, are typical of a general
> rule. The English administration was made by administrators
> throwing out their lines until they met and formed a system.

Essex had been amongst the first counties to set up a force
under the Rural Constabulary Acts and M'Hardy was its first
Chief Constable. At the outset he had to contend with widespread distrust, but eventually he won the full support of both
the magistrates and the community. In many respects his contribution to the establishment of county police forces throughout the country was comparable to that of Mayne and Rowan in
the establishment and development of the Metropolitan Police,
which had served as a pattern and inspiration for many of the
large provincial boroughs.
    On the basis of thorough local knowledge the county was split
up into divisions, each of these into detachments, and these
again into guards or beats. The total force of just over two
hundred men was thus distributed over the county, carrying
out a regular system of patrols. Horse patrols were avoided
where possible, except for supervisory purposes, since M'Hardy
considered them 'most inefficient in the detection of crimes;
the very noise of a horse's feet upon the road will disturb a
depredator, and he will conceal himself; it is a beacon for him
to avoid.' Station houses, strong rooms and barracks for the
men were gradually provided in each division.
    As in the metropolis, special stress was laid upon securing
the goodwill and co-operation of those living in the areas where
the police had to operate. The fear of rendering them unpopular
led M'Hardy to prohibit the training of constables in the use of
arms, even though he was anxious to avoid, so far as possible,
the employment of the army in lieu of police to deal with disorders. He held that the police were a more flexible body for
this purpose, since they could act singly or in twos or threes
whereas army detachments could function only as a body. It was

with an eye both to the popularity of the police and to its
efficiency that he strictly enforced the rule under which constables were forbidden to accept rewards without his special
permission, a permission which he normally gave only when a
man had risked his life. It was, he believed, the principal evil
of the old parochial system that constables had 'an interest in
the increase of crime'. One of the great benefits of the county
constabulary system, on the contrary, was that 'the poor man
is protected, and the same interest is taken to follow up any
injury he may receive as in the case of a rich man: whereas
in the older system, unless the party can produce the funds
the parochial officer will not follow up the case, and it cannot
be expected that he should do so at his own expense.' The scale
of fees for such special duties as attendance at Quarter Sessions
was strictly regulated.

Another method of gaining public support by increasing
police efficiency, and incidentally reducing the burden on the
rates, was much favoured by M'Hardy. This was the practice
of assigning to the rural constable a number of incidental duties
not directly connected with the prevention or detection of
crime or the maintenance of public order. The constable could
be employed as an inspector of weights and measures, perhaps
also to inspect highways, collect taxes and act as postman.[30]
Above all, and more closely in line with his police duties, he
could act as an assistant relieving officer, helping to repress
vagrancy and supervise the lower type of lodging house.

Early hopes that the New Poor Law would solve the problem
of vagrancy had been disappointed. Far from being discouraged
by the hardships of the Union Workhouses, habitual tramps
had come to regard them as a chain of free hostels. Such
additional deterrents as separate wards, tasks of work before
leaving, orders to relieving officers to hand wastrels and
impostors over to the police, were equally ineffective.[31] Up to
1848 the numbers of vagrants had continued to multiply. Poor
Law inspectors said that vagrants courted imprisonment by
refusing to work or committing other offences. A closer link
between poor law, police and prison authorities was called for;
it was even suggested that the whole care of vagrants should
be handed over to the police. Short of this, the employment of
police as assistant relieving officers was welcomed by the
President of the Poor Law Board. With the more stringent
enforcement thus introduced, the number of vagrants applying
for relief was reduced to a tenth between 1848 and 1853.[32]

One effect of the success of M'Hardy in organising the Essex
police against crime and vagrancy was the adoption of the
Rural Constabulary Acts in most of the adjoining counties also –
Suffolk, Cambridgeshire, Hertfordshire, though not Kent – as
well as further afield.[33] In other areas, where forces were
already established, poor law guardians adopted with enthusiasm
the idea of appointing police as assistant relieving officers.
When Colonel Oakes in Norfolk withdrew his co-operation from

such a scheme at Downham the guardians appealed to the
Home Secretary to make the practice general and compulsory,
so certain were they that it offered the only chance of breaking
up organised vagrancy and that it would 'also tend very
materially to aid the Police in the performance of other Parts
of their duty by bringing under their observation a large
number of the most worthless characters'.[34]

Though not all M'Hardy's ideas were accepted for general
application there can be no doubt that the recommendations
of the Select Committee appointed in March 1852 'to consider
the Expediency of adopting a more Uniform System of Police
in England and Wales, and in Scotland' were dominated by his
evidence and his experience.[35]

Not all was well, however, even in M'Hardy's Essex. It was
soon clear that one of the greatest obstacles to efficient
county forces was the independent borough force. This was
especially true of the smaller boroughs, but many of the larger
were little better. Neither in 1842 nor in 1848 had the borough
forces been able to make an effective stand against the
Chartists.[36] Durham in 1848 had a force of seven men. In some
cases, as at Bolton, it was the Watch Committee itself that
had opposed extension of the police even when danger was
imminent.[37] In Essex, M'Hardy complained, such towns as
Maldon, Saffron Walden, Harwich and Colchester wanted help
from the county when they got into difficulties but would not
take advantage of the provisions which would have allowed
them to amalgamate their forces with the county constabulary.
He quoted especially the example of Maldon, with its one
policeman, where 'at the last election, for want of proper peace
officers, there were a number of boxers brought from London
to protect one party, whilst the gipsies protected the other.'[38]
His experience led him to recommend strongly that borough
forces should be compulsorily amalgamated with those of the
counties.

Subsequent enquiries went far to show that the problem
was widespread. As Sir John Pakington observed in 1853,
'some of the larger towns had, at great expense, organised
an admirable police, but there were others of them whose
arrangements in this respect were wretched beyond description.'[39] Sir George Grey confirmed this in detail in 1856; he
was convinced that the problem of the reform of the provincial
police as a whole could not be separated from that of the
borough police, and especially of the smaller boroughs.[40] Eight
boroughs, with an aggregate population exceeding thirty-two
thousand, had still only one policeman for duty by day and
night. In each of twenty others, whose population totalled
eighty-two thousand, there were two. As regards individual
towns of moderate size, the information given to the House by
Grey may be summarised as in Table 4.1. In twelve more towns,
densely populated centres of social unrest with a large concentration of the labouring and poorer classes, containing

nearly half a million inhabitants, the total strength of the
police force amounted to two hundred and forty-six.

Table 4.1

Towns	Population	Number of police
Ashton-under-Lyne	30,500	17
Berwick	15,000	4
Blackburn	47,000	26
Bolton	61,000	27
Coventry	37,000	21
Oldham	53,000	32
Preston	70,000	37
South Shields	29,000	14
Stockport	54,000	24
Tynemouth	29,000	15
Warrington	23,000	10
York	36,000	29

As many as sixty-four of the boroughs coming within the
scope of the Municipal Corporations Act had populations of
under five thousand. They nevertheless almost all remained
independent of the counties, and though their police forces, if
any, could operate in the county area, the county police had
no powers within their boundaries. Only thirteen boroughs
had taken advantage of the provision for voluntary amalgamation between their forces and those of the adjacent counties,
though the weakness of borough forces was proved by the frequent applications for outside help. Nor was inadequacy of
numbers their only fault. The powers of the Watch Committee
to appoint and dismiss police of all ranks, the influence of
local political rivalries and trade interests upon their decisions,
the division of responsibility between them and the magistrates -
all these undermined the integrity and efficiency of borough
police organisations.[41] The very existence of many of them
hampered the development of the county police.

The implications of this situation had already been noticed
in the press. 'Crime concerns, not only the individual, the
parish, or the county, but the nation generally.' On this
ground the 'Edinburgh Review' demanded in 1852 that 'the
effort for its extirpation should be national likewise.' Criminals
went freely from one district to another, and for a county, let
alone a parish, to insist upon its right to independent and
isolated action was nothing less than to claim the privilege of
giving impunity to crime. The police system would not be perfect until the criminal population was placed under effective
supervision everywhere and all the time, until police information
was available to all, until there was an efficient organisation
in each district for local purposes, and the whole was directed,

in harmonious co-operation, to the common purpose of detecting
and repressing crime.[42]

The same outlook found expression in Parliament, where the
Earl of Ellenborough questioned the wisdom of leaving the
establishment of county police to the discretion of magistrates,
pointing out that 'variations in the size of forces in different
counties' bore no relation to the exigencies of each case. Drawing upon the example of the Irish police and the metropolitan
establishment, he again emphasised the desirability of sub-
sidising the police out of the Consolidated Fund.[43] It was with
similar ideas that E.R. Rice had moved for the appointment
of a Select Committee to consider the expedience of adopting
a more uniform system of police in England and Wales.[44] He
believed that the mixed system of constabulary, with a different
kind of police in almost every county, had failed wherever it
had been tried. He was convinced that there existed at last
throughout the country, particularly since the establishment
of railroads, 'a strong feeling in favour of a well-considered
measure of national police'. His motion was seconded by J.
Hume and the brief debate that followed was highly characteristic of the changed outlook. The statement by Viscount
Palmerston, Home Secretary in Lord Aberdeen's cabinet, that
'this was undoubtedly a matter which fell within the legitimate
range of the government's duty, and one in respect of which
they would be prepared to take an active and decisive part',
would have provoked a storm of acrimonious protest ten years
before. Now it was accepted as self-evident, and by this time
Disraeli, once so fiery an opponent, did not raise a murmur.
The contention that a more unified and centralised system of
rural police was essential to the better prevention of crime
and the more effective maintenance of public order was hardly
challenged, and the motion, altered only by extending the
Committee's inquiry to Scotland also, was duly adopted.

The resolutions of the Select Committee, given in their
Second Report published in July 1853, were strong and definite.[45]
Though not all were unanimously adopted, there were never
more than two dissentients amongst the fifteen members.

First, they reported that the Rural Police Acts of 1839 and
1842 had, because of their permissive character, 'failed to
provide such a general and uniform Constabulary Force as is
essentially required for the prevention of crime and security
of property'. Where the Acts had been put into operation, the
Committee were satisfied that the new police had made the
detection and apprehension of offenders more certain, had
'tended to the maintenance of order, and the improved habits
of the population', had been accompanied by the reduction or
even suppression of vagrancy, and had so effectively protected
property peculiarly exposed to depredation as to have increased
land values in the areas concerned. 'The adoption of the Rural
Police', they concluded, 'has proved highly advantageous to
these districts, whether tested by moral, social, or economical

considerations.'

No such approval could be given to efforts to improve the old parochial system under the 5 & 6 Vict., c. 109. Though superintending constables might be useful in virtue of their individual police service, they provided no remedy for the inefficiency of the parish constables as a whole. Indeed the Committee were definite in their opinion that 'any system of Police mainly dependent on the aid of Parochial Constables, must prove ineffectual for the protection of property, more especially that of the poorer classes, for the prompt detection and pursuit of offenders, the maintenance of order, and other duties of a Police Force, for which their necessary avocations and local connexions entirely disqualify them.' Moreover, though the real cost of parish constables was less easy for ratepayers to assess than that of a county police, the Committee was satisfied that it had been proved that the former was much greater than was generally estimated, whereas the latter effected savings which were not so widely known or appreciated. There were objections to the adoption of the Rural Police Acts on the ground that the cost was not equitably distributed between different parts of a county which might have varying needs for police according to density of population or nature of employment, but this could be met by statutory provision for the adjustment of the police rate to meet such cases.

The Committee made no direct comment on the police of the boroughs as such, but observed that the efficiency of all existing police forces was materially impaired by the want of co-operation between the rural constabulary and the police under the control of boroughs or other local jurisdictions. They firmly recommended that the smaller boroughs should be consolidated with districts or counties for police purposes, and that the police in the larger boroughs should be under a similar system of management and control to that of the adjoining district or county, where practicable under the same superintendence. This would serve the purposes of uniformity, co-operation and economy.

Of crucial importance was the observation that the county constabulary forces performed functions vital to the nation as a whole as well as to their particular localities. They had rendered valuable services in the protection of revenue, in the maintenance of order, in promoting law observance, in reducing the cost of prosecutions, and in protecting the lives and property of many who contributed nothing to the police rates. The House should therefore consider 'whether some aid should not be afforded by the Government towards defraying the cost of an improved and extended system of Police, without essentially interfering with the local management of that Force'.

Having thus cleared the way, the Committee concluded that the government should at once introduce legislation making 'the adoption of an efficient Police Force on a uniform principle imperative throughout Great Britain.' Their unqualified

rejection of the parochial system and of the idea that partial
reforms could ever make it effective, gave support to those
who believed that a police force suitable for nineteenth-century
needs could not be built on the foundations laid in much earlier
times for a very different society. Their recommendations
that the establishment of police on a uniform basis throughout
the country should be made compulsory, and that borough and
county forces should as far as possible be amalgamated in the
interests of crime prevention, public order and economy, reinforced the growing belief that some measure of central control was essential, though there were still doubts about how
this could be introduced without undermining local government.
  The conviction that there were some local matters, affecting
the well-being of the whole nation, in which it was necessary
for the central government to intervene, had already asserted
itself in factory legislation, in public health, in the poor law
and in the prison system. Though the liberties and freedom of
choice of individuals and local authorities were still fiercely
defended, it had been recognised that in such fields laissez-
faire was not enough and that the government must secure
essential reforms and set minimum standards for the whole
country. This advance in legislative regulation had a double
effect on the criminal law. First, it led directly to the emergence of a code of new offences, many of them non-indictable,
thus profoundly affecting both the content of the law and the
structure of the courts and the penal system. Second, it led
to the recognition that the state must assume more responsibilities for regulating not merely the treatment of convicted
offenders but the whole system of crime prevention and law
enforcement. To borrow a succinct phrase used in the debate
on the Police (Counties and Boroughs) Bill in 1856, 'It was
quite as much the duty of the Government to prevent crime
as to punish it.'[46]

THE COMPROMISE

It might seem that progress towards a uniform and radical
reorganisation of the provincial police, embracing counties
and boroughs alike, would now be comparatively smooth. But
there were still obstacles and delays. Such reform was closely
linked with an issue which weighed as heavily upon the public
mind at this time as the fear of central despotism as a threat
to individual liberty had done in the period before 1840. Then
the chief emphasis amongst opponents of police reform had been
on the danger of spies and of a mercenary force at the disposal of the central power. Now it had largely shifted to the
related, and no less deeply-rooted, fear that local autonomy
would be undermined by government regulation and inspection.
The very fact that permissive legislation had not been sufficient
to secure the adoption of paid police forces throughout the

country implied that the powers now being sought would impose such forces against the will of many local authorities. Would this not weaken, and ultimately destroy, the whole tradition and structure of local government? And was not local self-determination a heritage too precious to be sacrificed for the convenience of a more efficient police? The expansion and enforcement of public health legislation was being resisted on the same grounds. Such attempts to impose the control of the central government in traditionally local concerns were seen as the thin end of a wedge which would eventually destroy local autonomy altogether. Once more there appeared the argument, accepted even by Chadwick in the First Report of the Constabulary Commissioners, that any delay in securing uniformity through awaiting the consent of the local authorities would be more than compensated by the eventual whole-hearted support of the localities concerned, a support which Home Office circulars and inspectors alone could not hope to secure.

The sincerity of those using this argument was not always unimpeachable. It was often an attempt to conceal or justify local administrative inertia, indifference to the well-being of the community, or selfish and narrow vested interests. Moreover, experience had hardly justified it. Though a few progressive counties had made marked advances since the permissive legislation was introduced others had progressed hardly at all, and many appeared simply to have ignored it. Even mandatory legislation had, in the absence of inspection or sanctions of any kind, made little impression on many of the boroughs. The argument in itself cannot be disregarded. Distrust of the central government, on both political and financial grounds, was profound and of long standing, and so were local pride and the traditions of local government, which had contributed much to the greatness of the country. But the issue, as Macaulay stressed, was not whether belief in local government should be abandoned, or its constitutional foundations destroyed, but rather where the line should be drawn to enable new social needs and interests to be met.[47]

Attempts to draw the line reflected this underlying struggle. The first, made in June 1854 by Lord Palmerston, who was not then in office was, however, characteristically bold and went further than the Committee in invading local tradition. He introduced his 'Bill to render more effectual the Police in the Counties and Boroughs in England and Wales' with the statement that, looked at simply from the point of view of prevention, a force modelled on the Irish or metropolitan police would be the most effective, acting 'under the orders of Government, and uniform in its organisation and in the principle of its operation.' But he hastened to add that he attached great importance to the principle of local self-government. 'He thought it was quite impossible to over-rate the great national importance of employing the persons connected with the different districts of the country in administering the affairs of those districts so far as

it was possible to do so.' For this reason he would be very
sorry to extend the metropolitan principle of direct central
control to the whole country.[48]

This one concession made, however, his proposals were
sweeping. All boroughs with populations of less than twenty
thousand were to consolidate their police forces with those of
the counties in which they were situated. Five counties were
to amalgamate for police purposes with those adjoining them.
The powers given to justices in Quarter Sessions by the Rural
Constabulary Acts of 1839 and 1840 were to be transferred
to new County Police Boards. The Queen in Council was to be
entitled to order the appointment of additional constables and
to appoint four inspectors to watch over the general efficiency
of the provincial police.

There was a storm of protest. Over sixty mayors travelled
to London to demand that the Bill should not be applied to
their boroughs. As soon as Palmerston had agreed to remove
the boroughs from its scope, he found himself facing equal
opposition from county members. Eventually he withdrew the
Bill altogether, on the ground that no good purpose would be
served by forcing it upon people against their will. As he
ruefully confessed some time later, he had 'had no more chance
of passing the Bill in that House than a parish constable in
Somersetshire had of apprehending a thief'.

His retreat did not wholly escape censure. He was accused
of yielding, against his own conviction, to 'senseless and
interested clamour'. He was urged to go further rather than
draw back: 'The heart that Russia could not terrify, nor
Austria beguile, had quailed before the "bureaucracy" of
Manchester, Birmingham, Chester, and a deputation of county
wisdom.' The whole burden of the opposition had been the old
cry against centralisation. Yet the Post Office was centralised,
the railways, the electric telegraph; so was the administration
of the law by judges on circuit, and the whole sheriff system.
Why, then, should not such executive functions as crime
prevention and thief-catching also have the efficiency and
uniformity resulting from central organisation? Some matters,
like the health, cleanliness and comfort of local communities,
were proper subjects for local government 'but the repression
and punishment of crime is a national, and not a local question;
and the machinery employed for the purpose should be commensurate with the requirement, and co-extensive with the
field over which it spreads.'[49] Palmerston repeatedly spoke of
bringing in another measure but he never did so.

The following year even saw a final attempt to bolster up the
parochial system. A private member's Bill to amend and consolidate the law relating to parish constables, proposed, amongst
other things, the compulsory appointment of a superintendent
constable for each petty sessional division.[50] Even this slight
threat of compulsion provided opportunity in the subsequent
debate for an outburst against the 'general tendency to take

the management of the gaols, police, and all matters connected
with jurisprudence out of the hands of the local authorities
and centralise it in the government'. It also gave another opening for pressure on the government to take the initiative by
establishing a national constabulary force, partially subsidised
from exchequer funds. A chastened Lord Palmerston, however,
reminded the House that 'if the government were let in as pay-
master, it must be let in as commander in chief'. In his opinion
the question was too difficult for them to deal with. This provoked from Sir John Pakington the riposte that 'it was the duty
of Government to deal with difficult questions'.

In 1856 Sir George Grey came forward with an answer. A
man of unimpeachable integrity, he was a sincere Whig and
Liberal, profoundly attached to the tradition of local government, suspicious of rigid centralisation, abhorring arbitrary
methods and wedded to the maxim of legality in criminal justice.
He had already been Home Secretary in Lord John Russell's
first Cabinet, from July 1846 to February 1852, and was so
again under both Palmerston and Russell. He held the office
for a total of nearly fourteen years, ranging over a twenty-
year period, some of it tense with social unrest and marking
crucial stages in the development of the administration of
criminal justice. It was he who at last succeeded in breaking
the deadlock and helping forward the expansion of the police.

The Bill he introduced blended a minimum of direct compulsion with considerable indirect pressure. Its guiding principle
was to increase the efficiency of the police within the established
framework of local government. It required County Quarter
Sessions to take action under the Rural Constabulary Acts to
provide police forces for the whole of their counties where they
had not already done so. It made no direct attack on the right
of boroughs to retain their separate forces, but it facilitated
unions with the surrounding counties and, in the case of the
smaller boroughs, supplied a financial incentive. The device of
the Treasury grant, subject to efficiency and linked with
inspection, was calculated at a single blow to reduce local fears
of the expense of organised police forces and to forge a flexible,
reasonably unobtrusive instrument of central pressure.[51]

When Grey first asked leave to introduce this measure his
proposals were received with enthusiasm. But it was too much
to hope that hostility would not mount. As before it came
primarily from the boroughs, the City of London joining in
although it was expressly excluded from the scope of this Bill.[52]
Grey was obliged to withdraw clauses proposing that borough
police, as well as those of the counties, should be subject to
general regulations concerning their government and pay drawn
up by the Home Secretary, and that they should be appointed
by Chief Constables rather than the Watch Committees, again
on the county model. One member reproached him with trying
to deprive England of the municipal corporations given her by
a member of his own family. Several others saw the clauses as

blows at the independence of municipal institutions, calculated
to lessen self-reliance and self-government.[53]

Soon the debate passed from the vested interests of the
boroughs to the wider debate about the proper roles of central
and local government. It was maintained that those who had
petitioned against the Bill had rightly seen it as 'a stepping
stone to that system of centralisation which, however it might
suit the Governments of the Continent, was repugnant to the
habits and feelings of Englishmen.' The government was
accused of 'an indecent lust for power' and old threats were
raked up: 'England would soon be overrun by 20,000 armed
policemen - perhaps Irishmen or foreigners - upon whom a bad
Government could rely for the perpetration of acts of oppression.' Magistrates who voted for it would be 'digging their own
graves', for it was 'part of a plot to sweep away the unpaid
magistracy and replace them by stipendiaries.' Alternatively
'it was manifestly the purpose of the Home Office to take the
conservancy of the peace out of the hands of the magistracy,
and to transfer it to the police.' One member went so far as to
prophesy, with considerable accuracy, that the existing President of the Poor Law Board would be followed by a Minister
of Public Health with his inspectors, the Vice-President of
the Council charged with education by a Minister of Education,
also complete with inspectors. His foresight faltered only in
his deduction that, if the present Bill became law, 'the country
would soon be cursed with a Police Minister'.[54] For all this
outcry, the Bill passed through the Commons, and the clauses
tending to extension of central control were not much criticised
in the Lords. The principle that the country should be endowed
with a uniform system of police was at last accepted, even
though the machinery for securing it still fell far short of what
was needed.[55] The measure was a compromise, but it was also
a great step forward in the movement for police reform. The
choice between county police and parish constables had at last
been irrevocably taken.

Though the statute marked an advance in the development of
the police, it extended rather than altered the patterns of
organisation already laid down in the Municipal Corporations
Act and the Rural Constabulary Acts. The method of establishing a force remained as prescribed in 1839 and 1840. Grey
steadfastly resisted attempts to get him to include stipulations
as to the minimum number of police to population either in.
municipal or county areas. This was because he held that the
proportion of police needed varied too greatly in different
districts for a satisfactory figure to be assessed, and because
of his fear that any statutory minimum would come to be thought
of as a maximum. His opinion was borne out to some extent by
the very wide variations between counties that had already
adopted the Acts: Southampton approached the statutory maximum for the counties of one policeman to a thousand of the
population, whilst Cumberland was content with less than one

to five thousand. Nor did those who favoured a minimum agree amongst themselves as to what it should be. So it was still left to the justices to decide the strength of their forces, though approval was required for proposals to increase or diminish them once established.

The provision that the Treasury should contribute a fourth of the cost of police pay and clothing provided a lever which could be used to induce laggard authorities to bring their forces up to an appropriate strength. The grant was conditional upon a certificate from the Secretary of State that the police of the county or borough concerned had been 'maintained in a State of Efficiency in point of Numbers and Discipline' during the preceding year. Section 15 of the Act gave the Crown power to appoint three inspectors to visit and enquire into the state and efficiency of the police in both counties and boroughs, and to see whether the provisions of the Act were being duly carried into effect. The inspectors were also to enquire into the state of police stations, charge rooms, cells, lock-ups and any other police premises. They were to report on all such matters to the Secretary of State, who was to lay the report before Parliament.

Whilst some objectors saw the conditional grant as undermining the independence of local authorities, others thought it too small, prophesying that it would still be cheaper for really niggardly authorities to appoint hardly any police at all. During the debates there were attempts to get the Government to increase it to as much as a half, but they failed in face of Exchequer opposition. On the other hand, pressure to ensure that local police authorities should be given the opportunity of refuting any charges against the efficiency of their forces before a certificate was finally refused, led to the addition of a clause which entitled the justices or Watch Committee in such a case to receive a copy of the inspector's report and submit a statement upon it. If it were nevertheless decided not to allow the grant, the statement from the justices or committee, as well as a statement from the Secretary of State, was to be laid before Parliament.

Though the principle of inspection was already accepted in other fields - factories, the poor law, prisons - its extension to police did not escape attack. It was suggested that some of the reports by the prison inspectors upon gaols had been unfair and that these new inspectors would be likely to clash with the magistrates and create a difference of opinion between them and the Secretary of State. Grey was adamant on this point. He claimed that there had been no complaint about the exercise of the powers given to the Secretary of State in the management of prisons and no cause for such exaggerated apprehension of the powers he was now to exercise in the case of police.

Prisons [he pointed out] were placed also within the control of the municipal authorities in boroughs, giving the Secretary

of State supervision over the local control of prisons. That
was a precaution adopted by Parliament to secure an important public object. It was easy to talk of centralisation: but
it should not be forgotten that in matters of this kind the
principle involved did not apply solely to particular localities,
but the benefit sought to be obtained was one in which the
whole country at large was interested.
The appointment of inspectors was, in his eyes, 'the most
material provision of the Bill'.

One of the most unsatisfactory aspects of the Act was the
failure to deal more drastically with the problem of the separate
borough police. This omission may have been necessary to buy
off the opposition of borough members and secure the passage
of the Bill, but it gravely weakened the move towards greater
efficiency which was its avowed object. The exclusion of the
smallest boroughs from the Treasury grant put some pressure
upon them to merge their forces with those of the counties,
but they were not compelled to do so. The police of towns that
were not boroughs were to be gradually absorbed into the
county forces, but if they had populations of fifteen thousand
or more chief constables now had to get prior authority from
the Secretary of State before taking them over.

On the other hand the central authority was given certain
rights to intervene to encourage amalgamations. The Queen in
Council, on the advice of the Secretary of State, could fix the
date and terms of a merger where a borough could not come to
terms with a county. No amalgamation could be terminated
without the consent of the Secretary of State. He could intervene, on the application of ratepayers, to oblige magistrates
to form police districts, with varying proportions of police
and corresponding variations in the police rates.

There were a few provisions designed to bring county and
municipal police more into line. County constables were given
the same powers and duties within boroughs as borough constables already had in the counties. The rule excluding county
police from voting at parliamentary elections was extended to
the boroughs, with the additional provision that borough constables could not vote in municipal elections either, nor (in a
phrase which recalled many a tumultuous scene in the past)
could they 'endeavour to persuade or dissuade any Elector'.
Borough and county police alike were prohibited from receiving
for their own use any fees for acts done in the execution of
their duties. But the process of bringing borough and county
forces together went no further.

A brief but good analysis of the effects and implications of
the successive Police Acts of 1839, 1840 and 1856 upon the
provincial police was produced two years later by the Recorder
of Dartmouth. He referred to old fears that police powers
might be misused by an arbitrary government, or that the
pecuniary sacrifice required would be too high, as things of
the past:

> Under that popular system of Government which now for
> many years has happily obtained in this country, a con-
> fidence and belief have sprung up in the public mind that
> whilst nothing injurious to public liberty is to be appre-
> hended from the institution of a system of police which shall
> embrace the entire kingdom, the ends of good government
> imperatively require its adoption.

Upon examination it would be found that the three statutes
which regulated the county police, were 'framed upon principles
essentially popular, the magistrates of each county being the
body who are to exercise a controlling discretion, whilst to
the Secretary of State is alone confided such small functions as
are requisite for insuring uniformity of detail and action.'[156]

So complacent an attitude was hardly likely to satisfy Chadwick. To him the Act of 1856 was less the triumphant conclusion
of a long struggle than the beginning of a new phase in it.
So far, he pointed out, the Home Office had played little part
in helping counties with the implementation of the Constabulary
Acts.[57] County magistrates, inexperienced in matters of police
and now called upon to lay the foundations of a new system
without delay, would do much that would subsequently need
to be undone. Where efficient forces had been established
there had been much prior consultation with experienced people
like Rowan and himself, but the county magistrates in general
were all at sea on the subject and needed information on every
point. There was already much lack of uniformity amongst
existing forces which would need to be corrected. The great
value of the new inspectors would lie, he hoped, in the fact
that they could not only report on the defects of the police to
the Home Secretary but could also discuss the needs and
possibilities of the local forces with authorities in boroughs
and counties, influence the appointments of chief constables,
suggest collateral duties which would increase the usefulness
of the police, and encourage amalgamations between counties
or between counties and boroughs where these were likely to
improve efficiency.[58]

Events proved that even he was unduly optimistic. In 1861
it was reported that in the counties and most of the larger
boroughs the police were considered to be efficient in numbers
and discipline and equal to the duties required. 'Some of the
smaller Boroughs, however, give cause of complaint, where
the authorities, by neglecting to amalgamate for Police purposes with the surrounding county, appear to be opposed no
less to the public benefit than to their own advantage and
security.'[59] Not only did this problem in itself prove an
obdurate one, but, as a Royal Commission of our own day has
put it, 'although Government intervention was constantly
increasing, the leading characteristic of police conditions of
service was diversity . . . it is difficult to talk in the same
terms about the bewildering patchwork of local units that existed
before 1919 and the standardised service to which the country

has since become accustomed.[160] The Statute of 1856 fell far
short of providing a basis for the coherent and unified system
of police for the whole country of which reformers had dreamed.
Yet in its time it marked a decisive advance. At least the
local authorities were required to provide professional forces.
At least the central government, through inspection and the
grant, could accumulate closer knowledge and experience of
the nation's police, could bring some pressure to bear upon
those who lagged furthest behind. For the first time it became
possible to collect and publish on a national scale statistics
of the offences known to the police. A break had been made in
the long tradition that the provincial police was a wholly local
concern. The passing of the Act implied acceptance of Grey's
contention that the local police 'could not be considered as an
isolated question, but that it affected the whole community and
not alone the county or borough in which crime was allowed
to be undetected or unrepressed'. The expenses of maintaining
prisons and prosecuting prisoners had already been thrown
upon the community at large: the public had thus to pay for
any failure in the repression of crime in a particular locality.
It was logical that national as well as local interests should be
recognised.

Awareness of the police as a national responsibility was
sharpened by the ending of transportation, which was abolished
for the great majority of criminals in 1853. The cost of gaols
and police to deal with transported offenders in Australia had
been a heavy charge on the national exchequer for over half
a century. Now such offenders would have to be controlled
at home. This was one of the reasons advanced by Grey for the
Treasury grant towards the cost of provincial police.

The ending of transportation, however, influenced more than
the financial aspect of the Bill. It played a major part in securing the acceptance of a measure of compulsion which would have
been rejected out of hand in the 1830s or the 1840s. Much might
be ascribed to the success of those police forces that had
already established themselves. Much might also be due to the
liberal attitude maintained by recent governments, even in face
of grave threats to public order. Much, too, must be attributed
to the growing familiarity of legislative intervention in the
common affairs of life. Important, in their time, had been the
fears aroused by the belief that crime was increasing fast and,
even more so, to the alarm occasioned by ill-controlled outbreaks of rioting and disorder. Yet none of these had brought
public opinion and Parliament to the point of conceding any
general compulsion upon local authorities to provide efficient
police.

When acceptance came at last, it came during a period of
growing prosperity, when disorder was becoming rarer, when
Chartism had ceased to be a menace, when even the levels
of crime were believed to be falling. The peaks of commitments
reached in 1842 and 1848 seemed things of the past. From 1849

to 1853 the figure hovered around twenty-seven thousand and after a rise in 1854 dropped to below twenty-six thousand in 1856. The reduction was partly due to extensions in summary jurisdiction, especially in 1855,[61] but the editor of the Judicial Statistics was satisfied that this was not the only explanation. In particular he noted that the end of the Crimean War had brought no increase in crimes of violence comparable with that following the Napoleonic Wars.[62]

It was the new factor, the ending of transportation, that introduced into this apparently satisfactory situation a sense of deep insecurity, all the more potent because it was a fear of the unknown. Chadwick had foreshadowed disastrous consequences when he gave evidence earlier to the Select Committee: 'We have now constantly under confinement, in the prisons of Great Britain, a force of able-bodied men, equal to an army of about 30,000, numerically greater than the British force which fought at the battle of Waterloo.' Many of them were depredators who would eventually be transported. But resistance to transportation, already building up, would eventually succeed. Then 'these numbers of convicts, heretofore regularly shifted from this country, will be discharged with the almost certainty that the greater proportion of them must renew their careers, which they will have extensively open to them for renewal unless preventive measures of a general and complete nature be adopted.' Superior officers of the police and other competent persons, he added, viewed the prospect of an unguarded change of practice with very serious alarm.[63]

Some of the offenders transported in earlier times had been mere boys or others guilty only of comparatively minor crimes. But over the past thirty years the use of the death penalty for the more serious offences had been more and more restricted, both by legislation and by administrative discretion. Transportation had provided a reassuring alternative. So long as it had been available, dangerous or persistent criminals could still be eliminated. It had removed that section of the criminal classes which caused the greatest public anxiety. In future such offenders would remain in this country on their release. Certainly those discharged after serving part only of their sentences of penal servitude were to be subject to supervision under the 'ticket of leave' system, but the value of this must itself depend largely on the adequacy and efficiency of the police.[64] If the country must, for the future, learn to live with its criminals, it must pay the price of protection against them.

References

1 See First Report from the Select Committee on the Police (603), 1853, 'Parl. Papers' (1852-3), vol.36, p.1, Minutes of Evidence, No.1621, at p.102. See also letter from Home Office to Gorsts and Birchall (deputy clerks of peace, Preston), July 14 1842, in H.O. 65/4.
2 See letters of S. Horrocks to the Home Office, August 13

and 15 1842, in H.O. 45/249A.

3 See Barracks at Bolton, H.C. (March 1843), 'Parl. Debates' (1843), 3rd ser., vol.67, col.748. On the state of the police in this area see letter of Colonel W. Wemyss to the Home Office of October 14 1841, in H.O. 45/43.

4 See letters from Sir Charles Shaw to Home Office, May 3 1842, in H.O. 45/249E and August 11 1842, in H.O. 45/249C.

5 This letter was alleged by the prosecution at his trial to have been found in Thomas Cooper's pockets, and is reproduced in the 'Annual Register' (1843), vol.85, Chronicle, pp.36-7.

6 See letters from T. Bayley Rose (Stipendiary Magistrate) to Normanby, June 23 1841, in H.O. 45/51. T.B. Rose to Sir James Graham, August 3 1842, in H.O. 45/260; Lord Talbot to Graham, January 5 1842, in H.O. 45/260; W. Forrester to Loftus Lowndes, July 12 1842, in H.O. 45/260; W. Warre to Dartmouth, July 19 1842, in H.O. 45/268; Dartmouth to Home Office, August 11 1842, in H.O. 45/260; T.B. Rose to Home Office, August 15 1842, in H.O. 45/260; and again T.B. Rose, November 18 1842, ibid.

7 See 'Annual Register' (1842), vol.84, Chronicle, pp.133-4.

8 See letter from Lord Derby to Home Office, August 18 1842, in H.O. 45/249; also letter from Thomas Bennett Capt. R.N., Mayor of Hereford, to Sir James Graham, August 26 1842, in H.O. 45/247.

9 See D. Maude and R. Gladstone to Home Office, March 9 1848, in H.O. 45/2410A; Mayor of Liverpool, ditto, July 26 1848, in H.O. 45/2410A; T.B. Rose, ditto, March 30 1848, in H.O. 45/2410Y; Home Office to Clerk of Magistrates, Coventry, April 11 1848, in H.O. 41/19.

10 Home Office to Mayor of Liverpool, July 10 1848, in H.O. 41/19.

11 See letter from magistrates of Blackburn to Home Office, August 19 1842, in H.O. 45/249; W.B. Taylor, ditto, August 19 1842, in H.O. 45/260; Lord Talbot, ditto, August 25 1842, ibid.; H. Potts, ditto, August 24 1842, in H.O. 45/242.

12 See letter from Graham to Peel, August 15 1842, Peel's Papers, Add. MSS. (British Museum) 40, 477.

13 See draft from Home Office to the Hon. G. Rice Trevor (Deputy Lieutenant of Carmarthenshire), September 18 1843, in H.O. 45/454; Home Office to Rice Trevor, September 28 1843, in H.O. 41/18; ditto, October 5 1843, ibid., and Rice Trevor to Home Office, October 10 1843, in H.O. 45/454.

14 See The Metropolitan Police, H.C. (August 4 1848), 'Parl. Debates' (1848), 3rd ser., vol.100, col.1153, at col.1154.

15 See Graham to Peel, August 28 1842, Add. MSS. (British Museum) 40, 447, f. 108 r. and v.

16 See Lloyd Davies to Home Office, April 21 1843, in

H.O. 45/454.
17 Report of Inspector G. Martin to the Magistrates, January 2 1843, in H.O. 45/454.
18 See Colonel W.E. Powell to Home Office, July 27 1843, in H.O. 45/454 (Part 1) and Home Office to Powell, July 31 1843, in H.O. 41/18.
19 See Rice Trevor to Home Office, September 4 and 10 1843, in H.O. 45/454.
20 See Rice Trevor to Home Office, August 7 1843, in H.O. 45/454.
21 See, for instance, the case of Cardiganshire, Home Office to Powell, November 13 1843, in H.O. 41/18; Trevor to Home Office, March 2 1844, in H.O. 45/642, and Hugh Owen to Home Office, April 10 1844, in H.O. 45/642.
22 See Home Office to Powell, November 21 1843, in H.O. 41/18.
23 J.A. Wise to Home Office, September 2 1842, in H.O. 45/260. See also J. Wood to the Home Office, September 3 1842, in H.O. 45/260.
24 Brotherton to the Home Office, October 1 1842, in H.O. 45/264A.
25 Letter of Home Office to Lord Wharncliffe, September 30 1842, in H.O. 41/17, and Wharncliffe to Home Office, October 3 1842, in H.O. 45/264.
26 See E. Welbourne, 'The Miners' Union of Northumberland and Durham' (1923), p.73. Also Sidney and Beatrice Webb, 'The History of Trade Unionism' (1902 ed.), pp.164-5.
27 See letter from Lord Londonderry to Home Office, October 6 1844, in H.O. 45/636; Lord Londonderry to Home Office, June 19 1844, in H.O. 45/644, and Sir Thomas Arbuthnot to Home Office, June 13 1844, in H.O. 45/650.
28 Supply - Army Estimates, H.C. (March 10 1849), 'Parl. Debates' (1849), 3rd ser., vol.103, col.964, at col.1016.
29 See G.M. Young, 'Victorian England: Portrait of an Age' (1936), p.39.
30 See First Report from the Select Committee on the Police; with the Minutes of Evidence (603), 1853, 'Parl. Papers' (1852-3), vol.36, evidence of Captain J.B.B. M'Hardy, p.50, at pp.55-9.
31 Power to detain vagrants for up to four hours to perform tasks of work was given by the 5 & 6 Vict., c.57, s. 5 (1842). On the handing over of impostors to the police see Appendix to the Fourth Report of the Commissioners under the Poor Law Amendment Act, 'Parl. Papers' (1837-8), vol.28, p.246. Correspondence between the Commissioners of the Metropolitan Police and the Poor Law Commissioners, relative to the Relief of Persons casually found in a state of destitution.
32 See Report from the Departmental Committee on Vagrancy, Cd 2852. 'Parl. Papers' (1906), vol.103, p.1, at p.16; ibid., Appendix 3, Minute of the Poor Law Board, p.661, at p.662.

33 See, for example, Report of the Committee of Justices - on
 a plan for extending the protection of a Police Force to
 that portion of the County of Surrey beyond the limits of
 the Metropolitan Police District, printed leaflet published
 in 1850, in H.O. 45/3308.
34 See Memorial from G. Wood, Chairman of the Board of
 Guardians of the Downham Union, to the Secretary of State,
 April 26 1849, in H.O. 45/2986.
35 See First Report from the Select Committee on the Police;
 with the Minutes of Evidence (603), 1853, 'Parl. Papers'
 (1852-3), vol.36, p.1; Second Report from the Select
 Committee on the Police; with Minutes of Evidence (715),
 1853, ibid., p.161; see also the excellent Index to Reports
 from the Select Committee on Police (715-I), 1853, ibid.,
 p.345. On M'Hardy's evidence see especially First Report,
 Evidence nos 676-819, ibid., pp.50-61, and Second Report,
 Evidence nos 3809-14, ibid., at p.267. In addition, the
 Appendix to the Second Report contains nearly 30 pages
 of papers laid before the Committee by M'Hardy, including
 his reports to Essex Quarter Sessions of April 5 1842, with
 19 tables and returns, and of October 15 1850, with 8 tables
 and returns: see Second Report, ibid., Appendix, pp.300-29.
 It includes a paper against public executions.
36 See, for examples, J. Tiplady, March 28 1848, in H.O.
 45/2410G; S. Stone, May 21 1848, in H.O. 45/2410R; Mayor
 and Magistrates of Ashton, August 15 1848, in H.O.
 45/2410A, and Mayor of London, August 18 1848, in H.O.
 45/2410A.
37 See Mayor of Bolton, July 29 1848, in H.O. 45/2410A.
38 First Report from the Select Committee on the Police; with
 the Minutes of Evidence (603), 1853, 'Parl. Papers'
 (1852-3), vol.36, p.1, Minutes of Evidence at p.61.
39 See National Police, H.C. (April 26 1853), 'Parl. Debates'
 (1853), 3rd ser., vol.126, col.545, at col.549.
40 See Police (Counties and Boroughs) Bill, H.C. (February
 5 1856), 'Parl. Debates' (1856), 3rd ser., vol.140, col.229
 at col.232.
41 See First Report from the Select Committee on the Police;
 with the Minutes of Evidence (603), 1853, 'Parl. Papers'
 (1852-3), vol.36, p.1, at p.86; Evidence nos 1470-90,
 ibid., at pp.94-5; Evidence nos.1606-15, at p.101;
 Evidence nos 1949-53, at p. 120; Evidence nos 1983-2028,
 at pp.123-5.
42 The Police System of London, 'Edinburgh Review' (July
 1852 to October 1852), vol.96, pp.1-33, at p.27.
43 See The Rural Police in England - Volunteer Rifle Corps,
 H.L. (March 18 1852), 'Parl. Debates' (1852), 3rd ser.,
 vol.119, col.1226, at cols 1226-7.
44 See National Police, H.C. (April 1853), 'Parl. Debates'
 (1853), 3rd ser., vol.126, col.545, at col.548.
45 Second Report from the Select Committee on the Police;

with Minutes of Evidence (715), 1853, 'Parl. Papers'
(1852-3), vol.36, p.1.

46 See Police (Counties and Boroughs) Bill, H.C. (February
5 1856), 'Parl. Debates' (1856), 3rd ser., vol.140, col.243.

47 On this subject of the limits of state interference there is
no comparison more instructive than that between Burke's
famous passage in his Thoughts and Details on Scarcity,
written in 1795, in 'Collected Works' (Bohn's ed. 1854-89),
vol.5 (1855), p.83, at pp.107-8 and the no less famous
speech by Macaulay on Fielden's Ten Hours Bill of 1846,
'Collected Works' (ed. Lady Trevelyan, 1866), vol.8,
p.360 passim.

48 See Bill to render more effectual the Police in Counties
and Boroughs in England and Wales (Bill 127), 1854,
'Parl. Papers' (1854), vol.5, p.467; Counties and Boroughs
Police, H.C. (June 2 1854), 'Parl. Debates' (1854), 3rd ser.,
vol.133, col.1266, at col.1267.

49 See Police Bill - Question, H.C. (June 27 1854), 'Parl.
Debates' (1854-5), 3rd ser., vol.134, col.750; ditto, H.L.
(June 30 1854), ibid., col.957; Rural Police H.C. (July
3 1854), ibid., col.1073; Parish Constables Bill, H.C. (May
17 1855), 'Parl. Debates' (1855), 3rd ser., vol.138, col.702.

50 See Bill to amend the Laws relating to the Appointment and
Payment of Superintendents and Parish Constables, and to
dispense with the Services of High Constables and Petty
Constables in certain Cases (147), 1855, 'Parl. Papers'
(1854-5), vol.5, p.13, brought in on April 26 1855. See
also Parish Constables Bill, H.C. (May 17 1855), 'Parl.
Debates' (1855), 3rd ser., vol.138, cols 702-14 (Debate
on the Second Reading of the Bill). By 1854 twenty-five
counties in England had adopted Lord John Russell's Acts
of 1839-40 (some of them partially) and five counties in
Wales; see Return of the Several Counties of England and
Wales, their Population, the Number of Rural Police under
the Acts of 2 & 3 Vict., c.93 and 3 & 4 Vict., c.88, etc.
(211), 1854, 'Parl. Papers' (1854), vol.53, p.617.

51 A Bill to render more effectual the Police in Counties and
Boroughs of England and Wales [Bill 18], 1856, 'Parl.
Papers' (1856), vol.5, p.397; see also Police (Counties
and Boroughs) Bill, H.C. (February 5 1856), 'Parl. Debates'
(1856), 3rd ser., vol. 140, cols 229-45; ditto, H.C.
(February 13 1856), ibid., cols 690-7; ditto, H.C. (March
1856), ibid., cols 2113-90.

52 Ibid., cols 690-7, 2151, 2159 and 2144-5.

53 Ibid., cols 251-2, 2150, 2159-60, 2180, 2183 and 2186.

54 For discussion and amendments to the Bill see Police
(Counties and Boroughs) Bill, H.C. (May 9 1856), 'Parl.
Debates' (1856), 3rd ser., vol.142, col.293; ditto, H.C.
(May 23 1856), ibid., col.605; ditto, H.L. (June 13 1856),
ibid., col.1398; ditto, H.L. (June 19 1856), ibid., col.1673;
ditto, H.L. (June 24 1856), ibid., col.1894; ditto, H.L.

(June 27 1856), col.2048. On the amendments effected in
the Bill see Bill as amended in Committee (71), 1856,
'Parl. Papers' (1856), vol.5, p.407; Bill as amended . . .
on Re-Commitment, and on Consideration of Bill as amended
(Bill 145), 1856, ibid., p.417; and Bill as amended by the
Lords (Bill 215), 1856, ibid., p.429.

55 19 & 20 Vict., c.69 - An Act to render more effectual the
Police in Counties and Boroughs in England and Wales
(1856).

56 Thomas William Saunders, 'The Counties Police Acts', etc.
(1856).

57 Paper by Chadwick (undated) on the ignorance of the Home
Office, Chadwick Box 23 (marked Box 4, Paper 7).

58 Notes by Chadwick (undated) on the clauses of the Act of
1856, Chadwick Box 28 (marked Box 5, Paper 4).

59 Judicial Statistics, Part I, England and Wales, Returns
for the Year 1861 (3025), 'Parl. Papers' (1862), vol.56,
p.491, at p.496.

60 'Interim Report from the Royal Commission on the Police'
(1960), Cmnd 1222, p.7.

61 18 & 19 Vict., c.126 - An Act for diminishing Expense and
Delay in the Administration of Criminal Justice in certain
Cases (1855).

62 Judicial Statistics, Part I, England and Wales, Police -
Criminal Proceedings - Prisons, Returns for the Year 1856
(2246), 'Parl. Papers' (1857), vol.35, p.1, at pp.7-8.

63 See Second Report from the Select Committee appointed
to consider the expediency of adopting a more Uniform
System of Police in England and Wales, and in Scotland;
with Minutes of Evidence (715), 1853, 'Parl. Papers'
(1852-3), vol.36, p.161, evidence of E. Chadwick, p.253,
at p.259.

64 See Parish Constables Bill, H.C. (May 17 1855), 'Parl.
Debates' (1855), 3rd ser., vol.138, col.702, at cols 711-12.

5 The plague of the blue locusts: police reform and popular resistance in Northern England, 1840-57

Robert D. Storch

> Because the English Bourgeois finds himself reproduced
> in his law, as he does in his God, the policeman's trun-
> cheon [...] has for him a wonderfully soothing power.
> But for the workingman quite otherwise!
>
> F. Engels[1]

The implantation of a modern police in the industrial districts
of Northern England resulted from a new consensus among the
propertied classes that it was necessary to create a professional,
bureaucratically organized lever of urban discipline and permanently introduce it into the heart of working-class communities. The coming of the new police represented a significant
extension into hitherto geographically peripheral areas of both
the moral and political authority of the state. This was to be
accomplished by the creation of a powerful and quite modern
device - a bureaucracy of official morality. By 1840 it came to
be 'an axiom in police that you guard St. James by watching
St. Giles'.[2] This was a novel attitude. Eighteenth-century
governments and the upper classes in general were surely
apprehensive of the movements of the lower orders, but did
not consider it either useful or necessary to watch St Giles
all the time. One could learn what one needed to know about
what was on the collective mind of St Giles when it rioted; one
might even use or manipulate its riots in useful ways as the
reform movement of 1830-2 did with great success. Previous
to the nineteenth century urban disorder was not necessarily
perceived as subversive of the social order. 'Provided that the
ruler did his duty, the populace was prepared to defend him
with enthusiasm. But if he did not, it rioted until he did. This
mechanism was perfectly understood by both sides, and caused
no political problems beyond a little occasional destruction of
property [...] Since the riots were not directed against the
social system, public order could remain surprisingly lax by

Source: 'International Review of Social History', 20, 1975,
pp.61-90.

modern standards'.[3]

The mission of the new police was a symptom of both a
profound social change and a deep rupture in class relations
in the first half of the nineteenth century. By this time, both
the actions and the 'language' spoken by urban masses were,
if intelligible at all, deeply frightening. The notion that movements of the lower orders had comprehensible or 'legitimate'
objectives - cheaper gin, the deposition of a hated minister,
lower bread prices - was replaced by the feeling that they
aimed somehow at the utter unravelling of society. By the 1830s
and 1840s dread of the 'dangerous classes' could be transformed into near hysteria at times of great social and political
tension. Many members of the propertied classes were now
prepared to argue that unless new agencies of social discipline
were created, 'secret societies [...] working in the gloom of
night, may surprise us when surrounded by the noblest, the
best, the fairest of our land, when music floats through our
halls - may even strike us in the house of God on that day
devoted to prayer, may render our homes desolate, and involve
country and city in one common ruin'.[4] By the 1840s this type
of rhetoric was not uncommon among the bourgeoisie. Under
such circumstances not the military, nor a band of special
constables, but only a strong police securely lodged in the
working-class neighborhood 'could preserve property - the
countless millions possessed by the wealthy, the industrious,
the prudent; the trade of the merchant; the works of artists;
the factories of manufacturers; [...] the hospitals for the
sick; [...] the schools; [...] lastly those sacred edifices from
which flow those pure streams which prepare man for a future
and eternal home'.[5] In short the very fabric of society was
thought to be threatened. By this period popular disorder
of any type, even manifestations usually devoid of overt political
content - public-house affrays, dog-fights, races, popular
fêtes of any type - seemed to constitute a clear and present
danger to the social order.

Such apprehensions were often expressed in a concern that
the masses had totally eluded all contemporary mechanisms of
social control, or worse that they had somehow broken down.
For this reason the doings of the working class after release
from the salutary industrial discipline of the mill or workshop
became a matter of pressing interest. It was clear that what
workers did after passing out through the factory gates in the
evening into the *terra incognita* of the working-class neighborhood was both unwholesome and potentially dangerous. Joseph
Livesey, a Preston cheese merchant and temperance reformer,
wrote: 'My most anxious wish is to see this country peaceful,
prosperous and happy. Whatever other changes take place, we
shall never realize this till all the people are morally reformed.
Whilst trade and commerce, arts and sciences are rapidly
advancing, I think it will be conceded on all hands that the
morals of the great bulk of the people have not made equal

progress. [...] Unless the people are morally improved, being
now brought into large masses, and possessing increased
facilities for mischief, the result [...] may sooner or later,
be internal commotion if not a national wreck'.[6]

The industrial city, classically described by Engels, separated
class from class and eroded away older, more personal mechanisms of social control. 'Unhappily,' wrote a Liverpool businessman, 'it is true that, with the growth of wealth and population,
the wall of moral separation appears to have become broader,
higher and more impassible. The rich see less of the poor than
they used to do, know less of their habits, their feelings,
and their wants. [...] So far as our towns are concerned,
the cases are few [...] in which there is any personal tie
between rich and poor - any recognition [...] of a connexion
that does not end with working hours, or of any [...] claim
on an individual for anything besides fair wages and honest
work. [...] The subdivision of labour [...] sever[s] the
personal connexion which established an evident mutual claim
between master and servant. Regard to history confirms the
fears of common sense that a state of national life, in which
the moral unity of the nation is broken [...] is the sure forerunner [...] of rapid national decay'.[7] This kind of analysis -
paralleling that of Marx and Engels in significant ways -
expressed itself in bourgeois hands either in the language of
middle-class benevolence or else in the rhetoric of 'dangerous
classes'.

The 'licentiousness which prevails among the dense population of manufacturing towns is carried to a degree which is
appalling to contemplate [...]. And in addition to overt acts
of vice, there is a coarseness and grossness of feeling, and an
habitual indecency [...]. They are exempt from the restraints
of other classes'.[8] Because moral reform and social discipline
could only be generated - it was thought - from above, the
rupture of traditional lines of authority and deference was much
lamented. The Liverpool businessman quoted above remembered
with great feeling and nostalgia that his father 'knew every
one of the [...] hands whom he employed, they lived in their
employer's cottages, close to his house and mill, within reach
of the daily visits of his family'.[9] Because those threads could
never again be pieced together in the new environment of
Liverpool or Salford or Bradford, because the physical and
spiritual withdrawal of the upper classes was seemingly so total
and permanent, the way was open for the introduction of novel
types of surrogates - modern bureaucracies of official morality:
Somerset House and the new police.

For these reasons the police received an omnibus mandate:
to detect and prevent crime; to maintain a constant, unceasing
pressure of surveillance upon all facets of life in working-class
communities - to report on political opinions and movements,
trade-union activities, public house and recreational life. The
upper classes were not totally agreed on the ideal administrative

structure of the police nor on the precise relations between
the localities and central authority, and there continued to
be considerable local resistance to any highly centralized
model;[10] but there were few quibbles about the mission the
police were created to carry out in working-class districts.

By 1830 the deficiencies of the army in order keeping were
manifest. The inflexibility of the military, its inability to act
with anything less than the maximum of force when compelled
to intervene, and the consequent and frequent refusal of its
commanders to act; but more important its inherent unsuit-
ability to the task of providing the type of daily protection now
demanded[11] made its use increasingly inappropriate except in
pressing emergencies. Similarly, the old parish constable
system was now considered worse than useless. Thomas Ashton,
a Lancashire millowner, complained: 'Residents have their
relations or friends interested and you cannot get them to
act [...] The leet constables [...] are all connected by family
or some other way, they are of no use; we never could get a
protecting force from the neighbourhood'.[12] A Norwich manufacturer pleaded for a force under 'independent control'. The
local police would not protect industry 'from ignorant and
unlawful violence' - i.e. trade unionism - being under the
control of local tradesmen dependent on the working classes
and under the necessity to 'bid for popularity to the very
lowest of the voters'.[13] A Lincolnshire magistrate urged a
reformed police, pointing out that local constables were unable
or unwilling to suppress undesirable popular recreational
activities: 'If any active, influential individual is wanted to
interfere amongst the disorderly beerhouses, to suppress cock-
fightings, drunkenness, pugilistic combats [...] or any other
outrage, there is none to be found. [...] Our present constable [...] has never acted, and declines to act: he has been
sent for to quell riots in the streets, to take up drunken
brawlers, fighters, etc., but to no purpose'.[14]

As far as the working class and its political movement was
concerned, whatever reformed police structure was to be imposed,
it seemed certain that the new demands being raised among
the propertied for surer preservation of civil order and social
discipline would determine that the new police would inevitably
personify both alien values and an increasingly alien law in
the inner core of the modern industrial city.[15] Whatever power
the new policeman's truncheon might be invested with, it was
sure to be 'wonderfully soothing' - as Engels pointed out - to
the bourgeoisie; but 'for the working-man quite otherwise'.
The 1839 Constabulary Force Commissioners were ironically
well aware that the implantation of a modernized police structure
necessitated the overt cooperation and the moral assent of the
community.[16] This paper deals with the question of the degree
to which that moral assent was received. It proposes to examine
the impact the imposition of the police had upon working-class
communities; to discuss the threats working men perceived the

coming of the police to contain; to detail the attitudes and responses of the working-class political movement; and to reveal a hitherto undiscussed history of riotous protest against a reformed police structure.

Working-class political leaders consistently suspected that the new police was 'a *political*, not a *protective* force - that its object is not so much to prevent thieving as to watch political feeling, and give reports to the Ministers of the political movements of the working classes'.[17] The attitude of the working-class political movement in the eighteen thirties and forties toward a reformed modernized police system had solid roots in political experience: the days of Sidmouth, Oliver and Castle were not far behind after all.

E.P. Thompson has written that the radical populace viewed any police as a potential engine of political oppression until Chartist times.[18] In fact this attitude persisted past the Chartist period. Much of the hostility directed against the police from within working-class communities resulted as much from their interference in neighborhood and recreational life as from the suspicion that they had been implanted to carry on political surveillance. A great deal of the bitterness against the new police was a consequence of the fact that they were placed among the working classes to monitor all phases of working-class life - trade-union activity, drinking, gambling, sports as well as political activity. The overall mission of the police was to place working-class neighborhoods under a constant and multifaceted surveillance. The police, wrote one working-class leader, were 'really soldiers; it was no matter whether they were clothed in blue or red. [...] They were a set of blood-seeking vermin [...] They must exercise their strength to put down this blue-bottle force, or this country will soon be like Venice, governed by a little band of tyrants. [...] Was it not shameful [...] that they must be watched. [...] A man could not talk to his neighbour without one of these blue devils listening'.[19] The abolition of the London police became a prominent plank in the radical platform. Hetherington felt that a reform in the representation would guarantee only partial freedom. Englishmen could not be free until 'the police, like the rotten boroughs are abolished'.[20] London radicals in the 1830s pointed to the danger that the traditional liberties of the subjects would be eroded, as well as the prerogatives of the old parishes; sentiments which appealed to both the working classes and the rate-conscious London lower middle classes.

The example of Manchester is interesting in this regard. In the struggle of Cobden and his supporters to obtain a municipal charter and a borough police, radicals and trade unionists aligned themselves with the Tory anti-incorporators. A poster of 1838 printed by the trade-union leader John Doherty read:[21]

Men of the Borough
Be Up and Stirring Betimes on Friday
  Morning, by Ten o'Clock,
  Be at the
Manchester Town Hall
Remember! The Penalties for Non-Attendance are
  Whig Misrule
New and Oppressive Taxes
  A Bourbon Police.

Doherty and the Manchester trade unionists were perhaps less
quixotic than they seemed. When Sir Charles Shaw the government police commissioner told Sir Charles Napier that the
Manchester police were finally to be turned over to the town,
the latter seriously feared that they would become 'a means
for oppression in the hands of faction. A large town like that
requires a police, but ought to be ruled and paid for by a
responsible chief unconnected with [...] manufactories. He
ought to [...] keep the rich manufacturers from grinding the
poor to powder when raw cotton is falling in price; such
people naturally desire a police paid and governed by themselves'.[22]
    The idea that any significant change in England's police
structure would be unconstitutional and might pose a multiple
threat to working-class political and trade-union activity and
to the entire fabric of local neighborhood life ran deeply
through the writings and speeches of radical leaders[23] from the
time of the establishment of the London police to the attempt
by Russell to extend the new police to the manufacturing
districts of the North.
    In London the radical vestries of Marylebone and St Pancras
became the foci of anti-police propaganda after 1829. A pamphlet
distributed in Marylebone in 1830 urged the public to consider
the constitutional question as well as the awful expense involved
and then to 'UNITE in removing such a powerful force
from the hands of Government, and let us institute a police
System in the hands of the PEOPLE under *parochial* appointments'.[24] The same arguments advanced in London during the
1830s were repeated by northern radicals when the Whig
government carried the County Constabulary Act of 1839 and
created a new police force in Lancashire. Peter Bussey the
Bradford Chartist charged that the government 'appeared bent
on a destructive system of centralisation, which tended to
destroy the last vestige of the liberties of the working men of
the kingdom'. 'Would the people,' he asked, 'submit to 27,000
rural police being placed all over the kingdom [...] in effect,
another standing army, - to make the people submit to all
the [...] oppressions which Government comtemplate forcing
on them'.[25]
    J.R. Richardson raised the frightening prospect that the
government by establishing a 'depot for *gend'armerie*' in every

town might use the police to carry the New Poor Law into effect 'by first overawing the people, and then thrusting it down their throats'.[26] Richardson felt the time was approaching when every Poor Law union workhouse would have barracks for policemen beside it.[27] Oastler accused the Hyde magistrates of begging for a county police, 'a frenchified gens d'armie [sic], in order to help MR MARCUS to creep into the cradle of the babes and poison them with gas'.[28] The spectre of a government plot to make the new police an auxiliary of Somerset House was less fanciful than may be imagined. Oastler and the Chartists were merely taking Chadwick and the Poor Law Commissioners at their own word.[29] Nor should it be forgotten that at Huddersfield and Dewsbury anti-poor law manifestations were met by disciplined and efficient detachments of London police who stayed and fought the crowds in marked contrast to the local constables.[30] The fierceness of the London police on these occasions was surely in the minds of working men and their leaders when the government began to press for a county constabulary in 1839.

Resistance to a reformed police had roots in a number of fears: the traditional fear of a standing army; of the political uses which might be made of such a force; of the effects of police intrusion upon daily neighborhood life; and fear of the police as an agency which might be used to enforce the New Poor Law. There were also great apprehensions about the role the police might play in trade-union affairs and strikes. The Constabulary Force Commissioners had spoken of the 'need of an efficient police for the protection of the greater interests of the community of labourers against violence' as well as the need to afford protection 'to the use of machinery', which is 'protection to the great source of the manufacturing prosperity of the country'. The new police would be used to frustrate the attempts of strikers 'to deprive the capitalist of his free choice of agents for the employment of capital'.[31] The leaders of the working-class political movement were concerned that the police would become the guardians of unfettered capitalist economic development and of a free labor market as defined by orthodox political economy.

Testimony before the Constabulary Force Commissioners by a parade of northern millowners redoubled these suspicions. Thomas Ashton of Hyde said that 'in case of turns-out it would be desirable to have a force to protect the people that are willing to work'.[32] Henry Ashworth of Turton pleaded for a county force and described the difficulties he encountered importing blacklegs into the district during the spinners' strike of 1830. Ashworth's mills were situated at the junction of three townships. When he called upon the constables those belonging to two townships refused to appear at all; the third offered his services but was later discovered to be an intelligence agent of the unionists.[33] Sheriff Alison of Glasgow saw the establishment of a new police as the only efficient counter to trade-union power. His remedy for what he called 'intimidation' was to station forty to fifty police night and day around a struck mill to protect the manufacturer's property and the right of entry of blacklegs.[34] Chadwick himself felt that a new-style police might be useful in dealing with trade disputes. He argued that even in Sheffield in 1868 a force of 245 was insufficient to cope with a 'turn out of associated trades'. He urged that flying squads of London police be used to deal with 'picketting and terrorism' anywhere in England. This would strike a useful blow against the 'pot-house conclaves' who he felt ran the trade unions.[35]

Mr John Foster has ably illustrated how important a concern control over the police was to the working-class movement in Lancashire.[36] In Oldham, local constables were subjected to popular pressure both when they were controlled by the vestry and later by the police commission. The County Police Act of 1839 represented a great political defeat. State intervention and the increased power of the JPs which it entailed transformed the police into a weapon of the employers. Henceforth they could be more freely used as both political spies and escorts for strikebreakers.

In the spring of 1840, detachments of the new Lancashire police began to arrive in the localities amid cries of execration from the working-class press and from local communities whose initial contacts with the police had been shocking and disturbing. From Middleton: 'Blue Devils: We have now got four of those blue plagues, called new police, to torment [...] the virtuous part of the [...] inhabitants of this town, and it is afloat that we are to have two more'.[37] The arrival of the police in the Rochdale district threw many of the poor into consternation by busying themselves monitoring and harassing street traders, peddlers and match-sellers.[38]

The appearance of the new police contributed to the shock of initial contact. They were described as 'well clothed and shod, with a pair of white gloves [...] and a great coat for bad weather. They go strutting about [...] armed [...] with a bludgeon, striking terror through all the old women and children, who see them with 18s per week [...] while the labourer toils from morning till night for 10s'.[39] There were complaints from Mansfield, where a detachment of Metropolitans had been sent, that they were forbidding working men from chatting together in groups in the road 'while a set of idle drones are lounging about our streets'.[40] The epithets used to describe the new police - 'blue bottles', 'blue idlers', 'blue drones', 'hired mercenaries', 'unconstitutional bravoes' - reveal one of the most profound sources of resentment against them. The police were hated because they were felt to be unproductive parasites. Most of the terms used to describe them were synonyms for men who do not really work for a living. A meeting at Middleton was called in February 1841 to memorialize the Lancashire magistrates to abolish the new police. The

meeting was attended not only by workers but by small shop-
keepers upset about rate increases. All applauded when a
weaver asked: 'Who sent for the police? The middle class. The
middle class chose the men who concocted and passed the law
empowering the police to become in society nothing but out-
laws'.[41]
A significant item in the plans of a number of Chartist ris-
ings in 1840 was the outright murder of the police. This was
the case at Newcastle until cooler heads prevailed and at Sheffield where the 'policemen were special objects of vengeance.
all the conspirators having instructions to murder every policeman they met with'.[42] The radical and Chartist leaders of the
1830s and 1840s articulated the resentment felt against the
police on a day-to-day basis in working-class neighborhoods.
The phenomenon of anti-police resistance and its manifestation
in its most exacerbated form - the anti-police riot - was directly
linked to the sentiment that the police were intruders and
represented a threat to many aspects of community life. In a
significant number of cases episodes of violent resistance were
directly traceable to police interference with established or
customary leisure activities or with pub or beerhouse life.[43]
Most of the major anti-police riots are concentrated in the period
1839-44; however it should be noted that even in the relatively
calmer 1850s similar incidents, though on a smaller scale, took
place in the West Riding when county police were introduced
in 1857.

So far an approach has been made to a number of questions.
Some insight has been gained into the reasons working-class
leaders were suspicious of the police before their actual introduction. By outlining contemporary statements made by
magistrates, millowners and others, the conclusion has been
reached that those fears were not the result of demagogic
impulses but were, considering the historical context, reasonably legitimate. Second, some understanding has been gained
of the real shock experienced on the local or neighborhood
level once the police were placed on duty.
It remains now to detail and analyze a number of specific
episodes of anti-police resistance in the 1840s and to examine
their causes and course. Seven incidents, four in Lancashire
(Middleton, Manchester, Lancaster, Colne), two in Yorkshire
(Hull, Leeds) and one in the Potteries (Lane End), have been
selected for discussion. In most of these instances anti-police
activities were prolonged and extensive, often covering a large
portion of town. It is useful to remember however that the
anti-police riots of the 1840s represented an exacerbated form
of a common, even daily, phenomenon in every industrial town
at almost any time. The more routine, circumscribed disturbances which one might pull at any time from police records or
the local press are equally important pieces of data for the
social historian. Incidents which in the 1850s or 1860s might

have remained confined to one neighborhood, one street or
one pub, often resulted in the mobilization of a whole town in
the more tense 1840s.

The purposes or objectives of the participants varied. In
some cases - above all where police were newly implanted - the
chief objective was broad in scope: to permanently drive the
police out of the community by force. In places which had been
policed for some time anti-police eruptions had more limited
aims: to preserve popular recreations or customs, prevent
interference in strikes, protect wanted individuals, protest
against police interference in political activities, protest against
instances of police brutality, rescue arrested persons etc. In
a number of cases - Leeds, Manchester, Hull - local crowds
appeared against the police only after a confrontation between
the latter and a group of outsiders to the community - off-duty
soldiers on liberty in the town. The local populace entered at
first in solidarity with the soldiers - though with their own
set of grievances - and often stayed out against the police long
after the troops had been subdued or removed by their officers.
Off-duty soldiers often acted as the spark which ignited a
local working-class crowd and encouraged them to engage in
a disturbance. In such incidents the grievances of the latter
were 'mediated' through the discontents of an outside group.
At Lane End, Middleton, Lancaster and Colne this phenomenon
was not observed. The response of the working-class community
was unmediated and direct.

The major examples of the first type of disturbance in the
1840s occurred at Manchester and Leeds; however, a smaller
precursor of the same kind took place at Hull in July 1839. A
private in a regiment of foot stationed there was arrested by a
borough policeman for being drunk and disorderly. As he was
being taken off his mates turned out of a beerhouse to assist
him.[44] More police arrived on the scene and a large civilian
crowd gathered. In this case the police were driven off when
the civilians entered the affray on the side of the troops.[45]
The incidents at Manchester and Leeds were much more serious
and wider in scope.

During the evening of May 22 1843, police arrived to quell
a minor row between two soldiers at a beerhouse in Bengal
Street. The soldiers' mates and local workers in the beerhouse
closed ranks to prevent the arrest. The police retreated to
the station house, called out reinforcements and returned. The
arrest was successfully made, but not without a rescue attempt
being made by a large civilian crowd armed with stones.
Rumors flew about the next morning that hostilities would be
resumed. That evening an immense crowd led by soldiers
emerged from Bengal Street and converged on the police office.
The police barricaded themselves inside and waited for reinforcements, but by the time they arrived the crowd had broken
in to another police office in Kirkby Street and severely beaten
a number of constables. In Port Street five soldier leaders

were captured, but local residents turned out of their homes
to battle the police and effect a successful rescue. At 6.30 p.m.
an inspector walking along Oldham Road in search of a cavalry
unit saw a large crowd of perhaps 1000 led by nine soldiers
heading towards Piccadilly. The evidence suggests that this
crowd was separate from the one reported in Port Street at
about the same time. One must conclude that anti-police activities
had spread by this hour over a significant portion of the
Ancoats district. By about 10.00 p.m. order was finally restored
with the help of troops under officers.[46]

The Leeds police riot of 1844 was an even more serious affair.
Once again the immediate cause was the arrival of the police
at a working-class recreational center to deal with a minor
incident; once more off-duty soldiers were directly involved.
The appearance of the police at the Green Man beerhouse in
York Street on Sunday evening June 9 1844 touched off a series
of massive confrontations lasting three days, involving an
extremely large number of local civilians. By anyone's standards what ensued must be considered nothing less than a
mass uprising against the Leeds Corporation Police. At 8.00 p.m.
two policemen on duty in Kirkgate interviewed an individual
who complained that some soldiers at the Green Man had beaten
him and taken 2½d from his table. The constables went to the
beerhouse and apprehended a number of soldiers, but on the
way to the lock-up they were fallen on by the soldiers' mates
and beaten with fists and military belt buckles.[47] More policemen arrived and a general melee ensued confined - for the time
being at least - to police and soldiers. No local civilians took
any part in these events except to cheer the soldiers on. The
next evening (Monday) some forty soldiers belonging to the
70th Regiment of Foot assembled in the Green Parrot beerhouse
in Harper Street to further revenge themselves on the Leeds
police. They issued from the pub armed with bludgeons and
belts and attacked a number of policemen in Vicar Lane. As
they entered Briggate they encountered a huge crowd of local
civilians estimated by the press at more than a thousand. The
soldiers raised the cry 'Down With The Police!' and the crowd,
which had been giving way - not exactly knowing the soldiers'
intentions - moved to join them. The civilians according to
the local press followed the soldiers not 'out of love to the
soldiers themselves, but from [...] feelings of hatred towards
the police'.

Why were there so many civilians assembled in Briggate? Were
they originally simply onlookers gathered to watch the police
and soldiers fight things out? If so, why were they in Briggate
when the 'action' was taking place in Vicar Lane? Or were
there perhaps two anti-police crowds out, one military and one
civilian, each with its own grievances? This question is difficult
to answer, but some evidence exists to support the latter view.
These events took place in the midst of a campaign by the Leeds
magistrates and police to stop Sunday political meetings in the

Free Market on ostensibly sabbatarian grounds. There is also
evidence to suggest that on the previous day (Sunday) the
police had tried to stop a meeting in the Free Market.[48]

The Briggate crowd now led by soldiers marched together
down Kirkgate forcing the police to break and scatter. As in
Ancoats one year earlier, the disturbances spread rapidly. By
the time the evening's proceedings had terminated and the
streets of central Leeds swept entirely clear of any police
presence, four separate groups of local civilians had been
reported out against the police: the original Briggate crowd,
one composed of Leeds Irish in York Street, another in Park
Row and a fourth, which had gathered at the barracks in
Woodhouse Lane to cheer the soldiers. What is of most interest
in the rioting of Monday evening is that rather early most of
the soldiers involved were rounded up by other troops under
officers and marched back to barracks. With the soldiers
removed from the scene, local workers remained to battle the
police alone and on their own account. This was the case as
well the following night. All soldiers were strictly confined to
barracks and did not appear at all. In the battles of Tuesday
night a local working-class crowd faced the Leeds police
unaccompanied and unled by any outsiders. The magistrates
and police had prepared themselves well however. The police
were densely concentrated - making it difficult for the rioters
to isolate them in small groups or as individuals on their beats -
and armed with cutlasses. By about 10.00 p.m. order was
finally restored and calm returned to the center of the city
for the first time in three days.[49]

As far as the participation of local civilians was concerned,
no doubt the anti-police uprising of June 1844 was in part a
result of factors which must remain hidden. Yet this affair is
extremely instructive. Surely the decision of the magistrates
to suppress Sunday meetings and the implementation of this
policy by the police created a separate and volatile focus of
civilian discontent, which erupted in violence once the lead
was given in another quarter. Probably this does not go far
enough in accounting for the extreme violence nor the long
duration of the reaction. It seems likely that the Leeds anti-
police riot was the end result of a very long history of accumulated grievances and resentments against the corporation police
going back to their introduction in 1836. Ultimately it was the
quality of day-to-day police-community relations on the neighborhood level over a nine-year period which resulted in this
episode.

The final model-examples of community resistance to the police
in the 1840s did not conform exactly to the pattern of Hull,
Ancoats and Leeds. No soldiers were involved at any time,
except insofar as they were employed by the authorities;
resistance from local residents was direct and not mediated
through the grievances of any outside group. What accounts

for the marked difference in pattern observed at Hull, Manchester and Leeds and the outbreaks at Middleton, Lancaster and Colne?

In Hull, Manchester and Leeds a new police had been well implanted by the early 1840s. Leeds possessed a modern uniformed police since 1836. Certainly few people entertained the idea that it was possible to rid the locality of the police. The fact that the police had time to sink roots in these communities during a period of relative political calm may be linked to the fact that outbreaks, when they occurred, required some kind of outside catalyst. Instances of direct, unmediated resistance took place in communities in which the police were novelties, and usually occurred upon the introduction of the police in the first instance. In Middleton, Lancaster, Colne and the Potteries the main issue was not police brutality, interference with popular leisure patterns, interference in strikes or with popular political meetings, but the presence of the police itself.

In mid May 1840 at Middleton - the scene of much previous anti-police agitation - a number of new police went to serve an assault warrant on a young miner. He could not be located but a row ensued between the police and the suspect's mates. As one man was being led to the station house a crowd of some hundreds of people slowly began to gather. The police, fearing a rescue attempt, tried to rush their captive out of town. 'Marching through the Little Park [...] the road was crowded with men, women and children. A hooting was set up, and striking with bludgeons and fists, kicking with clogs and shoes, and throwing stones and brickbats became the order of the day'.[50] In the confusion the prisoner made his escape. The whole of the new Middleton police were forced to make their own escape and took refuge in Manchester. They were ultimately reinstalled only with the help of a strong contingent of Manchester police.

One year earlier, immediately after the introduction of new police in the Potteries, a similar incident took place. On May 7 1839 the police entered a beerhouse in Lane End to quell a typical row. When they arrived they were insulted by all parties to the dispute. Five persons were arrested, but as the police tried to leave the scene with their prisoners, they were met by a speedily assembled crowd. The police succeeded in reaching the lock-up, however the next morning a full-scale riot erupted. A large crowd congregated around the lock-up, stoned the police and threatened to effect a rescue at nightfall. People milled about the jail all day long while the magistrates called for police reinforcements from Stoke and Fenton and for the yeomanry. Under an escort of troops the prisoners were transferred to Newcastle while a furious battle raged in the streets. Barricades were erected out of earthenware crates, the Riot Act was read and the yeomanry ended by firing on the crowd with ball cartridge. For the next few days the district

resembled an armed camp. Regular troops were brought up
from as far away as Liverpool. One report stated that the
origin of the riot was in no way connected with politics 'but
appears to have arisen solely from a hatred of the [...]
police'.[51] Relations between the lower classes of the Potteries
and the police did not improve, prompting local respectables,
clergy, etc., to emphasize the constant danger to the lives
of the police 'lately established in the Borough of Stoke' and
to plead with Russell for a permanent force of troops to be
stationed in the district.[52]

At Lancaster serious disturbances took place on the race-
course with the first appearance of the new rural police at the
annual races holiday.[53] Here feeling against the implantation
of the police had been running high for some time not only
among the lower classes but among middling rate-payers as
well. In July 1840 the High Constable of the hundred complained that he was unable to file his police rolls; rate-payers
were adopting the 'impediment system' as a technique of passive
resistance and refusing to pay the police rate.[54] Many felt that
in the hundred of Lonsdale South there 'was no need for an
organized force, as was needed in the more industrial and
more heavily populated parts of the County [...] The establishment of the rural police [...] had more than doubled the
County-rate. In many townships the police-assessment exceeded
the poor-rate'.[55]

Even before the creation of the rural police Lancaster Races
were not totally unpoliced. Up to that point, they had been
monitored by the borough police of Lancaster. It is not certain
whether the Lancaster police had traditionally behaved with
more indulgence towards gambling, drinking and other normal
concomitants of popular fêtes. In any event, the roots of the
anti-police outbreak in 1840 do not lie entirely in the manifestation of a harder attitude; on the contrary the new rurals
were under orders to behave with restraint.[56] It was not the
overt behavior of the new police which gave offense; it was
their presence itself. Lancaster Races not only attracted persons from the city but farmers and tradesmen from the surrounding areas. It was probably the feelings of people such
as these which created the smouldering atmosphere at the opening of the meeting. One witness later testified: 'Heard many
people calling out against the police - "We want no police here",
"Go home to your own country".[57] There were many farmers
on the course. They were loud in expressing their feeling
against the rural police. They were respectable farmers'.[58]

On the first day of the Lancaster Races, July 22 1840, a
detachment of Lancashire rurals under Inspector Walters moved
up to the racecourse with orders to assist the borough constables in dispersing gambling tables and preventing breaches
of the peace. After the last race the county police were attacked
by a large crowd. A sergeant reported that the people 'called
the police "Bloody Rurals"' and threatened to break their

heads if they returned to the races the following day.[59]

On the following evening, the Chief Constable of the Lancashire force arranged to send up 24 reinforcements on the morning train. On Thursday Captain Ridge was able to appear on the course with 34 men. At about seven p.m. there was a scuffle on the racecourse, which the police diagnosed as a 'sort of sham fight' meant to provoke them. Ridge asked the crowd to disperse but was met by 'a general shower of sticks and stones', which nearly unhorsed him. The police then charged, took three prisoners, commandeered an omnibus and made for the safety of Lancaster. The crowd followed 'hooting and pelting with stones, and everything they could lay their hands on'. At a quarry near Highfield the police were ambushed by an even larger crowd forcing them off the road and into the fields. They reformed on the road further along and successfully entered the city still holding their prisoners.[60]

The resistance to the introduction of the new police at Colne was the most prolonged and serious of all Victorian anti-police episodes. The events at Colne from April through August 1840 were not so much riots - by definition ephemeral phenomena - as a bitter war of attrition against the new police. In mid April 1840 sixteen constables and a superintendent Macleod were introduced to Colne. Colonel Constance, a military officer sent to deal with the violence of April, provided us with a most intelligent and sensitive description of the shock of initial contact between the lower classes of an old weaving community and a modern uniformed police:[61]

> The lower orders of Colne are a particularly uncouthly set, and have hitherto been in entire possession of the place, occupying the streets, footpaths, and public places in groups at nearly all hours to the great inconvenience of the more respectable part of the inhabitants [...] who in moving about were obliged to thread their way [...] through the general obstruction. I consider this uncivilised and rude manner is more from habit than from any real intention to incommode or be uncivil - a want of civilisation, a want of example in so old, and remote a place. The police in correcting an inconvenience of so long a standing, may do well at first to correct it gradually, and by quiet measures [...] The ignorant will resist [...] if driven to it by harsh measures in introducing it.

Instead, the response of the police - total strangers to the district and including a substantial number of Scots - was the imposition of the 'move-on system'. One newspaper reported that the Colne police had instituted 'a regular system of thrashing and running the people', and that they uniformly responded to the groans and jeers with which they were greeted in the streets with bludgeon attacks. Sir Charles Napier noted that police conduct was extremely offensive, one constable in particular having 'prided himself on what he termed "slating them", i.e. breaking their heads with his staff. The people in [...]

Colne are said to be a rough and resolute set of men, and not likely to bear this sort of treatment'.[62]

By April 24 1840 a flash-point was reached. During the afternoon small knots of men began to collect in different parts of town; by sundown a large crowd numbering several hundreds had congregated. The events of that evening showed evidence less of a 'spontaneous' riot than of real tactical planning. Every lamp in Colne was put out. At about 9 p.m. the police formed up to clear the streets. One segment of the crowd pretended to flee ahead of them to the east. At length on a given signal this group turned 'and in a disciplined manner' began to stone those policemen who had been lured away from the main body. The police, split into two bodies, were driven from the streets.[63] The press feel that the decision to mount a concerted offensive against the police was taken at a Chartist meeting during Easter week. This cannot be either substantiated or disproved. What lends some credence to the theory is the fact that the crowd displayed great discipline and employed sophisticated tactics which may well have been the result of advance planning; Colne was not without a reputation for being a center of physical-force Chartism.

The following morning a fresh superintendent with twenty reinforcements was sent from Burnley. They found the town in 'a state of the utmost alarm and excitement'. The magistrates also requested the immediate despatch of troops. At about 9 p.m. a detachment of foot and some cavalry entered Colne, too late to prevent the police from being cleared from the streets once again. They were greeted cordially and with cheers. 'These fellows', one man told a reporter, 'know how to behave themselves, but the police don't'.[64] Colonel Constance at Burnley reported to Colonel Wemyss that many people at Colne told him that they were 'glad to see the soldiers but were determined not to have the police'.[65] Constance accurately assessed the chief objective of the Colne riot: to permanently rid the town of the police ('expulsing them from that part of the country'). Constance kept his men in Colne for a few days in order to monitor a monster Chartist meeting planned for April 27th. The meeting took place without incident and the troops were withdrawn to Burnley on April 28th.

Upon their departure the Lancashire police authorities more than tripled the number of constables assigned to Colne. Rioting did not recur, and between May and the end of July the police reduced their manpower to the level established by their regulations.[66] During the last week in July anti-police activities began to revive. At night the windows of prominent anti-Chartists and supporters of the police were smashed and volleys of stones were launched at patrolling constables from housetops. One of the chief targets was a Mr Bolton, a solicitor and clerk to the local magistrates, a vociferous anti-Chartist and the man locally considered most responsible for the appearance of the new police at Colne.[67]

On Tuesday evening August 4th Bolton's house was surrounded by a mob which smashed his windows. A general attack
was then launched against the police driving them from the
streets. The following evening saw another pitched battle in
the marketplace. On Thursday evening another assault was made
on the police with military order and precision. Early in the
evening a crowd armed with pistols, bludgeons, pokers and
other weapons mustered on the outskirts of town. There seemed
to be a commander who gave orders and directed the proceedings. At about 10 p.m. the streets suddenly became quiet
and there was a 'perfect lull'. Soon hundreds of men marched
into town 'in regular order'. A command was then given: 'All
cowards remain where you are, and the remainder march to
attack the police.' 'Then', one report ran, 'followed the most
hideous yells, showers of stones, and the crashing of windows.
The town next morning looked more like a besieged place than
anything else'. The police were once again routed and fled out
of town in all directions. Once more as in April troops arrived
on the scene from Burnley. Again they found Colne quiet.
The military officers protested that there was nothing for
them to do and immediately withdrew their men.[68]
    The next day the 'respectable inhabitants' called a meeting
at the grammar school[69] to consider what could next be done
to preserve both order and property, but when they assembled
they found the room already occupied by an angry meeting
of Chartists. Thoroughly frightened, a deputation led by a
magistrate hurried to Burnley to plead again for military
protection. Once more a detachment of foot and cavalry came
over to invest the town and again the army found itself at a
loss for something to do. In fact during the entire history of
anti-police resistance in Colne no confrontation with the army
ever took place. It was a prominent and intelligent part of
the strategy of the resisters never to engage the army, but to
wait until they had gone before dealing with the police. On
Sunday evening, arguing that calm had prevailed for some
days and that the troops required barracks, the army left
again. This of course was the signal for the resurgence of
anti-police activities.
    On Monday the magistrates, sensing this, swore in seventy
special constables drawn from among the 'respectable inhabitants' and convinced the police authorities to double the force
in Colne. That evening the Riot Act was read several times
and the police and specials paraded the town dispersing conclaves of civilians. Between 10 and 11 p.m. a large crowd
rallied at a newly erected church east of Colne, armed themselves with long spear-like iron palisades left over from the
construction of the church railings, and entered Colne from
Keighley Road. The battle was joined in one of the main streets
of Colne. The resisters were again described as marching 'in
military array, four abreast, each man carrying a bludgeon' or
other weapon. In the struggle Joseph Halstead, a special

constable and local millowner, was struck in the head with an iron palisade and killed. Yet again the police were swept from Colne and again troops from Burnley were called in only to find all calm. No doubt there would have been further anti-police eruptions but for the fact that Sir Charles Napier was finally ordered to have barracks built and establish a permanent military force at Colne. Ultimately the new police had to be installed in Colne by a resident military presence.[70]

There was a poignant sequel to the Colne police riots. The chief defendant in the murder of Halstead was a twenty-year old weaver, Richard Boothman. Boothman was tried at the assizes and sentenced to death in March 1841.[71] His sentence was later commuted to transportation for life to Van Diemen's Land. Boothman maintained to the end that he did not murder Halstead. He claimed he had never been a part of the crowd that night, had been arrested after just returning from a neighboring local feast and that he had been a victim of a case of mistaken identity. An attempt to reopen his case by his family in 1860 was unsuccessful, and he died still in exile in 1877 at the age of fifty-seven.[72]

To recapitulate thus far. The imposition of a modern police was opposed for a number of reasons and by different groups of people. Radicals argued against the police on the grounds that it constituted a break with the valuable English tradition of resistance to the concept of a standing army or in terms of the rhetoric of 'ancient rights and liberties'. Middle-class people often objected on similar grounds as well as out of rate consciousness. Farmers and others living in rural areas often argued that police might be necessary in cities such as Manchester or Leeds, but the expense of keeping them in the countryside far outweighed their potential usefulness. In addition working-class radicals and Chartists feared that the state might use the police to enforce the New Poor Law, employ them to break strikes and interfere in trade disputes, or use them to repress or spy upon working-class political movements.

Once actually deployed in the streets the police offended the lower classes in very concrete ways. The look of the police, their dress, the fact that to many workers' eyes their chief function was to merely walk about all day, gave rise to the accusation that government had saddled the country with well-paid idlers, 'blue locusts' who devoured tax money and produced nothing of use in return. Most disturbing of all was the imposition of the hated 'move-on system' as a standard item of police policy. The coming of the police also signalled a closer monitoring of working-class drinking patterns, the openings and closings of pubs and beerhouses, and an entirely novel and uncustomary surveillance of the entire range of popular leisure activities: drinking, brutal sports, footracing, fairs, feasts and other fêtes. The police came as unwelcome spectators into the very nexus of urban neighborhood life.

When the phenomenon of resistance was discussed, especially
in its most exacerbated form - the anti-police riot - two main
types of disturbance were discerned. These have been examined.
One further question suggests itself at this point. All the
incidents described so far occurred at a time of heightened
political and social tension and economic distress. Were these
eruptions simply a function of the heyday of Chartism or mere
concomitants of a period of ferment? It may be of use here to
analyze a 'control' situation, observe what happened when
the county police appeared in the West Riding during the
relatively calm year 1857, and compare the pattern to Lancashire
in 1839-40.

By the end of December 1856 the new West Riding police had
been deployed into most districts not policed by the muni-
cipalities. The reaction was as immediate and in some cases as
intense as in Lancashire sixteen years previously. The police
instantly made themselves obnoxious by mounting a concerted
campaign against customary patterns of working-class recreation. By the end of December the roads on the outskirts of
Wakefield, habitually 'infested [...] with young men given to
foot racing', were being cleared by the new police. In the same
area gambling on the public highway - a traditional Sunday morning activity of working-class youth - was severely repressed.[73]
In future weeks and months incidents of a similar nature were
frequently reported, often accompanied by affrays or attacks on
the police.

The police imposed an increased and more efficient supervision of the pubs and beerhouses. In the West Riding, drinking places on the outskirts of large towns had been virtually
immune to prosecution for keeping illegal hours. Out-townships
of Leeds such as Pudsey or Armley were not policed by the
borough and did not pay the Leeds police rate. Consequently
they had long been favorite retreats of Leeds workers, who
knew that they were unlikely to be turned out into the streets
when others went to church or chapel. A detachment of West
Riding police appeared suddenly in Pudsey in December 1856
and forced pubs to close during divine service. For this they
were complimented by Edward Baines, who saw them 'doing
good in several ways - not least in the cause of morality'.[74]
A similar situation existed on the outskirts of Huddersfield.
Beershops in the out-townships had never regularly observed
the Sunday closing times even under unusually severe pressure from the parochial constables. Now under a redoubled
police surveillance they were forced to shut down during
prohibited hours.[75] This generated great resentment in the
drink trade and among their patrons in the district.

Almost immediately a rash of assaults on the new police was
reported in the vicinity of Huddersfield. The offenders were
treated with great severity by the magistrates. At Deighton
in March 1856 fines totalling over £13 - an amount well beyond
the means of working-class pocket-books - were imposed for

the beating of two policemen.[76] Consider the case of Wibsey
near Bradford. From January to July 1857 a state of open
warfare existed between the local inhabitants and the new police.
At the end of January there was a crackdown on cockfighting.
A number of men were arrested and fined 5/- for cruelty to
animals.[77] Beerhouses and pubs were closely watched, and
gambling in the fields and on the roads was impeded. Relations
between the police and the community deteriorated, culminating
in the serious affair of Sergeant Briar.

Briar was known as 'one of the most active officers in the
West Riding Police' and was held chiefly responsible for most
of the unpleasant changes which had occurred in Wibsey since
the police arrived. In early May Briar was marked for elimination from the Wibsey scene. On some pretext he was enticed
to a beershop owned by a Mrs Thornton. The latter accused
him of an indecent assault. The magistrates would not entertain
the charge and instead committed Mrs Thornton on a charge
of perjury. At this the entire neighborhood erupted. On the
evening of June 3 1857 Briar was surrounded by a local crowd,
beaten with sticks and deprived of his staff and clothes. Naked
and nearly unconscious he was to be dragged the entire round
of Wibsey beerhouses to be exhibited to the patrons. Three
men were arrested in connection with this incident and fined
£5 each. The fines 'were immediately paid, the court was
crowded by the inhabitants of the Wibsey district [...] and
one of them boasted [...] that they could have raised ten
times the amount'.[78] No doubt the Briar incident was part of
a community vendetta against the new police most probably led
by local beerhouse keepers and their patrons; in other words
the majority of the male population of the district.

As in the case of Lancaster in 1840 the time of a local fête
was often the occasion for dealing with the new police. Colliers
from Thornhill and other mining communities near Wakefield
traditionally had enjoyed unrestricted holiday at Middlestown
Feast. In 1857 the West Riding police turned up in force to
prevent the usual excesses. The miners 'paraded the village
in bodies, shouting and getting up sham fights for the purpose
of provoking the police'.[79] The feast ended with a pitched battle
between police and colliers. Those arrested were warned by
the magistrates that before 'the establishment of the rural
police these practices [drinking and rowdyism] were winked at,
but in future they would be prevented'.[80] Henceforth, they
promised, the feast would be a closely monitored affair. Near
Halifax an incident similar in nature to the one which sparked
the Potteries riot of 1839 occurred. A row started in a beerhouse and the landlord ejected everyone into the road. When
two policemen attempted to stop the affair the whole neighborhood turned out of their houses to thrash the police.[81]

Often mobbings and assaults on the police were, on the surface at least, completely unprovoked.[82] The frequency of such
incidents indicates that people reacted not only to what the

police did but to their very presence in the community itself.
All of the classical reasons for distrusting or detesting the
police surfaced in Yorkshire in the late 1850s, most prominently
the theme of the 'blue locusts' or 'idle drones'. One Halifax
area beerhouse keeper called a particularly hated member of
the force 'an idle scroll [sic]'. Assailing the whole of the West
Riding police, he remarked: 'they were too idle to work, and
such as himself had to keep them'.[63] One of the defendants at
Lancaster in 1840 complained that 'every morning before he
got his breakfast the police took 10 per cent of it'.[84]

One must conclude from the example of Yorkshire in 1857
that the imposition of a modern uniformed police called forth
a bitter and often violent response, and that this reflex took
place despite the general state of the economy or the level of
political or social tension. The nature of the resistance - though
perhaps not the intensity - in the West Riding followed a pattern generally similar to Lancashire in the more turbulent
year 1840. The impression is left that once the police were
successfully entrenched the open warfare of initial contact
was replaced by a state one may characterize as armed truce.
In many instances however the truce would be broken and
more or less open warfare would resume for awhile. This might
occur when over-diligent police supervision of customary patterns of popular leisure infuriated people, when the police
openly protected or escorted blacklegs during strikes, or
when it was felt that the police were behaving in a brutal or
disrespectful manner. Police discourtesy or brutality,
especially during a time of distress or unemployment, could
generate a large riot reminiscent of Lancashire in the spring
and summer of 1840.

It may be of use to briefly discuss one instance of the
resumption of open warfare. At Lees near Oldham during the
cotton famine a crowd, estimated at about 150, gathered on
Saturday night January 23 1864, threatening to kill a certain
police constable Dermody. Dermody and another policeman with
him were assaulted, the police office was besieged and considerable damage was done. Most of the individuals involved
were unemployed workers. The immediate cause of the riot
was the serving of summonses on nine factory workers for
being drunk and disorderly. The underlying problem however
was police intimidation and harassment. Relations between the
police and working men, not friendly in 'normal' times, worsened
perceptively when the male population of a town was unemployed
and in the streets and pubs both day and night. Under such
circumstances the police were tempted to redouble the 'move-
on system' and indiscriminately break up casual assemblies
of men in the streets or in front of beershops and pubs.

At the trial of the Lees rioters the court received a memorial
drawn up by the vicar, the Rev. Mr Whittaker, stating that
the assault on the police was 'mainly attributable to the
injudicious and offensive intolerance of [...] constable

Dermody'. The memorial sheds valuable light on the local background to this incident: 'The other day a few men were returning from the working men's school, when they had occasion
to stop in the road [...] Police-constable Dermody instantly
ordered them off. At the same moment a man [...] returning
from the same place [...] stopped to see what was to do,
when, without the slightest provocation, said officer took
him by the back and pushed him violently along'.[85] Whittaker's
document concluded that the magistrates must take steps to
remove Dermody or there could be no peace in the town. Dermody was not removed. The matter was referred to the Superintendent of Police, who was assured by 'many of the respectable inhabitants of Leeds' that Dermody was 'more deserving
of commendation than blame'.[86] Similarly in Leeds anti-police
eruptions, often quite violent but on a more restricted scale,
continued to occur. One such episode, in which an entire
neighborhood turned out to shield a resident from arrest, tied
up nearly the entire Leeds force for a whole night in October
1848.[87]

Ultimately a modern, efficient bureaucratic police imposed by
the fiat of the state could not be driven out of the communities
into which they had been implanted – as the Colne, Lancaster
and Wibsey rioters had wished – any more than the new
machinery could be gotten rid of a few decades earlier. In this
respect they were perhaps quixotic efforts. More accurately,
they seem quixotic in retrospect only. Even the magistrates
of Lonsdale South (Lancaster) were under the impression that
the police could be withdrawn, in 1840, resolved that an
effort be made to withdraw from the operation of the Act of
Parliament, and appointed a committee to represent the matter
at the annual sessions.[88] In contrast, at Leeds in 1864, the main
demand of both rioters and memorialists was not the abolition
or withdrawal of the police, but the removal of an obnoxious
policeman. By this date nobody considered the possibility of
ridding a district of the police a realistic one. After initial
attempts to remove the police proved fruitless, anti-police
outbreaks took on more limited objectives: to preserve popular
customs and recreations; to prevent police interference in
labor disputes;[89] to protest police brutality; and to protect
or rescue members of the community wanted or arrested. Anti-
police violence did not disappear after the 1850s; it assumed
a more restricted shape and became (like prostitution) a typical
component of the undercurrent of everyday Victorian life.
   Moderation in the frequency of large-scale anti-police eruptions in no way signified that the authorities had succeeded
in obtaining the full moral assent of the community. On May 20
1872 (to take a random example) the following exchange took
place in a Leeds working-class street: 'When spoken to, [Holmes]
placed himself in a fighting attitude [...] and said [...] if he
did not leave the fold he would kick him out of it. The officer

told him he was on his beat. Holmes's wife then came up and [...] would not allow him to go around the fold saying *such like was not wanted there'*.[90] Over thirty-five years after the appearance of the Leeds Corporation Police, they were still regarded as unwelcome intruders in working-class neighborhoods, and were informed of the fact with some frequency.

The 'first thing a policeman ought to know', an informant told Stephen Reynolds at the beginning of this century, 'is when to let well alone'.[91] Reynolds found as much resentment against being moved-on in the streets, being interfered with in family affairs and in the pub as the present writer discovered in Colne in 1840 or Leeds in 1864.

Flora Thompson's Candleford Green people still regarded the police in the 1870s and 1880s as 'a potential enemy, set to spy on them by the authorities'.[92] Nor could it have been otherwise. The police were charged 'with the enforcement of a whole mass of petty enactments, which are little more than social regulations bearing almost entirely on working-class life. [...] In every direction, inside his own house as well as out, the working-man's habits and convenience are interfered with [...]. Whether or no he comes into collision with them is more a matter of good fortune than of law-abidingness [...] a working man may easily render himself liable to arrest [...] without in the least doing what is wrong in his own eyes or in the eyes of his neighbours'.[93] 'Nobody', wrote Robert Roberts of the same period, 'in our Northern slum [...] ever spoke in fond regard, then or afterwards, of the policeman as a "social worker" and "handyman of the streets". Like their children, delinquent or not, the poor in general looked upon him with fear and dislike. When one arrived on a "social" visit they watched his passing with suspicion and his disappearance with relief. [...] The "public" (meaning the middle and upper classes), we know well enough, held their "bobby" in patronising "affection and esteem", which he repaid with due respectfulness; but these sentiments were never shared by the undermass, nor in fact by the working class generally'.[94]

If one of the functions of the new police was to act as a 'domestic missionary', translating and mediating bourgeois values in working-class communities, they were notoriously unsuccessful in the task. Working-class culture persisted in possessing a flexibility and impermeability which conferred a degree of immunity upon its bearers. In class society, the fact of working-class alienation from the law was not so easily overcome, and the moral assent which the commissioners of 1839 hoped to obtain continued to be withheld into the twentieth century.

References
 1 The Condition of the Working Class in England, in 'Marx and Engels on Britain' (Moscow, 1962), p.263.
 2 The Police System of London, in 'Edinburgh Review',

July 1852, p.5.
3 E.J. Hobsbawm, 'Primitive Rebels' (New York, 1965), p.116.
4 E.A. Antrobus, 'London: its Danger and its Safety' (London, 1848), p.22.
5 Ibid., p.21.
6 'Livesey's Moral Reformer', January 6 1838.
7 'A Man of Business' [William Rathbone], 'Social Duties Considered With Reference to the Organisation of Effort in Works of Benevolence and Public Utility' (London, 1867), pp.2-14, Cf. J. Foster, 'Class Struggle and the Industrial Revolution' (London, 1974), pp.22-6.
8 J. Wade, 'History of the Middle and Working Classes', 3rd ed. (London, 1835), p.582.
9 'A Man of Business', op. cit. For other nostalgic glances back in a similar vein see N. Scatcherd, 'The History of Morley' (Leeds, 1830), p.180; Past And Present Times at Gildersome, 'Leeds Times', February 4 1843.
10 See L. Radzinowicz, 'History of the English Criminal Law' (London, 1968), 4, pp.215-21; H. Parris, The Home Office and the Provincial Police 'Public Law', autumn 1961, pp.230-55; J. Hart, The County and Borough Police Act, 1856, 'Public Administration', 34, (1956), pp.405-17.
11 F.C. Mather, 'Public Order in the Age of the Chartists' (Manchester, 1959), pp.153-81; F. Darvall, 'Popular Disturbance and Public Order in Regency England' (Oxford, 1969), pp.80, 262, 267; First Report, Royal Commission on Constabulary Force, 'Parliamentary Papers', 1839, XIX, p.83; Foster, op. cit., pp.66-7. Supt. Martin, who led the London police in the 1837 Poor Law riot at Huddersfield, the 1838 Poor Law riot at Dewsbury and the Birmingham Bull Ring Riots of 1839, pointed out that police can act individually in a crowd. Troops have both hands full and cannot leave their ranks without orders. Moreover they must either charge or fire and indiscriminately kill: Second Report, House of Commons Select Committee on Police, 'PP', 1852-3, XXXVI, p.92. The Colne anti-police riots discussed below perfectly illustrated the inadequacies of the military.
12 First Report, Royal Commission on Constabulary Force, p.82. The Manchester police were careful to draw the force from outside the community. See remarks of Capt. Willis in Second Report, House of Commons Select Committee on Police, p.23.
13 First Report, Commission on Constabulary Force, pp.75-6; cf. Foster, op. cit., pp.56-61.
14 First Report, Royal Commission on Constabulary Force, pp.104-5.
15 See the remark of E.P. Thompson, 'Rough Music': Le Charivari Anglais, 'Annales', 27, (1972), p.310: 'Une des formes les plus extrémes d'aliénation qu'on puisse trouver dans les sociétés capitalistes et bureaucratiques est l'aliénation de la Loi. Le fonctionnement de la Loi cesse

d'être assumé par ceux qui dirigent des communautés; elle
est déléguée, monopolisée, et utilisée par d'autres [...]
contre eux, à tel point qu'il ne reste plus dans la com-
munauté que la convention ou la peur d'être remarqué.' Cf.
for generalized working-class mistrust of all agencies of
authority H. Pelling, 'Popular Politics and Society in Late
Victorian Britain' (London, 1968), pp.1-6, 16-18, 62-71.

16 Radzinowicz, op. cit., p.229; First Report, Royal Commission on Constabulary Force, pp.12-13.

17 'Destructive and Poor Man's Conservative', November 2
1833.

18 E.P. Thompson, 'The Making of the English Working Class'
(London, 1963), p.82.

19 'Poor Man's Guardian', April 7 1832.

20 Ibid., November 5 1831.

21 A. Redford, 'History of Local Government in Manchester'
(London, 1939-40), I, opposite p.16.

22 Sir W. Napier (ed.), 'The Life and Opinions of General
Sir Charles Napier' (London, 1857), II, p.146.

23 An exception of course was Francis Place. See C. Reith,
'British Police and the Democratic Ideal' (London, 1943),
pp.72-3. Radzinowicz, op. cit., p.179; S.E. Finer, 'The
Life and Times of Sir Edwin Chadwick' (London, 1952),
p.30. Place was enthusiastic about Chadwick's seminal
essay, Preventive Police (1829). He was a friend of Supt.
Thomas of the London police and advised him on methods
of crowd control in the 1830s. For resistance to the London
police in the early 1830s see Radzinowicz, op. cit.,
pp.167-89; W.A. Lee, 'A History of Police in England'
(London, 1905), pp.245-61; G. Thurston, 'The Clerkenwell
Riot: the Killing of Constable Culley' (London, 1967),
passim; T.A. Critchley, 'A History of Police in England
and Wales 1900-66' (London, 1967), pp.54-5; H. Vizetelly,
'Glances Back Through Seventy Years' (London, 1893),
pp.58-65; Reith, op. cit., pp.54-77, 90-8.

24 Quoted in Reith, op. cit., pp.51-2, 68. The fear of the
cost of the new police sometimes tended to draw working-
class and lower-middle-class elements together in opposition,
cf. the situation in Lancaster, pp.99-100 below.

25 'Northern Star', March 9 1839.

26 Ibid. It should be noted that behind at least some of the
rhetoric about the threat to the good old constitution lay a
social tactical consideration: parish constables were much
easier to live with, and if need be to intimidate.

27 Ibid., August 3 1839.

28 Ibid., March 2 1839. Thomas Ashton of Hyde had indeed
appeared before the County Constabulary Force Commissioners to plead for a new police. It was not for the reason
Oastler cited, but to break the power of trade unionism.

29 Report from His Majesty's Commissioners for Inquiring into
the Poor Laws, 'PP', 1834, XXVIII, Appendix A, pp.197,579.

30 For these episodes as seen by the London police see Second Report, House of Commons Select Committee on Police, pp.61-92.
31 First Report, Royal Commission on Constabulary Force, p.70.
32 Ibid., p.82.
33 Ibid., p.85.
34 Ibid., p.84.
35 E. Chadwick, On the Consolidation of the Police Force and the Prevention of Crime, 'Fraser's Magazine', January 1868, pp.11-12, 18.
36 Foster, op. cit., pp.56-61.
37 'Northern Star', May 2 1840.
38 Ibid., June 6 1840. Cf. R. Cobb, 'The Police and the People (Oxford, 1970), passim; Henry Mayhew, 'London Labour and the London Poor' (London, 1851), I, p.16: 'To serve out a policeman is the bravest act by which a costermonger can distinguish himself. Some [...] have been imprisoned upwards of a dozen times for this offence [...] When they leave prison [...] a subscription is often got up for their benefit'.
39 'Northern Star', June 6 1840.
40 Ibid., March 27 1841.
41 Ibid., February 20 1841.
42 Thomas A. Devyr, 'The Odd Book of the Nineteenth Century' (Greenpoint, 1882), pp.199-200; cf. R.E. Leader, 'Reminiscences of Sheffield' (Sheffield, 1876), p.273.
43 The present writer is currently preparing a paper dealing with the role of the policeman as 'domestic missionary', with the question of daily relations on street level between the police and working-class communities up to 1900, and with the problem of the impact of the police on popular leisure patterns.
44 Police intervention at the pub often ended all rows, but sometimes in ways not pleasant for the police. For a random example see 'Leeds Times', December 19 1835; Constable Pullan came to the White Horse to quell a row between a group of woolcombers and sailors. When he entered, the combers and sailors closed ranks and thrashed him.
45 Napier, op. cit., p.56; 'Hull Advertiser', July 26 1839.
46 'Manchester Guardian', May 24 1843. Engels saw this incident as more than of passing interest: The Condition of the Working Class in England, p.263.
47 Belt-buckles were the favorite weapons of off-duty English soldiers and were noted to have been liberally employed in the Manchester riots a year earlier.
48 'Leeds Mercury', June 15 1844.
49 J. Mayhall, 'The Annals and History of Leeds' (Leeds, 1860), pp.505-6; 'Leeds Mercury', June 15 1844.
50 'Northern Star', May 16 1840. This detachment of rural police had arrived at their posts only two weeks earlier;

none was 'connected' with the town.

51 This account is based on reports in 'Leeds Times', May 18 1839, and 'Northern Star', May 18 1839, drawn from 'The Times' of London. If the chief objective of the rioters was to drive off the new police, they were nearly successful, at least in the short run. One local magistrate, pleading with the government to permanently station troops in the district, wrote that police morale had been so shaken by the riots that mass resignations from the force were expected. Copeland (?) to Russell, May 27 1839, Public Record Office, HO 40, 48.

52 Memorial of the Clergy, Chief Constables, Churchwardens, and Individuals of the Staffordshire Potteries, HO 41.15. On the continued inability of the police to cope with popular disturbances in this district see Radzinowicz, op. cit., pp.265, 278-9.

53 Some writers have correctly noted the intimate connection between popular protest and popular fêtes. See N.Z. Davis, The Reasons of Misrule: Youth Groups and Charivaris in Sixteenth-Century France, 'Past & Present', no.50 (1971); N.Z. Davis, Religious Riot in Sixteenth-Century France, ibid., no.59 (1973); E.P. Thompson, 'Rough Music': Le Charivari Anglais. In some English towns Guy Fawkes celebrations were often strongly tinged with overtones of popular protest. Guy Fawkes could be both a ritualized day of licence as well as an annual opportunity to have a 'legitimate' go at the police. See 'Leeds Times', November 11 1848 and November 8 1851 for Huddersfield; 'York Herald', November 7 1863 and November 15 1873 for Richmond and Malton; J.K. Green, 'Fireworks, Bonfires, Illuminations and the Guy Riots' (Guildford, 1952). For a similar day of licence at Leicester, see W. Kelly, 'Notices of Leicester Relative to the Drama' (London, 1885), p.177, and 'Leicester Journal', February 19 1847.

54 Even some of the magistrates were personally holding back payment: 'Lancaster Gazette', July 25 1840. Cf. proceedings of a ratepayers' meeting at Clayton in the West Riding to petition against the introduction of county police, in 'Northern Star', September 12 1840.

55 'Lancaster Gazette', July 25 1840.

56 Ibid., August 1 1840.

57 From the names of the police mentioned later at the trials it appears the force had a healthy complement of Scots and Welsh. One of the usual sources of mistrust of the police was their lack of connection with the local populace.

58 'Lancaster Gazette', August 1 1840; 'Preston Chronicle', August 15 1840. Other familiar epithets used were 'rural rascals', 'Blue bottles', 'soldiers in disguise'.

59 'Lancaster Gazette', August 1 1840.

60 Ibid., 'Preston Chronicle', August 15 1840.

61 Constance to Napier, April 28 1840, HO 40.58.

62 'Leeds Times', May 2 1840; Napier to Home Office, August 15 1840, HO 40.58. The 'move-on system' was so uniformly employed and constituted such a nuisance to the policed that it was duly noted in the broadside literature. See Manchester's An Altered Town (probably Preston-printed in the early 1840s), in 'Curiosities of Street Literature' (London, 1871). See account of a near riot in Leeds occasioned by the overzealous use of this device. The entire Marsh Lane district turned out at 1.00 a.m. to defend a group of men who had been chased away from a pub entrance by the police. A serious riot was only averted by the intervention of a middle-class witness who happened to be an overseer of the poor; 'Leeds Times', September 9 1843.

63 Based on accounts in 'Preston Chronicle', May 2 1840; 'Blackburn Standard', April 29 1840; 'Leeds Times', May 2 1840.

64 'Leeds Times', May 2 1840.

65 The attitudes of the military officers were remarkably humane and perceptive. They had a certain sympathy for the miserable condition of the inhabitants of Colne and were quick to grasp that the behavior of the police was brutal and insensitive. Napier wrote to the Home Office: 'I am quite certain that great forbearance on the part of the police is necessary not only at Colne but everywhere' (August 15 1840, HO 40.58). On the relations between urban rioters and the army later on, see Marx's article on the London Sunday trading riots, 'Marx and Engels on Britain', p.445. Here too the crowds shouted 'Long live the army! Down with the Police!' The army preserved a popular and not completely unjustified - reputation for behaving with some rectitude in civil disturbances.

66 'Blackburn Standard', August 12 1840.

67 Bolton, Halstead and other figures in the Colne riots are treated fictionally in Robert Neill, 'Song of Sunrise' (London, 1958); published in the USA as 'The Mills of Colne' (New York, 1958).

68 The army deliberately never sought confrontation with civilians at Colne. They refused to remain on the pretext that there were no barracks to accommodate them.

69 The grammar school was of course a middle-class institution and almost certainly not the usual meeting place of local Chartists. There is little doubt that in August - whatever the situation in April - the local Chartist infrastructure played a considerable role.

70 My account of the August riots is based on reports in 'Leeds Times', August 15 1840, 'Blackburn Standard', August 12 1840, 'Preston Chronicle', August 15 1840, and on the following despatches: Bolton to Home Office, August 7 1840, HO 40.45; Wemyss to Home Office, August 11 1840, HO 40.58; Napier to Home Office, August

15 1840, HO 40.58.

71 Boothman's family left a body of correspondence (Boothman
Correspondence, Lancashire Record Office, DDX 537)
preserved at Preston. His letters trace out the remainder
of his life from his trial and sentence, to his transfer to
the hulks to his death in the colonies. Boothman, though
he maintained he had nothing to do with the mob, was no
friend of the police. In a letter to his father from Lancaster
Castle, December 31 1840, he wrote: 'I find the conduct of
the Colne police to be most ridiculous and brutal but it is
nothing more or less than what we all know to be the case
not only with you but in all places where they have got
appointments'. Boothman Correspondence, DDX 537/7.

72 He left a rather respectable estate of £559 4/10d at his
death. Boothman Estate, Last Will and Testament, ibid.,
DDX 537/16.

73 'Leeds Times', December 27 1856.

74 'Leeds Mercury', January 20 1857.

75 Ibid., February 10 1857.

76 Ibid., March 10 1857. It is interesting to note that often
fines for assaults on the police were paid by collections
taken among friends and neighbors – an indicator of the
strength of feeling against the police. Publicans and beerhouse keepers were no doubt prominent contributors to
these subscriptions.

77 Ibid., January 24 1857.

78 Ibid., June 9 1857.

79 'Leeds Times', June 6 1857.

80 Ibid. Cf. the account of a riot against police interference
at Hunslet Feast in ibid., August 19 1843. It was noted that
'great animosity appears to exist against the police at
Hunslet'.

81 'Leeds Mercury', July 2 1857.

82 A representative incident from the Barnsley district: at
1.30 a.m. Constable Cherry and Sgt Hey were on duty at
Skelmanthorpe when suddenly a large crowd materialized
and pelted them with stones. 'Leeds Mercury', June 13
1857. It may be that the provocation was given some time
before, in which case this incident may have been in the
nature of 'squaring accounts'.

83 'Leeds Mercury', June 18 1857.

84 'Lancaster Gazette', August 1 1840.

85 'Oldham Standard', January 30 1864. Like most policemen
in Lancashire, Dermody was a stranger to the district with
no local ties. Even worse he was an Irishman, a fact much
emphasized by the crowd.

86 Ibid.

87 'Leeds Times', October 14 1848.

88 'Lancaster Gazette', August 1 1840.

89 A typical example: the severe beating of a policeman was
reported near Barnsley in December 1859. His current duty

was acting as escort to scabs at the struck Wharncliffe
Silkstone Colliery. Those arrested for the assault were
fined a total of £20, which was immediately paid by the usual
subscription. 'Leeds Mercury', December 20 1859. For the
continuing police role in strikebreaking, see R. Roberts,
'The Classic Slum: Salford Life in the First Quarter of the
Century' (Manchester, 1971), p.71.

90 Occurrence Book, Beeston Police Station (Leeds), entry
  May 20 1872. My emphasis.
91 Reynolds and B. & T. Woolley, 'Seems So' (London, 1911),
  p.91.
92 F. Thompson, 'Lark Rise to Candleford' (Oxford, 1954),
  p.553.
93 Reynolds and Woolley, op. cit., pp.86-7.
94 Roberts, op. cit., pp.76-7. The incident at Leeds illustrates
  one of Roberts's points. There were two schools of thought
  regarding PC Dermody. To a large degree, class determined one's opinion of his actions.

6   Policing the working-class city

Phil Cohen

CUFFS AND CAPES

The modern police force emerged out of the crisis of urban administration in the Victorian city. It was the first branch of the British state to develop an ideological as well as a purely repressive function. As such, the official task of policing was both to protect the institutions of private property, and to enforce statutory norms of public order primarily designed to ensure the free circulation of commodities, including the commodity of labour power.

In London especially, the metropolitan force was both the strong arm and the advance guard of municipal reform.[1] As a population formed by pre-industrial and rural conditions crowded in and colonized the archaic urban infrastructure, it became less a question of enforcing their segregation from the upper classes than of policing their usage of social space and time so that it did not obstruct the traffic of industry and commerce. The potential sources of obstruction included not only strikes, political mobilizations and organized crime, but also the development of street cultures and their irregular economies, upon which whole working-class communities came to depend as a means of local livelihood and identity against the anarchy of impersonal market forces. In such areas as these, the question 'Who rules around here?' was no mere metaphor of a class struggle waged essentially elsewhere: it was itself that struggle. For here the new instruments of bourgeois law and the traditional instruments of popular order became quickly locked in a brutal, if everyday, confrontation. Inevitably the slum neighbourhoods adjoining the inner industrial perimeter, with their volatile, visible and organized social systems, mounted the most violent and sustained opposi-

Source: National Deviancy Conference/Conference of Socialist Economists, 'Capitalism and the Rule of Law', London, Hutchinson, 1979, extracts from pp.120-36.

tion to these new urban reformers in blue. Islington was no exception.[2]

Henry Mayhew noted in the 1850s that the costermonger community was in the vanguard of resistance. To 'have' a policeman was the bravest act a coster could perform, and those who were sent down were regarded as local martyrs and heroes. When they came out of prison, subscriptions were organized. Coster boys adopted 'guerrilla' tactics based on superior knowledge of the local terrain, waiting hidden down an alleyway until the policeman came past, lobbing their stone or brick, and then just as quickly disappearing. Mayhew suggests that the costers' hatred of the police was due to a residual Chartist influence amongst them, but his own evidence suggests that the main motive was economic rather than political. As one coster told him:

> They drive us about, we must move on, we can't stand here and we can't pitch there: they are trying to drive us out of business. (Mayhew, 1851, p.22)

Resistance was not confined to the coster colony around Chapel Street market and the Pentonville Road. From the 1880s onwards, as Islington became increasingly proletarianized in the south and the middle class retreated northwards behind the barriers of property and income, it was those traditional occupational groups concentrated geographically and socially between the two, still tied to the irregular street economy, its seasonal patterns of casual labour and drift migration, who became the special targets of policing. For nearly half a century Popham Street and Packington Street off Essex Road, and Gifford and Bemerton Streets off the Caledonian Road, saw numerous affrays between constabulary and local populace. The local press records 146 such incidents in these areas between 1880 and 1920 - inevitably only those leading to arrest, and hence presumably only a fraction of the real number of cases. [...]

The ancient tradition of collective self-defence still existed in this area two generations later, as shown by a report ('Islington Gazette', June 1924) from the 1920s. A policeman arrested a local woman in the Caledonian Road, when a large hostile crowd - but this time *mainly of youths* - gathered round to rescue her. Stones, cans, bottles began to fly, and one nimble 16-year-old errand boy wriggled his way through the crowd and tripped up the policeman. However, the police had become increasingly efficient at dealing with these situations: reinforcements were summoned, and several more arrests were made.

Even arrest might not be the end of the story. One Islington resident (Mr Malone: oral testimony) recalled how in his youth, before the First World War, the police would strap a particularly obstreperous offender on to an open stretcher and wheel him back, still followed by the crowd, to the station. Once there,

the crowd would wait outside and, if they heard a noise, claim
the police were beating up the man, even on occasion retaliat-
ing by stoning the windows. He also remembered how during
this period, in the tenements where he lived, the arrival of
the police on what was regarded as the residents' own territory
would be greeted by a hail of flower pots, and this was not an
infrequent occurrence of his childhood!

What outraged these communities was not just the law's attack
on what they regarded as legitimate means of livelihood or
secondary income - these were in any case being increasingly
eroded by wider and purely economic forces - but the
criminalization of traditional street pastimes which were solely
recreational. From the 1870s onwards, it was young people
who were particularly singled out on this front. Mayhew (1851)
noted that street gambling, in the form of pitch and toss,
held a special fascination for the costers, Kings Cross being
a popular venue:

> It is difficult to find in the whole of this numerous class a
> youngster who is not a desperate gambler . . . every attempt
> by the police to check this ruinous system has been unavail-
> ing and rather given a gloss of daring and courage to the
> sport.

In the 1850s, men as well as boys had been addicts of pitch and
toss, but by the 1920s adults had taken to other forms of
betting, notably of course horse-racing, while pitch and toss
had retained its popularity as an integral part of general street
youth culture, now reinforced by the imposed leisure of
unemployment. Secondly, while pugilism was being taken off
the streets and refined in the boxing club, the rise of the
professional football club had given a powerful impetus to its
amateur emulation in the back alley.

During the 1920s, Islington police seem to have made a special
drive against these two sports, and it is therefore not surprising to find that they account for over half the reported
arrests of juveniles during this period. Given the scale of these
activities and the local police's limited manpower, there was no
attempt at mass roundups. Instead the police attempted a more
selective strategy of arrest. They concentrated harassment in
those streets associated by reputation or tradition with *adult*
crime. The geographical distribution of arrests for street
football (which has no possible criminal connotations) closely
follows that of youngsters for playing pitch and toss, which
may conceivably have been used as a cover for working as
bookies' runners. Policing tactics thus consisted of general
physical intimidation coupled with systematically arbitrary
arrests.

Another Islington resident, Mr Spendriff, remembers:

> If we'd been playing football or something in the street,
> there used to be a policeman - we used to call him Flash
> Harry - and he used to throw his cape at you as you'd run
> away. He'd throw it right between your legs. Yes. He'd

just cuff you round the ears and let you go. [oral
testimony]

Cuffs and capes seem to have been the favourite methods of
discipline, as they could be applied apparently randomly against
isolated kids. Officers who specialized in such attacks were of
course especially feared and hated. [...] The sense of shock
registered is not at the actual violence meted out. That is
accepted as a normal feature of relations between adult
authority and youth. What does hurt is the sudden and arbitrary nature of its occurrence.

Nevertheless, in the decade after the First World War, the
whole pattern of relations between the police and the working
class in North London had begun slowly, but subtly, to change
from outright physical confrontation to an unwritten system
of tacit negotiation. The antagonism was not resolved, but
it was pursued by means other than street beatings and set-
tos. The reasons for the change are complex: they are partly
to do with changes in the conditions and composition of the
local working class, partly with the position of youth within
the generational division of labour, and partly the result of
the changing function of the police force in the developing
structure of the capitalist state. Let us look at each in turn.

The years after 1919 saw the disintegration of many of the
material supports of traditional street culture. The casual
labour market generated by the irregular economy declined;
while the associated criminal subculture split off and became
the preserve of an increasingly professional fraternity, whose
scale of operations and organization embraced not just Islington
but also Kentish and Camden Town. Secondly, access to
job opportunities was no longer so dependent on highly localized
social networks of information and patronage. Apart from odd
jobs, the street corner labour exchange was actually less
efficient than the official version under conditions of widespread, and not just local, unemployment. Thirdly, the local
Irish presence had tended to become both geographically more
dispersed and culturally more entrenched, largely through its
involvement in trade unionism and local labour politics. The
traditional techniques of hardness and brawling expertise,
while still called on, tended to play a supporting rather than
a leading role. Concentrations of the old 'dangerous class'
had been broken up through sustained harassment or rebuild-
ing. Campbell Road was demolished to make way for a factory.
Slum tenements began to give way to municipal housing. Clis-
sold and Finsbury Parks, Highbury Fields, various youth
clubs, uniformed organizations, all claimed a share of youthful
energies from the overpoliced streets. Finally, the expanding
lower middle class consolidated *their* presence in residential
neighbourhoods previously monopolized by the carriage trade,
and added to the weight of civic consciousness in numerous
local institutions patronized by manual workers and their
families. Furthermore, the sheer physical fact that large numbers

of the men and boys, who had previously dominated the traditional street culture, were away from it during the war years, meant that women and children were left in charge and, in a sense, domesticated some of its functions.

All these changes, small in themselves, uneven in their development, nevertheless combined to alter the contexts of policing and the practices of social control at street level. In the process, the local working class had become more sedimented, less autonomous, their public behaviour to an extent domesticated by an urban environment which was beginning to bear the first marks of properly capitalist planning. But this does not mean that it had become sedentary, dependent or privatized.

In part, the patterns of street and neighbourhood usage remained remarkably consistent, given the changes in economic infrastructure. It was the moral ideologies associated with that use which were modified, harnessed to specific working-class notions of *public propriety*.

The notion was one of the great distinguishing characteristics of the labour aristocracy; and by the 1870s it was firmly established as an active principle amongst the large colonies of skilled print and railway workers in Islington. Nor was it just a notion, for these groups spun a whole cocoon of institutions around themselves to make substantive, and to preserve, the connection between superior occupational and moral status. What this in practice meant was a more or less ritual avoidance of contact with street cultures, a preference for more rational recreation over its popular diversions. It meant drawing a socially, and often geographically, visible line between the two habitats of working-class subjectivity - here the workshop, there the street - serving as a principle of territorial affinities and enmities. But if the skilled worker drew a line under his own feet, it was not always so neat or so visible for his children. Nevertheless, up until the First World War there were two quite clear-cut apprenticeships into working-class masculinity and manual labour. Those for whom apprenticeship was a material institution were kept firmly under the patriarchal thumb of the master craftsman in the workshop and, because of their prolonged financial dependence, kept under the parental thumb as well. From this basis, the parent culture had little difficulty in extending its strategy of social closure to embrace the free time of its youth. Those new institutions of public property, the woodcraft organizations and the boys' clubs, were dominated by the children of skilled workers - and of course in many cases it was only they who could afford the cost of membership.

There is no greater contrast than with the way coster boys and girls were informally apprenticed to their street trade. The aristocracy of the irregular economy ensured that their children started learning the trade almost as soon as they could walk. By the time they were 12 or 13, girls as well as boys had familiarized themselves with all the essential tricks of the trade, as well as having learned how to negotiate the local underlife and still stay out of trouble with the law. Just as importantly, they were often able to save enough from what they earned on the family barrow and through odd jobs to hire a pitch of their own, and set up in competition with their parents. Even more scandalous in the eyes of juvenile reformers, almost as soon as they reached puberty coster boys and girls could afford to leave home, rent lodgings and live as husband and wife. With money in their pockets, their own bosses, free from irksome family constraints (which did not, however, mean that they were not part of a close network of kin and could not rely on it for support when times were hard), no wonder coster youth were often the envy of their peers, the local youth style leaders, and their style was dead set against public propriety and all it stood for!

In between these two extremes stood the mass of unskilled and semi-skilled manual workers and their families. It was this stratum which now began to move away from the moral econo- mies of street culture, and find in the institutions of public propriety a means, not just of respectability, but of material advancement.[3] For them, involvement in trade unionism and local labour politics has been the great pathway to these twin goals. Labourism is the working-class politics of public propriety and conscience, and it is no coincidence that its spokesmen have always been in the vanguard of those advocating the strictest legal repression of 'hooliganism', 'juvenile crimes', and working-class youth cultures in general. In Islington, the rise of the New Unionism and, after the war, of the Unemployed Workers Movement not only organized the hitherto unorganized, but helped give them a stake in the new urban order that was taking shape. Unemployed men still gathered at the un- official labour exchange on the High Pavement of Essex Road, but to talk politics or racing results rather than to jeer at passing toffs or spit at the police, as was their regular habit in the 1890s. Their courting children no longer scandalized the older citizenry by obscene catcalls or by jostling them off the pavement, as they were recorded as doing up until 1914. By the 1920s, the monkey parade had retired to the greater privacy - if not decency - of Highbury Fields.

A railway porter summed up the span of change neatly enough, comparing his own childhood before the First World War with that of his son before the second:

When Johnny was growing up in the flats, people had started using flower pots to grow flowers in. When I was a lad there, they kept them empty to throw at the Law. [Mr Elder, oral testimony]

But perhaps the most sensitive indicator of change comes from comparing the accounts given by mainstream-strata young workers about their encounters with the law before and after the war. In the descriptions on the pre-1914 period, the

policeman remains a shadowy almost anonymous figure. A van
driver recalls one such childhood encounter:
> They were generally all stereotyped. Big black moustaches –
> you couldn't tell one from the other. All we knew was they
> was all down on us the same. We never got a chance to recog-
> nize them; we were too busy running away. [Mr Freeman,
> oral testimony]

But in the accounts of the 1920s and 1930s the portraits are
filled in. Personal idiosyncrasies are mercilessly characterized,
not least in nicknames. Wee Willy Winkie, Droopy Dan, Flash
Harry, King Kong. Terms, certainly not of endearment, but
of some familiarity. These are no longer shadows, but larger
than life figures in the scenarios of youthful experience. This
growing personification is one index of the gradual ideological
penetration of 'The Law' into the basic conditions of working-
class life during the period.

Another is the way certain aspects of routine policing
became perceived as part of public ceremonial, a legitimate
drama punctuating working-class life, as in this account *circa*
1920 by a warehouseman, then in his late teens:
> Well, the police, you could tell the time by them. The posse
> we used to call them. At ten o'clock at night you'd see them
> marching down the road, relieving the various beats...
> Course, Saturday nights, if you wanted to enjoy yourself,
> you'd go down with your mates to see the drunks being
> brought in to the station. [Mr Jackson, oral testimony]

So instead of an angry crowd representing a whole neighbourhood, solid with one of their own in the nick – a not
infrequent occurrence in the earlier period – here, a quarter
of a century on, we have a group of footloose youngsters
enjoying the spectacle of arrest as a free Saturday night entertainment.

It is impossible to be absolutely certain how typical these
different responses were, or how accurate the accounts. But
since they are all drawn from the mainstream elements, rather
than from the extremes of rough or respectable, it seems
likely that they do register substantive qualitative changes in
popular attitudes to policing over this period. Given that police
and court records were not available, it is difficult to construct any precise quantitative index of change. However, by
comparing local press reports of 'disturbances' from 1880 to
1935, a distinct pattern begins to emerge:

1 After the First World War the number of reported incidents
per year drops considerably. On the other hand, there were
episodic disturbances associated with local political activity –
meetings and marches against unemployment and fights with
local fascists.

2 After 1919 the reported size of the crowds involved in
'non-political' disturbances falls, sixty to eighty being a pre-
war figure and twenty to thirty post-war. The ratio of reported
arrests rises as the size of the crowds falls.

3 The age and sex composition reported also changes, men, women and children figuring in the pre-war reports, while in the 1920s and 1930s the accounts increasingly mention the predominance of male youths. This is also reflected in the details of those arrested, the age distribution progressively narrowing over time to the 14- to 18-year-old band, with a complement of slightly older, often unemployed lads.

4 The most frequent places of disturbances remain remarkably consistent across the whole period; but in the post-war reports a number of new landmarks of confrontation make their appearance - for example, the Carlton Club, and the Coffee Stall in Essex Road, both of which are described as hangabout centres for youth and the unemployed.

5 In the 1920s and 1930s disturbances were almost exclusively concentrated at weekends and public holidays, whereas in the earlier period they show a slightly broader distribution through the week and throughout the year, though here again weekends and holidays show a peak concentration.

6 More significant was the fact that the reported occupations of juveniles arrested shows a higher concentration of those in 'street trades' in the later period than in the earlier.

This evidence points both to the changing configuration of the parent cultures and the changing pattern of juvenile employment. Increasingly it was wage-earning and unemployed boys who were left behind on the front lines of street confrontation with the law, as their parents increasingly identified the etiquette of public propriety with the exercise of parental responsibility. But the visibility factor is not enough in itself to explain the concentration of police activity on street-corner youth. The introduction of legislation against street-trading by juveniles, the stricter enforcement of elementary school attendance after the war, separated them conspicuously from their younger brothers and sisters at the same time as their elders and betters retreated from the scene. Second, the creation of new categories of juvenile offence also created greater pressure on the police to enforce them. Third, the polarizations within the local youth constituency between the apprenticeships of the workshop and those of the street was diminishing. Not only was the irregular economy in decline, but the interwar years saw the decline of many of the Finsbury workshop trades, and the migration of skilled labour to the new light industries being set up in West London. Juvenile labour became increasingly concentrated in shop and distributive trades, a small army of messenger boys was taken on by the post office, while the railway continued to employ a considerable number of van boys. Office work in the City claimed many girls from domestic service and laundry work. These jobs were still often dead-end and low-paid, but at least they were *decasualized*, even if the attitude of young workers to them was not.

All of this served to articulate the conditions of juvenile

labour more closely to the institution of juvenile delinquency,
to make substantive in policing practice the imaginary connection between a dangerous place (the streets of the working-
class city) and a dangerous time (youth).

Of course it also gave impetus to those who were busy constructing safe places (youth clubs and organizations) where
working-class youth could have safe times (rational recreation). But here it must be noted that Islington was not
penetrated nearly so early or so thoroughly by the agencies
of religious evangelism and philanthropy, as many other
working-class areas (MacLeod, 1974). Here, for a long time,
the police were the sole agency of urban reform. This factor,
coupled with the survival of the irregular street economy, and
the presence of a well-organized criminal community, explains
why it took the police much longer to establish public propriety
in Islington than many other inner cities. The great watershed, which occurred in the 1914-18 period for Islington,
undoubtedly occurred in many industrial areas by the 1870s
and 80s (Storch 1976).

That this could happen at all is due to the decentralized
nature of the apparatus of enforcement; its key particularisms -
the logistics of police operations, and the cultures of local
resistance - interact to determine the actual tempo of change
in different urban contexts. However, if we want to underline
the 'law' of this uneven and combined development, we will have
to look in more detail at the structural processes which underlie the constraining variables of policing the working-class
city.

RELATIONS OF FORCE

The picture given so far has been no simple one of urban
pacification. We have seen that the limits imposed on policing
by working-class resistance were as significant as those imposed
on street cultures in the name of public propriety. The proletarian public-realm retained its historical individuality as a
nexus of institutions and practices, through the very means
of its accommodation to the capitalist city.

But what effect did these relations of force have on the internal development of police structures and functions? It seems
to me that the British police have become, almost uniquely,
a dependent part of a wider apparatus; we might call this the
'educational state system' - the system which educates the
subjects of capital about the state, and about their legal conditions of existence as 'individuals' in 'civil society'. It is no
coincidence that working-class kids call police 'The Law'
because it is from them that they receive their physical and
moral education about the place they occupy as legal subjects
in class society. Especially where 'father's word is law', it
is the policeman whose name is taken in vain as its support.

As for those who refuse to learn their lesson, they are
notoriously confused about which or whose law they have
transgressed - the law of patriarchy or of propriety. For in
the institution of public propriety, the two are indeed chronic-
ally conflated.

But this in turn has imposed a peculiarly contradictory role
on the police themselves. The British bobby is called upon to
perform two basic and distinct tasks:

As the moral entrepreneur of public propriety, and by implication arbiter of deviance, he performs a purely expressive
   function of community welfare and is expected to do so
   impartially, as a public servant, in contexts occupied solely
   by what appear to be individual citizens in need or distress.
   This aspect of the job is necessarily very labour intensive.

As the administrator of a juridical ideology of crime, in which
   the bourgeoisie has enshrined its version of the rights of
   capital and the obligations of labour, he performs a repressive
   function in a policing context where there are two categories
   of client - the legitimate and the illegitimate possessors of
   property. This aspect of the job has become increasingly
   capital intensive. [...]

Normally a capitalist state develops forms of representative
democracy and public accountability, which reproduce the conditions of bourgeois hegemony through a process of active
consent. Normally, therefore, its powers of physical coercion
are called on as a last resort, and against those who have
first been publicly outlawed as legal subjects by a variety of
ideological mechanisms. But the police force is in a peculiar
position here, as an agency of the state which has to penetrate
into the heart of civil society if it is to be effective, which
has to win active consent to its presence if it is to do so, but
which both directly and immediately represents the state's
powers of physical coercion. The situation is critical when it
comes to policing the working-class city. For, as we have seen,
in those areas which were characterized by a backward, small-
scale economy, the police force was charged with introducing
elements of urban discipline into a population which had not
yet fully experienced industrial discipline. And these districts
sustained popular cultures which incorporated quite highly-
developed countervailing norms of law and order, which could
only be totally eliminated by outright repression. It was thus
decisive that police intervention in the life of these areas
should be seen as the neutral administration of a rational
system of justice, rather than the brutal extension of bourgeois
class power; if the police were to be seen as legal subjects,
not as class subjects, it was necessary to evolve for these
'difficult' neighbourhoods a policing strategy which would
maintain the legitimacy of the force's role, as much to the world
outside as within itself, by representing the illusory unity
of its functions against the manifest reality of their contradictions.

The routine practices of policing were, therefore, designed
to conform to the same principles of formal legal rationality[4]
as the judicial system they serviced with 'offenders'. Only this
kind of bureaucratic accountability could give the appearance
of the police and the judiciary being independent of each other,
and both being independent of political pressure and vested
interest. So the policeman on the beat was trained to apply
standard protocols of surveillance, investigation and arrest
to all citizen subjects, irrespective of class, colour or creed;
just as the magistrate was supposed to apply universalistic
rules of evidence, definitions of crime and punishment, with
similar impartiality in the court.

As we have seen in Islington, however, the universality
of the legal subject could only be substantiated by systematically
violating the due process of law in the manner of its enforcement: which, in turn, undermined the whole enterprise of
legitimation. The alternative strategy, observing the full letter
of the law, would only generate mass arrests, which would
overstretch limited manpower resources and threaten the
bureaucratic system of processing offenders. The case of street
football and gambling illustrated how concretely the problem
arose, and also how the police evolved a method of dealing
with it: by a partial suspension of formal legal rationality, turning half a blind eye to the rule book; and by the partial suspension of statutory norms of public order, turning the other
half of the blind eye to a good deal of minor infringements.
Such a strategy enlarged the autonomy of the rank-and-file
police over and against the higher white-collar echelons whose
job is to maintain the bureaucratic accountability of the organization as a whole. But equally, the calculated use, or abuse,
of discretionary powers produces a highly arbitrary system of
policing, which undermines the official posture of the force
as neutral arbiters of justice. The force is still confronted with
the impossible choice of enforcing law *or* order.

In the event, an answer was found by modifying the operational definition of public order, thus producing mediation from
within the police apparatus itself.

The statutory definitions, as we have seen, consisted of
universalistic rules of public behaviour applied to isolated
economic agents going about their lawful business, which in
practice meant going from A to B in the shortest possible time.
These norms enter into a whole series of legal regulations
which criminalize any other kind of public behaviour - the laws
against being a suspected person, loitering with intent, causing an obstruction, behaviour likely to cause a breach of the
peace, insulting behaviour, definitions of riot and affray. These
rules and regulations are, therefore, especially strategic in the
city centre, where the symbolic institutions of power are concentrated and where different social classes - elsewhere
residentially segregated - congregate in large numbers. Their
function here, then, is to outlaw the social promiscuity of the

urban crowd, as well as its potential political thread, by reinforcing its characteristics as an atomized mass.

Now initially, and at the time when large numbers of the so-called 'dangerous and perishing' classes still lived crowded together in close proximity to the citadels of power, the police attempted to apply the same norms of public order to these residential areas as to the central place itself. As the problems of enforcing these norms became apparent, and as the urban poor were evicted from the city centre, the policing strategy changed. The innovations consisted precisely in differentiating between the two urban contexts. While statutory norms were still routinely enforced in the centre, in the new heartlands of the working-class city they were increasingly used only as an emergency measure, to justify the last resort of physical repression. In their place, a system of informal, tacitly negotiated and particularistic definitions of public order were evolved which *accommodated* certain working-class usages of social space and time, and *outlawed* others. What were ratified were those practices which articulated the institutions of patriarchy and public propriety, within the class habitat; what were outlawed were those practices of women and children which challenged the monopoly of those institutions over the working-class city and its legitimate usage. The new norms in effect imposed a system of unofficial curfew, informal out-of-bounds, to define what were the wrong people, wrong age, wrong sex, in the wrong place and the wrong time. And 'wrong' was defined in the simultaneous terms of a moral ideology of deviance and juridical ideology of crime. A kind of guilt-by-association was insinuated into these norms: if you were a legal subject caught following a less than pedestrian line of desire,[5] or a class subject caught out of your legal place, you were not only out of (statutory public) order, but had broken a moral code of respectable public behaviour. The first condition supplied the criminal offence, the second justified arrest. [...]

The principles of variation are rigorously determined by the strategic priorities of policing under different sets of circumstances, and those priorities are in turn determined by the need to maintain a balance between the conflicting demands of observing the letter of the law and the organizational maintenance of public order. The new methods set out to impose a principle of negotiation between the external policing of the neighbourhood and its internal systems of social control. More concretely, it was an attempt to forge an alliance between the spokesmen of proletarian patriarchy and propriety and the enforcers of bourgeois law and order. Here, uniquely, the police force and the labour movement perform complementary functions of political socialization - though, from a socialist standpoint, entirely negative ones. For the combined effect is to limit the access of working-class polity, while outlawing as potentially deviant the very 'public realms' they have had to

construct to reaffirm some kind of social existence in the face
of their disenfranchisement as speaking subjects within the
class habitat. But more recently, in a period which has seen
a general weakening of the links between sexual and generational
relations in the reproduction of labour-power, their massive
reinforcement at this superstructural level of 'community relations' has, if anything, served to sharpen working-class perceptions of the situation.

If the alliance at the top has been remarkably successful,
the negotiation of informal norms at the grass-roots has been
far less smooth. Firstly, because the constant drive towards
increased accumulation of capital demands the continual recom-
position and relocation of its labour force. Not only is this process resisted, thus unleashing community struggles which go
far beyond the confines of public propriety, but it throws up
new social forces (for example, immigrant workers) whose
material cultures also challenge these constraints. If outsiders
are to become established, informal norms must be negotiated
anew. The fact that their very presence threatens the delicate
equilibrium of existing tolerances means that the police normally
respond by falling back on the more or less brutal reimposition
of statutory public order when policing these groups.

A degree of immunity from this kind of direct legal repression has been won by the more sedimented sections of the class;
but only by surrendering some of the means by which they
once policed themselves. And these welfare functions, once
confiscated, become the cutting-edge of the police campaign
for active consent and public support. In many of the rougher
inner-city neighbourhoods, however, and despite everything
that municipal reformers can do, a strong countervailing sense
of moral and social cohesion has survived. In these conditions,
if the local police show one very public face in defence of order
and another, more private one, in the enforcement of the law,
they are likely to be condemned as two-faced.

Far from disappearing, the contradictions between the two
sides of police work have intensified. They continue to undermine each other, while taking on new, more mediated forms.
For example, the welfare function only remains credible if
its implication for law enforcement (that is, the scrupulously
impartial adherence to due process of law) is also observed.
But in criminal work the emphasis is inevitably on productivity,
increasing the ratio of arrests, and this in turn means bending
the rules. This is also a problem for organizational maintenance.
The more resources allocated to increasing the efficiency of
repressive policing, the more manpower has to be poured into
'community relations' to restabilize the public image of the
force. The more technologically sophisticated, and hence
impersonal, the systems of surveillance, the more home-beat
coppers are needed on the ground. The more manpower is
drained here, the more rationalization is needed in policing
methods in the other departments. The more this push-me-pull-

you process accelerates, the more essential and the more
impossible becomes the task of representing the repressive
edge as a natural extension of the welfare wedge - the Sweeney
as the legitimate offspring of Dixon of Dock Green.

In the post-war period, and especially during the last decade
and in the inner city, the situation has come to a head. Increasingly in these areas the police have had to rely on apparatuses
outside their control - notably, the mass media - to construct
local emergencies which would sanction the reimposition of
statutory norms through the systematic violation of the due
process of law. If it was so easy to fabricate imaginary scenarios
of lawlessness, hooliganism, mob violence and general rampage,
we should remember that the survival of distinctive habitats
of class subjectivity is necessarily a scandal, as well as a source
of secret fascination and fear, in a Welfare State dedicated to
equality of opportunity. Whatever social or political force
manages to emerge from its invisibility, to break through the
cover of routine surveillance and control, is by definition an
emergency. And if it is 'bad' news, it is because it is always
news from nowhere, a non-sense as well as a *non sequitur*
from this vantage point. The restoration of order simply demands
that this bad news return back into nowhere as quickly as
possible. The separate tempos of police and media intervention
thus work in counterpoint to each other, never in simple
harmony.[6] If the police were relatively successful in isolating
and attacking the new dangerous classes, they had also to pay
the price of increased dependency on sources of legitimation
in civil society. It was to prove a costly trade-off; for, as
their own behaviour came increasingly into the public limelight,
so many of the carefully negotiated norms and other special
arrangements which constituted time-honoured station practice
came suddenly to be redefined as 'corruption' because they
did indeed violate principles of neutral administration and due
process.

Yet the suppression of these practices could only endanger
the organizational maintenance of local forces, already heavily
under strength. The only alternative short-cut to getting
results consisted in reverting to the more overt techniques of
physical intimidation. Either way the image of public service
and accountability was damaged, and exposed the force to even
greater political pressure from watch-dog groups. Inevitably,
the push-me-pull-you process took its toll of the internal
command structure of the force. The division of police labour
became ever more specialized, and generated tensions between
rival departments, each jealously guarding its professional
autonomy. But the conflicts that have begun to shake the
foundations are not merely institutional: they have distinct
class connotations.

We have already noted the latent antagonism between the local
beat coppers and their superior officers. The former are
naturally concerned to safeguard their discretionary powers

which alone allow them to gain intimate working knowledge of neighbourhood underlife, and to successfully perform the delicate balancing act between productivity and acceptability. But however they negotiate their presence in the community, they are still accountable to their superiors. These latter are usually college-trained administrators (Trenchard's Boys) who are pre-occupied with a different set of priorities, above all the need to balance the demands of organizational maintenance with the observance of procedural norms. This is only one instance of a wider conflict between those whose conditions of police work require that they take account of the existence of 'the working-class city', and those whose position of public accountability requires that they do not. So, for example, a basic antagonism quickly developed between station staff, in charge of maintaining negotiated order in their local manor, and the new elite cadres like the Special Patrol Group and Regional Crime Squads, organized on paramilitary lines, whose explicit and peripatetic function was precisely to restore statutory order without regard for any of the factors constraining the operations of the local force.

Increasingly then, a split has tended to develop in the occupational socialization of the police force between its professional ideology and its material cultures. This too has a history (see Pilling, 1971).

Even as late as the Edwardian period, especially in industrial areas, policing was still regarded as a normal working-class job. Artisans and skilled men would get a job on the local force when times were hard, and return to their 'real' trade when seasonal or cyclical demand picked up. Police culture was that of a working class temporarily in uniform. But with the growing professionalism of police work, the growing diversification of skills based on mental as well as manual labour, a quite distinctive occupational culture emerged. The force now tended to attract working men whose aspirations, for whatever reason, fell short of their long-term prospects in the labour market. Recruits were mainly married men, often with considerable work experience in civilian life - but their entry into the force signified a far more permanent shift. This was reflected in the fact that police work had come to be seen as a highly deviant occupational choice within the range of working-class job opportunities. Police PROs tried to turn this to good account by promoting a middle-class image of the force as a 'vocation' and a 'career'. But, for the raw recruit, the reality was of course quite otherwise, and so very different working-class paradigms were brought to bear. The trade magazine of the force is still obstinately called 'The Job', and, as its pages stress, it is one of society's dirty jobs and pretty underpaid at that. The ideology of public service, as in other sectors, backfired and produced growing trade-union militancy amongst the rank and file. Paradoxically, this militancy is an effect of the social isolation of the policeman from the mainstream of

working-class life. The extent of social closure within this
occupational community is indicated by the tendency of police
work to become a family tradition - son succeeding father from
generation to generation. There are other, no less idiosyncratic,
factors at work in recruitment. Chief among them in the post-
1945 period is the increasing *juvenilization* of the force. National
service in the 1950s was an important feeder here, and so of
course was the mounting level of youth unemployment in the
1970s. But cultural factors are equally important. The effect
of such mass phenomena as the Teds, the Mods and Rockers,
and the Skinheads on those young people who remained within
the confines of parent cultures wedded to public propriety,
should not be underestimated. In working-class districts where
subcultures were strong, ultra-conformists could easily be
isolated from the mainstream of local peer-group life. It may be
significant then that those young constables I spoke of in
Islington,[7] who had all joined the force after 1965, though they
gave very disparate and personal reasons for doing so, were
almost unanimous in saying that what they liked best about
the job, what they had missed previously, was the sense of
comradeship - the fact that you had mates you could depend
on, who would back you up no matter what. This peer group
ideal, seemed, by all accounts, most strongly exemplified in
the section house where the single lived; here horseplay, petty
pilfering and strenuous parties seemed the order of the day.
While they displayed deference to the symbolisms of Authority,
these working-class youth were quite active in a whole culture
of insubordination, with its own quite elaborate rituals of
misrule. All this seemed to be officially tolerated, though not
encouraged, as a necessary safety valve for young men subject
to rigorous discipline at the bottom of the command structure -
good for bonding them into an efficient crime-fighting unit.
Just as it served as a defence against what was perceived as
social ostracism by the local community.

The result had been to narrow the scenario of law and order
down to a battle between two rival gangs, both composed of
young, single, working-class males, each seeking territorial
control over the class habitat - but with this difference, that
one mob have the full weight of the state behind them, the
other only themselves and their mates to fall back on. The
scores they have to settle still revolve around the question
'Who rules?' But they no longer revolve around the material
stakes of a class struggle, as it was with the costers in the
1880s. Now the struggle is purely symbolic. Nevertheless, it
is one which has all too real a consequence for those who are
on the losing side. [...]

To sum up, I have tried to suggest that the structural contradictions in policing practice derive from the force's peculiar
historical position within the British state. In Gramsci's terms,
it was the first branch of the state to exemplify a shift in
ruling-class strategy from a war of manoeuvre to a war of

fixed position (see Anderson, 1977). This pioneering role was
forced upon it by the underdeveloped nature of the local state
administration in a period of rapid urbanization, and at a time
when long-established structures of popular recreation and
justice retained powerful material supports. The response of
the police to its predicament partially succeeded in imposing
the elements of a properly capitalist urban discipline in the
name of public propriety, but signally failed to resolve its own
contradictions. These have sharpened into chronic conflicts
within the force itself, and in its relations to a whole series of
environing institutions. The current crisis in the policing of
the working-class city has become a crisis of legitimacy for
the bourgeois public realm as a whole.

Notes
1 See Storch (1976) for an empiricist reading of Victorian
  policing.
2 All historical material refers to the London borough of
  Islington. This research was carried out under the auspices
  of a grant from the Leverhulme Trust. It consisted of an
  analysis of local newspaper reports from 1875 and 1935 and
  of oral testimony collected from residents who grew up in
  Islington between the world wars. I am grateful to Lucy
  Bland for collecting much of this material and also to the
  staff of the Islington Library service for their help. The
  Islington Bus Company is collecting oral testimony on the
  political history of Islington during the inter-war period,
  and I am grateful to Neil Martinson for enabling me to
  consult that material.
3 See Walters (1975), an autobiographical account of working-
  class life in Islington between the wars. It gives a very
  good picture from the point of view of a spokesman of
  public propriety who lived in the 'notorious' Popham Street.
4 For a full discussion of this concept see Balbus (1973).
5 A comment on the ironic fact that urban planners use the
  term 'line of desire' to indicate the direction of maximum
  pedestrian flow between fixed points, for example from
  tube station to office, or from home to shops.
6 The objective effect of so-called 'moral panics' is therefore one of *reassurance* that the bourgeois public realm is
  alive and well and has triumphed once again over adversity.
  This aspect is ignored by Cohen (1973).
7 I gathered this information through participant observation
  while a youth worker in Islington between 1971 and 1974.

Bibliography
Anderson, P. (1977), The Antinomies of Gramsci, 'New Left
  Review', no.100.
Balbus, I. (1973), 'Dialectics of Legal Repression', Russell
  Sage Foundation, New York.
Cohen, S. (1973), 'Folk Devils and Moral Panics', Paladin,London.

MacLeod, H. (1974), 'Religion and Class in the Victorian City', Croom Helm, London.

Mayhew, H. (1851), 'London Labour and the London Poor', vol.1, George Woodfall.

Pilling, C. (1971), Police and Working Class Community, unpublished PhD thesis, Cambridge University.

Storch, R. (1976), The Police as Domestic Missionaries, 'Social History', no.4.

Walters, H. (1975), 'The Street', Centreprise Publishing Project, London.

7   White-collar crime and the institutionalisation of ambiguity: the case of the early Factory Acts

W. G. Carson

British factory legislation dates from 1802 when an enactment known as the Health and Morals of Apprentices Act was passed.[1] This statute purported to curtail some of the worst abuses practised against the large numbers of pauper children who, during the closing decades of the preceding century, had been shipped from major centres of population to become apprenticed to cotton-masters whose early water-powered mills had been erected in remote locations where water, unlike labour, was in plentiful supply. Although space precludes description of the privations endured by these 'pauper-apprentices', some idea of their plight can be gained from the terms of the enactment itself. Thus, for example, it banned their employment for more than twelve hours per day, provided for the eventual cessation of all night work by this class of employee and insisted on the provision of separate sleeping accommodation for males and females, not more than two apprentices being allowed to share one bed. Some rudimentary provision was also made for their physical and intellectual well-being by requirements covering such matters as clothing, ventilation, cleanliness and educational instruction.[2]

The limited measure of protection afforded, at least on paper, to the parish apprentices in the textile industry was little enough reward for the part which they played in the early stages of industrialisation. Their plight, however, was soon superseded by other developments stemming from further technological change. With the introduction of steam for the generation of rotary power, it became possible for manufacturers to abandon their remote locations and establish themselves in the towns where increasing economic pressure was rendering the labouring classes more amenable to factory employment, both for themselves and for their children. Although the transition to steam was a gradual one and much less rapid in branches of

Source: G. Geis and E. Stotland (eds), 'White-Collar Crime', Beverly Hills, Calif., Sage Publications, 1980, pp.142-73.

the industry other than cotton, the pattern of child-employment
had radically altered by 1819 when, as a result of the enthusiastic efforts of Robert Owen and the rather less fervent parliamentary sponsorship of Peel, further legislative intervention
took place. According to the latter, there were by then ten
times as many 'free' children employed in the cotton industry
as there had formerly been apprentices[3] and, accordingly,
it was to this class of labour that the Act of 1819 offered some
measure of protection. Restricted to cotton factories, this
enactment fixed the minimum age for employment at nine years
of age and prohibited the employment of those under sixteen
for more than twelve hours per day (excluding meal times) or
after 9.00 p.m. Subsequent measures, in 1825 and 1831,
extended these provisions as to night-working and, in the case
of the second, enlarged the age-group limited to twelve hours'
daily work to include all under the age of eighteen.[4]

The next major step in the development of this body of
legislation was taken in 1833 when, after two protracted and
contentious official enquiries, a further enactment was passed.[5]
Applying to a range of textile industries where steam, water
or other mechanical power was in use, this statute prohibited
the employment of children under nine years of age, limited
the labour of those between nine and thirteen to nine hours
per day, and restricted the employment of young people between
thirteen and eighteen to twelve hours daily. For all under the
age of eighteen, a ban was imposed - with some special exceptions - on their employment between 8.30 at night and 5.30 a.m.
Children in the younger age-group were to receive some
elementary education, vouchers to that effect being made a
prerequisite of their employment each week. A complex system
of age-certificates was also established in order to facilitate
enforcement of the various provisions and, most important of
all, four full-time Inspectors of Factories were to be appointed.

The history of factory legislation during the ten years following 1833 is largely dominated by the difficulties which the
latter officials encountered when, after initial and substantial
recalcitrance in the matter, they set out to enforce the law. A
Select Committee which reported in 1840 examined these problems in some detail[6] and, despite a further delay occasioned
largely by controversy over the vexed question of education,
a further measure was placed on the statute book in 1844.[7]
Apart from going some way towards removing some of the more
obvious practical obstacles confronting the Inspectors, a matter
to which we shall return, this enactment was notable for its
restriction of women to the same working-hours as young
persons, and for introducing requirements as to the fencing
of dangerous machinery. As far as child employees were concerned, while the minimum age for employment was reduced
to eight, it became illegal to employ them for more than six and
a half hours per day or during both the morning and afternoon
work-periods. The working hours of both children and young

persons were also to be reckoned from the time when any child
or young person commenced labour in the morning, the time
to be regulated by a public clock.

From the early 1830s onwards, however, another and more
drastic form of regulation had been canvassed by the Ten
Hours Movement, a loose-knit organisation comprising both
humanitarian reformers, like Ashley, and many operatives who
had formed themselves into Short-time Committees.[8] As the
title suggests, this body favoured a limitation of restricted
labour to ten hours per day, even though and, indeed, largely
because the interdependence of different classes of labour
within a mill would mean that such a step would necessarily
curtail the hours worked by all. A proposal of this kind was
defeated in 1844,[9] but pressure for such a measure continued
to mount in the years immediately following. In 1847, just one
year after the repeal of the Corn Laws, this pressure finally
achieved some measure of success through an enactment which
restricted women and all under the age of eighteen to a maximum
of ten hours' work per day and fifty-eight per week.[10] But
the 'normal working day', as it came to be known, was not quite
so easily secured. Many manufacturers, availing themselves
of statutory complexity combined with a legal decision to the
effect that 'reckoning' time did not have to mean that it was
reckoned continuously from the time of first starting work,[11]
successfully contrived to continue working their factories for
more than ten hours by employing women and young persons
in staggered relays.[12] When this loophole was removed by an
amending Act in 1850, it was only at the cost of accepting a
sixty-hour week (ten and a half per weekday, and seven and
a half on Saturday) in return for a provision that women and
young persons should not be employed outside the fixed hours
of 6 a.m. and 6 p.m. during the week, nor after 2 p.m. on
Saturdays, including a weekly total of eight hours allowed for
meals.[13] Even then the matter was not closed, for the government of the day had declined to include the children in the
fixed time restrictions which were imposed in 1850. As a result,
the last abuse with which the struggle for a standard working
day had to contend was the unseemly one of mills continuing
to work beyond 6 p.m. with relays of children taking the place
of women and young persons. It was not until 1853 that a
further enactment put an end to this practice.[14] [...]

Most authorities on the initial phase in the history of factory
legislation are in agreement that the early laws were violated
with impunity, largely because of inadequacies in the enforcement machinery provided.[15] Whatever the explanation, however,
it seems clear that the first enactments were contravened on a
substantial scale. Thus, for example, the evidence given before
a Select Committee in 1816 left little doubt that the Apprentices
Act of 1802 had long been a dead letter.[16] Visitors had rarely
been appointed from among the local Justices[17] and, according
to one Lancashire witness, it was the general understanding

in that county that the enactment was quite neglected.[18] Several
others had never even heard of its existence.[19] 'In this inquiry',
the 'Westminster Review' later recalled, 'it came out ... that
the provisions of the Apprentices Act were evaded and set
at nought.'[20]

Nor do things seem to have improved substantially in this
respect after the passage of the 1819 Act. Indeed, it was
largely the extent to which the terms of that statute were
violated that provided the immediate rationale for further legislative effort in 1825. According to Sir John Cam Hobhouse,
parliamentary sponsor of the Bill which was passed in that
year, his proposal for further regulation rested squarely on
a desire 'to carry into effect that excellent statute which had
long been shamefully evaded'.[21] But his efforts then and some
six years later do not appear to have produced the desired
effect. Setting aside the hotly contested evidence given before
the allegedly partisan Committee of 1832,[22] the more sanguine
proceedings of the Royal Commission established in the following year left little doubt that violation of the law was both
widespread and unchecked. In country districts, said the
Report, even attempts to enforce the law were seldom or never
made; in several of the principal manufacturing towns it was
openly disregarded; in others its operation was extremely
partial and incomplete. 'On the whole,' concluded the Commissioners, 'we find the present law has been almost entirely
inoperative with respect to the legitimate objects contemplated
by it'.[23]

Even after the appointment of four Inspectors and a number
of Superintendents to work under them, in 1833, there was no
immediate change. Acting under instructions to be 'in communication exclusively with the employers, with a view to
making the law acceptable to them',[24] the new officials were
extremely loath to prosecute and, indeed, even joined with
some of the more influential manufacturers in calling upon the
government to repeal the final stages of the Act's implementation.[25] It was only when this plea was rejected, in 1836, that
they were unquivocally instructed to put the law into effect.[26]
That the ideological implications of such dilatoriness in enforcing
factory legislation did not pass unnoticed at the time is
apparent in the following extract from the Memorial which the
Manchester Short-time Committee sent to the Home Office in
February 1837:[27]

> Your memorialists deeply regret that the due fulfilment of
> the intentions of the Legislature has hitherto, by one exped-
> ient or another, been delayed and postponed, causing
> extreme dissatisfaction to prevail among the operative clas-
> ses in the manufacturing districts, and an impression (dan-
> gerous and alarming at any time, but especially so in a case
> like the present, where the evidence on which the feeling is
> founded is not obscure, and accessible to few, but clear and
> palpable, and within the reach of all) that justice, where the

poor are concerned is no longer even handed, and that, in deference to the understood wishes of more opulent and therefore more influential parties, the law is in very numerous instances perverted and abused, and its more benevolent provisions trampled under foot.

From evidence such as this, it is clear that factory legislation which continued to be a complete sham could have had highly detrimental effects upon the capacity of the new industrial order to maintain its legitimacy. Thus, to the other forces which I have advanced as generating an impetus towards, rather than away from, regulation in this period, must be added the growing pressure of another logic which necessitated not only legislation, but enforcement. The role of factory legislation in reproducing the totality of the social order within which it was located could not be played entirely with the rhetoric of empty phrases. As we shall see, however, the assiduous efforts which, from 1836 onwards, did indeed go into the attempt to make regulation a reality collided head-on with other intransigent forces embedded in the social organisation of factory production in this period, a collision which culminated in ambiguity becoming the salient feature of factory crime.

FACTORY PRODUCTION AND EARLY FACTORY CRIME

In the preceding section of this paper it was argued that, in addition to the specific social movements pressing for factory legislation during the first half of the nineteenth century, there was an underlying impetus towards regulation within the system itself. Moreover, from the nature of the evidence adduced, it seems plausible to suggest that this argument need not simply be couched in terms of ex post facto theorisation which posits some unseen hand inexorably guiding law towards the fulfilment of its role in reproducing social order; effective factory legislation was frequently seen, albeit unevenly and sometimes only dimly, as having a potentially important part to play in this process. Because such underlying forces were at work, however, does not mean that the realisation of their potential was automatic, as if a relationship of mechanistic equivalence prevailed between the different elements which conjoined to produce the totality of nineteenth-century society. For one thing, such an argument would be difficult to sustain in the light of the very real and substantial resistance offered to most legislative proposals in this period; for another, it would drastically underestimate the extent to which violation, particularly with regard to over-working, was functionally integrated with the structure, organisation and ideology of the productive process during these years. In this section, I wish to focus primarily upon the latter point as a prelude to discussion of attempts to enforce the law.

The attractiveness of juvenile and female labour to the textile manufacturers of this period is well known. Not only were such workers seen to be more tractable and therefore more easily disciplined to factory routine, but also, of course, their labour came cheaper than that of adult males.[28] Moreover, by depressing the wage-levels of the male adult and, indeed, by diminishing his chances of factory employment just when exigency was driving him to it, the extensive employment of women and, particularly, of juveniles formed part of a vicious circle which maintained pressure on the workforce as a whole.[29] According to some commentators, it was precisely this adverse effect which the hiring of juveniles had on adult employment that provoked working-class demands for legislative restrictions on child labour.[30]

Whatever the accuracy of this assessment, however, there is no doubt as to the pattern of the employment structure which characterised the textile industry during the first half of the nineteenth century. By 1819, as we have already seen, it was claimed that there were ten times as many 'free' children employed in cotton factories as there had formerly been 'pauper apprentices'.[31] In the early 1830s, one estimate put the proportion of employees in cotton mills who were under twenty-one at between one-third and one-half, while women were calculated to constitute well over half of all workers in the entire textile industry.[32] When the recently appointed Factory Inspectors compiled figures on employment in 1839, the results showed that there were still more than 33,000 children between nine and thirteen (around 8 per cent of the entire labour force) and nearly 161,000 young persons between thirteen and eighteen (approximately 38 per cent) employed in textile factories coming within the provisions of the 1833 Act.[33] According to the statistics extrapolated by Professor Blaug from Chapman's earlier work on the cotton industry, about one-quarter of the workers in English cotton mills between 1834 and 1847 were adult men, more than half were women and girls, and the remainder boys below the age of eighteen.[34] As Blaug himself remarks, 'the tendency to replace dear adult labour by cheap juvenile labour resisted the efforts of factory reformers until the last decades of the nineteenth century'.[35]

Straight away then, it is apparent that the factory legislation which emerged during the first half of that century purported to impinge, not upon some insignificant and coincidental aspect of the productive process, but upon one of its most crucial features. However, it was not just by sheer force of numbers that juvenile labour - which, it will be recalled, was the sole focus of regulation up till 1844 - was an integral factor in production. Additionally, because the tasks performed by children were regarded as vital to the working of the machinery by adults, their labour was taken to be inextricably linked with the very operation of the mill itself. Thus, for example, when a wealthy cotton manufacturer called Robert Greg came to write a spirited attack on the progress of factory legislation up to 1837, he could find only one important defect in the factory system as such: the 'necessary union of the labour of adults and children'.[36] Only a year earlier Gaskell had inveighed in similar terms against the absurdity of the restrictions which the Act of 1833 had imposed upon child labour. The statute had been founded upon 'a singular ignorance of the interior economy of mills', he asserted, and had in consequence failed to appreciate that the child performed an essential part in their operation. 'There is a mutual dependence of the entire labourers one upon the other; and if the children who are employed principally by the spinner are dismissed, his work ceases and the mill is at a standstill.'[37]

What such mutual dependence of labour within the internal economy of the factory meant, of course was that any particular class of worker was exposed to the employer's views as to the role of labour, as a whole, in the productive process. And here, the arithmetic was sanguinary indeed. Obsessed with the extent of their capital investment in fixed plant and machinery, most entrepreneurs assumed both that output varied commensurately with the length of time worked, and that the cost of their investment fell as output was extended.[38] Hence, the 'interdependency' of labour all too easily became fused with a broader calculus which led ineluctably to overworking. The convergence was put cogently by one manufacturer when he was asked whether his desire to restrict even 'absolutely necessary' legislation to certain trades was grounded upon a belief that these involved harder physical work:[39]

No; it arises from the tendency which I conceive to exist in businesses where much capital is sunk in buildings and machinery for production to be pushed (for the sake of diminishing cost) to an extent inconsistent with the permanent welfare of the operatives. In such establishments the subdivision of labour causes the different classes of workpeople to be dependent upon the aid of each other. The greater proportion must act simultaneously and work the same number of hours; hence the weak and the strong, the old and the young, must of necessity conform to the established duration of labour, which, in the absence of legislative restriction, would be regulated most probably more by the physical capability of the vigorous and robust than by the necessities of the far greater proportion of the operatives of comparatively weaker powers of endurance.

In the context of the present discussion, the significance of such thinking lies not so much in the resistance that it generated to each successive proposal for further regulation as in the motivation which it provided for violation of the law. Whatever the advantages of effective restriction in the long term, in the short run the most obvious solution to problems of increased competition or declining profitability seemed to involve an extension of the hours of work; and because of the way in which the 'internal economy' of the typical mill was organised, such a strategy entailed a constant temptation to overwork the restricted classes of labour. As Hobsbawm and others have pointed out, low productivity and inefficient labour management were not generally seen as the key to such problems until well into the 1840s or even later, employers in the earlier period preferring to exhaust the possibilities of cutting costs by increasing hours and reducing money wage-rates.[40] In consequence, there was a recurrent incentive to law-breaking, particularly when – as in the case of the cotton industry during the 1830s and 1840s – fluctuations in trade concealed a progressively downward trend in rates of profitability.[41] When times were bad, some employers with stocks in hand would try to survive by going for long hours and increased output, thereby adding to the pressure on their competitors.[42] More commonly, when trade thrived, attempts would be made to meet the demand of relatively full orderbooks on the basis of existing plant and machinery, necessitating, once again, extended hours.

Throughout this entire period there is ample evidence to show that violation of the law relating to hours of labour was a calculated response to the perceived exigencies of the trade. In the earliest days, employers seem to have increased working hours at will, and indeed, by 1833 it could still be claimed that the law had any semblance of efficiency only in 'circumstances under which *it* conformed to the state of things already in existence' (my emphasis).[43] In the more fully documented years following 1833, the newly-appointed Inspectors greeted every downward trend in violation with diffident disclaimers of credit, almost invariably pointing out that it was the slackness of trade rather than their effort that was responsible.[44] Conversely, when things picked up, they would note the increased incentive to violation and counsel themselves to greater vigilance.[45] Even though manufacturers may have begun to turn towards other strategies during the 1840s[46] – partly as a result of the slump at the beginning of that decade, partly as a consequence of the passage of the Ten Hours Act in 1847, and partly because they were gradually learning that reduced hours did not necessarily entail proportionately reduced output[47] – the Inspectors remained convinced that violation of these provisions was largely a function of the state of trade. As surviving records of prosecuted offences involving overwork show, moreover, the pattern of their enforcement activity was substantially in keeping with such an interpretation. Dropping fairly sharply with the recession which followed the boom of 1836,[48] such prosecutions reached their lowest point with the depression that became most acute in 1842, picked up again with the slow recovery which produced prosperity in the greater part of 1845, only to decline with the subsequent recession that lasted until 1848 (see Table 7.1).

A plausible case can be made out, then, for suggesting that violation of the law's pivotal provisions with regard to hours of labour in this period was a calculated response to economic exigency, a response which reflected perfectly rational, if illegal, choices from within a range of possibilites ordained by the industry's employment structure, organisation and economic reasoning. Indeed, 'calculational' was precisely the term that was used in protracted evidence to the Select Committee of 1840 in relation to both overworking and many other kinds of offence against the Act.[49] According to Superintendent Trimmer, for example, some mill-occupiers had even told him that it answered their purpose better to pay the occasional fine rather than to obey the law.[50] It is important, moreover, to realise that the competitive and other pressures that could generate such responses were not restricted to a minority of so-called 'less respectable' employers. Even some of the most ardent of reforming masters, like John Fielden, could feel compelled to increase their hours in order to match their trade rivals.[51] Similarly, from 1833 onwards, there was a constant stream of protests from law-abiding employers in which they not only complained about the illegal activities of competitors, but also stated their own intention of following suit if the offenders were not restrained. As Messrs Sidgwick, employers of more than 1,000 workers at Skipton, explained in 1849, for example, the use of illegal relays in their area left them little choice but to engage in the same practice, 'in defence of our own interests (as regards the competition of parties who have increased their time of working)... to enable us to offer our goods on the same terms as they do'.[52]

Table 7.1 Prosecutions for overworking 1836-49

Year	No.	Year	No.
1836	356	1843	89
1837	253	1844	86
1838	246	1845	520
1839	105	1846	150
1840	65	1847	63
1841	101	1848	204
1842	36	1849	258

Figures compiled from the annual returns of prosecutions which each Inspector was required to submit (Reports of Inspectors).

The factory crime of this period was calculated and, as occasion demanded, pervasive. As Leonard Horner, one of the first and arguably the most important Inspector in this period, ruefully reflected after more than fifteen years' experience, 'we unfortunately know too well that all mill-owners are not to be trusted; that many of them have a very loose kind of morality

in regard to evasions of the factory law'.[53] Despite open admission of the grounds on which they might violate, however,
employers were frequently none too willing to assume personal
responsibility for the law having been broken. More often than
not, juvenile labour was hired directly by the skilled adult
operatives themselves, the industry's employment structure
again intruding, this time to lend superficial credibility to
claims that the master was not the really culpable party.
Moreover, as the law was framed at the point when Inspectors
were first appointed and some measure of real control became
a possibility for the first time, it was legally permissible to
shift responsibility from the mill-occupier to the employee,
where the magistrates were satisfied that the offence had been
committed without the personal consent, concurrence or knowledge of the master.[54]

By all accounts, this loophole was frequently not far from
the minds of offending employers in the years following 1833.
In some areas, for example, many masters put up notices saying that the law was to be obeyed and all penalties borne by
the spinners, overlookers and others who hired employees in
the restricted classes.[55] Not infrequently, too, there would
be active collusion in the matter, the servant agreeing to admit
the offence and the master agreeing to reimburse the minimal
fine which, in view of the offender's professed or genuine
poverty, the court would be likely to inflict.[56] While the
Inspectors may have attempted to follow the maxim *qui facit per
alium facit per se*,[57] their efforts were frequently of little
avail:[58]

> It not infrequently happens that the workman is paid by the
> piece and not by the day; and in this case the workman hires
> the children ... The tendency of this opening for shifting
> the responsibility from the master to the workman is to induce
> the former, the man of education, character and station, to
> represent himself, in case of prosecution, as having no know-
> ledge of the proceedings of his work-people ... so that he
> may escape from legal responsibility himself, although he is
> the person who ultimately profits by the evasion of the law,
> who can hardly be really ignorant of the acts of his work-
> people, and who ought to be responsible that the business
> of his factory is conducted according to the law.

What was at issue here was more than a legal nicety. More
significantly, it was a case of the carryover of traditional
relationships into factory production - an overlap which Bendix
and others have rightly interpreted as facilitating labour
management in the early stages of industrialisation[59] - being
used to surround violation of the law with structurally embedded patterns of rationalisation. On such grounds could super-
ficially plausible excuses of ignorance be advanced even though,
as Inspector Howell complained, the employer could hardly fail
to know 'how much material was worked up in an extra half-
hour, or could fail to note to a nicety the extra profit accruing

from even a few minutes extra work'.[60]

Displacement of responsibility onto others was not, however, the only strategy used by employers in this period to deny any real criminal guilt on their own part, while continuing to profit from factory crime. Some, of course, deemed it sufficient to follow the letter of the law even though its spirit was grossly abused - Ashworth, for example, maintained that even if a child was actually and patently under the permitted age, once an employer had paid sixpence for a certificate of age, however false, he had a licence to work the child.[61] Others contended that although they might indeed be in breach of the law, their delinquencies were merely formal or even technical offences involving no substance of moral responsibility commensurate with conviction on a criminal charge. Reluctant to accept the obligation to oversee the detailed operation of the law's provisions with respect to their premises, some conceded that offences might occur without their knowledge.[62] The mill-owner, as it was archly explained to Nassau W. Senior, for example, had other things on his mind than the prevention of eighty urchins from truancy.[63] Still others maintained that they were liable to prosecution simply because one out of a number of children remained on the premises for a few extra minutes, perhaps to escape the cold, or because one child, on one day, started work at a time different from that shown in the time-book.[64] For such violations, they insisted, they should hardly be held responsible in any real sense. Even less should they be criminally accountable for mere irregularities in the maintenance of the various records and registers required by the Inspectors under their power to promulgate administrative regulations.[65] On such plausible grounds it could even be conceded that the 'forms of the Act' were systematically disregarded in some areas, 'the master, relying on his general high character, and not fearing to be suspected of having intentionally violated its substance'.[66]

Once again, however, there is reason to suggest that there was more to the matter than mere inadvertence, understandable preoccupation or clerical oversight. For one thing, the Inspectors were convinced that so-called 'formal offences' often betokened the commission of substantive contraventions as well; that, as Inspector Saunders put it in 1838, 'neglect upon this head almost invariably proves that some other provisions of the Act have also been neglected or wilfully violated'.[67] Equally, it must be remembered that employers' protests in this context very much reflected as yet untransformed patterns of control, organisation and authority in industry.[68] If control over workers could be left largely in the hands of the sub-contracted employee, why not responsibility for their illegal mistreatment? Similarly, the Factories Acts and, in particular, their administrative machinery necessitated an unprecedented degree of internal bureaucratisation within the factory, and as such, were resisted on the grounds of unfamiliarity, inconvenience and expense. Moreover, since the administrative regulations tended towards the separation of ownership from control over the means of administration within a firm, they were seen as an expropriation of ultimate entrepreneurial authority and power. [69] In this as in other aspects of early factory crime, there was a strong element of resistance to interference in established entrepreneurial practice: [70]

> The Inspectors' regulations are founded upon the principle of the master being a tyrant and a cheat; and that the operatives must look to the Inspector rather than to him for justice and protection ... Regulations, framed in such a spirit, necessarily throw the master into a false position ... and throw power into the hands of the work-people, of which, it is too much to suppose, they will not sometimes avail themselves.

Notes

 1 42 Geo. III, c.73.
 2 Ibid., Sections 2, 3 and 6.
 3 'Hansard', 27 April 1818, p.342.
 4 59 Geo. III, c.66; 6 Geo. IV, c.63; 1 & 2 Will. IV, c.39.
 5 3 & 4 Will. IV, c.103.
 6 'P.P', 1840, X; 'P.P.', 1841, IX.
 7 7 & 8 Vict., c.15.
 8 For a good description of the Factory Movement, see J.T. Ward, 'The Factory Movement 1830-55', London, Macmillan, 1962.
 9 'Hansard', 1844, LXXIV, p.1104.
10 10 & 11 Vict., c.70.
11 Ryder v. Mills, 'P.P.', 1850, XLII.
12 See M.W. Thomas, 'The Early Factory Legislation', London, Thames Bank, 1948, ch.18.
13 13 & 14 Vict., c.54.
14 16 & 17 Vict., c.104.
15 See, for example, Thomas, op. cit., chs 1 and 2.
16 'P.P.', 1816, III.
17 See, for example, the evidence given by Richard Arkwright, ibid., p.515.
18 Ibid., p.555.
19 See, for example, the evidence of Wm Sidgwick, ibid., p.349.
20 'Westminster Review', vol.26, 1836, p.179.
21 'Hansard', 1825, XIII, p.644.
22 'P.P.', 1831-2, XV.
23 'P.P.', 1833, XX, p.36.
24 'P.P.', 1849, XXII, p.230.
25 See Thomas, op. cit., p.85 ff.
26 'P.P.', 1837, XXXI, pp.123-4.
27 'P.P.', 1837, L, p.203.
28 See, for example, R. Bendix, 'Work and Authority in Industry', New York, Wiley, 1956, p.34 ff.
29 On the disincentive to employ adult males, see E.P. Thomp-

son, 'The Making of the English Working Class', Penguin Books, 1968, p.341.

30 Bendix, op. cit., p.39.
31 'Hansard', 27 April 1818, p.342.
32 Thompson, op. cit., p.341.
33 Figures compiled from individual Inspector's returns published as an appendix to the First Report of the Select Committee of 1840. 'P.P.', 1840, X, p.154 ff.
34 M. Blaug, The Productivity of Capital in the Lancashire Cotton Industry during the Nineteenth Century, 'Economic History Review', vol.XIII, 1961, p.368; S.J. Chapman, 'The Lancashire Cotton Industry', Manchester, 1904, p.12.
35 Blaug, op. cit., p.368.
36 R.H. Greg, 'The Factory Question', London, 1837, p.125.
37 P. Gaskell, 'Artisans and Machinery', London, 1836, p.168.
38 Such assumptions were, for example, central to Senior's famous calculation that the entire net profit made by a mill working for $11\frac{1}{2}$ hours daily was earned in the last hour, any reduction to 10 hours therefore being disastrous. 'Letters on the Factory Act', London, 1837, p.12 ff.
39 'P.P.', 1833, XX, p.852.
40 E.J. Hobsbawm, 'Labouring Men', London, Weidenfeld & Nicholson, 1964, pp.352-6.
41 See, for example, J. Foster, 'Class Struggle and the Industrial Revolution', London, Methuen, 1977, pp.20-1.
42 Inspector Saunders, for example, noted in 1841 that 'on former occasions of commercial difficulty, some of the large capitalists have had recourse to longer hours of work, in order to avail themselves of the reduced wages of the operative, in anticipation of better times'. 'P.P.', 1841, VI, p.227.
43 First Report of Factories Inquiry Commission, 'P.P.', 1833, XX, p.36.
44 Such disclaimers were common in the early reports. As late as 1847, Inspector Saunders could still say that 'the great reduction in prosecutions would be much more satisfactory ... if I could have considered it the result of greater desire and endeavour to obey the law; but I fear it is even still more indicative of bad times ... which remove all inducement'. Reports of Inspectors, May-October, 1847, 'P.P.', 1847-8, XXVI, p.28.
45 See, for example, Reports of Inspectors, May-October 1849, 'P.P.', 1850, XXIII, p.37.
46 Hobsbawm, loc. cit.
47 From the mid-forties onwards, the Inspectors began to notice a change in this respect. Reports of Inspectors, passim.
48 The figure for 1836 would almost certainly have been even higher had it not been for the fact that, in anticipation of the law being changed, the Inspectors suspended their visits for much of the first half of that year.

'P.P.', 1837, XXXI, p.55.
49 See, for example, the evidence of Superintendent Heathcote; 'P.P.', 1840, X, p.135.
50 'P.P.', 1841, IX, p.191.
51 John Fielden, 'The Curse of the Factory System' (1836),
   ed. J.T. Ward, London, Frank Cass, 1969, p.XI.
52 Reports of Inspectors, November 1848-April 1849, 'P.P.',
   1849, XXII, p.14.
53 Reports of Inspectors, May-October 1848, 'P.P.', 1849,
   XXII, p.6.
54 3 & 4 Will. IV, c.103, Section XXX.
55 See, for example, Inspector Howell's report of 30 September
   1837; 'P.P.', 1837-8, XXVIII, pp.109-10.
56 'P.P.', 1840, X, p.121.
57 Ibid., p.10.
58 'P.P.', 1841, IX, p.578.
59 Bendix, op. cit., p.46 ff.
60 Reports of Inspectors, November 1851-April 1852, 'P.P.',
   1852, XXI, p.15.
61 'P.P.', 1841, IX, p.312.
62 Inspector Howell was particularly incensed by such excuses
   which he roundly dismissed as 'nonsense'. Reports of
   Inspectors, November 1851-April 1852, 'P.P.', 1852,
   XXI, p.15.
63 Nassau W. Senior, op. cit., p.21.
64 Ibid., p.20.
65 3 & 4 Will. IV, c.103, Section XVIII.
66 Senior, op. cit., p.21.
67 'P.P.', 1837-8, XXVII, p.124.
68 See, for example, Bendix, op. cit., p.58.
69 This was one of the objections underpinning many of the
   criticisms raised by Greg, op. cit., p.127 ff.
70 Ibid., p.127.

Dangerous Classes

8   A visit to the rookery of St Giles and its neighbourhood

Henry Mayhew

In company with a police officer we proceeded to the Seven
Dials, one of the most remarkable localities in London, inhabited
by bird-fanciers, keepers of stores of old clothes and old
shoes, costermongers, patterers, and a motley assemblage of
others, chiefly of the lower classes. As we stood at one of
the angles in the centre of the Dials we saw three young men -
burglars - loitering at an opposite corner of an adjoining dial.
One of them had a gentlemanly appearance, and was dressed
in superfine black cloth and beaver hat. The other two were
attired as mechanics or tradesmen. One of them had recently
returned from penal servitude, and another had undergone a
long imprisonment.

Leaving the Seven Dials and its dingy neighbourhood, we
went to Oxford Street, one of the first commercial streets in
London, and one of the finest in the world. It reminded us a
good deal of the celebrated Broadway, New York, although
the buildings of the latter are in some places more costly and
splendid, and some of the shops more magnificent. Oxford Street
is one of the main streets of London, and is ever resounding
with the din of vehicles, carts, cabs, hansoms, broughams,
and omnibuses driving along. Many of the shops are spacious
and crowded with costly goods, and the large windows of
plate-glass, set in massive brass frames, are gaily furnished
with their various articles of merchandise.

On the opposite side of the street, we observed a jolly, com-
fortable-looking, elderly man, like a farmer in appearance, not
at all like a London sharper. He was standing looking along the
street as though he were waiting for someone. He was a magsman
(a skittle-sharp), and no doubt other members of the gang were
hovering near. He appeared to be as cunning as an old fox in
his movements, admirably fitted to entrap the unwary.

A little farther along the street we saw a fashionably-dressed

Source: P. Quennell (ed.), 'London's Underworld', London,
Spring Books, pp.170-83.

man coming towards us, arm-in-arm with his companion, among the throng of people. They were in the prime of life, and had a respectable, and even opulent appearance. One of them was good-humoured and social, as though he were on good terms with himself and society in general; the other was more callous and reserved, and more suspicious in his aspect. Both were bedecked with glittering watch chains and gold rings. They passed by a few paces, when the more social of the two, looking over his shoulder, met our eye directed towards him, turned back and accosted us, and was even so generous as to invite us into a gin-palace near by, which we courteously declined. The two magsmen (card-sharpers) strutted off, like fine gentlemen, along the street on the outlook for their victims.

Here we saw another young man, a burglar, pass by. He had an engaging appearance, and was very tasteful in his dress, very unlike the rough burglars we met at Whitechapel, the Borough and Lambeth.

Leaving Oxford Street we went along Holborn to Chancery Lane, chiefly frequented by barristers and attorneys, and entered Fleet Street, one of the main arteries of the metropolis, reminding us of London in the olden feudal times, when the streets were crowded together in dense masses, flanked with innumerable dingy alleys, courts and by-streets, like a great rabbit-warren. Fleet Street, though a narrow, business street, with its traffic often choked with vehicles, is interesting from its antique, historical and literary associations. Elbowing our way through the throng of people, we passed through one of the gloomy arches of Temple Bar, and issued into the Strand, where we saw two pick-pockets, young, tall, gentlemanly men, cross the street from St. Clement's Church and enter a restaurant. They were attired in a suit of superfine black cloth, cut in fashionable style. They entered an elegant dining-room, and probably sat down to costly viands and wines.

Leaving the Strand, we went up St. Martin's Lane, a narrow street leading from the Strand to the Seven Dials. We here saw a young man, an expert burglar, of about twenty-four years of age and dark complexion, standing at the corner of the street. He was well dressed, in a dark cloth suit, with a billicock hat. One of his comrades was taken from his side about three weeks ago on a charge of burglary.

Entering a beershop in the neighbourhood of St. Giles, close by the Seven Dials, we saw a band of coiners and ringers of changes. One of them, a genteel-looking, slim youth, is a notorious coiner, and has been convicted. He was sitting quietly by the door over a glass of beer, with his companion by his side. One of them is a moulder, another was sentenced to ten years' penal servitude for coining and selling base coin. A modest-looking young man, one of the gang, was seated by the bar, also respectably dressed. He is generally supposed to be a subordinate connected with this coining band, looking out, while they are coining, that no officers of justice are near, and carrying the bag of base money for them when they go out to sell it to base wretches in small quantities at low prices. Five shillings' worth of base money is generally sold for ten-pence. 'Ringing the changes' is effected in this way:- A person offers a good sovereign to a shopkeeper to be changed. The gold piece is chinked on the counter, or otherwise tested, and is proved to be good. The man hastily asks back and gets the sovereign, and pretends that he has some silver, so that he does not require to change it. On feeling his pocket he finds he does not have it, and returns a base piece of money resembling it, instead of the genuine gold piece.

We returned to Bow Street, and saw three young pickpockets proceeding along in company, like three well-dressed coster-mongers, in dark cloth frock-coats and caps.

Being desirous of having a more thorough knowledge of the people residing in the rookery of St. Giles, we visited it with Mr. Hunt, inspector of police. We first went to a lodging-house in George Street, Oxford Street, called the Hampshire-Hog Yard. Most of the lodgers were then out. On visiting a room in the garret we saw a man, in mature years, making artificial flowers; he appeared to be very ingenious, and made several roses before us with marvellous rapidity. He had suspended along the ceiling bundles of dyed grasses of various hues, crimson, yellow, green, brown, and other colours to furnish cases of stuffed birds. He was a very intelligent man and a natural genius. He told us strong drink had brought him to this humble position in the garret, and that he once had the opportunity of making a fortune in the service of a noble-man. We felt, as we looked on his countenance and listened to his conversation, he was capable of moving in a higher sphere of life. Yet he was wonderfully contented with his hum-ble lot.

We visited Dyott House, George Street, the ancient manor-house of St. Giles-in-the-Fields, now fitted up as a lodging-house for simple men. The kitchen, an apartment about fifteen feet square, is surrounded with massive and tasteful panel-ling in the olden style. A large fire blazing in the grate - with two boilers on each side - was kept burning night and day to supply the lodgers with hot water for their tea and coffee. Some rashers of bacon were suspended before the fire, with a plate underneath. There was a gas-light in the centre of the apart-ment, and a dial on the back wall. The kitchen was furnished with two long deal tables and a dresser, with forms to serve as seats. There were about fifteen labouring men present, most of them busy at supper on fish, and bread, and tea. They were a very mixed company, such as we would expect at a London lodging-house, men working in cab-yards assisting cabmen, some distributing bills in the streets, one man carrying adver-tising boards, and others jobbing at anything they can find to do in the neighbourhood. This house was clean and comfortable, and had the appearance of being truly a comfortable poor man's home. It was cheerful to look around us and to see the social air of the inmates. One man sat with coat off, enjoying the warmth of the kitchen; a boy was at his tea, cutting up dried fish and discussing his bread and butter. A young man of about nineteen sat at the back of the apartment, with a very sinister countenance, very unlike the others. There was something about him that indicated a troubled mind. We also observed a number of elderly men among the party, some in jackets, and others in velvet coats, with an honest look about them.

When the house was a brothel, about fifteen years ago, an unfortunate prostitute, named Mary Brothers, was murdered in this kitchen by a man named Connell, who was afterwards executed at Newgate for the deed. He had carnal connexion with this woman some time before, and he suspected that she had communicated to him the venereal disease with which he was afflicted. In revenge he took her life, having purchased a knife at a neighbouring cutler's shop.

We were introduced to the landlady, a very stout woman who came up to meet us, candle in hand, as we stood on the staircase. Here we saw the profile of the ancient proprietor of the house, carved over the panelling, set, as it were, in an oval frame. In another part of the staircase we saw a similar frame, but the profile had been removed or destroyed. Over the window that overlooks the staircase there are three figures, possibly likenesses of his daughters; such is the tradition. The balustrade along the staircase is very massive and tastefully carved and ornamented. The bed-rooms were also clean and comfortable.

The beds are furnished with a bed-cover and flock-bed, with sufficient warm and clean bedding, for the low charge of 2s. a week, or 4d. a night. The first proprietor of the house is said to have been a magistrate of the city, and a knight or baronet.

Leaving George Street we passed on to Church Lane, a by-street in the rear of New Oxford Street, containing twenty-eight houses. It was dark as we passed along. We saw the street lamps lighted in Oxford Street, and the shop-windows brilliantly illuminated, while the thunder of vehicles in the street broke on our ear, rolling in a perpetual stream. Here a very curious scene presented itself to our view. From the windows of the three-storied houses in Church Lane were suspended wooden rods with clothes to dry across the narrow streets - cotton gowns, sheets, trousers, drawers, and vests, some ragged and patched, and others old and faded giving a more picturesque aspect to the scene, which was enhanced by the dim lights in the windows, and the groups of the lower orders of all ages assembled below, clustered around the doorways, and in front of the houses, or indulging in merriment in the street. Altogether the appearance of the inhabitants

was much more clean and orderly than might be expected in
such a low locality. Many women of the lower orders, chiefly
of the Irish cockneys, were seated, crouching with their
knees almost touching their chin, beside the open windows.
Some men were smoking their pipes as they stood leaning against
the walls of their houses, whom from their appearance we took
to be evidently out-door labourers. Another labouring man
was seated on the side of his window, in corduroy trousers,
light-gray coat and cap with an honest look of good-humour
and industry. Numbers of young women, the wives of costermongers, sat in front of their houses in the manner we have
described, clad in cotton gowns, with a general aspect of
personal cleanliness and contentment. At the corners of the
streets, and at many of the doorways, were groups of young
costermongers, who had finished their hard day's work, and
were contentedly chatting and smoking. They generally stood
with their hands in their breeches pockets. Most of these
people are Irish, or the children of Irish parents. The
darkness of the street was lighted up by the street lamps as
well as by the lights in the windows of two chandlers' shops
and one public-house. At one of the chandlers' shops the
proprietor was standing by his door with folded arms as he
looked good-humouredly on his neighbours around his shop-
door. We also saw some of the young Arabs bareheaded and
barefooted, with their little hands in their pockets, or squatted
on the street, having the usual restless, artful look peculiar
to their tribe.

Here a house was pointed out to us, No. 21, which was
formerly let at a rent of £25 per annum to a publican that
resided in the neighbourhood. He let the same in rooms for
£90 a year, and these again receive from parties residing in
them upwards of £120. The house is still let in rooms, but they
are occupied, like all others in the neighbourhood, by one
family only.

At one house as we passed along we saw a woman selling
potatoes, at the window, to persons in the street. On looking
into the interior we saw a cheerful fire burning in the grate
and some women sitting around it. We also observed several
bushel baskets and sacks placed round the room, filled with
potatoes, of which they sell a large quantity.

In Church Lane we found lodging-houses, the kitchens of
which are entered from the street by a descent of a few steps
leading underground to the basement. Here we found numbers
of people clustered together around several tables, some reading the newspapers, others supping on fish, bread, tea, and
potatoes, and some lying half asleep on the tables in all imagin-
able positions. These, we were told, had just returned from
hopping in Kent, had walked long distances, and were fatigued.

On entering some of these kitchens, the ceiling being very
low, we found a large fire burning in the grate, and a general
air of comfort, cleanliness and order. Such scenes as these

were very homely and picturesque, and reminded us very
forcibly of localities of London in the olden time. In some of
them the inmates were only half dressed, and yet appeared to
be very comfortable from the warmth of the apartment. Here
we saw a number of the poorest imbeciles we had noticed in the
course of our rambles through the great metropolis. Many of
them were middle-aged men, others more elderly, very shabbily
dressed, and some half naked. There was little manliness left
in the poor wretches as they squatted drearily on the benches.
The inspector told us they were chiefly vagrants, and were
sunk in profound ignorance and debasement, from which they
were utterly unable to rise.

The next kitchen of this description we entered was occupied
by females. It was about fifteen feet square and belonged to
a house of ten rooms, part of which was occupied as a low
lodging-house. Here we found five women seated around a
table, most of them young, but one more advanced in life. Some
of them were good-looking, as though they had been respectable servants. They were busy at their tea, bread and butcher's
meat. On the table stood a candle on a small candlestick. They
sat in curious positions round the table, some of them with an
ample crinoline. One sat by the fire with her gown drawn over
her knees, displaying her white petticoat. As we stood beside
them they burst out in a titter which they could not suppress.
On looking round we observed a plate-rack at the back of
the kitchen, and, as usual in these lodging-houses, a glorious
fire burning brightly in the grate. An old chest of drawers,
surmounted with shelves, stood against the wall. The girls
were all prostitutes or thieves, but had no appearance of
shame. They were apparently very merry. The old woman sat
very thoughtfully, looking observant on, and no doubt won-
dering what errand could have brought us into the house.

We then entered another dwelling-house. On looking down
the stairs we saw a company of young women, from seventeen
to twenty-five years of age. A rope was hung over the fire-
place, with stockings and shirts suspended over it, and clothes
were drying on a screen. A young woman, with her hair net-
ted and ornamented, sat beside the fire with a green jacket
and striped petticoat with crinoline. Another good-looking
young woman sat by the table dressed in a cotton gown and
striped apron, with coffee-pot in hand, and tea-cups before
her. Some pleasant-looking girls sat by the table with their
chins leaning on their hands, smiling cheerfully, looking at us
with curiosity. Another coarser featured dame lolled by the
end of the table with her gown drawn over her head, smirking
in our countenance; and one sat by, her shawl drawn over
her head. Another apparently modest girl sat by cutting her
nails with a knife. On the walls around the apartment were
suspended a goodly assortment of bonnets, cloaks, gowns and
petticoats.

Meantime an elderly little man came in with a cap on his head and a long staff in his hand, and stood looking on with curiosity. On the table lay a pack of cards beside the bowls, cups, and other crockery-ware. Some of the girls appeared as if they had lately been servants in respectable situations, and one was like a quiet genteel shop girl. They were all prostitutes, and most of them prowl about at night to plunder drunken men. As we looked on the more interesting girls, especially two of them, we saw the sad consequences of one wrong step, which may launch the young and thoughtless into a criminal career, and drive them into the dismal companionship of the most lewd and debased.

We then went to Short's Gardens, and entered a house there. In the basement underground we saw a company of men, women, and children of various ages, seated around the tables, and by the fire. The men and women had mostly been engaged in hopping, and appeared to be healthy, industrious, and orderly. Until lately thieves used to lodge in these premises.

As we entered Queen Street we saw three thieves, lads of about fourteen years of age, standing in the middle of the street as if on the outlook for booty. They were dressed in black frock-coats, corduroy, and fustian trousers, and black caps. Passing along Queen Street, which is one of the wings of the Dials, we went up to the central space between the Seven Dials. Here a very lively scene presented itself to our view; clusters of labouring men, and a few men of doubtful character, in dark shabby dress, loitered by the corners of the surrounding streets. We also saw groups of elderly women standing at some of the angles, most of them ragged and drunken, their very countenances the pictures of abject misery. The numerous public-houses in the locality were driving a busy traffic and were thronged with motley groups of people of various grades, from the respectable merchant and tradesman to the thief and the beggar.

Bands of boys and girls were gamboling in the street in wild frolic, tumbling on their head with their heels in the air, and shouting in merriment, while the policeman was quietly looking on in good humour.

Around the centre of the Dials were bakers' shops with large illuminated fronts, the shelves being covered with loaves, and the baker busy attending to his customers. In the window was a large printed notice advertising the 'best wheaten bread at 6d.' a loaf. A druggist's shop was invitingly adorned with beautiful green and purple jars, but no customers entered during the time of our stay.

At the corner of an opposite dial was an old clothes store, with a large assortment of second-hand garments, chiefly for men, of various kinds, qualities, and styles, suspended around the front of the shop. There were also provision shops, which were well attended with customers. The whole neighbourhood presented an appearance of bustle and animation, and omnibuses and other vehicles were passing along in a perpetual stream.

The most of the low girls in this locality do not go out till late in the evening, and chiefly devote their attention to drunken men. They frequent the principal thoroughfares in the vicinity of Oxford Street, Holborn, Farringdon Street, and other bustling streets. From the nature of their work they are of a migratory character. The most of the men we saw in the houses we visited belong to the labouring class, men employed to assist in cleaning cabs and omnibuses, carriers of advertising boards, distributors of bills, patterers, chickweed sellers, ballad singers, and persons generally of industrious character. They are willing to work, but will steal rather than want.

The lodging-house people here have not been known of late years to receive stolen property, and the inhabitants generally are steadily rising in habits of decency, cleanliness and morality.

The houses we visited in George Street, and the streets adjacent, were formerly part of the rookery of St. Giles-in-the-Fields, celebrated as one of the chief haunts of redoubtable thieves and suspicious characters in London. Deserted as it comparatively is now, except by the labouring poor vagrants and low prostitutes, it was once the resort of all classes, from the proud noble to the beggar picking up a livelihood from door to door.

We have been indebted to Mr. Hunt, inspector of the lodging-houses in this district, for fuller information regarding the rookery of St. Giles and its inhabitants twenty years ago, before a number of these disreputable streets were removed to make way for New Oxford Street. We quote from a manuscript nearly in his own words:

The ground covered by the Rookery was enclosed by Great Russell Street, Charlotte Street, Broad Street, and High Street, all within the parish of St. Giles-in-the-Fields. Within this space were George Street (once Dyott Street), Carrier Street, Maynard Street, and Church Street, which ran from north to south, and were intersected by Church Lane, Ivy Lane, Buckeridge Street, Bainbridge Street, and New Street. These, with an almost endless intricacy of courts and yards crossing each other, rendered the place like a rabbit-warren.

In Buckeridge Street stood the 'Hare and Hounds' public-house, formerly the 'Beggar in the Bush'; at the time of which I speak (1844) kept by the well-known and much-respected Joseph Banks (generally called 'Stunning Joe'), a civil, rough, good-hearted Boniface. His house was the resort of all classes, from the aristocratic marquis to the vagabond whose way of living was a puzzle to himself.

At the opposite corner of Carrier Street stood Mother Dowling's, a lodging-house and provision shop, which was not closed nor the shutters put on for several years before it was pulled down, to make way for the improvements in New Oxford Street...The shop was frequented by vagrants of every class, including foreigners, who, with moustache, well-brushed hat

and seedy clothes - consisting usually of a frock-coat but-
toned to the chin, light trousers, and boots gaping at each
lofty step - might be seen making their way to Buckeridge
Street to regale upon cabbage, which has been boiled with a
ferocious pig's head or a fine piece of salt beef. From 12 to
1 o'clock at midnight was chosen by these ragged but proud
gentlemen from abroad as the proper time for a visit to Mrs.
Dowling's.

Most of the houses in Buckeridge Street were lodging-
houses for thieves, prostitutes, and cadgers. The charge
was fourpence a night in the upper rooms, and threepence
in the cellars, as the basements were termed. If the beds
were occupied six nights by the same parties, and all dues
paid, the seventh night (Sunday) was not charged for. The
rooms were crowded, and paid well. I remember seeing fourteen women in beds in a cellar, each of whom paid 3d. a
night, which, Sunday free, amounted to 21s. per week. The
furniture in this den might have originally cost the proprietor £7 or £8. At the time I last visited it, it was not worth
more than 30s.

Both sides of Buckeridge Street abounded in courts, particularly the north side, and these, with the connected back-
yards and low walls in the rear of the street, afforded an
easy escape to any thief when pursued by officers of justice.
I remember on one occasion, in 1844, a notorious thief was
wanted by a well-known criminal officer (Restieaux). He was
known to associate with some cadgers who used a house in
the rear of Paddy Corvan's, near Church Street, and was
believed to be in the house when Restieaux and a sergeant
entered it. They went into the kitchen where seven male and
five female thieves were seated, along with several cadgers
of the most cunning class. One of them made a signal, indicating that someone had escaped by the back of the premises,
in which direction the officers proceeded. It was evident the
thief had gone over a low wall into an adjoining yard. The
pursuers climbed over, passed through the yards and back
premises of eleven houses, and secured him in Jones Court.
There were about twenty persons present at the time of the
arrest, but they offered no resistance to the constables. It
would have been a different matter had he been apprehended
by strangers.

In Bainbridge Street, one side of which was nearly occupied
by the immense brewery of Meux and Co., were found some of
the most intricate and dangerous places in this low locality.
The most notorious of these was Jones Court, inhabited by
coiners, utterers of base coin, and thieves. In former years
a bull terrier was kept here, which gave an alarm on the
appearance of a stranger, when the coining was suspended
till the course was clear. This dog was at last taken away by
Duke and Clement, two police officers, and destroyed by an
order from a magistrate.

The houses in Jones Court were connected by roof, yard, and cellar with those in Bainbridge and Buckeridge Streets, and with each other in such a manner that the apprehension of an inmate or refugee in one of them was almost a task of impossibility to a stranger, and difficult to those well acquainted with the interior of the dwellings. In one of the cellars was a large cess-pool, covered in such a way that a stranger would likely step into it. In the same cellar was a hole about two feet square, leading to the next cellar, and thence by a similar hole into the cellar of a house in Scott's Court, Buckeridge Street. These afforded a ready means of escape to a thief, but effectually stopped the pursuer, who would be put to the risk of creeping on his hands and knees through a hole two feet square in a dark cellar in St. Giles's Rookery, entirely in the power of dangerous characters. Other houses were connected in a similar manner. In some instances there was a communication from one back window to another by means of large spike nails, one row to hold by, and another for the feet to rest on, which were not known to be used at the time we refer to.

In Church Street were several houses let to men of an honest but poor class, who worked in omnibus and cab-yards, factories, and such other places as did not afford them the means of procuring more expensive lodgings. Their apartments were clean and their way of living frugal.

Other houses of a less reputable character were very numerous. One stood at the corner of Church Street and Lawrence Street, occupied by the most infamous characters of the district. On entering the house from Lawrence Lane, and proceeding upstairs, you would find on each floor several rooms connected by a kind of gallery, each room rented by prostitutes. These apartments were open to those girls who had fleeced any poor drunken man who had been induced to accompany them to this den of infamy. When they had plundered the poor dupe, he was ejected without ceremony by the others who resided in the room; often without a coat or hat, sometimes without his trousers, and occasionally left on the staircase naked as he was born. In this house the grossest scenes of profligacy were transacted. In pulling it down a hole was discovered in the wall opening into a timber-yard which fronted High Street - a convenient retreat for any one pursued.

Opposite to this was the 'Rose and Crown' public-house, resorted to by all classes of the light-fingered gentry, from the mobsman and his 'Amelia' to the lowest of the street thieves and his 'Poll.' In the tap-room might be seen Black Charlie the fiddler, with ten or a dozen lads and lasses enjoying the dance, and singing and smoking over potations of gin-and-water, more or less plentiful according to the proceeds of the previous night - all apparently free from care in their wild carousals. The cheek waxed pale when the

policeman opened the door and glanced round the room, but
when he departed the merriment would be resumed with
vigour.

The kitchens of some houses in Buckeridge Street afforded
a specimen of life in London rarely seen elsewhere even in
London, though some in Church Lane do so now on a smaller
scale. The kitchen, a long apartment usually on the ground-
floor, had a large coke fire, along with a sink, water-tap,
one or two tables, several forms, a variety of saucepans,
and other cooking utensils and was lighted with a gas jet.
There in the evenings suppers were discussed by the cadgers
an alderman might almost have envied - rich steaks and
onions, mutton and pork chops, fried potatoes, sausages,
cheese, celery, and other articles of fare, with abundance
of porter, half-and-half and tobacco.

In the morning they often sat down to a breakfast of tea,
coffee, eggs, rashers of bacon, dried fish, fresh butter,
and other good things which would be considered luxuries
by working people, when each discussed his plans for the
day's rambles, and arranged as to the exchange of garments,
bandages, etc., considered necessary to prevent recognition
in those neighbourhoods recently worked.

Their dinners were taken in the course of their rounds,
consisting generally of the best of the broken victuals given
them by the compassionate, and were eaten on one of the
doorsteps of some respectable street, after which they would
resort to some obscure public-house or beer-shop in a back
street or alley to partake of some liquor.

Heaps of good food were brought home and thrown, on a
side-table, or into a corner, as unfit to be eaten by those
'professional' cadgers - food which thousands of the working
men of London would have been thankful for. It was given to
the children who visited these lodging-houses. The finer
viands, such as pieces of fancy bread, rolls, kidneys, mutton and lamb, the gentlemen of the establishment reserved
for their own more fastidious palates.

On Sunday many of the cadgers stayed at home till night.
They spent the day at cards, shove-halfpenny, tossing,
and other amusements. Sometimes five or six shillings were
staked on the table among a party of about ten of them at
cards, although coppers were the usual stakes.... The life
of a cadger is not in many instances a life of privation. I do
not speak (says Mr. Hunt) of the really distressed, to whose
wants too little attention is sometimes paid. I allude to beggars by profession, who prefer a life of mendicancy to any
other. There are among them sailors, whose largest voyage
has been to Tothill Fields prison, or to Gravesend on a pleasure trip. Cripples with their arms in slings, or feet,
swathed in blood-stained rags, swollen to double the size,
who may be seen dancing when in their lodging at their
evening revels. You may see poor Irish with from five to

thirty sovereigns in a bag hung round their necks or in the waistband of their trousers; women who carry hired babes, or it may be a bundle of clothing resembling a child, on their back or breast, and other such-like impostors.

Between Buckeridge Street and Church Lane stood Ivy Lane, leading from George Street to Carrier Street, communicating with the latter by a small gateway. Clark's Court was on its left, and Rats' Castle on its right. The castle was a large dirty building occupied by thieves and prostitutes, and boys who lived by plunder. On the removal of these buildings, in 1845, the massive foundations of an hospital were found, which had been built in the 12th century by Matilda, Queen of Henry the First, daughter of Malcolm, King of Scotland, for persons afflicted with leprosy.

At this place criminals were allowed a bowl of ale on their way from Newgate to Tyburn.

Maynard Street and Carrier Street were occupied by costermongers and a few thieves and cadgers. George Street, part of which still stands, consisted of lodging-houses for tramps, thieves, and beggars, together with a few brothels.

From George Street to High Street runs a mews called Hampshire-Hog Yard, where there is an old established lodging-house for single men, poor but honest.

The portion of the rookery now remaining, consisting of Church Lane, with its courts, a small part of Carrier Street, and a smaller portion of one side of Church Street, is now more densely crowded than when Buckeridge Street and its neighbourhood were in existence. The old Crown public-house in Church Lane, formerly the resort of the most notorious cadgers, was in 1851 inhabited by Irish people, where often from twelve to thirty persons lodged in a room. At the back of this public-house is a yard, on the right-hand side of which is an apartment then occupied by thirty-eight men, women, and children, all lying indiscriminately on the floor.

Speaking of other houses in this neighbourhood in 1851, Mr. Hunt states: 'I have frequently seen as many as sixteen people in a room about twelve feet by ten, these numbers being exceeded in larger rooms. Many lay on loose straw littered on the floor, their heads to the wall and their feet to the centre, and decency was entirely unknown among them.'

Now, however, the district is considerably changed, the inhabitants are rapidly rising in decency, cleanliness, and order, and the rookery of St. Giles will soon be ranked among the memories of the past.

9 On the number of costermongers and other street folk

Henry Mayhew

The number of costermongers, - that it is to say, of those
street-sellers attending the London 'green' and 'fish' markets,
- appears to be, from the best data at my command, now
30,000 men, women and children.

The costermongering class extends itself yearly; and it is
computed that for the last five years it has increased considerably faster than the general metropolitan population. This
increase is derived partly from *all* the children of costermongers
following the father's trade, but chiefly from working men,
such as the servants of green-grocers or of innkeepers, when
out of employ, 'taking a coster's barrow' for a livelihood; and
the same being done by mechanics and labourers out of work.
At the time of the famine in Ireland, it is calculated, that the
number of Irish obtaining a living in the London streets must
have been at least doubled.

During the summer months and fruit season, the average
number of costermongers attending Covent-garden market is
about 2,500 per market-day. In the strawberry season there
are nearly double as many, there being, at that time, a large
number of Jews who come to buy; during that period, on a
Saturday morning, from the commencement to the close of the
market, as many as 4,000 costers have been reckoned purchas-
ing at Covent-garden. Through the winter season, however,
the number of costermongers does not exceed upon the average
1,000 per market morning.

OF THE VARIETIES OF STREET-FOLK IN GENERAL AND
COSTERMONGERS IN PARTICULAR

Among the street-folk there are many distinct characters of
people - people differing as widely from each in tastes, habits,

Source: P. Quennell (ed.), 'Mayhew's London', London,
Spring Books, pp.30-46.

thoughts and creed, as one nation from another. Of these the
costermongers form by far the largest and certainly the most
broadly marked class. They appear to be a distinct race - perhaps, originally, of Irish extraction - seldom associating with
any other of the street-folks, and being all known to each
other. The 'patterers,' or the men who cry the last dying-
speeches, &c. in the street, and those who help off their wares
by long harangues in the public thoroughfares, are again a
separate class. These, to use their own term, are 'the aristocracy of the street-sellers', despising the costers for their
ignorance, and boasting that they live by their intellect. The
public, they say, do not expect to receive from them an
equivalent for their money - they pay to hear them talk. Compared with the costermongers, the patterers are generally an
educated class, and among them are some classical scholars,
one clergyman, and many sons of gentlemen. They appear to be
the counterparts of the old mountebanks or street-doctors. As
a body they seem far less improvable than the costers, being
more 'knowing' and less impulsive. The street-performers differ
again from those; these appear to possess many of the characteristics of the lower class of actors, viz., a strong desire to
excite admiration, an indisposition to pursue any settled occupation, a love of the tap-room, though more for the society and
display than for the drink connected with it, a great fondness
for finery and predilection for the performance of dexterous
or dangerous feats. Then there are the street mechanics, or
artisans - quiet, melancholy, struggling men, who, unable
to find any regular employment at their own trade, have made
up a few things, and taken to hawk them in the streets, as the
last shift of independence. Another distinct class of street-
folk are the blind people (mostly musicians in a rude way), who,
after the loss of their eyesight, have sought to keep themselves
from the work-house by some little excuse for alms-seeking.
These, so far as my experience goes, appear to be a far more
deserving class than is usually supposed - their affliction, in
most cases, seems to have chastened them and to have given a
peculiar religious cast to their thoughts.

Such are the several varieties of street-folk, intellectually
considered - looked at in a national point of view, they likewise
include many distinct people. Among them are to be found the
Irish fruit-sellers; the Jew clothesmen; the Italian organ boys,
French singing women, the German brass bands, the Dutch
buy-a-broom girls, the Highland bagpipe players, and the
Indian crossing-sweepers - all of whom I here shall treat of in
due order.

The costermongering class or order has also its many varieties.
These appear to be in the following proportions: - One-half of
the entire class are costermongers proper, that is to say, the
calling with them is hereditary, and perhaps has been so for
many generations; while the other half is composed of three-
eighths Irish, and one-eighth mechanics, tradesmen, and Jews.

Under the term 'costermonger' is here included only such
'street-sellers' as deal in fish, fruit, and vegetables, purchas-
ing their goods at the wholesale 'green' and fish markets. Of
these some carry on their business at the same stationary stall
or 'standing' in the street, while others go on 'rounds'. The
itinerant costermongers, as contradistinguished from the stationary street-fishmongers and greengrocers, have in many
instances regular rounds, which they go daily, and which extend
from two to ten miles. The longest are those which embrace a
suburban part; the shortest are through streets thickly peopled
by the poor, where duly to 'work' a single street consumes, in
some instances, an hour. There are also 'chance' rounds.
Men 'working' these carry their wares to any part in which
they hope to find customers. The costermongers, moreover,
diversify their labours by occasionally going on a country round,
travelling on these excursions, in all directions, from thirty
to ninety and even a hundred miles from the metropolis. Some,
again, confine their callings chiefly to the neighbouring races
and fairs.

OF COSTERMONGERING MECHANICS

From the numbers of mechanics [said one smart costermonger
to me] that I know of in my own district, I should say there's
now more than 1,000 costers in London that were once mechanics or labourers. They are driven to it as a last resource,
when they can't get work in their trade. They don't do well,
at least four out of five, or three out of four don't. They're
not up to the dodges of the business. They go to market with
fear, and don't know how to venture a bargain if one offers.
They're inferior salesmen too, and if they have fish left that
won't keep, it's a dead loss to them, for they aren't up to
the trick of selling it cheap at a distance where the coster
ain't known; or of quitting it to another, for candle-light
sale, cheap, to the Irish or to the 'lushingtons', that haven't
a proper taste for fish. Some of these poor fellows lose
every penny. They're mostly middle-aged when they begin
costering. They'll generally commence with oranges or herrings. We pity them. We say, 'Poor fellows! they'll find it out
by-and-bye.' It's awful to see some poor women, too, trying
to pick up a living in the streets by selling nuts or oranges.
It's awful to see them, for they can't set about it right;
besides that, there's too many before they start. They don't
find a living, *it's only another way of starving*.

THE LONDON STREET MARKETS ON A SATURDAY NIGHT

The street-sellers are to be seen in the greatest numbers at
the London street markets on a Saturday night. Here, and in

the shops immediately adjoining, the working-classes generally
purchase their Sunday's dinner; and after pay-time on Saturday night, or early on Sunday morning, the crowd in the
New-cut, and the Brill in particular, is almost impassable.
Indeed, the scene in these parts has more of the character of
a fair than a market. There are hundreds of stalls, and every
stall has its one or two lights; either it is illuminated by the
intense white light of the new self-generating gas-lamp, or
else it is brightened up by the red smoky flame of the old-
fashioned grease lamp. One man shows off his yellow haddock
with a candle stuck in a bundle of firewood; his neighbour
makes a candlestick of a huge turnip, and the tallow gutters
over its sides; whilst the boy shouting 'Eight a penny, stunning pears!' has rolled his dip in a thick coat of brown paper,
that flares away with the candle. Some stalls are crimson with
the fire shining through the holes beneath the baked chestnut
stove; others have handsome octahedral lamps, while a few
have a candle shining through a sieve: these, with the
sparkling ground-glass globes of the tea-dealers' shops, and
the butchers' gaslights streaming and fluttering in the wind,
like flags of flame, pour forth such a flood of light, that at
a distance the atmosphere immediately above the spot is as
lurid as if the street were on fire.

The pavement and the road are crowded with purchasers and
street-sellers. The housewife in her thick shawl, with the
market-basket on her arm, walks slowly on, stopping now to
look at the stall of caps, and now to cheapen a bunch of greens.
Little boys, holding three or four onions in their hands, creep
between the people, wriggling their way through every
interstice, and asking for custom in whining tones, as if seeking charity. Then the tumult of the thousand different cries
of the eager dealers, all shouting at the top of their voices,
at one and the same time, is almost bewildering. 'So-old again,'
roars one. 'Chestnuts all 'ot, a penny a score,' bawls another.
'An 'aypenny a skin, blacking,' squeaks a boy. 'Buy, buy,
buy, buy, buy, bu-u-uy!' cries the butcher. 'Half-quire of
paper for a penny,' bellows the street stationer. 'An 'aypenny
a lot ing-uns.' 'Twopence a pound grapes.' 'Three a penny
Yarmouth bloaters.' 'Who'll buy a bonnet for fourpence?' 'Pick
'em out cheap here! three pair for a halfpenny, bootlaces.'
'Now's your time! beautiful whelks, a penny a lot.' 'Here's
ha'p'orths,' shouts the perambulating confectioner. 'Come and
look at 'em! here's toasters!' bellows one with a Yarmouth
bloater stuck on a toasting-fork. 'Penny a lot, fine russets,'
calls the apple woman; and so the Babel goes on.

One man stands with his red-edged mats hanging over his
back and chest, like a herald's coat; and the girl with her
basket of walnuts lifts her brown-stained fingers to her mouth,
as she screams, 'Fine warnuts! sixteen a penny, fine w.r-r-
nuts.' A bootmaker, to 'ensure custom,' has illuminated his
shop-front with a line of gas, and in its full glare stands a

blind beggar, his eyes turned up so as to show only 'the whites,' and mumbling some begging rhymes, that are drowned in the shrill notes of the bamboo-flute-player next to him. The boy's sharp cry, the woman's cracked voice, the gruff, hoarse shout of the man, are all mingled together. Sometimes an Irishman is heard with his 'fine ating apples'; or else the jingling music of an unseen organ breaks out, as the trio of street singers rest between the verses.

Then the sights, as you elbow your way through the crowd, are equally multifarious. Here is a stall glittering with new tin saucepans; there another, bright with its blue and yellow crockery, and sparkling with white glass. Now you come to a row of old shoes arranged along the pavement; now to a stand of gaudy tea-trays; then to a shop with red handkerchiefs and blue checked shirts, fluttering backwards and forwards, and a counter built up outside on the kerb, behind which are boys beseeching custom. At the door of a tea-shop, with its hundred white globes of light, stands a man delivering bills, thanking the public for past favours, and 'defying competition.' Here, alongside the road, are some half-dozen headless tailor's dummies, dressed in Chesterfields and fustian jackets, each labelled, 'Look at the prices,' or 'Observe the quality.' After this is a butcher's shop, crimson and white with meat piled up to the first-floor, in front of which the butcher himself, in his blue coat, walks up and down, sharpening his knife on the steel that hangs to his waist. A little further on stands the clean family, begging; the father with his head down as if in shame, and a box of lucifers held forth in his hand - the boys in newly-washed pinafores, and the tidily got-up mother with a child at her breast. This stall is green and white with bunches of turnips - that red with apples, the next yellow with onions, and another purple with pickling cabbages. One minute you pass a man with an umbrella turned inside up and full of prints; the next, you hear one with a peepshow of Mazeppa, and Paul Jones the pirate, describing the pictures to the boys looking in at the little round windows. Then is heard the sharp snap of the percussion-cap from the crowd of lads firing at the target for nuts; and the moment afterwards, you see either a black man half-clad in white, and shivering in the cold with tracts in his hand, or else you hear the sounds of music from 'Frazier's Circus', on the other side of the road, and the man outside the door of the penny concert, beseeching you to 'Be in time - be in time!' as Mr. Somebody is just about to sing his favourite song of the 'Knife Grinder'. Such, indeed, is the riot, the struggle, and the scramble for a living, that the confusion and uproar of the New-cut on Saturday night have a bewildering and saddening effect upon the thoughtful mind.

Each salesman tries his utmost to sell his wares, tempting the passers-by with his bargains. The boy with his stock of herbs offers 'a double 'andful of fine parsley for a penny'; the man

with the donkey-cart filled with turnips has three lads to shout
for him to their utmost, with their 'Ho! ho! hi-i-i! What do
you think of this here? A penny a bunch - hurrah for free
trade! *Here's* your turnips!' Until it is seen and heard, we
have no sense of the scramble that is going on throughout London for a living. The same scene takes place at the Brill - the
same in Leather-lane - the same in Tottenham-court-road - the
same in Whitecross-street; go to whatever corner of the metropolis you please, either on a Saturday night or a Sunday morning, and there is the same shouting and the same struggling
to get the penny profit out of the poor man's Sunday's
dinner.

THE SUNDAY MORNING MARKETS

Nearly every poor man's market does its Sunday trade. For a
few hours on the Sabbath morning, the noise, bustle, and
scramble of the Saturday night are repeated, and but for this
opportunity many a poor family would pass a dinnerless
Sunday. The system of paying the mechanic late on a Saturday
night - and more particularly of paying a man his wages in a
public-house - when he is tired with his day's work, lures
him to the tavern, and there the hours fly quickly enough
beside the warm taproom fire, so that by the time the wife
comes for her husband's wages, she finds a large portion of
them gone in drink, and the streets half cleared, so that the
Sunday market is the only chance of getting the Sunday's
dinner.

Of all these Sunday-morning markets, the Brill, perhaps,
furnishes the busiest scene; so that it may be taken as a type
of the whole.

The streets in the neighbourhood are quiet and empty. The
shops are closed with their different-coloured shutters, and
the people round about are dressed in the shiney cloth of the
holiday suit. There are no 'cabs,' and but few omnibuses to
disturb the rest, and men walk in the road as safely as on the
footpath.

As you enter the Brill the market sounds are scarcely heard.
But at each step the low hum grows gradually into the noisy
shouting, until at last the different cries become distinct, and
the hubbub, din, and confusion of a thousand voices bellowing
at once again fill the air. The road and footpath are crowded,
as on the over-night; the men are standing in groups, smoking
and talking; whilst the women run to and fro, some with the
white round turnips showing out of their filled aprons, others
with cabbages under their arms, and a piece of red meat
dangling from their hands. Only a few of the shops are closed;
but the butcher's and the coal-shed are filled with customers,
and from the door of the shut-up baker's, the women come
streaming forth with bags of flour in their hands, while men

sally from the halfpenny barber's smoothing their clean-shaven
chins. Walnuts, blacking, apples, onions, braces, combs,
turnips, herrings, pens, and corn-plaster, are all bellowed
out at the same time. Labourers and mechanics, still unshorn
and undressed, hang about with their hands in their pockets,
some with their pet terriers under their arms. The pavement
is green with the refuse leaves of vegetables, and round a
cabbage-barrow the women stand turning over the bunches,
as the man shouts, 'Where you like, only a penny.' Boys are
running home with the breakfast herring held in a piece of
paper, and the side-pocket of the appleman's stuff coat hangs
down with the weight of the halfpence stored within it. Pre-
sently the tolling of the neighbouring church bells breaks
forth. Then the bustle doubles itself, the cries grow louder,
the confusion greater. Women run about and push their way
through the throng, scolding the saunterers, for in half an
hour the market will close. In a little time the butcher puts up
his shutters, and leaves the door still open; the policemen in
their clean gloves come round and drive the street-sellers before
them, and as the clock strikes eleven the market finishes, and
the Sunday's rest begins.

HABITS AND AMUSEMENTS OF COSTERMONGERS

I find it impossible to separate these two headings; for the
habits of the costermonger are not domestic. His busy life is
passed in the markets or the streets, and as his leisure is
devoted to the beer-shop, the dancing-room, or the theatre,
we must look for his habits to his demeanour at those places.
Home has few attractions to a man whose life is a street-life.
Even those who are influenced by family ties and affections,
prefer to 'home' - indeed that word is rarely mentioned among
them - the conversation, warmth, and merriment of the beer-
shop, where they can take their ease among their 'mates'.
Excitement or amusement are indispensable to uneducated men.
Of beer-shops resorted to by costermongers, and principally
supported by them, it is computed that there are 400 in London.
  Those who meet first in the beer-shop talk over the state of
trade and of the markets, while the later comers enter at once
into what may be styled the serious business of the evening -
amusement.
  Business topics are discussed in a most peculiar style. One
man takes the pipe from his mouth and says, 'Bill made a
doogheno hit this morning.' 'Jem,' says another, to a man just
entering, 'you'll stand a top o' reeb?' 'On,' answers Jem, 'I've
had a trosseno tol, and have been doing dab.' For an explanation of what may be obscure in this dialogue, I must refer my
readers to my remarks concerning the language of the class. If
any strangers are present, the conversation is still further
clothed in slang, so as to be unintelligible even to the partially

initiated. The evident puzzlement of any listener is of course gratifying to the costermonger's vanity, for he feels that he possesses a knowledge peculiarly his own.

Among the in-door amusements of the costermonger is card-playing, at which many of them are adepts. The usual games are all-fours, all-fives, cribbage, and put. Whist is known to a few, but is never played, being considered dull and slow. Of short whist they have not heard; 'but,' said one, whom I questioned on the subject, 'if it's come into fashion, it'll soon be among us.' The play is usually for beer, but the game is rendered exciting by bets both among the players and the lookers-on. 'I'll back Jem for a yanepatine,' says one. 'Jack for a gen,' cries another. A penny is the lowest sum laid, and five shillings generally the highest, but a shilling is not often exceeded. 'We play fair among ourselves,' said a costermonger to me - 'aye, fairer than the aristocrats - but we'll take in anybody else.' Where it is known that the landlord will not supply cards, 'a sporting coster' carries a pack or two with him. The cards played with have rarely been stamped; they are generally dirty, and sometimes almost illegible, from long handling and spilled beer. Some men will sit patiently for hours at these games, and they watch the dealing round of the dingy cards intently, and without the attempt - common among politer gamesters - to appear indifferent, though they bear their losses well. In a full-room of card-players, the groups are all shrouded in tobacco-smoke, and from them are heard constant sounds - according to the games they are engaged in - of 'I'm low, and Ped's high.' 'Tip and me's game.' 'Fifteen four and a flush of five.' I may remark it is curious that costermongers, who can neither read nor write, and who have no knowledge of the multiplication tables, are skilful in all the intricacies and calculations of cribbage. There is not much quarrelling over the cards, unless strangers play with them, and then the coster-mongers all take part one with another, fairly or unfairly.

It has been said that there is a close resemblance between many of the characteristics of a very high class, socially, and a very low class. Those who remember the disclosures on a trial a few years back, as to how men of rank and wealth passed their leisure in card-playing - many of their lives being one continued leisure - can judge how far the analogy holds when the card-passion of the costermongers is described.

'Shove-halfpenny' is another game played by them; so is 'Three up'. Three halfpennies are thrown up, and when they fall all 'heads' or all 'tails', it is a mark; and the man who gets the greatest number of marks out of a given amount - three, or five, or more - wins. 'Three-up' is played fairly among the costermongers; but is most frequently resorted to when strangers are present to 'make a pitch' - which is, in plain words, to cheat any stranger who is rash enough to bet upon them. 'This is the way, sir,' said an adept to me; 'bless you, I can make them fall as I please. If I'm playing with Jo, and a stranger bets with Jo, why, of course, I make Jo win.' This adept illustrated his skill to me by throwing up three half-pennies, and, five times out of six, they fell upon the floor, whether he threw them nearly to the ceiling or merely to his shoulder, all heads or all tails. The halfpence were the proper current coins - indeed, they were my own; and the result is gained by a peculiar position of the coins on the fingers, and a peculiar jerk in the throwing. There was an amusing manifestation of the pride of art in the way in which my obliging inform-ant displayed his skill.

'Skittles' is another favourite amusement, and the coster-mongers class themselves among the best players in London. The game is always for beer, but betting goes on.

A fondness for 'sparring' and 'boxing' lingers among the rude members of some classes of the working men, such as the tanners. With the great majority of the costermongers this fondness is still as dominant as it was among the 'higher clas-ses', when boxers were the pets of princes and nobles. The sparring among the costers is not for money, but for beer and 'a lark' - a convenient word covering much mischief. Two out of every ten landlords, whose houses are patronized by these lovers of 'the art of self-defence', supply gloves. Some charge 2d. a night for their use; others only 1d. The sparring seldom continues long, sometimes not above a quarter of an hour; for the costermongers, though excited for a while, weary of sports in which they cannot personally participate, and in the beer-shops only two spar at a time, though fifty or sixty may be present. The shortness of the duration of this pastime may be one reason why it seldom leads to quarrelling. The stake is usually a 'top of reeb', and the winner is the man who gives the first 'noser'; a *bloody* nose however is required to show that the blow was veritably a noser. The costermongers boast of their skill in pugilism as well as at skittles. 'We are all handy with our fists,' said one man, 'and are matches, aye, and more than matches, for anybody but reg'lar boxers. We've stuck to the ring, too, and gone reg'lar to the fights, more than any other men.'

'Twopenny-hops' are much resorted to by the costermongers, men and women, boys and girls. At these dances decorum is sometimes, but not often, violated. 'The women,' I was told by one man, 'doesn't show their necks as I've seen the ladies do in them there pictures of high life in the shop-winders, or on the stage. Their Sunday gowns, which is their dancing gowns, ain't made that way.' At these 'hops' the clog-hornpipe is often danced, and sometimes a collection is made to ensure the performance of a first-rate professor of that dance; sometimes, and more frequently, it is volunteered gratuitously. The other dances are jigs, 'flash jigs' - hornpipes in fetters - a dance rendered popular by the success of the acted 'Jack Sheppard' - polkas, and country-dances, the last-mentioned being generally demanded by the women. Waltzes are as yet unknown to them.

Sometimes they do the 'pipe-dance'. For this a number of
tobacco-pipes, about a dozen, are laid close together on the
floor, and the dancer places the toe of his boot between the
different pipes, keeping time with the music. Two of the pipes
are arranged as a cross, and the toe has to be inserted between
each of the angles, without breaking them. The numbers present at these 'hops' vary from 30 to 100 of both sexes, their
ages being from 14 to 45, and the female sex being slightly
predominant as to the proportion of those in attendance. At
these 'hops' there is nothing of the leisurely style of dancing -
half a glide and half a skip - but vigorous, laborious capering.
The hours are from half-past eight to twelve, sometimes to one
or two in the morning, and never later than two, as the costermongers are early risers. There is sometimes a good deal of
drinking; some of the young girls being often pressed to drink,
and frequently yielding to the temptation. From £1 to £7 is
spent in drink at a hop; the youngest men or lads present
spend the most, especially in that act of costermonger polite-
ness - 'treating the gals'. The music is always a fiddle, sometimes with the addition of a harp and a cornopean. The band
is provided by the costermongers, to whom the assembly is
confined; but during the present and the last year, when the
costers' earnings have been less than the average, the landlord
has provided the harp, whenever that instrument has added
to the charms of the fiddle. Of one use to which these 'hops'
are put I have given an account, under the head of 'Marriage'.

The other amusements of this class of the community are the
theatre and the penny concert, and their visits are almost
entirely confined to the galleries of the theatres on the Surrey-
side - the Surrey, the Victoria, the Bower Saloon, and (but
less frequently) Astley's. Three times a week is an average
attendance at theatres and dances by the more prosperous
costermongers. The most intelligent man I met with among them
gave me the following account. He classes himself with the
many, but his tastes are really those of an educated man:-

Love and murder suits us best, sir; but within these few
years I think there's a great deal more liking for deep tra-
gedies among us. They set men a thinking; but then we all
consider them too long. Of *Hamlet* we can make neither end
nor side; and nine out of ten of us - ay, far more than that
- would like it to be confined to the ghost scenes, and the
funeral, and the killing off at the last. *Macbeth* would be
better liked, if it was only the witches and the fighting. The
high words in a tragedy we call jaw-breakers, and say we
can't tumble to that barrikin. We always stay to the last,
because we've paid for it all, or very few costers would see
a tragedy out if any money was returned to those leaving
after two or three acts. We are fond of music. Nigger music
was very much liked among us, but it's stale now. Flash
songs are liked, and sailor's songs, and patriotic songs. Most
costers - indeed, I can't call to mind an exception - listen

very quietly to songs that they don't in the least understand. We have among us translations of the patriotic French
songs. 'Mourir pour la patrie' is very popular, and so is
the 'Marseillaise'. A song to take hold of us must have a
good chorus.
'They like something, sir, that is worth hearing,' said one of
my informants, 'such as the "Soldier's Dream", "The Dream
of Napoleon", or "I'ad a dream - an 'appy dream".'
The songs in ridicule of Marshal Haynau, and in laudation of
Barclay and Perkin's draymen, were and are very popular
among the costers; but none are more popular than Paul Jones -
'A noble commander, Paul Jones was his name.' Among them
the chorus of 'Britons never shall be slaves', is often rendered
'Britons always shall be slaves'. The most popular of all songs
with the class, however, is 'Duck-legged Dick', of which I give
the first verse.

> Duck-legged Dick had a donkey,
>   And his lush loved much for to swill,
> One day he got rather lumpy,
>   And got sent seven days to the mill,
> His donkey was taken to the green-yard,
>   A fate which he never deserved.
> Oh! it was such a regular mean yard,
>   That alas! the poor moke got starved.
> Oh! bad luck can't be prevented,
>   Fortune she smiles or she frowns,
> He's best off that's contented,
>   To mix, sirs, the ups and the downs.

Their sports are enjoyed the more, if they are dangerous
and require both courage and dexterity to succeed in them.
They prefer, if crossing a bridge, to climb over the parapet,
and walk along on the stone coping. When a house is building,
rows of coster lads will climb up the long ladders, leaning
against the unslated roof, and then slide down again, each one
resting on the other's shoulders. A peep show with a battle
is sure of its coster audience, and a favourite pastime is fighting with cheap theatrical swords. They are, however, true to
each other, and should a coster, who is the hero of his court,
fall ill and go to a hospital, the whole of the inhabitants of
his quarter will visit him on the Sunday, and take him presents
of various articles so that 'he may live well'.
Among the men, rat-killing is a favourite sport. They will
enter an old stable, fasten the door and then turn out the rats.
Or they will find out some unfrequented yard, and at night
time build up a pit with apple-case boards, and lighting up
their lamps, enjoy the sport. Nearly every coster is fond of
dogs. Some fancy them greatly, and are proud of making
them fight. If when out working, they see a handsome stray,
whether he is a 'toy' or 'sporting' dog, they whip him up -

many of the class not being very particular whether the animals
are stray or not.

Their dog fights are both cruel and frequent. It is not uncommon to see a lad walking with the trembling legs of a dog
shivering under a bloody handkerchief, that covers the bitten
and wounded body of an animal that has been fighting at some
'match.' These fights take place on the sly - the tap-room or
back-yard of a beer-shop, being generally chosen for the
purpose. A few men are let into the secret, and they attend
to bet upon the winner, the police being carefully kept from
the spot.

Pigeons are 'fancied' to a large extent, and are kept in lath
cages on the roofs of the houses. The lads look upon a visit
to the Redhouse, Battersea, where the pigeon-shooting takes
place, as a great treat. They stand without the hoarding that
encloses the ground, and watch for the wounded pigeons to
fall, when a violent scramble takes place among them, each bird
being valued at 3d. or 4d. So popular has this sport become,
that some boys take dogs with them trained to retrieve the
birds, and two Lambeth costers attend regularly after their
morning's work with their guns, to shoot those that escape
the 'shots' within.

A good pugilist is looked up to with great admiration by the
costers, and fighting is considered to be a necessary part of
a boy's education. Among them cowardice in any shape is
despised as being degrading and loathsome, indeed the man
who would avoid a fight, is scouted by the whole of the court
he lives in. Hence it is important for a lad and even a girl to
know how to 'work their fists well' - as expert boxing is called
among them. If a coster man or woman is struck they are
obliged to fight. When a quarrel takes place between two boys,
a ring is formed, and the men urge them on to have it out, for
they hold that it is a wrong thing to stop a battle, as it causes
bad blood for life; whereas, if the lads fight it out they shake
hands and forget all about it. Everybody practises fighting,
and the man who has the largest and hardest muscle is spoken
of in terms of the highest commendation. It is often said in
admiration of such a man that 'he could muzzle half a dozen
bobbies before breakfast.'

To serve out a policeman is the bravest act by which a costermonger can distinguish himself. Some lads have been imprisoned
upwards of a dozen times for this offence; and are consequently
looked upon by their companions as martyrs. When they leave
prison for such an act, a subscription is often got up for their
benefit. In their continual warfare with the force, they resemble many savage nations, from the cunning and treachery
they use. The lads endeavour to take the unsuspecting 'crusher'
by surprise, and often crouch at the entrance of a court until
a policeman passes, when a stone or a brick is hurled at him,
and the youngster immediately disappears. Their love of
revenge too, is extreme - their hatred being in no way

mitigated by time; they will wait for months, following a policeman who has offended or wronged them, anxiously looking out
for an opportunity of paying back the injury. One boy, I was
told, vowed vengeance against a member of the force, and
for six months never allowed the man to escape his notice. At
length, one night, he saw the policeman in a row outside a
public-house, and running into the crowd kicked him savagely,
shouting at the same time: 'Now, you b——, I've got you at
last.' When the boy heard that his persecutor was injured for
life, his joy was very great, and he declared the twelvemonth's
imprisonment he was sentenced to for the offence to be 'dirt
cheap'. The whole of the court where the lad resided sym-
pathized with the boy, and vowed to a man, that had he escaped,
they would have subscribed a pad or two of dry herrings, to
send him into the country until the affair had blown over, for
he had shown himself a 'plucky one'.

It is called 'plucky' to bear pain without complaining. To
flinch from expected suffering is scorned, and he who does so
is sneered at and told to wear a gown, as being more fit to be
a woman. To show a disregard for pain, a lad, when without
money, will say to his pal, 'Give us a penny, and you may have
a punch at my nose.'

They also delight in tattooing their chests and arms with
anchors, and figures of different kinds. During the whole of
this painful operation, the boy will not flinch, but laugh and
joke with his admiring companions, as if perfectly at ease.

10 The threat of outcast London

Gareth Stedman Jones

In the period after 1850, fears about the consequences of urban
existence and industrial society centred increasingly on London.
For London, more than any other city, came to symbolize
the problem of the 'residuum'. As the 'Quarterly Review'
remarked in 1855:[1]

> the most remarkable feature of London life is a class decidedly
> lower in the social scale than the labourer, and numerically
> very large, though the population returns do not number
> them among the inhabitants of the kingdom, who derive their
> living from the streets...for the most part their utmost efforts
> do little more than maintain them in a state of chronic starva-
> tion...very many have besides their acknowledged calling,
> another in the background in direct violation of the eighth
> commandment; and thus by gradations imperceptibly darken-
> ing as we advance, we arrive at the classes who are at open
> war with society, and professedly live by the produce of
> depredation or the wages of infamy.

London was regarded as the Mecca of the dissolute, the lazy,
the mendicant, 'the rough'[2] and the spendthrift. The presence
of great wealth and countless charities, the unparalleled
opportunities for casual employment, the possibility of scrap-
ing together a living by innumerable devious methods, all were
thought to conspire together to make London one huge magnet
for the idle, the dishonest, and the criminal. All the features
of self-help that had begun to manifest themselves so strikingly
in the north were conspicuously absent from the poorer quarters
of London. As Beatrice Potter on a visit to Lancashire later
noted in a letter to her father:[3]

> One sees here the other side of the process through which
> bad workmen and bad characters are attracted to the large
> town. In East End life one notices this attraction, here one

Source: 'Outcast London: a Study in the Relationship between
Classes in Victorian Society', Oxford, Clarendon Press, 1971,
extracts from pp.12-16, 281, 284-97.

can watch the outcasting force. In the first place there are
no odd jobs in a small community which depends on productive industries. Unless a man can work regularly he cannot
work at all. Then a bad character is socially an outcast, the
whole social life depending on the chapel and the co-op.

The location of the 'residuum' in London was particularly
unsettling if only because of the immense size of the city and
its national importance. Twentieth-century urban sociologists
have enumerated some of the most distinctive features of city
life:[4] the substitution for primary contacts of secondary ones,
the weakening of bonds of kinship, the decline of the social
significance of the family, the undermining of the traditional
basis of social solidarity and the erosion of traditional methods
of social control. Districts of the city acquire specialized functions. Class divisions become geographical divisions. Social
contrasts become more dramatic and abrupt. The neighbourhood loses its significance; people can live in close physical
proximity but at great social distance; the place of the church
is taken by the press; custom gives way to fashion. Above all
the city is more volatile, its social stability can never be
assumed. In a striking juxtaposition, Robert Park linked the
stock exchange and the mob as two homologous urban symbols.[5]
'It is true of exchanges, as it is of crowds, that the situation
they represent is always critical, that is to say, the tensions
are such that a slight cause may precipitate an enormous effect.'

In a more protean form, all these characteristics had been
perceived by nineteenth-century observers as reasons for
concern about the future development of the metropolis.[6]
Victorian London was by far the largest city in the world, over
twice as large as Paris, its nearest rival in 1851. In face of a
city of over two million people, a city which was to exceed five
million by the end of the century, articulate contemporaries
wavered between feelings of complacent pride in the sheer size
and wealth of an immense human artifact, and feelings of dread
at the terrible threat that such an aggregation represented.
But the problem was not simply one of size. In the course of
the nineteenth century, the social distance between rich and
poor expressed itself in an ever sharper geographical segregation of the city. Merchants and employers no longer lived above
their places of work. The old methods of social control based
on the model of the squire, the parson, face to face relations,
deference, and paternalism, found less and less reflection in
the urban reality. Vast tracts of working-class housing were
left to themselves, virtually bereft of any contact with authority
except in the form of the policeman or the bailiff. The poor
districts became an immense *terra incognita* periodically mapped
out by intrepid missionaries and explorers who catered to an
insatiable middle-class demand for travellers' tales.[7] These
writers sometimes expressed apprehension about the large
and anonymous proletarian areas of South London, but the most
extensive and the most feared area was the East End, a huge

city itself in all but name. In a typical description, Walter Besant observed:[8]

> The population is greater than that of Berlin or Vienna, or St. Petersburg, or Philadelphia...in the streets there are never seen any private carriages; there is no fashionable quarter...one meets no ladies in the principal thoroughfares. People, shops, houses, conveyances - all together are stamped with the unmistakable seal of the working class... perhaps the strangest thing of all is this: in a city of two million people there are no hotels! That means, of course, that there are no visitors.

The presence of an unknown number of the casual poor, indistinguishable to many contemporaries from criminals, apparently divorced from all forms of established religion, or ties with their social superiors, inhabiting unknown cities within the capital, constituted a disquieting alien presence in the midst of mid-Victorian plenty: especially in the light of the growing importance of London in relation to the rest of the country after 1850. For London was no longer simply the home of the Court, the Parliament, and the national government; it had also become the capital of a vast new empire. Contemporaries grew increasingly fond of comparing the grandeur of London with that of ancient Rome. But that comparison was itself disquieting. For just as Rome had often been at the mercy of its mob, so London, impregnable from without, might become vulnerable to an even more potent and volatile threat from within.

It was in the 1860s that this contradictory configuration of complacency and fear about the metropolitan condition was first fully articulated, and in other ways also the 1860s represented a watershed in the social history of London. The last cholera epidemic took place in 1866 and was followed soon after by the beginnings of a continuous decline in the death rate. The mid-1860s also witnessed the first serious legislative attempts at sanitary and housing regulation, while the institution of a metropolitan common poor fund in 1865 inaugurated a new chapter in the history of urban poor relief which culminated in the 1870s in the abrasive attempt to abolish all forms of outdoor relief. Closely connected with this development came the first vigorous attempts to systematize charitable relief in an effort to moralize the casual poor - a vast expansion in the range and objects of benevolence which derived in part from the same impulses which were to produce the new liberalism of the 1870s.[9] Finally, the collapse of the Thames ship-building industry in 1867 firmly established in the public mind the image of the East End as a nursery of destitute poverty and thriftless, demoralized pauperism, as a community cast adrift from the salutary presence and leadership of men of wealth and culture, and as a potential threat to the riches and civilization of London and the Empire.

In the late 1860s and early 1870s, the liberal utopia had

never seemed nearer. The bulk of the middle and upper classes had never felt more secure or confident in the future. But there remained the slight but disturbing possibility that the forces of progress might be swamped by the corrupting features of urban life, that, unless checked or reformed, the 'residuum' might overrun the newly built citadel of moral virtue and economic rationality. [...]

The social crisis which beset middle-class London in the 1880s was far more serious than the disorders which had punctuated the 1860s. In the 1860s, the distress which followed the slump of 1866 had to a great extent been localized in one corner of London. With the exception of ship-building and to a lesser extent the construction industry, skilled trades had been only mildly affected. At the political level, although alarm had been expressed during the passage of the Second Reform Bill, the crisis quickly passed. The working class were not united behind an ideology which offered any serious challenge to the dominant orthodoxies, and once reform had been won, the movement petered out. Pessimistic and sometimes hysterical diagnoses of the condition of the London poor were still pro-duced. But, as has been shown, these were mainly the products of a comparatively narrow section of the professional classes; except for a short period of time, they did not accurately reflect any general feeling of anxiety on the part of middle and upper-class London as a whole.

In the 1880s on the other hand, the crisis was both more deep-rooted and more comprehensive. Basically the crisis was composed of four elements: a severe cyclical depression as the culmination of six or seven years of indifferent trade; the structural decline of certain of the older central industries; the chronic shortage of working-class housing in the inner industrial perimeter; and the emergence of socialism and various forms of 'collectivism' as a challenge to traditional liberal ideology. [...]

Almost equally ominous from the viewpoint of the middle class, was the evidence of growing disaffection among the higher sections of the London working class. The enthusiastic recep-tion given by artisans to the works of Henry George[10] and the activities of the newly founded Social Democratic Federation were seen as disturbing symptoms of a change in popular tem-per. In the 1870s the London artisan had been thought to be getting better off and better housed. Despite its radicalism, there seemed little danger that this stratum would identify with the submerged groups beneath it. In the early 1880s, however, it was revealed that insanitary housing, overcrowding, and high rents afflicted not only the casual poor but also the artisan. The appeal of Henry George, as Arnold Toynbee noted,[11] was not fortuitous, for George's theory of rent provided an arresting and convincing explanation of housing conditions in London. Even more serious was the suggestion that the growing housing

shortage was pushing the respectable working class into the
same living quarters as the disreputable poor. Thus, while the
geographical separation of rich and poor was becoming ever
more complete, the poor themselves were becoming more closely
crammed together regardless of status or character. In this
situation, the onset of cyclical depression was particularly disturbing. For, as the depression deepened, signs of distress
began to appear in the ranks of the respectable working class.
'Agitators'[12] were already beginning to blur the distinction
between the respectable working class and the 'residuum' by
appealing to both under the slogan of 'relief to the unemployed'.
The dangerous possibility existed that the respectable working
class, under the stress of prolonged unemployment, might
throw in its lot with the casual poor.

The 1880s have usually been described in terms of a rediscovery of poverty and a decline of individualism.[13] But the
context of this rediscovery and the manner in which individualism was challenged have sometimes been misunderstood. Historians have tended to follow Beatrice Webb and talked of 'a
new consciousness of sin among men of intellect and property'.[14]
While this 'new consciousness' no doubt existed, and to some
extent accounted for the rapid expansion of the settlement
movement and the epidemic of 'slumming' in the mid-1880s, the
more predominant feeling was not guilt but fear. There was
little empathy or even sentimentality in the descriptions of the
poor that came out of the growing literature on 'Outcast London'. The poor were presented as neglected, and even to a
certain extent exploited (by irresponsible landlords, sweating
employers, and publicans). But they did not emerge as objects
of compassion. They were generally pictured as coarse, brutish,
drunken, and immoral; through years of neglect and complacency they had become an ominous threat to civilization.
Secondly, the idea of a decline of individualism in the 1880s
can be maintained only if the nature of the challenge to it is
defined more precisely. For, to use another phrase of Beatrice
Webb, however much[15] 'individualism run wild' came to be blamed
for the condition of the London poor in the course of the 1880s,
the traditional distinction between deserving and undeserving
poor remained a central tenet of middle-class social philosophy
both in its individualistic and in its collectivistic forms. What
distinguished the 1880s was not the break-down of this distinction, but rather a dramatic re-interpretation of it.

The theory of 'demoralization' which had prevailed among
charity workers and social thinkers in the 1860s and 1870s
was a moral non-sociological type of explanation relying in the
last resort upon hedonistic premises. It is significant that it
purported to explain not poverty but pauperism. The implication was that pauperism, poverty's visible form, was largely
an act of will. It had been freely chosen and was therefore
sinful. This pauper way of life had been chosen because the
negligence and thoughtlessness of the rich had made the state

of mendicancy more agreeable than the state of labour. By
ensuring, through the tightening up of charity and poor law,
that mendicancy was made less eligible than labour, pauperism,
and economic immorality among the London working class, it
was assumed, would be gradually eliminated. In the 1880s
however, the effect of the literature of the housing crisis was
to divert attention from 'pauperism' to chronic poverty. The
theory of poverty that emerged from this literature differed
significantly from the literature of the 1860s and 1870s. As in
previous accounts, the poverty of the poor was associated
with drink, early marriage, improvidence, irreligion, and
idleness. But these were now seen as symptoms rather than
causes. At the root of the condition of the poor lay the pressures of city existence. Crammed together in filthy, airless,
and noisy one-room tenements, it was inevitable that the poor
would be brutalized and sexually immoral and that they should
seek to escape the dreadful monotony of their conditions of
existence by craving the 'cheap excitements' offered by the
pubs, the low music-halls, and streets. It was further inevitable that generations which had been born and nurtured in
such conditions should inevitably 'degenerate' both physically
and morally. Poverty was no longer pauperism in disguise;
the savage and brutalized condition of the casual poor was the
result of long exposure to the degenerating conditions of city
life.

The theory of urban degeneration has already been discussed.
In the 1880s this theory, in its various forms, came to colour
all social debate on the condition of the casual poor. Connected
with the theory were two other fears which further accentuated
anxiety. The first of these was that the effect of the agricultural depression had been to produce a massive influx from
the countryside into the towns. If the theory of urban degeneration was correct, then the long-run consequences of the migration into the towns would be a progressive deterioration of
the race. A second assumption made this prophecy appear both
more weighty and more urgent. Formerly, it was claimed, a
balance of vigour had been preserved, because Darwinian laws
of nature had weeded out the unfit products of urban life. But
these laws had been increasingly violated. Medical science,
sanitary improvement, and humanitarian legislation were now
enabling an ever greater proportion of the 'unfit' to reach
maturity and multiply their kind. As one popular pamphleteer
put it:[16]

> Freely undertaking the responsibilities of marriage, the
> population is more freely replenished from the unfit than
> from the healthy and energetic elements of the electorate.
> It is monstrous that the weak should be destroyed by the
> strong. How much more repugnant is it to reason and to
> instinct that the strong should be overwhelmed by the
> feeble, ailing and unfit!

It was generally believed that the casual poor were largely

composed of this growing degenerate stratum of city life. If
this were so, then the ultimate causes of their poverty and
distress were neither economic nor moral but biological and
ecological. The chronic poverty of the casual residuum was due
not to the conditions of casual employment but to their 'feeble
and tainted constitutions', the product of generations of decaying slum life. The prevalence of casual employment was determined primarily not by a demand for irregular work but by
the ready availability of a supply of degenerate labour which
was lazy, shiftless, and incapable of regular work.

In this context, the onset of cyclical depression in 1884 was
disquieting. For signs of distress were beginning to appear
among the respectable working class, and 'agitators' were
beginning to confuse the 'exceptionally' unemployed respectable working class with the under-employed casual residuum
under the general title of 'the unemployed'. For informed
observers, however,[17] there could be no confusion between
cyclical depression and the fruits of urban degeneration.
Cyclical depressions, at close hand, might appear cruel and
harmful. But in the long term they were not malignant. They
might then, as Booth put it,[18] 'be considered as the orderly
beating of a heart causing the blood to circulate - each throb a
cycle'. Even wage earners in the long term benefited from
'the invigorating influence of periodic distress'. 'As to character', wrote Booth,[19] 'the effect, especially on wage earners,
is very similar to that exercised on a population by the recur-
rence of winter as compared to the enervation of continual
summer'. On the other hand the distress and unemployment
which was associated with casual labour and urban degeneration
was not only malignant but also threatening. Describing this
group of the population, Booth wrote,[20] 'I do not doubt that
many good enough men are walking about idle; but it must be
said that those of their number who drop low enough to ask
charitable aid, rarely stand the test of work... the unemployed
are, as a class, a selection of the unfit, and on the whole those
most in want are the most unfit.'

Booth's distinction between the 'true working classes' and
the casual residuum was central to the crisis of the 1880s, and
in varying forms it was present in the social attitudes of every
grouping from the COS to the SDF. Arnold White in an article
on[21] 'the nomad poor' in 1885 divided the unemployed into three
categories. Twenty per cent were 'genuinely unemployed';
another forty per cent were 'feckless and incapable'. The
remaining forty per cent however were wholly degenerate:[22]
'physically, mentally and morally unfit, there is nothing that
the nation can do for these men except to let them die out by
leaving them alone'. From a different perspective H.M. Hyndman
made the same distinction. 'Everywhere no doubt', he wrote,[23]
'there is a certain percentage who are almost beyond hope of
being reached at all. Crushed down into the gutter, physically
and mentally by their social surroundings, they can but die out,

leaving, it is hoped, no progeny as a burden on a better state
of things'. According to 'The Times', the residuum was the
'great storehouse of the unemployed';[24] thus, while relief funds
might be suitable for alleviating genuine distress, it was essential that no encouragement should be given to casual residual
class,[25] 'For adult members of the class the old remedy would
have been a sound whipping at the cat's tail; and it might have
been worthwhile to try one or two experiments of the kind on
bodies proverbially suited to them.' The same point was made
by one writer in the 'Charity Organisation Review', with the
suggestion of a yet more final solution to the problem of chronic
poverty:[26]

> It must be admitted that the residuum is hopeless: the loafer
> and the casual can be benefitted by no philanthropy...if a
> man who winter after winter betakes himself to the house
> were on the third occasion to be kept there permanently, he
> might well be forced to repay a considerable part of the cost
> of his maintenance and at least he would be compelled to
> cease from further propagation of his own species.

The residuum was considered dangerous not only because of
its degenerate nature but also because its very existence served
to contaminate the classes immediately above it. For a while a
portion of this class belonged there by inheritance, its numbers
were continually being supplemented by new recruitments from
the[27] 'incapable and immoral who have fallen out of the classes
above them'. A Mansion House Committee, formed to investigate
the causes of distress in 1885, concluded that the existence
of the residuum was one of the major causes of the crisis:[28]
'This class', it stated, 'is a dead weight on the labour market,
and interferes with the opportunities of the better classes of
more willing and worthy labourers, upon whom moreover, its
contagious influence has a wide and degrading effect.' If this
situation were allowed to continue,[29] if the cyclical depression
grew worse and provincial immigration continued to push
Londoners downwards to the bottom of the labour market, then
the size of the residuum would grow still further and the
respectable working class would be eaten away from below.

It has been argued that the predominant reaction to the rediscovery of poverty in the early 1880s was not so much guilt
as fear. The discovery of a huge and swelling residuum and
the growing uncertainty about the mood of the respectable
working class portended the threat of revolution. Discussions
of the condition of the London poor which in the 1870s had
been confined to experts within the pages of specialized journals,
now became the subject of urgent general debate. From 1883
onwards[30] the quarterly journals and the press were full of
warnings of the necessity of immediate reform to ward off the
impending revolutionary threat. Samuel Smith, the 'philanthropist', struck a note typical of this genre when he stated in
1885,[31] 'I am deeply convinced that the time is approaching

when this seething mass of human misery will shake the social
fabric, unless we grapple more earnestly with it than we have
yet done...The proletariat may strangle us unless we teach it
the same virtues which have elevated the other classes of
society.'

But the real extent and depths of these fears were most
strikingly illuminated by the events of 1886 and 1887. The
winter of 1885-6 was exceptionally severe. Not only was the
depression at its height, but the February temperatures were
the coldest for thirty years. Out-door work was practically
brought to a standstill, and distress was particularly intense
in the docks and the building industry. This was the background to the famous riot of 8 February.[32] On the afternoon
of the 8th a meeting of the unemployed was called by the Fair
Trade League in Trafalgar Square to demand public works and
protective tariffs as a solution to unemployment. The audience
of around 20,000[33] was composed predominantly of unemployed
dock and building workers. This meeting was interrupted by
the SDF who denounced the Tory exploitation of unemployment
and put forward a programme of socialism and revolution. After
some scuffling between the two groups, the SDF leaders led
part of the crowd out of the Square with the intention of dispersing in Hyde Park.

In Pall Mall however, after some provocation from club-men,
stones were thrown at the Carlton Club. After this, the march
turned into a riot. All forms of property were assailed, all
signs of wealth and privilege were attacked. In St James's
Street all the club windows down one side of the street were
broken, and in Piccadilly looting began. By this stage the SDF
had lost control of the crowd, and after a hasty meeting at
the Achilles Statue by Hyde Park Corner, the leaders retired.
The crowd did not disperse however. In Hyde Park they over-
turned carriages and divested their wealthy occupants of their
money and jewellery. They then moved on to South Audley
Street looting every shop along their route, and from there
returned via Oxford Street to the East End. The progress of
the crowd had been virtually unhampered since a misheard
order had despatched the police to guard Buckingham Palace
and the Mall. 'In a word', as 'The Times' put it,[34] 'the West End
was for a couple of hours in the hands of the mob' and it considered the event more alarming than 1848. Not since 1832[35]
had private property in London been so disturbed.

The real significance of the riot lay not so much in what
happened as in the strength of the middle-class reaction to it
and the extent of the fear of the casual residuum that it
revealed. This will become clear once the events of the immediate
aftermath of the riot have been described. For while historians
have written detailed accounts of the riot of 8 February, they
have virtually ignored the events of the two succeeding days.

On the morning of 9 February, a dense fog descended upon
London. 'Roughs' again gathered in Trafalgar Square, and

the West End remained in a state of near-panic.[36] Shops were closed and boarded up, and the police went round warning tradesmen to expect new attacks. Although the square was cleared in the afternoon, the rumour spread that[37] 'some 100s of the dock labourers proposed to join others from the East End in further attacks upon the property in the West', and that the military had been called out to counter them.[38] 'Such a state of excitement and alarm has rarely been experienced in the Metropolis', wrote 'The Times'.

But the panic of 9 February was insignificant beside that of the following day. On 10 February, London was visited by something akin to the *grande peur*. In the morning the confidence of the West End had been slightly restored and some shops had begun to re-open. But from mid-day the fog thickened,[39] 'the disorderly classes' again began to assemble in Trafalgar Square and the panic grew. The rumour spread that '10,000 men were on the march from Deptford to London, destroying as they came, the property of small traders'. The story originated from a jeweller who informed the Southwark police that he had seen 'roughs' gathering in Deptford. The police alerted Southwark shop-keepers, and from there the panic spread throughout South London. All over South London, 'the shops closed and people stood at their doors straining their eyes through the fog for the sounds of the 10,000 men who were stated to be marching either to Clapham Common or to the City.' By mid-afternoon, 'the terror was so general in South London that the board schools were literally besieged by anxious parents eager to take their children home under their protection.' But similar situations existed elsewhere. In Whitechapel a mob was said to be marching down from the Commercial Road; at Bethnal Green the mob was said to be in Green Street; in Camden Town there was a rumour that the mob would go from Kentish Town to the West. In the City and the West End, all approaches were guarded. Banks and private firms closed down. Shops were shuttered and fortified, and the bridges were protected. The gates of Downing Street were shut and special precautions were taken at government offices to ward off sudden attack. Troops were confined to barracks in the company of magistrates who were to read the riot act when the mob approached.

But just as those with property prepared to defend it, so those without prepared to join the revolutionary horde. At about 1 p.m. a crowd began to assemble at the Elephant and Castle in the expectation of joining the mob from Deptford - 'the great majority of those present were loafers and loungers of a pronounced type'. By 4.30 p.m. the crowd had grown to around 5,000, and was beginning to make assaults on local shops. The tension increased as it was rumoured that a rising had already taken place in Bermondsey and that the mob had split into two - one part proceeding via the Old Kent Road, and the other via Southwark Park Road. At 5.25 p.m. 'The Times' received a

telegram from inhabitants of the Old Kent Road stating: 'Fear-
ful state all around here in South London. 30,000 men at Spa
Road moving to Trafalgar Square. Roughs in 1000s trooping
to West. Send special messenger to Home Office to have police
in fullest force with fullest military force also to save London.'
But while the residents of the Old Kent Road awaited the
arrival of the rioters from Deptford, the Deptford people were
apprehensive of a visit from the rioters said to be at the
Elephant and Castle and the Old Kent Road. Shops were closed
down and barricaded in Deptford Broadway and New Cross
Road in anticipation of the approaching mob, and the police
who had heard some reports that the mob was meant to be
coming from Blackheath, hastened to investigate the situation
there. Again, as at the Elephant and Castle, a crowd of around
2,000 'rough' assembled in Deptford High Street to await the
arrival of the mob.

By the middle of the evening the police had dispersed the
crowds in Deptford and the Elephant, and some measure of
confidence had been restored in South London. But elsewhere
in London, rumours continued to fly. A socialist meeting was
alleged to have been arranged for the evening in Cumberland
Market, and by 8 p.m., 2,000 persons had gathered in the
dense fog to await the non-existent speaker. 'Many rough-
looking characters were revealed by the light of the lamps.'
Four hundred police stood by, 'and it was understood that the
soldiers at adjacent barracks were in readiness in case their
aid should be required.' At about 8.30 p.m. the police began
to break up the crowd, and there was some sporadic street
fighting before it finally dispersed. There were similar rumours
of meetings at Hampstead and elsewhere. It was not until the
following morning that the panic fully subsided.

The events of 10 February not only bore witness to the reality
of the fear of an uprising of the casual poor, but also showed
that this was not entirely without justification. While the mob
from Deptford was a product of frenzied imagination, the crowds
of unemployed who gathered to join it, were not. For William
Morris, the February scare was[40] 'the first skirmish of the
Revolution', and Aveling contended[41] that a revolutionary situation would have existed, had the socialists been able to prepare
for it.

Throughout the rest of 1886 and 1887 fear of a 'sansculottic'
insurrection remained strong. The police were sharply attacked
in the middle-class press[42] for spreading panic and allowing
property to be attacked. Sir Edmund Henderson, the chief
commissioner of the Metropolitan Police, was dismissed to[43]
'quiet the disturbed nerves of the well-to-do'. His successor,
Sir Charles Warren, a hero of the Egyptian campaign, would,
it was hoped,[44] infuse a more military spirit into the handling
of the unemployed. Large demonstrations continued, but they
were subjected to increasing provocation and harassment by

the police,[45] and on occasion intimidated by the ostentatious
presence of armed Life Guards. Inhabitants of the West End
remained scared, and shop-keepers[46] continued to petition the
government to close Trafalgar Square.

Social tension came to a climax once more in the autumn of
1887. The background to it was described by Booth:[47]

> In 1887 trade did not improve, but as the year wore on, less
> food and money were given. It was the year of the Queen's
> jubilee, remarkable for its long spell of splendid summer
> weather. The 'unemployed' were very numerous, and more
> than ever habituated to idleness. The fine weather made
> camping out pleasant rather than otherwise, and Trafalgar
> Square and St. James's Park were occupied nightly...When
> October came, the weather changed suddenly, and the nights
> were frosty. But already camping out had grown into a habit
> and the expense of the night's lodgings had been dropped
> out of the budget. The poor folk still slept out, and were
> content to lie with only a newspaper between them and the
> cold stones. This state of things attracted attention. The
> newspapers published accounts of it and the public imagina-
> tion was aroused. Here at any rate was genuine distress.
> Some charitable agencies distributed tickets for food or lodg-
> ing, others the food itself, taking cart-loads of food into the
> square.

The spectacle of concentrations of the outcast camped on the
border of the West End produced growing middle-class alarm.[48]
'The finest site in Europe'[49] had been turned into a 'foul camp
of vagrants'; and tension mounted considerably when the SDF
began to organize the unemployed in the square under the
slogan, 'not charity, but work'. The police cleared the square
with a considerable show of force on the pretext that it was
crown property. But after threatening demonstrations in Hyde
Park and Whitehall on 20 October, and a march of the unemployed
on Westminster Abbey, the Government rescinded its order.
This however produced panic among West End shop-keepers
who threatened[50] that if the police did not clear the Square, they
would employ armed bands to clear it themselves.

A few days later the police again cleared the square, and
meetings were forbidden. The result was the famous battle of
'bloody Sunday' on 13 November.[51] 'No-one who saw it will ever
forget the strange and indeed terrible sight of that grey winter
day, the vast, sombre-coloured crowd, the brief but fierce
struggle at the corner of the Strand and the river of steel and
scarlet that moved slowly through the dusky swaying masses,
when two squadrons of the life-guards were summoned up from
Whitehall.' For weeks afterwards, the West End remained in a
state of crisis.[52] Mounted police patrolled the Square, the military was kept in a state of readiness and special constables
were enrolled. Propertied London was attempting to re-enact
its successes at Kennington Common.

Notes

1 The Charities of London, 'Quarterly Review', no.cxciv (1855), p.411.

2 See Henry Solly, 'A Few Thoughts on how to deal with the Unemployed Poor of London, and with its "roughs" and criminal classes', Society of Arts, 1868.

3 Beatrice Webb, 'My Apprenticeship', 1926, p.166; see also p.151: her interest in this dramatic contrast led her to write her first book on the history of Co-operatives.

4 See, in particular, Robert E. Park, The City: Suggestions for the Investigation of human behaviour in the Urban Environment, in Park, Burgess and McKenzie, 'The City' (1925). Louis Wirth, Urbanism as a way of Life, in Wirth, 'On Cities and Social Life' (1964).

5 Park, op. cit., p.20.

6 A general typology of nineteenth-century attitudes to the City is to be found in Françoise Choay, 'L'Urbanisme: utopies et réalités', (Paris, 1965).

7 In the 1870s, perhaps the most characteristic author of this genre was James Greenwood; see for instance, 'The Seven Curses of London' by the 'Amateur casual' (1869), 'In Strange Company' (1873), 'The Wilds of London' (1874), 'Low Life Deeps and an Account of the Strange Fish to be Found there' (1876). Impelled by a mountain of debts and his growing poverty, the ageing Mayhew catered for this appetite for the quaint, the picturesque, and the grotesque in 'London Characters' (1870)- a sad decline from his former plan to complete a comprehensive social survey of London, of which 'London Labour and the London Poor' was to form a part.

8 Walter Besant, 'East London', 1901, pp.7-9.

9 This new charitable impulse was channelled through the Charity Organization Society, founded in 1869. It would be incorrect however to situate the COS either in the old or the new liberalism. For the society itself was a heterogeneous collection of individuals whose reasons for participation varied greatly. Thus while Sir Charles Trevelyan clearly belonged to the older generation of political economists, Samuel Barnett was much closer in thought to Green and Marshall. Other early founding figures were formed by a syncretic admixture of intellectual influences. Thus Octavia Hill combined a political economy worthy of Mrs Marcet, with an emphasis on the beautification of the environment of the poor that derived from Ruskin. Edward Denison on the other hand combined an equally strict political economy with a Carlylean distaste for the 'cash nexus' and an emphasis upon the regenerative powers of an urban gentry. It might be suggested that in the late 1860s and early 1870s classical political economy with its hedonistic psychology, and the various emerging views of the new liberals occupied two areas of a wide arena of

social and political positions which allowed for innumerable different but related attitudes.

10 See Paul Thompson, 'Socialists, Liberals and Labour: the struggle for London, 1885-1914' (1967), p.113.

11 Arnold Toynbee, 'Progress and Poverty: a Criticism of Henry George' (1883), p.34.

12 See R.H. Gretton, 'A Modern History of the English People', vol.1, '1880-98' (1912), p.199.

13 See, for instance, Helen Lynd, 'England in the 1880s: Towards a Social Basis for Freedom' (1945), ch.xi and passim; Herman Ausubel, 'In Hard Times: Reformers among the Late Victorians' (1960), passim.

14 Beatrice Webb, 'My Apprenticeship' (1926), pp.179-80.

15 Charles Booth, 'Life and Labour of the People of London', 1st series, vol.4, p.33.

16 Arnold White, 'The Problems of a Great City' (1887), p.30. See also Alfred Marshall's comment, 'There are no feeble people in the prairies. Some feeble people go there, but they either get back quickly to a large town, or else they die. Charity and sanitary regulations are keeping alive, in our large towns, thousands of such persons, who would have died even fifty years ago. Meanwhile economic forces are pressing heavily on them, for they can do nothing but easy monotonous work, most of which can be done as well or better by machinery or children. Public or private charity may palliate their misery, but the only remedy is to prevent such people from coming into existence...persons in any rank of life who are not in good physical and mental health have no moral right to have children.' Industrial Remuneration Conference, 'The Report of the Proceedings and Papers', presided over by Sir Charles Dilke (1885), p.198.

17 See, for instance, Charles Booth, op. cit., 1st series, vol.1, p.155. 'The question of those who actually suffer from poverty should be considered separately from that of the true working classes, whose desire for a larger share of wealth is of a different character. It is the plan of agitators and the way of sensational writers to confound the two in one, to talk of "starving millions" and to tack on the thousands of the working classes to the tens and hundreds of distress. Against this method I protest.'

18 Booth, op. cit., 2nd series, vol.5, p.73.

19 Ibid., p.73.

20 Booth, op. cit., 1st series, vol.1, p.149.

21 Arnold White, The Nomad Poor of London, 'Contemporary Review' (May 1885), vol.xlvii, pp.714-27.

22 White, op. cit., p.715.

23 H.M. Hyndman, English Workers As They Are, 'Contemporary Review' (July 1887), vol.lii, p.129.

24 'The Times', 6 Feb. 1886, p.8.

25 Ibid.

26 Anon, Permanent Distress in London, 'Charity Organisation Review' (Mar. 1886), p.86.
27 'Report on the Mansion House Committee, appointed in March 1885 to enquire into the causes of permanent distress in London and the best means of the remedying the same' (1886), p.11.
28 Ibid., p.11.
29 Ibid., p.10.
30 See, for instance, Ellice Hopkins, Social Wreckage, 'Contemporary Review', xliv (July 1883), p.98; Brooke Lambert, The Outcast Poor, Esau's Cry, 'Contemporary Review', xliv (Dec. 1883), p.916; Joseph Chamberlain's, Labourers' and Artisans' Dwellings, 'Fortnightly Review', no.CCIV. new series (Dec. 1883), pp.3-4; F. Peek, Lazarus at the Gate, 'Contemporary Review', xlv (Jan. 1884), p.83; Frank Harris, The Housing of the Poor in Towns, 'Fortnightly Review', xlxix (Oct. 1883), p.596; 'Daily News', 19 Oct. 1883; Samuel Smith, The Industrial Training of Destitute Children, 'Contemporary Review', vol.xlvii (Jan. 1885), p.110; Lord Brabazon, State-directed Colonisation; its Necessity (reprinted from 'Nineteenth Century', Nov. 1884), in 'Social Arrows' (1886), p.149; Walter Besant, The People's Palace, 'Contemporary Review', vol.li (Mar. 1887), p.229; G. Osborne Morgan, Well Meant Nonsense about Emigration, 'Nineteenth Century', vol.xxi (Apr. 1887), p.610; H.P. Tregarthen, Pauperism, Distress and the Coming Winter, 'National Review', (Nov. 1887), p.393; Samuel Barnett, A Scheme for the Unemployed, 'Nineteenth Century', vol.xxiv (Nov. 1888), p.754; Bennet Burleigh, The Unemployed, 'Contemporary Review', vol.lii (Dec. 1887), p.772; H. Evans, The London County Council and its Police, 'Contemporary Review', lv (Mar. 1889), p.448; Archdeacon Farrer, The Nether World (Gissing), 'Contemporary Review', lvi (Sept. 1889), p.376; see also sources cited in Anthony S. Wohl, The Bitter Cry of Outcast London, 'International Review of Social History', vol.xiii (1968), pt.2, pp.222-5.
31 Samuel Smith, op. cit., pp.108, 110.
32 For accounts of this riot, see H.M. Hyndman, 'The Record of an Adventurous Life' (1911), pp.400-7; Joseph Burgess, 'John Burns: the Rise and Progress of a Right Honourable' (Glasgow, 1911), pp.45-85; 'Tom Mann's Memoirs' (1923), pp.59-60; Engels, 'Correspondence with the Lafargues' (1959), vol.1, pp.333-7; E.P. Thompson, 'William Morris, Romantic to Revolutionary' (1955), pp.480-4; Bentley B. Gilbert, 'The Evolution of National Insurance in Great Britain, the Origins of the Welfare State' (1966), pp.33-8; Origin and Character of the Disturbances in the Metropolis on 8th February, and the Conduct of the Police Authorities, 'P.P.', 1886, XXXIV,LIII.
33 'The Times', 9 Feb. 1886, p.6.

34 'The Times', 9 Feb. 1886, leading article, p.9.
35 'The Times', 10 Feb. 1886, 'Rioting in the West End', p.5.
36 Ibid.
37 Ibid.
38 Ibid.
39 All the quotations that follow come from 'The Times', 11 Feb. 1886, p.6.
40 'Commonweal' (Mar. 1886), vol.2, no.14, p.17.
41 Ibid., p.21. Such preparations had been entirely absent. As Hyndman justly put it, in an interview with the 'Pall Mall Gazette' (9 Feb., p.4), 'No-one knows what we shall do...not even ourselves'. The attitude of the SDF towards the rioters was equivocal. On the one hand, they wished to maintain that unemployment was a product of the beginnings of the breakdown of Capitalism, and that attacks upon property were a natural consequence. But on the other hand, as has already been argued, even the SDF maintained a certain distinction between the working class and the residuum. This came out in Champion's comments about the looting ('Pall Mall Gazette', 9 Feb.), 'If I had a revolver and I saw the mob looting a shop, I would shoot the fellows down right and left with my own hand'.
42 See 'Pall Mall Gazette', 10 Feb., p.11; 11 Feb., p.1; 12 Feb., pp.1-2.
43 Lord George Hamilton, 'Parliamentary Reminiscences and Reflections, 1886-1906', vol.2 (1922), p.14.
44 See Lieutenant-Colonel Spencer Childers, 'The Life of the Right Honourable Hugh C.E. Childers' (1901), vol.2, pp.241-4.
45 See 'Commonweal', (Mar. 1886), p.23; 28 Aug., p.171; 20 Nov., p.265; Burgess op. cit., pp.94-6; 'Pall Mall Gazette', 22 Feb., p.3.
46 'Commonweal', 1 Jan. 1887, p.5.
47 Booth, op. cit., 1st series, vol.1, p.231.
48 See (James Allman), The Truth about the Unemployed, by one of them, 'Commonweal', 26 Nov. 1887, p.381.
49 Bennet Burleigh, op. cit., p.72.
50 'Commonweal', 12 Nov. 1887, p.360.
51 J.W. Mackail, 'The Life of William Morris' (1899), vol.ii, p.191.
52 See E.P. Thompson, op. cit., pp.568-88.

Criminalization and Youth

11   The street children of London

Henry Mayhew

The Causes which fill our streets with children who either
manifest the keen and sometimes roguish propensity of a
precocious trader, the daring and adroitness of the thief, or
the loutish indifference of the mere dull vagabond, content if
he can only eat and sleep, I consider to be these:
1.   The conduct of parents, masters, and mistresses.
2.   The companionship and associations formed in tender
years.
3.   The employment of children by costermongers and others
who live by street traffic, and the training of costermongers'
children to a street life.
4.   Orphanhood, friendlessness, and utter destitution.
5.   Vagrant dispositions and tastes on the part of children,
which cause them to be runaways. [...]
Concerning cause 1. [...] The brute tyranny of parents,
manifested in the wreaking of any annoyances or disappoint-
ments they may have endured, in the passionate beating and
cursing of their children, for trifling or for no causes, is
among the worst symptoms of a depraved nature. This conduct
may be the most common among the poor, for among them are
fewer conventional restraints; but it exists among and debases
other classes. Some parents only exercise this tyranny in their
fits of drunkenness, and make that their plea in mitigation;
but their dispositions are then only the more undisguisedly
developed, and they would be equally unjust or tyrannical when
sober, but for some selfish fear which checks them. A boy
perhaps endures this course of tyranny some time, and then
finding it increase he feels its further endurance intolerable,
and runs away. If he have no friends with whom he can hope
to find a shelter, the streets only are open to him. He soon
meets with comrades, some of whom perhaps had been circum-
stanced like himself, and, if not strongly disposed to idleness

Source: 'London Labour and the London Poor', London, Griffin,
Bohn, 1861, vol.1, extracts from pp.468-79.

and vicious indulgencies, goes through a course of horse-
holding, errand-running, parcel-carrying, and such like, and
so becomes, if honestly or prudently inclined, a street-seller,
beginning with fuzees, or nuts, or some unexpensive stock.
The where to buy and the how to sell he will find plenty to
teach him at the lodging-houses, where he must sleep when he
can pay for a bed.

When I was collecting information concerning brace-selling
I met with a youth of sixteen who about two years previously
had run away from Birmingham, and made his way to London,
with 2s. 6d. Although he earned something weekly, he was so
pinched and beaten by a step-mother (his father was seldom
at home except on Sunday) that his life was miserable. This
went on for nearly a year, until the boy began to resist, and
one Saturday evening, when beaten as usual, he struck in
return, drawing blood from his step-mother's face. The father
came home before the fray was well ended; listened to his
wife's statement, and would not listen to the boy's, and in his
turn chastised the lad mercilessly. In five minutes after the
boy, with aching bones and a bitter spirit, left his father's
house and made his way to London, where he was then vending
cheap braces. This youth could neither read nor write, and
seemed to possess no quickness or intelligence. The only thing
of which he cared to talk was his step-mother's treatment of
him; all else was a blank with him, in comparison; this was
the one burning recollection.

I may here observe, that I heard of several instances of
children having run away and adopted a street life in consequence of the violence of step-mothers far more than of step-
fathers. [...] Had this Birmingham boy been less honest, or
perhaps less dull, it would have been far easier for him to have
become a thief than a street-trader. To the gangs of young
thieves, a new boy, who is not known to the police is often
(as a smart young pickpocket, then known as the Cocksparrow,
described it to me) 'a God-send'. [...]

I did not hear of any girls who had run away from their
homes having become street-sellers merely. They more generally
fall into a course of prostitution, or sometimes may be ostensibly street-sellers as a means of accosting men, and, perhaps,
for an attractive pretence to the depraved, that they are poor,
innocent girls, struggling for an honest penny. If they resort
to the low lodging-houses, where the sexes are lodged indiscriminately, their ruin seems inevitable.

2.   That the companionship and associations formed in tender
years lead many children to a street life is so evident, that I
may be brief on the subject. There are few who are in the
habit of noting what they may observe of poor children in the
streets and quieter localities, who have not seen little boys
playing at marbles, or gambling with halfpennies, farthings,
or buttons, with other lads, and who have laid down their
basket of nuts or oranges to take part in the play. The young

street-seller has probably more halfpence at his command, or, at any rate, in his possession, than his non-dealing playmates; he is also in the undoubted possession of what appears a large store of things for which poor boys have generally a craving and a relish. Thus the little itinerant trader is envied and imitated.

This attraction to a street career is very strong, I have ascertained, among the neglected children of the poor, when the parents are absent at their work. On a Saturday morning, some little time since, I was in a flagged court near Drury-lane, a wretched place, which was full of children of all ages. The parents were nearly all, I believe, then at work, or 'on the look out for a job', as porters in Covent Garden-market, and the children played in the court until their return. In one corner was a group of four or five little boys gambling and squabbling for nuts, of which one of the number was a vendor. A sharp-looking lad was gazing enviously on, and I asked him to guide me to the room of a man whom I wished to see. He did so, and I gave him a penny. On my leaving the court I found this boy the most eager of the players, gambling with the penny I had given him. I had occasion to return there a few hours after, and the same lad was leaning against the wall, with his hands in his pockets, as if suffering from listlessness. He had had no luck with the nut covey, he told me, but he hoped before long to sell nuts himself. He did not know his age, but he appeared to be about eleven. Only last week I saw this same lad hawking a basket, very indifferently stocked with oranges. He had raised a shilling, he said, and the 'Early Bird' (the nick-name of a young street-seller) had put him up to the way to lay it out. On my asking if his father (a journey-man butcher) knew what he was doing, he replied that so long as he didn't bother his father he could do what he pleased, and the more he kept out of his (the father's) way the better he would be liked and treated.

The association of poor boys and girls with the children of the costermongers, and of the Irish fruit-sellers, who are employed in itinerant vending, is often productive of a strong degree of envy on the part of unemployed little ones, who look upon having the charge of a basket of fruit, to be carried in any direction, as a species of independence.

3.   'The employment of children by costermongers, and others who live by street traffic; and the training of coster-mongers' children to a street life, is the ordinary means of increase among the street-folk.'

The children of the costermongers become necessarily, as I have already intimated, street-dealers, and perhaps more innocently than in any other manner, by being required, as soon as their strength enables them, to assist their parents in their work, or sell trifles, single-handed, for the behoof of their parents. The child does but obey his father, and the father does but rear the child to the calling by which his daily bread is won. This is the case particularly with the Irish, who often have large families, and bring them with them to London.

There are, moreover, a great number of boys, 'anybody's children', as I heard them called, who are tempted and trained to pursue an open-air traffic, through being engaged by coster-mongers or small tradesmen to sell upon commission, or, as it is termed, for 'bunse'. In the curious, and almost in every instance novel, information which I gave to the public concern-ing the largest body of the street-sellers, the costermongers, this word 'bunse' (probably a corruption of *bonus*, *bone* being the slang for good) first appeared in print. The mode is this: a certain quantity of saleable, and sometimes of not very saleable, commodities is given to a boy whom a costermonger knows and perhaps employs, and it is arranged that the young commission-agent is to get a particular sum for them, which must be paid to the costermonger; I will say 3s., that being some-where about the maximum. For these articles the lad may ask and obtain any price he can, and whatever he obtains beyond the stipulated 3s. is his own profit or 'bunse'. The remunera-tion thus accruing to the boy-vendor of course varies very materially, according to the season of the year, the nature of the article, and the neighbourhood in which it is hawked. Much also depends upon whether the boy has a regular market for his commodities; whether he has certain parties to whom he is known and upon whom he can call to solicit custom; if he has, of course his facilities for disposing of his stock in trade are much greater than in the case of one who has only the chance of attracting attention and obtaining custom by mere crying and bawling 'Penny a piece, Col-ly-flowers', 'Five bunches a penny, Red-dish-es', and such like. The Irish boys call this 'having a back', an old Hibernian phrase formerly applied to a very different subject and purpose.

Another cause of the abundance of street-dealers among the boyish fraternity, whose parents are unable or unwilling to support them, is that some costers keep a lad as a regular assistant, whose duty it is to pull the barrow of his master about the streets, and assist him in 'crying' his wares. Some-times the man and the boy call out together, sometimes separ-ately and alternately, but mostly the boy alone has to do this part of the work, the coster's voice being generally rough and hoarse, while the shrill sound of that of the boy re-echoes throughout the street along which they slowly move, and is far more likely to strike the ear, and consequently to attract attention, than that of the man. This mode of 'practising the voice' is, however, perfectly ruinous to it, as in almost every case of this description we find the natural tone completely annihilated at a very early age, and a harsh, hoarse, guttural, disagreeable mode of speaking acquired. In addition to the costers there are others who thus employ boys in the streets: the hawkers of coal do so invariably, and the milkmen - espec-ially those who drive cows or have a cart to carry the milk-pails in. Once in the streets and surrounded with street-associates, the boy soon becomes inured to this kind of life, and when he leaves his first master, will frequently start in some branch of costermongering for himself, without seeking to obtain another constant employment.

This mode of employing lads, and on the whole perhaps they are fairly enough used by the costermongers, and generally treated with great kindness by the costers' wives or concubines, is, I am inclined to think, the chief cause of the abundance and even increase of the street-sellers of fish, fruit and vegetables.

4. To 'orphanhood, friendlessness, and utter destitution', the commerce of the streets owes a considerable portion of its merchants. A child finds himself or herself an orphan; the parents having been miserably poor, he or she lives in a place where street-folk abound; it seems the only road to a meal and a bed, and the orphan 'starts' with a few lucifer-matches, boot-laces, nuts, or onions. It is the same when a child, without being an orphan, is abandoned or neglected by the parents, and, perhaps without any injunctions either for or against such a course, is left to his or her own will to sell or steal in the streets.

5. The vagrant dispositions and tastes of lads, and, it may be, now and then somewhat of a reckless spirit of adventure, which in our days has far fewer fields than it once had, is another cause why a street-life is embraced. Lads have been known to run away from even comfortable homes through the mere spirit of restlessness; and sometimes they have done so, but not perhaps under the age of fifteen, for the unrestrained indulgence of licentious passions. This class of runaways, however, do not ordinarily settle into regular street-sellers, but become pickpockets, or trade only with a view to cloak their designs of theft. [...]

The propensities of the street-children are the last division of my inquiry, and an ample field is presented, alike for wonder, disgust, pity, hope, and regret.

Perhaps the most remarkable characteristic of these wretched children is their extraordinary licentiousness. Nothing can well exceed the extreme animal fondness for the opposite sex which prevails amongst them; some rather singular circumstances connected with this subject have come to my knowledge, and from these facts it would appear that the age of puberty, or something closely resembling it, may be attained at a much less numerical amount of years than that at which most writers upon the human species have hitherto fixed it. Probably such circumstances as the promiscuous sleeping together of both sexes, the example of the older persons indulging in the grossest immorality in the presence of the young, and the use of obscene expressions, may tend to produce or force an unnatural precocity, a precocity sure to undermine health and shorten life. Jealousy is another characteristic of these children, and perhaps less among the girls than the boys. Upon

the most trivial offence in this respect, or on the suspicion of
an offence, the 'gals' are sure to be beaten cruelly and savagely
by their 'chaps'. This appears to be a very common case. [...]

In addition to the licentious, the vagabond propensities of
this class are very striking. As soon as the warm weather
commences, boys and girls, but more especially boys, leave the
town in shoals, traversing the country in every direction; some
furnished with trifling articles to sell, and others to begging,
lurking, or thieving. It is not the street-sellers who so much
resort to the tramp, as those who are devoid of the commonest
notions of honesty; a quality these young vagrants sometimes
respect when in fear of a gaol, and the hard work with which
such a place is identified in their minds - and to which, with
the peculiar idiosyncrasy of a roving race, they have an
insuperable objection.

I have met with boys and girls, however, to whom a gaol
had no terrors, and to whom, when in prison, there was only
one dread, and that a common one among the ignorant, whether
with or without any sense of religion - superstition. 'I lay
in prison of a night, sir', said a boy who was generally among
the briskest of his class, 'and think I shall see things'. The
'things' represent the vague fears which many, not naturally
stupid, but untaught or ill-taught persons, entertain in the
dark. A girl, a perfect termagant in the breaking of windows
and such like offences, told me something of the same kind.
She spoke well of the treatment she experienced in prison, and
seemed to have a liking for the matron and officials; her conduct there was quiet and respectful. I believe she was not
addicted to drink.

Many of the girls, as well as the boys, of course trade as
they 'tramp'. They often sell, both in the country and in town,
little necklaces, composed of red berries strung together upon
thick thread, for dolls and children: but although I have
asked several of them, I have never yet found one who collected
the berries and made the necklaces themselves; neither have I
met with a single instance in which the girl vendors knew the
name of the berries thus used, nor indeed even that they *were*
berries. The invariable reply to my questions upon this point
has been that they 'are called necklaces'; that 'they are just
as they sells 'em to us'; and they 'don't know whether they
are made or whether they grow'; and in most cases, that they
'gets them in London, by Shoreditch'; although in one case a
little brown-complexioned girl, with bright sparkling eyes,
said that 'she got them from the gipsies'. At first I fancied,
from this child's appearance, that she was rather superior in
intellect to most of her class; but I soon found that she was
not a whit above the others, unless, indeed, it were in the
possession of the quality of cunning.

Some of the boys, on their country excursions, trade in
dominoes. They carry a variety of boxes, each differing in
size and varying accordingly in price: the lowest-priced boxes

are mostly 6d. each (sometimes 4d., or even 3d.), the highest
1s. An informant told me that these boxes are charged to him
at the rate of 20 to 25 per cent less; but if, as is commonly
the case, he could take a number at a time, he would have them
at a smaller price still. They are very rudely made, and soon
fall to pieces, unless handled with extreme care. Most of the
boys who vend this article play at the game themselves, and
some with skill; but in every case, I believe, there is a willingness to cheat, or take advantage, which is hardly disguised;
one boy told me candidly that those who make the most money
are considered to be the cleverest, whether by selling or
cheating, or both, at the game; nor can it be said that this
estimation of cleverness is peculiar to these children.

At this season of the year great numbers of the street-
children attend the races in different parts of the country,
more especially at those in the vicinity of a large town. The
race-course of Wolverhampton, for instance, is usually thronged
with them during the period of the sport. While taking these
peregrinations they sometimes sleep in the low lodging-houses
with which most of our provincial towns abound: frequently
'skipper it' in the open air, when the weather is fine and warm,
and occasionally in barns or outhouses attached to farms and
cottages. Sometimes they travel in couples – a boy and a girl,
or two boys or two girls; but the latter is not so common a case
as either of the former. It is rare that more than two may be
met in company with each other, except, indeed, of a night,
and then they usually herd together in numbers. The boys who
carry dominoes sometimes, also, have a sheet of paper for
sale, on which is rudely printed a representation of a draught-
board and men – the latter of which are of two colours (black
and white) and may be cut out with a pair of scissors; thus
forming a ready means of playing a game so popular in rustic
places. These sheets of paper are sold (if no more can be got
for them) at a penny each. The boy who showed them to me
said he gave a halfpenny a piece for them, or 6d. for fifteen.
He said he always bought them in London, and that he did not
know any other place to get them at, nor had 'ever heard any
talk of their being bought nowhere else'.

The extraordinary lasciviousness of this class which I have
already mentioned, appears to continue to mark their character
during their vagabondizing career in the country as fully as
in town; indeed, an informant, upon whom I think I may rely,
says, that the nightly scenes of youthful or even childish
profligacy in the low lodging-houses of the small provincial
towns quite equal – even if they do not exceed – those which
may be witnessed in the metropolis itself. Towards the approach
of winter these children (like the vagrants of an older growth)
advance towards London; some remain in the larger towns,
such as Liverpool, Manchester, Birmingham, Sheffield, &c.,
but the greater proportion appear to return to the metropolis,
where they resume the life they had previously led, anything

but improved in education, morals, manners, or social position generally, by their summer's excursion.

The language spoken by this rambling class is peculiar in its construction: it consists of an odd medley of cockneyfied English, rude provincialisms, and a large proportion of the slang commonly used by gipsies and other 'travellers', in conveying their ideas to those whom they wish to purchase their commodities.

Among the propensities of the street-boys I do not think that pugnacity, or a fondness, or even a great readiness, for fighting, is a predominant element. Gambling and thieving may be rife among a class of these poor wretches; and it may not unfrequently happen that force is resorted to by one boy bigger than another to obtain the halfpence of which the smaller child is known to be possessed. Thus quarrels among them are very frequent, but they rarely lead to fighting. Even in the full swing and fury of their jealousy, it does not appear that these boys attack the object of their suspicions, but prefer the less hazardous course of chastising the delinquent or unjustly suspected girl. The girls in the low lodging-houses, I was told a little time since, by a woman who used to frequent them, sometimes, not often, scratched one another until the two had bloody faces; and they tried to bite one another now and then, but they seldom fought. What was this poor woman's notion of a fight between two girls, it may not be very easy to comprehend.

The number of children out daily in the streets of London, employed in the various occupations I have named, together with others which may possibly have been overlooked - including those who beg without offering any article for sale - those who work as light porters, as errand boys and the like, for chance passengers, has been variously calculated; probably nothing like exactitude can be hoped for, much less expected, in such a speculation, for when a government census has been so frequently found to fail in correctness of detail, it appears highly improbable that the number of those so uncertain in their places of resort and so migratory in their habits, can be ascertained with anything like a definite amount of certainty by a private individual. Taking the returns of accommodation afforded to these children in the casual wards of workhouses, refuges for the destitute and homeless poor; of the mendicity and other societies of a similar description, and those of our hospitals and gaols - and these sources of information upon this subject can alone be confidently relied upon - and then taking into the calculation the additional numbers, who pass the night in the variety of ways I have already enumerated, I think it will be found that the number of boys and girls selling in the streets of this city, and often dependent upon their own exertions for the commonest necessaries of life, may be estimated at some thousands, but nearer 10,000 than 20,000.

The consideration which I have devoted to this branch of

my subject has been considerable, but still not, in my own opinion, commensurate to the importance of its nature. Steps ought most unquestionably to be taken to palliate the evils and miseries I have pointed out, even if a positive remedy be indeed impossible.

Each year sees an increase of the numbers of street-children to a very considerable extent, and the exact nature of their position may be thus briefly depicted: what little *information* they receive is obtained from the worst class – from cheats, vagabonds, and rogues; what little *amusement* they indulge in, springs from sources the most poisonous – the most fatal to happiness and welfare; what little they know of a *home* is necessarily associated with much that is vile and base; their very means of existence, uncertain and precarious as it is, is to a great extent identified with petty chicanery, which is quickly communicated by one to the other; while their physical sufferings from cold, hunger, exposure to the weather, and other causes of a similar nature, are constant, and at times extremely severe. Thus every means by which a proper intelligence may be conveyed to their minds is either closed or at the least tainted, while every duct by which a bad description of knowledge may be infused is sedulously cultivated and enlarged. Parental instruction; the comforts of a home, however humble – the great moral truths upon which society itself rests; – the influence of proper example; the power of education; the effect of useful amusement; are all denied to them, or come to them so greatly vitiated, that they rather tend to increase, than to repress, the very evils they were intended to remedy.

The costers invariably say that no persons under the age of fifteen should be allowed by law to vend articles in the street; the reason they give for this is – that the children under that period of life having fewer wants and requiring less money to live than those who are older, will sell at a less profit than it is fair to expect the articles sold should yield, and thus they tersely conclude, 'they prevents others living, and ruins themselves.'

There probably is truth in this remark, and I must confess that, for the sake of the children themselves, I should have no objection to see the suggestion acted upon; and yet there immediately rises the plain yet startling question – in such a case, what is to become of the children?

12 Vagrancy and delinquency in an urban setting

Ivy Pinchbeck and *Margaret Hewitt*

[... It] was voluntary enterprise which, in 1815, set on foot the first systematic investigation into the contemporary causes of juvenile delinquency under the auspices of the Society for Investigating the Causes of the Alarming Increase of Juvenile Delinquency in the Metropolis. [...]

It was the Committee's comments on the auxiliary causes of juvenile delinquency [...] which were to prove the most important in influencing contemporary attitudes to the problem of juvenile delinquency. Together with similar statements from a variety of other sources, these were both to encourage more voluntary effort in providing institutions whose aim was to reform, not merely punish, delinquent youth, and also to inspire attempts radically to reform the law regarding juvenile crime. According to the Committee, the severity of the existing criminal code, with its two hundred offences liable to capital punishment, was itself a cause of juvenile crime, and 'acts very unfavourably on the mind of the delinquent, for while the humanity of the present age forbids the execution of the greater part of these laws, the uncertainty of their operation encourages the offender to calculate, even if convicted, on a mitigated punishment'. Further, they claimed that 'the vicious inclinations of the delinquent' were directly facilitated by the consequence of the system of offering rewards to police officers on a sliding scale, which made it advantageous to overlook the minor depredations of the incipient thief, and thus fail to check him in the early stages of a criminal career, since 'it is in the officer's interest that the young criminal should attain to maturity in crime, when he will get more money for arresting him'. As their Report very clearly demonstrated, the consequences of the system of rewarding the police for actual conviction in addition to the practice of paying for information

Source: 'Children in English Society', London, Routledge & Kegan Paul, vol.2, 1973, pp.431, 436-8, 441-4, 460-6, 472-9, 480, 482-5, 487-90, 492.

leading to conviction, not merely inhibited them from the
uniform and full performance of their duty, but led to some of
them actually inciting young people into crime: 'Many a poor
unsuspecting and even guileless youth was enticed into crime...
by the police themselves, who then gave information of, and
received a bounty for, the very offences which they have
conceived, planned, suggested, aided and secured the commission of'.[1]

Impressed by the failure of the law and its officers to restrain
the young delinquent from a career of increasingly serious
crime, the Committee were no less concerned with the disastrous
effects of punishments meted out to those already embarked.
Their frequent visits to the London prisons prompted them to
quote from Howard's original 'Report on the Condition of
Prisons': 'if it were the aim and wish of magistrates to effect
the destruction present and future, of young delinquents, they
could not devise a more effectual method than to confine them
so long in our prisons, those seats and seminaries, as they have
been properly called, of idleness and vice' [...]

The belief that juvenile delinquency could be substantially
reduced by establishing separate prisons for the young offender
with 'a system adapted to the reformation of youth' which
should combine all the advantages of education, classification
and employment, prompted Peter Bedford and his friends to
found in May 1818 the Society for the Improvement of Prison
Discipline and for the Reformation of Juvenile Offenders. This
was to [...] undertake more detailed study in this country of
the effects of contemporary prison conditions on the young
people committed to them; and also to make extensive visits
to the special juvenile prisons and reformatories already established on the Continent. Convinced that independent, voluntary effort was insufficient to the task, and using the information they had collected, the Society then submitted to the
Home Secretary a plan for a reformatory for boys, which they
suggested should accommodate six hundred delinquent boys
and combine in its organisation and structure all the advantages
of regular inspection, classification, education and employment.
Every class was to have its own dining-room, workshop and
'airing ground'. Each prisoner was to have his own cell. For
many years, however, it proved impossible to convince successive parliaments of the desirability of state support for schemes
such as this. Thus, the development of reformatory, as distinct from punitive, institutions for the juvenile delinquent
was left to a number of enthusiasts such as Peter Bedford, and
later Mary Carpenter, and the voluntary societies which helped
them in their work. [...]

By the 1840s it is possible clearly to distinguish two schools
of reformers regarding the nature of the institutions to which
the juvenile offender might properly be committed; one advocating the establishment of separate juvenile prisons, the other
educational and home-like reformatories. Before the position

became clarified, however, the whole subject was again inten-
sively investigated by two committees, sitting about the same
time and covering very much the same ground: the Select
Committee on Criminal Commitments and Convictions, which
issued two Reports, the first in 1827 and the second in the
following year; and the Select Committee on the Police of the
Metropolis which reported in 1828.

Both these Committees were appointed to enquire into the
increase in the number of criminal commitments and convictions,
the former dealing with England and Wales and the latter, as
its name suggests, restricting its investigations to the Metropolis. Both were at pains to point out that, to some degree,
the 'increase' in juvenile delinquency was more apparent than
real, the numerical increase in commitments being related to
changes in criminal procedure which allowed prosecutors'
expenses, and more especially to the replacement of the old
night-watchman by a more efficient, regular and professional
police force. As to the causes of juvenile delinquency, both
were also in agreement in listing, among others, the low price
of spirits which encouraged heavy drinking at an early age
for both parents and their offspring; the general want of
employment; the parental neglect of children, increasingly
large numbers of whom were said to be abandoned at an early
age. They also pointed to the change in the apprenticeship
system which now allowed 'outdoor' apprentices; the maladministration of the Poor Law under which less and less attention had been paid to the law's continuing requirement that
the young should be adequately trained and disciplined to fend
for themselves; and the failure of the penal system to provide
suitable methods of treatment.

On this last point, the Select Committee on Criminal Commitments and Convictions found that[2]

> they cannot doubt that the present system of long imprison-
> ments for young offenders, besides the expense and incon-
> venience attending it, greatly promotes the growth of crime
> ...a boy is committed to prison for trial, the degradation
> and the company he meets there prepare his mind for every
> vice; after long delay, he is sentenced to six months' or a
> year's imprisonment, he herds with felons, and comes out an
> accomplished thief, detesting the laws of his country, and
> prepared with means to evade them.

Very cautiously they commended the experiment of giving the
justices powers of summary jurisdiction with regard to certain
petty offences of juveniles under sixteen or seventeen years
of age so as to avoid the moral dangers of detaining them in
prison for long periods. The only effective alternative, they
argued, was to hold the Sessions at much shorter intervals of
three or, at the most, four weeks. This particular recommendation was accompanied with the affirmation that, for thefts
'under a certain...value', swift justice should be followed by
short periods of imprisonment and whipping: 'Great advantage

may be derived from the application of corporal punishment to boys.[3] In fact, private whipping and short periods of solitary confinement seemed to be the only proper punishment for boys guilty of petty thefts for the first offence. One witness had gone so far as to state unreservedly: 'I think it [summary jurisdiction] would be imperfect, unless you give them powers of ordering whipping or solitary confinement; I think solitary confinement for a fortnight with a boy for his first offence is much the best possible punishment'. After which, he hastened to add: 'I do not mean to say solitary confinement in the dark, but that they should see no one but the chaplain and the officers of the prison during that time'.[4]

Their obvious attachment to certain old, 'well-tried' methods of punishment for the petty criminal did not, however, blind the Committee to certain advantages of more recent methods of dealing with the young offender which had been tried out with success on the Continent, particularly in France. Thus they enthusiastically endorsed the French principle of 'treating boys differently from men', and were deeply interested in their system of bringing together all those convicted under the age of twenty into one prison where methods of reform were adopted. It was this which influenced them to recommend the establishment of a House of Correction for Young Criminals with a system of management totally different to that operating in adult prisons.

This particular recommendation was reinforced by the Report of the Select Committee on the Police of the Metropolis, which advocated a separate prison for juvenile delinquents, specially built for the purpose or, if the cost of such a scheme be thought prohibitive, the stationing of a convict ship in the Thames, specially fitted up for the reception of boys.

In addition to advocating a special prison to which young offenders might be committed, this Committee was also concerned for the effective after-care of children released from prison, realising that without this many would inevitably return time and again. Like others before them, they believed that the solution to this particular problem was to send boys to sea, either on the men-of-war of the Royal Navy or on merchant vessels. 'If, on their discharge from prison, they could thus be separated from their former associates and weaned from their former habits, a better security against the repetition of offence would be provided than could be hoped for from any improvement of their morals that could be effected by the discipline of prison'.[5] Alternatively, they recommend that young offenders should be sent after their discharge from prison to some institution similar to the Refuge for the Destitute, at Hoxton, where they could be trained in some employment and thus diverted from the necessity of returning to a life of crime. [...]

For over twenty years the merits of the rival systems of separate juvenile prisons and the reformatory school system had been argued by the protagonists of the two schools of

thought, the one more concerned that anti-social groups
should be deterred, the other that the malleable young offender
should be reformed. Despite the considerable success of the
reformatory schools it was, however, the deterrent principle
which now temporarily secured ascendancy in the Parkhurst
Act which established for the first time in England a separate
prison for juvenile offenders.

From the outset Parkhurst was the subject of criticism. Among
its more formidable detractors was Mary Carpenter, the famous
advocate of the reformatory system. One of Miss Carpenter's
many criticisms of the Parkhurst Prison was that it represented
an essentially negative approach to the problem of juvenile
delinquency. At first glance, the actual wording of the Act
might make such a criticism seem far from just. The explanatory
preamble to the Act begins: 'Whereas it may be of great public
advantage that a Prison be provided in which young Offenders
may be detailed and corrected, and may receive such Instruction and be subject to such Discipline as shall appear most
conducive to their Reformation and to the Repression of
Crime...' As is often the case, however, the real flaw in the
Act was not so much to be found in its individual clauses but
in what was not explicitly laid down in any one of them. Although the idea of a separate prison for juveniles had been
canvassed and debated in England for some considerable time,
the legislation on which the first such prison was based was
curiously vague about the system on which the prison was to
be run. [...] Offenders who proved too difficult or 'incorrigible' were to be removed from Parkhurst and returned to an
ordinary prison, there to serve the full period of their original
sentence. Clauses VI, VII and VIII, however, which purported to lay down the way in which the prison was actually
to be run, are a good deal less precise. The Governor was to
have 'the same powers...as are incident to the Office of a
Sheriff or Gaoler'; the Secretary of State was empowered 'from
time to time to make rules for the Government and Regulation
of Parkhurst Prison, and for the Discipline of the Offenders
imprisoned therein, and to subscribe a Certificate that they are
fit to be enforced'. Moreover: 'It shall be lawful for the
Secretary of State from time to time to specify...such offences
which, if committed in Parkhurst Prison by Male Convicts,
shall appear to him deserving of corporal Punishment...and
the Governor...shall have Power to inflict such Punishment'. [...]

In effect, therefore, Parkhurst was left to approach the
problem of how the objects of the Act might be achieved in
practice in a largely empirical manner, the success or failure
of which necessarily depended on the sympathy and flexibility
of mind of those who held office in the prison.

The earliest reports do not encourage much optimism on this
score. In December 1838 102 boys arrived in Parkhurst drawn
from hulks and Metropolitan prisons and serving sentences

varying from two years' imprisonment to fifteen years' transportation. 'The Penal Discipline', reported the Governor,
Robert Woolcombe, 'consists of deprivation of liberty, wearing
an iron on the leg, a strongly marked prison dress, a diet
reduced to its minimum, the enforcement of silence on all
occasions of instruction and duty and an uninterrupted surveillance by officers'.[6] The first four 'fit and discreet' men
appointed under the Act to visit the prison at least once a
month and enquire into the behaviour and conditions of the
prisoners did not seem disposed to adopt a less negative
approach, although one of them was William Crawford of the
Philanthropic Society. Despite an expression of the belief that
'the utmost care must be taken to avoid any species of discipline
which is inconsistent with the habits and character of youth
or calculated in any degree to harden and corrupt', they were
quite clear about their major objectives. The prison, they
suggested, should provide 'a judicious course of moral, religious
and industrial training; but the means adopted for this purpose
should not be of such a nature as to counteract the wholesale
effects of corrective 'discipline'. Further they argued 'that
every comfort and indulgence' which was not essential to preserve health of mind and body should be excluded, and that
there should be nothing in the arrangements of the prison which
might tend to 'weaken the terror of the law or to lessen in the
minds of the juvenile population at large, or of their parents,
the dread of being committed to prison'.[7]

Almost immediately, however, attempts were made to modify
and improve the régime. In February 1839 the Home Office
instructed the Governor that leg-irons could be removed for
good conduct and in September 1840 leg-irons were abolished
altogether. It took rather longer to improve the prison diet,
concerning which successive Annual Reports are curiously
reticent, but in the Report for 1844 it is noted that 'the previous
diet had not been considered sufficiently nourishing to sustain
the vigour of growing boys kept in continual and active employment', and that a new diet had been introduced in November
1843 and an improvement in the boys' 'health and energy' was
recorded.[8] Meantime, while the chaplain endeavoured to discover what type of boy found his way into prison, the Governor
set out to discover some principles which might be applied in
the management of his institution. He divided his charges into
three classes:

1. Probationary class. Boys were not permitted 'that intercourse with each other which is inseparable from youthful
exercise'. Whilst in this class a boy's capabilities and habits
were noted and he was treated accordingly.

2. Ordinary class. Boys in this class were not subject to
corporal punishment.

3. Refractory class. Received very rough treatment.

By 1842 numbers in the prison were growing so rapidly that
new constructions were begun and additional staff drafted to

the prison. The first groups of boys were sent on conditional
pardon to Western Australia where they were apprenticed to
settlers. But the boys were restless, the treatment uncertain,
and the results doubtful. A few boys attempted to escape from
the prison each year and the numbers in the Refractory Ward
increased. In spite of solitary confinement, bread and water,
extra drill and whipping, some boys proved too tough to handle
and were either transported as convicts or returned to ordinary prisons.

A good deal of the difficulty experienced in handling the
boys arose from the very crude nature of the classification
which the first governor had adopted. In 1843, the new
Governor, Captain George Hall, embarked on a more sophisticated scheme. The prison was now divided into:[9]

1.   The General Ward for boys of 14 and over.

2.   The Junior Ward for boys below 14.

3.   The Probationary Ward for boys for the first four months
after admission.

4.   The Refractory Ward for punishment.

5.   The Infirmary Ward for boys needing in-patient
treatment.

The boys worked an average of seven hours a day, mainly
indoors, and almost half their time was spent in classrooms,
a fact which Captain Hall believed contributed in no small
measure to the restlessness of many of the boys in his care
who had never been accustomed to so sedentary and confined
an existence. He advised the visitors that the 'physical and
moral advantages of giving to the prisoners healthful and
interesting employment in the open air and training them to
handicrafts whereby they may readily earn for themselves a
comfortable subsistence in the Colonies, are too obvious'. In
their Report for 1849 the visitors expressed dissatisfaction with
the general progress of the prison and introduced a number
of changes, including several suggested by the Governor himself, which greatly changed the approach to the management
of the boys. Boys were to be graded into first, second, and
third class prisoners; schooling was to be cut and emphasis
was to be placed on outdoor, agricultural, training. This last,
entirely desirable, development was to have disastrous consequences. When the new scheme was put into practice, and
the boys sent to work outside the prison walls for the first
time, the largest number ever (thirty-four) attempted to
escape. In order to allay public anxiety, a small military guard
was provided to check escapes from the farm. Although it
remained for no more than four years, this guard, together
with the leg-irons used in the first two years, became the
symbols of Parkhurst not merely for its critics in the nineteenth
century but for a large number of twentieth-century writers
on the treatment of juvenile delinquency.[10]

The responsibility for this must rest largely with Mary
Carpenter herself and is mainly due to the influence her books

wielded and still wield today. [...]

Mary Carpenter, the eldest child of a Unitarian Minister,
already had a wide range of experience of work among children
long before she developed a particular interest in juvenile
delinquency. While still a girl she assisted her father in teaching the pupils in his private school. In 1831 when she was
twenty-four, she became superintendent of a Sunday School
in Bristol, and it was there that she first became aware of
the problems of the poor. Four years later she became secretary
of the Working and Visiting Society which her father had
established in Bristol for visiting the homes of the poor of the
Sunday school. The plight of those children continued to
engage her interest after her father's death and, in 1846,
having studied the results of John Ponds' Ragged School Movement and the success of Sheriff Watson's Industrial Feeding
School in Scotland, she decided to open a Ragged School at
Lewin's Mead, Bristol. Experience at Lewin's Mead convinced
Miss Carpenter that this type of school needed supplementing
by an altogether different type; a school where young criminals
could be kept under some form of detention and trained by a
mixture of discipline and kindness.

[...] She made a clear distinction between destitute,
neglected and criminal children, and suggested free day schools,
compulsory industrial feeding schools and reformatory schools
as the best method of dealing with the three groups. These
proposals attracted the attention of a large number of people
who had been conscious of the need for action and who had
been waiting for just such a comprehensive and able review
of the situation. The response to her book encouraged Mary
Carpenter, with the support of Matthew Davenport Hill, now
a resident of Bristol and a personal friend, to call a conference
of like-minded people in December 1851, in Birmingham, for
the purpose of considering 'the condition and treatment of the
Perishing and Dangerous Classes of Children and Juvenile
Offenders', and the remedies which their condition demanded.
The Conference did not attract as much attention as she had
hoped and the attendance was small, but it did lead to a
Resolution advocating the threefold system of schools being
laid before the Secretary of State for Home Affairs (Sir George
Grey) who told a deputation from the conference that there
was not sufficient interest to warrant legislation. To prove him
wrong, the principal figures of the conference formed a permanent committee to carry on the work and to form a lobby to
press their cause 'throughout the length and breadth of the
land'.

In May 1852 Mr Adderley (later Lord Norton) moved in the
House of Commons for a Committee of the House to enquire into
the treatment of criminal and destitute juveniles. [...] A
Committee was indeed appointed and presented its Report in
the year following. Mary Carpenter herself gave evidence. 'I
do not believe', she stated, 'that reformation is compatible with

the general system adopted at Parkhurst', explaining that she had never visited the prison personally. She agreed that particularly difficult boys should be sent there, but denied all knowledge of the major changes which had been introduced in 1849.[11]

While the Committee continued its laborious task of sifting the mass of evidence presented to it, Mary Carpenter was anxious herself to demonstrate the advantages of the reformatory schools she so vigorously advocated. The opportunity came to her to set up such a school on her own lines when some vacant buildings, situated near the village of Kingswood, four miles from Bristol, came on the market. The house had been built by Wesley himself and twelve hundred children could be accommodated in the buildings which were surrounded by many acres of land. The place seemed to Mary Carpenter to be an ideal background for her work with delinquent city children. The property was purchased for her by Mr Russell Scott of Bath, who had been much impressed by a visit to the 'Rauhe Haus', the cottage-village for juvenile delinquents founded in 1833 by Emmanuel Wichern at Hamburg and the model for the juvenile prison at Mettrai. Other friends helped with gifts of money, furniture and fittings. In September 1852 Kingswood School was opened as a mixed reformatory.

Mary Carpenter was to outline the principles on which she worked at Kingswood in her new book 'Juvenile Delinquents, their Conditions and Treatment', which appeared early in 1853:[12]

The child...must be placed where the prevailing principle will be, as far as practicable, carried out, - where he will be gradually restored to the true position of childhood. He must be brought to a sense of dependence by re-awakening in him new and healthy desires which he cannot by himself gratify, and by finding that there is a power far greater than his own to which he is indebted for the gratification of those desires. He must perceive by manifestations which he cannot mistake, that this power, whilst controlling him, is guided by wisdom and love; he must have his affections called forth by the obvious personal interest felt in his own individual well-being by those around him; he must, in short, be placed in a *family*. Faith in those around him being once thoroughly established, he will soon yield his own will in ready submission to those who are working for his good; it will thus gradually be subdued and trained, and he will work with them in his reformation and training, trusting, where he cannot perceive the reason of the measures they adopt to correct or eradicate the evil in him. This, it is apprehended, is the fundamental principle of all true reformatory action with the young, and in every case where striking results have followed such efforts, it will be traceable to the greater development of the principle, to a more true and powerful action on the soul of the child, by those who have assumed the holy duties of a parent.

The purpose of 'Juvenile Delinquents' was not, however, merely to outline more clearly the principles on which she herself worked, but once more to attack the Parkhurst system. Other workers in the field of juvenile delinquency had been advocating to the House of Commons Committee a term of imprisonment prior to admission to reformatories; in fact, draft legislation was being prepared to this effect. This plan 'filled her with alarm' and in her book she not only supported the results of her own experience with accounts of the successful reformatories in America, on the Continent and at Redhill, in England. She also wrote of the 'failure' of Parkhurst, referring to 'those unhappy young persons who have become, to their unspeakable misfortune, the children of the State'. She made particular play on the account sent to her by a gentleman who had recently spent all of five hours at Parkhurst in which he vividly referred to the armed guard which had been introduced to allay local anxiety at the employment of the boys outside the prison, and who walked along the hedges of the fields in which the boys were at work 'muskets loaded, and bayonets fixed'. She concluded that Parkhurst was 'most costly, most inefficacious for any end but to prepare a child for a life of crime'.[13] [...]

Some little while after the publication of 'Juvenile Delinquents', the House of Commons Committee presented their Report in which the case for the voluntary reformatories as suitable institutions to which juvenile offenders might be committed by the courts was generally admitted. The legislation which embodied this and related proposals reached Parliament too late in the session for it to be successful, but the encouragement given to the reformatory movement, both by the Committee's Report and the draft legislation, gave a fresh impetus to its activities. A second Conference was called in November 1853. [...] Since the aim of the Conference was to gain publicity and public support, the number of people invited was very much larger than before and included both the expert and the amateur as well as those who were more generally interested in the problem of juvenile delinquency. 'We are here to correct public opinion', Davenport Hill told them. 'It requires even more reformation than the children of whom we have been speaking. It is to this ignorant and cruel public opinion that the existence of the vice of thousands of our fellow creatures in prison is owing'.[14] Fired by his enthusiasm, the Conference proceeded to discuss and adopt various suggestions which were incorporated into a Bill which Mr Adderley introduced into the next session of Parliament under the title of the Youthful Offender's Act[15] which, in an amended form, became law in 1854.

Under the Act, voluntary societies were authorised to establish reformatory schools which were to be allowed the necessary powers of compulsory detention. Each school was to be

governed by the 'Managers', the body of subscribers who were
to frame their school's rules. The Home Secretary was to
certify the schools as satisfactory, and was given the right to
veto any rules he thought undesirable and the power to withdraw certification if the Managers, after due notice, failed to
meet any request with regard to the modification of their
rules. Wherever possible, parents were to be required to
make some financial contribution to the upkeep of their children whilst in the school.

During its passage through Parliament the draft Bill had been
subject to the very amendment which Mary Carpenter had most
feared. Although the general tenor of the Act was to substitute
reformatory treatment for retributive punishment, a concession
was made to the older principle by including in its final provisions a clause under which children were to serve a fourteen
days' period of imprisonment, an expiation for their crime
before they were remitted to the custody of a reformatory.
Nevertheless, Matthew Davenport Hill hailed the Act as the
Magna Carta of juvenile delinquents. He wrote enthusiastically
on 2 August 1854 to William Miles, M.P.:[16]

> You have established three great principles. First, the value
> of voluntary action in the institution and conduct of Reforma-
> tory Schools. Secondly, the substitution of reformatory treat-
> ment for retributive punishment as the rule, subject, how-
> ever, to exceptions which may or may not, if I had been a
> dictator, venture to go as a first step. Thirdly, you have
> recognised the duty of the parent to maintain his offspring,
> and not to cast the burden on the public. These, my dear
> sir, are great principles. Although little thought of now by
> the world at large, I firmly believe that their solemn recogni-
> tion and confirmation by the Legislature will be considered in
> future times to form a great epoch in the jurisprudence of
> this country.

Within four years of the Act authorising their establishment
there were over fifty reformatory schools, almost the highest
number at any time in the nineteenth century. Since offenders
were now legally detained, the schools no longer exerted themselves to attract children to stay by the facilities and provisions they offered. 'There is [now] little of the petting and
bribery which at the outset obtained here and there', wrote
the Inspector of Reformatory Schools in 1859. 'The principle
of duty is more clearly insisted on: persuasions less trusted
to'.[17] [...]

Once the voluntary principle had been accepted it was open
to any respectable person in the country to establish a reformatory school. Most of the early managers disregarded the problem
of suitability of staff and appear to have assumed that any
calibre of staff under proper supervision would be sufficient
to the task. The very first report of the Inspector of Reformatory Schools made particular reference to this, remarking on

the lack of efficient staff and noting that 'some have still to be retained who are but ill-suited to the work'.[18] Some institutions experienced a continuous series of staff changes and the difficulties associated with it, while others were more fortunate in appointing, more or less by chance, officers with a natural inclination for residential work, who then assumed real control of the institution. The inspectorate saw clearly the importance of defining the respective roles of voluntary managers and paid staff, but it was a long time before they felt sufficiently strong and influential to intervene with bad management on behalf of good staff.[19]

Even when the staff employed was of the right quality, they came without training, very often without experience and sometimes with very rigid ideas. As a result, the discipline in the reformatories became very quickly more and more penal and restrictive, some schools introducing the barred windows, locked doors and cropped hair which continued to be a feature of some schools until the 1920s, thus making a mockery of the bitter battle which had been fought by some pioneers against the use of an exclusively restrictive policy in training children.

It had been the intention of the pioneers that the voluntary reformatories should independently and individually develop their systems of reformation, but at the same time they were well aware of the advantage of the exchange of information and experience between those engaged in the day to day operation of the schools. To achieve this, the Preventative and Reformatory Schools Committee, which had met for the first time during the 1851 Birmingham Conference, promoted five years later the Reformatory and Refuge Union with the threefold object: [20]

1. To collect and diffuse information as to the operations and results of all such Institutions: to afford a means of communication between their promoters, and of concerted action with reference to the Government, the Legislature, and public bodies in general.
2. To facilitate the establishment of new Institutions, the selecting and training of efficient masters, matrons and assistants, the procurement of books and school material for educational or industrial work, and the ultimate provision for inmates by emigration or situations of permanent employment.
3. To promote the religious, intellectual, and industrial education of such Institutions and, without interfering in their management, to encourage those who conduct them in every effort to elevate and reclaim the neglected and criminal class, by educating them in the fear of God and the knowledge of the Holy Scriptures.

The energy with which the Union set to work, no less than the piety of its objects, did a great deal to influence public opinion in favour of the reformatories and to encourage magistrates to use them. In November 1857 after correspondence with

the managers of the reformatory schools, the Management
Committee of the Union found themselves in a position to be
able to advise the magistrates as to which reformatories were
ready to receive and were most suitable for the various classes
of 'criminal children', and a communication was addressed to
the Metropolitan magistrates to that effect, offering to help
them in the matter. The offer was accepted, and over the
years the Reformatory and Refuge Union (after 1933 known as
the Children's Aid Society) co-operated with magistrates all
over the country in placing juvenile delinquents in the voluntary reformatory schools. [...]

The movement for the establishment of voluntary reformatory
schools was at its strongest some twenty years before the
establishment of compulsory education in England, and at a
time when the children of very large sections of the population
lived in states of extreme poverty and social deprivation. It
was not surprising that a constantly recurring criticism of the
provisions for young delinquents was based on the argument
that it was only by committing a crime that a child could gain
access to education and industrial training. Lord Chief Justice
Denman expressed a widely felt attitude when he said: 'I am
myself extremely jealous of the gratuitous instruction of the
young felon in a trade, merely because he is a felon'.[21] The
managers of the reformatories were always acutely aware of
this difficulty and endeavoured to find a practical solution by
providing what they did in a manner unlikely to attract and
be pleasant to the offender. Thus, the education provided was
often poor in quality, the work hard, the bulk of the money
earned by the children retained by the institution, and the
buildings, food and clothing left much to be desired. Some
managers took this attitude even further by denying the right
of any former inmate of a reformatory to achieve a 'specially
good appointment in the world'.

Once compulsory education was established, however, and
all children of the lower classes had been afforded access to
elementary education, there was a pronounced and continuous
process of change for the better in the material, educational
and industrial facilities offered by the reformatories.[22]

The pioneers of the reformatory schools were pioneers in the
sense that they were responsible for the formulation and introduction of social change, but once compulsory education had
been introduced, their ideas which had once been revolutionary
tended to become reactionary, and from the mid-seventies
onwards the founders of the reformatories and the many who
had followed in their wake were overtaken by social forces
which some of them could not accept. The central issue in
which the managers became involved was the question of whether
or not a convicted juvenile delinquent should undergo a short
period of imprisonment before entering a reformatory. Three
reasons were usually offered to justify preliminary imprisonment. One was simply administrative. It took some time after

a committal to find a school and ascertain if the managers were prepared to accept the particular child. During this time the child had to be detained somewhere, and prison seemed the obvious choice; indeed, in the absence of remand homes, often the only choice. A second reason was that a reformatory was concerned only with reforming offenders. Since a crime had been committed, there should also be a punishment. If it was not the business of the reformatory to punish, then punishment must be carried out prior to admission - in prison. Thirdly, it was argued that a young offender, following his committal, would be in a state of 'high excitement', which was not conducive to the start of reformation. Hence, it was argued, a calming period in prison would create in him a proper state of mind receptive to what the reformatory itself had to offer.[23]

These considerations had lain behind the insertion of the previous imprisonment clause in the Youthful Offenders Act of 1854. Increasingly, however, their wisdom came into question. Those who were opposed to the principle of previous imprisonment put forward counter-arguments. They said that the practice deprived prison of its terrors; that it corrupted children by bringing them into contact with older, more experienced criminals; that it cast a taint on their characters and added to the offender's difficulties when he resumed life in the community. By the 1880s the judiciary, the inspectorate, the managers of Scottish schools and public opinion had hardened considerably against the continuation of the practice of previous imprisonment for youthful offenders. The managers of the English reformatories, however, held out with surprising obstinacy. Speaking at the Conference of Managers of Reformatory and Industrial Institutions in 1881, the Rev. S.C. Baker declared himself as in no doubt as to the advisability and necessity of retaining the practice:

'My experience of thirty years (eight years as a Chaplain of a County Prison and twenty-two as a Reformatory manager) gives me an ever strengthening conviction that there is no punishment for a juvenile offender whom you want to reform like imprisonment in a separate cell in a well-ordered prison'. It was good, he argued, because it was prolonged, unlike flogging, which could be braved out. Referring to magistrates whom he had heard object to imprisonment as 'enough to break the poor boy's heart', which, 'practically means to break down his rebellious spirit', he declared, 'such breaking down is most disagreeable in the boy's view of it, but most desirable in *ours*. We want that wicked spirit of his broken; and if any contrition is added to its brokenness, then he becomes, so far, that "broken and contrite heart" which God does not "despise"...[124]

Year after year, when the imprisonment clause of the Youthful Offenders Act came up for discussion at the Conferences of the Reformatory and Refuge Union, similar opinions were voiced and even in the 1890s the majority of those attending such

conferences, were prepared to accept them as valid. Outside
the Union, however, their validity was seen more and more as
dubious.

Concern at the complacency of the Union, hints that conditions
in the schools were sometimes far from satisfactory, and
attempts by such men as Sir William Harcourt to amend the
Youthful Offenders Act so as to abolish the imprisonment
clause - all these contributed to the appointment of the Reformatory and Industrial Schools Commission in 1883.

The object of the Commission was 'to enquire and report
upon the operation management, control, inspection, financial
arrangements and conditions generally of certified Reformatories...in order to run such institutions more efficiently for
the object with which they were established.' The Report of
the Commission, published in 1884, was surprisingly weak and
indecisive, and stands in marked contrast to that of the Commission which sat and reported twelve years later. After considering a substantial amount of evidence, it was reported[25]
that the

> effect...has on the whole been very satisfactory. They are
> credited we believe justly, with having broken up the gangs
> of young criminals in the large towns; with putting to an end
> the training of boys as professional thieves; and with rescu-
> ing children fallen into crime from becoming habitual or har-
> dened offenders, while they have undoubtedly had the effect
> of preventing large numbers of children from entering a life
> of crime. These conclusions are confirmed by the statistics
> of the juvenile commitment to prison in England and Wales
> since 1856...in 1856, the number of these commitments was
> 13,981; in 1866, 9,356; in 1876, 7,138. Since that time, the
> number has decreased regularly and had fallen in 1881 to
> 5,483.

[...] Inevitably confronted with the much debated issue of
the previous imprisonment clause, the Commissioners drew
attention - not, one suspects, without some relief - to the sharp
division of opinion amongst those who had presented evidence
on the desirability of its retention. In the absence of a consensus of opinion favourable to change, the Commission were able
to commend a policy of the least possible interference. Children should, they believed, be subjected to some short but
sufficiently sharp punishment before the reformatory treatment
began. In most cases this would continue to take the form of
a term of imprisonment, but for boys under the age of fourteen they recommended that magistrates should have the alternative of ordering them to be whipped at the police station.
As for girls, they might have a period of solitary confinement -
seven days for those under twelve, fourteen for those aged
twelve and upwards - which could be passed in properly fitted
cells in or near to the reformatory to which they had been
committed. In addition they expressed the belief that when a
child under fourteen, or on a first conviction, was sent to a

reformatory, a special report should be submitted by the con-
victing magistrates to the Home Secretary, stating their reasons for such a step, and such children should only be committed up to the age of sixteen or for a period of from three to
five years.

Finally, the Commissioners made six recommendations designed
to restrict the use of punishment in reformatories and advocated the establishment of special reformatories for 'refractory
cases' with a proviso that children sent to such schools must
be paid for by the reformatory sending them there, so as not
to swamp the new institutions with all the children who might
be expected to present any form of difficult behaviour. They
also wanted to see more half-way hostels for children discharged on licence, and they wanted more care and accuracy in
the returns submitted by the managers in the disposal and
success of the inmates.

The Royal Commission of 1884 did not question the need for
the kind of schools they were dealing with. The 1896 Departmental Committee, on the other hand, tackled their job very
much more thoroughly and at considerably greater depth. [...]

The other outstanding feature of the 1896 Report was the
importance which it attached to the child. The previous Commission took the view that the reformatory and industrial
schools were essential to the protection of the community. While
they recognised that the offender had a right to be fairly and
properly treated in the institution, they nevertheless regarded
the institution as being more important in relation to society
than the child itself. The 1896 Committee on the other hand,
anticipating twentieth-century practice, regarded the child
and his welfare as the most important single factor in the operation of these schools, and viewed the schools primarily as
instruments for offering children a happy and constructive
environment.[26]

Precisely because they differed from the managers in their
understanding of the function of reformatories, the Committee
decided that reformatory and industrial schools should be
treated as one because 'there is no substantial difference in
the discipline and regime beyond what can be accounted for by
difference of age'.[27] While the Committee's observations were
undoubtedly correct, they were nevertheless based on a confusion of principle. The reformatories had been established in
1854 to deal with young offenders: industrial schools were
added three years later to absorb 'those who have not yet fallen
into actual crime but who are almost certain from their ignorance,
destitution, and the circumstances in which they are growing
up, to do so if a helping hand be not extended to them'. Industrial schools, that is to say, were intended for what Mary
Carpenter called children of the 'perishing classes'; vagrant
and destitute children, not convicted of any criminal offence.

By the end of the nineteenth century, therefore, the trend of
development in the institutional care of the young delinquent

was the opposite of what the original schools had found to be effective. Whereas they had introduced a division of intake and management for their populations, the system now moved towards unification. With the abolition of imprisonment before admission to the reformatories in 1899, the external differentiation between the two types of school disappeared.[28]

The vigour with which the abolition of the previous imprisonment clause was resisted by the schools themselves had meanwhile only added to the doubts entertained by magistrates, judges, philanthropists and politicians regarding the desirability of such institutions, and prompted them to seek alternative ways of dealing with young offenders.

The Summary Jurisdiction Act of 1879[29] had allowed one possible alternative to either imprisonment or institutional treatment in that it had provided that a juvenile could, for petty offences of which he was undoubtedly guilty, be let off with an 'admonition' instead of a formal conviction. Subsequently the growing conviction of the futility of short sentences of imprisonment and of the undesirability of committing children to prison at all brought the 'admonitary method' into prominence in discussions of the treatment of juvenile delinquents.

Four years later a different though related alternative was provided by the Probation of First Offenders Act, 1887.[30] Colonel Vincent, who introduced the Bill, explained his motives for doing so to the Fifth Conference of the National Association of Certified and Industrial Schools (scarcely the most sympathetic of audiences, judging by the Council's Report which inveighs against 'the growth of that morbid sentimentality which so often manifests itself in sympathy with the individual wrongdoer at the expense of public morality').[31] 'I have always felt', declared the Colonel, undeterred, 'that imprisonment with all its lifelong taint, its never-ending self-reproach, its unnecessary torture of possible denunciation to a trusting employer, an unsuspecting wife or family, is to be avoided, so far as is practicable, in the young'.[32] His Bill, therefore, gave magistrates discretionary powers to release, on his own recognisance, any delinquent convicted of an offence punishable by not more than two years' imprisonment.

Important in principle, since it provided a middle course between admonition and imprisonment, the Probation of First Offenders Act nevertheless had two substantial drawbacks, compared with the system of probation operating today. First, its application necessarily involved the formal conviction of the offender. Second, unlike the system of probation which had been operating in the United States for some years in Massachusetts and Michigan, where the offender was returned to his family under the supervision of a specially designated probation officer, no provision was made in England for the supervision of those on probation. Because of this, magistrates were, in practice, reluctant to invoke the Act and preferred to send offenders to industrial schools.

It was to this particular deficiency of the Act that the Howard Association made repeated reference in its campaign to keep juvenile offenders not merely free from the taint of imprisonment but out of the reformatory schools of which they were no admirers. [...]

On grounds of economy as well as efficacy, the best alternative, both to imprisonment and to committal to a reformatory was, in the view of the Howard Association, a properly organised and supervised system of probation. In this they had the strong support of Mr Stewart, stipendiary magistrate for Liverpool, who had himself used the services of local school-board officials to gain information concerning the social background of the offenders who appeared before him, thus avoiding sentences inappropriate to the individual child. The result, he claimed, was beneficial both to the child and to the community.

Increasing advocacy of the merits of the probation system for the young offender; strong opinion against the desirability of imprisonment of children; growing criticisms of the reformatory schools in which, according to a letter in 'The Times', 'Most of us are losing faith...by herds and battalions',[33] paved the way for further reforms. [...] Not only was the previous imprisonment clause withdrawn in 1899,[34] but the Youthful Offenders Act of 1901[35] and the Probation Act of 1907[36] effectively established the form of probation urged by the Howard Association, and which is familiar to us today. The following year, the monumental Children Act,[37] in establishing separate juvenile courts, confirmed the ascendancy of the view that juvenile delinquents were not most appropriately or most effectively dealt with by the same processes of law and the same punishments as adult criminals, and, by so doing, reflected a revolutionary change of attitude from the days when the young offender was regarded as a small adult, fully responsible for his crime.

References

1 'Report of the Committee of the Society for Investigating the Causes of the Alarming Increase of Juvenile Delinquency in the Metropolis', 1816, p.23.
2 Report from the Select Committee on Criminal Commitments and Convictions, 'PP', 1828, VI, p.12.
3 Ibid., p.13.
4 Ibid.
5 Report from the Select Committee on the Police of the Metropolis, 'PP', 1828, VI, p.8.
6 Quoted in J. Carlebach, 'Caring for Children in Trouble', 1970, p.27.
7 Ibid., p.26, n.3.
8 Ibid., p.28.
9 Ibid., pp.28-9.
10 Cf. H.T. Holmes, 'Reform of the Reformatories', Fabian Tract no.3, 1906, p.2; C.E.B. Russell and L.M. Rigby,

'The Making of the Criminal', 1906, pp.207-8; M.C. Barnett, 'Young Delinquents: a Study of Reformatory and Industrial Schools', 1913, p.18; M.A. Speilman, 'The Romance of Child Reformation: London Reformatory and Refuge Union', 1921, pp.61-2.
11 'PP', 1825, VII, p.102.
12 M. Carpenter, 'Juvenile Delinquents, their Conditions and Treatment', 1853, p.298.
13 Ibid., p.202.
14 R. and F. Davenport Hill, 'The Recorder of Birmingham: a Memoir of Matthew Davenport Hill', 1878, p.166.
15 17 & 18 Vict., c. 86.
16 Davenport Hill, op. cit., pp.168-9.
17 Second Report of the Inspector of Reformatory Schools, 'PP', 1859, XIII pt II, pp.15-16.
18 Quoted in Carlebach, op. cit., p.66, n.2.
19 Ibid., p.67.
20 'Fifty Years Record of Child Saving and Reformatory Work (1856-1906), being the Jubilee Report of the Reformatory and Refuge Union', p.7.
21 Quoted in Carlebach, op. cit., p.71.
22 Ibid.
23 Ibid., p.73.
24 'Report of the Conference of Managers of Reformatory and Industrial Institutions', 1881, p.14.
25 Report of the Reformatory and Industrial Schools Commission, 'PP', 1884, XLV, p.x.
26 Carlebach, op. cit., p.80n.
27 Ibid., p.80.
28 Ibid.
29 42 & 43 Vict., c. 49.
30 An Act to Permit the conditional Release of First Offenders in Certain Cases, 50 & 51 Vict., c. 25.
31 'Report of the Fifth Conference of the National Association of Certified and Industrial Schools', 1891, p.13.
32 Ibid., pp.89-90.
33 'Annual Report of the Howard Association', 1899, p.4.
34 Reformatory Schools Act, 62 & 63 Vict., c. 12.
35 64 Vict., c. 20.
36 7 Edw. VII, c. 17.
37 8 Edw. VII, c. 67.

PART II   THEORY:
Introduction

In this part of the Reader, problems to do with the nature of
crime and the identification of criminals are treated through
the assessment of *criminological theories*. Each article addresses
specific themes in the sociological or psychological literature
on crime, with a view to highlighting the theoretical complemen-
tarity or antagonism between the various approaches. Consequently, this part is more expository and analytical than
the 'history' section. These essays are specially written over-
views rather than selections from existing detailed work.

Nevertheless, it would be wrong to think that there is little
or no connection between 'history' and 'theory'. For example,
the notion of the city as the ground and context of modern
criminal subcultures cuts across convenient disciplinary
boundaries. Similarly, issues to do with the role of the state
in matters of law and order can only be adequately raised if
historical and theoretical approaches complement one another.
More generally still, it might be asked whether a fully historical
and social approach to crime lessens the need for the kind of
criminological analysis which concentrates on the responsibility
or pathology of particular individuals or groups. That question,
too, straddles debates in history, sociology and psychology.
While it is now generally recognized that theory can only be
fully understood in its historical and social context, it is also
the case that historical studies employ theoretical frameworks.
Historians have often been less than explicit about their
theoretical standpoints, but much contemporary work shows an
increasing awareness of the interconnections between history
and theory. To take just a couple of recent examples, David
Philips, in analysing (in close detail) crime in the nineteenth-
century Black Country, explicitly adopts an 'interactionist'
approach. And E.P. Thompson, in a conclusion to a book about
eighteenth-century poachers, defends the universal qualities
of law.

The following articles are designed to achieve two things.
First, they try to depict the overall shape that theoretical

debates about crime have assumed in the last century. Clearly, this task carries the risk of over-generalization, but it is important to illustrate and investigate the key characters of competing perspectives or 'paradigms' - for instance, of positivism, of 'interactionism', of marxism. Moreover, we have also sought to exhibit and assess differences *within* paradigms. Eysenck's recent work, for example, shares common methodological ground with Lombroso's early theories of the deviant personality. While there are differences in technical sophistication and substantive causal explanation, both see the criminal as having discoverable constitutional imbalances which explain social deviance.

Again, there are theorists working within the marxist tradition who would nevertheless disagree fairly strongly about the role of law in society or about the relation between crime and political disorder. These theoretical differences must be respected, though they may count for less when argument is confined to outlining the *general* principles of studying crime and society.

The second aim is to raise questions about the relative merits of sociological and psychological approaches. In fact, within both disciplines, crime, crime control or treatment can seldom be regarded as autonomous areas of study in their own right. The emphasis has often been to reflect upon crime or deviance as a test or exemplification of more general social or psychological theories. Durkheim's 'Suicide' (a key text in developing explanations of deviance) was largely the vehicle for his typologies of different kinds of social system. If only because of this feature of the literature, the reader must work through general propositions about society or the human personality in order to understand the possible meanings of criminality promoted by each particular theoretical approach.

It is useful to think of the relationship between sociology and psychology as forming a 'tension'. This notion suggests some shared areas of interest between the disciplines, as well as the theoretical preferences which divide them, and is reflected in the alternations in emphasis between Readings 15 and 16. Thus Sapsford's article on the search for the deviant personality projected by positivistic psychologies contrasts with Heathcote's subject: the handling of social 'pathology' in terms of collective norms and urban ecology. Readings 17 and 18 consider deviance from the perspective of the relation between socialization and moral choice. This emphasis reveals a distance from the more 'scientific' (possibly pseudo-scientific) approaches characteristic of the first 'tension'. Dallos examines the bearing of family influences and learning theory on explanations of moral choice and criminality. Some sociological theories of a humanist character also share an interest in socialization but place greater value on the voluntary character of moral and cultural 'affiliation'. As illustrated by Muncie and Fitzgerald the role of peer groups, subcultures and the tendency to live up to the 'labels' issued by authorities are thought to be more pertinent to understanding deviant motivations.

A third possible 'tension' concerns collective action and social control. Dallos and Sapsford chart the key developments in social psychology which bring together group structures, social authority and individual consciousness as important elements in theories of human action. Hall and Scraton, in their article, guide us through the various approaches to crime and deviance which share the marxist thesis that crime (and criminology) must be examined from the analytical vantage points of class conflict, historical process and the rule of law itself.

Certain themes have been touched on here which run through the articles and the different academic specialisms, especially problems to do with forms of explanation and the relevance of theory to institutions, policy and treatment. Both themes deserve sustained attention, since they continue to direct criminological research and argument. In this context, Young and Cohen contribute wide-ranging assessments of the field today. Young provides an exposition of the central theoretical 'models' and suggests how debate might be advanced. Cohen's paper - developing and updating the themes of his influential (1974) article - reminds us that theoretical points of departure have political conditions and implications as well as intellectual criteria of adequacy. This also serves to reinforce the claim that historical and theoretical perspectives must be more thoroughly integrated.

13 Footprints on the sand: a further report on criminology and the sociology of deviance in Britain

Stanley Cohen

The development of social scientific theory and knowledge takes place not just within the heads of individuals, but within particular institutional domains. These domains, in turn, are shaped by their surroundings: how academic institutions are organized, how disciplines are divided and subdivided, how disputes emerge, how research is funded and how findings are published and used. In criminology, an understanding of these institutional domains is especially important for knowledge is situated not just, or not even primarily, in the 'pure' academic world, but in the applied domain of the state's crime control apparatus.

Indeed, if we are to follow Foucault, the *whole content* of criminology - with its 'garrulous discourse' and 'endless repetitions' is to be explained with reference to its application by the powerful: 'Have you ever read any criminology text?,' he asks.[1] 'They are staggering. And I say this out of astonishment, not aggressiveness, because I fail to comprehend how the discourse of criminology has been able to go on at this level. One has the impression that it is of such utility, is needed so urgently and rendered so vital for the working of the system, that it does not even need to seek a theoretical, justification for itself, or even simply a coherent framework. It is entirely utilitarian.'

The delicate question of the relationship between knowledge and power receives explicit attention in many parts of this Reader - notably in Jock Young's overview of the development of criminological theory, in the chronology of eighteenth- and nineteenth-century crime control, and in exploring some of the 'tensions' in the rest of Part 2. As a guide to further reading about this and related issues, this paper reports on a brief interlude in the criminological enterprise in Britain: the state of 'mainstream criminology' at the end of the 1960s, the

Source: article commissioned for this volume. Stanley Cohen is Professor of Sociology, University of Essex.

evolution at that point of the 'new deviancy' school and some of the consequent developments in the next decade.

My aim is confined to mapping the place in which the more interesting ideas of this period have been produced and disputed. The enterprise is thus complementary to - and must be read in conjunction with - Jock Young's overview of the ideas themselves and with other similar projects.[2]

The first and longer part of the paper is an edited and abbreviated version of a report prepared for the annual conference of the British Sociological Conference in 1971.[3] The second part - more a guide to reading than a substantive report - brings that chronicle up to date by listing some later developments.

1 AT THE END OF THE 1960s

In 1968, the ineptly named National Deviancy Conference - the major institutional vehicle through which new deviancy theory was developed and diffused in Britain - was founded. Its major ideas - as formulated initially through its own internal discussion and soon a series of publications[4] - were largely programatic. They took the form, that is, of placing on the agenda a number of items self-consciously different from those which appeared on the agenda of mainstream British criminology at the time. These included: (i) a reconstitution of criminology as part of the 'sociology of deviance' and its reintegration into mainstream sociology; (ii) an elevation of social control (or 'societal reaction') as a question of central concern and a consequent adoption of a structurally and politically informed version of labelling theory; (iii) a determination to 'appreciate' deviance in the senses of granting recognition to the deviant's own subjective meaning and of not taking for granted the control system's aim of eradicating deviance; (iv) an emphasis on the political nature of defining and studying crime and deviance.

These ideas served to demarcate significantly one set of collective self definitions from another. They were not so much novel in abstract as in their determined insertion into, and opposition towards, the existing criminological discourse. This type of negative construction is, of course, typical in the history of ideas[5] and to understand its form, we must reconstruct the main features of established criminology at the time. This established paradigm was fairly secure, with an integrity of its own, a certain impressive weight and an umbrella-like quality which was able to absorb all sorts of ideas, even those potentially threatening. I argued at the time that this paradigm would be difficult to reform: the new sociology of deviance would have to develop a critique of a structure on which it would also be partially parasitic. A rough analogy was the relationship between the sociology of industry on one hand, and industrial relations on the other.

The three headings from the following summary of my original
BSA report (mainstream criminology; sociology; the National
Deviancy Conference) will be used again in Part 2 to categorize
the post-1970s developments.

Mainstream British criminology
The main institutions I reviewed in 1971 were: (a) the Home
Office, and particularly the Home Office Research Unit set up
in 1957 to carry out a long-term research programme, mainly
concerned with the treatment of offenders and to act as a
'centre of discussion with universities and other interested
organizations'; (b) the Institute for the Study and Treatment
of Delinquency (ISTD), set up in 1931, and crucial in that it
directly produced the British Society of Criminology (BSC)
and the only criminological journal in the country, the 'British
Journal of Criminology' (BJC); (c) the Institute of Criminology
at Cambridge, set up under Home Office sponsorship in 1958
and (d) the teaching of criminology in London, particularly
the work of Hermann Mannheim. These institutions and individuals by no means represented a monolithic establishment,
and there were many cross links, for example, the Cambridge
Institute had close links with the Home Office (but not until
recently with the 'British Journal of Criminology' group).
   Four characteristics common to these institutions - pragmatism,
the interdisciplinary conception, correctionalism and positivism -
were then identified:

Pragmatism The pragmatic approach had become an indisputable
feature of British criminology. This was not a characterization
made in retrospect by current observers[6] but one that had been
proudly proclaimed by the leading representatives of the
indigenous British criminological tradition. Thus Radzinowicz,
after surveying what he calls the 'liberal' and 'deterministic'
theories of crime, ends up by endorsing what he himself terms
the 'pragmatic position'. This he sees as a 'new realism'; there
is no single purpose of punishment, there is no single causal
theory of crime, therefore any or all perspectives, from Burt
to Merton, have something to recommend themselves and in this
'lies the strength and promise of the pragmatic position'.[7]
   The pragmatic frame of reference was the one that shaped
the few general text-book-type works produced by British
criminologists[8] as well as the organization of research and
teaching. One finds an overall distrust of theory or of any
master conception into which various subjects can be fitted.
The impediments to a theoretical criminology are easier to find
than account for. One major reason is alluded to at several
points by Radzinowicz;[9] the fact that the whole idea of 'schools'
of criminal law and criminology in the Continental sense is
quite alien to the British legal tradition. On the Continent,
major schools of criminal law - liberal, classical determinist,
positivist, social defence - flourished for decades, partly

because of the powerful position of professors of criminal law in the legal system. In England such positions of influence were the prerogative of the judiciary, the makers and interpreters of the law, 'to them the formulation of an all-embracing doctrine and the emergence of a school was something quite alien'.[10] Criminology had to take root in this pragmatic legal tradition.

In America, by contrast, although an autonomous criminology also developed, it was much more firmly located among the social sciences. As Radzinowicz[11] among others has suggested, this location was partly due to the American ideology of optimism in which crime could be seen as the product of remediable social forces. American legal training had also been different: unlike Britain, lawyers had, for a long time, been exposed to the social sciences in their undergraduate training. The strong American socio-legal tradition was virtually absent in Britain. There was, thus, little opportunity for either a legally or sociologically based theoretical criminology to emerge.

In a much wider sense, the pragmatic tradition could be seen as part of the national culture; the amateur, muddling-along ethos of British life, combined with the Fabian type of pragmatism in which disciplines with obvious practical implication like criminology are located. Behind many enterprises in such fields, the attitude is: find out the right facts, then let the well-meaning chaps (for example, in the Home Office) make the obvious inferences and do the rest. Contrast, for example, the highly professional and research-based collection of information for policy-making in an American official commission with the typical Royal Commission - with its motley collection of peers, bishops, judges, very part-time experts and 'informed laymen', and its unbelievably slow rate of productivity.

Although I did not accept the drift of his whole argument, these points need to be put into a broader context such as the one suggested by Anderson.[12] His argument is that there is not just an absence of a tradition of revolutionary thought in Britain, but an absence of major intellectual traditions at all. Thus the weakness of sociology (which he overstates) is diagnosed in terms of its failure to produce any classical tradition and its historical dependence on the charity, social work and Fabian institutions. Significantly, from the point of this report, Anderson finds one reason for the absence of a separate intelligentsia in a factor I have already mentioned - the absence of Roman law in England and the blocking of an intelligentsia based on legal faculties, teaching abstract principles of jurisprudence. Another - somewhat less secure - plank of his argument is the influence of European émigrés (Popper, Wittgenstein, Berlin, Eysenck, et al.). These were 'intellectuals with an elective affinity to English modes of thought and political outlook' who found British empiricism and conservatism - the way it shunned theories and systems even in its rejection of them - quite congenial.[13]

It is (aesthetically at least) appealing to apply much of this analysis to British criminology. To give a specific parallel, the careers of the major founders of contemporary British criminology - Mannheim, Radzinowicz, Grunhut - were not too far removed from those of the émigrés Anderson considers. Mannheim, for example, after a distinguished judicial career in Germany, came to London in 1934, where - according to all his biographers and ex-students - his natural empiricism and tendency to relate his teaching to practical work in the courts found an affinity in 'the ideas of English social reformers, the work of the probation service and expedients in the after care of prisoners'.[14] To point to this pragmatic frame of mind does not, of course, detract from the contributions, for example in teaching or reform, of figures such as these. Indeed, this might be their strength. But it does provide a necessary lens through which to view their work.

The interdisciplinary conception   Pragmatism and empiricism are perspectives which often go hand in hand with the interdisciplinary ideology. Criminology cannot be other than interdisciplinary in the sense that it has to draw on the findings of what Morris[15] refers to as the 'strange motley of investigators who have, at some time or another, borne the title of criminologist' - doctors, lawyers, statisticians, psychiatrists, clinical psychologists and others more bizarre than these. It would be a waste of time, then, to labour this point, if not for two additional turns this feature took in British criminology - the first was to make a religion out of the necessity of drawing on different disciplines and the second was to play down the sociological contributions to this pantheon, pushing criminology either in the legalistic direction or (more frequently and more unfortunately) towards the clinical/psychological/forensic ideology.

Again, let me start with an assertion from Radzinowicz[16] to the effect that progress in criminology can be made only by the interdisciplinary approach: 'a psychiatrist, a social psychologist, a penologist, a lawyer, a statistician joining together on a combined research operation'. In the British context, the fact that a sociologist is not even mentioned was predictable. By the end of the 1950s the major figures in teaching and research were Radzinowicz (legal), Grunhut (legal), Mannheim (legal training and later psychiatric and sociological interest). The major institutions directly or marginally contributing - the Maudsley Hospital, the Tavistock Institute, the ISTD, the BSC and the BJC - heavily weighted the field towards psychology and psychiatry. This weighting remained despite the later contribution by sociologists such as Mays, Morris, and later Downes.

This multidisciplinary image was reflected at a number of levels. It was part of the criminologists' presentation of self to the public.[17] It could be found in criminological conferences, in textbooks and in lecture courses. Thus in Walker's textbook, out of the fifty-seven pages devoted to the topic of explaining crime, seven are given to 'constitutional theories', fifteen to 'mental subnormality and illness', twenty to psychological theories of 'maladjustment, the normal offender, and psychopathy' and fifteen to 'environmental theories' (including 'economic theories', 'topographical aspects' and the 'human environment'). Mannheim's work is more difficult to characterize in this way because, although he clearly sees criminology as multidisciplinary and his own training was legal, he made significant sociological contributions in such books as 'Social Aspects of Crime in England between the Wars' and his treatment of most sociological theories is as comprehensive as the rest of his 1965 text.

A clear statement of the interdisciplinary commitment was provided by another leading British criminologist, Gibbens, at a Council of Europe Criminological Conference:[18]

> most of the important ideas and research hypotheses in
> criminology still come from the parent disciplines of law,
> social science, psychology and psychiatry ... major contri-
> butions to criminology continue to come from studies which
> are not originally designed to come within its scope. Geneti-
> cists stumbled upon the significance of the XYY syndrome,
> the Danish twin study was a by-product of medical study,
> the English study of a sample of the population born on the
> same day was originally designed to study midwifery and
> infant mortality...

Other institutions revealed much the same, with an even more striking weighting towards the legal or clinical disciplines. The twelve research reports published then by the Home Office Research Unit contain mainly topics of a statistical, social administrative type, together with highly technical psychological research.

The character of British criminology is seen very distinctively in the ISTD, BSC, BJC axis. The Institute for the Scientific Treatment of Delinquency, set up in 1931, was the only one of its kind until the establishment of the Cambridge Institute. Its original aims included: 'to initiate and promote scientific research into the causes and prevention of crime', to provide educational and training facilities and 'to establish observation centres or other auxiliary services for the study and treatment of delinquency'.

The essentially clinical nature of its approach was not altogether removed after its 'Psychopathic Clinic' was taken over by the National Health Service in 1948 and the phrase 'Scientific treatment' was changed to 'study and treatment'. Thus in its 1957-8 'Annual Report' the case was stated against handling crime from the penal end of the system and just using outside scientific information. One should rather move towards 'extending the principle of treating offences whenever possible as behaviour disorders calling for appropriate psycho-social measures'. Clinical positivism was stressed as the scientific ideal.

In the following year's Report the phrase 'the root problem of
delinquency, viz. the condition of "pre-delinquency"' appeared.
The possibility of predicting delinquency - an obsession in
British criminology - was always stressed. The 1960-1 Report
complained that there were still resistances to dealing with
crime as a 'behaviour problem with characteristic antecedents
... Judging by comparative study of *other* forms of mental
disorder, it is in the highest degree probable that in all cases
the existence of a "predelinquent" stage can be established ...'
(emphasis mine).

It is of course true that the ISTD was uniquely dominated by
psychiatrists (Edward Glover and Emmanuel Miller being the
most notable), but Mannheim was a leading member from the
outset and a scrutiny of the Annual Reports from 1950 onwards
shows that virtually every leading British criminologist (with
the exception of Radzinowicz) held some office in it. The
parent organization had considerable importance through its
educational activities, but also through its offshoots: - the
BJC, started in July 1950 as the 'British Journal of Delinquency', with Glover, Miller and Mannheim as its editors (the
name was changed in July 1960), and the BSC, which started
off life within the ISTD in 1953 as the Scientific Group for the
Discussion of Delinquency Problems. The contents of the BJC
over its twenty years reflected fairly accurately the discipline's
concerns. A detailed classification of these contents[19] and a
closer textual reading show: a very wide interdisciplinary
spread, considerable attention is given to clinical and applied
penological matters (classification, prediction, treatment,
etc.); concern with penal and legal reform, a representation
of non-academic correctional interests (e.g. reprinting a
Metropolitan Police Commissioner's talk). Despite what looked
to an outsider a fair proportion of space given to clinical
material, an editor complained in 1970, 'Where, we may ask,
are the brave, resourceful, and imaginative clinical papers of
yesterday?'[20]

An examination of the British Society of Criminology revealed
a similar pattern. The backgrounds of both the Organizing
Committee and the guest speakers over twenty years show a
commitment to the interdisciplinary spread, with a heavy bias
in the clinical direction.[21]

This type of analysis of the disciplinary content and the preoccupations of British criminology's main institutions at the end
of the 1960s was not meant to imply that sociologists were
excluded for conspiratorial professional reasons. The imbalance
was there partly because sociological criminology had not
demonstrated any practical potential, and also - more simply -
because there was so little of it. As the editors of a collection
on the sociology of crime and delinquency put it at the time:[22]

Our reliance upon theories developed in other countries and
particularly in the United States is sometimes so pronounced
in the teaching context, that students gain the impression of

an almost complete hiatus in British research. Erroneous as such an impression may be the fact remains that the heavy traffic in ideas about delinquency has tended to flow almost exclusively in one direction.
As I will show in the next section, the impression of a hiatus in sociological attention to crime is not all that erroneous. With the notable exceptions of Morris's ecological study and its predecessors (Mays, Sprott, Jephcott, Carter and Kerr), the Morrises' sociological studies of prison, and some work on sentencing, there was virtually nothing before the post-1965 wave following Downes's book 'The Delinquent Solution'. Two of the most frequently cited works of sociological relevance before the 1960s - Sainsbury's study of the ecological patterns of suicide in London and Scott's description of delinquent gangs - were in fact both done by psychiatrists.
While it is difficult altogether to blame British sociology for paying so little attention to indigenous sociology, it cannot be exonerated easily from two further charges: a certain parochial- ism which wilfully excluded American sociology of crime and deviance for so long and, then, a clear misunderstanding as to what sociology is about. Mannheim was partly guilty on the first charge, with his apparent policy of selecting for his text- book American work only when British or European work could not be found; while the work of West was a clear example on both these counts. Curious notions about sociology being con- cerned with 'area' or 'environmental' factors appear, sociology is identified with statistics, and concepts such as anomie, sub- culture or deprivation are distorted.
In summary, the objectionable features of the interdisciplinary commitment appeared as: (i) the rigidity with which it was defended; (ii) the way it was skewed to exclude sociology and to lean in the clinical direction; (iii) its parochialism and (iv) its actual misunderstanding of sociology.

Correction, reform and the problem of values British crimin- ology has always been tied to two explicit interests: the first, the managerial interest in making the correctional system more efficient and the second, the humanitarian interest in reform- ing the system. These interests are often incompatible - but they might not be so, when they are rationalized jointly in terms of the medical or psychiatric model, or its softer version, the rehabilitative ethic. 'Treatment' can be seen both as more efficient and more humanitarian.
These relationships are complex enough in the day-to-day functioning of the system. What is more at issue here is the way in which British criminology had compromised itself by an unreflexive espousal of both these interests. There appeared to be a certain awareness that this was even a matter to worry about. Either correctional aims were taken for granted:[23]
Criminology, in its narrow sense, is concerned with the study of the phenomenon of crime and of the factors or circum-

stances ... which may have an influence on or be associated
with criminal behaviour and the state of crime in general. But
this does not and should not exhaust the whole subject matter of criminology. There remains the vitally important problem of combating crime ... To rob it of this practical function, is to divorce criminology from reality and render it
sterile.

Alternatively, attempts were made to divorce criminology
from such 'practical functions'. Walker, for example, states:
'Perhaps the hardest impression to eradicate is that the
criminologist is a penal reformer' and concedes that although
his findings might form the basis of reform campaigns, such
campaigns are humanitarian not scientific in nature:[24]

> it is no more his [the criminologist's] function to attack or
> defend the death penalty than it is the function of the
> political scientist to take part in an election campaign. The
> confusion, however, between criminologists and penal re-
> formers has been encouraged by criminologists themselves,
> many of whom have also been penal reformers. Strictly
> speaking, penal reform is a spare time occupation for cri-
> minologists just as canvassing for votes would be for political
> scientists. The difference is that the criminologists' spare
> time occupation is more likely to take this form, and when it
> does so it is more likely to interfere with what should be
> purely criminological thoughts.

It was to Walker's credit that he stated his resolution of the
problem so clearly. In contrast, the major institutions of
British criminology apparently quite unself-consciously accepted
the official system's aims - and took up, within these limits,
various correctional ('hard') or reformative ('soft') stances.
Most criminological contributions were made by those who were
actually employed by the system (i.e. as prison doctors or
psychologists); those who were sponsored by the system (i.e.
doing research financed by the Home Office) or through the
numerous institutions which organize co-operation between so-
called 'scientific' and so-called 'practical' objectives.

The stances appeared in differing guises among the institutions under review - ranging from a bland dominance of correctional interests and personnel to a sophisticated attempt to
involve 'practitioners' with the academic enterprise. At the more
sophisticated end of this spectrum, clearly there must have
been some awareness of the potential tensions and conflicts of
interest. But this awareness was seldom expressed in any public way. And if Walker's solution was clear, it was also over-
simplified and untenable. What had been problematic to
generations of social scientists - the question of values and
commitment - could hardly be resolved by asserting that there
could be such things as 'purely criminological thoughts'. The
constraints that operate in the very selection of certain subjects as being worthy of research; the methods chosen by the
investigator; the way the project is funded and sponsored;

the question of access to confidential data; whether findings
have to be vetted before publication; how results will be used:
all these and related matters could not be ignored.

This is not, of course, a problem peculiar to criminology.
The 1960s saw a growing questioning of traditional positions
across the range of the social sciences. And on matters about
crime and deviance – where the hierarchies of moral credibility
are normally so taken for granted – the issues took on a
dramatic form. Becker's partly rhetorical, but justly celebrated,
1967 question, 'Whose side are we on?'[125] was to become a major
focus of debate. But within the institutions of British criminology and the official or quasi-official grant giving bodies on
which individual researchers were dependent, the question
was simply not on the agenda.

The positivist trap   The heavy and anachronistic dominance of
clinical interests within the interdisciplinary rubric of British
criminology ensured a total acceptance of the positivist
paradigm. As my report is concerned not with the content of
the theories themselves, readers are referred to the standard
accounts of positivist thought (such as Matza's) and the theoretical sections of the rest of Part 2 in order to understand
this dominant paradigm. At the level of abstract ideas, it was
certainly the perceived (or caricatured) features of criminological positivism (the search for clinical or statistical proof of
causation, the commitment to scientific determinism, the denial
of authenticity and meaning to deviance) which were inverted
in the embryonic counter-theories of the time.

In my original report, I used one example to epitomize the
characteristics of British criminology at the time. This was
West's 1969 first Report of the Cambridge Study of Delinquent
Development.[26] At the time, this was one of the largest single
pieces of criminological research ever carried out in this
country, financed by the Home Office (£70,000 to March 1968)
and with an eminent Consultative and Advisory Committee
(including only two out of eleven with more or less sociological
backgrounds). In his preface to his Report, Radzinowicz
hailed the research as being 'in the great tradition of explorations of the springs of delinquency. Although on a smaller
scale, it will ultimately claim a place alongside such classics
as the work of Robbins, the Gluecks and the McCords. All too
little of this sort has been attempted in England'.

This assertion was correct: in methodology and conception
this research went no further than the extraordinary jumble
of eclectic positivism that had already rendered the work of
the Gluecks such an anachronism. Sociologists could hardly
be expected to be impressed with a study which states that
although it is more concerned with individual characteristics,
it is also interested in the 'demonstration' of the extent to
which troublesome boys and other family problems are concentrated among the very poorest: 'It may be that the next stage

of the inquiry will go some way to answering the question of
whether these problems spring from poverty or whether poverty
itself merely reflects an underlying individual inadequacy'.

The design involved an eight-year follow-up of some 400 boys
selected at the age of eight or nine. Did some overall conception inform the selection of dimensions to be studied? West
answers: 'The aim was to collect information on a large number
of items, all of them said to have relevance to the development
of juvenile delinquency and to see in the event which items
or which combination of items would prove to be the clearest
determinants of future delinquency.' Social factors such as
television were excluded because these were too 'universal' and
of course neighbourhood influences could be excluded because
these were 'constant'. Besides such indices as teachers' ratings
and psychological dimensions of the family, items were included
such as height, weight, body-type and various tests of psy-
chomotor habits.[27] The preliminary findings suggested that the
social level of the family was the most important single factor
in discriminating poorly behaved boys from the rest. From an
actuarial point of view, the most efficient prediction might be
based on a few easily registered and objective social facts. The
index 'family income inadequate' was 'remarkably effective'
in identifying the 'problem-prone minority'. If this is so (and
of course such a finding was the basis of Toby's devastating
critique of the Gluecks, six years previously), then what was
the point of a study like this? Why use the opportunities
provided by a long-scale longitudinal design in such a way?
Leaving aside any theoretical payoff (which the researchers
might want to say did not concern them) the practical advantages of such individualistic prediction studies - as numerous
critics have shown - are highly dubious.

This, then, was the sort of research which appeared typical
of mainstream/British criminology at the time. Besides the
'internal' critique to which projects like this were open, they
clearly could not have been expected to command much sociological credibility or interest. To talk of 'mainstream' criminology in this way, is of course to ignore the numerous side-
streams which were yielding interesting work at the time. Morris,
Downes and Trasler had all produced books connecting criminological interest to core social science theories (ecology, subculture, behaviourism); Tony Parker had begun publishing
his series of vivid life histories; and in related areas such as
the study of legal institutions, the police and the mass media,
work had already begun which implicitly rather than program-
matically was very different from established criminology as I
have characterized it. We need now to consider how sociology
as a whole had responded to the insulation of criminology.

The response from sociology
In 1966, Morris argued that even if British criminology had *not*
moved in its neo-Lombrosian direction away from the concerns

of such amateur Victorian sociologists as Mayhew, it 'would
still not have been able to gain much from association with the
social sciences in British Universities'.[28] Without pioneers
such as Mannheim, he suggested, criminology would still have
been where it was in the thirties. But what were sociologists
doing during all this time? This question is important because
new deviancy theory was a response to a lack of sociological
belonging nearly as much as it was to perceived defects of
criminology.

Sociologists of the period were clearly not particularly interested in the subject matter and preoccupations of criminology.
Few would have shown (or admitted) a comparable unfamiliarity
with other areas such as education or industry. For the most
part - given the nature of British criminology at the time - this
indifference was quite justified, but this does not account for
the absence of interest in the actual 'stuff' of crime and deviance.
On the surface, this was surprising, as the study of deviance
was rooted in the classic sociological tradition. As Becker,
among others, had pointed out, to theorists like Durkheim,
'problems of deviance were problems of general sociology'.[29]

The reasons for severing these connections are complex and
beyond my scope in this report. On the side of sociology, they
include a sophisticated version of the sort of philistine distrust which greets, say, Durkheim's 'Suicide' and the whole
work of Freud. How can looking at suicide explain how societies
work 'normally'? How can the interpsychic conflicts of a few
middle-class Viennese Jews explain how the 'normal' mind works?
Studying deviance is seen as an esoteric and marginal occupation.[30] Crucial, too, has been the development of consensual
theories in sociology, in the more mechanistic versions of which
crime and deviance are simply the results of the machine going
wrong. It was precisely this sort of conception which new
deviancy theory reacted against. The major barriers, though,
had been created on the other side: the moralistic, non-
abstract ways in which deviance was studied and the early
identification of this field with social work, reformative or
correctional concerns. As Polsky noted, criminology was the
least successful of all subfields of sociology in freeing itself
from these concerns. He comments on Merton's condemnation
of the 'slum-encouraged provincialism of thinking that the
primary subject matter of sociology was centred on such
peripheral problems of social life as divorce and delinquency'
that, 'Given the perspectives within which delinquency and
crime are always studied, it is obvious why Merton might regard
them as peripheral problems of social life rather than fundamental processes of central concern to sociology.'[31] Polsky might
be caricaturing criminology and is wrong if the old Chicago
School studies of crime and deviance are considered. But clearly
the development of criminology had little to recommend itself
to sociology.

Returning to the institutional level, would one not expect the reverse in Britain; that the pragmatic Fabian stream in sociology would find criminology and related fields highly congruent with its self-image? To some extent, this was true, but this stream had already started running in different directions. On the one hand, sociology developed scientific, academic or professional self-images into which certain topics were not respectable enough to be fitted. On the other, soft, liberal attitudes became anathema to the hard radicals of sociology to whom deviants were not really political. Both these developments, but particularly the first, which was the more dominant, led to those sniggerings about 'girls who want to do sociology because they like people'.

Elsewhere, in trying to describe the sort of attitudes that were prevalent in the profession, I wrote:[32]

In terms of having congenial people to discuss our work with, we found some of our sociological colleagues equally unhelpful. They were either mandarins who were hostile towards a committed sociology and found subjects such as delinquency nasty, distasteful or simply boring, or else they were self-proclaimed radicals, whose political interests went only as far as their own definition of 'political' and were happy to consign deviants to social welfare or psychiatry. For different reasons, both groups found our subject matter too messy and devoid of significance. They shared with official criminology a depersonalized, dehumanized picture of the deviant: he was simply part of the waste products of the system, the reject from the conveyer belt.

For such reasons, then, the institutional domain of British sociology found little room for crime and deviance. The major journals (compared, say, to the American ones over the same period) contained a very low proportion of articles even remotely connected to the subject. Whole substantive areas - such as sexual deviance, drug-taking and mental illness - were virtually completely missing and there were no specialist journals (like the American 'Social Problems') to cover these areas. Until the 1971 Conference, at which this Report was presented, the British Sociological Association had shown very little interest in the area. Various professional surveys at the time confirmed that despite the sociological explosion in Britain (one university chair before the war and over forty in 1967), sociological interest in crime and deviance was insignificant and well below most other specialist fields.

Sociology, at the time, seemed to show a basic divide between those who, to use Horowitz's terms, thought that the discipline should be 'impeccable' and those who thought it should be 'important': 'The aesthetic vision of the impeccable sociologist ... preserves him from the worst infections of "helping people".' The gap was more than a matter of aesthetic styles, though 'it demands a specific decision on the part of scholars and researchers as to where they will place their intellectual bets: on scientific autonomy or on social relevance.'[33]

While the search for impeccability might have shut deviance out of sociology, the obvious political question remains as to what is 'important' and 'socially relevant' - and to whom? In left-liberal thought as a whole, the potential relevance of crime and deviance was not yet recognized. In liberal rhetoric, deviants were consigned to the non-political categories of welfare and reform, while for orthodox Marxists, criminals were part of the lumpen proletariat and of little political impor- tance. Of radical political theories, only anarchism - later of indirect influence on the new deviancy movement - had room on its agenda for the question of crime.

By the end of the 1960s, though, all these walls insulating crime and deviance - from academic sociology and from left or radical political thought - were beginning to crack.

The evolution of the National Deviancy Conference
By the middle of the 1960s, there were a number of young sociologists in Britain attracted to the then wholly American field of the sociology of deviance. The ideas in such works as Becker's 'Outsiders' and Matza's 'Delinquency and Drift' seemed to make sense across a whole range of teaching and research interests, particularly in 'marginal' areas such as drugs, sexual deviance, youth culture and mental illness. Official criminology was regarded with attitudes ranging from ideological condemnation to a certain measure of boredom. But being a sociologist - often isolated in a small department - was not enough to get away from criminology: some sort of separate subculture had to be carved out within the sociological world. So, ostensibly for these reasons (though this account sounds suspiciously like colour-supplement history), seven of us met in July 1968, fittingly enough in Cambridge in the middle of the Third National Conference of Teaching and Research on Criminology, organized by the Institute and opened by the Home Secretary. We decided to form a group to provide some sort of intellectual support for each other and to cope with collective problems of identity. Friends and colleagues were to be sounded out, ideas about circulating reading lists and research plans were discussed and it was proposed to arrange a symposium.

Before picking up the group's subsequent development, it is important to speculate on the less than purely academic reasons for its formation and rapid growth.[34] The first is that we all sensed something in the sceptical, labelling, and societal reaction perspectives, the anti-psychiatry school and similar currents, which struck a responsive political chord. The stress on labelling, injustice, scapegoating, stigmatizing, the implicit underdog sympathy, the whole 'central irony' (as Matza called it) of the neo-Chicago School and its recogni- tion of Leviathan, the implications of Laing's work - these were all sympathetic ideas.

Later, the perceived limitations of these common strands

(outsiders' sympathy and the critique of social control institutions) were to provide the basis for division within the group. But at the time, such interests were appealing for reasons strongly related to the personal background of the group's original members and the overall political climate. A degree of involvement with left/radical political movements (anarchist, socialist, CND) had been followed by a certain disillusionment with such 'conventional' political activity. Contemporary commentators such as Jeff Nuttall[35] captured well this generational experience. Talking or doing something about deviance seemed to offer a form of commitment, a way of staying in, without on the one hand selling out, or on the other playing the drab game of orthodox politics.

Such commitment was easier because the historical period was one of growing and visible militancy of deviant groups working outside the political structure. The hope for real social change (or any event, where the action was) seemed to be with the hippies, druggies, squatters and, above all, everything that was happening in the American campuses and ghettos. These identifications were facilitated by personal involvement in some of these marginal groups. Some of the original members, and even more of the later members of the Deviancy Conference, were on the fringes of what Jock Young nicely called 'the Middle Underground'. Involved as participants, we couldn't resist the lure to be also observers - and make a decent living from it! The romantic, voyeur-like appeal of the subject matter was thus important; one doubts whether a similar group could have sprung up around, say, industrial sociology, educational sociology, or community studies.

I have speculated on this sort of reason because it would seem implausible to suggest that only some sort of disinterested quest for knowledge drew people to the field. As in all such causal stories, the matter is over-determined, and from its early years onwards the organization began to mean many things to its members at different states of their involvement. While these real differences and incipient tensions were already noted in my 1971 Report, the story, none the less, was one of some success. The original group of seven increased at the first Conference in York to about twenty, and this number rose to 130 by the seventh Conference in October 1970. In 1971, the paid-up membership was 230. Social workers and other groups outside academic sociology were actively recruited and various social activists and commentators were drawn in as speakers. A forum, as well as support (financial and moral) were given to radical groups such as tenants' associations, claimant unions, Case Con (the militant social work organization) and RAP (Radical Alternatives to Prison). Plans were discussed to formalize contact with such groups and allow them to shelter under the NDC umbrella.

The actual substantive papers at the Conference could be grouped into four categories: ethnographies of deviant groups

and activities; studies of social control agencies; critiques of
existing criminology or deviancy theory; attempted connections
with fields such as social work, psychiatry and the mass
media. The discussions in these early years reflected with
reasonable fit the original agenda items: developing an alternative or counter-criminology; applying the new American
sociology of deviance ideas to the British scene; establishing
a critical and committed sociology. As the group expanded,
alternative (and, somewhat later, potentially divisive) directions began to appear: academic versus activist; liberal,
libertarian and Marxist; hard and soft. I ended my 1971 Report
by listing some differences manifest at that point:

(a) Should the group just drift along, amplifying and if need
be changing, or should some attempt be made at tightening up?

(b) Should one tighten up in the direction of demanding
greater commitment to social action?

(c) Should one tighten up in the direction of demanding
greater theoretical sophistication, making everything more
impeccable? As a corollary, does this mean excluding or
limiting the numbers of non-sociologists?

(d) To what extent should the perceived limitations of the
theories which originally looked so attractive lead to an immer-
sion in 'harder' and ostensibly more political theories?

Such differences were, indeed, to become important later.
So, too, were some other problems which I raised in trying to
make a provisional comparison between the positions of mainstream criminology and the deviancy group at the beginning
of the 1970s. One was the strength which criminology could
draw from concentrating on areas most likely to be defined as
'relevant' and 'important'. In contrast, sociologists of deviance
often dealt with catchy, esoteric and hip areas which seemed
of less public relevance. This was due partly to personal
preference, but more to the fact that the interactionist approach
seemed better suited to forms of deviance such as drug-taking,
homosexuality and mental illness, which are ambiguous,
marginal and already subject to widespread normative dis-
sensus. An allied problem was the value commitment being
developed in opposition to criminology's compromised identification with the official system. There was a danger here of a
self-indulgent romanticism - a tendency to oversimplify matters
by simply 'changing sides'.

But whatever these internal tensions and potential problems,
the lines of confrontation between the rival discourses seemed
well defined. The next decade promised some interesting movements.

2 AT THE END OF THE 1970s

The ten years since my original Report was compiled have been
extraordinarily rich and interesting ones, both in the study of

crime and deviance, and in sociology as a whole. It was as if
the explosions in the wider cultural and intellectual world of
the late 1960s had left behind all sorts of mutations and
fall-outs which now had to be contemplated and classified. To
a large extent, especially in the social sciences, the centre did
not hold - and fission, diversity and crisis-talk became the
commonplaces of the decade. For this reason, the more or less
clear patterns of ten years ago are now much harder to
find. And for the same reason, there is some danger in
attributing causal significance to one force - say, the growth
of the National Deviancy Conference - when the developments
in question would have occurred anyway under the influence
of this wider movement. None the less, the visible influence
of the new deviancy theories - both within the field (centri-
petal) and spreading outwards (centrifugal) - was remarkable.
Let me report briefly on some of these developments, following
the headings used in Part 1.

Mainstream criminology
There are more corners and cavities than ten years ago, but
for the most part the institutional foundations of British
criminology remain intact and unaltered. As I originally suggested, the Establishment saw the new theories as simply a
fashion which would eventually pass over or as a few interesting ideas which could be swallowed up without changing the
existing paradigms at all. If we are talking about the centre
of Foucault's 'power-knowledge spiral' - the point where the
utilitarian connection between ideas and policy is most transparent - this is hardly surprising. Indeed, this decade has
seen a *reinforcement* of this connection: the Home Office
Research Unit, the research branches of the Prison Department, the Metropolitan Police and allied state agencies have all
expanded and become more professional and productive. This
is particularly notable given the overall decline of government
support for social science research. In line with what happened
in the United States over this decade, the content of this
type of criminology has switched (and is likely to switch even
more) in the direction of 'criminal justice'; that is to say, an
exclusive concern with the operation of the system. Research
deals mainly with matters of decision-making, manpower,
evaluation and classification.
    As we move to those institutions on the periphery of power -
those ostensibly concerned, that is, with knowledge - the
picture is a little more diverse. The various quasi-academic
bodies reviewed in Part 1 (such as the ISTD, the BSC and
the BJC) have become more catholic and a little more receptive
to the newer sociological currents. The uneven nature of this
receptivity, though, is shown nicely in the pages of the
'British Journal of Criminology' between 1970 and 1980. The
papers themselves reflect only a slight change from the previous
decade, while the book review section (under a series of

sociologically-minded review editors) became fully tuned in to
the whole range of 'new' and 'radical' theory.

Moving even further from the power-knowledge centre and
towards the more unambiguously-academic settings, the decade's
fall-out is much more visible. Even in 1971 I reviewed a textbook in my original report - Hood and Sparks's 'Key Issues in
Criminology'[136] - which was already perceptibly different from
its predecessors: more sociological, more theoretically aware
and more questioning of correctional interests. Over the
decade, changes such as these became taken for granted in
official criminological circles - though more, I suspect, in
teaching than in research and policy-making. A 1979 textbook
such as Bottomley's,[37] while emerging from well within the
mainstream criminological consensus, gave explicit and coherent
recognition to potentially threatening ideas. And in the mild
boom in post-graduate criminology studies, (a trend unlikely
to continue) the old and the new were shuffled around together
in curricula, examination papers and reading lists. Edinburgh
Keele, Hull, Middlesex and Sheffield were all added to Cambridge as centres for specialist criminology MAs. While some
allowed one tendency rather than another to dominate, the
most notable pattern was Sheffield's, where the old and the new
criminologists lay side by side.

Let me take the 1977 inaugural lecture by A.E. Bottoms, the
Director of the newly-established Centre for Criminological
Studies at Sheffield, to illustrate this accommodation.[38] His
subject matter - the dangerous offender - derives clearly from
the agenda of the old criminology. It conjures up images of
the traditional obsessions of positivism and social defence, it
seems clearly 'correctional', it raises the spectre of clinical
prediction. But while Bottoms certainly addresses himself to
these issues, the paper is informed by a sceptical and theo-
retically-minded attempt to understand the current revival of
interest in the *concept* of dangerousness itself. The question
is not simply whether or not dangerousness can be predicted
and legislated about, but how the idea relates to current
changes in penal thought, such as the emergence of neo-
classicism. Yet other examples might be found within criminology of influence and accommodation of this sort. Policy
debates in such areas as parole have thrown up much more
fundamental controversies than would have been possible in the
older liberal reform consensus.[39] Consideration of such matters
as sentencing and the aims of punishment are more theoretically
informed and less insular. And while longitudinal studies such
as West's still continued, they were sometimes presented in
a framework which took cognizance of such views as labelling
theory.[40]

At the centre of the criminological enterprise though, it is
business as usual. At the academic edges, those more sensitive
to changing currents (in thinking, publication, conference
papers, student interests), a pattern of accommodation is

taking place. What clearly has not happened, is any sort of
collective crisis of self-confidence. In allied fields elsewhere,
such shifts have indeed taken place in response to the power
of ideas.[41] But there is no reason to suppose that the institutions of British (or any other) criminology will crumble in
the face of any ideas - let alone the vague, inconsistent and
incomplete alternative offered by the new theories. As I have
suggested elsewhere,[42] the reluctance of the new theories to
inhabit the same areas as the old, has left behind an ambiguous
no-man's-land, on either side of which the protagonists can
still carry on with their private preoccupations.

The response from sociology
The centrifugal forces dispersed by the new deviancy theories
and their later marxist versions have undoubtedly had more
effect on sociology than on criminology. This, of course, is
predictable given sociology's largely academic and non-political
base - and also its intrinsic and pathetic vulnerability to intellectual fashions, blackmailings and hijackings of one sort or
another. In any event, these have been exciting years in what
is still seriously called the 'discipline'. And while most of this
excitement was in response to the more sweeping cultural
changes of the last two decades, the NDC can justifiably claim
some share of the fall-out in Britain. The inhospitable terrain
I described at the end of the 1960s has changed dramatically.
The sociological landscape has been fenced off into separate
territories, and whether due to an indirect stimulation from the
new deviancy work or to an actual migration of the group
members to these territories, a whole range of sociological
connections have now appeared for students of crime and
deviance. I can do little more than list the more interesting
ones:

Education   These years have seen a major interest in the
control functions of the educational system. The equation
'education equals social control' has usually been extremely
crude, but the by-products of this work have been of considerable intrinsic interest as well as relevance to the sociology of
deviance. These include studies of: the control element in the
historical development of state educational systems; the ideology
of the curriculum; the microdynamics of deviance and control
in the classroom[43] and - perhaps most importantly - a focus
on the oppositional relationship between working-class culture
and the school.[44]

Mass media   Sociologists associated with the NDC were interested from the outset in the selection, presentation and effects
of images of deviance in the media.[45] This interest has since
been pursued on a large and productive scale by individuals
and by institutions such as the Centre for Mass Communication
Research at Leicester. A substantial body of work now exists

on the social production of news and on media portrayals of crime, deviance and other social problems such as race and industrial conflict.[46]

Cultural studies   Two prominent elements in the new deviancy theory's critique of concepts such as the delinquent subculture were an insistence on seeing cultural forms as meaningful in their own right and on locating these forms structurally and historically. These two ideas - combined with cross-currents from European Marxist and structuralist thinking - found their most fertile ground in the work of the Centre for Contemporary Cultural Studies at the University of Birmingham. This work on popular culture, working class culture and various deviant youth subcultures has been of major intellectual importance.[47]

Medicine and psychiatry   At the end of the 1960s, the sociology of medicine had only just begun developing in Britain. Psychiatry and mental illness had received virtually no sociological attention. During the decade, though, a number of interests voiced in the early years of NDC meetings were soon to be found in the various institutional homes in which medical sociology developed, particularly the research centres in Aberdeen, Bedford and Warwick. New journals in the field were started and courses in 'medicine and society' organized. Disability and handicap were studied as forms of deviance;[48] the notion of medicine as social control (again!) and allied ideas about the 'medicalization of life' and the 'therapeutic state' became common and so did a sociological version of anti-psychiatry and a transfer of Scheff's type of labelling theory of mental illness.

Law   My original Report noted promising developments in the sociology of law, which were of obvious interest to students of crime and deviance. These have now been greatly extended - both through the institutionalization of empirically-based 'socio-legal studies' and by a theoretical interest in the sociology of law. A flourishing new journal was started ('British Journal of Law and Society') and an older one republished (the 'International Journal for the Sociology of Law'). A substantially funded SSRC research centre (the Centre for Sociological Studies), which was set up in Oxford in 1972, now has a staff of twenty-five. The study of law as a social institution has moved both in a micro direction[49] (e.g. research on the language and interaction of the courtroom) or towards more macro concerns (e.g. historical and theoretical work on law and the state).[50] In comparison with America, though, (see, for example, the journal 'Law and Society' over the last ten years) the study of law as a social institution has barely begun.

Social policy and welfare   It is extremely difficult to determine whether the new theories have had much effect on the actual

practice of social welfare in Britain - on the welfare-state
level, on individual agencies or on professional social work.   .
There is little doubt, however, that the decade has seen a
major revision in the way social policy has been conceptualized
at all these levels. There has been a growing disillusionment
with the achievements of state welfare in advanced capitalist
societies. This disillusionment has taken a conservative form
in the discrediting of humanitarianism, benevolence and state
intervention, but it has also led to a popularization of the
more radical (including feminist) views of 'welfare as control'.
This takes the form of a debunking of the pretensions of the
welfare apparatus or else (in combination with Marxist type
analysis of state expenditure) theorizing about welfare as
part of the state's programme of legitimation and pacification.
As one recent observer notes, this social control view of social
policy is of particular interest not in areas like crime and
deviance, where the control function is obvious, legitimate
and open - but in areas seen as more covert, mystifying and
illegitimate.[51]

The evolution of the National Deviancy Conference
The last decade's developments in crime and deviancy theory -
heralded probably by the publication of 'The New Criminology'
in 1973 - form the subject matter of much of Hall and Scraton's
article and are not my business here. I will indicate merely
the places where readers might follow the story.
    As I have already suggested in the previous section, various
core ideas from the new deviancy paradigm found their way
into already-established sub-fields of sociology. Certain institutional areas in particular - education, medicine, mass media,
welfare - provided hospitable ground for re-analysis in terms
of the master conception (vague and woolly as it is) of social
control. In yet other areas - such as youth cultures - the master conceptions of meaning and authenticity became dominant.
And actual substantive areas of deviance not initially given
much attention, were absorbed into the new theories.[52]
    As to the original group's own internal trajectory, the most
remarkable thing, perhaps, is its continued existence. Despite
schisms, defections, recriminations, collective boredom, chronic
illnesses and premature burials, the organization has survived
for twelve years. And despite migration to the academic sub-
fields described earlier and to more political groupings (especially on the left, in civil liberties, the women's movement,
radical social work, the prison movement), the membership
number remains respectable and there is a regular attendance
at the annual or bi-annual conferences which remain the
group's main intellectual and social activity. Perhaps the most
notable institutional achievement was the NDC's role in creating (in 1974) the European Group for the Study of Deviance
and Social Control.[53] The European Group has met annually
for six years and has become an influential force in bringing

together like-minded sociologists and activists in Western
Europe.

The group's current concerns reflect the changing cultural
and political mythology through which its dominant members
choose to understand themselves. The loose cultural relativism
of the euphoric late 1960s gives way to the more brutal economic
realities and diminished expectations of the late 1970s. A
large measure of the diversity and eccentricity which were so
characteristic of the group's early years has now been exported
out. And consequently, the hard core of the remaining group
has become more orthodox and homogeneous. In line with the
master theoretical move (explained in article no.20 by Hall
and Scraton) from interactionism to Marxism, a number of consequent changes have been apparent in the type of papers
given, encouraged and published under the group's official
sponsorship. For example: a move away from ethnographies
(of deviant types, life-styles, subcultures) and towards
structural or historical work; a similar move away from empirical
studies of control agencies towards macro-analysis of overall
political tendencies; a disinheritance of the wider 'sociology
of deviance' rubric in favour of a concentration on 'crime, law
and the state'; the beginnings of a keener interest in problems
of women and crime.

These tendencies can be observed in the two most recent
NDC publications.[54] They have not, of course, gone uncriticized
and recent years have seen more or less clear divisions appearing between the orthodox Marxist vanguard, an older liberal
tradition (still interested, for example, in labelling theory) and
a maverick libertarian group. Current doubts about the new
orthodoxy - coming from unconvinced insiders or sympathetic
outsiders - take the form of accusation of closure: a premature
burial of the problems inherited from 1960s deviancy theory
and a premature dismissal of the agenda of mainstream criminology.[55]

Leaving aside the existence of such interesting disputes and
divisions, it is clear that the new perspective overall has now
become established and institutionalized. In the same way as
initially outrageous art movements (such as Dada and surrealism)
eventually become respectable, so too has the new deviancy
and criminology become part of the accepted order of things.
Its practitioners are ensconced in orthodox academic departments, journals, examining boards and publishing companies.
No booklist would be complete without one.

Finally, what about the world outside universities and
polytechnics - the crime control system, welfare agencies,
professional social work? Here patterns of influence are much
harder to detect. Making an impact of this sort was very high
on the group's original agenda, though this commitment was,
I think, eventually compromised by a certain ambiguity about
whether any short-term or reformist objectives were worth
supporting in the face of known structural obstacles towards

any change of the existing social order. There have been 'interventions' (to use the code word) in various policy debates over the last decade, but I doubt whether many direct lines of influence can be traced. This is not to say that some key ideas have not percolated through and informed important institutional changes. It is clear, for example, that early theories of stigma, secondary deviation, amplification and the like were taken up in the various movements over the last decade against closed institutions such as mental hospitals and prisons. It is equally clear, though, as some writing on decarceration and community control is beginning to suggest, that these policies often originated for quite different reasons and – moreover – are producing results not always in line with the theory from which they are supposedly derived.[56] The exact lines of influence in areas like this have yet to be understood.

The same could be said for the connections with social work practice. Here, though, after some early warnings about the ambiguity of new deviancy theory's practical implications,[57] the direct interest in establishing an 'alternative' or 'radical' social work has been considerable. And much of this interest has been consonant with, if not directly influenced by, the type of perspective on social work common in the ranks of the NDC. There has been a great deal of work – initially programmatic[58] or theoretical,[59] but increasingly descriptive,[60] about the prospects for radical social work in Britain. In addition, specific social work settings such as probation and the juvenile court have been analysed in quite new terms. A number of papers in a recent collection on social work and the courts, for example,[61] reproduce quite exactly the directions suggested by new deviancy theory. One paper demystifies the court process by analysing the micropolitics of its flow ('exposing ... the underbelly of the magistrates' courts', as the editor claims);[62] another examines the construction of 'practice theory' by probation officers[63] and another looks at the clients' own perceptions of the court routine.[64]

There are a number of other sectors of the control and welfare system in Britain – notably prisons, police, juvenile institutions – where an equivalent list could be produced of work directly carried out or influenced by the new deviancy theorists.

In some cases, this work has been mainly analytic, in others it has been sponsored by explicit policy interests – for example, civil liberties or prison abolition. Certain current tendencies in the new criminology – especially the interest in abstract and historical issues – do not lend themselves to such immediate policy connections. There is little doubt, however, that the global fall-out from the last decade's ideas have profoundly influenced the ways in which middle level control and welfare institutions are being conceptualized. Whether this has, or will, change their practice is another story.

CONCLUSION

At the end of my original BSA paper, I queried the whole purpose of this type of exercise in collective self-consciousness.
What is the point of all the historical and institutional reflection
embodied in reports of this sort? The dangers of obsessive
self-reflection are even more apparent now than they were ten
years ago. A great deal of thinking in the social sciences –
mirroring the whole intellectual culture's narcissistic contempla-
tion of itself – has been devoted to an examination of its own
origins, crises and reasons for existence.
  Much of this thinking is patently unproductive. And readers
might well wonder why, in a course about crime – a subject
so obviously grounded in the real world – so much effort has
been expended in mapping out the histories and present contexts in which knowledge is produced, rather than in getting
along with the real business. The answer is paradoxical: some
measure of self-consciousness about how knowledge is produced and diffused is needed to assess what proportion of
this knowledge speaks only to itself. This is true even for the
natural world, as the astronomer Sir Arthur Eddington tells
his scientific colleagues: 'We have found a strange footprint
on the shores of the unknown. We have devised profound
theories, one after another, to account for its origins. At last,
we have succeeded in reconstructing the creation that made
the footprint. And Lo!, it is our own.'[65]

Notes
  1 M. Foucault, Prison Talk, in C. Gordon (ed.), 'Power/
    Knowledge: Selected Interviews and Other Writings, Michel
    Foucault, 1972-1977', Brighton, Harvester Press, 1980,
    pp.47-8.
  2 Most notably, David Matza's analysis of criminological
    positivism in 'Delinquency and Drift', New York, Wiley,
    1964, and his definitive sociology of knowledge in 'Becoming
    Deviant', Englewood Cliffs, N.J., Prentice-Hall, 1969.
      A great deal of the 'new' criminology and sociology of
    deviance of the 1970s has been marked by such self-
    reflexive theory; for one of the more interesting attempts
    to relate theory to its policy implications, see G. Pearson,
    'The Deviant Imagination', Macmillan, 1975.
  3 Subsequently published as Criminology and the Sociology
    of Deviance in Britain: a Recent History and a Current
    Report, in P. Rock and M. McIntosh (eds), 'Deviance and
    Social Control', Tavistock, 1974, pp.1-40.
  4 S. Cohen (ed.), 'Images of Deviance', Penguin Books,
    1971, and 'Folk Devils and Moral Panics', MacGibbon & Kee,
    1972, and J. Young, 'The Drugtakers', MacGibbon & Kee,
    1971.
  5 And accounts for the important point made in Jock Young's
    subsequent auto-critique: that the new theories were

largely an idealist inversion of the old: Working-Class
Criminology, in Taylor I., Walton, P. and Young, J.
'Critical Criminology', Routledge & Kegan Paul, 1975.
6 For example, W.G. Carson and P. Wiles (eds), 'Crime
and Delinquency in Britain: Sociological Readings', Martin
Robertson, 1971, p.7.
7 L. Radzinowicz, 'Ideology and Crime: a Study of Crime in
its Social and Historical Context', Heinemann, 1966, p.128.
8 The standard examples at that time being: N. Walker,
'Crime and Punishment', Edinburgh University Press, 1965;
H. Jones, 'Crime and the Penal System', University Tutorial
Press, 1965; H. Mannheim, 'Comparative Criminology',
Routledge & Kegan Paul, 1965 and D. West, 'The Young
Offender', Penguin Books, 1967.
9 op. cit., (1966) and 'In Search of Criminology', Heinemann,
1961.
10 Radzinowicz, op. cit. (1966), p.21.
11 Radzinowicz, op.cit. (1961), p.119.
12 P. Anderson, Components of the National Culture, 'New
Left Review', vol.50, 1968, pp.3-57.
13 Ibid., pp.18-19.
14 J. Croft, Hermann Mannheim: a Biographical Note, in T.
Grygier et al. (eds), 'Criminology in Transition: Essays
in Honour of Hermann Mannheim', Tavistock, 1965, p.xvi.
For further accounts of Mannheim's work, see Lord Chorley,
Hermann Mannheim: a Biographical Appreciation, 'British
Journal of Criminology', vol.10, 1970, pp.324-47, and
T.P. Morris, Comparative Criminology: a Text Book,
'Howard Journal', vol.XII, 1966, pp.61-4.
15 Ibid., p.62.
16 Radzinowicz, op. cit. (1961), p.177.
17 See, for example, the collections of papers published to
mark the centenary of the Howard League of Penal Reform:
H.J. Klare (ed.), 'Changing Concepts of Crime and its
Treatment', Oxford, Pergamon, 1966, and H.J. Klare and
D. Haxby (eds), 'Frontiers of Criminology', Oxford,
Pergamon, 1967.
18 T.C.N. Gibbens, 'Identification of Key Problems of
Criminological Research', Strasbourg, Council of Europe,
1970, p.5.
19 M. Wright, Twenty Years of the 'British Journal of
Delinquency/Criminology', 'British Journal of Criminology',
vol.10, 1970, pp.372-82.
20 E. Glover, 1950-1970: Retrospects and Reflections,
'British Journal of Criminology', vol.10, 1970, p.315.
21 Here - as elsewhere - see my original B.S.A. report for
more details.
22 Carson and Wiles, op. cit., p.48.
23 Radzinowicz, op. cit. (1961), p.168.
24 Walker, op. cit., preface.
25 H.S. Becker, Whose Side Are We On?, 'Social Problems',

vol.14, 1967, pp.239-47.
26 D.J. West, 'Present Conduct and Future Delinquency',
   Heinemann, 1969.
27 Such as the Gibson Maze Test; the Body Sway Test (most
   of the boys apparently hardly swayed at all, while others
   found this test unpleasant and anxiety provoking); and
   the Tapping Test (tapping a pencil on a blank piece of
   paper for 10 seconds; this apparently reveals extra-
   punitive personality types and it could be expected that
   'boys with delinquent personalities would tend to scatter
   their dots more widely'. Sceptics will note that the scores
   did reveal a slight but significant positive correlation with
   bad conduct as rated by teachers: $r = 0.17$).
28 Morris, op. cit., p.61.
29 H.S. Becker (ed.), 'The Other Side: Perspectives on
   Deviance', New York, Macmillan, 1964, p.4.
30 The classic demonstration of this remains C. Wright Mills,
   The Professional Ideology of Social Pathologists, 'American
   Journal of Sociology', vol.49, 1945, pp.165-80.
31 H. Polsky, Research Method, Morality and Criminology,
   in 'Hustler's Beats and Others', Chicago, Aldine, 1967,
   p.142.
32 Cohen, op. cit. (1971), p.6.
33 I.L. Horowitz, 'Professing Sociology: Studies in the Life
   Cycle of Social Science', Chicago, Aldine, 1969, p.99.
34 See Pearson, op. cit., for a complementary account of these
   wider reasons.
35 J. Nuttall, 'Bomb Culture', MacGibbon & Kee, 1968.
36 R. Hood and R. Sparks, 'Key Issues in Criminology',
   Hutchinson, 1971.
37 A.K. Bottomley, 'Criminology in Focus', Oxford, Martin
   Robertson, 1979.
38 A.E. Bottoms, Reflections on the Renaissance of Dangerousness, 'Howard Journal of Penology and Crime Prevention',
   vol.16, no.2, 1977, pp.70-96.
39 For example, R. Hood, 'Tolerance and the Tariff', NACRO,
   1974.
40 D. Farington, Longitudinal Research on Crime and Delinquency, in N. Morris and M. Tonry (eds), 'Crime and
   Justice: an Annual Review', University of Chicago,
   vol.1, 1979.
41 For a model account of just such a crisis of confidence in
   the 'law and development' movement, see D.M. Trubeck
   and M. Galanter, Scholars in Self-Estrangement: Some
   Reflections on the Crisis of Law and Development Studies
   in the United States, 'Wisconsin Law Review', vol.1974,
   no.4, 1975, pp.1062-102.
42 S. Cohen, Guilt, Justice and Tolerance: Some Old Concepts
   for a New Criminology, in D. Downes and P. Rock (eds),
   'Deviant Interpretations', Oxford, Martin Robertson,
   1979.

43 For example, D. Hargreaves et al., 'Deviance in Classrooms', Routledge & Kegan Paul, 1975.
44 Especially P. Corrigan, 'Schooling the Smash Street Kids',
   Macmillan, 1979, and P. Willis, 'Learning to Labour: How
   Working Class Kids Get Working Class Jobs', Saxon House,
   1978.
45 S. Cohen and J. Young (eds), 'The Manufacture of News:
   Deviance, Social Problems and the Mass Media', Constable,
   1973.
46 See the work over the last five years of Stuart Hall,
   Graham Murdock, Philip Elliott, Steve Chibnall, Paul
   Hartman, the Glasgow Media Group, et al. For a recent
   review and bibliographical guides see 2nd edition of 'The
   Manufacture of News', and G. Murdock, Misrepresenting
   Media Sociology, 'Sociology', vol.14, no.3, August 1980.
47 The initial work was collected in S. Hall and T. Jefferson
   (eds), 'Resistance Through Rituals: Youth Subcultures
   in Post-War Britain', Hutchinson, 1976. For a later review
   see S. Cohen, Symbols of Trouble, Introduction to new
   edition of 'Folk Devils and Moral Panics', Oxford, Martin
   Robertson, 1980.
48 For example, M. Voysey, 'A Constant Burden; the Reconstitution of Family Life', Routledge & Kegan Paul, 1975.
49 Most notably, P. Carlen, 'Magistrates' Justice', Martin
   Robertson, 1976.
50 An allied development (from history rather than sociology)
   has been the massive interest, associated with the name
   of E.P. Thompson, in law, crime and the state in 17th- to
   19th-century England. As Block II of this Course shows,
   this work has been of major stimulus to some contemporary
   criminologists. See also G. Pearson, Goths and Vandals:
   Crime in History, 'Contemporary Crises', vol.2, no.2,
   April 1978, pp.119-39.
51 J. Higgins, Social Control Theories of Social Policy, 'Journal
   of Social Policy', vol.9, no.1, January 1980.
52 For a notable example in the area of sexual deviance, see
   the papers and bibliographical guides in K. Plummer (ed.),
   'The Making of the Modern Homosexual', Hutchinson, 1980.
53 For a selection of papers from the first European Group
   conference, see H. Bianchi et al. (eds), 'Deviance and
   Control in Europe', Wiley, 1975.
54 'Permissiveness and Control', Macmillan, 1979, and 'Capitalist
   Discipline and the Rule of Law', Hutchinson, 1979.
55 See the papers in Downes and Rock, op. cit.
56 A. Scull, 'Decarceration: Community Treatment and the
   Deviant', Englewood Cliffs, Prentice-Hall, 1977, and
   S. Cohen, The Punitive City: Notes on the Dispersal of
   Social Control, 'Contemporary Crises', vol.3, 1979,
   pp.339-63.
57 For example, S. Cohen, It's All Right for You to Talk:
   Political and Sociological Manifestos for Social Work Action,

in R. Bailey and M. Brake (eds), 'Radical Social Work',
Edward Arnold, 1975.

58 Bailey and Brake, op. cit.

59 P. Corrigan and P. Leonard, 'Social Work Practice under
Capitalism', Macmillan, 1978.

60 For example, M. Brake and R. Bailey, 'Radical Social
Work and Practice', Edward Arnold, 1980.

61 H. Parker (ed.), 'Social Work and the Courts', Edward
Arnold, 1979.

62 P. Carlen and M. Powell, Professionals in the Magistrates'
Courts: the Courtroom Lore of Probation Officers and
Social Workers, ibid., pp.97-117.

63 P. Hardiker, The Role of the Probation Officer in Sentencing, ibid., pp.117-34. See also her paper, Social
Work Ideologies in the Probation Service, 'British Journal
of Social Work', vol.7, no.2, 1977, pp.131-54.

64 H. Parker, Client/Defendant Perceptions of Juvenile and
Criminal Justice, ibid., pp.135-52.

65 A. Eddington, 'Space, Time and Gravitation', New York,
Harper, 1959, p.201.

14　Thinking seriously about crime: some models of criminology

Jock Young

Crime is a subject of perennial interest, and in recent years it has once again become a topic of major public debate. We are likely to encounter the 'conversation about crime' wherever we turn - in conversations at a bus stop, or in the pub, reading the 'News of the World' or the 'Guardian' or listening to a phone-in on the radio. These conversations will not only reflect the concern with what is commonly perceived as the ever-rising rate of crime, our feelings about what this means, and what ought to be done about it. They will also draw on a range of implicit explanations as to what causes crime, and a range of implications as to how to deal with it, even though we are not aware that we are using criminological theories and explanations of crime at all.

But there are important differences between 'popular theories' of crime and criminology. In particular, the latter:

(a) attempts to ground itself in an empirical knowledge of the patterns, incidences and variations in criminal behaviour, drawing on more systematic information;

(b) attempts to build a theoretical position systematically, so that the different parts of the theory fit coherently, ironing out inconsistencies and contradictions of position;

(c) attempts to be as comprehensive as it can - dealing with the different aspects and drawing these into a systematic account.

This does not mean that it is only criminologists who are capable of 'thinking seriously about crime'. Popular or lay discussions of crime may be well-ordered and thoughtful, and most criminological theories are better at explaining some aspects (or types) of crime than others.

In more popular discussions, we can often identify the points where people switch theories in mid-argument. For example, they sometimes define vandalism as a 'wilful act of damage'

Source: article commissioned for this volume. Jock Young is Reader in Sociology, Middlesex Polytechnic.

(implying conscious intent), but go on in the next breath to *explain* vandalism as a product of the vandal's poor home background (implying that the behaviour is determined). Another common 'switch' is between the explanation of crime and the policy conclusions that are drawn. For example, if it is true that vandalism is the product of poor family and home circumstances, then is it logical to propose that vandals should be harshly punished for acts which are determined by circumstances? If the principal cause of vandalism is 'bad home conditions', we should logically 'treat' the circumstances, not the individual vandal, if we want to get to the root of the problem.

Using criminological theories can be equally problematical. It is not uncommon for theories of crime to adopt different explanations for different types of crime and offender. Thus white-collar crime is theorised differently from working-class petty property crime. Indeed the variability of what is defined as crime has led some criminologists to question the search for a single, all-embracing theory which will explain all criminal activity. What is considered to be crime differs between and within societies over time. For example, the sale of alcohol was a legitimate activity in the USA at the turn of the century, was effectively criminalised during the Prohibition period, and is once more legitimate again. Throughout this period the activity remained the same, it was the legal status of the sale of alcohol that changed. It may well be that we should not require a single theory, no matter how systematic in form, to account for *all* the many different types of crime within a single explanatory framework. Criminological theories indeed differ precisely as to whether or not they assume a *single* explanation of crime in general to be either conceivable or useful.

In this article I shall introduce and consider six of the major paradigms within criminological theory. I shall show how some theories explain particular types of crime more adequately than others - and need not necessarily be faulted on this ground alone. The proposition that, though crime-in-general is universal, the types and patterns of crime are specific to particular societies at particular times is central to some of the theories we review. The test of this *general* applicability may not be relevant for judging their value as it would for theories, for example, on a set of universal psychological or physiological features.

Each of the paradigms I shall consider has certain features or elements in common. For example, they all have a particular view of human nature or of social order, even though this may not be especially stated. In examining the six paradigms, then, I shall ask a number of questions about each one.

(A) What is their view of *human nature* in general?
(B) What picture do they present of the *social order* which crime challenges, abrogates or deviates from?

(C) Do they define crime as a 'natural', 'social' or 'legal' phenomenon?
(D) What is the *extent* and *distribution* of crime - is it general and 'normal', in all societies, or is crime a marginal and exceptional activity? Do all people commit crime or are there particular groups or individuals who engage in criminal activity?
(E) What are the principal *causes* of crime?
(F) What *policy deductions* do they draw as to how crime should be dealt with?

I shall ask these six questions to each of the major paradigms - classicism, positivism, conservatism, strain theory, new deviancy theory and marxism - which we examine in this article. The answers to questions which are provided by each paradigm will enable us to distinguish clearly between them.

It is important to remember that we are using these questions as a device for organising one's thoughts about crime. In posing them as dichotomies (Is the view of human nature a voluntaristic or deterministic one? Is the view of social order based on consensus or coercion?), we are deliberately applying the question to draw out and emphasise the differences between paradigms. Posing the questions as dichotomies does not necessarily mean that each theory wholly answers the questions with one alternative or the other.

It is also worth noting that the six paradigms are not of the same kind. Conservatism, for example, has been generally ignored in academic criminology, being regarded largely as a pragmatic and unelaborated way of thinking. The paradigms also have different historical developments; classicism dates back to the eighteenth century, while interest and work in new deviancy theory stems from the 1960s.

In this article, paradigms are presented ideal-typically. Just as I have emphasised differences between the paradigms, so I have minimised the variety of position *within* six theoretical models. Positivism, for example, contains many other strands besides that of 'individual positivism' on which this article focuses. Although the paradigms are presented sequentially, this does not imply that they have been developed in a series of discrete historical stages from classicism to marxism. Nor does it suggest that they were developed in a unilinear fashion. They are *competing* paradigms, each with its own intellectual history and each flourishing, with powerful support and a substantial body of research work, at the present time.

THE DICHOTOMIES

(A) Human nature: voluntarism versus determinism
At the point of committing a crime, is the offender perceived as acting out of free-will (voluntarism) or is she/he seen as propelled by forces beyond his or her control (determinism)?

This can be conceived of as a question of either whether the act was committed wilfully as part of a process of reasoning (i.e. was it a rational act, whether or not correct in its reasoning) or whether it was non-rational, invoking determining factors outside rational control. (Such factors can be either genetically or environmentally/determined.)

(B) Social order:consensus or coercion
Theories of crime are the other side of the coin to theories of order. All criminological theory, at least implicitly, involves a theory of social order. Order in our society can be understood as based either on the consent of the vast majority (although a minority may be coerced by this consent) or largely by the coercion - subtle or blatant - of the majority by a powerful minority.

(C) Definition of crime: legal versus social
The definition of crime may be seen as obvious and taken for granted: it is behaviour or activities which break the legal code. Alternatively it may be argued that a more appropriate measure would be behaviour or activities that offend the social code of a particular community. The legal and social codes do not always coincide and can often conflict. One might argue that tax-evasion is illegal only on paper; in reality it is a normal activity indulged in by a large part of the population. Similarly, vandalism may be seen simply as a crime by virtue of the act of being illegal or else it may be seen as part and parcel of the spirited behaviour of young adolescent boys.

(D) The extent and distribution of crime: limited versus extensive
Is crime, as the official statistics suggest, a limited phenomenon committed by a small number of people, or are the statistics misleading in that law-breaking is an extensive phenomenon engaged in by a large proportion of the population? All criminological theories start from this key problem, although, as we shall see, they differ markedly in their use and interpretation of official crime statistics.

In Figure 14.1 I have constructed a series of Aztec pyramids, each representing the likelihood of going to prison depending on class, age, race and sex. As can be seen, the social characteristics which greatly increase the risk of incarceration are to be lower working class rather than middle class, young rather than old, black rather than white, and male rather than female. Thus - to take an example - whereas on an average day in 1960 only one in 450 Americans were in prison: one in 26 black men aged between twenty-five and thirty-four were behind bars. Serious crime, according to the statistics, is a minority phenomenon within which certain social categories most marginal to society are vastly over represented. We have used American statistics here because

252   *Jock Young*

comparable British figures on race are non-existent and, on class, extremely limited (although one British study, interestingly, indicates that the likelihood of a labourer going to prison is identical to that in the USA - see Banks (1978)).

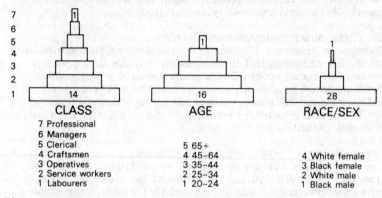

7 Professional
6 Managers
5 Clerical   5 65+
4 Craftsmen   4 45-64
3 Operatives   3 35-44   4 White female
2 Service workers   2 25-34   3 Black female
1 Labourers   1 20-24   2 White male
                                             1 Black male

Figure 14.1 Odds on going to prison by class, age, race and sex. Source: American data derived from Wright (1973).
Note: a labourer is fourteen times more likely to go to prison than a professional; a 20- to 24-year-old is sixteen times more likely than a 65-year-old; a black male is twenty-eight times more likely than a white female.

The prisoner is thus seen to be on the fringe of the economy - unemployed or a casual labourer, to have missed out on the educational system, to belong to a minority group.

(E) The causes of crime: individual versus society
The causes of crime may either be located primarily within the individual, whether in his or her personality, biological make-up or powers of reasoning, or be seen as essentially the product of the wider society within which the individual exists. For example, rape might be viewed either as a product of a gross genetically-determined personality disorder, or as a mode of conduct which is a direct product of the sexist nature of a patriarchal society and the way in which sexual encounters are usually understood and conducted by men.

(F) Policy: punishment versus treatment
Such a series of propositions regarding the nature of the criminal, the way social order is to be maintained, the definition and extent of crime and its root causes has, of course, implications for public policy. If, for instance, we view crime as a voluntary act of the individual, we would tend towards a policy of punishing him or her, whereas, if she/he is seen as acting under the compulsion of individual or social forces, the treatment of the criminal might seem to be inappropriate.

CLASSICISM

Classicist theories of crime and punishment developed out of the Philosophy of the Enlightenment which swept Europe in the second half of the eighteenth century. Within a hundred years, most of the legal and penal systems of administration in Europe had been thoroughly remodelled in the light of classicist principles. Enlightenment thinkers were reacting strongly against the arbitrary systems of justice which prevailed during the ancien régime, and the severe and 'barbarous' codes of punishment by which the law was upheld in the period of feudalism and the absolutist monarchies. The rise of classicism is closely associated with the emergence of the free market and the beginnings of agrarian capitalism, and is best thought of as the philosophical outlook of the emerging bourgeoisie – the class that was rising to prominence in this new social order. The members of this new rising class not only sought to secure a privileged position for themselves in society, but aspired to refashion society itself along new lines. They demanded political rights hitherto denied them – they were political, as well as legal reformers in England, at the forefront of the movement to extend the franchise to the new propertied classes. They also demanded a legal system that would defend their interests and protect their 'rights and liberties' against the arbitrary power hitherto wielded exclusively by the aristocratic landed classes and the Crown. In England, they were the principal inheritors of the English Revolution of 1644 which limited the prerogative of the monarchy, and, even more, of the 'Glorious Settlement' of 1688 which settled the country under a constitutional monarchy and undermined the last vestiges of feudal power and authority.

The legal system they proposed had at its centre the concept of the 'free' and legal contract between free and equal individuals. 'Contract' for them was a practical necessity, for it was the relation which allowed men to hire the labour of others, to sell goods and acquire property, not according to rank and statute, but according only to the dictates of a free market. Modern civil law, which revolves around the concept of the contract, was first elaborated under these auspices. But 'contract' was also a grand conception of how society itself arose and how individuals were bound to one another within it, and therefore how their conduct ought to be regulated (i.e. the foundations of a new system of law).

Enlightenment philosophy centred on the 'sovereign individual'. Individuals were conceived as free and rational agents, capable of defining their own self-interests and of choosing rationally to temper their actions according to the dictates of Reason, a faculty lodged in each individual. They therefore thought of society, not as something sovereign which pre-dated the individual, but as something which individuals had contracted to establish for their own individual and mutual benefit.

They expressed their legal claims in terms of the 'rights and liberties of the individual' - and sought to limit the power and prerogative of the state (which, in previous times, had been powerfully identified with aristocracy and Crown) to the defence of the rights, liberties and property, as well as the safety and security, of the individual. The preoccupation with individual rights and duties, and with the limited conception of the state, together with the centrality of property and the market, make Enlightenment classicism the source of many ideas and conceptions that were subsequently to be elaborated within liberal political theory and constitutional doctrine. Their influence has been carried into our own times within the 'liberal tradition'. Individuals were therefore 'free' to act according to the dictates of Reason and self-interest, except in so far as their actions limited the freedom of others, equally free, citizens. They should be rewarded proportionately to their energy, skill and efforts - and, conversely, punished proportionately, according to the social harm which they inflicted on other individuals.

The rights, liberties and freedoms which had previously belonged to the very few by virtue of birth, rank and title were now claimed by this rising class. But they laid claim to them, not in their own name, but as a 'universal' right. The American Declaration of Rights, a classic Enlightenment constitutional document, is entirely cast in this language of 'universal rights' - though there were many classes of persons (for example, the labouring poor and women) to whom, in fact, they did not conceive that they could apply. They were opposed to the arbitrary administration of justice in earlier times, which depended on the discretions and exceptions which 'great men' could make according to personal whim or inclination. They wanted, instead, a *universal* system of justice that would apply equally to all men. They wanted it to be a 'rational' system, derived not from the jumble of precedent and custom and tradition but from clearly-defined rational first principles, and set out in a systematic form. Its operations should be certain and predictable, so that men could calculate the 'benefits' and 'costs' of wrong-doing as they did the profit and loss of a financial transaction. They wished to abolish the irrational discrepancy between petty crimes, punished by the terrible engines of capital statute and torture, and devised in their place a scale of punishment proportional to the severity of the crime. Just as men were governed by Reason, so too ought the systems of government, legislation and law by which their common conduct was governed. The application of Reason, calculation and predictability to matters of legislation and law made them the forerunners of modern systems of administration.

The most celebrated classicist theorist is the eighteenth-century Italian writer, Cesare Beccaria; his work was enormously influential on Enlightenment thinkers, including English legal reformers like John Howard, whose writings led to the

construction of new penal regimes based on imprisonment,
Romilly, who led the attack on the capital statutes, and the
founder of Utilitarianism and leading figure among the
'philosophical radicals', Jeremy Bentham. The first chapter
of Beccaria's classic work, 'An Essay on Crimes and Punishments',
serves well to introduce us to classicist principles in criminological theory (1801, pp.5-6):

> Laws are the conditions, under which men, naturally inde-
> pendent, united themselves in society. Weary of living in a
> continual state of war, and of enjoying a liberty which
> became of little value, from the uncertainty of its duration,
> they sacrificed one part of it, to enjoy the rest in peace and
> security. The sum of all these portions of the liberty of each
> individual constituted the sovereignty of a nation; and was
> deposited in the hands of the sovereign, as the lawful admin-
> istrator. But it was not sufficient only to establish this
> deposit; it was also necessary to defend it from the usurpa-
> tion of each individual, who would always endeavour not only
> to take away from the mass his own portion, but to encroach
> on that of others. Some motives, therefore, that strike the
> senses, were necessary to prevent the despotism of each
> individual from plunging society into its former chaos. Such
> motives are the punishments established against the trans-
> gressors of the laws. I say, that motives of this kind are
> necessary; because experience shows that the multitude
> adopt no established principle of conduct; and because society
> is prevented from approaching to that dissolution (to which,
> as well as all other parts of the physical and moral world, it
> naturally tends), only by motives that are the immediate
> objects of sense, and which being continually presented to
> the mind, are sufficient to counter-balance the effect of the
> passions of the individual, which oppose the general good.
> Neither the power of eloquence nor the sublimest truths, are
> sufficient to restrain, for any length of time, those passions
> which are excited by the lively impressions of present objects.

This passage is based on several fundamental premises of the
classicist school: the 'natural independence' and sovereignty
of the individual; the binding together in society under the
'social contract', which yielded power to the monarch or state
only in return for the protection of rights and the security
of person and property; the 'associationist' psychology of
human motivations which underpinned their legal and social
theories; the need for law to prevent the pursuit of naked
self-interest from plunging society into a competitive struggle
- a 'war of all against all', as the political philosopher, Hobbes,
put it. Beccaria's leading disciple in England was Bentham,
who applied the rational calculus of his Utilitarian philosophy
extensively to questions of law and punishment. Bentham sought
to reform the archaic English system of justice according to
rational principles, systematically applied. The legal code should
be formalised, punishment made to bear directly on the

individual, predictable and proportional to the offence. He
reduced the complex issues concerning criminal motivation to
the simple terms of his 'pleasure/pain' continuum. Punishment
should be rational and impersonal. Bentham said of Beccaria
that his was the 'first of any account which is uniformly
censorial'.

Classicist thinking has been immensely influential on legal
and criminological reasoning over the past two centuries: many
modern ideas about crime – for example, the centrality in
English law of the concept of individual responsibility – can be
traced to classicist roots. It was rarely, however, anywhere
put into practice in its pure form. Its implementation within
the reform of both the criminal law and the administration of
justice was more piecemeal and governed by pragmatic considerations than the pure classicists would have wanted. Classicism was subsequently further modified by the introduction,
within its framework, of some principles drawn from positivism,
the second major paradigm we shall examine: for example, a
wider number of groups – children, the insane and feeble-
minded – were recognised as being incapable of full rational
responsibility for their actions, and the law was required to
take some circumstantial factors and influences into account,
modifying the pure classicist doctrine of 'free will'. The resulting amalgam of classicism and positivism – often labelled 'neo-
classicism' – has, however, constituted the dominant criminological paradigm in Anglo-Saxon legal thought and practice,
and is the main source of the eclectic synthesis which, as
Radzinowicz and others have observed, has dominated British
and North American criminology since (see, for an elaboration,
Stan Cohen's article no.13 in this volume).

What is interesting about the classicist paradigm is that it has
the largest history of any contemporary criminological theory
but still continues to be a major influence both on institutions
of social control and in controversies in criminology. For example, a major debate within the last decade has been over the
necessity of re-establishing classicist principles in terms of
adult offenders (e.g. N. Morris, 1974; Fogel, 1975) and in the
juvenile courts (e.g. A. Morris, 1978).

(A) Human Nature

Although free will may not exist perfectly, the criminal law
is largely based upon its presumed vitality and forms the
only foundation for penal sanctions. (Fogel, 1975, p.183)

Within classicism, human nature is concurred as rational, free
and governed by self-interest. Human beings are considered
'equal' in that they are all endowed with free-will and with the
faculty of Reason. When cast in this universal framework, the
theory disclaims distinctions of birth and aristocratic lineage,
making its claims in the name of universal Man. In terms of its
origins, this fitted well with the rising ambitions and fortunes
of the emergent bourgeoisie who most fiercely espoused its

principles. In practice, significant sections of the population –
women, the labouring poor, the insane (even, at times, the
great majority) – have not been assumed to meet the criteria
of the full citizenship accorded only to the fully rational
individual. Such exceptions are justified on the grounds that
they are either *pre*-rational (e.g. children and juveniles) or
sub-rational (the aged and infirm). The precise constituency
of those excluded from the category of rational equals
varies historically. The issue was and continues to be politically
significant, since it related to the question of how far the
reform of the franchise should go in extending full citizenship
to the un-enfranchised.

There is a tension in the classicist conception of human
nature between the rational self and the pursuit of self-interest.
Using self-interest as a basic reference point in the analysis
of human motivation gave the theory a firm, realistic – perhaps
even materialistic – foundation: 'society' arose because the
self-interest of individuals in the security of life and property
over-rode the competitive drive to gain maximum advantage –
there was no need to posit some wider, 'social' instinct or
ideal. But, in order that individuals, all seeking to realise
their interests, did not bring society to ruin, self-interest had
to be tempered by Reason, which was something more than
mere 'rational calculation'. This tension was never adequately
resolved. Nevertheless, writers like Bentham believed that
the motivation to commit or not to commit a crime for personal
advantage could be so weighted – provided punishment was
sufficiently severe and certain – that 'choosing to obey the
law' would come to be seen as the most rational of the available
choices. Punishment – or, as he called it, the 'science of pain'
– should be so severe that the 'benefits' of crime were far
outweighed by its 'costs'. Classicists are little concerned with
the complexities of human motivation. They believed motivations
could be calculated and influenced by external, objective
arrangements.

(B) Social order
In the classicist conception, social order is based on the
Social Contract. In their view, society did not pre-date the
individual. Instead, individuals rationally calculated that they
could best secure their mutual advantage by 'contracting
together' to establish a sovereign state or power. In the face
of the threat from external conquest or the 'war of all against
all', they were prepared to sign away some part of their
sovereign liberties to 'the Sovereign', in return (the basis of
the contract) for the protection of person and property against
crime and usurpation. But they believed that this sovereign
power, the state, should play a limited role – accorded only
that power necessary to protect individuals' rights and liberties.
Coercion by the state should be limited to this minimum, based
on a consensus between rational citizens. The exercise of power

by the state is therefore justified only in so far as it satisfies the interests of its citizens by facilitating and maintaining justice – that is, by protecting the just rewards of labour and punishing justly those who offended against this order. In a modified form, this conception of a social order based on the Social Contract continues to be influential in contemporary thought and, together with the emphasis on the individual's rights and civil liberties and the doctrine of the limited state (itself constrained by the 'rule of law') forms the cornerstones of modern legal and constitutional traditions within the liberal perspective.

The classicist conception of social order assumed, of course, the formal equality of status between all individuals who merited the honour of full citizenship. However, the emphasis on private property, on the just rewards for entrepreneurial skill and the 'right' to accumulate wealth produced an actual social structure in which the basis of rights and benefits was very unequally distributed throughout society. This formal universalism underpinned the notion that 'all men' should be equal under the 'rule of law'. Classicism, however, failed both in theory and practice to square the significant divergencies between *formal* and *substantive* equality.

The rights which the law protected stemmed from and, ultimately, reverted to the individual citizens – the foundation stone of social order. Consent, once given, could also be withdrawn (though classicists differ as to the conditions under which the overthrow of the Sovereign or state is justified). In this sense, the bourgeois classes who subscribed to 'social contract' doctrine remained faithful to the Whig Revolutionary tradition that had overthrown the absolute monarchy in the 1640s – though they were rapidly gaining ascendency in the new social order which emerged in the wake of the Hanoverian settlement.

(C) Definition of crime

Crime is defined as that which violates the Social Contract: in this definition, behaviour which is detrimental, not to the state as such, but to the personal safety and property of those individuals in society whose decision to 'contract in' founded the authority of the state. This, and not the question of whether such behaviour is widespread or 'normal', is the main criterion. Thus, for Social Contract theorists, tax-evasion might be widespread and generally condoned as 'normal', but it would be necessary to legislate against it because it is anti-social and against social justice as they defined it. For them, 'legal' rather than 'natural' definitions are paramount in the definition of crime. They do not, therefore, subscribe to relativist conceptions of crime. They concentrate, not on circumstances and influences, but on the criminal *act* itself. If illegal, judged as the law defines it in the light of the Social Contract, then the act should be punished proportionally – with unwavering

certainty, severity and impartiality. Neither the arbitrary
exercise of terror nor the discretionary application of justice –
so much a feature of judicial administration under the ancien
régime or discretionary justice as practised in the modern
courts – are acceptable to them.

The law, however, though certain and predictable, should
not be involved in the control of any activities which do not
harm others, do not contradict their self-interest or threaten
the Social Contract. From this stems the long tradition in Anglo-
Saxon law that, far from prescribing what the individual can
and cannot do, it allows citizens to be free to do anything they
like, provided only it is not proscribed by law. Liberty was
sovereign: subject only to the law's constraints. Thus the
law should not be extended to so-called 'consensual crimes' –
crimes which are 'without identifiable victims' (e.g. prostitution, as it is viewed from their highly masculine-oriented
world). Law and morality should be regarded as separate
spheres: the one regulating public concerns, the sphere of
the social contract; the other, the proper sphere of individual
judgment and private reasoning. The civilised state is that
which defines the minimal number of activities as crimes, and
which permits moral diversity and individual variation – provided only that the Social Contract is protected.

(D) The extent and distribution of crime
Crime is the infringement of a *legal code*, not of a behavioural
or social norm. The only acceptable method of ascertaining
whether a particular act is, in fact, 'criminal' is *within* the
legal process – that is, by 'due process of law'. 'Due process'
was a founding conception of classicism because it preserved
the rights of an ascendent class against the arbitrary exercise
of justice and coercion by the state. Provided 'due process'
is observed, and the certainty of detection improved (classicists strongly favour a regular and improved police), the
criminal statistics can be taken as an accurate guide as to the
true extent of criminality in a society. As Paul Tappan forcefully puts it (1970, p.47):

> The behavior prohibited has been considered significantly
> in derogation of group welfare by deliberative and repre-
> sentative assembly, formally constituted for the purpose of
> establishing such norms; nowhere else in the field of social
> control is there directed a comparable rational effort to ela-
> borate standards conforming to the predominant needs,
> desires and interests of the community ...
> Adjudicated offenders represent the closest possible
> approximation to those who have in fact violated the law,
> carefully selected by the sieving of the due process of the
> law; no other province of social control attempts to ascer-
> tain the breach of norms with such rigor and precision.

This process of adjudication by due legal procedures represents
the judgment by the court, not only as to whether in fact the

act was committed by an individual, but - of crucial importance
to classicism - whether the individual intended to commit the
act, whether the accused was in his or her right mind (*mens
rea*) and could thus be held responsible for his or her actions
as a rational individual.

(E) Causes of crime

In the classicist paradigm, the whole conception of the 'causes
of crime' relates to the question of rational motivation. Within
the consensual majority, where Reason and self-interest are
in a proper balance and the 'costs' of crime clearly outweigh
the 'benefits', no one should ideally be tempted to commit crime
since, by definition, this would be an *irrational* calculation. But
for the labouring poor of the nineteenth century, for example,
many instances could be conceived where 'benefits' were greater
than 'costs', and crime was the result of a rational calculation -
though harmful to the Social Contract. For this reason, punishment is at the centre of the classicist conception of justice:
through legislation and the reform of penal regimes, punishment
must be made so strict that the individual would be deterred
from committing crime again.

To this rational calculus, significant exceptions are made,
along the continuum of Reason. Rationality in its full sense -
and hence full responsibility - could not be present where
Reason is impaired (e.g. insanity) or where no 'intent' can be
shown (accident). Somewhat against the main thrust of this
thinking, certain marginal exceptions through mitigating
circumstances can also be allowed as marginal excuses (e.g.
under duress or provocation). Even so, they are attributed
to errors or absence of Reason, rather than to the positive
force of circumstances. The source of criminality is thus located
within the rational, 'reasoning' individual.

Nevertheless, unsatisfactory laws, or a legal system lacking
clear principles, can create crimes which should never be
labelled as such, and unjust laws or inequitable punishments
can exacerbate the extent of crime. The systematisation and
proportionality of law and punishment - the reforms which the
classicists champion - are supported as much for these as for
more strictly 'humanitarian' reasons.

(F) Policy

Principles guiding the decision to imprison should be these:
  1. *Parsimony*: the least restrictive (punitive) sanction
     necessary to achieve defined social purposes should be
     imposed.
  2. *Dangerousness*: prediction of future criminality should
     be rejected as a base for determining that the convicted
     criminal should be imprisoned.
  3. *Desert*: no sanction should be imposed greater than
     that which is 'deserved' by the last crime, or series
     of crimes, for which the offender is being

sentenced. (N. Morris, 1974, p.xi)

Here we will suggest that the law should deal only with a narrow aspect of the individual, that is, his criminal act or acts. We will urge that the law be applied uniformly to all offenders. We will spell out our principles of restraint, urging that criminal sanctions be imposed only when other remedies have proved inadequate.

The whole person is not the concern of the law. Whenever the law considers the whole person it is more likely that it considers factors irrelevant to the purpose of delivering punishment. The other factors, by and large, have been and will certainly continue to be characteristics related to influence, power, wealth, and class. They will not be factors related to the needs or the treatment potentialities of the defendant. (American Friends Service Committee, 1971, pp.146-7)

The central focus of classicist criminal policy is the criminal act itself. Criminals must 'choose' within the certain knowledge of detection - hence the requirement of a modernised and regular police force. Punishment must bear down directly on the responsibilities and calculations of the individual. Since the purpose of punishment is *not* to inflict arbitrary pain, or to make public retribution, but so to arrange things as to make obeying the law the most rational of choices, punishment must be made proportional to the actual social harm it causes, and limited to only that required to deter further criminal acts. Previous convictions of the actor are to be judged irrelevant to the particular act being judged by judicial process, since he or she must be punished only in relation to the specific action for which an accusation has been laid. The notion of using punishment to make a *general* example is anathema to classicism: the process must bear directly on the individual and the act. General deterrence puts the principle of social order (a subordinate or derived principle, a classicist doctrine) *above* that of justice to the individual (the sovereign or founding principle). Classicism is, of course, concerned to preserve the Social Contract: but, it argued, the most effective way of doing this is through the resolute pursuit of individual justice. Within 'due process', there should be a strict defence of the individual's legal rights - classicism strongly defends the 'presumption of innocence', for example. This concern for 'due judicial process' extends to the proportionate penalties in sentencing. Bentham hoped for a strict 'economy' of punishment - penalties and sentences strictly proportional to the offence. Thus modern neo-classicists strongly favour a fixed 'tariff system' of sentencing, as against the more discretionary system which prevails in, for example, English and American courts at this moment. (American Friends Service Committee, 1971, p.124):

We submit that many distortions and corruptions of justice -

such as the discriminatory use of penal sanctions and the
use of the criminal justice system to promote conformity
and control classes of person – depend upon the existence
of wide margins of discretionary power in the hands of
police, district attorneys, judges, correctional administrators, parole boards, and parole agents. Therefore, discretion is at the core of the problem.

According to the principles of legal equality, crimes should
be judged by a jury of one's peers – that is, by other rational
and equal individuals. Judges should be guided by a clear and
systematic legal code. And sentencing should be limited to
applying a prior, agreed and fixed set of penalties – a tariff
system – equally across the board, allowing only minor adjustments and discretions for 'mitigating circumstances'. Thus
(Fogel, 1975, p.254):

We propose to inform the convict at the outset of the penalties for his crime. We would replace the present law with
a series of determinate sentences, keyed to the present
felony classification system. For each felony class, a fixed
sentence is proposed, with a narrow range in mitigation or
aggravation allowed around that definite figure to permit
adjustments either for the facts of a particular case or for
the seriousness of the offense as compared to others in the
same class. In effect, then, a relatively small range of
allowable prison terms would be associated with each offense.
Whenever the court found imprisonment to be the appropr-
riate disposition, it would select a fixed sentence from within
that range and impose it. When a convicted person left the
courtroom, he would know his actual sentence to be served
less good time.

Neither inappropriate leniency nor undue harshness are
permissible in the classicist economy of punishment. The first
fails to achieve its effect; the latter introduces a personal and
emotional element into a system which should be rational and
impartial. Punishment should therefore be strictly applied,
irrespective of the status or background of the accused, but
also applied efficiently and effectively. Bentham, indeed, hoped
to impose within the new penal regimes a very strict criterion
of efficiency and cost-accounting: he was, for example, in
favour of prisons which 'paid', but of regular public inspection
as well. Punishment should be seen to be 'just' – but it should
also be strict, regular and disciplined. Justice should be doled
out without delay and to the maximum of offenders the police
can apprehend. The law is an instrument, not only of control,
but also of education. And 'educating the public' into the
calculus of law-abidingness requires that irregularities, due
to either lack of detection or evasion of penalties or irrational
prison regimes, should be eliminated. Any deviation from strict
disciplinary uniformity simply encourages crime, either through
ineffective control or by propagating injustices which cause
citizens to question the justice and impartiality of the Social

Contract. In particular, modern classicists have directed their wrath against the prison regime on two counts: that prison life does not embody principles of justice and/or that it attempts to treat the individual rather than to punish him. David Fogel notes this in two of the central parts in his demands for justice (1975, p.184):

The entire process of the criminal law must be played out in a milieu of justice. Justice-as-fairness represents the super-ordinate goal of all agencies of the criminal law.

When correction becomes mired in the dismal swamp of preaching, exhorting, and treating ('resocialization') it becomes dysfunctional as an agency of justice. Correctional agencies should engage prisoners as the law otherwise dic-tates - as responsible, volitional and aspiring human beings.

Thus N. Morris notes sadly: 'The prison should, were the world not full of paradox, be a very paradigm of the rule of law' (1974, p.21). Instead, due process ends at the point of imprisonment and the prison has become a lawless institution. The lawful educational role of the lawful prison is viewed by David Fogel as the central keynote of the neo-classicist 'justice model' (1977, pp.126-7):

The period of incarceration can be conceptualized as a time in which we try to reorient a prisoner to the lawful use of power. One of the more fruitful ways the prison can teach nonlaw-abiders to be law-abiding is to treat them in a lawful manner. The entire effort of the prison should be seen as an influence attempt based upon operationalizing justice. This is called the 'justice model.'

It is a sad irony in our system of criminal justice that we insist on the full majesty of due process for the accused until he is sentenced to a prison, then justice is said to have been served. The entire case for a justice model rests upon the need to continue to engage the person in the quest for jus-tice as he moves on the continuum from defendant-to-convict-to-free citizen.

Nor is justice achieved in the modern prison by instituting seemingly progressive treatment or rehabilitation processes. For these involve a dishonesty which conceals disproportionate punishment. (American Friends Service Committee, 1971, p.24):

Thus the sleight of hand that transforms prisons into some-thing else, such as 'civil institutions' for addicts and re-formatories for juvenile delinquents, does not alter the coer-cive reality....

We believe there is much to be gained from honesty in our semantics. By characterizing all penal coercion as punishment, we emphasize rather than dilute the critical necessity of limit-ing it as much as possible.

Thus it is the twin obstacles to justice of arbitrary punishment or scientific treatment which classicism opposes.

PROBLEMS OF CLASSICISM

The classicist contradiction

The principal contradiction at the heart of classicism has already
been indicated. It is, in essence, the contradiction between
formal and substantive equality. Classicism assumes that all
'men' are free, rational and equal. An impartial and universal
system of justice can operate 'rationally' in such circumstances, where none has priority of rank or status, and no
prior handicaps or advantages. But the real world does not
in any way resemble this ideal model. Indeed, it cannot by
definition, since classicism is rooted in a competitive model
of man, where seeking advantage is precisely the most
rational of motivations; and the principal purpose of the Social
Contract is to defend the rights and liberties of 'men', above
all the liberty to employ the labour of others, to acquire property and accumulate wealth. These generate, as the necessary consequence of a competitive system, massively unequal
distribution of advantages and disadvantages. But classicism
attempts to abstract from these real material conditions, and
to posit a state of formal equality. It has therefore constantly to confront all the contradictions that flow from a legal
philosophy based on formal equality which is required to
operate 'justly' in conditions of substantive inequality. Many of
the other problems in classicism flow from this central contradiction.

The necessity of punishment

If men are free, sovereign and rational, and the contract
just, we may ask why individuals persist in violating the law
at all? Should not Reason regularly prevail? The fact that it
does not, necessitating just and swift, but also extensive and
severe, punishment, means that the motivations and incentives
to commit crime are arising from some aspect of society not
accounted for within the rationalist calculus. One source is that
very structure of substantive inequalities which the paradigm
finds so difficult to explain or take into account. Another may
be that the Social Contract is, in reality, more 'just' for some
than it is for others - the others being, perhaps, the majority
of those lacking an advantageous position within the system.
The premise that what is good and just for individuals corresponds to the 'collective good' is assumed, not demonstrated.

The pyramid of crime

If all individuals are equally endowed with Reason, why is the
incidence of criminal irrationalities not random? Why do the
statistics take the shape of that pyramid shown in Fig.14.1,
with the poor regularly committing so much more crime than
the rich? Perhaps, in the light of this, formal equality is a
sham, imposing a form of legal fairness on a system which
regularly generates substantive inequalities: a world where,

as Anatole France cynically put it, the 'law in all its majesty forbids both the rich and poor from sleeping under the bridges of the Seine'. Both may be equal 'in the sight of the law' - but nowhere else.

The problem of rational abstraction

Many of the problems with classicism derive from its tendency to abstract out the individual act from its circumstantial conditions and contexts. This tendency parallels that of attempting to isolate formal equality from its substantive circumstances. But men and women rarely make such strictly isolated individual calculations into which no trace of surrounding conditions enter. It is not only that we often act 'irrationally'. It is also that what is and is not 'rational' depends on the prevailing conditions and the circumstances from which calculations about human actions are made. Goals are very rarely formed in a void; and they are hardly ever motivated by pure self-interest. Classicists tend to resolve all these factors into the general faculty of Reason, but apart from a sort of built-in philosophical guarantee, they produce no convincing explanation of what this general faculty is or where it came from or how it modifies and tempers the competitive drive to self-advantage. Moreover, though they claim a universal Reason, their actual social calculations are based on a highly particular and differentiated notion of which groups in society are endowed with this universal faculty. In fact, it has often excluded a wide range of people in the population - the vast majority, including the lower orders and outcasts of society, women and children. They speak of Reason and Men as abstract universals, but they often mean the reasons of a very particular and limited number of particular men.

The problem of equivalence

In particular, no matter how one tries in abstract reasoning, in concrete terms, it is impossible to squeeze 'equivalence' out of the poor, who were clearly not equal. Beccaria himself touched upon the problem when he attempted to elaborate a punishment suitable for robbery (1801, pp.80-1):

He who endeavours to enrich himself with the property of another, should be deprived of part of his own. But this crime, alas! is commonly the effect of misery and despair - the crime of that unhappy part of mankind, to whom the right of exclusive property (a terrible and perhaps unnecessary right) has left but a bare existence. Besides as pecuniary punishments may increase the number of robbers, by increasing the number of poor, and may deprive an innocent family of subsistence, the most proper punishment will be that kind of slavery, which alone can be called just; that is, which makes society, for a time, absolute master of the person, and labour of the criminal, in order to oblige him to repair, by this dependence, the unjust despotism he

usurped over the property of another, and his violation
of the social compact.
Thus equivalence is impossible to squeeze out of the poor -
indeed any attempt makes matters worse. Thus, the classicist
justification of imprisonment arises as a solution to this problem
of how to extract equivalence out of those who possess no
property. Namely, that we equate the extent of property violation with its equivalence in time, and deprive the person of
his or her liberty proportionally. But, however, ingenious
Beccaria's formulation and its repeated invocation through the
centuries, it scarcely solves the problem of the impoverished
dependents. For imprisonment likewise increases the number
of poor but, more than this, by stigmatising the prisoner, it
often denies him future employment, thus exacerbating his
poverty. The equivalent formal punishment has, therefore,
real substantive consequences in the lives of the offender and
his dependents. For whereas the rich offender may be cushioned
by his or her wealth, the poor offender, with the *same* sentence but little to fall back on, is punished *in fact* disproportionately.

POSITIVISM

We speak two different languages. For us, the experimental
(i.e. inductive) method is the key to all knowledge; to them
everything derives from logical deductions and traditional
opinion. For them, facts should give place to syllogisms; for
us the fact governs and no reasoning can occur without
starting with facts, for them science needs only paper, pen
and ink and the rest comes from a brain stuffed with more
or less abundant reading of books made with the same ingre-
dients. For us science requires spending a long time in examining the facts one by one, evaluating them, reducing them
to a common denominator, extracting the central idea from
them. For them a syllogism or an anecdote suffices to demo-
lish a myriad of facts gathered through years of observation
and analysis; for us the reverse is true (Ferri, 1901, p.244)

Psychology is no longer a subsidiary of philosophy, it refers
no longer on common sense reflections of life, or on armchair
theorizing; by becoming experimental it has made the first
faltering steps towards becoming scientific ... Admittedly
these theories are much less powerful than those of physics,
or astronomy, or chemistry, and they command less universal
agreement; nevertheless they cannot be dismissed out of
hand as useless and premature. Consider how quickly the
older and more mature sciences outgrew their earlier theories,
and how, almost unnoticed, they changed the face of the
world. Psychology has set out on the same road, and sooner
or later society will have to take heed of its views....

Sooner or later, society will have to replace its happy-go-lucky, unreasoning ways of dealing with offenders by rational, scientific methods, firmly founded on painstaking observation and empirically-based theory; three thousand years of failure to solve the problem of crime would suggest even to the most conservative that the old ways might not be the best!
(Eysenck, 1977, pp.212-13)

Emerging in the nineteenth century, positivism attempted, under the influence of Darwinism, to carry through a radical change in the conception of man's place in nature. For just as Darwin's theories served to displace the human species out of the unique category of a divine creation into the wider evolutionary context of life on this planet, positivism's task was to show that human behaviour was understandable by the same scientific laws that governed all living activity. This 'positivist revolution' has seen a continuing struggle against 'metaphysical', 'pre-scientific' conceptions of human behaviour - in particular as represented by classicism and its notions of human rationality, equality and free-will.

Positivism's major attribute - from which its major characteristics may all be deduced - is in its insistence on the unity of the scientific method. That is, the premises and instruments which are so demonstrably successful in the study of the physical world and of animal biology are seen to be of equal validity and promise in the study of society and humans. Insisting on this premise, positivists have proceeded to propound methods for the quantification of behaviour, to acclaim the objectivity of the scientific expert and to assert the determinate, law-governed nature of human action. In so doing, positivist criminology creates almost a mirror image of classicism: free-will disappears under determinancy, equality bows before natural differences and expert knowledge, and human laws that are created become scientific laws that are discovered.

There have been many varieties of positivism both in criminology and in the social sciences in general. The particular version I wish to focus on in this section is by far the most prominent example, both in positivist theory and in practice. This theory admits that biological, physiological, psychological and social influences all contribute to the creation of the criminal but that it is in the *individual* that the fundamental predisposition to crime is situated. Furthermore, that the social order is consensual and that crime is a product of the under-socialisation of the individual into this consensus. This type of positivism - what could be termed individual positivism - is the focus of this analysis. It owes its prominence not only to its theoretical dominance but, even more, because it is the paramount type of theory used by practitioners. I will refer to other varieties of positivism at the end of this section.

(A) *Human nature*

I think the major objection to the proposals I have outlined

> is that they smack of treating human beings as if they were
> nothing but biological organisms subject to strictly deter-
> ministic rules; this Pavlovian revolution, coming on top of
> the Copernican and Darwinian ones, is too much for the self-
> esteem of many people. Undesirable the fact may be, but that
> is not sufficient reason for rejecting it as a fact, one would
> need better reasons to change one's scientific judgment. And
> where there is (1) a recognised social need, and (2) a recog-
> nised body of scientific knowledge which looks likely to be
> able to create a technology to cope with that need, it needs
> little in the way of precognitive ability to forecast that in due
> course society will use this knowledge and create this tech-
> nology. (Eysenck, 1969, p.190)

All individual behaviour - however much this may violate human
conceit - is a determined product of circumstances. Human
beings have a basic animal nature which is more or less socialised
into the values of society so that the line from the criminal to
the law-abiding citizen is a continuum of degrees of socialisation. Therefore it is not a question of the 'criminal' and the
'normal' existing as separate categories of humanity but rather
of everyone being a determined being, the major variable being
the degree and efficacy of socialisation.

(B) Social order
Individual positivists would hold that there is a consensus in
society which corresponds to the needs of the system. That is
the values into which individuals are socialised are necessary
to the orderly maintenance of the total society. Coercion should
be limited to a minimum of cases where recalcitrant, 'undersocialised' individuals refuse to recognise their problems and
are unwilling to be integrated into society.

To the positivist, the classicist contradiction between substantive and formal equality is a fiction based on the preposterous assumption of formal equality. People are substantially different - not in the sense of status - but in terms of
their individual abilities and degree of socialisation. Here
again, as with determinism, there is much resistance to scientific reality (Eysenck, 1977, p.75):

> This general attitude is often supported by reference to
> political notions. It is said that all men are born equal and
> it is deduced from this that indeed all men have the same
> innate ability, the same good or poor degree of personality,
> the same propensity to crime, and so on. This, of course,
> is a misinterpretation of the old saying. What it means is
> simply that all men are equal before the law ... It does not
> say anything whatsoever about their strength, their health,
> or other features in which they may differ from each other,
> and in which, as we know perfectly well, they do in fact
> differ. However, the fact that this is a misunderstanding
> has in no way lessened the impact of the saying on the
> great majority of people who are strongly convinced that

any innate differences in ability or in propensity to crime
would set some kind of limit to the working of modern democracy.
In reality, an individual's final place in the social order reflects
more or less the compound of his or her potentiality and the
social skills which have been inculcated into them.

(C) Definition of crime
A hallmark of such positivism is the belief that there is a consensus of value in society that can be scientifically ascertained.
Against this it can be judged whether an act is deviant or not.
The word 'deviant' is preferable to 'criminal', as the latter
merely refers to violations of legal codes which (a) may not
reflect consensual values at all (e.g. tax-evasion as normal
behaviour), (b) do not encompass all acts of deviance (e.g.
sexual promiscuity may be deviant but perfectly legal), or
(c) are based on legal concepts which are unscientific reflecting metaphysical concepts of free-will and intent (i.e. they are
classicist).

(D) The extent and distribution of crime
However much the positivists would be sceptical of the crime
statistics in that they are a product of an unscientific conceptualisation collected in a process which is unsystematic
and non-exhaustive, they would not doubt their basic pyramidal shape and the variations indicated between different
groups of people. That is, that the incidence of crime is indeed
greater among blacks than whites, young than old, male than
female, and is inversely proportional to class and education.
Thus they would regard the official statistics as 'poor' data,
yet data of relevance all the same. Whatever his or her scientific scruples, it is a rare positivist who will not make direct
use of the criminal statistics.

(E) Causes of crime
Every crime is the resultant of individual, physical and
social conditions. (Ferri, 1893, p.161)
Crime is a product of the undersocialisation of the individual.
This can be a result of (a) an innate genetic or physiological
incapacity of the individual to be easily socialised; (b) a family
background which was ineffective in the use of socialisation
techniques in its child-rearing practices; (c) a social milieu
which lacked coherent and consistent consensual values. Each
of these levels - the physical, the family and the social - will
be seen to compound with each, to determine the socialisation
of a specific individual. And it is noted that it is at the very
bottom of the class structure, where the incidence of crime is
greatest, that such 'defects' are most likely to occur. For it
is there that the least capable individuals accumulate and pass
on their inadequacies from generation to generation in a cycle
of deprivation.

The causes of crime are thus rooted in defects in the past of the actor, in his or her determined antecedents. Crime itself is a reflection of these; as a product of undersocialisation it is an activity without meaning, a non-rational outburst of pre-social impulses.

None of this falls into the trap of suggesting that the *direction* or *shape* that crime takes is a biological pre-given. As Hans Eysenck astutely notes (1977, pp.77, 79):

criminality is a social concept, not a biological one. Indeed, what is criminal in one country may not be criminal in another; homosexuality is a crime in some American states but not in Germany. Similarly, what is a crime at one time may not be at another. It is a crime to kill people but only in peace time; during war time it becomes a citizen's duty to kill others ...

The very notion of criminality or crime would be meaningless without a context of learning or social experience and, quite generally, of human interaction. What the figures have demonstrated is that heredity is a very strong predisposing factor as far as committing crimes is concerned. But the actual way in which the crime is carried out, and whether or not the culprit is found and punished - these are obviously subject to the changing vicissitudes of everyday life. It would be meaningless to talk about the criminality or otherwise of a Robinson Crusoe, brought up and always confined by himself on a desert island. It is only in relation to society that the notion of criminality and of predisposition to crime has any meaning. While recognizing therefore, the tremendous power of heredity, we would by no means wish to suggest that environmental influences cannot also be very powerful and important indeed.

The criminal or deviant would be a rule-breaker in any culture - he would be a pacifist during wartime, an aggressor during peace. It is not necessary, therefore, for the positivist to explain the content of the norms that are violated, merely the propensity of the individual to violate them.

(F) Policy

The classical school exhort men to study justice; the positivist school exhorts justice to study men. (Hamel, 1906, p.265)

The criminal justice of the future, administered by judges who have sufficient knowledge, not of Roman or civil law, but of psychology, anthropology and psychiatry, will have for its sole task to determine if the defendant is the material author of the established crime; and instead of brilliant logomachies by the prosecution and the defence in an effort to trick one another, there will be a scientific discussion on the personal and social condition of the offender in order to classify him in one or another anthropological class to which

one or another form of indeterminate segregation will apply.
(Ferri, 1901, p.229)

If the criminal is determined and not responsible for his or
her actions, it makes no sense to punish cr¹me. Instead, we
must replace punishment by *treatment*. We must substitute for
the jury system of lay people a panel of experts who diagnose
the condition of the *individual* and prescribe the appropriate
treatment. The punitive response, as advocated by classicist
and conservative theorists, is not only inapplicable, it actually
exacerbates the socialisation problems of the deviant.

Prognosis for the criminal is based not so much on what he
or she did (the *act*), not on who he or she is (the *actor*) but
on his or her background (the *antecedents*). The vandal may
cause £5 worth of damage or £50 worth, but to sentence him
proportionately to the impact of the act (as the classicists
would) is meaningless. What is necessary is to see if the
vandalism sprang from a deep-seated malaise of socialisation
or if it was the mere experimentation of a normal youth. And
once diagnosis is made, the criminal must be treated for as long
as is necessary. Sentences are therefore indeterminate, just
as one's stay in hospital is indeterminate, and based on satisfactory treatment or 'cure' rather than on the fixed sentences
of the classicists. Rehabilitation rather than punishment must
be our priority. But to achieve this, it will be necessary to
discard outmoded prejudices and thinking. As Hans Eysenck
stridently put it (1977, p.213):

> Modern psychology holds out to society an altogether dif-
> ferent approach to criminality, an approach geared only to
> practical ends, such as the elimination of antisocial conduct,
> and not cluttered with irrelevant, philosophical, retributory
> and ethico-religious beliefs ... We have now reached the
> point where we can hope to combat crime effectively; shall
> we have the courage and the wisdom to give up our ancient
> hates and fears, and grasp the opportunity?

PROBLEMS OF POSITIVISM

The denial of authenticity

By asserting that deviancy is a non-rational, determinate
product of undersocialisation, the positivists take all human
volition and meaning away from activity. For example, they
would argue that in advanced capitalist societies, as property
ownership is the central cultural concern, then those who are
undersocialised will be thieves. In Puritan New England, on
the other hand, religious norms were paramount, and the undersocialised were adulterers and blasphemers. The danger here
lies in stressing a consensual culture when all deviation
is simply attributed to lack of socialisation. In reality the conflict over property in Western capitalism is not a function of
lack of culture; it relates to the inequitable distribution of

property in such societies. Sometimes such a conflict can be a
result of a fully-formed oppositional culture (e.g. revolutionary
socialism) or by an alternative culture which despises property
(e.g. bohemian countercultures). More often, it will involve
people accepting the dominant culture of success - yet, as they
have limited opportunities to acquire property, taking up
illegitimate means to achieve it (e.g. as depicted in strain
theory, see below) or accepting the prevalent culture of
individualism and engaging in a no-holds-barred competition
with their fellows ('the cult of the individual'). In all these
instances deviance is *cultural*, whether it is a deviant culture
set against the wider culture, or the dominant culture itself
encouraging deviance. One might not like the particular cultural
manifestation, but that is another thing; it is not sufficient
to label it a product of undersocialisation. Thus human deviance
may be the result of:

Alternative value systems - contradictions in value, cynicism
or hesitances about official values. Because positivism ignores
human choice and creativity it becomes myopic to the diverse
ways in which human beings cope with a given environment and
the different cultures which they create in response to it.

The normal criminal - Acceptance of the dominant culture of
success may exacerbate feelings of frustration as regards one's
lot in life, and acceptance of the cult of individualism may
encourage aggressive competition. Both these may lead to crime
- but not only in the lower reaches of society. For studies
of unreported crime invariably indicate that crime is widespread
throughout the social structure (see Pearce, 1976; Reiman,
1979). This suggests that it is not merely the 'undersocialised'
lower reaches of society which engender crime but also the
'socialised' top of the pyramid. This endemic deviancy would
point to the conclusion that the total society might be 'pathological' in positivist terms. That, for example, there might be
a close link between an acquisitive society and theft; between
patriarchal sexist values and rape. It is 'normal' socialisation,
then, that may lead to crime.
    Both these instances suggest that the equation utilised by
positivism, namely that crime equals the consensual society
defining the rules and the predisposed individual breaking
them, is woefully inadequate.

Denial of the classicist contradiction
By putting such an emphasis on the predisposed individual
as the source of crime, positivism defuses the problem of the
classicist contradiction. Thus it translates a major problem
of capitalist order - how to cope with the conflict between
the ideals of equal competition and the reality of unequal property distribution - into a function of the inequality of
individuals. No matter whether one agrees with such competition

or not, it is obvious that limitations in social mobility, access
to educational opportunities, differentially distributed career
prospects, etc., constantly belie the reality of such a meritocratic competition. It is substantive differences in *social* opportunities, as well as in individual capacities, that structure the
actual material possibilities constraining individuals in our
society. The insistence on equality in classicist thought is not
a mere metaphysical mistake - rather it is an ideal which is
constantly undermined by the reality of capitalist society.

Denial of freedom
The stress on determination denies the alternative possibilities
facing the majority of human beings at each juncture of their
lives. For although *total* determination is a human possibility,
for example in the case of a heavily tranquillised prisoner in
a high security prison, choices nearly always remain. Such an
overstress on determinacy denies the role of consciousness
in standing back and creating and assessing the means of
interpreting and manoeuvring a particular set of material conditions. For example, even if it is absolutely correct that there
is a high correlation between, for example, lower-working-class
backgrounds and delinquency, this does not imply that the
background *causes* delinquency. It merely implies that people
in such an underprivileged determinant position in our type
of society tend at a particular time to create a culture of
delinquency as a means of attempting to cope with their predicament. Sometimes, in fact, these cultural responses to
given conditions can rapidly change, witness the politicisation
of prisoners at Attica, or the way in which particular individuals
in their 'moral career' can explore different cultural means
of understanding their position. For example, note how individuals such as Malcolm X moved from being a thief, to being a
Black Muslim, to becoming a revolutionary, seeking actively
to understand and surmount his problems as a ghetto black.
    To prove that there are correlations between certain deter-
minant positions and certain types of crimes (e.g. company
directors and corporate tax-evasion) does not take meaning
away from these activities, it merely provides us with the facts
which we have to explain in terms of human choice and meaning.
    This is not to deny that human beings confront material
determinants which are experienced in the same way as the laws
of the natural sciences.

Varieties of positivism: a critical comment
At the close of this section there is an important comment to
be made which applies throughout the article. As noted in the
introduction, one of our tasks is to examine the inconsistencies
of structure in a theory. Now although the particular version
of positivism we have examined is often presented as an internally coherent structure, that is, in fact, debatable. For
example, starting from the central premise of the unity of

scientific method, it is frequently assumed that the other
characteristics of the theory are logically deducible - for
example, that human action is determined and that there is a
consensus of value in society. Now it is difficult to imagine a
positivist criminology which does not assume human behaviour
is determined - for it is not then predictably determined and
scientific laws are inappropriate. But it is quite possible to
imagine a positivism which denies the consensual nature of
social order. Indeed such positions exist, for example:

Radical positivism - where the total society is seen to be
disintegrating and a multiplicity of emerging cultures are
occurring to challenge the old order. In this instance some
types of crime could be construed as a 'healthy' innovative
adaption to a pathological society (see Taylor, Walton and Young,
1973, pp.14-19).

A pluralistic positivism - By a scientific survey of cultural
norms, a positivist may come to the conclusion that there
empirically exists in society a variety of normative standards.
Indeed some of these subcultures may seem to be supportive
of criminal behaviour. That is, a type of *sociological* positivism
may emerge which argues that, in these cultures, it is the
socialised, well-adjusted individual who is the criminal (e.g.
Miller, 1958).
   It is important to note, then, that certain aspects of the
above critique strike at the heart of positivist theory, whereas
others merely represent a critique of the specific variety presented here. Thus to argue that positivism denies the possibility
of a plurality of value applies only to species of 'individual
positivism', presented above, whereas criticisms regarding the
denial of human volition apply to the total spectrum of positivist
theories of human behaviour.

CONSERVATISM

A third approach that is often encountered in public discussion about crime is conservatism. In fact, conservatism as a
body of opinion is less openly theoretical or systematic than
our other 'paradigms'. Conservatism is directed *against*
liberalism and reformism, and its essentially pragmatic character
is a consequence of protracted historical resistance to the
reforming impulse. But the success of conservative arguments
also depends on their ability to convey a *positive* sense of
traditional, hierarchical forms of social organisation. In contrast to the 'golden age' of established values, proposals for
reform appear 'subversive' in the conservative scenario, and
the more radical the proposals are, the more dangerous and
'anarchic' they appear.
   It should be said that conservatism (with a little 'c') is not

co-terminus with Conservatism in its party-political sense. It is very likely (but not necessary) that Tory parties will offer variations on the basic conservative themes; but the latter might embrace other political views in specific circumstances, or form a part of 'common sense'.

(A) Human nature
The image of human nature in conservative theory is *homo duplex*. In this it is similar to classicism and positivism. In all three theories, an instinctual nature is directly opposed to a social self, but in each theory the resolution of this tension has a different status. In classicism, Reason is tempered by just punishment, while in positivism the conflict is analysed deterministically, and treated in terms of 'normal' socialisation. Conservative thought is distinctive in that it involves a voluntaristic notion of human action such that the tension remains potentially unresolved: the 'old Adam' remains within most of us, poised to break through the veneer of civilisation. However, we are also endowed with free choice and powers of restraint, and the responsible, fully social person must continually mobilise these human capacities in order to control the lower urges. Sacrifice, discipline and the submission to authority become, in this context, the foundations of conservative philosophy.

(B) Social order
Conservative theory arose as a reaction against the ideas of the French Revolution. Thus it has always stressed the organic nature of society, defending the traditional order against the individualism and rationalism of the emerging bourgeoisie (Nisbet, 1970, p.11):
   From conservatism's defence of social tradition sprang its emphasis on the values of community, kinship, hierarchy, authority and religion, and also its premonitions of social chaos surmounted by absolute power once individuals had become wrenched from the context of those values by the forces of liberalism and radicalism.
The evolution of human institutions goes beyond individual desires and Reason. Reason in itself, especially when harnessed to the egoism of individual desires, can lead directly to social disintegration. For social cohesion to be maintained, self-interest must be subordinated to the general good. However, unlike the liberal classicist approach, conservatives do not see the general good as being a contractual agreement. Conceptions of the family and of marriage are indicative here, and they also serve to remind us that, in several respects, conservatism is of current as well as of historical interest. For the conservative, the unity of the family, its harmonious but patriarchal structure, is a long-term social and moral good, transcending the vicissitudes of particular circumstances. Given liberal and classicist premises, the logic of marriage guidance

counselling is that it enables the parties rationally to re-draw
the terms of the marriage contract, thus re-establishing a
relationship between formally equal individuals. In the conservative vision, self-sacrifice and order, embodied in the family,
cannot be reduced to utilitarian calculations of individual
pleasure and pain, effort and reward.

In classicism, order is achieved through the pursuit of justice; in conservatism, the rational pursuit of fairness may be
thought to be counter-productive. Order must take precedence
over justice, for 'order is indispensable to justice because
justice can only be achieved by means of social and legal order'
(Haag, 1975, p.35). Van den Haag continues (p.46): 'objections to inequality of condition are objections as to the system
of distributive justice, unless they are objections to God.'

The author of 'Punishing Criminals' - the most forthright
presentation of a conservative criminology - notes how inequality
is a key part of our system. If we wish to maintain the capitalist
order then we must have inequality, since disproportionality
of reward is the most effective method of maintaining capitalism,
which is, in turn, held to be the most effective system of
production available to humanity. Such an order is therefore
ultimately in everyone's interests, and the short-term or
single-minded pursuit of individual justice must be seen as
being either naive or dangerous. Thus Van den Haag's clinical
dissection of the classicist contradiction (pp.45-6):

Since the law quite deliberately restricts the tempted, as
well as the untempted, there is a kernel of truth in the
belief, held by revolutionaries of various persuasions (most
elaborately by Marxists) that the law is a device of the rich
and powerful to keep the poor and powerless in check. The
threats of the law are meant to restrain those who would do
what the law prohibits. Obviously, the poor and powerless
are more tempted to take what is not theirs, or to rebel,
than the powerful and wealthy, who need not take what they
already have.

However, the discovery that the penal law restrains the
poor and powerless more than the wealthy and powerful who
are less pressed, or tempted, to do what it forbids is about
as revealing as the disclosure that the Prohibition laws were
meant to restrain drinkers more than the teetotalers who
imposed them. Obviously, the law restrains some groups
more than others and is violated by some groups more often
than by others ... So because the temptation to break the
laws is unequally distributed, because of different personalities and different living conditions, the laws -- and the
punishments for violating them -- must weigh or fall most
heavily on some persons and groups. Those less favored by
society are more tempted to violate laws and therefore suffer
punishment for doing so more often.

Coercion is an inevitable part of the system, and its focus
must of necessity be on those most tempted, namely the poor.

(C) Definition of crime

For the conservative it is those activities which threaten order
that should be criminalised. In contrast to classicism, this
includes acts which offend morality as well as those which endanger person or property. For attacks on tradition and the
people's respect for authority are a considerable threat to an
orderly society. Hence the extraordinary focus of Conservative
ideologues on the threat of pornography. Thus Mary Whitehouse
writes about BBC programmes: 'there is a developing trend ...
to undercut authority that is undermining the morals of the
British people ... Sex and four-letter words are just the tip
of the iceberg. It is the constant attack on morals and authority
that concerns us', and again: 'Dirty books and sleazy films
are as much a danger to Britain as enemy agents' (cited in
Manson and Palmer, 1973, p.94).

(D) Extent and distribution of crime

As we have seen from the discussion on Van den Haag's book,
the pyramid of crime is no surprise to the conservative criminologist. It is to be expected that crime is sometimes very widespread, and that the poor are tempted to commit more crime
than the rich.

(E) Causes of crime

The following quotations, very different in style, capture the
'associational' quality of conservative diagnosis. They also
indicate that the concern for moral degeneration frequently
paraded in conservative thought, should not be thought separate from the support of an economic order requiring considerable material deprivation.

All these things are shaking our society to its very roots ...
The old discipline of mass unemployment and grinding poverty
has largely been eliminated. Family ties and family discipline
are loosening. The influence of religion on social behaviour
seems to be fading. The sense of personal obligation to
society has been dimmed and dulled in a world that is changing so fast and in a society grown so complex that the individual feels helpless to influence his own destiny. (Reginald
Maudling, cited in Gamble, 1974, p.111)

Through television we are encouraging on the consumption
side, things which are entirely inconsistent with the disciplines necessary for our production side. Look at what TV
advertising encourages: immediate gratification, do it now,
buy it now, pay later, leisure time, hedonism. (Anthony
Downs, Consultant to Lyndon Johnson's Riot Commission)

For the conservative, the causes of crime lie in the pursuit
of individual gratification (usually incommensurate with effort),
the undermining of traditional loyalties and the consequent
unwillingness of the individual to accept discipline. This weakening of the social ties - itself encouraged by the liberal tradition

of rational individualism, of which classicist criminology is part - is exacerbated by the fact that both classicist and positivist influences undermine the necessity for coercion in the preservation of order. Classicism presses for the strict determination of punishment, emphasising legal rights and due process. Positivism insists on treating the offender rather than attempting to subdue the recalcitrant by means of 'short, sharp shocks'.

(F) Policy
The central goal of conservative control policy is the maintenance of order. To achieve this aim coercion is a necessity. It is not a marginal or minimal phenomenon as in positivism or classicism, but rather a central part of social control which is undermined if any laxity in the exertion of authority occurs. Furthermore, it is due to the very nature of human beings that such coercion is necessary and always will be necessary. Crime will never be eliminated either by the propagation of Reason or the most insistent socialisation process. A more pragmatic approach is therefore desirable. For the conservative, justice may be important but it must always be subsumed under the need to maintain order. This is best encapsulated in the notion of a 'dual track' system of punishment. That is, an offender is first judged strictly on his or her offence - as in classicist theory - but such a proportional punishment is then added to or substracted from by a series of criteria whose concern is order; for example:

Ascriptive criteria Who is the offender? Is the person in a position of responsibility whose defection and transgression threatens the fabric of authority (e.g. a police officer or an NCO, as compared with someone in the ranks)? If so, the punishment should be more severe.

Dangerousness Is the person a recidivist who is palpably of further danger to society and should therefore be incarcerated longer than strict justice requires? Important in this formulation is the notion of incapacitation as an added confinement beyond that strictly determined by the requirements of just punishment.

Deterrence Does the offence or the type of offender represent a particular threat to society at the time of arrest? Is it necessary in passing sentence to hold in mind the function of punishment in deterring similar offenders? Would clemency better indicate, and support, the majesty of the state? Conservative answers to these questions require considerations other than those of equivalence between offence and penalty.
As a converse of such 'additions' to justice, charity may be invoked where the individual poses no threat to order and where the infringement is seen as only a temporary failing.

Thus, in the business of maintaining order, proportionate justice may be added to or subtracted from; preferably at the point of sentencing. The judge's discretionary role is central here. It is the judge who must weigh both the dangers to order and the efficacy of charity. If conservatism is most often seen as involving the principle of deterrence incommensurate with desert, we must take note of the other side of its coin, namely the principles of pardon and of clemency.

If classicism insists on focusing on the *act* of crime and positivism on the biographical and determining *antecedents* of the criminal, conservatism would stress the *actor* him/herself. The person's relative position or reputation in the social order becomes of considerable importance. For here we are dealing with a school of thought which makes much of the symbolic and public nature of punishment. If classicism upholds a system of deterrence restricted to inhibiting the individual's future transgressions, conservatism insists upon a *general deterrence* which would punish the one individual to deter all others and would punish the individual according to the social significance of the crime. The conservative preference for the simple moral lesson, deriving from unchallengeable authority, is reflected in the residual (and obsessive) belief in the efficacy of physical punishment. Punishment should be expressed as publicly as possible, whether in the ceremonial of the courts (and its subsequent coverage in the mass media), or in the more direct ways in which, in the public view, the law is seen to be carried out. The limits of permissible behaviour are thus demonstrably drawn and the penalties for infractions are clearly spelt out.

If classicism would punish the intransigent in the privacy of the prison where the offenders might rationally dwell upon the consequences of their crime, and if positivism would treat the culprit in the hospital-like atmosphere of a therapeutic unit, conservatism would dispute that private and personal attention to criminals best serves the public order. The moral lesson of punishment for the individual must extend its salutary effects to the population as a whole, for it is here that the greatest social good can be achieved.

PROBLEMS OF CONSERVATISM

It is this awareness of man's weakness and folly, not class interest or any doctrinaire conception of how the state should be organised, that leads the conservative to distrust sudden and drastic change, and all policies which depend upon it. He recognizes that, once the structure of society has been weakened beyond a certain point, there is no crime too horrifying for human beings, even highly cultivated and intelligent human beings, to commit. Indeed, it is the danger of the total breakdown of civilisation which induces him to tolerate inefficiencies, and even injustices, rather than put social stability at risk ... (Lord Coleraine, in Buck, 1975, p.180)

For classicism, equal competition between individuals rewarded and punished on a just basis is the mechanism which would bind each citizen to society. I pointed to the problems of classicism which stem from the desire to maintain existing property relations at the same time as advocating a meritocratic race of rewards. The classicist contradiction of insisting on formal equality while maintaining substantive inequalities gives rise to the problems of how justly to punish the unequal equally and why the poor are more evident in the criminal statistics than the rich. For conservatives, such a predicament is a product of the naive rationalistic optimism of classicism. Instead, they would insist on a 'realistic' pessimism. They would note that (even in a world based on the most rational and just system of rules) human nature being such, many would inevitably cheat. Since people are *created* unequal, talk of equality merely incites envy and dispute. The conservative squarely accepts, and is bound to defend, the fact that the social order is not one of equality and justice. Two types of problem stem from this commitment.

First, the cause of crime, for conservatives, is the innate propensity of evil of the individual, combined with the weakening of social ties which allows such anti-social intransigence to break its bonds. There is thus little attempt to link the type of crime (e.g. stealing or rape) to the nature of particular societies. Conservatism posits a root cause of deviancy, but it has no explanation of why individuals or groups concentrate on certain crimes rather than others.

Second, the pessimism of conservative theory assumes that, to maintain the present social order, coercion is inescapable: reason and justice will not bind society together. In response to this, it is legitimate to counterpose the possibility of a society in which the incidence of crime would be minimised by creating real substantive equalities based on agreed principles of justice. The classicist contradiction, too, would appear to be resolved in the move from mere formal equality to equality both in form and substance.

STRAIN THEORY

The three perspectives we have discussed have all focused on the individual. Although crime is seen as arising from some weakness in the binding between the individual and society, the impulse to criminal or deviant behaviour is located firmly in the individual. In classicism, temptation to break, and infractions of, the law occur because the chains of reason which bind the individual to the social contract are insufficiently developed. Within positivism, the socialisation of the individual is seen to be insufficient to constrain his or her natural impulses; whereas in conservative thought, tradition has been undermined and discipline relaxed to the extent that the individual feels little need to have self-sacrifices and limitations on his or her desires. In each theory crime or deviancy arises from the natural impulses of the individual as a result of a process of 'leakage' or weakness in the social order. Strain theory breaks with such theories because it rejects the notion that crime arises from innate drives or instincts of the individual, and insists that the impulse to crime is normal and *socially* induced.

(A) Human nature

In rejecting the notion of an innate human nature, strain theory moves towards a position which emphasises the social nature of a person's individuality. Human nature is not a pre-social 'given', but is created by the particular society within which the individual lives. There is not, therefore, a tension within the individual between the 'natural' self and 'social' self – for the self is a product of social order.

It is not only in the focus on the total society rather than the individual which distinguishes strain theory from classicism, positivism and conservatism. In addition, while its main thrust remains determinist, it attempts to break out of the rigid either-or dichotomies of determinism or free will which beset the previous theories. This it endeavours to do by picturing the human situation as that of rational problem-solving individuals placed in determined frameworks. In particular, the individual is seen to be inculcated with cultural goals and with a range of appropriate means and opportunities of achieving them. These determined 'givens' are the framework within which rational people make choices and decisions in order to attempt to solve the particular predicaments they face in their part of the social structure.

(B) Social order

Social order is maintained by the socialisation of people into a consensus of values which corresponds to the needs of the social system. Society is a functioning entity in which each part interrelates and supports the other. Such a *functionalist* notion of social order does not, however, preclude the examination of its dysfunctions. As Robert Merton, the leading exponent of strain theory, explained (1966, p.817):

The study of social problems requires sociologists to attend to the dysfunctions of patterns of behavior, belief and organization rather than focusing primarily or exclusively on their functions. It thus curbs any inadvertent or deliberate tendency in functional sociology to reinstitute the philosophy that everything in society works for 'harmony' and the 'good'.

It is at this juncture that strain theorists make their major innovation, for they note how, in order that social order may function, dysfunctional consequences are inevitable. Richard Cloward and Lloyd Ohlin graphically locate this process in their book 'Delinquency and Opportunity' (1960, pp.81-2):

A crucial problem in the industrial world is to locate and
train the most talented persons in every generation irrespective of the vicissitudes of birth, to occupy technical work
roles. Whether he is born into wealth or poverty, each
individual, depending upon his ability and diligence, must
be encouraged to find his 'natural level' in the social order.
This problem is one of tremendous proportions ...
    ... One of the ways in which the industrial society attempts
to solve this problem is by defining success-goals as potentially accessible to all, regardless of race, creed or socio-
economic position. Great social rewards, it is said, are not
limited to any particular segment or segments of the population but are available to anyone, however lowly his origins
... The industrial society, in short, emphasizes *common* or
universal success-goals as a way of ensuring its survival.
If large masses of young people can be motivated to reach
out for great social rewards, many of them will make the
appropriate investment in learning and preparation, and a
rough correlation between talent and ultimate position in
the occupational hierarchy will presumably result.
    One of the paradoxes of social life is that the processes
by which society seeks to ensure order sometimes result
in disorder. If a cultural emphasis on unlimited success-
goals tends to solve some problems in the industrial society,
it also creates new ones. A pervasive feeling of position
discontent leads men to compete for higher status and so
contributes to the survival of the industrial order, but it
also produces acute pressure for deviant behavior.

But the emphasis on the possibility of success constantly
contradicts the actual opportunities facing people - particularly
those lower in the class structure. Thus Merton notes (1964,
p.214):

In this same society that proclaims the right, and even the
duty, of lofty aspirations for all, men do not have equal
access to the opportunity structure. Social origins do
variously facilitate or hamper access to the forms of success
represented by wealth or recognition or substantial power.
Confronted with contradiction in experience, appreciable
numbers of people become estranged from a society that pro-
mises them, in principle, what they are denied in reality.

It is out of such an estrangement that crime and deviance
are seen to arise.

(C) Definition of crime
It is at this point that we should note that strain theory does
not limit itself to mere economic crime. It has been applied not
only to thieving and robbery but to vandalism, truancy,
drug-addiction, mental illness, suicide and homicide (Clinard,
1964). The major thrust of the argument is that the means by
which an industrial society maintains itself create the circum-

stances by which a wide range of disorder occurs. Thus it is
in a plethora of indicators of dysfunction that strain theorists
are interested. Indeed as functionalists they note that some
examples of crime may be directly functional to the social order,
being the result of 'normal' behaviour rather than strain, and
should not be considered as major indications of disequilibrium.
Strain theorists do not therefore limit themselves to using the
official crime statistics, but rather see them along with other
social indices as useful and usable.

(D) Extent and distribution of crime
Despite reservations about the immediate use of official statistics
or studies limited to interpreting these figures alone, strain
theorists would accept the general pyramidal 'shape' of crime
and disorder: namely that there is an inverse correlation
between class position and crime. Indeed the pyramid of crime
is the basic empirical problematic of their theory. For it is
at the bottom of society that the strain of blocked opportunities
to shared cultural goals is greatest and where the highest
amount of crime and deviancy should take place. The classicist
contradiction regarding the fact that not all rational citizens
will equally embrace the Social Contract is not a problem for
strain theorists, rather the reverse: it is the basis of their
explanation of disorder. Differences in wealth and property
provide success goals and opportunities for their achievement
to a much greater extent for the wealthy than for the poor.
The classicist principles of a free and equal race for rewards
are seen as essential for an industrial society to function, but
the substantive inequalities of wealth give rise to frustration
and deviance among the poor.

(E) Causes of crime
Deviance then is seen to be the result of a disjunction between
the culturally induced aspirations of individuals and the
structurally determined opportunities. The focus is not at all
on the individual's antecedents, the actor, or the act, and it
is a tension not within the individual, but between culture and
structure. Such a tension is rooted in the total society, and
in pointing to this strain theory recognises a fundamental
irony in the social order (Matza, 1969, p.77):

> the irony of a virtue, ambition, promoting a vice, deviant
> behavior, contains an ellipsis. Ambition promotes deviation
> when it is institutionally frustrated. The latent feature of
> ambition that will yield a reversal and mock its virtue is
> the reality of class barriers and restrictions on social mobil-
> ity. Such barriers and restrictions inhere in the very idea
> of ambition; by definition its only possible aim is to over-
> come them. Thus, ambition contains within itself the seed
> of institutional frustration.

Irony, as David Matza puts it, becomes a central tenet of such
functionalist analysis.

But these dysfunctions are experienced not so much by isolated individuals as by whole groups of individuals in certain structural positions. It is here that strain theory introduces its concept of subculture. Thus David Downes (1966), in his study of working-class delinquency in Stepney and Poplar, invokes the definition of culture formulated by C.S. Ford, namely 'learned problem solutions'. That is, subcultural responses are jointly elaborated solutions to collectively experienced problems. Groups of people have both collective goals and legitimate means fixed for them by the determining agency of society. In their positions as housewives, or teenagers, or corporate executives, they evolve subcultures - specialised parts of the general culture suitable for their needs. Often these are deviant, but where there are significant discrepancies between aspiration and opportunity, deviant subcultures or *contracultures* occur. Deviant behaviour, then, is viewed as being a meaningful attempt to solve the problems faced by groups of individuals in particular structural positions - it is not a meaningful pathology. And here strain theory differs qualitatively from classicism, positivism and conservatism, for it *guarantees meaning to deviancy*.

(F) Policy
The policy arising from strain theory is to attempt to alleviate the disjunction between aspiration and opportunities, institutional means and structural goals. In its most characteristic form, this involves piecemeal social engineering in order to try and provide opportunities to lessen the 'strain'. Coercion should be at a minimum; what is necessary is to reform the structure of society so that a more egalitarian opportunity structure is engendered and the contradictions of classicism are lessened *in fact*.

In terms of treatment of the individual, punishment is obviously irreconcilable with this approach. What is necessary on the immediate level is to teach the individual skills that will allow people most profitably to use their opportunities and demonstrate that many subcultural 'solutions' are of limited usefulness.

PROBLEMS WITH STRAIN THEORY

Problems of middle-class crime
Strain theory accepts the pyramid of crime and sees the high incidence of lower-working-class crime as a product of the greater strain experienced by those at the lower end of the class structure. As with positivism, surveys of unreported crime which show that crime is ubiquitous would seem to undermine the causal basis of strain theory. Against this it can be countered that what is vital for strain theory is merely a disjunction between aspirations and opportunities - people do

not have to be *absolutely* deprived to suffer from feelings of frustration - they may be *relatively* deprived in terms of their aspirations and opportunities. Thus the income-tax fiddler may be middle class and relatively well-off - yet his aspirations may be still considerably higher than his opportunities. All this may be true, but what remains to be explained is why the powerful who make laws find it necessary to break them.

Denial of pluralism of value
Without our denying the existence in Western capitalist countries of a consensual ideology which stresses the equal possibilities of all to succeed, it is a fault in strain theory that it sees such values as monolithic and unquestioned. This is not to suggest, for example, a working-class consciousness which is clearly contrary to the status quo. It points to the widespread existence of contradictions in value, cynicism, fatalism, and disassociation from the major institutions - as well as outright rejection. Similarly, the attempt in strain theory to marry rational choice and determinacy fails because it allows human rationality only a foothold in the process. Rational problem-solving is seen to occur, first, in individuals attempting to link together the predetermined goals and opportunities that constrain them, and then, if this fails, in innovating means to achieve the same goals (e.g. stealing to acquire consumer goods, etc.), and only then, if all else fails, in the innovation of new goals and means (e.g. violent gangs, drug users with countercultural norms, etc.). The rational person is added onto the predetermined culture and structure - he or she is an added extra. Such a position considerably underestimates the rational undermining of accepted value and legitimate procedure which constantly occurs: negotiation of values, cross-cuts in means, reinterpretation of goals, cynical conformity, distancing of commitment, etc. In each case, human reason steps into the determining process - rebellion is rare, but so is the simple acceptance of the central values which the strain theorists describe. Normality and deviance are not separate watertight categories of behaviour, nor does normal behaviour automatically precede ventures into deviance. Rather, at times, they blend together, are mistaken for each other or are irrevocably interwoven into the actual patterns of social behaviour.

The limits of reform
It is important to ask how far opportunities can be provided to lessen 'strain' without necessitating a change in the system. The reformist principles of strain theory would suggest that widespread adaptation is possible - yet the actual experience of projects such as Mobilization for Youth would suggest that severe economic and social limits to such adaptations occur. The short-term goals of adjusting the individual to existing opportunity suggests strongly the adaptation of the individual to the status quo rather than an attempt at any fundamental

changes.

Why is the system there in the first place?
Strain theory explains the classicist contradiction as resulting
from the necessity for a high level of inculcated aspirations in
order for the social system to function. It is extremely doubtful if such a stratagem is an international ploy on the part of
the ruling class or – even if it were – if it would be the most
efficient method of solving the problem of the recruitment of
appropriate personnel to specific tasks. A system of selective
recruitment and cooling out would seem more adequate – and
is probably more accurate empirically.

The classicist contradiction between equality of opportunity
and inequality of wealth is a means of legitimating the system.
On a formal level it presents the notion of the open meritocratic
society, while on a substantive level it preserves the existing
class structure. This process of legitimation is, itself, a result
of political pressure and conflict – the compromise of a half-
finished struggle.

A satisfactory explanation of the structural roots of the
contradiction and the nature of the 'strain' eludes these theorists. As Laurie Taylor nicely puts it (1971, p.148):

> It is as though individuals in society are playing a gigantic
> fruit machine, but the machine is rigged and only some
> players are consistently rewarded. The deprived ones then
> either resort to using foreign coins or magnets to increase
> their chances of winning (innovation), or play on mindlessly
> (ritualism), give up the game (retreatism), or propose a
> new game altogether (rebellion). But in this analysis nobody
> appears to ask who put the machine there in the first place
> and who takes the profits. Criticism of the game is confined
> to changing the pay-out sequences so that the deprived can
> get a better deal (increasing educational opportunities,
> poverty programmes). What at first sight looks like a major
> critique of society ends up taking the existing society for
> granted. The necessity of standing outside the present
> structural/cultural configurations is not just the job for
> those categorized in the rebellion mode of adaptation – it is
> also the task of the sociologist.

NEW DEVIANCY THEORY

This theoretical position emerged primarily in the 1960s and
early 1970s, and has a close relationship with the libertarian
currents widespread within Western capitalism in that period.
Its influence was, and still is, widespread. Outside criminology
theoretical parallels occur, for example, within anti-psychiatry
and radical feminism. New deviancy theory was primarily a
radical response to positivist domination of criminology, and
attempted to recover the 'meaning' in human behaviour denied,

or reduced to biological and physiological imperatives, in positivism.

(A) *Human nature*

The new deviancy theorists' conception of human nature is one which emphasises free-will and creativity. People create meaning in the world, and they, in striving towards diverse numbers of cultural goals, impart a multitude of interpretations to the social and physical world around them. Human behaviour must be understood on the level of meaning imparted to it by the people involved. Reality is not 'given' or predetermined: it is socially constructed. Human rationality relates to the logic and norms of a particular culture; it is relative rather than absolute. Human nature is then constantly open and existentially boundless, and cannot be delimited in terms of a pre-given essence, for human beings make their own world and transform their own nature.

Like strain theory, new deviancy theory attempts to marry voluntaristic and deterministic notions of human nature, but does so in almost a reverse fashion. In strain theory, human beings were seen to improvise rationally within their pre-given social framework. In new deviancy theory, human beings are born free, but lose their voluntaristic capacity in the structures that society lays down in order to control their behaviour.

(B) *Social order*

The basic image that new deviancy theory has of social order is that of a pluralism of values. Individuals live in an overlapping world of normative ghettos. In contrast to all previous theories, the notion of a consensus in society is challenged and replaced by the concept of a diversity of values. Consensus is a mystification, an illusion foisted on the public by the powerful. More precisely, it is an attempt by the powerful to foist their own particular value system on the diversity of groups within society. This is achieved, on the one hand, by their control over the major ideological apparatus within society (e.g. the mass media, education) and on the other, by their control and use of the repressive apparatus (e.g. the police, courts). It is the particular nature of this illusion that new deviancy theorists stress. They argue that the illusion is constructed first, by securing general agreement that there is a consensus rather than a diversity of values within a particular social order, and second, by insisting that this consensus - which is, in fact, the particular values of the powerful - is not a human but a natural construct to which any well-socialised person would *naturally* adhere. Thus what is in fact a human construct, a system of values created by a specific group of people, is presented as a 'thing', a reification having existence outside and above human creation. Such a position, as we have seen, is most characteristic of positivism - the main ideological enemy of new deviancy theory – but both classicism and conservatism embrace a similar notion of natural consensual values which all fully social individuals would share.

(C) Definition of crime
The most characteristic conception of the new deviancy theorists is their notion of *labelling*. Society, they argue, does not consist of a monolithic consensus but rather of a pluralistic array of values. For an action to be termed criminal or deviant demands not one, but two, activities: a group or individual must act in a particular fashion, and, second, another group or individual with different values must label the initial activity as deviant. Human beings acting creatively in the world constantly generate their own system of values. Unfortunately within the pluralistic order of society certain groups – variously and vaguely termed 'the powerful', 'the bureaucracy', 'the moral entrepreneur' – with more power than others, *enforce* their values upon the less powerful, labelling those who infringe their rules with stereotypical tags. Thus, people who in fact are existentially free, and evolve different values or experiment with various forms of behaviour, are labelled by the authorities as *in essence* 'a homosexual', 'a thief', or 'a psychopath'.

(D) Extent and distribution of crime
At the same time as emphasising the diversity of behaviour, the new deviancy theorists stress the ubiquity of deviance. It is not merely the poor who commit crime. Exposés of corporate activities and self-report studies of middle-class youth indicate the widespread nature of crime. But the theorists go further than this, for they stress not merely ubiquity and diversity but also, paradoxically, *similarity*. And it is through this observation that new deviancy theory obtains its radical purchase on the world. That is, while it recognises that the norms of sexual intercourse vary from one social group to another, it notes how they all involve aggression and male domination. Similarly, while it is true that economic relations involve a great diversity, they also ubiquitously involve theft. All men are rapists, all people are thieves. Categories blend into one another: marriage and prostitution, rape and 'normal' sexual intercourse, corporate income-tax fiddling and robbery, street violence and the violence of unguarded machinery in factories, the vandalism of the 'redevelopment' of the city and the vandalism of the kid in the telephone kiosk.

Whereas previous theories make clear lines between conformity and deviancy, these theorists suggest that not only is deviance relative to the values of the beholder but that behind conformist appearances lies an underlife of deviance.

For conformity *involves* deviance, the everyday life of the deviant involves infraction, and, of particular importance, the sanctimonious conformity of the powerful involves the violation of the laws which they themselves create.

What, then, are the new deviancy theorists to make of the
pyramid of the official statistics? Simply, that it is a fabrication.
It is a result of the prejudiced fashion in which the police and
the courts discriminate against lower-working-class deviance
and ignore the crimes of the powerful. The classicist contradiction between equality and property is a reality which is
manifest not in the way in which the poor commit more crimes
than the rich, but rather in the fact that the poor are more
vulnerable to arrest and prosecution than the rich. The ubiquity of crime becomes a pyramid of official statistics because
of the differential reaction of authority.

(E) Causes of crime

In analysing cases of intended non-conformity, people usually
ask about motivation: why does the person want to do the
deviant thing he does? The question assumes that the basic
difference between deviants and those who conform lies in
the character of their motivations [...] Psychological theories
find the cause of deviant motivations and acts in the individual's early experiences ... sociological theories look for
socially structured sources of 'strain' in the society, social
positions which have conflicting demands placed upon them
such that the individuals seek an illegitimate way of solving
the problems their position presents them with. (Merton's
famous theory of anomie fits this category.)

But the assumption on which these approaches are based
may be entirely false. There is no reason to assume that
only those who finally commit a deviant act actually have the
impulse to do so. It is much more likely that most people
experience deviant impulses frequently. (Becker, 1963,
p.26)

If crime and deviancy are ubiquitous, it is not necessary to
explain their origin. If previous theories have focused on the
individual and structural antecedents of the criminal act
(positivism and strain theory, respectively), on the act itself
(classicism) and on the actor (conservatism), new deviancy
theory focuses on *reaction*. It is the administration of crime,
not its origins, which is the key to understanding the phenomena
(Duster, 1970, p.90):

The person described as deviant in society may be considered
deviant in only one way, but the community reaction to him
can be total. For example, a pregnant high-school senior may
be quite capable of finishing her studies successfully before
graduation, but the total response, stigma, and ridicule may
lead her to leave; a homosexual may be as competent as the
next person in the government bureaucracy and similar in
every other way except for his sexual appetite; but may be
treated as though he was *totally* different.

The labelling process has two consequences: ideological
and coercive. Troy Duster brings this out in his study of
heroin addicts at the California Rehabilitation Center. Certain

deviant aspects of the addict may be regarded as 'master statuses' from which a knowledge of the total identity of the individual, overriding all other characteristics of the person, may be deduced. The process is often self-fulfilling, for, once stigmatised, the heroin addict finds it very difficult to re-enter the ranks of normality. Further, Duster notes how the addicts, in order to be released at an early date, must in the therapeutic group accept the moral characterisation imposed by their attendant psychiatrists. Moreover, the identity and kinship which they develop in the institution reinforces their notion of themselves as men set apart from the normal by virtue of their postulated personality weaknesses. In fact, Duster argues, there is negligible difference between addict and normal, apart from social inferiority, *until* the deviancy amplification process occurs (1970, p.247):

> The point to be made is that the addict supplied a drug without stigmatisation would make the case that has been presented: that he cannot be identified among 'normal' men without a chemical test, and could therefore lead that kind of social life which would negate the charge of psychic weakness.

Duster, in common with other labelling theorists, implicitly holds a view of the world which suggests that there is a plurality of forms of behaviour in society and therefore definitions of deviancy. None of these deviant forms is, however, particularly extreme *until* social reaction occurs and spirals the deviant into a gross and unnecessary position. He would suggest that heroin addiction is initially a peripheral deviancy which, because of the blinkering effect of the notion of the 'dope fiend' as a 'master status', is reacted to in a totally miscued and unnecessary fashion. Thus the very act of labelling, by materially limiting the future choices of the person and by being presented to the person as being the truth about his or her nature with all the force of authority, has a self-fulfilling effect. The old adages, 'once a thief always a thief', 'once a junkie always a junkie', *become* true not because, as earlier criminologists had maintained, this was the essence of the person involved but because the power of labelling transformed and cajoled people into acting and believing *as if* they possessed no freedom in the world. This observation is a pointed criticism of positivist notions of scientific laws that govern human behaviour. These 'laws', far from holding sway outside human control and purpose, are a *creation* of human interventions. If there is a correlation between broken homes and delinquency, it is not because the former *causes* the latter, but rather that delinquents from broken homes are differentially selected over their 'normal' compatriots to be arrested, prosecuted and to end up in the statistics. They are preferentially chosen because of the stereotype of them as typical 'delinquents'. Thus they become like this stereotype through the process of labelling in both its coercive and ideological aspects. The criminal *career* is a function of social reaction rather than a result of a predisposed essence.

(F) Policy

In strain theory we saw the irony of how the pursuit of *conformity* gives rise to deviance. Counterposed against this, in new deviancy theory, is the irony of *social control* giving rise to gross deviance. For much social control is seen to be irrational and dysfunctional. The prisons do not work - they have a high recidivism rate. The stigmatisation of the delinquent leads, in a man-made progression, to the hardened criminal. Those in power are not only wrongly intolerant of diversity, their overreaction creates a more intransigent deviance which further threatens their image of the monolithic consensual world and raises the level of coercive strategies necessary to maintain control. The key to controlling the 'crime problem', then, lies in the control of reaction against deviance, rather than in structural change.

For example, in 1967 in the United States, the President's Commission published 'The Challenge of Crime in a Free Society'. Among other things, this report suggested that major causes of crime were poverty, slum conditions and blocked opportunities (i.e. a strain-theory approach). It was from the new deviancy perspective that Jack Douglas assembled a series of essays in a reader, 'Crime and Justice in American Society', which mounted a critique against this conventional wisdom (1971, pp.xix-xx):

> The authors of this book also share many ideas on how Americans must go about reconstructing the foundations of their laws and legal procedures in order to increase the safety of their person and their property while at the same time increasing the sense of social justice and the degree of social order. It is particularly noteworthy in this respect that none of the essays argues that we must have any kind of socio-economic reordering of our society to produce these results. Whereas the crime commission report continually insisted we must end slum living and every other form of social ill before we can solve our worst problems connected with crime and injustice, these essays have little to say about the social reorganization of priorities and resources. I suspect most of us are in favor of more equitable social policies in one form or another, yet it has been our implicit assumption that the critical, basic, problems with our laws and legal practices are causing our most severe problems of crime and injustice. The presidential commission's choice of placing the blame for these problems on social imbalances became a way of absolving legislators and legal authorities from responsibility for their own failures to create and administer practicable and just laws and legal procedures. We do not absolve them. We hold them to be most culpable, collectively and personally, for our most urgent problems of crime and

injustice. They will continue to be so as long as they continue to administer and support the present system of un-
workable and unjust laws and legal procedures. No amount
of rhetoric, mystification, denial, or blame-gaming can
change this fact.

What is to be done then about crime? Each of the two parts
of the control process – ideological and coercive – must be
tackled. Ideologically it must be recognised that advanced
industrial countries are diverse in value, and what is necessary
is what Becker and Horovitz (1971) termed 'a culture of
civility'. That is, tolerance must replace moral indignation,
and an awareness of the open nature of human action replace
essentialist stereotypes and reified notions of value. In terms
of coercion, there must be a de-escalation of punishment, a
realisation of the insignificant nature of most primary deviance
(deviance before it is amplified – when it is termed secondary
deviance) and a resistance to the creation of moral panics
over deviancy. This policy of *radical non-intervention* (E.
Schur 1973) involves the decriminalisation of many offences,
particularly the so-called 'crime without victims' (pornography,
prostitution, gambling, etc.) and severely lowers penalties
on most others. And for the remaining serious offenders
(Douglas, 1971, pp.42-3):

> it will probably be necessary to maintain a form of maxi-
> mum isolation from the rest of society simply because the
> offender cannot be controlled by any other means. In such
> instances, Americans should investigate the possibilities of
> 'banishment' in which the recalcitrant offenders are allowed
> to run their own society, providing humane living conditions
> are maintained; banishment would absolve the rest of us
> from the guilt of dehumanizing our fellow human beings.

PROBLEMS WITH THE NEW DEVIANCY THEORY

Denial of structural causes
By granting human beings freedom in an absolute sense without acknowledging any material constraints, human purpose
is reduced to the level of whimsy. By propounding a conception of human nature as being free and spontaneous before
the intervention of the state sullied it, these theorists threw
all the weight of their criticism on bad administration. It was
a romantic theory of the noble deviant, expressive and creative,
who was bowed under the fetters of state control.

Thus whereas positivist theory, however, distortedly, had
emphasised the make-up of the individual and the structure
of his or her social arrangements as generating deviancy (albeit
ignoring the effects of social reaction), new deviancy theory
accomplished precisely the reverse position. It romantically
suggested that nothing was wrong with the structure of society
and the individual psyche outside the maladministration of the

state and heavy-handed control agencies. In this manner, the conflict endemic in a class society was glossed over and the basic causes of crime ignored.

Inadequate explanation of social reaction
Paradoxically for a theory which prides itself on introducing social reaction into the explanation of deviant behaviour, it is extremely limited in this respect. For the emphasis on maladministration rather than on structures ignores the structural causes of reaction. Hence reaction is regarded as a simple irrationality in terms of administration, and politics is seen as showing up dysfunctions in the ruling class and clarifying mistakes in logic. Against this I would argue that the control system does involve a logic and that this logic relates to the total social order. Therefore the resistance of our rulers to the 'rational' logic of labelling theory is scarcely a mere whim of irrationality.

Problem of the ubiquity of crime
The stress on the ubiquity of crime and the denial of structural causes do not leave any possibility of explaining differences in human behaviour between subcultures, over time and between countries. For although it may be true that all people commit crime, it is palpably obvious that they do not commit the same kinds of crime or to the same extent. Even deviancy theorists who argue that middle-class and working-class juvenile delinquency is identical, as are the real crime rates of blacks and whites and even men and women, are stopped short when asked about old people compared with young people. Such a search for a democratic crime statistic may be a laudable pursuit of equality, but it is very bad criminology.

Furthermore, whereas the new deviancy theorists have importantly stressed the differential vulnerability of people to arrest, they are wrong to pose this as an *alternative* to the differential propensity of people to commit crime. Surely, a study of differences in vulnerability *and* propensity would take us some of the way towards understanding the official statistics on crime?

Problem of political intervention
The strategy of non-intervention has serious flaws. At the most obvious level, the emphasis on maladministration rather than structure as the cause of problems in society blinds the theory to the root causes of the various crimes without victims. Because of this there is little attempt to suggest structural *as well as* legislative solutions to the problems.

Even if we take the empirical incidents most tailor-made for new deviancy theory, namely 'crimes without victims', problems arise. For if we examine a list of these crimes - prostitution, drug use, illegal gambling, pornography, abortion, homosexuality - the first thing to be noted is that it is a mixed bag.

We are asked to agree in each case that there is no victim; we are asked to agree that it is irrational to intervene in so-called 'consensual crimes'. Why should we interfere, the new deviancy theorists ask us, with free individuals doing their own thing? Our answer to them must be clear: because individuals are not free, because it is precisely the structural determinants, which the labelling theorists chose to ignore, which imprison and enmesh human action and rationality. Furthermore, the exercise of power is not an inherent evil, for it can be used to combat the repressive institutions that surround us. It is because social intervention can have a progressive as well as a deleterious consequence that we must discriminate between 'crimes without victims' and separate these categories which are presented to us. To present consensus between partners as an argument for the innocuousness of an activity is to ignore that contractual agreement in a capitalist society is very often not an agreement between equals but one between those of unequal power. Nor is such a 'free contract' beset by merely material constraints; the ideological domination of bourgeois ideas and categories scarcely makes for a *rational* contract between free individuals.

If we turn then to the structural causes of 'crimes without victims', we shall be more capable of distinguishing between them. To do this we must place activities in their social and historical context, and not generalise upon such an abstract and spurious basis as 'consensual activities'.

When we move beyond 'crimes without victims', the problems become even greater. For although we might argue that we should leave the juvenile vandal alone, should we absolve the income-tax fiddler? And in discussing rape, we find a crucial contradiction in new deviancy theory. Consistent with their general theory, new deviancy theorists would argue that rape is ubiquitous and scarcely demands a causal explanation outside its assumption as normal male behaviour, but would, at the same time, hesitate to warn about false labelling or suggest that recent fears about rape are merely a moral panic which grossly over-estimates the threat.

At base, the politics of non-intervention overlook the genuine fears that people have about crime. By underplaying the dangers of crime in the streets and suggesting that all would be solved merely by the state de-escalating its reaction to the criminal, it ignores the profound malaise and destructive anti-social behaviour which exists in our cities and which is generated by the type of society we live in.

MARXISM

The sixth theoretical perspective to be discussed is marxism. Although marxism has developed more sophisticated analyses of human nature and social order than the other traditions,

its early contributions to the analysis of crime were limited.
During the last decade, a Marxist criminology has emerged
although the debates are at an early stage. In this development
there has been a tendency both to reject some of the conceptual gains and to ignore the rational kernel and insights of
non-marxist traditions in criminology.

(A) Human nature

Men make their own history, but they do not make it just as
they please; they do not make it under circumstances chosen
by themselves, but under circumstances directly encountered,
given and transmitted from the past. The tradition of all the
dead generations weighs like a nightmare on the brain of the
living. (Marx, 1969, p.360)

For marxists, the dichotomy between human beings being
depicted as having free-will (e.g. classicism or conservatism)
or as being determined (e.g. in positivism) is false. Also they
reject the notion of adding free-will at the end of a large series
of determinants (e.g. strain theory) or the depiction of determinancy as a monopoly of social reaction impacting on the pure
spirit (e.g. new deviancy theory). Human beings are both the
producers and the products of history; they create institutions
and meaning within a particular historical period which is,
in the last instance, determined by the mode of production of
the time. Furthermore, there is no pre-social essence of
humanity as is postulated in the majority of non-marxist theories.
The notion of an animal nature which will determine behaviour
if 'society' does not intervene, or of an *a priori* human reason
which exists outside of social context, is an absurdity. Rather,
in their deviant behaviour and in their normal behaviour, in
their reason or their unreason, in their individualism or in
their collectivism, human beings are social beings. Thus
(Marx, 1971, p.189):

Man is a *zoon politikon* in the most literal sense; he is not
only a social animal, but an animal that can be individualised
only within society. Production by a solitary individual outside society ... is just as preposterous as the development
of speech without individuals who live *together* and talk to
one another.

Statements concerning the particular characteristics of
social relationships, about, for example, the degree of individualism, rationality, freedom or determinancy must be historically grounded. That is, they must be generalisations not
about all humanity in the abstract, but about specific historical
periods. It is important to specify, then, problems of freedom
and determinancy within capitalism.

(B) Social order

In 'Capital' (vol.1), Marx characterises the transition from
feudalism to early capitalism as the imposition of the discipline
'necessary for the system of wage labour' (1976, pp.899-900):

The advance of capitalist production develops a working class which by education, tradition and habit looks upon the requirements of that mode of production as self-evident natural laws. The organization of the capitalist process of production, once it is fully developed, breaks down all resistance. The constant generation of a relative surplus population keeps the law of the supply and demand of labour, and therefore wages, within narrow limits which correspond to capital's valorization requirements. The silent compulsion of economic relations sets the seal on the domination of the capitalist over the worker.

The coercion necessary at the genesis of capitalism becomes supplanted by the silent compulsion of the market. The worker is doubly free - free to sell his labour and 'free' of the ownership of the means of production. That is, compared with feudal relationships, he is free - but it is a voluntary compulsion because he is forced to sell his labour in the market-place: he is free to be exploited. But not all the population are able to find employment; there is a 'relative surplus population' in capitalism which seem to maintain a market in labour - the ability of the employer to bid for labour among competing individuals selling their labour-power. Lastly, Marx notes how, through 'education, tradition, habit', people begin to accept this 'double freedom' as natural - as being an eternal part of human existence. The natural world of the voluntary compulsion of the market-place coupled with the daily discipline of the factory seal the fate of the worker. Marxism stresses the role of the work situation as the major focus of social control in capitalist society, while 'direct extra-economic force is still used only in exceptional cases'.

It is important to stress the double nature of freedom under capitalism. Marxism does not suggest that freedom is an illusion, but rather that the nature of capitalist reality is both opaque and contradictory. Unlike the new deviancy theory, it does not view support for the existing system as a mystification but as arising out of the nature of capitalist reality itself. As Maurice Godelier puts it (1972, p.337), in a capitalist society,

'It is not the subject who deceives himself, but *reality* which deceives him, and the appearances in which the structure of the capitalists' production process conceals itself are the starting-point for individuals' conceptions.'

In his discussion of the labour process in 'Capital', Marx outlines two contrasting spheres. On the one hand, the world as it appears from the level of the process of circulation (the market exchange of commodities, i.e. labour and wages) with the process of production (i.e. the production of surplus value); on the level of the sphere of circulation of commodities the worker freely sells his labour, he obtains the market equivalent for it, he is an equal before the law, he is not cheated by the individual capitalist. On the other hand, if we leave

'the noisy sphere of human rights' and enter 'the hidden abode
of production', we find a different story: coercion and necessity
replace freedom, substantive inequality replaces formal equality,
exploitation replaces equivalence. The market economy creates
of necessity real freedom, rationality and individualism, at least
in *certain sections* of the population. Thus the immediate
world of appearances (freedom, equality, equivalence) inverts
and obfuscates reality (servitude, inequality, exploitation),
but it is not a mere illusion. Such a double, opaque and contradictory structure of reality is characteristic of capitalism
and throws up theories which stress one-sidedly either free-
will or determinism. There is the rational basis of conformity
in our society (as one-sidedly depicted in classicism) and there
is the determinancy (as one-sidedly portrayed in positivism).

The dull compulsion of economic need, as an indirect coercion,
exists throughout the workforce. What of direct coercion and
the 'exceptional circumstances' of its use? Here, as Dario
Melossi puts it, the exceptions are in fact 'the sphere of penal
repression, that is, in the sphere of exceptions' (1976, p.32).
For the coercion at the genesis of capitalism continues with
its development (p.28):

> The way of the cross walked for some time by the pro-
> letariat punished for a social transition that they did not
> initiate or understand and which they opposed with all their
> force is, in a more developed moment, walked by the rebel,
> the criminal, by the ones Marx numbers among the lumpen-
> proletariat.

Thus the data presented to the President's Commission indicate that the labourer is fourteen times more likely to go to
prison than the professional, the person with less than four
years' education is eighteen times more likely to enter prison
than the postgraduate, and the black male is five times more
likely to go to prison than the white. Unemployment in particular correlates and covaries with imprisonment (Quinney,
1977, pp.131-40; Janovic, 1977).

The pattern is clear: the major focus of the prison (i.e. direct
coercion) is the workless, the reserve army of labour and
those marginal to the workforce. Indeed in New York one out
of every twenty blacks between the ages of 25 and 34 was
actually *in* prison on an average day (Wright, 1973, p.32).

The principles behind the control of the worker and the workless are the same. Whereas classicism portrays the history of
punishment as the tale of men of good-will advancing steadily
on humanitarian grounds under the banner of reason, marxism
notes how classicist ideals are historically situated. Central to
this debate is the work of the Bolshevik legal theorist Eugene
Pashukanis (1978), who pointed out that concomitant with the
rise of commodity production (involving the notion of abstract
labour, the free and equal worker, the proportional correspondence of labour reward, and the concept of time as an
abstract and general measure of values) arose precisely similar

concepts in punishment. Namely, the notion of the abstract, voluntaristic formally equal, legal actor who is punished proportionately to the cost of his crime by a fine or by the equivalent denial of his free time in prison. Thus the principles of reward which coax and give reason to the conformity of the worker in the factory are the same as the principles of punishment which are inflicted upon the recalcitrant. Just as the population must be convinced that utility to society is proportionately rewarded, they must also be made aware that lack of utility is effectively curbed and stigmatised. The pyramid of success must have a shadow of failure.

An image used by the new deviancy theorists was that of the iron fist and the velvet glove. Social control was at base naked coercion, a fist poised above the total population, but this was disguised and supplemented by a velvet glove of mystification. Material coercion and ideological delusion attempted to pacify the population, yet – and here was the irony of their critique – such a control mechanism was, in the last resort, dysfunctional. For labelling exacerbated rather than ameliorated deviancy.

How does marxism differ from this? I have pointed to its insistence on pinpointing the nature of coercion and consensus in a particular historical period – in this case capitalism – and on detailing how coercive means are differentially applied to the working population (the worker or the workless). Coercion is not a blanket category, but is directly applied to the workless while manifesting itself as an indirect pressure on those in work ('the dull compulsion of economic need'). Consensus is not a system of mystified ideas by which the ruling class deludes the population but arises out of the contradictory nature of reality itself. It is based on the *real* freedom and gains of capitalism that coexist and conceal coercion and exploitation; that is, the 'double freedom' of the worker under capitalism.

Marxists as well as new deviancy theorists are fascinated by the role of the prison as an instrument of social control.

What point, the new deviancy theorists ask, is there in such a *dysfunctional* system? It represents for them the prime symbol of administrative irrationality. But marxists, from the same empirical observation, come to exactly the opposite conclusion. They argue that the prison has two vital and efficient *functions* in capitalist society. The first is as a material deterrent, the second is as an ideological weapon. First, they point to the fact that although the focus of penal sanctions is on the workless, their real effort is on those in work. For the prisons do not control the future activities of their inmates; their presence controls the rest of the population. For the threat of being permanently excluded from reasonable work, of social stigmatisation and of immiseration holds the respectable working class, the honest citizen, constantly in check.

Second, by portraying crime as a monopoly of the emarginalised and the major problem of order in society, they deflect attention away from the crimes of the powerful and the exploitative nature of capitalism itself.

Marxist criminology does not only specify and differentiate the way in which coercive and consensual controls impact on the working and workless population; it views the system as an integrated whole. Thus:

(a) The 'reserve army of labour', a relatively immiserised pool of people out of work, affects the market position of those in work by posing a constant potential competition for jobs.

(b) The social conditions of the reserve army and the threat of those in work joining them allow the imposition of a rigorous discipline in the workplace.

(c) Both workless and those in work are rewarded and punished in terms of the same principles of proportionality; there is a continuum of reward and punishment within society.

(d) The prison's 'failure', in that it well-nigh irrevocably stigmatises the recalcitrant, serves as a first line of control for the workless and an important second line of control - after work itself - for those in work.

(e) The state in acting against the criminal serves to legitimate itself as the protector of universal interests in society.

(C) Definition of crime
With the exception of the new deviancy theory, all the theories discussed in this article assume that crime is any action which is severely against the interests of the majority of citizens. New deviancy theory disagrees here: crime is that behaviour which violates the interests of the powerful. How does marxism differ from this?

The basis for the political support of bourgeois society among the mass of the population is closely entwined with their fears of crime and disorder. Just as the ruling class takes working-class demands for justice and enmeshes them in the support of a class-ridden society, so, too, a real need for social order is similarly transmuted. The existence of a class society leads to desperation, demoralisation and a war of all against all. The working-class community suffers immensely from the criminals in its midst. Law gains its support not through a mere mystification of the working class, an ability to render people spellbound by its paraphernalia of pomp and authority. Legal institutions represent, it is true, the interest of the ruling class, but they are also much more than just this. As Herbert Marcuse put it (1971, p.101):

The state, being and remaining the state of the ruling class, sustains *universal* law and order and thereby guarantees at least a modicum of equality and security for the whole society. Only by virtue of these elements can the class state fulfil the function of 'moderating' and keeping within the bounds of 'order' the class conflicts generated by the pro-

duction relations. It is this 'mediation' which gives the
state the appearance of a universal interest over and above
the conflicting particular interests.

The class society which creates social disorganisation also
creates its partial palliative. Legal institutions also contain
within them gains and concessions wrested from the bourgeoisie
by the labour movement. Furthermore, they are a repository
for the ideals of equality, justice and liberty which, however
empty these remain as formal pronouncements outside the
economic and political basis necessary to realise them, remain
genuine ideals all the same. Conservative law-and-order campaigns therefore play on real needs for social order and embody
genuine ideals, albeit in a distorted form. In this fashion,
the criminal and the destructive elements of a class society are
presented not as *result* of the present society but as the *cause*
of its lack of harmony. The ideological impact of such an
inversion of the real world is considerable.

As with our discussion of the contradictory nature of the
work process in capitalism, we see in law similar opaque and
contradictory phenomena. Thus bourgeois law arises in order to
safeguard, contract and protect property: that is, to maintain
equality in the realm of exchange while perpetuating and
allowing for increasing accumulation at the level of production.
The law offering equality of judgment and protection to all
involves a contrast between formal equality on one level which
obscures and perpetuates substantive inequality on the other.
Thus, laws are passed which judge people as equal individuals,
obscuring the fact that their inequitable class position makes
them differentially vulnerable to commit crime in the first place.
The formal equality of protection which laws give in the
defence of the property of individuals, however, is simply
the right of one class to perpetuate and extend its ownership
of the means of production, thus rendering the working class
both propertyless and unequal. Therefore to judge people
equally is to act inequitably, to protect property equally is
to extend inequality. Here again, bourgeois society creates
crime which threatens the working class, and law maintains a
degree of protection against the criminal. Also legal rights
allow the individual to organise politically and they afford some
protection against the intrusions of the ruling class and the
state. Law not only legitimates ruling-class domination, it has
a legitimate component to it, in terms of the protection of
working-class interests. It is not, therefore, a mystification
of the real interests of the powerful, as new deviancy theorists
would maintain.

(D) The extent and distribution of crime
In marxist criminology, crime is seen to be endemic in the
social order. The explanation of how the pyramid of crime
emerges is, however, different from previous theories. In strain
theory, the classicist contradiction between property

(substantive equality) and formal equality of opportunity is seen to be the root cause of crime. With this, marxism would be in broad agreement. Contrary to this, new deviancy theory stresses that the main contradiction is between the formal equality of ideal justice and the substantive inequality of justice in practice. With this, no Marxist would quarrel. It must be stressed, however, that the two positions are not alternatives. For the pyramid of crime is not merely a figment of the differential reaction of the powerful. In a class society, despite the espousal of formal equalities of opportunity and of justice, substantive inequalities occur on *both* levels. As Jeffrey Reiman puts it (1979, pp.7-8):

> There is evidence suggesting that the particular pressures of poverty lead poor people to commit a higher proportion of the crimes that people fear (such as homicide, burglary, and assault) than their number in the population.
>
> ... if arrest records were brought in line with the real incidence of crime, it is likely that those who are well off would appear in the records far more than they do at present, even though the poor would still probably figure disproportionately in arrests for the crimes people fear. In addition to this, those who are well off commit acts that are not defined as crimes and yet that are as harmful or more so than the crimes people fear. Thus, if we had an accurate picture of who is really dangerous to society, there is reason to believe that those who are well off would receive still greater representation.

(E) Causes of crime

Contemporary capitalism makes a social contract based on effort and reward, the premise of citizenship being the provision of work and access to property and consumer goods. It is unable to employ the totality of the population: a proportion of individuals are marginalised. It is impossible to enmesh these people in the social control of the workplace as thus they are potentially a dangerous class. They have, unlike the stable workforce, little to lose from criminality. The judicial machinery must, therefore, be used to coerce them into subservience: it must fill the gap where work discipline is absent. The aetiology of crime and law-abiding behaviour has, therefore, the same root: the incorporation, or lack of it, of the population into the workforce. While this explains merely the propensity for crime among the workers, it does not root the actual motivation. Here again the motivation lies - as strain theory has indicated - in the classicist contradiction. The ever-present disparity between effort and reward, the emphasis on equal opportunities yet the unequal reality of a class society, the stress on individual competition yet the handicapped nature of the race - all militate to create a criminogenic milieu. Such contradictions are particularly hard on the marginalised groups who are denied full access to the consumer society. Thus,

the very process which binds the worker to his bench turns
the mind of the unemployed to forms of crime which have, in
fact, a high rate of surveillance and apprehension.

Such a root cause of crime must be combined with an analysis
of the effects of social reaction upon crime – as the new
deviancy theorists one-sidedly argue. In fact Marx himself,
in one of his rare discussions on crime, noted (1859):

There must be something rotten in the very core of a social
system which increases its wealth without decreasing its
misery, and increases in crimes even more rapidly than in
numbers ... Violations of the law are generally the offspring
of the economical agencies beyond the control of the legis-
lator, but, as the working of the Juvenile Offenders' Act
testifies, it depends to some degree on official society to
stamp certain violations of its rules as crimes or as transgressions only. This difference of nomenclature, so far from
being indifferent, decides on the fate of thousands of men,
and the moral tone of society. Law itself may not only
punish crime, but improvise it.

What of crimes of the powerful – how is it that those that
make the rules are also persistent rule-breakers? The solution
to this paradox is in the contradictory nature of law. Certain
laws are passed by pressure of subordinate classes which act
against the interests of the powerful (e.g. anti-monopoly
legislation, progressive income tax measures, factory safety
legislation). The extension of real power is exhibited in the
degree of their actual implementation: for, as Reiman has
indicated, the pyramid of crime is in part the product of the
differential immunity of the powerful to prosecution.

What of the element of volition or determinism in the criminal
act? Engels is quite clear about the nature of crime *in extreme
circumstances*. It evolves from the demoralisation and brutal-
isation of exploitation in which 'the working-man becomes
precisely as much a thing without volition as water ... at a
certain point all freedom ceases' (1969, p.159).

How does this differ from a positivist theory of crime, which
would invoke invariable laws of human behaviour? In the sense
that Engels specifies particular brutalising circumstances. As
Hall and Scraton indicate (see article no.20), however, Engels
is not consistent in his writings on crime. For it also constituted
the 'earliest, crudest and least fruitful form of rebellion'
(Engels, 1969, p.240). But even such an act of volition is soon
enveloped in determinants (p.240):

The workers soon realized that crime did not help matters.
The criminal could protest against the existing order of
society, only singly, as one individual; the whole might of
society was brought to bear upon each criminal and crushed
him with its immense superiority.

A marxist criminology also points to the existence of determinants which as a product of human creation are not natural
laws but at the same time come to dominate the lives of human

beings. It is here that positivism has its validity. It is at the
desperate end of the social spectrum where the overwhelming
milieu precipitates people into highly determined roles where
the tyranny of the organism is best displayed, and where the
positivists, whether psychologists or biologists, come into
their own. But this is a product of historical time and place -
it is *not* a part of 'human nature' or 'man's essence' in the way
that positivism might have us believe.

Such a position is critical of the manner in which the new
deviancy theory rejected positivism. That is, in suggesting
that positivism is wrong because it has an incorrect portrayal
of human capacity - it denies human creativity - and that
people who act in a determined fashion are acting like that
because they are acting *as if* they were determined. It is wrong
to confuse human potential with human reality or to regard the
determination of human beings as a mistake in thought.

(F) Policy
It may be true that there are correlations between broken
homes and vandalism - the task must be to remove the conditions that give rise to such associations. It may be true - as
strain theory argues - that the contradiction between the ideals
of equality and the reality of restricted opportunities gives
rise to delinquency. Yet this classicist contradiction between
formal equality and the substantive inequalities stemming
from property is not solved, as the strain theorists would have
it, by merely opening up more opportunities. For the unequal
distribution of property and power in capitalism will always
result in the privileged reproducing inequalities of opportunity
areas. For marxists, the solution to the contradiction of classicism is to abolish, that is to create a world where formal
and substantive inequalities disappear.

PROBLEMS OF MARXIST CRIMINOLOGY

Problem of specificity
The line of causality invoked by marxists is: capitalism leads
to crime, and creates a series of problems in terms of specific
times, places and groups. To say, for instance, that crime is
endemic among corporate elites does not explain which corporate executives commit criminal acts and under what specific
economic circumstances.

In part, this problem relates to the overconcentration of
marxism on the total society rather than on the individual or
group. Strain theory, with its emphasis on subculture as a
historical entity wherein a group of individuals faced a shared
set of circumstances, and new deviancy theory with its notion
of 'moral career' - the biographical interaction of the individual with society - are more readily capable of dealing with
the micro-level of analysis. In recent years the concept of

subculture has been recontextualised and integrated into marxist analysis, particularly of youth cultures - and this is a fruitful line of development.

Problem of functionalism

There is a tendency in much marxist criminology to take up a position which could be called *left functionalist*. That is, phenomena are 'explained' by the role they are seen to play in maintaining capitalism. Dysfunctions, effects which create imbalances and disequilibria, are played down. We have noted in our discussion of strain theory how Merton recommended the study of crime and social problems as a corrective to this tendency in bourgeois structural functionalism, but no such strictures have been applied to functionalist tendencies in marxist criminology.

Problems of dealing with non-economic crimes

There is a tendency in marxist criminology to assume an obvious economic motive for criminal activities. This is untrue, even in the case of a professional robber, and, of course, it is inadequate in terms of rape or vandalism. What is needed here is a widening of theory and further specification and contextualisation as discussed earlier. In terms of rape, for example, one would look for a marxist approach which was capable of analysing the notion of patriarchy and discussing the basis of gender differences and male aggression. In terms of juvenile delinquency one would look for a way in which economic deprivation is manifested in delinquent subcultures which involve vandalism and acts of physical violence. Once again, it is to subculture theory that one turns to find concepts that mediate between the study of the total society and the actual activities of delinquent individuals.

Problems of reform and strategy

Marxist criminology would argue that real progress in the elimination of crime will occur only if fundamental changes are wrought in the ownership of the means of production. Revolution, not reform, is the major item on the agenda. With this in mind, it is necessary to argue for changes in criminal justice which would help to transform rather than merely shore up the system. Such a strategy is difficult, for there is no such thing as a demand which is without contradictions. For example, we have shown elsewhere (Greenwood and Young, 1975) how the right to abortion as a formal demand conceals the substantial inequalities which force some women to have abortions. Progressive abortion legislation involves gain on the level of women's rights, but is simultaneously a control measure on the part of population-controllers. Reforms, because they emerge from a class-divided society, will always display such a two-sided nature. The strategic problem is how to discriminate systematically between 'negative reforms', which on the whole

serve to open up the system to fundamental change, and
'positive reforms', which merely give legitimacy to the system
and increase its stasis (see Mathieson, 1974).

Problem of crime under socialism
In classical marxism the excesses of deviance, and with them
the need for law and the state, are seen to 'wither away'. A
debate occurs within marxist criminology as to whether such a
position is utopian. Thus Paul Hirst writes (1975, p.240):
'One cannot imagine ... the absence of the suppression of
theft and murder, nor can one consider these controls as purely
oppressive.' Such a debate has relevance to the whole problem
of the causality of crime for, if it is true that all industrial
societies will produce 'excessive' deviance, then part of the
cause of crime is not only in capitalism but in the complex
nature of industrial societies *per se*.

CONCLUSION

I have presented in this article six theories of crime and
deviance, systematically comparing them on the central questions which any theory of order and of criminality must tackle.
By examining the paradigms in this way, it is possible to
differentiate clearly between them. But, as was suggested
in the introduction, one must be careful how we compare the
different theoretical approaches. In particular, we should
bear the following in mind.

Ideal-type theories
I have constructed 'ideal' theories which have, to an extent, a
high degree of internal consistency; so the answer to each
question should follow logically from the answer to the others.
In actual practice, however, one finds theorists who lack
consistency and, of course, others whose writings are *in
between* the theories so described.
    Thus in the early 1970s many theorists both in Britain and
the United States began to move from new deviancy theory
towards marxism. As a result, much of this transitional work
shows characteristics of both traditions (e.g. the essays in
Taylor, Walton and Young, 1975). The purpose of placing
theories into such ideal types is to create a usable vocabulary
so that we can argue about crime in a serious and systematic
fashion.

The myth of unilinear development
With the exception of conservatism - which strangely is
rarely discussed in books on criminological theory - we have
presented the theories in the order that is conventional in
textbooks on criminology. That is classicism, positivism, strain
theory, new deviancy theory and (perhaps) marxism. This

is not to make the common textbook mistake of believing that they developed in a series of discrete historical stages from classicism to marxism, each representing a step in the rational progress towards the solution of the crime problem.

This is palpably untrue, for the following reasons:

There are many unilinear lines - the one presented here is the one conventional in *sociological* textbooks on criminology. Different experts would have different unilinear lines and each unilinear line of development would be hotly disputed by experts from other disciplines; e.g. a biologist interested in crime might see biological positivism as the function of a line of scientific achievement - scarcely a stage at the beginning of criminology. Thus Hans Eysenck views himself as being at the end of a lengthy and distinguished lineage, but his line crosses the one presented above only at the point of positivism.

Lack of dominance of any one theory - Rarely, if at all, does a theory dominate even select parts of the Academy, as the notion of unilinear development suggests. Rather, the situation is more that of competing paradigms. For instance, at the moment, academic criminology is presented with a wealth of eminently viable positions and excellent theoreticians in each of the theoretical traditions I have presented here. All these positions are flourishing and have powerful support and sound and substantial work as their basis. They can hardly be considered remnants of bygone theoretical ages! They all have long intellectual histories and social bases which belie the notion of the revolutionary development of theory in which earlier forms are dismissed and become defunct.

The myth of the new theory
Criminology, like the rest of the social sciences, suffers from much forgetfulness of its history, and fresh theories are rediscovered with a surprising naiveté (see Young, 1979). A major case in point is the so-called positivist revolution at the beginning of the century presented by leading exponents such as Enrico Ferri as a Copernican transformation of notions of human nature, social order and criminal policy. But, in fact, a flourishing positivist school occurred in the middle of the nineteenth century (see Lindesmith and Levin, 1937; Pearson, 1975). Or, more recently, the distinguished American legal scholar Isaac Balbus in 1977 'discovered' the commodity fetishist theory of law only to admit ruefully at the end of his work that he had come across a more sophisticated version of this theory written in 1924 by Eugene Pashukanis!

Now the point of pouring scorn on the 'new discoveries complex' is not to say that nothing new ever happens in theory or to detract from the work of the recent theorists. Theories, however recurrent, emerge in particular historical periods with special emphasis and advantages of their own. They play important roles in revitalising past discoveries, putting new stress on the interpretation of events and relating these to current happenings. What is annoying is the amnesia regarding the past and the perennial tendency to one-sided interpretations of social reality: voluntarism versus determinism; biological versus sociological reductionism, etc. The problem facing a theorist is to transcend such dichotomies, yet the tendency in terms of the fashionable theory of the moment is to swing backwards and forwards, to bob from one position to the other. Thus in sociological circles in the late 1960s, positivism became démodé and was replaced by a new deviancy theory which, far from transcending the position put forward by its opponent, merely inverted every facet of positivist theory, so that a mirror image resulted.

Theory and the real world
At the beginning of this article I stressed how academic theorisation about crime is not separate from lay discussions by the public at large. It merely reproduces in a more systematic and consistent form the discussions occurring in pubs and at bus-stops. But there is another sense in which there is an intimate relationship between academic criminology and the real world. That is, these ideas very often have an only too real institutional basis. For instance, it may not have escaped the reader that the juvenile court is an arena where positivist theories of crime are dominant and that the adult courts are the realm where classicist principles often hold sway.

From the seating arrangement in magistrates' courts to the design and layout of prisons, fundamental ideas about the causation of crime and the nature of justice come into play.

I have indicated how the study of crime is not a marginal concern to the citizen but plunges us immediately into fundamental questions of order and morality in society and to the examination of the very basis of the civilisation we live in.

References
American Friends Service Committee (1971), 'Struggle for Justice', New York, Hill & Wang.
Balbus, I. (1977), Commodity Form and Legal Form, 'Law and Society Review', 11 (3), pp.571-88.
Banks, Charlotte (1978), 'Survey of the South-East Prison Population 1972', Home Office Research Bulletin, no.5.
Beccaria, C. (1801), 'An Essay on Crimes and Punishments', 5th ed., London, J. Bone.
Becker, H.S. (1963), 'Outsiders', New York, Free Press.
Becker, H.S. and Horovitz I.L. (1971), The Culture of Civility, in 'Culture and Civility in San Francisco', ed. H.S. Becker, Chicago, Aldine.
Buck, P. (ed.) (1975), 'How Conservatives Think', Penguin Books.
Clinard M. (1964), 'Anomie and Deviant Behavior', New

York, Free Press.

Cloward, R. and Ohlin, L. (1960), 'Delinquency and Opportunity', New York, Free Press.

Douglas, J., ed. (1971), 'Crime and Justice in American Society', Indianapolis, Bobbs-Merrill.

Downes, D. (1966), 'The Delinquent Solution', Routledge & Kegan Paul.

Duster, T. (1970), 'The Legislation of Morality', New York, Free Press.

Engels, F. (1969), 'The Condition of the Working Class in England', Panther.

Eysenck, H. (1969), The Technology of Consent, 'New Scientist', 26 (June).

Eysenck, H. (1977), 'Crime and Personality', Paladin.

Ferri, E. (1893), Sociologie Criminelle, Paris.

Ferri, E. (1901), Studi sulla Criminalita in Francia del 1826 al 1878, in 'Studi sulla Criminalita', ed. E. Ferri, C. Lombroso, R. Garofalo and G. Fioretti, 2nd ed., Turin, Bocca.

Fogel, D. (1975), 'We are the Living Proof', Cincinnati, W.H. Anderson.

Fogel, D. (1977), Pursuing Justice in Corrections, in 'Justice and Punishment', ed. J. Cederblom and W. Blizek, Cambridge, Mass., Ballinger.

Gamble, A. (1974), 'The Conservative Nation', Routledge & Kegan Paul.

Godelier, M. (1972), Structure and Contradiction in Capital, in 'Ideology in Social Science', ed. R. Blackburn, Fontana.

Greenwood, V. and Young, J. (1975), 'Abortion in Demand', Pluto Press.

Haag, E. van den (1975), 'Punishing Criminals', New York, Basic Books.

Hamel, G.A. van (1906), L'Opera di Cesare Lombroso nella scienza e nelle sue applicazione.

Hirst, P. (1975), Marx and Engels on Law, Crime and Morality, in 'Critical Criminology', ed. Taylor, Walton and Young, pp.203-32.

Janovic, I. (1977), Labor Market and Imprisonment, 'Crime and Social Justice' (fall-winter), pp.17-31.

Lindesmith, A. and Levin, Y. (1937), The Lombrosian Myth in Criminology, 'American Journal of Sociology', 42, pp.635-71.

Manson, I. and Palmer, J. (1973), Moralists in the Moron Market, in 'Contemporary Social Problems in Britain', ed. R. Bailey and J. Young, Farnborough, Saxon House.

Marcuse, H. (1971), 'Soviet Marxism', Penguin Books.

Marx, K. (1859), Population, Crime and Pauperism, 'New York Daily Tribune' 16 September.

Marx, K. (1969) The Eighteenth Brumaire of Louis Bonaparte, in F. Engels and K. Marx, 'Basic Writings on Politics and Philosophy', ed. L.S. Feuer, New York, Doubleday.

Marx, K. (1971), 'Contribution to the Critique of Political Economy', Lawrence & Wishart.

Marx, K. (1976), 'Capital', vol.1, Penguin Books.

Mathieson, T. (1974), 'The Politics of Abolition', Martin Robertson.

Matza, D. (1969), 'Becoming Deviant', Englewood Cliffs, Prentice-Hall.

Melossi, D. (1976), The Penal Question in 'Capital', 'Crime and Social Justice', no.5, spring-summer, pp.26-33.

Merton, R.K. (1964), Anomie, Anomia and Social Interaction, in 'Anomie and Deviant Behavior', ed. M. Clinard, New York, Free Press.

Merton, Robert (1966), Social Problems and Sociological Theory, in 'Contemporary Social Problems', ed. R. Merton and R. Nisbet, 2nd ed., New York, Harcourt, Brace & World.

Miller, W.B. (1958), Lower-class Culture as a Generating Milieu of Gang Delinquency, 'Journal of Social Issues', 15, pp.5-19.

Morris, A. (1978), 'Juvenile Justice?', Heinemann Educational.

Morris, N. (1974), 'The Future of Imprisonment', University of Chicago Press.

Nisbet, R. (1970), 'The Sociological Tradition', Heinemann.

Pashukanis, E. (1978), 'Law and Marxism', Inklinks.

Pearce, F. (1976), 'Crimes of the Powerful', Pluto.

Pearson, G. (1975), 'Deviant Imagination', Macmillan.

President's Commission on Law Enforcement and Administration of Justice (1967), 'The Challenge of Crime in a Free Society', Washington, D.C., Government Printing Office.

Quinney, R. (1977), 'Class, State and Crime', New York, McKay.

Reiman, J. (1979), 'The Rich Get Richer and the Poor Get Prison', New York, Wiley.

Schur, E. (1973), 'Radical Non-Intervention', Englewood Cliffs, Prentice-Hall.

Tappan, P. (1970), Who is the Criminal? in 'The Sociology of Crime and Delinquency', ed. M. Wolfgang, L. Savitz and N. Johnston, 2nd ed., New York, Wiley, pp.41-8.

Taylor, Laurie (1971), 'Deviance and Society', Michael Joseph.

Taylor, Ian, Walton, P. and Young, J. (1973), 'The New Criminology', Routledge & Kegan Paul.

Taylor, Ian, Walton, P. and Young, J., ed. (1975), 'Critical Criminology', Routledge & Kegan Paul.

Wright, E. Olin (1973), 'The Politics of Punishment', New York, Harper & Row.

Young, J. (1979), Left Idealism, Reformism and Beyond, in 'Capitalism and the Rule of Law', ed. National Deviancy Conference, Hutchinson.

15 Individual deviance: the search for the criminal personality

R. J. Sapsford

INTRODUCTION

During the eighteenth and early nineteenth centuries, crime
was regarded for the most part as the deliberately chosen
behaviour of rational actors; man has the ability to think and
choose, and those who break the law at the expense of others
do so wilfully and selfishly. The punishment of crime, therefore, considered the needs of the victim and, much more, the
need of the state to deter others from similar offences, and
could be as severe as was needed to achieve these ends, for
the criminal had forfeited his or her right to consideration. In
the second half of the nineteenth century, however, two broad
groupings of academics began to doubt the ability of the
criminal to choose and therefore the appropriateness of the
scale of punishment then in force. One, dominated by leading
psychiatrists in France and England, began to consider
criminality as a form of mental illness, and their speculations
led eventually to the strong line of research into the environmental and developmental antecedents of criminality, and into
its treatment, which is discussed by Rudi Dallos in article
17 in this book. The other looked more to man's physical nature
and came to believe that at least some criminals are *born* bad
and have little choice in the matter. One of the earliest exponents of this view was Caesare Lombroso.

Lombroso, a professor of psychiatry at the University of
Pavia, was researching in prisons and asylums to determine
the similarities and differences between criminals and the insane.
He describes, in the introduction to his daughter's book on
his work, how he was carrying out a post-mortem examination
of a famous bandit when he suddenly noticed a number of
anomalies in the skull which suggested regression to a less

Source: article commissioned for this volume. R.J. Sapsford
is Lecturer in Research Methods, Faculty of Social Sciences,
the Open University.

developed human form.

This was not merely an idea, but a revelation. At the sight
of that skull, I seemed to see all of a sudden, lighted up as
a vast plain under a flaming sky, the problem of the nature
of the criminal - an atavistic being who reproduces in his
person the ferocious instincts of primitive humanity and the
inferior animals.

His conclusions were not based on a single case, of course -
he and his students measured the skulls of many thousands of
men, including normal people as well as the criminal and the
insane. Combing these measurements with physiognomic and
behavioural observations, he reported

that many of the characteristics found in savages and among
the coloured races are also to be found in habitual delinquents.
They have in common, for example, thinning hair, lack of
strength and weight, low cranial capacity, receding foreheads,
highly developed frontal sinuses, a high frequency of medio-
frontal sutures, precocious synosteosis (especially frontal),
protrusion of the curved line of the temporal, simplicity of
the sutures, considerable thickness of the cranial bone,
enormous development of the jaws and the zygomata, obli-
quity of the orbits, darker skin, thicker, curly hair, large,
or handle-shaped ears, a greater analogy between the two
sexes, less pronounced genetic activity, a lower degree of
sensitivity to pain, complete moral insensitiveness, indolence,
the absence of any remorse, improvidence appearing at times
in the guise of courage, and courage alternating with base
cowardice, great vanity, facile superstition, exaggerated
susceptibility of the ego, and finally the relative concept of
the divinity and morals.

He was prepared to allow that not all criminals are born to the
role - some achieve it through mental disorder or the pressure
of the environment - but for others he saw crime as an inherited
and atavistic propensity towards behaviour which humanity as
a species has outgrown.

Lombroso is often considered a founding father of criminology
because of his rejection of the philosophical and speculative
approach to the nature of criminal man and his insistence on
empirical evidence. Actually, he was by no means the first to
take such a line. Primacy should perhaps be awarded to Franz
Joseph Gall some sixty years earlier. Gall's phrenological work,
seeking to relate character and abilities to the size and shape
of bumps on the skull, is nowadays often written off as the
speculations of a crank. However, it was actually a serious
scientific attempt to locate centres in the brain which were
primarily responsible for various activities; once Gall's pre-
supposition that the structure of the brain would be exactly
replicated in the shape of the skull had been discarded, this
line of research led to positive results, as we shall see in a
later section. (Gall's major work runs to four volumes, and
the English version runs to six; interested readers who want

a short summary and some further references should consult Savitz et al., 1977).

Gall and Lombroso are but two of a long line of investigators on the trail of the criminal personality, a search which still continues. Some have looked for social factors, particularly childhood experiences, which might turn a potentially ordinary human being into a criminal; these theories often stress the role of the social environment to the neglect of the person whose environment it is. Gall, Lombroso and their successors, however, take the opposite view that criminals are born, not made, and that criminality is inherited and/or physiologically determined.[1] It is this line of research which I shall be tracing in this article, through the ramifications of sociobiology and the eugenics movement, medicine and surgery, and the psychometric classification of human personality by academic psychologists.

For purposes of clear exposition I shall accept the axioms of this approach as given and as beyond the need for argument in the course of this article. Three of them need to be noted at this point as at least problematic, however:

(a) this kind of theory assumes that such complex and essentially social behaviours as the commission of crimes can be explained at the level of the individual, and

(b) it assumes that the explanation can relevantly be cast in terms of the individual's biology or experience, without reference to 'mind' or 'meaning' or how *social* reality is constructed by the individual. To an extent one may argue, quite cogently, that this kind of approach misses out most of what is distinctive about being human and of what makes sense of our experiences; Rudi Dallos and I have attempted to argue just this in article 19 in this Reader - The Person and Group Reality. On the other hand, one must admit that some of the limitations on our behaviour have a biological basis - we are not free to fly at will, having no wings - and it is legitimate to ask whether some at least of our supposedly mental and decisional life also has a biological basis. Thirdly,

(c) it is assumed by theorists in this area that we can be 'scientific' and stand back in a value-neutral pose from the consequences of our theories. This third assumption is explored, in a very introductory fashion, in the final section of the article. In particular one should note that the pose of value-neutrality must itself be open to discussion on ethical grounds in an area such as this, where theory leads almost inevitably to practical intervention in the lives of people and where the intervention may take such irreversible forms as psychosurgery or sterilization.

THE EVOLUTION OF THE CRIMINAL

The claim that human behaviour can best be understood as the outcome of a process of biological evolution is most strongly expressed in the work of a group of recent writers - among them ethologists and geneticists - who have come collectively to be known as 'sociobiologists'. For example, it is claimed that 'behaviour and social structure, like all other biological phenomena, can be studied as 'organs', extensions of the genes that exist because of their superior adaptive value' (E.O. Wilson, 1975, p.22). Even more dramatic is the way the idea is expressed by Tiger and Fox (1971, p.17): 'We have confidently asserted that identifiable propensities for behaviour are in the wiring. Unless we look to divine intervention, these got there by the same route as they got into the wiring of any other animal: by mutation and natural selection'. That *physical* characteristics are determined in this manner - given an appropriate environment for their development - is by now well established. What is the evidence, however, for the evolution of behavioural patterns?

The evidence tends to be of two kinds: studies demonstrating the influence of inherited traits on behaviour, and ethological field-studies demonstrating how adaptive behaviours become dominant in a species. (A third kind of evidence, fossils, is available for studying the transmission of physical characteristics, but behaviours do not often leave fossils.) The sociobiologists tend to specialize more in ethological studies which try to trace the survival function of behaviours and the ways in which they can be transmitted. We all know of examples of selective breeding for traits of behaviour, because we all know that dogs are selectively bred on this basis, but this kind of selectivity is contaminated by the environment, including the actions of the human handler - it is a problem of naturalistic research that it is very difficult to separate out the effects of heredity and early environment. However, controlled studies have been carried out in which the environment is made as similar as possible for different breeds, and human handlers are excluded, and the characteristic behaviours still emerge (Scott, 1972). Learning-theorists among psychologists are used to the notion of genetically pure strains of rats which show typical behaviours: strains have been bred successfully which show high ability at maze-learning (Tryon, 1940), high or low emotionality (see Scott, 1972), high or low incidence of avoidance behaviour (Brush et al., 1979) and even quite complex patterns of nest-building behaviour (see Pribram, 1971). Such ideas were long ago extended to the human species through works such as Galton's 'Hereditary Genius' (1869) which argue that high achievement within the well-educated stratum of society tends to be concentrated in families more often than might be expected by chance.

Such evidence is weak for three very closely related reasons.

First, the parallel between inheritance of non-physical characteristics in animals and such inheritance in man is a doubtful one: man's environment includes a language and a culture which can enforce a form of 'inheritance of acquired characteristics' in a way unknown in the animal world. Second, the cases examined by Galton included families where transmission of achievement by non-biological means - e.g. by being born to a position of privilege - is an extremely plausible alternative hypothesis. Third, Galton's definition of achievement can at best be described as a limited one; Samuel Smiles (1859) carried out a very similar study which included industrialists among the eminent and came to an entirely contrary conclusion - that many currently eminent men came from an undistinguished ancestry.

More fruitful may be the lines of research which link current human behaviour with that of species which may be considered our evolutionary ancestors, and which try to show the survival-value of given behaviours. In the latter genre we have the development by Hamilton (1964) and E.O. Wilson (1975) of the notion of 'inclusive fitness' (that a gene's success must be measured in terms of its dominance in a population, not just the survival of particular carriers of it) to explain altruistic behaviour: altruism is a survival characteristic, despite its potential cost to the individual, because it ensures the survival of near relatives, who share a proportion of the benefactor's genes.[2] Such thinking can also be used to explain our inappropriate behaviours, by showing their former survival potential (remembering that evolution is generally an *extremely* slow process). For example, many of the physiological signs of anger or fear clearly have the function of gearing the body for fight or flight, which would once have been appropriate ways of dealing with the environment, though now outdated in most contexts.

Some present behaviours can be seen in our evolutionary ancestors; for example, smiling occurs among chimpanzees in many of the situations where a human baby will also smile. Lorenz (1966) has suggested that human military gestures might usefully be seen as a redirected form of the aggression displays common to humans and chimpanzees, although culture gives them a different meaning. Criminal behaviour - aggression and acquisitiveness - would be seen by writers of this genre as of obvious survival value in more primitive societies, lingering on but now inappropriate. (Note that we are talking here not of a 'gene for crime', but of the transmission of generalized behavioural tendencies which may sometimes result in crime.)

From the last quarter of the nineteenth century well into the twentieth there has been a succession of studies purporting to show that various dysfunctional traits such as criminality and feeble-mindedness ran as much in 'blood-lines' as do haemophilia, eye-colour and blood-type. The first and most notorious is Richard Dugdale's rather extraordinary book 'The Jukes: a Study in Crime, Pauperism, Disease and Heredity', published in 1877. Visiting New York prisons in an official capacity, Dugdale came across six offenders - their crimes ranged from vagrancy to attempted rape and attempted murder - who were to some degree related by blood. In his own words:

> These six persons belonged to a long lineage, reaching back to the early colonists, and had intermarried [very] slightly with the emigrant population of the old world ... They had lived in the same locality for generations, and were so despised by the reputable community that their family name had come to be used generically as a term of reproach ... Out of twenty-nine males ... the immediate blood relations of these six persons, seventeen of them were criminal, or fifty-eight per cent.

Dugdale, and later Estabrook (1916), traced in all some twelve hundred ancestors of the Juke family back to their 'founding father', and documented what they considered an untypical and intolerable incidence of crime, pauperism, prostitution and illegitimate birth. (The pauperism and the criminality tended to run in different branches of the family.)

Another book early in this century, Henry Goddard's 'The Kallikak Family', documents the family line which sprang from the union of an American soldier with a feeble-minded tavern girl. Goddard traced 480 descendants, of whom 143 were feeble-minded, 36 illegitimate, 41 described by him as 'sexually immoral persons, mostly prostitutes', or keepers of 'houses of ill fame', 24 alcoholics and three criminals.

> We have here a family of good English blood ... throughout four generations maintaining a reputation for honour and respectability of which they are justly proud. Then a scion of this family, in an unguarded moment, steps aside from the paths of rectitude and, with the help of a feeble-minded girl, starts a line of mental defectives that is truly appalling. After this mistake, he returns to the traditions of his family, marries a woman of his own quality, and through her carries on a line of respectability equal to that of his ancestors.

(Note that we are now talking about the inheritance of strictly moral categories).

It is interesting to note the extent to which previously formed theory can be imposed on data by the determined researcher. In the report (Goddard, 1910) on the original work which later led to 'Kallikaks', where the data-base is rather more thoroughly documented, a substantial number of families are described in which some form of defect is described as 'running', and some of the attempts made to establish the connection are redolent of special pleading. There are several cases of 'skipped generations', and one classic family to whose three diagnosed feeble-minded cases we might also add the two others who died young, because, according to the definition of Tredgold, which describes an idiot as 'one who cannot avoid

ordinary dangers', these children were also defective, since
they were both killed at play, apparently not being able to
protect themselves in a usually harmless game (p.50).

The Kallikaks, as it happened, were more notable for their
feeble-mindedness than their criminality. In a later book (1916),
however, Goddard gives the results of applying intelligence
tests to a sample of imprisoned delinquents, where he classified
50 per cent of his subjects as feeble-minded. Thus he felt he
had established a connection between criminality and feeble-
mindedness: though not all of the feeble-minded were criminals,
50 per cent of criminals were feeble-minded. As he had already
established to his own satisfaction that feeble-mindedness was
an hereditable trait, he felt justified in arguing that criminality
was also hereditable. (It should be pointed out that many later
studies of prisoner intelligence, which include control-groups
from outside prison, fail to replicate his results - see, for
example, Healy and Bronner (1936), Tulchin (1939), Eissler
(1949), Cleckley (1964), Banister et al. (1973), Bolton et al.
(1976).)

Some of the best evidence that non-physical characteristics
may be genetically determined at least in part comes from
studies of 'identical' (monozygotic) and 'fraternal' (dizygotic)
twins. Not all twins are identical, even though they are
conceived at the same time: identical twins come from the same
fertilized ovum, which splits and develops into two children,
but fraternal twins result from simultaneous fertilization of
two ova, both of which develop independently. Thus identical
twins have an identical genetic make-up, but fraternal twins
share only a proportion of their genes. If we find that identical
twins resemble each other more closely than do fraternal twins
in some behavioural characteristic, we may reasonably assert
that the behaviour is genetically determined: both kinds of
twins would have similar environment and early experience, but
only the identical twins have precisely similar genes. Where the
twins are separated at birth, so that they have *different*
environments, and identical twins still show greater behavioural
similarity than fraternal ones, the case is virtually proved.

Unfortunately, twinning is a fairly rare phenomenon, and twins
separated at birth are even harder to find. None the less,
'twin studies' have been carried out. One of the earliest studies
is reported by Johannes Lange in 1929. Of a sample of 15 pairs
of identical twins one of whom was in prison, the other had
also been in prison in ten cases; one of the pairs was separated
at birth, and another not long after. Of 17 pairs of fraternal
twins where one brother was in prison, the other had been
inside in only two cases. The rate for the fraternal twins is
not significantly different from that for siblings who are not
twins, but the figure for identical twins is far too high to be
a coincidence, particularly as they tended to have been imprisoned for similar crimes. Subsequent studies of criminality,
discussed below, come to similar results. Among other evidence

for genetic transmission of non-physical states we might well
look at the impressive set of investigations of the mental health
of twins reported by Shields (1973, p.581): in six series of
monozygotic twins (one of whom was schizophrenic), in five
different countries and from periods differing by more than
thirty years, at least 58 per cent of the second twins were also
diagnosed schizophrenic; for series of fraternal twins reported
in the same studies the figure is never higher than 18 per
cent. Further evidence, also from Shields (1973, p.568), shows
that monozygotic twins are more similar than dizygotic ones
in their scores on the two principal scales of Eysenck's
Personality Inventory - i.e. in general temperament. Impressive
evidence for some effect of genetic similarity on criminality
does seem to be accumulating. Rennie (1978, p.80) cites
eight studies similar to Lange's, carried out between 1932 and
1976 in countries as diverse as England, the United States
of America and Japan, seven of which find a significant difference between likelihood of imprisonment for identical and
fraternal twin-pairs one of whom is in prison; the eighth
(Dalgard and Kringlen, 1976) shows a difference which does
not reach statistical significance but is in the same direction.[3]
Eysenck, in 'Crime and Personality', brought together figures
from a number of 'twin studies' involving deviance other than
conviction and imprisonment, and again there is a strong
suggestion of a genetic effect. In the first edition of the book
(in 1964) he had 65 per cent of monozygotic twin-pairs where
both had been diagnosed alcoholic, 71 per cent where both
were convicted of crime as an adult, 85 per cent where both
were labelled as juvenile delinquents, and 87 per cent where
both showed behavioural disorder in childhood; except in the
'juvenile delinquency' category, the figures for concordance
among fraternal twin-pairs were half this size. In the third
edition of the book, in 1977, he had added further studies to
the 'adult crime' category, roughly trebling the sample size,
and finds only 55 per cent of concordant pairs among monozygotic twins - but as few as 13 per cent of concordant pairs
among dizygotic ones, so the point which he is making is not
weakened.

  Some of the results are so strong that they must surely
cause some suspicion. For example, could some of the variance
still be explained by the environment? One might argue for
instance that identical twins have more similar environments
than fraternal ones, because of their perceived similarity.
This could be ruled out in part by studies of twins separated
at birth, but there have been few such studies. However,
Hutchings and Mednick (in Mednick and Christiansen, 1977)
looked at children (*not* twins) adopted at birth, and compared
them according to the reported criminality of both the adoptive
and the biological father. The interesting results are summarized in Table 15.1. The criminality of the adoptive father
seems to make little difference, but children whose biological

Table 15.1   The criminality of children adopted at birth

Nature of non-biological father	Nature of biological father	Percentage of children who had been convicted of a crime by adulthood
Non-criminal	Non-criminal	10.4
Criminal	Non-criminal	11.4
Non-criminal	Criminal	21.0

Source: Rennie (1978)

fathers were criminal were far more likely than others to become criminal themselves. This still fails to establish the case beyond doubt, because other variables not noticed by the researchers could in fact be causally related to the behaviour - for example, there is evidence that the proportion of males to females among one's siblings may affect one's deviant behaviour (Jones et al., 1980). Moreover, one should remember that people with some kinds of criminal record are rarely permitted to become adoptive parents. None the less, there seems a strong likelihood that one's genetic inheritance has some effect on one's behaviour.

A definitive answer would be provided if we could identify an actual pattern of genes and show its association with criminal behaviour, but biological science is not yet so far advanced. What we can do, however, is to identify the genetic determinants of sex and thence the genetic consequences of the chromosomes (strings of genes) which determine sex. The normal male has one full-length X sex-chromosome and one shorter Y chromosome, while the normal female has two X chromosomes, and we have long known that certain physical characteristics - tendency to baldness, to colour-blindness and to haemophilia, for example - are carried on the portion of the X chromosome which is not 'masked' by the shorter Y chromosome, so that these conditions are carried dormant by the female but are manifested most frequently (or, in the case of haemophilia, only) in the male. Now most of the population has this system of pairing among sex-chromosomes (XX for females, XY for males), but anomalies occur in which extra chromosomes, either X or Y, are present, and these (comparatively) easily identified anomalies have also been shown to have consequences for physical characteristics and for behaviour. For a while it was thought that the presence of an extra Y chromosome (giving an XYY pattern) might be associated with certain kinds of criminal behaviour, and this illusory hope caused a considerable stir in the criminological world.

The first report of this 'syndrome' was in 1961 (Sandberg et al., cited in Fox, 1971). Criminological interest was aroused in 1965, however, when Patricia Jacobs and her co-workers published a survey of 197 mentally subnormal male patients in the Scottish special hospital at Carstairs who had exhibited dangerous, violent or criminal propensities. Of these 197, twelve exhibited some chromosomal abnormality, and eight (3.5 per cent) had the XYY pattern - the extra Y chromosome. This may fail to catch your interest, but a survey of 1,709 randomly-chosen adult males and 266 new-born infants failed to show a single XYY male, so the difference in incidence is actually rather startling. This finding was followed up by researchers all over the western world - something like 200 papers were published in medical, psychological and criminological journals in the late 1960s and early 1970s - and at first it appeared a real 'find'. Several studies of males in maximum-security establishments confirmed the untypical incidence of the XYY pattern (see for example, Forssman, 1970; Griffiths et al., 1969; Kessler and Moos, 1972), and they seemed to identify the XYY male as prone to mental illness (particularly psychopathy), of lower IQ and achievement, with an anti-social personality, and probably with a history of offences against property, alcoholism and/or covert homosexuality. The syndrome was raised in courts as a medical defence several times in the late 1960s, though never successfully.

However, in later papers things started going wrong. For example, the XYY pattern may be common in maximum-security establishments but it is rare in ordinary prisons (Jarvik et al., 1973), and it is clear that most people who have it never finish up in an institution (Moor, 1972; Owen, 1972). Disagreements began to emerge on whether this type's proclivity was towards property offences or crimes of violence (Mulvihill and Tumin, 1969) and even on the characteristic temperament of the XYY male - whether he was masculine and aggressive or timid and passive (contrast Forssman (1970) and Jarvik et al., (1973) with Debray (1972) and Kessler and Moos (1972)). An alternative explanation for the higher incidence in security institutions has been offered by Fox (1971): their greater height and size increases the chance of them being labelled as dangerous by psychiatrists and the courts (though an association with criminality still remains after height is controlled - see Mednick and Christiansen, 1977). By now this discovery, which looked so promising in its early years, has more or less lost its interest for criminologists as the contradictions have mounted up.

Many, indeed most, geneticists have contended that inherited behavioural tendencies can readily be overcome, with training. Dugdale, for instance, believed in the power of education to reform even the depraved Jukes, if only they could be caught in time. By and large, however, this kind of study has often been taken as identifying a class of incurable deviants for whom segregation and confinement is the only 'treatment' of benefit to society - or even elimination, for 'evolutionary' thinking leads all too naturally to thoughts of selective breeding and the deliberate weeding-out of unfit genes. The effect of 'The Jukes' on European and American minds has been rightly described as a feeling of 'the dangerous classes as not only a physical but a *biological* threat - philoprogenitive, promiscuous and irresponsible. These were the people who, breeding like rats in their alleys and hovels, threatened, by sheer increase in numbers, to overwhelm the well-bred classes of society' (Rennie, 1978, p.79). Francis Galton, who was one of the earliest English 'eugenicists' (supporters of the proposition that human breeding should be controlled selectively in order to improve the race) speaks of 'the infamous Jukes family' in his 1883 book as one piece of evidence for this position. Tredgold (1910) speaks of feeble-mindedness as 'intimately ... connected with ... pauperism, prostitution and crime' and warns that 'the propagation of these persons is threatening to imperil the very life of the nation by inducing a widespread degeneracy'. Goddard speaks explicitly for the extinction of certain blood-lines: 'Careful studies have shown ... that at least two thirds of these mental defectives ... belong to the strains of the human family whose intelligence lies below that which is required for the performance of their duties as citizens' (1916, pp.106-7) - and argues that the feeble-minded should be prevented from breeding in order to help eliminate criminal propensities from the race. Havelock Ellis, a contributor to the study of crime in addition to his better-known work on the psychology of sex, regarded crime as one stage in the progressive deterioration of genetic lines and was quite explicit in recommending that such inferiors should not reproduce themselves: 'We must know what are those stocks that are unlikely to produce the worthy citizen of the future ... Those who uphold the ideals of eugenics are bound to proclaim the duty of all who are probably unfit to become the parents of a fine race to abstain from procreation', and he goes on to recommend the voluntary sterilization of criminals and the insane.

One might be inclined to write off the eugenicist movement as a historical curiosity, and many academic psychologists are inclined to dismiss the 'misuse' of their theories and tests by administrators as 'psychological illiteracy' unsupported by any reputable member of the 'profession'. However, this kind of disclaimer of the ethical implications of one's work are unconvincing for three reasons.

(a) Sterilization of the feeble-minded in order to preserve the quality of the gene-pool has continued to be advocated (and practised) by the medical profession long after the fashion for eugenics had died out elsewhere. In the 1930s and 1940s many thousands of mentally retarded people were sterilized in

Virginia with the explicit intention of improving the human species (Reinhold, 1980). In England such a sterilization was a cause celebre in 1975, and a Secretary of State made a tacit admission recently that the practice continues ('Hansard', 16 January 1980, 759-60).

(b) Theories with respectable antecedents may be used by practitioners in ways which their proponents might well consider abhorrent. Bernstein's research on educational disadvantage, for example, has been used or mis-used to declare working-class children *ineducable* (Bantock, 1965; Rosen, 1972). Although many of the academic 'fathers' of intelligence testing may have been genuinely interested in the structure of intelligence *per se* or in overcoming environmental handicap, their tests have been used (inappropriately, because of the culture-bound nature of all such tests) to debar low scorers from immigration to the United States along with coolies, convicts and prostitutes (see Kamin, 1974, for a review).

(c) Over and above the use of such work by practitioners there is a solid substrate of belief in the inheritability of 'nastiness and viciousness' in the popular culture of the Western world. One has only to point to the popularity of such books as 'The Naked Ape' by Desmond Morris to show that sociobiology has a ready market among educated and semi-educated non-specialists. This tends to mean that views which in calmer perspective may be seen as based on emotive and 'political' considerations may in times of crisis come to command support in 'reputable' academic circles. The debate over the inheritance of intelligence and thence over the educability of blacks and the working class, is one such case (again, see Kamin for a review). Another and more dramatic one is the theory of 'race' which underlay the Nazi 'final solution' to the 'problem' of Jews, Slavs, Gypsies and other minorites. One is tempted to believe that this line of theorization could never have commanded popular support, and to say that no competent scientist of the day could have endorsed the Nazi theories. Such endorsement is to be found, however, in Yerkes (1921, particularly the chapter edited by Boring, Brigham (1923) and Hirsch (1926, 1930), among others. Brigham at least was a fully convinced exponent of the difference between the Nordic, Alpine, Slav and Mediterranean races, and the others are at the least compatible with such a line of 'scientific theory'.

THE CURE OF CRIME

Apart from segregation or elimination, a further line of treatment suggested by the emphasis on biological factor is medication or surgery. If criminal behaviour (or behavioural traits which may lead to crime) is indeed the result of something

physical and structural, whether it be a hereditary defect or
the result of environmental trauma, then it would fall naturally
within the province of the medical profession. Physical illnesses
are cured by physical means.[4] So while one line of research
followed Lombroso in looking for the genetic origins of deviant
behaviour, another developed (out of Gall and the phrenologists)
which looked for the site of damage or deficiency in the brain,
with the aim of remedying the defect by drugs or surgery.

Attempts at localizing emotional function within the brain
have been carried out using either electrical stimulation via
implanted electrodes or surgical destruction of brain areas or
their connections to other parts of the brain. (Unremarkably,
such experiments have been carried out predominantly on
animals.) The human brain consists of three areas which succeed each other developmentally - a primitive brain-stem which
is also found in reptiles, a mid-brain which we share with the
lower mammals, and the *neocortex* of the higher mammals and
man - and the consensus now appears to be that emotions and
the regulation of voluntary behaviour are in some sense
'centred' in the midbrain: more specifically, attention has
focused on the limbic system, a large lobe surrounding the
primitive brain stem.

Work on electrical stimulation of the hypothalamus - an area
towards the top of the brain stem - suggests that full blown
attack behaviour could be elicited by this means in a wide
variety of species. Lesions (surgical damage) in this area
destroy the response. Greater interest has centred in two
other areas of the limbic system, however. The amygdala, an
almond-shaped nucleus to one side of this portion of the brain,
seems to produce hyperemotionality when stimulated, or the
reverse when damaged surgically (Papez, 1937; MacLean,
1949) and alteration to the control of fight and flight responses
(Egger and Flynn, 1963; G.V. Goddard, 1964, 1969; Schreiner
and Kling, 1953). The septal region, above the amygdala and
directly connected to it, produces something like opposed
effects under stimulation or lesion (Slotnick and McMullen,
1972; Slotnick et al., 1974) - though the effects even of lesion
may be only temporary (Gotsik and Marshall, 1972) - and the
suggestion that the two together act as a 'check and balance'
system has been raised explicitly by King and Meyer (1958).
Equally important from the point of view of human behaviour
is the extensive evidence that lesions in this area may disrupt
learning (Burkett and Bunnell, 1966; Butters and Rosvold,
1968; Schwartzbaum et al., 1964; Thompson and Langer,
1963).

What relevance this work, done predominantly on cats and
rats, has for the understanding of human behaviour is almost
entirely unclear. Classic studies on wounded soldiers after
the First World War (summarized in Mark and Ervin, 1970,
pp.56-7) certainly suggest that damage in these areas can lead
to violent or antisocial behaviour and to difficulty in the con-

trol of impulse. Various writers have reported violent or
psychopathic behaviour in previously normal subjects following
hypothalamic tumour (Reeves and Plum, 1969; Malamud, 1967)
or encephalitis (Brill, 1959; Himmelhoch et al., 1970). None
the less, there is no record of amygdaloid stimulation producing
assaultative behaviour in humans, except where there was
already a history of such behaviour (see Valenstein, 1973,
pp.240-7 and 253-4). The evidence is therefore ambiguous as
regards humans, to say the least - the more so because some
of the reported 'lessening of violence' in animals in fact
amounts less to a cure for a specific behaviour than to a total
flattening of all behaviour (Valenstein, 1973, passim).

None the less, surgical cure of human violence has been
attempted. Early work followed on experimental disruption of
the prefrontal cortex (the distinctively 'higher' part of the
brain) in monkeys at Yale University during the 1930s, where
rage responses appeared to be totally extinguished. During
the 1940s these 'lobotomies' were performed on some 40,000
severely disturbed mental patients in the United States, but
growing evidence of severe side effects in terms of gross
personality deterioration led to their virtual discontinuance
in the 1950s (Valenstein, 1973, p.55). However, lobotomy and
the related operation of leucotomy are performed from time to
time to this day; four 'aggressive' female patients were
leucotomized at Rampton in the 1970s ('Guardian', 17 October
1980). More recently there has been a strong vogue for more
precise surgical techniques destroying only a very few cells,
generally from the amygdala or hypothalamus, and marked
improvement in behaviour is reported by the surgeons in many
of these cases (see Valenstein, 1973, pp.54-5 and 213-24).
However, even the most passionate supporters of these surgical
procedures are unable to deny that 'unfortunate' side effects
such as impotence follow in a far from negligible proportion
of cases (see, for example, Mark et al., 1972). One American
State's courts ruled that any such procedure was unlawful
when applied to the incarcerated because they are in no
position to give an informed consent (Kamowitz vs Department
of Mental Health, described by Rennie, 1978, pp.236-42),
but there is no general agreement on this point and amygdalec-
tomies are still occasionally performed on prisoners and compulsorily hospitalized mental patients in this country and in
the United States. Figures for the incidence specifically of
amygdalectomy in England and Wales are not available to me,
but 88 patients underwent psycho-surgery of unspecified
kinds in 1977-8 ('Hansard', 16 January 1980, 759). In the only
case which I have myself encountered - described briefly in
an Appendix to Sapsford (1979a) - there was considerable
apparent improvement over the previously extremely disturbed
behaviour, and the patient himself believed in the efficiency
of the procedure, but the results were by no means
unambiguous.

The other and less drastic medical approach to the control of violent and impulsive behaviour is by the use of drugs - mostly tranquillizers. The major tranquillizers - serpasil, chlorpromazine, the phenothiazines and, more recently, lithium carbonate - are now well established in the treatment of various kinds of psychoticism (Goldberg, 1968; Gittleman-Klein and Klein, 1968; Cole and Davis, 1968; Schou, 1968). All of these drugs seem to have the effect of slowing electrical activity in the limbic system (see Leaton, 1971). They do not 'cure' the disorder, but merely suppress its symptoms. The prolonged suppression of acute anxiety and bizarre behaviour, however, can itself be of great therapeutic benefit to a disturbed patient by giving him a 'breathing space' in which to readjust to his family and the wider social world.

Milder drugs such as the barbiturates and their later cousins meprobromate (Miltown, Equanil) and chlorodiazepoxide hydrocholoride (Librium) are used for the relief of acute or chronic neurotic anxiety. They are more selective than the major tranquillizers, less likely to cause drowsiness, and quite useless for the treatment of the psychoses, but for the help of neurotics their efficacy is limited but well established (Rickels, 1968). Again, the effect appears to be mediated through the limbic system (Schallek et al., 1962).

Unfortunately, the usefulness of the major tranquillizers is at least partially offset by the range of side-effects which they sometimes produce, from drowsiness, depression, fevers, chills, skin rashes and nervous 'shaking' to anaemia, liver damage and (at large doses) shock, coma and respiratory collapse. Even the minor tranquillizers may cause the occasional skin rash, and perhaps slight cognitive impairment in elderly patients. Also, both classes are habituating, and withdrawal from them can cause considerable distress. None the less the use of minor tranquillizers in the general population is so widespread that many doctors have become alarmed by it; some are now refusing to prescribe them to patients who arrive in their surgeries with problems self-diagnosed as amenable to this treatment.

In prison the minor tranquillizers have been used very widely, partly for curative reasons but perhaps even more because tranquillized prisoners are easier to manage. There has been some degree of protest from prisoners at the apparent over-prescriptions in England and America, but also some degree of welcome; in some American prisons tranquillizers have been used as a black-market currency (Rennie, 1978, pp.194-5) and some prisoners who find prison a particularly threatening place may *demand* medication. One particularly harmful aspect of drug use may be over-prescription to men in the early stages of long and indeterminate sentences; their withdrawal as release comes nearer may badly unsettle the prisoner and thus prolong his term in prison. One man whom I met in 1975 - see Sapsford (1979a, pp.181-3) - certainly had his life-sentence prolonged because of disturbed behaviour after he was taken off Valium, after five years of its prescription, in preparation for possible release. (There was also a fashion in America during the early 1970s for the prescription of lithium to control recurrent violent behaviour. Its prescribers report that the prisoners certainly experienced less inclination towards violence, but a proportion of them also developed the symptoms of paranoia - see Tupin et al., 1973.)

Another way of controlling aggression in humans has been by tampering with the patient's hormone balance, hormones being chemical substances released into the bloodstream which have been shown to play a major directing role in the control of development and behaviour at all levels. Greatest interest has focused on the ones involved in sexual development, and particularly on the male hormone testosterone. In most species the male is more aggressive than the female, and castration usually reduces this aggressiveness. Rats castrated after puberty lose their natural aggression but can have it restored by injections of testosterone, though the injections have little or no effect on rats castrated before puberty. Among humans, substances which inhibit the production of testosterone have been injected, in prisons and mental hospitals, to control the behaviour of 'sexual deviates' prone to aggressive outbursts, with some reports of success (see, for example, Blumer and Migeon, 1975). In Denmark during the 1950s and 1960s some psychopaths were castrated (with their agreement) to reduce their violent tendencies; some success was claimed for the pro-gramme, but it has since been abandoned (Stürup, 1960, 1972; see also Conrad, 1965, pp.235-6). There has also been a fairly widespread use of 'female' hormones to reduce the masculinity of rapists, again with some success claimed, but with pre-dictable side-effects. 'This tends to have the effect in males of developing female characteristics, such as enlarged breasts, which may require surgery' (Hall Williams, 1975, pp.190-1).

'UNDERSTANDING' THE CRIMINAL

So far we have looked at genetic and ethological studies iden-tifying the 'born criminal' and at medical and surgical attempts to 'cure' the criminal. There is a third class of theorists who also locate criminality firmly as a property of the individual but who allow that individuals differ among themselves - though in predictable ways - and who proceed to develop classificatory schemes for the population in order to match appropriate treat-ment to appropriate psychological types of offender. They attempt, in a word, to 'understand' the criminal, but not in the sense in which the work is used in later articles in this Reader (to understand what criminal behaviour *means* to the criminal). Rather, they try to understand what *drives* the criminal to his behaviour, with the intention of tinkering with causes. Typically this approach works through a typology of behavioural styles grounded in physiology or even gross physique (Kretschmer, 1921; Sheldon, 1949). As the main example in this section we shall be looking at the research of Hans Eysenck and his colleagues, whose theories are about character-traits - enduring dispositions to behave in certain ways - but grounded in speculations about physiological mechanisms underlying and explaining these dispositions.

In early versions of his theory, Eysenck posited two basic 'dimensions' of personality which are statistically independent of each other - *neuroticism* (stability or instability of behaviour - the 'neurotic' label is something of a misnomer) and extra-version-introversion (impulsiveness, sociability and generally outgoing behaviour, versus shyness, control, withdrawal and inversion). He proceeded, with his colleagues, to construct a questionnaire measure - the MPI (Maudsley Personality Inventory, named after the hospital where it was developed) or in later versions EPI (Eysenck Personality Inventory) - by the usual method of getting groups of people who differ in known ways to answer a large number of questions about themselves, then keeping only those questions which differentiate the groups. The two scales as eventually produced appear validly to differentiate neurotics from normals and extraverts from introverts. Factor analysis demonstrates that the two scales are largely unrelated (Eysenck, 1960a).

The questionnaire was first intended as a diagnostic instrument for hospitals. All mental patients - or virtually all - score highly on N, but introverts and extraverts differ in the kinds of mental disturbance which they show: introverts tend to develop anxiety, depression, phobias, obsessions and compulsions, while extraverts are prone to personality disorders, mania and hysteria (Eysenck, 1960a). Interest soon focused on the high-NE quadrant, the people who score above the average on both neuroticism and extraversion, because of the wide range of 'deviants' to be found there. For example, people prone to traffic accidents tend to score highly on both scales (Fine, 1963). So do unmarried mothers (Sybil Eysenck, 1961), psychopaths (Eysenck, 1964), women criminals (Syed, cited in Eysenck, 1964) and male prisoners (Eysenck, 1964). Among short-term prisoners, it is the high-NE men who are most likely to be recidivists (Andry, 1963). On the other hand, there tends on the whole to be no effect of imprisonment, according to Eysenck (1964) - men are as likely to score within this quadrant on the first day of a long sentence as after ten years - so the figures demonstrate a personality difference, not an effect of environment. (Some doubts might be raised here; both Heskin et al. (1973) and Sapsford (1978, 1979b) found an increase of introversion with length of imprisonment).

From these findings, from physiological evidence and from some oddities of how people and animals learn, Eysenck has

built up a theory of how people come to have a behavioural
style which leads them to deviance. Eysenck's physiological
theories centre not upon the mid-brain and the limbic system,
but upon an even more primitive structure, the *reticular
formation*, which appears to act as a 'filter' for processes
involving 'motivation'. Now when animals and people are learning simple tasks or carrying out simple repetitive behaviour,
it has often been noticed that the behaviour may stabilize or
even deteriorate with repetition, but pick up at its old level
or even improve after a break from the task. This is interpreted
as evidence for 'inhibition' building up in the nervous system -
repetition is inherently de-motivating - to the point where it
overcomes 'excitation', the motivating force of the reward for
the task. People differ in the extent to which their performance
deteriorates under conditions of repetition. The degree to
which a given reward or punishment is motivating is another
way in which people differ, and again the balance of excitation
and inhibition may well provide an explanation.

Let us posit that inhibition builds up more swiftly in extraverts than in introverts (but also breaks down more quickly),
but that the reverse is true for excitation - extraverts are
slower to be aroused than introverts, but stay aroused longer.
We can then make four predictions: (i) that extraverts will
show less persistence in repetitive tasks than introverts
(because inhibition builds up) but will show higher improvement after a break (because it breaks down quickly); (ii) extraverts will be less vigilant than introverts (as watching for
irregular events is effectively a repetitive task); (iii) extraverts will find stronger stimuli more pleasant than weaker
ones, and the reverse for introverts (because excitation builds
up quickly in introverts), and (iv) extraverts will be less
conditionable than introverts, will learn less easily (because
rewards are not so rewarding for them and because inhibition
builds up quickly). All four of these predictions have been
borne out in practice. When required to tap a metal plate as
quickly as they can for a minute, extraverts have longer
periods between bursts of tapping, but their performance is
more strongly facilitated by a rest-break between sessions
than is that of introverts (Spielmann, cited in Eysenck, 1964).
Extraverts do far worse in vigilance tasks (Bakan, cited in
Eysenck, 1964). Introverts prefer lower levels of stimulation
than extraverts and are less disturbed by isolation and perceptual deprivation (Eysenck, 1960b). Extraverts learn more
slowly than introverts in conditioning experiments (Franks,
1960; Eysenck, 1962).

The importance of these findings, Eysenck argues in his
1964 book, is that the learning of 'conscience' may also be
a conditioning process. One may suppose that one thing which
stops the 'normal' person from indulging his or her (possibly
criminal) impulses is a feeling of fear or anxiety at the possibility of being caught and exposed or punished. This anxiety,

originally elicited by punishment or exposure when we were
children, comes by a process of conditioning to be attached
to the inevitable forerunner of the punishment - the delinquent
act, or perhaps even the intention to commit it. However,
extraverts do not condition well, so there is less likelihood of
this pattern building up. Also punishment occurs always *after*
the event - often quite a long time after - so the faster build-
up of excitation in extraverts means they are more likely to
be affected by the immediate reward than by the delayed punishment. Furthermore, they need higher levels of stimulation, so
they are likely quite simply to emit more, more dramatic and
more impulsive behaviour. More frequent dramatic and impulsive
behaviour, unhindered by the restraints of 'conscience', means
more potential crime.

Thus Eysenck's theory. Obviously there have been subsequent elaborations; time has not stood still since 1964. More
recently (Eysenck, 1967; see also Gray, 1967), he has stressed
the importance of autonomic arousal more highly than that of
inhibition. Other writers have suggested that a more complex
version of learning-theory should be applied; Loo (1979), for
example, suggests the need to distinguish between inhibition/
excitation at the 'stimulus' end of the process and at the
'response' end. More recently still (Eysenck and Eysenck,
1976), a third factor has been introduced: building on arguments by writers such as Wolpe (1970) that psychoticism is
both genetically and behaviourally distinct from neuroticism,
and on his own earlier work which can be reinterpreted as
arguing for a three-factor solution rather than a two-factor one
(Eysenck, 1955a, 1955b; Sybil Eysenck, 1956; Devadasan,
1964), Eysenck has introduced a new P scale which correlates
with psychoticism. However, the picture does not change:
psychotics, psychopaths, criminals and other 'deviants' are
still to be found clustered in one sector, with high scores on
P and E (see also Sybil and Hans Eysenck, 1970). He also
notes that mental patients who are high on all three traits are
resistant to therapy, which implies a poor prognosis for
prisoners.
    Various other psychometric questionnaires have been used
from time to time to locate the behaviour of offenders on a
psychological continuum which also includes the normal population, but without recourse to physiological explanations such
as those used by Eysenck or the physical somatotypes of
Sheldon or Kretschmer. Some, like the Authoritarianism Scale
(Adorno et al., 1950) or the Machiavellianism Scale (Christie
and Geis, 1970) are single-trait measures which make no attempt
to explain the whole of deviance but look simply for the predicted consequences of one hypothesized aspect of personality.
Some, like Cattell's 16PF (16 Personality Factor Questionnaire -
Cattell, 1965, 1973) are generalized descriptors of personality
with no single theorization underlying them, but still useful

as descriptions; the 16PF and the EPI are the two personality questionnaires most commonly used in prisons for assessment and classification. The MMPI (Minnesota Multiphasic Personality Inventory - Dahlstrom et al., 1972; Welsh and Dahlstrom, 1956) is another non-specific diagnostic tool, less fashionable in this country but with some history of use in the United States for predicting delinquency and assessing delinquents (see for example, Hathaway and Monarchesi, 1957, 1963).

As one example of the use of such non-specific tests to develop theories in forensic psychology we might take Megargee's theory of the control of violence. Megargee hypothesized that some people's violence is 'under-controlled' - they erupt at every little incident - but that others suffer from 'over-control' - their aggression and hostility is suppressed rather than expressed, and may build up into grotesquely exaggerated violence. Thus one should find both types among the most serious of violent offenders but only the 'under-controlled' among the more petty, giving the paradoxical result that apparent hostility and aggression *decreases* as offences become more serious. This paradoxical result has indeed been found in mental hospitals (Megargee, 1966; Blackburn, 1968, 1971, 1975) and in prisons (Molof, 1967; McGurk, 1978), with the MMPI used to detect and classify the two types. (Unfortunately, however, a recent paper by McGurk and McGurk (1979) casts some doubt on the theory's validity: both types are found among prisoners with no history of violence at all, and the 'over-controlled' type is also quite common among prison officers.)

CRIME RESEARCH AND SOCIAL ENGINEERING

The biological, psychological and ethological work which we have here been considering stems, much of it, from the academic study of the nature of man, but an important line of practical application underlies it: to varying degrees, all these techniques are for use by those with administrative responsibility for the control of crime. Many of the studies which we have considered have aimed originally at moderating the excesses of these administrators. One of Lombroso's main points, for example, was that the scale of punishment common in his day could not be justified by any supposed effect of such punishments, for the people most likely to commit crimes were precisely those whose behaviour is not changeable; they are the born criminals, the people who have regressed to an earlier state of behaviour, and they do so not by their *choice*, but by reason of their *biological constitution*. Heavy punishment, therefore, neither deters nor cures. Eysenck, in his more sophisticated way, is a close follower of Lombroso in this respect: he delineates a type of personality highly likely to come into conflict with the norms of 'respectable' society, and he points out that for this

type punishment and deterrence are likely to be particularly
ineffective – which is, after all, why they are found in penal
institutions in the proportions that they are. (He also points
out that prison may constitute far less of a punishment for
these extraverts than for introverts.) Dugdale's 'Jukes' were
thought to be susceptible to education, if caught early enough,
so the aim was reform, not castigation. For Goddard's
'Kallikaks' the best suggested solution was that they should
not breed, but even here there was little or no suggestion that
they should be sterilized by force or restrained from breeding
by the state. The Eugenics movement, then fashionable though
now largely in disfavour, numbered among the members many
whose greatest passion was the liberty of the individual.

None the less these good intentions in 'bio-psychological'
criminology have produced research whose major application is
to the identification of potential deviants and their cure,
handling, disposal, segregation or other forms of 'treatment'.
Inevitably this has been most definitely true of research into
the control and 'amendment' of human personality by means of
drug therapy or surgery – to conceptualize crime as an illness
with a cure is a very tempting line of thought – but Eysenck's
work on personality types and their implications for treatment,
for example, has been of quite as much interest to educated
prison administrators as to the academic psychologist. (Eysenck's
suggestions for the use of his own work have actually been
far from academic; he has advocated drug therapy rather than
punishment, to effect a change of personality.) This has meant
that the practical outcome of such work has been, by and
large, intensely conservative and highly supportive of the
state and social conditions *as they happen to be at any given
time*. This tendency is reinforced by the fact that the largest
customers for such work, and the largest providers of research
funds and access, are precisely those departments of government and the administration whose task it is to 'manage' or
'cure' the labelled deviant. Such work tends to take the social
milieu for granted, or regard it as 'someone else's specialism',
and concentrate on the treatment of deviants from it. To do
so can lead to just accusations of being blinkered, or worse:
quite typical of the paradoxical position which can arise is that
of the surgeon in H.G. Wells's story 'The Country of the Blind',
who proposes to remove the sighted visitor's eyes in order to
fit him for the society in which he finds himself. The example
is an extreme one – perhaps unnecessarily and ludicrously so –
but it is fair in that it draws a warning: the psychologist
who permits people to think of him as a social engineer must
not be surprised if he later finds himself practising social
engineering.

Furthermore, it cannot be denied that there has been a
resurgence of interest in biological bases of crime among
criminological psychologists in America during the late 1970s.
A recent article by Hirschi and Hindelang (1977) has sug-

gested again a link between crime and low intelligence, and it
has been suggested that the known association of crime and
social class should be reinterpreted in these terms (Jeffery,
1978). The breeding-out of feeble-mindedness has again been
advocated (W. Wilson, 1970). Criminal behaviour has also been
related to such diverse factors as malnutrition or diet deficiency,
epilepsy and perceptual difficulties (Hippchen, 1978; Lewis
and Balla, 1976; Williams and Kalita, 1977), and the use of
drugs to control behaviour is strongly advocated in some
quarters. To quote Jeffery (1978):

> The new model of treatment emerging in biological psycho-
> logy is one involving the biochemistry of the brain ... it
> goes without saying that a major research effort is needed
> ... We must recognize that the police courts and corrections
> cannot handle a genetic defect, hypoglycemia or learning
> disabilities any more than they can handle cancer or heart
> disease.

Two final caveats may usefully be made about the biological
approach to the study of crime:

(a) It should be noted - and will come as no surprise to the
reader - that 'crime' is a large, vague label for a wide range
of behaviours which may have little in common other than that
they happen to be proscribed. In the section on drugs, surgery and 'brain control', for example, we were looking for a
physiological basis for acts of uncontrolled violence or sexual
aggression, but few writers other than Eysenck have seriously
proposed a brain-centre which also controls petty theft. That
there has to be a single explanation for crime, and particularly
a single biological explanation, is by no means obvious.

(b) By and large, biological explanations are based on literally
captive populations - they seek to explain why certain 'types'
are common in prison. In its simple form this is very poor
research methodology, for (i) the 'type' in question may be
equally common outside prison, or (ii) some characteristic of
the 'type' other than its criminality may be responsible for the
high arrest-rate (the trait may be class-related, for example).
It was this kind of factor, among others, which discredited
the XYY research. However, even in better-controlled studies,
such as Eysenck's for instance, similar problems occur. People
high in both extraversion and neuroticism (and on the P-
factor, in his latest formulation) are far more common proportionately among prisoners and other 'deviant' groups than in
the general population, but such groups are a minority in the
population, so there may in fact be *more* high NE people outside
the labelled groups than inside them. Any determinist theory
which posits a single cause for crime faces extraordinarily
great difficulties in explaining why most people picked out as
potential criminals by possession of this causal factor never
in fact become habitual criminals. The problem is particularly
acute in periods when the fashionable stress is on the preven-

tion of crime rather than its punishment. Theories such as these can all too readily be used to take preventive action against groups of people most of whom would never have offended.

Notes

1 One should perhaps point out that the two positions are *not* in fact opposites; both could be true of different criminals or of the same criminals. In any case genetic factors might well show themselves as inherited tendencies – personality traits, perhaps – which affected the course of socialization.

2 One should remember that the 'survival of the fittest' refers to the fittest *species*, not necessarily the fittest *individual*. The cinnabar moth, for example, has a caterpillar which is instantly recognizable (bearing dramatic yellow and black bars) and tastes extremely nasty to predators. Thus a predator may eat one but will avoid others thereafter; the caterpillar's characteristics do not save the first one from being eaten, but they do help to preserve the species.

3 It should be noted, however, that the Dalgard and Kringlen study is methodologically superior to the others in several ways. For a review of 'twin studies', see Mednick and Christiansen (1977).

4 The medical profession has, of course, acquired responsibility for areas of deviance where no physical cause is known or suspected, such as some forms of mental illness, or where no 'cure' is mooted, such as mental handicap. The interested reader should see Szasz (1962), Heather (1976) and Scull (1975) for further discussion.

References

Adorno, T., Frenkel-Brunswick, E., Levinson, D.J. and Sanford, R.N. (1950), 'The Authoritarian Personality', Harper, New York.

Andry, R.G. (1963), 'The Short-Term Offender', Stevens.

Banister, P.A., Smith F.V., Heskin, K.J. and Bolton, N. (1973), Psychological Correlates of Long-Term Imprisonment. I: Cognitive variables, 'British Journal of Criminology', vol.13, pp.312-23.

Bantock, G.H. (1965), 'Education and Social Values', Faber & Faber.

Blackburn, R. (1968), Personality in Relation to Extreme Aggression in Psychiatric Offenders, 'British Journal of Psychiatry', vol.114, pp.821-8.

Blackburn, R. (1971), Personality Types among Abnormal Homicides, 'British Journal of Criminology', vol.11, pp.14-31.

Blackburn, R. (1975), An Empirical Classification of Psychopathic Personality, 'British Journal of Psychiatry', vol.127, pp.456-60.

Blumer, D. and Migeon, C. (1975), Hormone and Hormonal

Agents in the Treatment of Aggression, 'Journal of Nervous and Mental Disease', vol.160, pp.127-37.

Bolton, N., Smith, F.V., Heskin, K.J. and Banister, P.A. (1976), Psychological Correlates of Long-Term Imprisonment. IV: a Longitudinal Analysis, 'British Journal of Criminology', vol.16, pp.38-47.

Brigham, C.C. (1923), 'A Study of American Intelligence', University Press, Princeton.

Brill, H. (1959), Postencephalic Psychiatric Conditions, in Arieti, S. (ed.), 'American Handbook of Psychiatry', vol.2, Basic Books, New York.

Brush, F.R., Froehlich, J.C. and Sakellaris, P.C. (1979), Genetic Selection for Avoidance Behaviour in Rats, 'Behaviour Genetics', vol.9, pp.309-16.

Burkett, E.E. and Bunnell, B.N. (1966), Septal Lesions and the Retention of DRL Performance in the Rat, 'Journal of Comparative and Physiological Psychology', vol.62, pp.468-71.

Butters, N. and Rosvold, H.E. (1968), Effect of Septal Lesions on Resistance to Extinction and Delayed Alternation in Monkeys, 'Journal of Comparative and Physiological Psychology', vol.66, pp.389-95.

Cattell, R.B. (1965), 'The Scientific Analysis of Personality', Penguin Books.

Cattell, R.B. (1973), 'Personality and Mood by Questionnaire', Jossey-Bass, San Francisco.

Christie, R. and Geis, F.L. (1970), 'Studies in Machiavellianism', Academic Press.

Cleckley, H.M. (1964), 'The Mask of Sanity', Mosby, St Louis.

Cole, J.O. and Davis, J.M. (1968), Clinical Efficacy of the Phenothiazines as Antipsychotic Agents, in Efron, D.H. (ed.), 'Psychopharmacology: a Review of Progress', PHS Publication no.1836, U.S. Government Printing Office.

Conrad, J.P. (1965), 'Crime and its Correction: an International Survey of Attitudes and Practices', University of California Press.

Dahlstrom, W.G., Welsh, G.S. and Dahlstrom, L.E. (1972), 'An MMPI Handbook', rev. ed., University of Minnesota Press.

Dalgard, O.S. and Kringlen, E. (1976), A Norwegian Twin Study of Criminality, 'British Journal of Criminology', vol.16, pp.223-6.

Debray, Q. (1972), L'Apport de la génétique à la Connaissance du Criminel, 'La nouvelle Presse médicale', vol.1, p.2474.

Devadasan, K. (1964), Cross-Cultural Validity of Twelve Clinical Tests, 'Journal of the Indian Academy of Applied Psychology', vol.1, pp.55-7.

Dugdale, R.L. (1877), 'The Jukes: a Study in Crime, Pauperism, Disease and Heredity', Putnam, New York.

Egger, M.D. and Flynn, J.P. (1963), Effect of Electrical Stimulation of the Amygdala on Hypothalamically Elicited Attack Behaviour in Cats, 'Journal of Comparative and Physiological Psychology', vol.26, pp.705-20.

Eissler, R.R. (1949), Some Problems of Delinquency, in Eissler, K.R. (ed.), 'Searchlights on Delinquency', International Press, New York.

Ellis, H. Havelock (1890), 'The Criminal', Walter Scott, London (recent ed., Patterson Smith, Montclair (N.J.), 1973).

Estabrook, A.H. (1916), 'The Jukes in 1915', Carnegie Institution, Washington.

Eysenck, H.J. (1953), 'The Scientific Study of Personality', Routledge & Kegan Paul.

Eysenck, H.J. (1955a), Psychiatric Diagnosis as a Psychological and Statistical Problem, 'Psychological Reports', vol.1, pp.3-17.

Eysenck, H.J. (1955b), 'Psychology and the Foundations of Psychiatry', H.K. Lewis.

Eysenck, H.J. (1960a), 'The Structure of Human Personality', Methuen.

Eysenck, H.J. (1960b), 'Experiments with Drugs', Pergamon Press, Oxford.

Eysenck, H.J. (1962), Conditioning and Personality, 'British Journal of Psychology', vol.53, pp.299-305.

Eysenck, H.J. (1964), 'Crime and Personality', Routledge & Kegan Paul (see also 3rd ed., 1977).

Eysenck, H.J. (1967), 'The Biological Basis of Personality', Charles C. Thomas, Springfield (Ill).

Eysenck H.J. and Eysenck, S. (1976), 'Psychoticism as a Dimension of Personality', Hodder & Stoughton.

Eysenck, S. (1956), Neurosis and Psychosis: an Experimental Analysis, 'Journal of Mental Science', vol.102, pp.517-29.

Eysenck, S. (1961), Personality and Pain Assessment in Childbirth of Married and Unmarried Mothers, 'Journal of Mental Science', vol.107, pp.417-30.

Eysenck S. and Eysenck H.J. (1963), The Validity of Questionnaire and Rating Assessments of Extraversion and Neuroticism and their Factorial Stability, 'British Journal of Psychology', vol.54, pp.51-62.

Eysenck, S. and Eysenck, H.J. (1970), Crime and Personality: an Empirical Study of the Three-Factor Theory, 'British Journal of Criminology', vol.10, pp.225-39.

Fine, B.J. (1963), Introversion-Extraversion and Motor Vehicle Driver Behaviour, 'Perceptual and Motor Skills', vol.12, pp.95-100.

Forssman, H. (1970), The Mental Implications of Sex Chromosome Aberrations, 'British Journal of Psychiatry', vol.117, p.360.

Fox, R.G. (1971), The XYY Offender: a Modern Myth, 'Journal of Criminal Law, Criminology and Police Science', vol.62, pp.59-73.

Franks, C.M. (1960), Conditioning and Abnormal Behaviour, in Eysenck, H.J. (ed.), 'Handbook of Abnormal Psychology', Pitman.

Gall, F.J. and Spurzheim, J.G. (1810-19), 'Anatomie et physiologie du système nerveux en général et du cerveau en particulier', Paris, 4 vols (English ed. (1974), 'On the Function of the Brain and each of its Parts', 6 vols, AMS Press, New York).

Galton, F. (1869), 'Hereditary Genius: an Enquiry into its Laws and Consequences', Macmillan (recent ed. (1972) published by Peter Smith, Gloucester, Mass.).

Galton, F. (1883), 'Inquiries into Human Faculty and its Development', Macmillan (recent ed. (1950) published by AMS Press, New York).

Gittleman-Klein, R. and Klein, D.F. (1968), Long-Term Effects of Antipsychotic Agents: a Review, in Efron, D.H. (ed.), 'Psychopharmacology: a Review of Progress', PHS Publication no.1836, U.S. Government Printing Office.

Goddard, G.V. (1964), Functions of the Amygdala, 'Psychological Bulletin', vol.62, pp.89-109.

Goddard, G.V. (1969), Analysis of Avoidance Conditioning Following Cholinergic Stimulation of Amygdala in Rats, 'Journal of Comparative and Physiological Psychology' Monograph 68, pp.1-18.

Goddard, H.H. (1910), Heredity in Feeble-Mindedness, 'American Breeders Magazine', vol.1, pp.165-78.

Goddard, H.H. (1912), 'The Kallikak Family: a Study in the Heredity of Feeble-Mindedness', Macmillan.

Goddard, H.H. (1916), 'The Criminal Imbecile', Macmillan.

Goldberg, S.C. (1968), Prediction of Response to Antipsychotic Drugs, in Efron, D. (ed.), 'Psychopharmacology: a Review of Progress', PHS Publication no.1836, U.S. Government Printing Office.

Gotsik, J.E. and Marshall, R.C. (1972), Time Course of the Septal Rage Syndrome, 'Physiology and Behaviour', vol.9, pp.685-7.

Gray, J.A. (1964), Strength of the Nervous System and Levels of Arousal: a Reinterpretation, in Gray, J.A. (ed.), 'Pavlov's Typology', Pergamon Press, Oxford.

Gray, J.A. (1967), Strength of the Nervous System, Introversion-Extraversion, Conditioning and Arousal, 'Behaviour Research and Therapy', vol.5, pp.151-69.

Griffiths, A.W., Richards, B.W., Zaremba, J., Abramowicz, T. and Stewart, A. (1969), An Investigation of a Group of XYY Prisoners, in West, D.J. (ed.), 'Criminological Implications of Chromosome Abnormalities', Cambridge University Press.

Hall Williams, J.E. (1975), 'Changing Prisons', Peter Owen.

Hamilton, W.D. (1964), The Genetic Evolution of Social Behaviour, 'Journal of Theoretical Biology', vol.7, pp.1-16.

Hathaway, S.R. and Monarchesi, E.P. (1957), The Personality of Pre-Delinquent Boys, 'Journal of Criminal Law and Criminology', vol.48, pp.149-63.

Hathaway, S.R. and Monarchesi, E.P. (1963), 'Analysing

and Predicting Delinquency with the MMPI', G. Cumberledge.

Healy, W. and Bronner, A.F. (1936), 'New Light on Delinquency and its Treatment', Yale University Press.

Heather, N. (1976), 'Radical Perspectives in Psychology', Methuen.

Heskin, K.J., Smith, F.V., Banister, P.A. and Bolton, N. (1973), Psychological Correlates of Long-Term Imprisonment. II: Personality Variables, 'British Journal of Criminology', vol.13, pp.323-30.

Himmelhoch, J., Pineus, J., Tucker, G. and Detre, T. (1970), Sub-Acute Encephalitis: Behavioural and Neurological Aspects, 'British Journal of Psychiatry', vol.116, pp.531-8.

Hippchen, L. (1978), 'The Eco-Biological Approach to Treatment of Delinquents and Criminals', Van Nostrand Reinhold, New York.

Hirsch, N.D. (1926), A Study of Natio-Racial Mental Differences, 'Genetic Psychology Monographs', vol.1, pp.394-7.

Hirsch, N.D. (1930), 'Twins: Heredity and Environment', Harvard University Press.

Hirschi, I. and Hindelang, M. (1977), Intelligence and Delinquency, 'American Sociological Review', vol.42, pp.571-86.

Jacobs, P., Brunton, M. and Melville, M. (1965), Aggressive Behaviour, Mental Subnormality and the XYY Male, 'Nature', 25 December, pp.1351-2.

Jarvik, L.F., Klodin, V. and Matsuyama, S.S. (1973), Human Aggression and the Extra Y Chromosome: Fact or Fantasy?, 'American Psychologist', vol.28, pp.674-82.

Jeffery, C.R. (1978), Criminology as an Interdisciplinary Behavioural Science, 'Criminology', vol.16, pp.149-69.

Jones, M.B., Offord, D.R. and Abrams, N. (1980), Brothers, Sisters, and Antisocial Behaviour, 'British Journal of Psychiatry', vol.136, pp.139-45.

Kamin, L. (1974), 'The Science and Politics of IQ', Halstead Press.

Kessler, S. and Moos, R.G. (1972), Phenotypic Characteristics of the XYY Male, 'Comments on Contemporary Psychiatry', vol.1, p.107.

King, F.A. and Meyer, P.M. (1958), Effects of Amygdaloid Lesions upon Septal Hyperemotionality in the Rat, 'Science', vol.128, pp.655-6.

Kretschmer, E. (1921), 'Körperbau und Charakter', Hamburg. (English version (1925), 'Physique and Character', Harcourt Brace, New York.)

Lange, J. (1929), 'Verbrechen als Schicksal', Munich (English version (1931), 'Crime as Destiny', Allen & Unwin).

Leaton, R.N. (1971), The Limbic System and its Pharmacological Aspects, in Rech. R.H. and Moore, K.E. (eds), 'An Introduction to Psychopharmacology', Raven Press, New York.

Lewis, D. and Balla, D. (1976), 'Delinquency and Psychopathology', Grune & Stratton, New York.

Lombroso, C. (1876), 'L'Uomo delinquente', Hoepli, Milan
    (translation is from Sylvester, S.F. (1972), 'The Heritage
    of Modern Criminology', General Learning Press, Cambridge,
    (Mass.)).
Lombroso, G. (1911), 'Criminal Man According to the Clas-
    sification of Cesare Lombroso', Putnam.
Loo, R. (1979), Neo-Pavlovian Properties of Higher Nervous
    Activity and Eysenck's Personality Dimensions, 'International
    Journal of Psychology', vol.14, pp.265-74.
Lorenz, K. (1966), 'On Aggression', Harcourt Brace Jovanovich,
    New York.
McGurk, B.J. (1978), Personality Types among 'Normal'
    Homicides, 'British Journal of Criminology', vol.18, pp.146-61.
McGurk, B.J. and McGurk, R. (1979), Personality Types
    among Prisoners and Prison Officers, 'British Journal of
    Criminology', vol.19, pp.31-49.
MacLean, P.D. (1949), Psychosomatic Disease and the 'Visceral
    Brain': Recent Developments Bearing on the Papez Theory
    of Emotion, 'Psychological Medicine', vol.11, pp.338-53.
Malamud, N. (1967), Psychiatric Disorder with Intracranial
    Tumours of the Limbic System, 'Archives of Neurology',
    vol.17, pp.113-23.
Mark, V.H. and Ervin, F.R. (1970), 'Violence and the Brain',
    Harper & Row, New York.
Mark, V.H., Sweet, W.H. and Ervin, F.R. (1972), The Effect
    of Amygdalectomy on Violent Behaviour in Patients with
    Temporal Lobe Epilepsy, in Hitchcock, E. et al. (eds),
    'Psychosurgery', Charles C. Thomas, Springfield (Ill.).
Mednick, S.A. and Christiansen, K.O. eds (1977), 'Biosocial
    Bases of Criminal Behaviour', Gardner Press, New York.
Megargee, E.I. (1966), Undercontrolled and Overcontrolled
    Personality Types in Extreme Anti-Social Aggression,
    'Psychological Monographs', vol.80, whole no.611.
Molof, M.J. (1967), 'Differences between Assaultive and Non-
    Assaultive Juvenile Offenders in the California Youth
    Authority', State of California, Research Division of the Dept
    of Youth Authority, Research Report no.51.
Moor, L. (1972), Un gène de la Délinquance: Mythe ou Réalité?,
    'Annales Medico-Psychologigues', vol.2, p.521.
Morris, D. (1967), 'The Naked Ape: a Zoologist's Study of the
    Human Animal', Cape.
Mulvihill, D.J. and Tumin, M.M. (1969), 'Crimes of Violence:
    a Staff Report submitted to the National Commission on the
    Causes and Prevention of Violence', vols 11-13, U.S.
    Government Printing Office.
Owen, D.R. (1972), The 47, XYY Male: a Review, 'Psycho-
    logical Bulletin', vol.78, pp.209-33.
Papez, J.W. (1937), A Proposed Mechanism of Emotion, 'Archives
    of Neurology and Psychiatry', vol.38, pp.725-44.
Pribram, K.H. (1971), 'Languages of the Brain', Prentice-Hall,
    Englewood Cliffs.

Reeves, A.G. and Plum, F. (1969), Hyperphagia, Rage and
   Dementia following a Ventromedial Hypothalmic Neoplasm,
   'Archives of Neurology', vol.20, pp.616-24.
Reinhold, R. (1980), Virginia Sterilized the 'Retarded', 'New
   York Times', 23 February, p.6.
Rennie, Y. (1978), 'The Search for Criminal Man', Lexington
   Books, Lexington (Mass.).
Rickels, K. (1968), Anti-Neurotic Agents: Specific and Non-
   Specific Effects, in Efron, D.H. (ed.), 'Psychopharmacology:
   a Review of Progress', PHS Publication no.1836, U.S.
   Government Printing Office.
Rosen, H. (1972), 'Language and Class: a Critical Look at
   the Theories of Basil Bernstein', Falling Wall Press, Bristol.
Sapsford, R.J. (1978), Life-Sentence Prisoners: Psychological
   Changes during Sentence, 'British Journal of Criminology',
   vol.18, pp.128-45.
Sapsford, R.J. (1979a), Learned Helplessness, Reactance and
   the Life Sentence, PhD thesis, University of London.
Sapsford, R.J. (1979b), 'Life-Sentence Prisoners: Deterioration
   and Coping', The Open University, Social Science Publications,
   Milton Keynes.
Savitz, L., Turner, S.H. and Dickman, T. (1977), The Origin
   of Scientific Criminology: Franz Joseph Gall as the First
   Criminologist, in Meier, R.F (ed.), 'Theory in Criminology:
   Contemporary Views', Sage.
Schallek, W., Kuehn, A. and Jew, N. (1962), Effects of
   Chlordiazepoxide (Librium) and other Psychotropic Agents
   on the Limbic System of the Brain, 'Annals of the New York
   Academy of Science', vol.96, pp.303-14.
Schou, M. (1968), Lithium in Psychiatry: a Review, in Efron,
   D.H. (ed.), 'Psychopharmacology: a Review of Progress',
   PHS Publication no.1836, U.S. Government Printing Office.
Schreiner, L. and Kling, A. (1953), Behavioural Changes
   following Rhinencephalic Injury in the Cat, 'Journal of
   Neurophysiology', vol.16, pp.643-59.
Schwartzbaum, J.S., Kellicutt, M.H., Spieth, T.M. and
   Thompson, J.B. (1964), Effects of Septal Lesions in Rats on
   Response Inhibition Associated with Food-Reinforced
   Behaviour, 'Journal of Comparative and Physiological Psycho-
   logy', vol.58, pp.217-24.
Scott, J.P. (1972), 'Animal Behaviour', 2nd ed., University
   of Chicago Press.
Scull, A.T. (1975), Moral Entrepreneurs to Medical Men: from
   Madness to Mental Illness, 'European Journal of Sociology',
   vol.16, pp.218-61.
Sheldon, W.S. (1949), 'Varieties of Delinquent Youth: an
   Introduction to Constitutional Psychiatry', Harper, New York.
Shields, J. (1973), Heredity and Psychological Abnormality,
   in Eysenck, H.J. (ed.), 'Handbook of Abnormal Psychology',
   Pitman.

Slotnick, B.M. and McMullen, M.F. (1972), Intraspecific Fighting in Albino Mice with Septal Forebrain Lesions, 'Physiology
and Behaviour', vol.8, pp.333-7.

Slotnick, B.M., McMullen, M.F. and Fleischer, S. (1974),
Changes in Emotionality Following Destruction of the Septal
Area in Albino Mice, 'Brain Behaviour and Evolution', vol.8,
pp.241-52.

Smiles, S. (1859), 'Self-Help: the Art of Achievement Illustrated
by Accounts of Great Men', London. (Modern edition, J.
Murray, 1958.)

Stürup, G.K. (1960), Sex Offences: the Scandinavian
Experience, 'Law and Contemporary Problems', vol.25,
pp.361-75.

Stürup, G.K. (1972), Castration: the Total Treatment, 'International Psychiatry Clinics', vol.8, pp.175-96.

Szasz, T.S. (1962), 'The Myth of Mental Illness: Foundations
of a Theory of Personal Conduct', Secker & Warburg.

Thompson, R. and Langer, S.K. (1963), Deficits in Position
Reversal Learning following Lesions of the Limbic System,
'Journal of Comparative and Physiological Psychology',
vol.56, pp.987-95.

Tiger, L. and Fox, R. (1971), 'The Imperial Animal', Holt,
Rinehart & Winston, New York.

Tillman, W.A. and Hobbs, G.E. (1949), The Accident-Prone
Automobile Driver, 'American Journal of Psychiatry', vol.106,
pp.321-31.

Tredgold, A.F. (1910), The Feeble-Minded, 'Contemporary
Review', June, pp.717-27.

Tryon, R.C. (1940), Genetic Difference in Maze-Learning
Ability in Rats, in Anastasi, A. (ed.), 'Individual Differences', Wiley, New York.

Tulchin, S.H. (1939), 'Intelligence and Crime', University of
Chicago Press.

Tupin, J.P., Smith, D.B., Clanon, T.L., Kim, L.I., Nugent,
A. and Groupe, A. (1973), The Long-Term Use of Lithium
in Aggressive Prisoners, 'Comparative Psychiatry', vol.14,
pp.311-17.

Valenstein, E.S. (1973), 'Brain Control: a Critical Examination
of Brain Stimulation and Surgery', Wiley, New York.

Welsh, G.S. and Dahlstrom, W.G. (1956), 'Basic Readings on
the MMPI in Psychology and Medicine', University of
Minnesota Press.

Williams, R.J. and Kalita, D.K. (1977), 'A Physician Handbook
on Orthomolecular Medicine', Pergamon, Oxford.

Wilson, E.O. (1975), 'Sociobiology: the New Synthesis', Harvard University Press.

Wilson, W. (1970), Social Psychology and Mental Retardation, in Ellis, N.R. (ed.), 'International Review of Research in Mental Retardation', Academic Press, vol.4.

Wolpe, J. (1970), The Discontinuity of Neurosis and Schizophrenia, 'Behavioural Research and Therapy', vol.8, pp.179-87.

Yerkes, R.M., ed. (1921), 'Psychological Examining in the United States Army', Memoirs of the National Academy of Sciences, no.15, Washington, D.C.

16   Social disorganisation theories

Frank Heathcote

INTRODUCTION

In this article we shall look at the cluster of theories and
explanations of crime that come under the broad generic title
of 'social disorganisation'. Together they constitute a 'social'
approach to the study of crime and deviance. It must however
be emphasised that the social disorganisation theorists were
not primarily concerned with the study of crime itself, but
more with the sociological problems of urban living in periods
of rapid social change. They were almost as much concerned
with the study of social organisation as disorganisation,
which was seen and defined as the pathological and deviant
side of the overall organised society. The emphasis on 'social
factors' as the major explanatory approach to the study of
crime has always, to some extent, been developed in reaction
to prevailing individualistic psychologically-based notions,
and we shall see that the early impetus for the growth of the
concept of social disorganisation was no exception to this. In
revealing the roots of it, we must look first towards the French
'moral statisticians' in the early years of the nineteenth century,
and see how their work presaged the later pioneering 'social
poverty surveys' in Britain of such philanthropic campaigners
as Henry Mayhew, Charles Booth and Seebohm Rowntree.

Our theoretical route will be to trace the development of the
concept of social disorganisation as it relates to crime and
delinquency from its inception as a major structural variable
of the positivist school of social thought. The main tenets of
positivism were summarised by Jock Young in article no.14 in
this book. You will have noted that a major assumption of
this school was to conceive of a total society as a social system
determining the actions and attitudes of its individual members.

Source: article commissioned for this volume. Frank Heathcote is Staff Tutor, Faculty of Social Sciences, The Open
University.

This was supposedly achieved through their effective socialisation into a consensus of its 'shared value-system' of attitudinal and behavioural norms that the majority were alleged to accept. Deviants and criminals were seen in this world-view as a small minority occupying the margins of society principally because of their 'defective' socialisation, and were depicted as existing in a state of social disorganisation within these marginal areas.

From there we shall show how Emile Durkheim developed the theoretical notions of 'normal' and 'pathological' states of society, together with his related concept of 'anomie' as an abnormal or 'forced' social situation highly conducive to crime, deviance and other indices of social disorganisation. Like the other nineteenth-century social evolutionist Herbert Spencer, and like Comte and the moral statisticians, Durkheim viewed society as analogous structurally to a biological organism consisting of functionally interdependent parts and having attendant prescriptions for social 'health' (stability and order) and 'disease' (disorganisation and disorder).

We shall follow the development of this biological or 'organic' strand of theory into the 1920s with the emergence of the Chicago-based 'ecological' approach to crime, deviance and other forms of urban social disorganisation. Here again we shall note the continuing positivist influence of first, 'scientific' empirical methods of data-collection, and second, the refinement of spatially-bounded research into delineated urban zones and 'natural areas' exhibiting high rates of working-class crime and disorder which were similar in conception to the nineteenth-century 'criminal areas' of Henry Mayhew, Friedrich Engels, John Glyde and others which have been discussed in earlier articles. Third we shall chart the development of the Social Darwinian notion of natural selection and the struggle for space translated into the dynamic processes of urban communities in a period of remarkably rapid social and technological change.

It is worth emphasising at this point the continuing urban focus of concern about crime and disorder throughout the period of this article. The early positivists, the moral statisticians of the early nineteenth-century, Durkheim later in the same century and as we shall subsequently see, the Chicago School of Urban Ecology of the 1920s and 1930s shared the same apprehension of increasing working-class social disorganisation and disorder deriving from rapid industrialisation in the emerging towns and cities of Europe. This helped form and confirm their view of society as an external organic reality characterised by a constraining morality which determined social order. Early nineteenth-century statistical surveys all pointed to the unusually heavy incidence of crime and disorder among the working classes in the growing factory towns and cities. Explanations for this were constructed in terms of a wide range of social and environmental factors: for example poverty, ignorance, density of population, and the 'neighbourhood contagion' of criminals existing in overclose proximity to each other. As we shall see, the writers of most of these early environmental and statistical accounts, while viewing crime as a social fact endemic to the growing forms of industrial society, at the same time were by no means hostile to the positive values of industrial capitalist enterprise. They resolved this dissonance by feeling and expressing a sense of moral obligation to seek methods of lessening the evils seen as resulting from it - hence the statisticians' concern with patterns of 'moral' forms of behaviour.

From these antecedents emerged the development of the ecological approach to social disorganisation of the early Chicago School led by Robert Park and E.W. Burgess, which while retaining the positivist and 'functionalist' perspective of society as a consensus of shared norms and values, later moved into the more pluralistic worlds of Clifford Shaw and Henry McKay, with whom each area within the total society came to be seen as possessing its own set of norms, traditions and accepted behaviours. After making the necessary criticisms of this approach, we shall follow the translation of this ecological perspective into that of the British 'Area Studies' theorists from the 1940s to the present day and show how they reconstituted the Chicago perspective to take into it the wider and more dynamically-processual framework of cultural, socioeconomic and political variables. At the same time, however, they still retained the essentially ecological focus of seeking to understand the incidence of high working-class crime and disorder rates by investigating initially the structure and processes of specific urban zones. A final common theme to be noted in all the approaches and theories included in this section is their essentially 'correctionalist' stance. This embodies another positivist notion that since all forms of social disorganisation are abnormal and 'pathological' to a healthy society, they can by definition be largely eradicated by making planned adjustments to the structure and processes of that society, and thereby to the individuals within it.

The 'social' approach to explaining crime - the early years
In the early years of the nineteenth century, the social and philosophical thought of positivism, exemplified by the writings of Comte and Saint-Simon, flourished throughout Europe. Comte and, after him, Durkheim, provided sociological investigation with a positivist basis. Only observable and measurable facts and general propositions about them were felt to matter and it is these that they held to be the only proper concern of an objective and scientific sociology. It was in this sort of climate that the first attempts were made to tackle the problem of crime 'scientifically' - a growing and worrying problem in the expanding industrial European towns of the first decades of the nineteenth century.

In the 1820s a number of analyses of crime statistics were

made in different European countries. In England they first
appeared in 1857, and their appearance made certain factual
statements about social trends possible. This type of analysis,
revealing the predictability of the amount and types of crime
in relation to such social and demographic factors as region,
area, season, sex, age and education, contrasted strongly with
the predominant individualistic approach to crime of classical
liberal theory which, since the Enlightenment and following
Beccaria, Bentham and Carrara, had been based on the premise
of rational man possessing the freedom to make individual
decisions as to his choices of action in all situations. Now a
sociological approach was developing which clearly implied that
crime was a regular and normal feature of social activity, that
it was endemic to existing forms of social organisation and
that there must be distinguishable and measureable crime-
inducing - or 'criminogenic' - features of the existing forms of
society. Moreover it must therefore be theoretically possible,
by specifying the causes, to 'correct' the outcome - a method
and result completely at one with the positivist sociology and
the type of 'correctionalist' criminology that has largely prevailed in the western world until recent years.

The attraction of the 'moral statistic' approach in the 1820s
and 1830s is therefore clear: it not only utilised the 'scientific'
attractions of statistical method but also provided a basic thesis
in explaining why the growing social unrest and crime-rate was
happening where it was - in the rapidly growing and already
overcrowded urban industrial towns of Britain and the Continent.
For the next half-century, sociological analysis of this kind
dominated the study of crime. With it, the idea of social reform
alleviating the tensions and, hopefully, the aggression of the
urban poor and of 'the dangerous labouring classes' in the
industrial trouble-spots was very much to the fore.

*The nineteenth century English and American philanthropic
reformers*
The incidence, location and types of social unrest including
crime were markedly similar in urban Britain and urban France,
and it did not take long for the same 'moral statistics' approach
to develop here. It fitted in well with the English empirical
tradition: what Hermann Mannheim has described as 'the English
mind, with its practical rather than theoretical bias, has been
more interested in penological questions of treatment than in
the criminological and philosophical issues of causation and
responsibility' (1960, p.18).

England in the 1830s saw the growth of public reformist
and scholarly interest in crime not only as a growing social
problem of the industrial towns, but also in its geographical
distribution. In 1848, Joseph Fletcher, the secretary of the
Statistical Society in London, related crime-rates to the social
characteristics of geographical areas by his theory of neighbourhood contagion, viewing local crime as a profession that

attracted new recruits by contamination with existing criminals. In 1856 John Glyde published 'The Localities of Crime in Suffolk', based on the relation between population density and crime, and in 1863 John Burt produced work aimed at proving the reproductive nature of crime, and that habitual crime was the result of 'criminal classes already existing'. Although distinctly atheoretical, these early works were among the first English ecological studies. Similarly, as earlier articles have shown, philanthropic social observers such as Henry Mayhew and Charles Booth also identified a long list of criminogenic social factors emerging in the rapidly-expanding urban environment. These included such diverse phenomena as opportunity, over-crowding, disease, anonymity, the absence of social sanctions, the loss of community solidarity, the breakdown of the old feudal reciprocities and the growth of individual competitiveness.

In his detailed and painstaking investigations into the crime-rates, types of crime and the addresses of convicted and 'known' criminals in different areas and streets of London, and in exposing the 'rookeries' of specific types of crime in such areas as Spitalfields, St Giles, Westminster and the Borough, Mayhew in his four-volume work 'London Labour and the London Poor' (1861), produced what was the first truly eco-logical study of crime in Britain. In the later years of the century, following his example, Booth and Rowntree conducted large-scale surveys into urban poverty. Even though they claimed new levels of systematisation for their work, they were both indebted to the earlier pioneering work of Mayhew in pointing the way to detailed topographical studies of social investigation.

In nineteenth-century America in the same period, crime similarly attracted the attention of a collection of religious, humanitarian and utopian reformers who tended to equate it with sin, poverty and immorality - behaviour that totally opposed the American ideal. Crusades and movements flourished in the attack on such 'evils' as idleness, poverty, drunkenness, low education and mental illness. In this climate, crime began to be studied by such practitioners in prison and welfare work as Charles Loring Brace and Edward Crapsey, and social science was seen mainly as the means of accumulating a body of largely empirical knowledge for reformist purposes. Crime was invariably seen as a product of 'disharmony' in society, its institutions and social conditions, and deriving from the way of life of various groups of the urban underclass - its causes there being said to be a combination of a 'lack of community integration' and political corruption.

Yet despite the undoubted strengths of the 'social' approach to explaining crime and deviance of the moral statisticians and despite the support of such French environmentalists as Lacassagne - who argued that societies produced the type and number of criminals they deserved - and Tarde - who stressed imitation as a significant social factor in accounting for much

crime and deviance - in 1876, sociological explanations in
Britain and America became overshadowed and in decline. In
that year Lombroso published his influential 'L'Uomo Delinquente', and explanatory theories almost overnight became
'constitutional', hereditarian, and returned to the level of the
individual. It was around this time and in this climate that
Emile Durkheim, a critical philosopher who later became the
first professional sociologist, attempted to reassert the merits
of social explanation.

DURKHEIM AND THE STUDY OF CRIME

Durkheim and social disorganisation theory
Durkheim's contribution to the development of sociology is
immense. He directed his powerful intellect to a number of the
major theoretical questions of social science: how societies
cohere, what initiates major social change, where and what is
the social element in human life, can this be identified and
analysed? By no means all his large and complex sociological
theory is relevant to our purposes in this article, but his
social disorganisation theory should not be seen, as in many
criminological texts, as something separate from and unconnected with his main theoretical formulations.

The background to Durkheim's writings
Emile Durkheim, the son of a Jewish rabbi, was born in 1858
in Lorraine. As a teenager, he saw such traumatic events
befall France as defeat in the Franco-Prussian war, the setting
up of the Third Republic and the anti-semitism of the Dreyfus
Affair. There can be little doubt that his concern with social
cohesion and social order, and with the 'moral' nature of
society derives in part from the turmoil of these political struggles. Like Comte he initially maintained that only observable
'facts' and general propositions about them were the proper
concern of sociology, although his later writings showed a
considerable broadening of this initial theoretical position.
Although writing specifically about crime and deviance was not
a main concern of his, Durkheim, in showing the reductionist
flaws in individualistic theories of explanation, did find deviant
and criminal activity an appropriate area for demonstrating
that what were popularly seen as individually-motivated acts
in fact required sociological analysis as patterned social phenomena if their true causes were to be properly understood. In
this he was following essentially the methods of the then
temporarily eclipsed moral statisticians.

His contribution to the study of crime
In strengthening earlier accounts of the growth of crime in
modern industrial societies, Durkheim argued two points: first,
that modern industrial urban societies encourage a state of

'egoism' which is contrary to the maintenance of social solidarity and to conformity to law, and second, that in periods of rapid social change, 'anomie' occurs. By this he meant an 'anomic' disordered society lacking effective forms of social control, and thereby leading to a state of individually perceived 'normlessness' within it. This would be characterised by the deregulation of behaviour, a disruption of people's usual expectations, an absence of clear-cut moral rules and a lack of certainty as to the forms of behaviour required in the changed social circumstances. From this it will be clear that for Durkheim to conceive of a society as functional and healthy in a developing sense, it should possess a high degree of social solidarity which acts as a constraining moral force on the individual through its 'collective conscience' - the expression of the prevailing social morality of the time.

In his first major work, 'The Division of Labour' (1964, first published in 1893), Durkheim attempted to account for the presence of social solidarity in society. Briefly, his argument was that, in traditional primitive societies, men are similar to each other in ideas, outlook and experience. The common body of values and experiences oriented around similar life-styles induces a high degree of social solidarity of a 'mechanical' kind, and abnormal 'pathological' states of society such as revolution or widespread crime rarely exist. On the other hand, modern industrial societies are not at all like this. They are noticeable more for the differences between members caused by highly-differentiated patterns of experience, upbringing and training. This leads to the formation of a system of 'organic solidarity', and he stressed that its increasingly complex division of labour could lead to workers losing their sense of relationship to each other and to a lack of understanding of the nature and meaning of the tasks on which they were engaged. The individual thus becomes 'debased' and compelled to take part in a 'forced division of labour' where his 'natural faculties' are not being utilised. Under such conditions of potential anomie, the moral authority of society's 'collective conscience' would have little or no effect on the individual members, and conditions would become ideal for crime, deviance and disorder. Individual demands and appetites become unregulated, and 'egoism' prevails, ultimately even developing its own individualistic normative structure at variance to that previously held by the wider society.

In his study of 'Suicide' (1952, first published in 1877), Durkheim again used the concept 'anomie' but this time in relation to a specific deviant act. He noticed that the suicide rate rose not only in times of severe economic depression but also in periods of sudden prosperity. At such times, people's expectations again become deregulated and disrupted, and a number of those affected commit suicide. More supporting evidence for his concept of 'egoism' came from his finding that individuals lacking effective social or familial affiliations - for

example, widows, divorcees and the single - were more likely
to commit suicide than those possessing high levels of such
attachments. As will be seen in the article no. 18 by Muncie
and Fitzgerald, Durkheim's concept of 'anomie' was taken right
into the mainstream of American sociology and social disorganisation theory by Robert Merton, although in doing this he
transformed it along lines of development that became very far
removed from those of Durkheim.

Durkheim and the normality of crime
Crime for Durkheim is a 'social fact'. It is normal and universal
in its varying forms in all cultures and societies, at all stages
in their development, and is, thereby, endemic to social
organisation. This being so, the efforts of 'correctionalist'
criminologists to eradicate forms of crime and deviance are at
best misguided and inevitably fruitless. Durkheim, however,
like the moral statisticians, went further than this. Because
crime is universal in this sense and an integral part of social
organisation, it must, he reasoned, have a positive social
function. It shows the boundaries of morality and of toleration
for the 'collective sentiments' of a society and it indicates, where
it occurs, sufficient flexibility for adaptation in that society
to change. Criminals thus should be seen as men of ideas that
happen to be labelled illegitimate within the existing moral
framework of the society. For example, Socrates was seen by
Durkheim as a criminal in Athenian society because of the
'independence of his thought', a man ahead of his time. A
flourishing crime-rate therefore is a symptom of healthy progressive society - without it society would become conformist
and thereby stagnate. In this way Durkheim believed that crime
'keeps open the path to necessary changes' (1964, p.70).

The normal and the pathological
While Durkheim's major work 'The Division of Labour' was very
critical of Spencer's utilitarianism which he saw as highly
individualistic, he followed Spencer in his nineteenth-century
intellectual preoccupation with biology. Indeed Durkheim's
basic assumptions reflected those of the organicists in viewing
society as an entity 'sui generis' that was not reducible to its
constituent parts, except in fulfilling the basic functions or
needs of the whole. It was the notion of 'functional needs'
that reinforced his view of social systems as existing on a continuum between 'normal' and 'pathological'. Essentially, Durkheim defined these two different states as follows.

'Normal' society and repressive law - The extent and type of
social solidarity in a given society depends on its division of
labour. In simple traditional societies with little social differentiation, this took the form of mechanical solidarity in which
there was a functional fit between individual aptitudes and social
roles, and the division of labour was 'spontaneous'. This to

Durkheim was the perfect or 'normal' social order, in which the similarity of roles, activities and attitudes supplied the 'normative consensus' in the collective conscience of the society. The type of law necessary to underpin this general moral agreement he termed 'repressive law'. This was simply a punitive system not requiring any conceptual complexities such as 'restitution' or 'rehabilitation' to cloud its operation. Because such a society had general moral agreement on what constituted crime, there was a similar consensus on the nature of punishment – usually involving such 'negative reinforcements' as loss of liberty, prestige and privileges and/or the infliction of pain.

Pathological society and restitutive law – The forms of social order in modern complex 'organic' society were, to Durkheim, very different. A high degree of specialisation and differentiation operated in the major economic, political, religious and social institutional spheres of society. Individuals no longer performed the same, similar or even related activities – the division of labour had become complex, and now forced or constrained individuals into specialised roles that may or may not have been consonant with their personal skills and attributes. The forced nature of the division of labour under these conditions produced discontent with the social order, which in turn produced yet more constraint. In short, as Taylor, Walton and Young put it, 'occupational and social arrangements are out of accord with the demands of men's nature and needs, and the social system becomes in this sense "pathological"' (1973, p.84). The same authors go on to identify different types of deviant produced by this type of society: two major ones being:
the functional rebel: a normal person rebelling against the forced division of labour and its associated social inequalities and thereby drawing attention to the dissonance between biological needs and social roles in the society. Such a person, for Durkheim, expresses the true 'spontaneous' or 'normal' collective conscience as opposed to the artificial, 'forced' or 'pathological' one currently in operation.
the skewed deviant: this is the faultily socialised individual in a disorganised pathological society characterised by a weak 'anomic' and 'egoistic' collective conscience that allows, and in some cases encourages, unrestricted and unregulated individualism through the culture's dissonance with actual individual needs (Taylor, Walton and Young, 1973, pp.84-5).

It is important to note that Durkheim does not describe *individuals* as suffering from anomie or egoism – the terms are normative phenomena and refer to the type of society that produces a 'debased' human nature. Consequently the explanations and analyses of such states must be sociological. Another important qualification connected with this is that nowhere does he state that there is a direct or inevitable causal

determination between deviance and the reaction of individuals
to an anomic or egoistic society. He argues rather that such
social conditions may predispose or impel certain individuals
into deviance - particularly to the two types mentioned above.

The form of law which attempts to contain crime and deviance
in such an organic differentiated society is, like the society,
more complex. In calling it 'restitutive law', Durkheim held
true to his thesis that law reflected existing social organisation.
Being external and a tangible reality to the individual, it acted
as a visible expression of, and a maintenance system for, the
existing form of social solidarity and collective conscience of
the society. Restitutive law, therefore, unlike repressive law
in the simple mechanical societies, operated to maintain the
social, economic, political and religious differentiations of
organic society by focusing on restitution to the victim of crime
and deviance rather than on the punishment of the offender.
Punishments thereby become more lenient in this type of society.
Executions and the lesser physical punishments and tortures
of repressive law give way to individual loss of freedom through
imprisonment only, and to the monetary fines of our present-
day society.

Thus unlike individualistic and positivistic static interpretations of the relationship between individuals and their society,
Durkheim believed that man's nature is 'duplex': i.e. it is
formed by the dialectic between his biological endowments
(aptitudes and merit) and social processes (especially those
pertaining to control and constraint) deriving from the division
of labour. Unless individuals submit their individual will and
desires to the collective conscience of society, the dialectic
becomes dysfunctional and dissonant, and crime and deviance,
'normal' and endemic as it is to social organisation everywhere,
is likely to ensue. In locating his explanations of crime and
deviance in these social relationships, Durkheim's legacy has
been to confirm the validity and importance of a sociological
approach in what hitherto had been a largely analytically
individualistic field.

THE DEVELOPMENT OF SOCIOLOGICAL CRIMINOLOGY AND THE CHICAGO SCHOOL

Introduction
At the beginning of the present century, urban America became
the focus of and centre for the study of crime as a social
phenomenon. Before looking directly at the emergence and
work of the Chicago School of urban sociology in the 1920s,
1930s and 1940s, we should look briefly at the changes that
were taking place in American society and in the study of
criminology there during the pre-Chicago years.

As in Europe, Lombroso's biological and hereditarian theories
of the 'born criminal' were steadily discarded after the publica-

tion in America of Goring's statistical study of 'The English Convict' and Aschaffenburg's similar study using German data, 'Crime and its Repression' (1913). Social and environmental causal explanations of crime began to come more into prominence all the time. As in England, the dynamics of rapid social change – urbanisation, immigration, population growth and mobility – made the relation between social conditions and crime seem very direct, since most reported crime was revealed to be taking place in those areas and social groups most affected by these changes. As sociology departments began to open and develop in the American universities, so crime was included in their study of urban social problems. Thereby its study was placed more firmly within the mainstream sociological tradition. The theoretical orientations of a liberal social relativism gained ground, postulating first that ideas, events and behaviours have signification or meaning only in relation to their specific context. Second, and following from this, the behaviour of the offender should be seen as deriving from participation in one of several deviant social worlds, and third, that crime is the product of deleterious social forces that can be changed, 'corrected' and remedied by various forms of social engineering.

At the start of the twentieth century, evolutionary theory, and in particular Social Darwinism, became a potent influence not only in sociological thought generally – the classical sociologists Comte, Spencer, Pareto, Durkheim, Tönnies, Marx and Weber were all social evolutionists in depicting societies as dynamic permanently changing social systems evolving through predictable stages of development – but also in the emerging criminological theory of the time. The defining of certain behaviours as criminal and their perpetrators as 'the socially unfit' effectively disadvantaged them in the competitive struggle for existence and social approval, and placed them into the category of a deviant minority. Thereby the law-abiding majority were allowed to flourish and develop by following the prescribed norms and rules of their society. The publication in America of such sociologically-oriented works as Parmalee's 'The Principles of Anthropology and Sociology in their Relation to Criminal Procedure' (1908), Tarde's 'Penal Philosophy' (1912) and Bonger's 'Criminality and Economic Conditions' (1916) all served to advance the cause of the development of a sociological perspective to the study of crime. The groundwork had thereby been well laid for the emergence of the first truly sociological criminology at the University of Chicago in the 1920s.

The ecological approach to the study of crime

Human ecology refers to the spatial distribution of population: the relationships between people who share a local territory and which are affected by the nature of the territory. This style of approach became a significant feature in sociology and criminology in the 1920s with its development as a general social methodology by Park and Burgess at the University of

Chicago. The old early nineteenth-century ideas of 'criminal areas' featuring as we have seen in the work of Mayhew, Booth, Fletcher and Glyde in England, of Brace and Crapsey in America, and in the 'social physics' of the moral statisticians Quetelet and Guerry - involving the use of geographic maps showing the relationships between crime and selected urban social variables (for example poverty, overcrowding and dilapidation), were given new life by the work of Robert Park and his associates initially in Chicago itself, and later replicated by other adherents of the school in similar American cities. Thereby the focus of study turned for some time towards the physical environment.

Robert Park was reared in a Scandinavian immigrant community in Minnesota, was a member of a youth gang, and consequently developed an abiding interest in marginal worlds and deviant groups. He worked as a journalist and as a result experienced at first hand the intimate details of the different aspects of city life at the time when the effects of rapid social change on the mid-west American cities were at their most vivid. As a keen empiricist and an eager advocate of the field-work methods of participant observation, he employed and perfected the methods of documentary fact-gathering and campaign policy-urging journalism concerned with social conditions, especially housing, in the city. In 1914 he was a sociologist in the University of Chicago and for twenty years he and his colleagues and students amassed and published a wealth of detailed empirical social research data on urban society and its growth and development. Students were sent out with notebooks to record direct observations of the rich and varied cultural social life of Chicago's city areas. Among the most important works were McKenzie's 'The Neighbourhood: a Study of Columbus, Ohio' followed by Nels Andersen's 'The Hobo: the Sociology of the Homeless Man' (both 1923). Thrasher's classic study 'The Gang' came four years later, followed by Wirth's 'The Ghetto' (1928), Zorbaugh's 'Gold Coast and the Slum' and Shaw's 'Delinquency Areas' (both 1929). Three important theoretical works on the ecological approach appeared around the same time: 'Introduction to the Science of Sociology' (1924) - a textbook by Park and his colleague E.W. Burgess, and their collections of papers in 'The City' (1925) and 'The Urban Community' (1927).

Chicago in the 1920s was an ideal social laboratory for their work: a massive influx of European immigrants ever since the 1860s - a population growth from 10,000 in 1860 to 2 million in 1910 - much of it of such diverse nationalities as Germans, Poles, Italians, Lithuanians and Irish. The consequential problems of social change, culture conflict, and the competition for 'lebensraum' and scarce resources were extremely visible and acute. An unprecedented rate of crime and deviance was causing concern, and social disorganisation was no longer an abstraction. Moreover, the same phenomena were equally visible in the other growing manufacturing towns and cities of

the American mid-west. Durkheim's pronouncements about
the effects of an anomic society were, it seemed, becoming
only too true.

The major themes and concepts of the school
The biological analogy - 'Ecology' is a biological term borrowed,
according to Morris in what remains the most comprehensive
study of the ecological approach, 'The Criminal Area' (1957),
from European biologists such as Eugenius Warming and Ernst
Haeckel, who around the turn of the century themselves drew
analogies between plant and animal colonies and human communities. They stressed that human communities, like plants,
grew by experiencing the coming together of many different
individuals. They then changed over time, and ultimately
declined through being gradually superseded by other incoming
individuals who adopted different forms of social organisation.
As in plant and animal life, Park drew attention to the fact
that it is also a characteristic of human environments to find
an interdependence of species symbiotically sharing the same
habitat. He argued that social ecology should explain how
what he termed 'the biotic balance' of human communities was
maintained in a state of dynamic equilibrium. It should also
explain which other processes were involved when this state
was disturbed, conflict arose, and a new community with its
own social forms emerged and replaced the existing one. The
emphasis of the early social evolutionists, like Spencer and
Durkheim, in viewing society as a biological organism made up
of interdependent parts was also very marked in this perspective.
   Another major biological strand of influence on the school
and referred to in the previous section, was the Social Darwinian notion of natural selection and the 'survival of the
fittest', when new and stronger species supplant weaker existing ones. This was translated into 'the struggle for space',
which became a core concept of ecological theory. In this,
individuals are pushed out of their former habitat by an insur-
gent group and have to settle elsewhere - the city slum being
seen as 'the area of minimum choice'. Here the struggle is
expressed by the ecologists in economic as well as biological
terms.

The interactionist method - Park and Burgess publicly acknowledged their debt to the symbolic interactionist perspective
in sociology then recently developed by W.I. Thomas, Simmel,
Cooley and Mead. This was, first, in adopting their preoccupation with the effect on the forms and types of interaction
of the actors' perception of the outside cultural world through
their own 'definition of the situation'. Second, the participant
observation-style methods of the interactionists were adapted
especially by such Chicago School adherents as Shaw and
McKay, Thrasher, Whyte and Andersen into what Matza has

termed 'appreciative studies' of specific deviant worlds such
as delinquent boys, juvenile gang members, hobos, and 'taxi-
dancers' (1969, p.15). In these the researcher actually entered,
'appreciated', and participated in the world and life-styles of
the deviants themselves, with great emphasis being placed on
the deviant's 'own story'. These studies complemented the
school's other painstaking and varied methods of data collection,
ranging from official statistics to life histories and biographies.
With them all, ethnographic method combined with the ecological
approach: the concept of a deviant world, concentrated in a
particular locale, is securely anchored in the ecological segregation of what Matza calls the 'isolated cultural area' (1969,
p.26).

The empirical nature of the School's social research and its
concern with 'correctionalist' solutions to problems of urban
social disorganisation and disorder lay of course very squarely
within the positivist tradition of Comte and his advocacy of
the adoption of natural science methods for social research.
Indeed Taylor, Walton and Young go so far in this connection
as to indict the ecological tradition as being 'most responsible
for the continuing hold of positivistic assumptions in American
sociology' (1973, p.111).

The idea of 'natural areas' - Like the moral statisticians before
them, the Chicagoans, and especially Clifford Shaw and Henry
McKay (two avid researchers into urban crime and deviance),
could not help but notice in Chicago and other cities of the
American mid-west the similarity of behavioural patterns within
certain 'natural areas' of the cities. Here we see the merging
of the sociological model of plant life with its 'symbiosis' - the
living together of different organisms within the same habitat
in a 'biotic' state of equilibrium with their physical environment
- with the 'struggle for space' concept of Social Darwinism.
Park had observed how successive waves of new urban immigrants imploding into the developing urban areas had caused
different types of housing, living and working zones to emerge,
each having its own distinctive cultural as well as physical
pattern. As he put it, 'it is assumed (that) people living in
natural areas of the same general type and subject to the same
social conditions will display, on the whole, the same characteristics' (1929, p.36). The positivist overtones of social determinism, of inert human beings being acted upon and constrained
by their physical and social environment, are clear to see.

While the Chicagoans agreed that those occupying a natural
area ecologically comprise a community, they found some difficulty in arriving at an agreed definition of what this constituted. Zorbaugh considered the physical aspects and boundaries
of an observable territorial location to be paramount, while
McKenzie stressed cultural factors: the population, race,
language, income and occupational characteristics of a natural
area. Burgess, in an attempt at synthesis, detailed a natural

area as possessing *physical* or ecological aspects based on the interplay of locational and social relationships, *cultural* ones based on a social system peculiar to the locality, and *political* ones deriving from local political action (1929). There is clearly a problem here in expressing the relationship of physical and cultural variables within the confines of a delimited territorial area.

The zonal theory of city growth - Ecology is, as we have seen, essentially a biological organic theory that sees a hierarchical system of interdependent organs radiating out along nervous axes in decreasing functional order from a prime central organic system to the outer periphery. It is not, therefore, surprising that the sociological ecologists chose to depict their ethnographic maps of human communities in these terms. The Chicagoans adapted this system in their construction of the zones of the mid-west American city: the central business district dominating all other zones through its transport and communications system thereby integrating the component parts into the whole.

Basically, they found that the rapid industrialisation of the towns involved the settlement of poor immigrants in a near-central area. They then moved out to pleasanter suburbs as they became more settled and affluent, to be replaced by a new wave of immigrants - usually poor and in search of low-cost housing. Thereby large cities could be conceived eventually as having five major concentric bands. Following McKenzie's scheme at Columbus, Park and Burgess applied his analysis to Chicago where, starting from the centre, we have:

Zone 1: the central business district - large banks and commercial offices - busy by day but deserted at night.

Zone 2: the interstitial area - sometimes called the 'transitional zone' or 'twilight zone' - of now decaying but formerly opulent residential property, flats and hotels; the 'bed-sit' land of students, casual workers, new immigrants and deviant 'marginals' such as prostitutes, alcoholics and 'gays', and containing the 'underworld dens' of thieves and drug-pushers; also (in Chicago) the Chinatown, Little Sicily and 'the Ghetto' ethnic minority areas.

Zone 3: the respectable artisan district - streets of similar-looking working-class housing.

Zone 4: suburbia - middle-class white-collar private housing, larger and less densely situated homes, flats and residential hotels.

Zone 5: 'exurbia' - large individual residential properties of the relatively affluent right on the outer limits of the city and into the commuter zone.

The zones could be subdivided segmentally into the natural areas previously described. From our discussion of the problems of definition of the term and in particular of the difficulties of analytically retaining the cultural world of the inhabitants

of a given area within its physical locational boundaries, it is
not surprising that on occasions the same 'natural area' was
seen as occupying segments of different zones. Andersen, for
example, while postulating the ecological segregation within
the same natural area of the peculiar world of the hobo - which
he termed 'Hobohemia' - and showing that hobos comprised in
all only between 1 and 2 per cent of Chicago's population, also
stated that they were to be found primarily in three different
'narrow areas' in separate zones (1923, p.14).

The concept of 'delinquency area' - Clifford Shaw first used
the term 'delinquency area' to describe those 'natural areas'
of the city characterised by high crime-rates and patterns
of anti-social behaviour exhibited by a high proportion of its
inhabitants. Morris defines its formal characteristics as
'physical deterioration, overcrowding, a mobile population and
a proximity to the areas of industry and commerce'. He goes
on to describe its social characteristics as 'primarily a lack of
informal agencies of social control whereby the norms accepted
by the wider society may be maintained' (1957, p.19).

It was, of course, the second zone - the interstitial area
with its shifting population, squalid accommodation and high
incidence of crime and other forms of deviant social disorganisation that interested the Chicagoans - just as it had Mayhew
before them. Shaw, in particular, as a city probation officer,
followed Park in campaigning for pragmatic programmes of
social control within these twilight zones - which quickly become
labelled 'delinquency areas' - and obtained state funds for a
number of action-research projects in them. It was Shaw who
noticed that his delinquent clients tended to live close together
in areas characterised by a specific form of criminal activity -
for example 'shoplifting areas' or 'street robbery areas'. Shaw
found a direct conceptual link here not only with the 'rookeries'
of Mayhew but also with the 'anomie' of Durkheim. It seemed
clear to him that traditional social solidarities, values and modes
of control had broken down in the ambient social disorganisation
of these delinquency areas, undergoing as they were the
continuing ecological dynamic of 'invasion, dominance and
succession' by one generation after another.

Shaw also noticed two other related phenomena: first, that
the highest concentration of official delinquent homes was in
the interstitial zone. This continued over time, over considerable population change, and also over change in the dominant
cultural traditions of the zone. Second, he noted that the official
delinquency-rates declined in direct proportion to the distance
from the central business district.

The results of a series of case studies including 'The Jack
Roller' (1930), 'Natural History of a Deviant Career' (1931)
and 'Brothers in Crime' (1938) led Shaw to transfer the focus
of his investigations from physical aspects of the environment
to the relationships of known delinquents with others and the

methods by which delinquent attitudes and values were transmitted among them. A problem of definition, however, arose
here, caused, according to Morris, by Shaw's 'somewhat slip-
shod phraseology'. While he stated that the communities to be
studied for factors leading to delinquency were geographically
'areas in which delinquency occurs most frequently', his
primary interest was, as we have seen, with the genesis and
transmission of delinquent attitudes. He accordingly based his
statistics of 'the distribution of delinquency offences' on the
home addresses of known offenders rather than on the areas
of the actual commission of the offences as might reasonably
be implied by his definition itself. Given the physically criminogenic nature of, for example, the central business area, largely
deserted by night and containing much thievable property in
its offices, department stores and finance houses, it is clear
that the delinquency-rates produced by the two criteria are
very different conceptually as well as numerically.

Shaw and his associate Henry McKay developed the notion
of the delinquency area into what has become known as the
'cultural transmission theory of delinquency'. This held that
within the most socially disorganised city areas (i.e. the interstitial zones), particular forms of crime have become a tradition
or a 'cultural norm' which is transmitted from one generation
to the next. Successful criminals in the area, by what Veblen
termed the 'conspicuous consumption' of their extravagant
life-styles and symbols of affluence, demonstrated both the
success and the normality of their way of life. They thereby
became a model for ambitious youths, themselves lacking
legitimate opportunities to attain such wealth. Subsequently
a criminal tradition becomes normative to the area, and one
which approximates to a state of 'social disorganisation' in the
Durkheimian sense of a lack of a uniform set of cultural standards conforming to that of the wider society, and of a community thereby ceasing to act as an effective agent of social
control on its members. Under such circumstances, criminal
activity becomes tolerated and accepted. This was therefore
indicted by Shaw and McKay as a direct cause of the high rates
of criminal activity in these areas.

An important point should be noted here. By this formulation,
Shaw and McKay effectively moved ecological theory forward
from its early physical location and structural determinism.
Previously, such factors as overcrowding, slum housing and
poverty were cited as causal factors in themselves; now structural factors became relegated to the minor role of predisposing
symptoms of the more significant processes of social and cultural transmission of delinquent patterns of behaviour that formed the basis of the later cultural affiliation theories described
by Muncie and Fitzgerald. To Shaw's credit, he attempted
to combine a factor analysis of the physical variables with
a 'situational analysis' of the individual's reactions to
them achieved through a detailed life history of their be-

haviours and attitudes. But as Alihan, a contemporary critic
of the Chicagoans had noted, this theoretical formulation is no
longer strictly ecological: 'if the environment includes such
aspects as the social and the technological, the process of
competition loses its ecological significance' (1938, p.246).

This view, however, caused a theoretical problem for the
Chicagoans. On the one hand, they followed functionalist notions
of society as a consensus of shared norms and values, while
on the other, their interpretations stressed the diverse
'pathologies' of specific deviant worlds, inhabiting particularly
the 'delinquency areas' of the cities, and of different 'natural
areas' each having its own set of behavioural and cultural
norms. As Matza put it: 'they exaggerated the separation
between deviant and conventional worlds ... this was the vice
attending their ethnographic virtue' (1969, p.71). Shaw and
McKay solved this dilemma by rejecting the previously firm
Chicagoan notion of society as a consensus and substituting
for it a view of a pluralistic society - each area having its own
set of norms, traditions and accepted behaviours. Thereby
social disorganisation theory advanced into that of differential
social disorganisation, and this new emphasis, incorporating
as it does the important notion of 'conflict', is discussed in
Muncie and Fitzgerald's article. Meanwhile it remains for us to
review some of the major criticisms of the Chicago ecological
approach and to trace the effect of its tradition on British
criminology.

The ecological approach to crime: an assessment
As we have seen, the Chicago School with its ecological approach
to society and social issues in the 1920s was arguably the most
potent influence in developing a social perspective in these
areas at the time, so redressing the analytically individualistic
imbalance that had existed since the initial impact of Lombrosian
theory. A sociological tradition became established that had
the study of crime as one of its principal concerns but within
the framework of seeing criminal behaviour as analagous to
any other social behaviour. The main proponents of the School
in Chicago had a practical influence on social policy by ensuring, with journalistic zeal, that their studies received plenty
of publicity and by appointing themselves self-styled advisers
to the municipal policy-makers. They suggested, first, the
potentiality of the study of the spatial distribution of various
social indices within the city, second, that various deviant
behaviours may be ecologically associated with rapid urban
growth, and third, that the inhabitants of 'high-delinquency
areas' of the city adopted, by a process of learned cultural
transmission, a normatively reinforced life-style that condoned
criminal and anti-social behaviour - at least in terms of the
values of the wider city community. They developed and made
academically respectable their own form of empirical data-
collection by means of a unique blend of statistical and

cartographic methods and ethnographic 'appreciative' parti-
cipant-observational studies of particular deviant worlds. They
further refined the concept of 'social disorganisation' as an
analytic tool to come to mean 'the decrease of the influence of
existing social rules of behaviour upon individual members of
the group' (Thomas and Znaniecki, 1927), and this was undoubtedly useful in terms of the groups they were studying.

Yet there was an essentially theoretical difference between
the social disorganisation theories of the School and those
propounded earlier by Durkheim: whereas the focus of Durkheim's concern was *structural* - i.e. he wished to investigate
how a social structure initially generates pressures towards
deviance and why this occurs more in some structural sectors
rather than others - that of the Chicago School in all but its
earliest manifestations was, as we have seen, one of *transmission*. They accepted unproblematically the degree and forms
of social disorganisation present in a given urban location,
and directed their work towards revealing the processes and
systems by which these were actually transmitted among
affected social groups. As Muncie and Fitzgerald show, it was
the precise merging of these two theoretical strands that came
to characterise the later subcultural theories of crime and
deviance.

It was, however, when the attempt was made to apply this
same concept of social disorganisation to the study of crime
that we see its limitations. Its usage in this context not only
implied what Quinney and Wildeman termed 'a social absolutism
that regarded only one system as being the standard from
which all behaviour was evaluated' (1977, p.68) - which was
not at all consistent with the school's 'appreciative' strand of
theory based on the assumption of a peculiar deviant world
having its own normative structure - but became distinctly
tautologous. The same behaviour - for example, street crime
in the interstitial area - said to be explained by social disorganisation theory, was used also to prove its existence, and
crime became in a circular fashion an indicator of social disorganisation too. Similarly it must be said that the ecological
theory of the early Chicago School was over-deterministic in
its basic assumption that certain ecological situations must
inevitably produce crime, delinquency and other indices of
social disorganisation. Indeed the very term itself is pejoratively
used by Park and the early School leaders and reflects their
view of urbanism as essentially negative and alienative to the
development of human nature through its 'anomic' and pathological constraints. This assumption, of course, fitted well
with the correctionalist overtones of the early work of the
School, and tended to depict the deviants themselves as the
unfortunate creatures of urban circumstances.

On a more particularistic note, some serious criticisms can
be levelled at Shaw's concept of the delinquency area on which
a great deal of later ecological theory is built. His method of

computing the delinquency-rate itself has not remained free
from criticism. Essentially this was the ratio between the number
of offenders charged having home addresses in a given area
and the total population of the same sex and age group from
that same area. Sophie Robison, in 'Can Delinquency be
Measured?' (1936), argues that this measure cannot be valued
since it fails to take account of the 'dark number' of undetected
and 'unprocessed' offenders (for example those let off with a
caution) in the same area. It also fails to note the proven
effect of social class and family factors in deciding whether a
delinquent is in fact charged with an offence, and finally it
ignores the impact of local immigrant cultures on an area's
delinquency-rate. Negroes and Italians, for example, tend to
produce high rates of charged offenders compared with other
ethnic groups. Another later critic, Jonassen, underlined
this by suggesting that Shaw's square-mile-area rate system
is too large: the area is unlikely to be ethnically homogeneous
and the rate fails thereby 'to show not only the relative delinquency of specific groups, but that not all groups produce
delinquents under the same conditions' (cited in Morris, 1957,
p.89). Similarly Lander's later work in Baltimore with Japanese
immigrants (1954) and the British 'Radby' studies (Carter and
Jephcott, 1954) referred to in the next section show how Shaw
and the Chicagoans failed to note the existence of 'areas of
immunity' within a delinquency area: stable communities with
low delinquency rates can in fact exist within an area of high
social disorganisation.

We should also be aware of certain other more theoretical
criticisms that have been made of the ecological approach of
the Chicago School. Repeatedly the concepts of social organisation and disorganisation are used interchangably within the
same theoretical framework. Consequently it never becomes
clear, for example, whether the delinquency area represents
a normative culture of social disorganisation in its own right,
or whether it is a subverted area within an existing system of
social organisation. The essential Chicagoan dilemma remains
unsolved: that of wishing to emphasise at the same time the
'naturalism' and diversity of the specific deviant world with
its overtones of voluntarism of the individual in entering into
and remaining within that particular world - such as Andersen's
'Hobohemia' referred to earlier - and the correctional 'pathological' stance of Burgess and Shaw particularly in wishing
'to lose the deviation' or to reduce it, thereby asserting the
primacy of the normative law-abiding consensus of the wider
urban community. There is little doubt that the inward-turning
focus on the structural forces of a particular area - almost
invariably, as we have seen, this was the socially disorganised
interstitial zone where, as Laurie Taylor puts it, 'the criminal
environment hangs around in a rather uncomfortably autonomous
manner' (1971, p.129) - neglected not only the political,
economic and social forces of the wider society as they affected,

and in many ways maintained, the existing inequalities of the
zone, but also disregarded the dynamic processes of the zone's
interactive relations with other zones. As Matza said, 'the
Chicagoans suffered from a certain blindness to overlap'. They
attempted to solve the essential diversity-pathology dilemma
by using 'the conception of social disorganisation to relocate
pathology: it was moved from the personal to the social plane'
(1969, p.147); in other words, pathological communities suffered from social disorganisation and social disorganisation was
pathological: the old circularities are still there and the disparity is never satisfactorily resolved.

Finally we should note the criticisms of historical specificity
and of the unsophisticated and selective use of official statistics
in the work of the Chicago School. Historically the 'evidence'
relating to the formation of delinquency areas was specific to
the rapid urban growth of Chicago and other American manufacturing cities in the mid-west in the late 1920s and 1930s.
We should not therefore expect it to be necessarily valid in
other physical and cultural locations at other times. Statistically
the 'evidence' requires cautious interpretations, as we have
seen with Shaw's concept of the delinquency-rate. Certainly
at the time of the Chicago studies there was no consideration
of, for example, such statistical 'pollutants' as the role of
state agencies in the manufacture of these statistics, or of
different styles of policing in different areas leading in turn
to the construction of different official crime-rates for the
areas.

MORE RECENT BRITISH 'AREA STUDIES'

In Britain there have been a considerable number of 'area
studies' of delinquency which have attempted to demonstrate
the dimensions of the problem within a particular urban area,
but there has been little attempt to generalise and summarise
these in any coherent way. The study of criminology has
always been more of a marginal 'fringe' activity in British
universities, and the Chicago School traditions have not had
the same impact as in America. It is not too surprising, therefore, to find far fewer studies in Britain investigating delinquency that have an ecological framework; most have tended
to focus sociologically and empirically on the problem as it
pertains to specific towns and cities, viewing crime as being
sub-culturally determined by the frustrations of working-class
life.

Apart from a few statistical surveys of delinquency such as
Bagot's work comparing rates in Liverpool with the rest of
England and Wales (1941), and that of Carr-Saunders, Mannheim, and Rhodes in London (1942), little work of substance
in this genre was achieved until the 1950s. At this time, crime-
rates, particularly among juveniles, were rising substantially

and really challenging for the first time one of the enduring
basic assumptions of positivistic criminology. This was that
as poverty and social insecurity became reduced through post-
war full employment and increasing personal affluence, so the
crime-rate would progressively decrease. The provisions of the
Welfare State were supposedly the main causes of the erosion
of personal and social responsibility, and they proved an easy
scapegoat, especially among sections of the magistracy and
police, while the continuity and further decline of the pre-war
evils of slum housing and urban overcrowding, together with
the considerable family problems caused by the effects of the
war, were easily overlooked.

It was in this sort of climate that J.B. Mays's study of the
delinquent sub-culture of an inner city slum area in Liverpool,
'Growing Up in the City', was published in (1954). Although
the theoretical framework was that of sub-cultural sociology -
which is discussed in Muncie and Fitzgerald's article - rather
than ecology, it showed affinities to both Whyte's 'Street
Corner Society' and Shaw's 'situational analysis'. By interview-
ing boys from the Liverpool University Settlement project,
Mays produced a vivid picture of an area possessing a cultural
background in which shoplifting, malicious damage and petty
thieving constituted 'normal' behaviour for boys in certain
age groups which was passively accepted in the neighbourhood.
He discovered that almost all boys in the area had committed
similar types of offence as a result of conforming to the delinquency norm transmitted through membership of any of the
teenage gangs, but not all had been detected or prosecuted.
Mays therefore offered a solution to one of the problems that
worried other investigators: why every boy from a delinquency
area does not become a delinquent. He does, in Mays's view,
but is not necessarily caught and prosecuted. Perhaps the
most striking conclusion from this work for our purposes is
that it suggests quite strongly that sociological or cultural
factors as a cause of crime were relatively neglected by the
environmentalism of the ecological approach.

Shortly afterwards, the publication of the 'Radby' studies of
a Midland mining town by Carter and Jephcott (1954) suggested
that the idea of a delinquency area needed to be refined even
further. They found that different normative standards were
upheld in different streets within the same slum 'delinquency'
area. There would be 'black' streets containing a high concentration of cases of juvenile delinquency and adult crime,
together with considerable domestic violence, drunkenness,
street fighting and sexual promiscuity. Adjacent to them and
externally very similar in design and appearance were 'white
streets' with low rates of delinquency and crime, little or no
street disorder, 'house-proud mothers' and 'better controlled
children'. The clear inferences from this are that the family
and local street corner values are seen as the crucial factors
in determining whether juveniles become delinquent or not,

that families with similar normative outlooks and behaviours
are 'attracted' to live close to each other, and that Mays was
not correct in imputing a lack of continuity between juvenile
and adult attitudes and behaviours in relation to crime and
delinquency. These were all findings to be distinctively underlined a few years later in America in an important paper by
Walter Miller. In this he identified a number of 'focal concerns'
characterising the distinctive 'lower-class' cultural life of
urban slum areas which promoted a certain kind of localised
delinquency by street-corner groups. Such 'concerns' as
'toughness', 'smartness' (in the sense of gaining by one's wits),
'excitement' and an involvement with 'trouble' are mentioned
among others as the means by which the main emphases of
the local lower-class culture - adult as well as juvenile - can be
acted out and group or gang cohesion reinforced. We can clearly
detect here a movement towards seeing social class and cultural
factors as they affect family and local area values as important
determinants of delinquent behaviour.

In 1957 Terence Morris published 'The Criminal Area: a
Study in Social Ecology'. This has possibly remained the most
comprehensive and best-known area study in Britain, and is
centred on Croydon. Its importance can be judged from the
fact that its major findings constituted a turning-point in
British area studies. Its emphasis upon the importance of the
type and area of housing and of the housing policies of local
authorities as being more relevant to studying the dynamics of
delinquency than the previous concepts of ecological zones and
delinquency areas greatly affected, as we shall see, the direction and nature of British sociological research into the deprivations of urban areas. The concept of 'housing classes' took over
from that of 'delinquency area' as the focal concern of most
post-1960 work in this field. Morris concluded that the physical
characteristics of specific urban areas were not particularly
relevant to their delinquency-rates, nor were delinquency areas
likely to be socially, ethnically or culturally homogeneous. What
he found to be crucial was the combination of the effects of
low social class and planned housing policy. The areas of peak
crime and delinquency-rates in Croydon were found to be two
of the inter-war council housing estates, together with some
concentration in two older residential areas noted for slum
housing and physical deterioration. Within these estates and
areas, Morris's data supported the 'Radby' findings that areas
of delinquent residence were concentrated in small localised
sections. In Croydon at the time of Morris's study, the policy
of the housing authorities was to rehouse 'difficult' families
together in the older estates. From this Morris argues two
points: first, that the chances of any child becoming delinquent
seem related to the number and strength of the delinquent
influences operating in his immediate local environment, and
second, that the areas with lowest rentals - i.e. the older
estates - attract the lowest income groups within which most

offenders tend to be found. Both of these points are consonant with the premises of differential association theory that Muncie and Fitzgerald discuss. This implies, of course, that it is more a question of the inhabitants of the older estates taking their delinquent activities with them when they move rather than one of the poor housing and slum area corrupting the inhabitants as Shaw and McKay had argued.

Largely as a result of Morris's work, the focus of subsequent British area studies widened to include the study of differential access to housing space, of policies concerning the utilisation and allocation of publicly-owned housing, and of the effects on people compelled to live in low-grade housing in 'rough' areas with regard to criminal and delinquent behaviour. It can be seen that such first-order sociological concepts as social class and the differential access to power and influence feature more and more in such studies. In the late 1950s and 1960s, a growing number of area studies focused on the difference between publicly- and privately-owned housing in terms of delinquency-rates. The studies of Mannheim in Cambridge (1948), Ferguson in Glasgow (1952), Jones in Leicester (1958), Spencer in Bristol (1964), Wallis and Maliphant in London (1967), Patrick in Glasgow (1973) and, as recently as 1976, Bottoms and Baldwin in Sheffield all demonstrated the clear connection between inclusion in the official crime- and delinquency-rates and the occupation of publicly-owned housing, particularly on the older inter-war estates which tended to be used by local authorities for rehousing its various categories of 'problem families'.

It is at this point in our review of post-war British area studies that we find a core concept of Chicago ecology retained, revived and reconstructed. The competitive struggle for space, originally the legacy of Social Darwinism in human ecology, and dependent on the population sequences of invasion, dominance and succession, returns as the basis of the organisation of urban life and of many contemporary urban area studies. It has however now become transformed into the struggle for housing space. As Laurie Taylor succinctly puts it (1971, p.131):

> Whilst today there may be town planners, civic designers, and social reformers who modify the nakedness of such a struggle, this has not simply ended land speculation, Rachmanism, discriminatory housing policies, or prevented the formation of ghettoes. The housing estate is as much the product of competition as the slum and may evidence a similar if not greater degree of social disorganisation.

We must agree, but the important point to note in the context of ecological and area studies is that it is not the competition of either free market forces or indeed of natural selection, to use the biological analogy. Rex and Moore in 1967 published the results of their study of how Sparkbrook became an immigrant twilight zone of Birmingham, in which they dispensed entirely with the biological emphases in the ecological theory of the development of urban zones. They saw the structure of Birmingham, as determined by the 'class struggle for housing' expressed in Weberian terms, as being based on the differential access to and control of domestic property of different groups of the population. They argued that allocation policies are crucial in determining the social characteristics of both publicly- and privately-owned housing areas, and cited in evidence what they felt to be the discriminatory practices of the local authority against black families as a means of ensuring the perpetuation of the white working-class 'public suburbia' of its council estates. The result, of course, was that immigrant groups became forced into inhabiting privately rented multi-occupation twilight areas like Sparkbrook. In 1970, Lambert, using Rex and Moore's conflict model of housing classes competing for urban space, completed a study of race relations and crime in a different twilight area of Birmingham. He was able to define this area ecologically as a 'crescent-shaped zone consisting largely of older and larger types of houses, mostly now in multi-occupation and revealing a high rate of population change in the lodging-house zone' (1970, p.283). The area had a high crime-rate, but most of this was not committed by black immigrants who were arriving in the area without jobs in large numbers, but by white and black 'long stay' residents of the area. What Lambert found, however, was that the rate of crime among new immigrants gradually increased to match that of the area as a whole. Here again we note the location of the explanation for crime and delinquency not in the nature of the area itself, but in the difficulties of specific groups obliged to live in these areas because of their relatively lowly position in the competitive urban markets for houses and employment.

Recent developments of British area studies in the 1970s still focus on the housing area but with the somewhat changed emphasis of the manufacture of 'neighbourhood reputation': how a certain area becomes labelled 'bad' along with all the inhabitants within it, and how what Owen Gill terms 'hierarchies of desirability' develop both in relation to 'types' of housing area and 'types' of tenant (1977, p.5). A review of recent work in this field by Phil Scraton shows how the political conception of reputation held by decision-makers is linked directly to class and power relations in the area of housing allocation (1981, chapter 5). Questions now asked include: How should available public housing best be used? Who in the allocation system decides who should live where and how are such decisions made? These are the focal concerns of work in area studies still being developed but owing much to the labelling and social reaction perspectives of sociology and criminology that are considered in later articles of this book. Notable contributions to this genre have been made by the American sociologists Gerald Suttles and E.V. Walters. In 1968 Suttles, in his study

of the Addams slum area of Chicago, developed the concept of
the 'cognitive map' as a useful way of looking at the web of
social meanings or reputations that become attached to certain
neighbourhoods. He defines this as the means by which an
individual produces an internally consistent mental picture of
his complex urban environment and locates himself and his
roles within it. The cognitive maps of individuals living in the
same area and possessing similar outlooks and shared experiences – together with those of members of such public agencies
concerned with that area as the police and Social Services
officials – these combine to form a stereotyped public image
or reputation of the area. In a later work Suttles further
developed this concept to define what he termed a 'defeated'
neighbourhood: 'a community so heavily stigmatised and outcast
that its residents retreat from most forms of public participation
out of shame, mutual fear and an absence of faith in each others'
concern' (1972, p.239). In the same year, Walters extended
this with his concept of 'the dreadful enclosure': i.e. 'certain
milieux with reputations for moral inferiority, squalor, violence
and social pathology'. Walters is at pains to show that the
indices of pathology often cited as evidence of an enclosure's
negative reputation derive not from the ecological characteristics
of the area as in the Chicago model, nor from the working-class
life-styles featured by the sub-cultural school, but are essentially a product of the inhabitants' 'exclusions from power,
resources and honour' – i.e. from the socio-economic processes
related to power. In realistic terms, the stigma of living in
such areas can have a profound effect on an individual's
educational, housing and employment chances in life, and so
permanently obstruct him or her from making any real progress
in the competitive struggles not only for space, but for the
market resources affecting these essential life-chances.

In 1974 Sean Damer investigated a 'dreadful enclosure' in a
corporation slum-clearance estate in the Govan area of Glasgow.
The estate's negative reputation was firmly fixed by its local
unofficial name of 'Wine Alley', which was used by its inhabitants, the local corporation and police alike. Also that year,
Howard Parker published 'View from the Boys', his vividly
documented account of adolescent life in the Roundhouse
tenement area of inner Liverpool, and three years later Owen
Gill published his findings from a similar sort of investigation
in a different slum area of Merseyside in 'Luke Street'. The
theoretical aim of these later studies is primarily to provide
a radical-critical refinement of labelling, social reaction and
deviance-amplification theory by investigating beyond the
physical and ecological characteristics and the 'types' of
inhabitants of a twilight area – to use Gill's words: 'to see
how the conflict imagery and disharmony of urban society is
organised so that at the everyday and local level, delinquency
becomes a possibility' (1977, p.182). Yet all these studies still
retain the essentially ecological base of looking at a delineated

area - a neighbourhood - and begin by enumerating, just like
the Chicago School, the physical and ecological reasons for
its decline into its present slum and socially disorganised nature.
They also employ the Chicago method of 'appreciative' participant observation, together with the same liberal use of personal biographies of the area inhabitants.

From the perspective of this article, however, we must note
the essential reconstruction of Chicago theories, particularly
since the work of Rex and Moore, to include ways in which
relatively powerful interest-groups - such as the local housing
authority - can use political and economic power to manipulate
and maintain the disadvantage of other less powerful and less
well organised groups. Similarly the biological analogy of Park
and Burgess's population sequences of invasion, dominance
and succession has been adapted into one of class conflict or
'housing classes' moving into new areas and achieving positions
of control while at the same time forcing other weaker groups
to lose out in the struggle of the housing market. The struggle
for space of Social Darwinism and the early ecologists is still
there, but has become transformed into the socio-economic
class struggles of the 1960s and 1970s. Rex and Moore depict
this as 'a process of discriminative and de facto segregation
which compelled coloured immigrants to live in certain typical
conditions and which of itself exacerbated racial ill-feeling'
(1967, p.20). It remains at its roots still a struggle for space
in the city, but the original Chicago positivist static notion
of a consensual urban society unfortunately possessing a
minority of pathological deviants living in a correctable milieu
of social disorganisation has been widened and rendered dynamic
by the inclusion of the concepts of change, conflict and struggle within the reconstructed theoretical framework.

We have moved now well away from the original ecological
concepts of urban zones, delinquency-rates and 'natural'
'delinquency' or 'criminal' areas. Nevertheless this article has
tried to show that, in the reconstruction of urban theory, the
community and neighbourhood study remains the basic vehicle
for truly comprehensive understanding and 'appreciation' of
the urban condition - and the initial step in the analysis of
community structure is still the intensive observation of its
basic micro-units: the family and the age-graded groups. We
have made many criticisms of the Chicago School and its deterministic ecological approach. It would perhaps be fair, therefore, in view of the undoubted influence of its theories, which
continues in sociology and criminology to the present day, to
end this article with Laurie Taylor's very positive review of
a few of the School's achievements (1971, pp.130-1):

> The ecologists displayed a welcome readiness to provide
> quantitative and qualitative accounts of deviance. They
> were sympathetic observers *and* statisticians, practical
> reformers *and* theoreticians. To read their books is to ac-
> quire a sense of the ebb and flow of life in Chicago in the

1930s or to put it more forcefully, it is to appreciate the
dynamic elements which underlie the development of the
city.

References
Alihan, M.A. (1938), 'Social Ecology: a critical analysis',
Columbia University Press.
Andersen, N. (1923), 'The Hobo: the Sociology of the Homeless
Man', University of Chicago Press.
Aschaffenburg, G. (1913), 'Crime and its Repression' (trans.
Albrecht), Boston, Little, Brown.
Bagot, J.H. (1941), 'Juvenile Delinquency: a Comparative Study
of the Position in Liverpool and England and Wales', London,
Cape.
Bonger, W.A. (1916), 'Criminality and Economic Conditions'
(trans. Horton), Boston, Little, Brown.
Bottoms, A.E. and Baldwin, J. (1976), 'The Urban Criminal',
Tavistock.
Burgess, E.W. (1929), in 'Basic Social Data in Chicago',
ed. Smith and White, University of Chicago Press.
Carr-Saunders, A.M., Mannheim, H. and Rhodes, E.G. (1942),
'Young Offenders', Cambridge University Press.
Carter, M.P. and Jephcott, P. (1954), The Social Background
of Delinquency, unpublished, University of Nottingham
Library.
Damer, S. (1977), Wine Alley: The Sociology of a Dreadful
Enclosure, in 'The Sociology of Crime and Delinquency in
Britain', ed. W.G. Carson and P. Wiles, vol.2, Martin
Robertson.
Durkheim, E. (1952), 'Suicide: a Study in Sociology', Routledge
& Kegan Paul.
Durkheim, E. (1964), 'Rules of Sociological Method', New York,
Free Press.
Durkheim, E. (1964), 'The Division of Labour in Society', New
York, Free Press.
Ferguson, T. (1952), 'The Young Delinquent in his Social
Setting', Oxford University Press.
Fletcher, J. (1848), Moral and Educational Statistics of England
and Wales, 'Journal of the Statistical Society' (London),
vol.2.
Gill, O. (1977), 'Luke Street: Housing Policy, Conflict and the
Creation of the Delinquency Area', Macmillan.
Glyde, J. (1856), Localities of Crime in Suffolk, 'Journal of
the Statistical Society' (London), vol.19.
Goring, C. (1913), 'The English Convict', London, HMSO.
Jones, H. (1958), Approaches to an Ecological Study, 'British
Journal of Delinquency', vol.8, no.4, pp.277-93.
Lambert, J.R. (1970), 'Crime, Police and Race Relations',
Institute of Race Relations/Oxford University Press.
Lander, B. (1954), 'Towards an Understanding of Juvenile
Delinquency', Columbia University Press.

Lombroso, C. (1876), 'L'Uomo delinquente', Milan, 5th ed, Turin, Bocca.

Lombroso, C. (1913), 'Crime: its Causes and Remedies' (trans. Horton), Boston, Little, Brown.

McKenzie, R.D. (1923), 'The Neighbourhood: a Study of Columbus, Ohio', Chicago University Press.

McKenzie, R.D. (1933), 'The Metropolitan Community', New York, McGraw-Hill.

Mannheim, H. (1948), 'Juvenile Delinquency in an English Middletown', Routledge & Kegan Paul.

Mannheim, H., ed. (1960), 'Pioneers in Criminology', Stevens.

Mannheim, H. (1965), 'Comparative Criminology', Routledge & Kegan Paul.

Matza, D. (1969), 'Becoming Deviant', Englewood Cliffs, Prentice-Hall.

Mayhew, H. (1861), 'London Labour and the London Poor', 4 vols, London, Griffin.

Mays, J.B. (1954), 'Growing Up in the City', Liverpool University Press.

Miller, W.B. (1958), Lower Class Culture as a Generating Milieu of Gang Delinquency, 'Journal of Social Issues', vol.14, pp.5-19.

Morris, T.P. (1957), 'The Criminal Area: a Study in Social Ecology', London, Routledge & Kegan Paul.

Park R.E. (1929), Sociology, in 'Research in the Social Sciences', ed. W. Gee, New York, Macmillan.

Park, R.E. (1936), Human Ecology, 'American Journal of Sociology', no.42 (1), p.15.

Park, R.E. and Burgess, E.W. (1924), 'Introduction to the Science of Sociology', University of Chicago Press.

Park, R.E. and Burgess, E.W. (1925), 'The City', Chicago University Press.

Park, R.E. and Burgess, E.W. (1927), 'The Urban Community', Chicago University Press.

Parker, H. (1974), 'View from the Boys', David & Charles.

Parmalee, M. (1918), 'Criminology', New York, Macmillan.

Patrick, J. (1973), 'A Glasgow Gang Observed', Eyre Methuen.

Quetelet, A. (1942), 'Treatise on Man', Paris, Bachelier.

Quinney, R. and Wildeman, J. (1977), 'The Problem of Crime', New York, Harper & Row.

Rex, J. and Moore, R. (1967), 'Race, Community and Conflict: a Study in Sparkbrook', Institute of Race Relations/Oxford University Press.

Robison, S.M. (1936), 'Can Delinquency be Measured?', Columbia University Press/Oxford University Press.

Scraton, P. (1981), 'Class, Marginality and State Control', Macmillan.

Shaw, C.R. (1930), 'The Jack Roller', Chicago University Press.

Shaw, C.R. (1931), 'Natural History of a Deviant Career', Chicago University Press.

Shaw, C.R. (1938), 'Brothers in Crime', Chicago University Press.

Shaw, C.R. et al. (1929), 'Delinquency Areas', University of Chicago Press.

Shaw, C.R. and McKay, H.D. (1942), 'Juvenile Delinquency in Urban Areas', University of Chicago Press.

Spencer, J. (1964), 'Stress and Release on an Urban Estate', Tavistock.

Suttles, G.D. (1968), 'The Social Order of the Slum', University of Chicago Press.

Suttles, G.D. (1972), 'The Social Construction of Communities', University of Chicago Press.

Tarde, G. (1912), 'Penal Philosophy', Boston, Little, Brown.

Taylor, I., Walton, P. and Young J. (1973), 'The New Criminology', Routledge & Kegan Paul.

Taylor, L. (1971), 'Deviance and Society', Michael Joseph.

Thomas, W.I. and Znaniecki, F. (1927), 'The Polish Peasant in Europe and America', 2 vols, 2nd ed., New York, Knopf.

Thrasher, F.M. (1927), 'The Gang', University of Chicago Press.

Wallis, C.P. and Maliphant, R. (1967), Delinquent Areas in the County of London, 'British Journal of Criminology', vol.7, no.3, pp.250-84.

Walters, E.V. (1972), Dreadful Enclosures: Detoxifying an Urban Myth, unpublished paper.

Whyte, W.F. (1943), 'Street Corner Society', University of Chicago Press.

Wirth, L. (1928), 'The Ghetto', University of Chicago Press.

Zorbaugh, H. ed. (1929), 'Gold Coast and the Slum', University of Chicago Press.

17 Moral development and the family: the genesis of crime

Rudi Dallos

APPROACHES TO THE STUDY OF THE FAMILY

In this article I shall explore explanations which consider
crime in relation to the individual's environment, as opposed
to heredity, as described by Sapsford in article no.15. More
specifically, the focus here will be on the social learning
experiences of the individual in the context of a primary
socializing group in our society, namely, the family. Criminologists have been well aware of the significant contribution that
a study of the family situation offers to an explanation of
crime. In the 1950s, in particular, a large number of descriptive
or 'naturalistic' studies were carried out on the families of
'criminals' and 'delinquents', the aim being to establish factors
in the criminal's family life, or so-called 'under-the-roof culture', which were responsible for their later criminal or delinquent activity. There was an abundance of folk wisdom to
suggest that factors such as physical abuse and erratic discipline might be responsible; so by studying large numbers of
'criminal' families it was hoped that such causative factors
could be clearly identified and differentiated.

In fact, the data from such studies did at first appear to
corroborate much of the 'folk wisdom'. A popular conclusion
drawn was that the parents of delinquents and criminals were
statistically more likely to employ methods of discipline involving an assertion of power; in particular, physical forms of
punishment. More generally, they were also more likely, in the
investigator's view, to be 'erratic' in their disciplining of the
children and to show a lack of affection for them. These studies,
though making contributions to an understanding of the family's
influence on subsequent criminality, had serious methodological
and conceptual deficiencies which limit their validity.

Following a review and critique of these 'naturalistic' studies,

Source: article commissioned for this volume. Rudi Dallos is
Staff Tutor, Faculty of Social Sciences, the Open University.

their findings are considered in terms of, and extended by, three major lines of theorizing in criminal pathology: psychoanalytic, learning and cognitive developmental theory. Historically, these represent not only the major theories in criminal psychology but also significant intellectual developments within psychology.

The *psychoanalytic explanations* derive from clinical psychiatry and hence have been essentially concerned with explanations employing a 'medical illness model'. That is, due to certain difficulties in the child's early sexual development, he/ she has in a sense become ill, the 'symptoms' of such an illness being the committing of crimes such as arson, theft, sexual attacks and murder. Since individuals are seen as 'sick', they are consequently regarded as being not fully 'responsible' for their actions. This view has had considerable impact on sentencing and treatment policies (Wootton, 1959; West, 1973) and facilitated the rise of psychiatric treatment for offenders, therapeutic communities and schools.

The emergence of Behaviourist psychology in the 1950s and 1960s brought a challenge to and sought to reject psychoanalytic theory because of its 'unscientific' nature: predominantly, its lack of rigorous testability. Metaphysical poking around inside people's heads in the search for unconscious processes was regarded as unnecessary in order to 'predict' actions, so by the principle of Occam's razor the concepts of consciousness and the unconscious, too, were abolished as unnecessary (Skinner, 1953). The Behaviourist *learning theories* proposed instead that people's actions were controlled by a system of rewards and punishments. Such an analysis suggested that crime was due to inappropriate learning experiences or social mis-programming. Criminals were no longer seen to be ill but suffering from mis-learning.

The 1960s and 1970s have seen a reaction to and shift away from simple Behaviourist explanations towards cognitive developmental theories. These represent a return to a consideration of 'internal processes' that Behaviourism sought to reject. Fundamental to the cognitive developmental approach is a consideration of the child's understanding and 'inner representation' of its world, particularly its social world in the case of moral development. Most importantly Piaget's and Kohlberg's contributions are to view predisposition to commit crime in predominantly 'cognitive' rather than emotional terms. That is to say, a person's actions are regarded as guided by their level of moral development or awareness which reflects their ability to undertake *reasoning* concerned with issues of 'right' and 'wrong', 'goodness' and 'badness' of actions.

The emphasis of the studies which will be covered in this article is essentially *deterministic*; that is, a search for *causes* of criminal activity within the family environment, this being seen in terms mainly of the influences of the parents' child-rearing practices in determining the child's predisposition to criminal activities. This *asymmetrical* pattern of influence is questionable in that the influence is more likely to be *symmetrical* or mutual. These issues are taken up specifically in article no.19 by Dallos and Sapsford.

THE FAMILY ENVIRONMENT: UNDER-THE-ROOF CULTURE

There is an abundant store of 'folk wisdom' regarding what aspects of the family environment are conducive to criminal or delinquent development: bad parental example, lack of discipline, lack of affection, parental irresponsibility, physical abuse, broken homes, deprivation, lack of contact with parents and influence of media/television. These ideas still have common currency, partly as a legacy of the thinking of the early criminologists studying the influence of the family environment on criminal development. Of note also was the notion, deriving from Cyril Burt's influential work for the Home Office (1923), that delinquency was related to mental deficiency (see p.321 in Sapsford's article). Since he also regarded mental deficiency as hereditary and related to class, this implied a 'pool' of mentally deficient, largely working-class, sections of the population from which criminals could be expected to emerge. Burt did discover, though, and emphasized, that many delinquents came from economically 'comfortable' homes. In his view, delinquency resulted from a plurality of converging factors so that the juvenile criminal is far from constituting a homogeneous psychological class. Since he considered bad homes, defective discipline, vicious home atmosphere, defective family relationships and constitution as the major causes of crime, rather than poverty, his work was and still is influential in promoting the family as a prime target for social interventions, such as institutional care for children 'at risk' and home visits by child and social workers.

Child-rearing practices
The primary emphasis of the influential 'pioneering' studies conducted in the 1950s was *descriptive*, the aim being to identify and differentiate aspects of 'under the roof culture' which were conducive to subsequent criminal activity, rather than to propose rigorous theoretical accounts. The approach was essentially normative in that, for example, one of the aims was to identify patterns of child-rearing which were 'likely' to lead to criminal activity.

The child-rearing studies fall into two broad areas: *naturalistic* and *experimental*. The former were concerned with relating child-rearing practices in actual families to incidence of criminality or delinquency. Typically, the approach taken was to compare the family features of a pre-labelled group such as delinquent children (in terms of convictions) with those of a 'normal' group. By contrast, the *experimental* studies attempted to establish a measurable, though hypothetical, entity (known in psychology as an intervening variable, like IQ, for example), namely, moral development or strength of conscience, which were seen to be related to the individual's predisposition to commit crimes. *Moral development* was defined as the extent to which individuals have developed an awareness and understanding of the moral codes of society as well as that of their immediate social groups, friends, family and colleagues.

Retrospective studies

The studies by the Gluecks serve as an example of the naturalistic retrospective approach. In one study (1950), they attempted to assess the influence of the family environment by examining the families of 500 'proven delinquent' boys from two correctional schools in Massachusetts in comparison with the families of 500 'non-delinquents', the boys being carefully matched on the basis of age, IQ, ethnic-racial origins and type of locality they lived in. The method then involved: the collection of 'field data' from the child's school, social work agencies involved and courts and, second, intensive home interviews with the parents. Their over-riding finding was that the parents of the delinquent group were statistically more likely to employ methods of disciplining of their children deemed, by the investigators, to be unsuitable: lax, over-strict or erratic. Both parents were more likely to use physical punishment and be indifferent or hostile towards their children. The Gluecks (1950, p.282) summarized their findings by stating that delinquent children were different

in having been reared to a greater extent than the control group in homes of little understanding, affection, stability, or moral fibre by parents usually unfit to be effective guides and protectors or desirable sources for emulation and the construction of a consistent, well-balanced and socially normal superego during the early stages of character development.

Not surprisingly, in a later study (1962), they also found that the hostility became reciprocal, so that delinquent children were found to develop feelings of indifference and hostility towards both parents and to regard them as unacceptable figures for emulation.

More recently, a study by Andry (1971) suggests that the fathers of 'delinquent' children are particularly significant in that they show less affection, have less contact with and are identified with, less than the fathers of 'normal' children. This presents something of an apparent paradox, since children have also been found to follow their parents into criminal careers (Feldman, 1976).

Experimental studies

An alternative type of research in this area is exemplified by the experimental studies of moral development carried out by

Sears and colleagues (1957). They considered whether criminal activity was a result of the acquisition of a faulty morality or of conscience. Fundamental to this approach was the quantification of moral development, as mentioned earlier, in order to enable comparisons of the effects of different types of child-rearing. Such a measure was seen to be valuable for enabling a more refined analysis of the effects of child-rearing practices in delinquent and non-delinquent families, since it indicated 'latent' predisposition to crime as well as actual 'performance'. In other words, children treated in certain ways in non-delinquent families may become equally (latently) 'immoral', but various other factors have suppressed their performance of delinquent/criminal acts. A lack of predictive power regarding actual behaviour, however, makes such a measure of little value and questions its basic validity. In order to assess the child-rearing problems, mothers were interviewed extensively about the behaviour of their children generally, their child-rearing practices and, most significantly, how the child acted in a number of standard situations of interest to the experimenters, such as after he had deliberately done something known to be naughty behind his mother's back. The general pattern of findings from these studies was that psychological techniques of discipline - praise, withdrawal of love and isolation (sending a child to his/her room) - were positively associated with moral development. On the other hand, physical techniques such as withdrawal of tangible rewards, deprivation of privileges and physical punishment were negatively associated with it, and, of all the techniques used, physical punishment was found to be most detrimental.

Hoffman and Saltzsein (1967), however, point out the need to make a distinction between two different aspects of psychological techniques of discipline: *love-withdrawal* is viewed as a purely emotional but non-physical response as opposed to what they called *induction* or reasoning. That is, techniques in which the parent points out the painful consequences of the child's act for the parent or for others. In a study of socio-economic differences, they found very little evidence of the use of induction as a technique in working-class families, but in the middle-class group it was associated with highest moral development. Such studies 'smuggle' in suggestions of class differences in morality which may not be valid; rather the parenting differences may merely reflect differences in 'style' of communication, such as talking less to the children. In turn, these may be a result of differences in education of the parents and 'socio-economic' constraints such as the financial need for working-class mothers to work and consequently having less time and energy available for their children.

These studies had various methodological drawbacks, including the use of reports of child-training practice as opposed to actual observation. However, they were carried out before the sophistication of video and observation screens were commonly

introduced (though this does not excuse more recent studies).
Similarly, apart from actual records of offences, the activity
of the children was not usually observed but again was assessed
by reference to parents' reports. Such reporting is prone to
considerable bias, since parents have wildly different ideas
of what is 'normal' and may conceal or distort evidence, particularly if they are of a different class background from the
essentially middle-class interviewers whom they may be trying
to please. To their credit, the Gluecks did not rely entirely
on parents' (usually mother's) reports, but also gathered as
much 'field data' as possible. This, in fact, often showed
gross incompatibilities between parents, school and welfare
organization accounts of the child's disciplining.

Some studies such as those by MacKinnon, which will be
described later, did in fact examine actual behaviour of the
children such as resistance to temptation. However, discipline
was still assessed in terms of self-reports of the subject's
childhood experiences. In addition, there was a frequent tendency to view morality as general as opposed to multi-dimen-
sional; that is, though someone may steal, for example, they may not
necessarily commit acts of violence, for example. The predictive power of such a general measure of morality is therefore
highly questionable (Pittel and Mendelsohn, 1966).

A further and very serious failing of these studies is that
they predominantly employed pre-labelled populations. Becker
has suggested that individuals of families may come to accept
the definitions imposed on them by the defining class and
subsequently act accordingly. Hence such retrospective studies
of families who have been *labelled* as criminal or delinquent-
prone may be distorted by the family's internalization of such
labels and the expectations, in the form of types of behaviour
towards their children, associated with them (see article no.18
by Muncie and Fitzgerald).

Prospective studies

One approach designed to avoid the last of these problems is
to undertake studies which take not a pre-labelled group as
the starting-point but a 'normal' population of children who are
then followed through their development in order to see which
ones become 'delinquent' and which do not. A study by West
(1969), for example, examined a sample of 411 boys, aged
eight to nine years, from six junior schools in an area in
London described as 'a typically working-class neighbourhood
in the process of slow physical and cultural change'. A wide
range of information was gathered on the children, including
their economic status, housing, personality and parenting.
The researchers observed the boys from the ages of eight and
nine to fourteen. By then, some 7.3 per cent had been convicted
by a juvenile court at least once, and a higher proportion were
'known' by the police or teachers to be offenders. The results,
with regard to parenting, were that 'socially deprived, unloving,

erratic, inconsistent and careless parents tend to produce
badly behaved boys.' However, it is important to mention that
in this and their following reports (Knight and West, 1975)
the most important indicators of delinquency were poor income,
poor housing and a large number of children. For example, of
the 83 most delinquent of the sample by the age of eighteen to
twenty, the main difference between those who stopped offending (termed 'temporary delinquent') and those who were still
offending ('continued delinquent') was the latter's lower socio-
economic background and greater incidence of previous family
criminality.

A major criticism of the studies described so far is that they
have great difficulty in accounting for within-family differences;
that is, why one child rather than another becomes delinquent.
The response from such normative approaches is that all children from criminogenic families would be more 'likely' to commit
crimes, though other varying factors such as school, friends
and opportunity could mitigate the family influence. Second,
as was stated earlier, these approaches imply an *asymmetrical*
or unilateral pattern of influence, that is, parents acting upon
the children. Philosophically, this represents a view emanating
from John Locke of the newborn infant as a 'tabula rasa' or
blank board upon which experience is written to form its
personality. The Gluecks were to some extent aware of the
shortcomings of this view, and in their later studies their
stated aim was 'to ascertain the involvement of socio-cultural
influence (largely in the most intimate environmental circle,
the home with its under-the-roof culture) in laying down and
moulding of delinquency-related traits both in general and
with respect of boys of *various physique types*' (1962), their
suggestion here being that the effects of the family situation
vary according to the type of physique of the child. This is
suggestive of a mutual influence effect and provides some
explanation of within-family differences; however, it is still
essentially unilateral. Children are born with merely physical
differences, and thus different types of discipline produce
different types of character development.

Reciprocal influences
More recently, Bell has taken up the issue of genetically-based
constitutional differences in children but significantly proposed
that these can determine the type of discipline employed by
the parents. Children have been found to differ particularly
in their level of activity, assertiveness and need for others.
Bell proposes (1968, p.88) that in order 'to predict the nature
of the parent-child interaction, it is necessary to know the
behaviour characteristics of the child, the cultural demands
on the parents and the parents' own individual assimilation of
these demands into a set of expectations for the child'. Two
types of parent control are suggested to be related to this:
upper-limit-control behaviour which is intended to *reduce* and

redirect activity of the child which exceeds the parents' expectations, and lower-limit-control behaviour which *stimulates* the child's activity level. For example, highly assertive and active children are likely to 'pull' physical punishment from parents, since the child's activity is likely to exceed their expectations of what is normal. That is, they will be trying, sometimes desperately, to quieten the child down.

This differs from the Gluecks' account in that it suggests that the type of parenting employed is not a fixed feature of the parents but arises from the *dynamic/interactive* relationship between the child's constitution, cultural demands and parental expectations. Hence siblings in the same family may be treated *differently* according to their constitution, and the manner of this treatment will be influenced by the parents' expectations. The relative importance of the three factors is not seen to be readily quantifiable and is seen to vary between families.

Bell does not appear to consider, however, whether the parental expectations eventually act to assimilate the constitutional differences. For example, boys are likely to be treated differently from girls, since the parents are influenced by the different expectations for them prevalent in society. It is possible, though, that in a similar way, specific expectations may develop for each child; for example, one boy may be seen as 'artistic' as opposed to a brother seen as 'practical', 'sensitive' as opposed to 'tough', and so on. These perceptions or 'constructs' (see p.434 in Dallos and Sapsford's article no.19) may have different expectations associated with them and consequently result in different ways of treating the children.

Summary
The findings of these studies in this section have been that the use of psychological techniques, and in particular the technique of induction, is associated with the highest moral development or strength of conscience and hence the lowest predisposition to commit crimes. The use on the other hand, of physical techniques involving an assertion of 'power' - in particular, physical punishment - is associated with the poorest moral development and highest predisposition to commit crimes. It is salutary to note just what excessive use of physical punishment may involve in some families. The following is a description by a sex-offender of his childhood disciplinary experience (West, Roy and Nichols, 1978, p.10):

> He remembers savage beatings from both parents for the most trivial reasons. 'Coming home late from school, dirty clothes, worn shoes, whatever the excuse, the result was the same, a clenched fist over the head. I remember being strapped by my mother for some similar reason and ending up cowering on the floor being punched and kicked. Another time, as I was the last of the three children due to get the strap on that occasion, I got panicky and attempted to run from her after the first few hits. She caught me and pushed

me hard into the corner of a door. My face struck and blood spurted from a cut near my eye. She followed me up to the bathroom and kicked me from behind in her anger when she saw the mess of blood everywhere. Then I was made to clean up the bathroom and to go to bed with no treatment for the cut.'

These studies provided considerable data, albeit some of dubious validity, of the 'family life' of delinquent children and 'criminals'-to-be. Some of the material is highly emotive, as in the above example, and makes it easy to see why there can arise a 'missionary zeal' to protect children seen to be at grave risk from their parents. Not surprisingly, the family became a prime target for social intervention in the 1950s and 1960s. Unfortunately, the nature and rationale that was behind such intervention is questionable. It is apparent that these studies employed certain moralistic ideologies which essentially served to 'blame' parents for their treatment of their children and their subsequent criminal activity. However, this begs the question of where the causal chain starts. That is to say, why are the parents behaving in such a way? Is it the influence of their parents? (That is, the child's grandparents.) The notion of family systems scripts for parenting acquired from one's own parents is taken up in the article by Dallos and Sapsford.

Such a focus on the family also contained class and cultural-bound assumptions of what a 'good family' life is like. Living in a working-class community, however, necessitates different patterns of thought and action (see also the notion of a 'defining class' responsible for the establishment of the law and morality in Hall and Scraton's article no. 20, pp. 460-98). Of course, Burt makes the point that it is not merely poverty which is the cause of crime, and this has been supported by West and his colleagues. Hence blame or responsibility for crime is shifted from social causes and the individual criminal to the influence of the parents upon the child.

Nevertheless, such a view did not lead to simple treatment policies, since placing children at risk into institutional care was complicated by evidence from the psychoanalytically-oriented literature (e.g. Bowlby - see section on Maternal Deprivation) that separation of children from their parents, particularly the mother, was damaging. Intervention policy appears, therefore, to have been essentially at a stalemate in that, though the family was identified as a major criminogenic factor, disruption of the child's family life for purposes of retribution and rehabilitation or in order to 'protect' it from its family was also seen to be harmful.

The following sections will consider the three main styles of child training which have been identified. They can be seen to correspond broadly to the three main psychological paradigms introduced earlier:

(a) love withdrawal - this stresses the importance of emotional contact between the child and its parents, particularly the mother, which is a central concern of the psychoanalytic approach;

(b) power assertion – these techniques involve the use of power and tangible rewards/punishments as the outcome of the child's actions, which is consistent with a learning theory approach;

(c) induction – here the emphasis is on explanation and reasoning with children in order to make them aware of the consequences of their actions, and thereby a promotion of moral development, this essentially representing a cognitive-developmental approach.

PSYCHOANALYTIC EXPLANATIONS

As mentioned earlier, psychoanalytic theory guided the early naturalistic studies and, together with the data from these, was employed to develop explanations of crime as caused by the family environment and, subsequently, prescriptions for its prevention and treatment. Two main views of family influence can be distinguished: one concerned with 'normal' development and proposing a quantitative approach, with strength of conscience as a continuum from low-high (e.g. little-great resistance to temptation).

The second approach involves the use of the 'medical illness' model in that disturbances in child development, such as those due to 'bad' parenting, can produce 'ill' or 'neurotic' individuals who commit crimes as a symptom of their illness.

Freud (1930), in fact, had very little to say about criminal behaviour as such, but his general theories on the development of conscience and the acquisition of feelings of guilt in the child have provided the focus and the theoretical structure for a large number of studies. Many Freudian concepts are by now so familiar that they have become part of common language – unconscious need, death wish, repression, guilt complex, Oedipus complex – to such an extent that it is easy to lose sight of their originality and the controversy that they aroused, particularly regarding the proposal that a child's love for its parents contains definite sexual aspects. Apart from the many emotive and sensational aspects of his theory, one of its major achievements was to produce a plausible and comprehensive model of man which links the conscious, cognitive (rational) processes (ego) and the unconscious, emotional forces (id). Unlike many later psychological theories, it does not cleave man into an emotional and rational half.

Freud proposed a model of man which is a system consisting of three main components. The *id* represents a set of dynamic unconscious forces made up of the individual's biological needs: thirst, hunger, sex and warmth. This forms the 'squirming power-house' of the individual's psyche. The *ego* is the

conscious component and represents the individual adapting
to external reality. The conscious processes - memory, perception, language, thinking, learning and so on - comprise the
ego and are employed in the service of the id to provide ways
of satisfying the biological needs. The ego, then, is a sort of
balancer of the instincts, reality and social restrictions of the
superego. The *superego* represents the individual's internalization of society's demands and restrictions which are predominantly handed on to the child by its parents. Freud constantly revised his theory, and his later version involved two
distinct groups of instincts within the id. The 'life instincts'
were to do with preserving life (libido), and frustration of
these causes a conscious experience of emotional tension which
is painful and unpleasant. The removal of this tension is
accompanied by a *conscious* experience of pleasure - *pleasure
principle*. The second group of instincts was concerned with
destructive forces such as aggression, masochism and death -
death instincts. Freud (1970) saw death as the neutral state
or equilibrium around which the life and death instincts swayed.

Freud's model is essentially developmental. The child passes
through a number of important sexual stages which are concerned with its erogenous zones: oral, anal, phallic and genital.
A disturbance of development at any of these stages can lead
to serious problems in later life. For example, over-restraint
at the anal stage (from eighteen months to three years) was
seen to lead to an overly mean, fastidious, obsessional personality, whereas over-indulgence led to a messy and disorganized,
though generous and creative one.

Later Freudians such as Erikson have been concerned with
elaborating these stages and considering the role of the ego
in the associated conflicts more specifically (ego-psychology).
Erikson (1950) proposes eight ages, or stages of development,
of man, running from infancy to old age, each stage being
seen to have associated conflicts which need to be worked
through before the next stage can be entered: infancy (oral
stage) - trust vs. mistrust ... old age (maturity) - ego
integrity vs. despair. According to Erikson, the structure of
the stages is due to a combination of three factors: the biology
of the child (somatic), the structure of the society (cultural),
which in turn is determined by the practical realities of
climate, resources, means of livelihood, and so on (environmental). However, Erikson proposed that cultural differences
in treatment of children at each stage produce characteristic
cultural personality types. For example, he observed that
Sioux children who were treated very generously at the oral
stage but severely dealt with for any biting, developed accordingly into generally warm, generous adults, though with
occasional vicious sadistic tendencies, such characteristics
being appropriate to their communal but harsh nomadic life as
hunters. In any particular culture, though, there are differences in how the parents act towards the child at the various

stages with resulting differences in personality; some obviously producing a predisposition to activity which the society may regard as deviant.

Strength of conscience

A vital element in this is the resolution of the child's incestuous longings for its parents during the phallic stage (from three to five years). In the case of the boy, guilt arises from the wishes to destroy the father, who is seen to threaten him with castration as a punishment for the boy's desire for his mother (Oedipus complex). The onset of this fear is seen to result from boys' and girls' realization of the differences in their sexual organs. For the boy, the realization makes acute the threat of castration, and for the girl is seen to produce 'penis envy' and a feeling that she has already been castrated, for which she blames her mother. The boy is seen to resolve his fears by a process of repression; that is, pushing the feelings back into the unconscious and by *identification* with the father so that, by becoming like him, his threat is reduced. The process in the girl is less clear, but she is seen to transfer her affections from the mother to the father and wish to acquire or control his penis and then to have a baby from him as a substitute for one. Subsequently, boys and girls develop their sexual identities as result of an identification biased towards mother or father. The direction of this identification was also seen to depend upon the relative degree of masculinity or femininity already present or latent in the child. (In single-parent families, the identification may be with someone outside the home when parent and child are of different sex, otherwise problems may develop.)

Conscience was seen as developing from this process of identification. Generally, however, the boy's need for identification with the father, due to his 'great guilt', was greater than the girl's with the mother, because of her less intense feelings of 'blame' (though why this feeling of deprivation for the castration of the 'magnificent' penis should be less intense is not clear). Hence boys were seen as developing stronger superegos or consciences and as a result of this a more intense identification. This proposition has been severely criticized by feminist writers such as Kate Millett (1970) in terms of the lack of evidence for such a moral superiority and for the basis of the concept of penis envy.

Rather than seeing a girl's penis envy as inevitable due to 'the boy's superior equipment' (Freud, 1964, p.126), Millett argues instead that it represents an aspect of the inferior status imposed upon and generally accepted by women in a patriarchal society. Hence the concept of penis envy does not justify the idea of male moral supremacy, nor does it in fact provide an adequate account of female sexual development and the basis for the identifications with parents seen by Freud to be necessary for the development of conscience. It might be facetiously suggested that one reason why women are still supposed to be morally inferior is because Freudian theory does not adequately explain their process of moral development!

In this way, the strength of conscience was seen to be directly derived from that of the parents. Freud had little to say about the influence of different types of parenting, though he did state that conscience develops out of 'the dread of losing love' (1930, p.107). From this it follows that the use of physical discipline and lack of love does *not* facilitate the development of a strong superego or conscience since the first requirement is for a strong loving attachment of the child to its mother. As Freud remarked, 'experience has shown, however, that the severity with which a child's superego develops in no way corresponds to the severity of the treatment it has itself experienced. It seems to be independent of the latter; a child who has been very "leniently" treated (physically) can acquire a very strict conscience' (1930, p.117).

Resistance to temptation: the 'normal' delinquent
A study typical of the experimental approaches which attempted to test the psychoanalytical model is illustrated by the work of MacKinnon (1938). The aim was to test whether action behaviour such as resistance to temptation agreed with psycho-analytic predictions. In one study, subjects were secretly observed while they attempted to solve problems for which the answer booklets were left available, though they had been instructed that it was permissible to look at answers to only some of the problems. Nearly half of the subjects cheated and when asked if they had felt guilty, 25 per cent said they had. However, of those who had not cheated, 84 per cent said they would have felt guilty. Accordingly, of the 'cheaters', only 39 per cent said they normally felt guilt, whereas 75 per cent of the non-cheaters did.

Such findings were taken to suggest that guilt is somehow a permanent state and, according to the Freudian model, resisting temptation, rather than reducing guilt, somehow feeds energy to the conscience.

There was further incidental evidence of this in that the violaters tended to swear more, pound the desk and kick the table. This expressed energy was seen as subtracting from that made available to the conscience. The childhood experience of their subjects was also explored, particularly in terms of the types of punishment usually employed on them. Of the cheaters, 78 per cent reported some physical punishment, as opposed to 48 per cent of non-cheaters. On the other hand, some psychological punishments were characteristically employed for 22 and 52 per cent of them respectively.

MacKinnon concluded that Freud's view (that the severity of punishment was inversely related to the guilt produced in a child) was correct if severity of punishment was taken to mean physical punishment. However, they made the point that it is the quality of the pain which is important. Physical punishment tends to arouse anger and feelings of revenge, whereas a mother telling a son with tears in her eye that he has disappointed her can arouse intense guilt and shame.

These studies, then, indicate how different patterns of child-rearing appear to produce differences in strength of conscience. An individual may, therefore, develop 'normally' but have low resistance to temptation. Simply, this is seen as a badly socialized individual, otherwise normal but having acquired less socially desired self-restraint.

The 'neurotic' criminal

One approach which has been extremely influential in criminal psychology and has had considerable influence upon sentencing and treatment (Friedlander, 1947; Feldman, 1976) is to consider some types of criminal and delinquent behaviour as symptoms of 'mental illness' or 'neurosis' respectively. Fundamentally, this has employed the medical 'illness' model upon which psychoanalytic theory is based. This proposes that the result of serious unresolved unconscious conflicts arising from faulty psychosexual development, mainly prior to and following the oedipal stage, can produce a 'mental illness'.

A great anxiety can be built up in that the child fears that it will be unable to control its emotional urges: sexual and hostile towards mother and father respectively. Considerable psychic energy is used to repress these feelings (prevent them from entering consciousness), but this may become self-perpetuating and damaging if the conflicts are not resolved, because of factors such as family conflicts, excessive punishment, personalities of the parents or excessive sibling rivalries.

A later difficulty may occur if, following the resolution of this conflict, the child develops a very punitive superego from the parent. This is the case where a child feels strongly hostile towards the parent and the subsequent superego developed is all the more severe towards the forbidden desires of the child. In short, if things go wrong, a condition very like a physical illness is seen to develop for which the 'patient' needs treatment.

The *neurotic criminal*, then, is regarded as essentially suffering from the same unconscious conflicts as a non-delinquent neurotic, but the expression is in terms of action rather than a fantasy. The essential difference is regarded (by Friedlander, 1947; Aichorn, 1935) to be in terms of the lack of development of the ego and the superego so that the instinctive urges are not repressed but are 'acted out'. The pattern of parenting is seen as one in which the child's initial instinctive needs are rather inconsistently handled, since the child's demands, even if initially rejected, would eventually be met. Hence, ego is governed by the 'pleasure principle' rather than the reality principle, in that there is no effective adaptation to the demands of reality. There is an accompanying problem at the oedipal stage when, since resolution of guilt through the process of identification does not satisfactorily take place, the superego develops inadequately. Hostility is also maintained (in the case of a boy) towards the father, and resentment towards the mother (in the girls), as are unexpressible sexual feelings for the mother and father respectively. The solution often is to return to a former level of development, usually the 'anal-sadistic'. The pattern of personality development has been called 'latent delinquency' (Aichorn, 1935) or the 'anti-social character' which was believed to manifest itself in activities such as kleptomania, psychopathic behaviour, arson and embezzlement. The pattern of development is illustrated by the following case study, which I have paraphrased from Friedlander (1947, pp.123, 244).

Mary, a ten-year-old, was caught stealing chocolate cigars from a shop. She took them while the assistant's back was turned, and she then made no attempt to hide them, or to justify her action. She had previously been known to pilfer in a school gang but her activities were treated leniently, so her parents never came to know of it. However, she became extremely guilty about her activities, and the conviction of an eighteen-year-old cousin for stealing appeared to upset her stability completely so that she developed fantasies that her cousin would betray her and that this would spoil her chances of equalling her brother's successes at school. The incident with the cigars was significantly in the same shop where she had previously been caught with the gang, and where the assistant was a close friend of her mother.

Her childhood showed a mixture of anti-social character development and neurosis, the main source of conflict apparently arising from her feelings of rejection as a result of her mother's preference for her brothers (sibling rivalry). In addition, there was considerable tension between her parents, and her mother was prone to manic depression. Although outwardly attached to her mother, she did express hostility, in particular by stealing from her purse. During periods of separation from her mother, she showed great longing which, taken with her misbehaviour, suggested guilt feelings about her hostility.

The case was taken to show how a neurotic problem of unresolved guilt could reveal itself in terms of criminal activity, the source of guilt being her stealing in the gang and from her mother's purse, this being finally relieved by her mother's scolding after the cigar incident. Such stealing can be seen, then, as symbolic of a need for love not given, which showed itself in this way due to her 'anti-social character' development; that is, a giving way or 'acting out' her conflicts rather than internalizing these into neuroses. Examples of a similar nature appear with remarkable regularity in the papers; for example, shoplifting of wealthy and respectable persons and a range of crimes which have such an aura of self-destruction about them (see Friedlander, 1947; Feldman, 1976).

Disturbed identification

Attempts have been made to interpret the actions of sexual offenders such as rapists in terms of disturbed psychosexual development. In an intensive study of the childhood and development of rapists, West, Roy and Nichols (1978) discovered that one of the main features of the men was an inferiority complex regarding their masculinity. Many of the offenders had come from such disruptive and emotionally damaging homes (see p.378 above) that they had never received the support required to establish a male identity through identification with their fathers and consequently lacked any feelings of self-confidence or security regarding sex. Society, particularly working-class society, is seen to require a show of masculinity from young men in terms not only of sexual virility and copulatory expertise but also of competitiveness, courage and strength. Rape, then, could be considered to be a desperate attempt to assert power over a woman and try to gain the emotional boost to their masculinity that a 'conquest' was seen by them to give. The treatment and view of women as objects to be used in this 'alienated' way is considered in Dallos and Sapsford's article no.19 (p.452).

In fact, though many of the offenders were married, there was found to be gross imbalance in their relationships with their wives, appearing to be either overly dominant or submissive. Both of these were seen to be ways of coping with their deep insecurities, since when wives began to show dissatisfaction with the relationship, the men felt betrayed and resentful. Though their marriages were not seen as the cause of their acts, neither had marriage really alleviated their deep problems, nor were they in a normal sense successful marriages.

Maternal deprivation

Frequently, in cases of children and adults who seem to be suffering from kinds of neurotic delinquency or criminality, evidence has been found of 'grossly' disturbed relationships with their mothers in their early years (Bowlby, 1946); in particular, this was revealed in children who appear to be 'psychopathic' (that is, affectionless personalities with no apparent sense of right or wrong). Bowlby conducted a number of retrospective studies to examine the nature and effects of breaking or disruption of the tie between mother and child. In one study of children attending a child guidance centre, a group of forty-four who had stolen were compared with a control group who had not. The two groups were matched on the basis of age, sex and the fact of being emotionally disturbed. The 'thieves' were distinguished from the others in that fourteen of them were seen as 'affectionless' characters (compared to none in the control group) and seventeen had suffered prolonged separation (six months or more) from their mothers or foster-mothers in their first five years of life as compared

with only two in the control group. In addition, the affectionless characters almost always had a history of separation and
they were far more delinquent than any of the others (Bowlby,
1946).

To Freud, the mother-child bond was seen as extremely
important. In his view, a form of bonding took place through
the satisfaction of physiological needs by the mother, initially
through breast-feeding, and subsequently as a result of
stimulation of the erogenous zones when changing, bathing and
generally caring for the baby. However, the crucial aspect
of this bonding was initial satisfaction through the breast;
mother becomes associated with this satisfaction and takes on,
for the child, the satisfying aspects of it. Freud later saw
the bonding as operating through a number of component
instincts including the need to tug and grasp as well as suck.
Evidence for the strength of such components can be found in
the work of Harlow (1958), where baby chimps in stress situations showed a preference for a soft, furry mother-surrogate
as opposed to a wire frame but milk-giving mother surrogate.
In addition, the criticism has been raised by Bowlby and others
that bottle-fed children develop strong ties to their mothers,
as do children who have been quite severely abused. Schaffer
and Emerson (1964) have also shown that children form strong
attachments to fathers and other relatives even though they
rarely engage in such basic physical caretaking.

Though such criticisms have been raised, breast-feeding
appears to enjoy 'in vogue' periods which may, like the concept
of penis envy, be governed by social learning resulting from
shifting political forces rather than by biological discoveries.

Bowlby (1970) proposes that the bonding is better explained
in terms of a view of man (and child) as essentially social and
having a primary need for company and dislike of isolation,
which predominantly the mother satisfies (Harlow, 1958). In
addition, he also considers his findings in terms of a biologically-
based process of 'imprinting' developed from animal studies
which suggest an irreversible bonding mechanism between
parent and child. Young animals such as goslings, for example,
have been found to have such a strong instinct to attach themselves to 'something' in early life that they will even adopt
moving cardboard boxes as mothers (Lorenz, 1971).

Though very suggestive and important, this work has produced considerable controversy. As was mentioned in the work
by Schaffer and Emerson, children form attachments to a
range of adults and are seen as actively initiating and guiding
as well as being guided by the parents. It has been shown,
besides, that children do not require a unique mother-figure
as such, but can cope with up to about eight consistent care-
takers (Rutter, 1971). Supporting evidence also comes from
children who have grown up satisfactorily in the kibbutz and
communes, though it has been suggested that even in these
situations, a form of mother-child bonding is usually maintained.

Tiger and Shepher (1975) make the important point that women
(and men) in the kibbutz, though probably influenced by their
biological characteristics, have and make a *choice* whether to
be constantly with their children. This, of course, produces
a very different kind of mother-child (or father-child) relationship and one which may well be more satisfactory. In conclusion, it is probably not merely the break in the mother-child
bond which is damaging, but the fact that the child subsequently
has no stable bond with any adult/s, as in institutional care
where there is a continual change of staff and consequently
disruption of any relationship the child has formed.

Treatment

The two main views of the criminal or delinquent as normal but
possessing a weak conscience, as opposed to basically 'ill' in
a medical sense, suggest quite different implications for treatment and how we view the criminal. In order to consider the
first of these views, it is necessary to understand that psychoanalytic theory was very much a product of, and in some ways
served to legitimize, nineteenth-century middle-class patriarchal
societies.

Phil Brown (1974) suggested that though Freud revolutionized
awareness of childhood sexuality, his views on women were
quite counter-revolutionary in assuming a male supremacy.
His views of anthropology were also culture-bound, assuming
the development of a family structure as an inevitable response
to the oedipal conflict. A number of anthropological studies,
however, have found little or no evidence of oedipal conflicts:
for example, Margaret Mead's studies of Samoa (Millett, 1970;
Tiger and Shepher, 1975). According to Freud, the laws of
society have developed from a need to resolve the Oedipus complex in primitive man by means of incest taboos. Otherwise
the 'father' would monopolize the women and be in a continual
deadly sexual-based conflict with the sons. In *Totem and Taboo*,
he considered the 'primal horde' and the family in terms of
the sons banding together to slay the father and eat his flesh.
In his views, only with the introduction of incest taboos was
it possible for males to live peacefully together in the family.
(This, of course, regards women's roles as secondary in the
evolution of 'civilization'.) The natural instincts have to be
sublimated or redirected to more acceptable activities, such as
work and creativity. Hence the theory justifies the need for
the repression of our basic nature and freedom since, in
Freud's view, we have instincts to kill and destroy - death
instincts. His view of man is clearly not an optimistic one; in
fact, 'Freud saw only the increasing burdens that modern
society was placing on the ego, burdens that would create an
ever-increasing measure of guilt and aggression' (Miller,
1962, p.266).

Perhaps this explains the appeal of the freedom of the
criminal seen as archetypal 'folk hero' or heroic outlaw, figures

such as Jesse James, in that they represented our fantasy escape from such repression. (See also the 'trickster' archetype as hero in Carl Jung, 1953.) Such popular admiration is double-edged, though, since captured heroes must pay the full penalty for their crimes, and perhaps if they have caught the public eye they may be made examples of by the defining class, so that we realize 'crime doesn't pay': that is, repression must be accepted.

The second and most pervasive impact of psychoanalytic theory has been to establish the medical-illness model of crime. Thomas Szasz (1961) in an influential criticism of the mental illness model describes how, in the history of medicine, conditions such as hysteria which have no identifiable physical/ neurological basis became medically accepted in the late nineteenth century as a matter of faith or more specifically due to the status of the powerful psychiatrist, Charcot, rather than any medical evidence. Similarly, he maintains that Freud did not 'discover' that hysteria or other such conditions were mental illnesses; merely, he advocated that the sufferers be declared 'ill'. The list of so-called illnesses increased in the early twentieth century and, as Szasz suggests (1961, p.58):

> Then, with increasing zeal, physicians and especially psychiatrists began to call 'illness' (that is, of course, 'mental illness') anything and everything in which they could detect any sign of 'malfunctioning', based on no matter what norm. Hence, agoraphobia is illness because one should not be afraid of open spaces; homosexuality is illness because heterosexuality is the social norm; divorce is illness because it signals failure of marriage. Crime, art, undesired political leadership, participation in social affairs or withdrawal from such participation – all these things and many more are now said to be symptoms of mental illness.

The effect of labelling various kinds of deviants as ill makes it easier for the deviant to be deviant. That is, a less harsh treatment may be accorded them. However, Szasz accuses the medical profession here of engaging in a process of narcotization rather than liberation, in that use of the medical model distracts us from searching for the possible social and psychological causes. In a sense, the psychiatrists 'collude' with society in producing an acceptable human image of themselves in regard to treatment of offenders, but also conveniently avoid any reflexive and possibly painful examination of their own and society's contribution to the problem. Though humanely treated, the criminal is ultimately at fault and not aspects of society. Even this 'humane' treatment has pernicious aspects in that labelling as ill as opposed to criminal may result in longer and wider deprivations and constraints of the individual's freedom.

West (1967, p.262) nicely illustrates the difficulty that psychotherapy has faced with the treatment of delinquency. Though they may be regarded as ill, many delinquents do not see it that way. When sent for psychotherapy, they are apt to say: 'There's nothing wrong with me. I don't know why you sent me here.' As Szasz suggests, their conflicts are with society, not with themselves, and their resistance poignantly illustrates that the medical model is inappropriate. Hence West concludes that while individual-based psychotherapy with criminals and delinquents has been less than successful, group-based psychotherapeutic techniques have been more useful, partly because they don't insist on the individual accepting a 'sick' role. Finally, an approach to treatment which combines many strands of Freudian theory is seen in that offered by therapeutic communities or schools. One of the most famous was Aichorn's School for Boys, started in the 1920s, which was founded on the view that delinquency was primarily due to lack of love and constant care during the formative years in childhood. Aggression and provocative acts were a way of fighting back against a world which they had come to see as rejecting and hostile. The boys' aggression was allowed to take its course to the point where their rooms, furniture and possessions might be destroyed. Having 'acted out' their tensions and broken the 'emotional ice' with the staff, they were then exposed to discipline as well as love. Aichorn's School, and others, have met with considerable success but are seen to be expensive, and hence the future of such approaches is threatened (West, 1967).

LEARNING-THEORY-BASED EXPLANATIONS

Behaviourism represented a reaction to psycho-analytic and other intra-psychic theories in psychology. Considerable scorn was poured on psychoanalytic theory, particularly in relation to its lack of empirical testability, though some studies such as that of MacKinnon did, in fact, attempt to do this. More specifically much criticism was voiced as to the lack of demonstrable effectiveness of psychoanalytically-based treatments (Eysenck, 1964). In psychology, then, behaviourism represented a move towards an apparently more 'scientific' approach. Freudian theory was regarded as too vague and imprecise, since very few specifically testable hypotheses could be drawn from it. Behaviourists, however, wanted to ape and gain the respectability of nineteenth-century physical scientism. Central to such a reactionary movement was an attempt to discredit the previous 'mentalistic' approaches such as psychoanalysis which involved a dualist philosophy that distinguishes between mind and matter. Instead Behaviourists viewed man as a 'black box', and if from input (stimulus) output (response) could be predicted, then in their view it was unnecessary to consider mind as a separate entity (Skinner, 1953).

Among the contributions of this approach to criminology was the consideration of moral development or conscience as a learning process or 'social programming' throughout childhood.

Such learning is essentially regarded as being based on a
system of rewards and punishments administered primarily by
the parents. The child's development is seen essentially in
terms of its efforts to maximize rewards and minimize or avoid
punishment. This Behaviourist approach derives its empirical
foundation primarily from studies of learning in animals. The
work to be described in this section deals with applications
to child development which have 'softened' such a Behaviourist
approach by including 'mentalistic' concepts such as imitation
and internalization.

The basis of these approaches stems from the work on conditioning in animals and humans. This embodies two approaches
to learning: classical and operant conditioning. Both approaches
are deterministic in their accounts of learning. *Classical conditioning* is concerned with the simple physiological reflex type
of learning in that a certain stimulus is seen as *eliciting* a
physiological response. For example, a loud noise *elicits* an
arousal response. However, the interesting part is that a
neutral stimulus, if frequently paired with the physiologically
active one, will take on its properties and will also elicit a
response. The 'father' of behaviourism, J.B. Watson, demonstrated this in his famous experiment with a little boy named
Albert who liked furry white rats but not loud noises. After
several pairings of the loud noise in the presence of the rat,
little Albert developed a fear of furry white rats. The experimenters had considerable difficulty in getting Albert to like
rats again (extinguishing his fear). If the intensity of the
initial conditioning is traumatic, then the fear response can
become virtually permanent (Mowrer, 1960). *Operant conditioning*, on the other hand, is concerned with the consequences
following the *emitting* of a response; if these are favourable,
then the act is more likely to be repeated in the future. This
process, then, requires activity on the part of the child as
a prerequisite; waiting for the correct response to occur
spontaneously, however, is inefficient, so that a vital technique
called 'shaping' is employed in which, initially, actions approxi-
mating to the desired one are rewarded and gradually the
margin of difference is reduced.

Internalization
These approaches are deterministic and do not require any
reference to consciousness in order to explain learned behaviour.
The process whereby the child is socialized is considered to
consist of two stages:

(a) A child seeing a piece of chocolate (stimulus) in a
supermarket might reach and take it. If this leads to punishment, such as shouting or a smack, then the pairing of chocolate in a supermarket and a smack leads to a learned anxiety
such that, in future, the sight of a bar of chocolate in a
supermarket causes anxiety. This is essentially classical conditioning whereby anxiety is learned to an initially rewarding

stimulus - chocolate.

(b) The second stage is operant conditioning. Responses are emitted, and those which are effective in reducing anxiety (and therefore rewarding) are learned. Such responses can include walking away from chocolate in shops on subsequent occasions or making sure that one is not caught!

Such explanations have been extended by Aronfreed (1968), who argues that it is necessary to consider the symbolic conscious representations that the child may have of its actions. Otherwise it can be credited with having only a limited number of internalized responses to specific cues which represent a very narrow form of socialization. By 'symbolic representation' is meant a conscious linking, as verbal thoughts, of the sequences and outcomes in reward/punishment terms, which are likely to follow certain actions: for example, 'He has suggested that we steal that car; we might get caught and punished'. The end of this 'chain' of verbal thought is accompanied by an emotional experience, such as fear (stage (a) above), then subsequent rewarding action (stage (b) above), such as that directed towards reducing this fear.

Aronfreed has employed the internalization model to explain a number of interesting responses to transgressions: *confession and reparation* are explained as occurring because the parents have instructed the child: 'Tell us, and you won't be punished' - hence the child comes to adopt such a response if this succeeds in reducing punishment.

Self-criticism is seen as a response one step back in this chain; that is, the child reduces the state of anxiety produced by anticipating punishment such as 'being told off' by inflicting this on itself; this in turn triggers off the feeling of relief that follows 'actual' punishment.

Fundamental to learning-theory explanations is that actions are controlled by the rewarding or punishing consequences of the act. In the case of confession, this reward is seen to be implicit or self-induced. Since, however, this is not directly observable, it can be seen as a retreat to mentalistic explanations which behaviourists initially sought to reject. A greater difficulty for such explanations is the paradox of children who are physically beaten for showing violence and become *more* rather than less violent since, after punishment, such behaviour should show a decline. An attempt has been made to introduce the concept of imitation through observation, also apparent in the phenomena of self-criticism, to explain the child's process of socialization. The influence of parental models has been indicated in studies by the Gluecks (1962) and Osborn and West (1979), where it was found that boys, for example, appeared to imitate their fathers in embarking upon criminal careers (see also Andry, 1971).

At first sight, imitation appears to occur without any intention on the part of the learner or teacher, though adults and adolescents may, in fact, be well aware of the 'idols' that they are 'imitating' in dress and manner. Like the process of internalization, the explanations of imitation involve reference to 'internal representation', though this is concerned now with the actions of *others* and their consequences rather than the child's own.

Bandura and his colleagues (1963) have carried out much innovative work in the area. In one experiment, young children watched films in which an adult behaved in a strikingly aggressive way. This behaviour was followed by one of three options: (a) generous praise and food, (b) severe punishment, and (c) no consequences. Not surprisingly, the children who saw endings (a) or (c) tended to imitate the actions of the adult most in a test setting later on. Children watching such films have been reported to say: 'He's a good fighter, like daddy', and so on. Girls, however, were seen to be generally less likely than boys to imitate violence.

An interesting follow-up to the first study described is that if, when the children were given a second opportunity to reproduce the behaviour of the adult in the film, they were all offered attractive incentives, this completely cancelled out the differences between the various groups. The children had learned and remembered the aggressive actions of the adult, even if he had been punished. What was affected by the consequences for the adult was the willingness of the children to risk the same actions. This has interesting implications for the affects of television viewing, for example, in that children are learning the techniques of violence, whether the actors appear to be rewarded or not.

The learning-theory-based explanations are rather similar to those for internalization, except that the consequences following the imitated person's actions are seen to be applied by the child to itself: in other words, 'If I act like he/she does, I shall also be rewarded' (vicarious reward). Further to this, it is proposed that some of the reward rubs off (secondary reward) from the 'idolized' adults, so that the very actions of doing what they do become self-rewarding to the child. Once emitted, these actions may also, of course, be directly rewarded by parents or others. It is important to consider that, despite the punishment that may follow imitation of parental aggression, the vicarious and secondary reward aspects must *outweigh* the direct punishment value! In addition, the Bandura study reveals that vicarious reward may influence performance of the act but not actual learning. At this point, learning-theory-based explanations appear rather shaky.

A consideration of the factors which influence the imitability of the adult models sheds some light on this picture. One simple factor is whether they are of the same sex. In one of the Bandura studies, girls were found to imitate violence more from a female than from a male model, though the boys commented that a woman should not behave like that and imitated her less than the girls. Imitation seems to involve notions of role-appropriate behaviour. The studies seem to have rather played down the extent to which imitation involves the 'style' of actions and not merely the bare essentials of the act. This links into other factors such as prestige, socio-economic status, sexual desirability, power, charisma, which strongly influence whether the model will be imitated. It seems, then, that imitation involves the child having a sophisticated set of values and social norms regarding desirability in adults; however, for the young child in particular - as Piaget suggests (1932) - most adults can do no wrong and therefore there is a great tendency to imitate them.

Learning-theory-based approaches have had considerable applications to crime and delinquency. Some approaches such as aversion therapy employ (as in the film and book 'Clockwork Orange') essentially classical learning; that is, a fear response is conditioned to the initially pleasant stimulus - for example, requesting homosexuals to fantasize naked men, followed by electric shock - and eventually the fear response replaces excitement. These techniques are in decline, but the use of operant approaches (behaviour modification) is not. In particular there has been much use of 'token economies' where only appropriate or desirable behaviour credits a 'token' which can be used to buy whatever consumables the inmate wants. The giving of tokens is very tightly controlled (their use prohibits the distraction of money from outside the token economy situation), the intention being that individuals eventually learn to act in 'appropriate' ways, such as not stealing and non-abusive behaviour (Feldman, 1976, Hoghughi, 1979).

COGNITIVE APPROACHES TO MORAL DEVELOPMENT

The social learning and psychoanalytic explanations offered of moral development within the family have considered such learning in terms of a linear causability, namely the influence of parenting on the child. Cognitive approaches, on the other hand, regard the child as *actively constructing* its morality through an *interaction* with its social world. The concern is not with simple causal explanations of behaviour but with a consideration of the growing stages of moral awareness. The effects of different types of parenting are seen to be mediated by the child's developing ability to understand the meaning of the parent's actions and statements. Hence different types of parenting suggest rather than predict particular outcomes for the child's moral development.

Genetic epistemology
Piaget's (1929) approach is to regard intellectual and moral development in terms of a 'genetic' epistemology: the acquisition of knowledge and the child's biological development being perceived as inseparable. He regards development of the

intellect as proceeding through distinct stages which are
governed by biological developments such as the onset of
imagery and language. Based on extensive detailed observation
of children, including his own, Piaget differentiated four stages
of intellectual development which are dependent upon the
child's ability to represent its external material and social
world. These briefly are: Sensory Motor (0 to 18 months) -
in this, intelligence is expressed in the form of physical action:
that is, thinking is doing. Pre-operational (18 months to 7
years) - this stage is accompanied by the onset of language
and iconic representation of the world. The most outstanding
feature of this stage is the child's cognitive and emotional
egocentricity. Concrete Operational stage (7 to 11 years) -
there is a move away from egocentricity towards the development of transformational abilities leading to the ability to comprehend 'quantity' and 'number'. Formal Operations (11 to
adult) - this is essentially the ability to undertake a scientific,
hypothesis-testing-type of thinking. This was less well charted
than the others, and other studies have shown that in fact
very few adults reach this stage.

Piaget (1932) innovated two approaches for the study of
moral development: first, he examined how children learn and
create rules, through a process of negotiations, in games such
as marbles that were considered to be analogous to the learning
of moral rules. Second, he gave children pairs of short stories
concerned with stealing and lying that contained different
emphases on *intention* as opposed to *material damage* caused.

(a) Alfred meets a friend who is very poor. This friend tells
him that he has had no dinner that day because there was
nothing to eat in his home. Alfred has no money, so he goes
into a baker's shop and steals a roll, then he runs out and
gives the roll to his friend.

(b) Henrietta goes into a shop. She sees a pretty piece of
ribbon on a table and thinks to herself that it would look nice
on her dress. So while the shop-lady's back is turned, she
steals the ribbon and runs away at once.
Children were then asked which child was naughtier and should
receive the sterner punishment: responses included, for
example, 'The boy must be punished more. Rolls cost more',
as opposed to responses such as: 'The girl, because she took
it for herself.'

Based on the reactions to these stories, and his observations
on rule-learning in children's games, Piaget distinguished two
main stages of moral development: adult constraint (4 to 8
years) - fundamental to this stage was a belief in the sanctity
of adults' rules such that wrong is defined in terms of that
which adults punish. The egocentricity characteristic of the
pre-operational stage was apparent in the child's play in which
he shows no hesitation in breaking rules which later in this
stage they are able to learn. Similarly, the child shows an
inability to take into account the *intentions* behind the actions

of the children in the stories, though they do have some ability to do this with their own actions. They appeared to be 'perceptually centred' upon the material consequences of the acts: 'Alfred was naughtier because the roll cost more than a ribbon.'

Co-operation justice (8 years onwards) - morality is now based on co-operation and reciprocity, since children acknowledge the need for rules in the games and stick to them scrupulously so that there is justice and fairness for all. This is regarded as a step towards the ability to 'take the role of the other'; that is, seeing the infraction from the other child's point of view. This reflects the intellectual development of the Concrete Operational stage and is also shown in the child's ability to take account of intentions: 'Henrietta was "naughtier" because her act was selfish.'

Piaget distinguished a number of sub-stages including the concept of *equity* or over-riding sense of fairness, generally seen around the ages of 13 to 14.

Parental influence on moral development

Piaget suggested that though, of necessity, the parent-child relationship contained asymmetrical control due to the need for the parents to impose some fundamental duties on the child, this should be reduced to a minimum in order to facilitate moral development. In his view, a relationship based on mutual control facilitates moral development: 'one must place oneself on the child's own level and give him a feeling of equity by laying stress on one's obligations and one's deficiencies.' However, this could be difficult, since Piaget felt that parents have such prestige in the child's eyes that their wishes are taken as laws (Piaget, 1932). Nevertheless, if parents taught children to attach greater importance to intentions than to rules, the transition from the morality of adult constraint to co-operation could be facilitated, though this was taken to be a result not of adult teaching but of assisting the child to understand his social/moral world.

Kohlberg's moral stages

Kohlberg's contribution was to consider rigorously and in greater detail the stages of moral development described by Piaget. In his view, the major motivational source for moral development was the need for acceptance and self-realization, these requiring the child to formulate, on the basis of its social interactions, what appears to be *mutually acceptable*. The major aspects of moral development were regarded as universal, since all societies were seen to have common sources of social interaction, role-taking and conflict. In his view, it is the general range and quality of such experiences rather than specific experiences of punishment/reward with others, such as parents, that influence moral development. As with Piaget, the major concept is that of children *and adults* continually developing moral structures in order to make sense of their social world. Kohlberg, though, emphasized that moral development continues into adulthood, and he devised a range of stories - moral dilemmas - that aimed to study not only child but also adult morality: for example (1963, pp.18-19):

> In Europe, a woman was near death from a special kind of cancer. There was one drug that the doctors thought might save her. It was a form of radium that a druggist in the same town had recently discovered. The drug was expensive to make, but the druggist was charging ten times what the drug cost him to make. He paid $200 for the radium and charged $2,000 for a small dose of the drug. The sick woman's husband, Heinz, went to everyone he knew to borrow the money, but he could only get together about $1,000 which is half of what it cost. He told the druggist that his wife was dying and asked him to sell it cheaper or let him pay later. But the druggist said, 'No, I discovered the drug and I'm going to make money from it.' So Heinz got desperate and broke into the man's store to steal the drug for his wife. Should the husband have done that? Why?

He was interested in the responses people gave to such a story in terms of the arguments they used to justify their choice. Based on these answers, Kohlberg suggested that moral development consists of six stages ranging from a morality which resides in a blind acceptance of authority to one involving conscience and a respect for the individual: a typical stage 1/2 (*preconventional*) answer might be: 'He should steal the drug. It isn't really bad to take it. It isn't like he didn't ask to pay for it first. The drug he'd taken is only worth $200, he's not really taking a $2,000 drug.' (Stage 1)

This implies a deference to authority and materialistic orientation, whereas stages 3/4 (conventional) involve an apparent concern with pleasing others and doing one's duty. 'He should steal the drug. He was only doing something that was natural for a good husband to do. You can't blame him for doing something out of love for his wife; you'd blame him if he didn't love his wife enough to save her.' (Stage 3)

Finally, stages 5/6 (post-conventional) initially involve a concern with contractual/legalistic obligations and then with self-chosen 'universal moral principles'. 'This is a situation which faces him, to choose between stealing and letting his wife die. In a situation where the choice must be made, it is morally-right to steal. He has to act in terms of the principle of preserving and respecting life.' (Stage 6) (All the examples of the stages are taken from Kohlberg, 1969, pp.379-80.)

Kohlberg has found that children and adults have a characteristic stage of moral development which is roughly the one within which 50 per cent of their answers fall, and that that development is linear. So that in order to reach a particular stage, e.g. 4, one must have developed through the earlier ones (1, 2, 3). Moral reasoning in addition is viewed as a form of reasoning, so that advanced moral reasoning depends upon advanced intellectual abilities (Kohlberg, 1976). The reverse, though, is not seen to be true, in that advanced intellectual reasoning abilities are not necessarily accompanied by advanced moral development, since this also requires experience and exposure to moral explanations. Note that this implies that people who have 'low' moral development may be constrained from achieving higher stages by their intellectual limitations.

It is arguable that Kohlberg's stages contain implicit moral norms and values which are essentially those of white middle-class Americans. In different societies, state 6 could be anarchistic and insensitive to others. It necessitates the assumption that the 'universal moral principles' are essentially 'good' ones, otherwise a Nietzscheian destructive anarchy is a logical possibility. In support of this criticism is Kohlberg's own finding of cross-cultural differences, with Americans possessing the highest moral development!

The role of education and the family is seen to be influential. Holstein (in Kohlberg, 1976) suggests, as does Piaget, that parents can advance moral development by encouraging discussion of moral issues. An exchange of viewpoints is regarded by Kohlberg as essential for the fostering of 'role-taking' abilities and the mutuality of such view-taking is seen as important; adults should consider the child's point of view or children may not take and communicate theirs. Evidence in support of this comes from a study in which children raised in orphanages were found to show the lowest levels of moral development as compared with Israeli kibbutz children who showed the highest (Kohlberg, 1976). Although both groups had little interaction with parents, the role-taking opportunities, through supervised peer-group discussion, for example, were much greater in the kibbutz. Kohlberg has applied such findings for rehabilitation purposes, believing that exposure to higher stage (than one's own) moral reasoning will eventually lead to development (Kohlberg et al., 1975).

A necessary question is to what extent such a normative approach of developmental stages predicts actual behaviour. Kohlberg offers as a 'real-life' example an American officer serving in Vietnam who moved from 'conventional to principled' thinking due to his realization of the conflict between 'law and order', 'army morality' and the 'more universal rights of the Vietnamese'. However, it is not reported whether he subsequently changed his behaviour. Support for his view that the stages do predict behaviour comes from behavioural tests of resistance to temptation, on which stages 5 and 6 subjects have been found to be less likely to obey authority figures if this involves a lack of concern for other people (Kohlberg, 1976).

It is not unusual, though, for individuals such as some leaders, for example, to express views indicating stage 6 morality without necessarily acting accordingly. The stages, then, imply a form of moral superiority related to intelligence which rather ignores the possibility of individual choice that is taken up in article no.19 by Dallos and Sapsford. Certainly it is possible that individuals may 'choose' to operate at a lower moral stage if this appears more appropriate. In prisons, for example, the inmates tend to perceive the prison rules and morality of the staff as a stage below their own, and hence act accordingly. Though Kohlberg proposes a model of man as actively constructing his/her morality, he nevertheless places the emphasis on the stages as fixed in the individual at any given time.

A SUMMING UP

An alternative that is considered in Dallos and Sapsford's paper is to regard morality as continually negotiated anew according to the situational demands. Kohlberg's view, however, is fundamentally normative and deterministic rather than truly interactional. Similarly, learning-theory approaches view the criminal's actions as determined by their prior family history. But the possibility remains that individuals have decision points in their lives and are able to make 'free' though constrained choices.

Finally, the family here has been chosen as the focus of causal agency. This stops short of two main questions: How did the parents come to act the way they do? What is the wider influence of society? As we have seen, Erikson proposes a tentative explanation of the way society and institutions such as the family develop in response to materialistic as well as human constraints. Yet the assumption throughout - of the many observers of the family discussed in this article - is that it is an indispensable institution. A number of writers such as Laing and Cooper, and Reich, have questioned this, suggesting that the family is a constraining institution with an economic rationale which is intended to support patriarchal and capitalist societies. Reich, in particular, argues that its major oppressive function is by means of sexual repressions and the subsequent installation of societal norms. As has been discovered, in terms of the development of conscience this is not to say that families do not offer a degree of support and potential for growth of the individual. However, group living is a viable alternative, as are extended family structures. It needs to be borne in mind that some of the problems which appear to be generated by the family are a function of its basic nature as a structure for living in our society. The article by Dallos and Sapsford considers some of the ways in which the family operates to *constrain* and *construct* individual choice rather than how it determines action, as has been the main concern of these approaches. It is possible that attempted explanations in simple causal terms are naive. Bowen (1960) suggests that it takes three generations to produce a

schizophrenic: a mother who manoeuvres acrobatically in interpersonal relationships coupled with a stubborn, exasperating
father and a do-gooder brother or sister. The grandparents
in turn had lain the seeds in their relationship, which is typi-
fied by rigidity and repetitiveness. So, too, with criminogenic
families. The range of influence may extend quite far, so that
ways of being a family and its influence on the members is
complex and cannot adequately be explained in simple causal
terms.

References
Aichorn, H. (1935), 'Wayward Youth', Viking, New York.
Andry, R.G. (1971), 'Delinquency and Parental Pathology',
   Staples Press.
Aronfreed, J. (1968), 'Conduct and Conscience', Academic
   Press, New York.
Bandura, A., Ross, D. and Ross, S.A. (1963), Imitation of
   Film-Mediated Aggressive Models, 'Journal of Abnormal and
   Social Psychology', vol.66, pp.3-11.
Bell, R.Q. (1968), A Reinterpretation of the Direction of Effects
   in Studies of Socialization, 'Psychological Review', 75, p.81.
Bowen, M. (1960), A Family Concept of Schizophrenia, in
   Jackson, D.D. (ed.), 'The Etiology of Schizophrenia',
   Basic Books, New York.
Bowlby, J. (1946), 'Forty-Four Juvenile Thieves', Baillière,
   Tindall & Cox.
Bowlby, J. (1970), 'Attachment and Loss', vol.1, Penguin
   Books.
Brown, Phil (1974), 'Toward a Marxist Psychology', Harper
   & Row, New York.
Burt, C. (1923), 'The Young Delinquent', University of London
   Press.
Erikson, E. (1950), 'Childhood and Society', Penguin Books.
Eysenck, H.J. (1964), 'Crime and Personality', Routledge &
   Kegan Paul.
Feldman, M.P. (1976), 'Criminal Behaviour: a Psychological
   Analysis', Wiley, Chichester.
Freud, S. (1930), 'Civilization and its Discontents', Hogarth
   Press.
Freud, S. (1964), Femininity, in 'New Introductory Lectures
   on Psychoanalysis', Norton, New York.
Freud, S. (1970), 'An Outline of Psychoanalysis', Norton,
   New York.
Friedlander, K. (1947), 'The Psycho-Analytic Approach to
   Juvenile Delinquency', Routledge & Kegan Paul.
Glueck, S. and Glueck, E.T. (1950), 'Unravelling Juvenile
   Delinquency', Harvard University Press.
Glueck, S. and Glueck, E.T. (1962), 'Family Environment and
   Delinquency', Routledge & Kegan Paul.
Harlow, H.F. (1958), The Nature of Love, 'American Psycho-
   logist', vol.13, pp.678-85.

Hoffman, M.L. and Saltzsein, H.D. (1967), Parent Discipline and the Child's Moral Development, 'Journal of Personality and Social Psychology', vol.5, p.45.

Hoghughi, M. (1979), The Aycliffe Token Economy, 'British Journal of Criminology', vol.19, no.2.

Holstein, T. (1976), in Lickona, T. (ed.), 'Moral Development and Behaviour', Holt, New York.

Jung, C. (1953), On the Psychology of the Trickster Figure, in 'Collected Works', vol.9, Pantheon, New York.

Knight, B. J. and West, D.J. (1975), Temporary and Continuing Delinquency, 'British Journal of Criminology', vol.15, p.43.

Kohlberg, L. (1963), Moral Development and Identification, in National Society for the Study of Education, 62nd Yearbook, 'Child Psychology', University of Chicago Press.

Kohlberg, L. (1969), State and Sequence: the Cognitive Developmental Approach to Socialization, in Goslin, D.A. (ed.), 'Handbook of Socialization Theory and Research', Rand McNally, New York.

Kohlberg, L. et al. (1975), 'Just Community Approach to Corrections', Harvard Graduate School of Education Press, Cambridge, Mass.

Kohlberg, L. (1976), in Lickona, T. (ed.), 'Moral Development and Behavior', Holt, New York.

Lorenz, K. (1971), 'Studies in Animal and Human Behaviour', Methuen.

MacKinnon, D.W. (1938), Violation and Prohibitions, in Murray, H.A. (ed.), 'Explorations in Personality', Oxford University Press, New York.

Miller, G.A. (1962), 'Psychology: the Science of Mental Life', Penguin Books.

Millett, K. (1970), 'Sexual Politics', Fontana.

Mowrer, O.H. (1960), 'Learning Theory and Behaviour', Wiley, New York.

Osborn, S.G. and West, D.J. (1979), Conviction Records of Fathers and Sons Compared, 'British Journal of Criminology', vol.19, no.2.

Piaget, J. (1932), 'The Moral Judgment of the Child', Routledge & Kegan Paul.

Piaget, J. (1929), 'The Child's Conception of the World', Routledge & Kegan Paul.

Pittel, S.M. and Mendelsohn, G.A. (1966), Measurements of Moral Values, 'Psychological Bulletin', vol.66, no.1, p.22.

Rutter, M. (1971), 'Maternal Deprivation Reassessed', Penguin Books.

Schaffer, H.R. and Emerson, P.E. (1964), The Development of Social Attachments in Infancy, 'Monographs of the Society for Research in Child Development', vol.29, no.3.

Sears, R.R., Malloby, E.E. and Levin, H. (1957), 'Patterns of Child-Rearing', Harper & Row, New York.

Skinner, B.F. (1953), 'Science and Human Behavior',

Macmillan, New York.

Szasz, T.S. (1961), 'The Myth of Mental Illness', Harper, New York.

Tiger, L. and Shepher, J. (1975), 'Women in the Kibbutz', Penguin Books.

West, D.J. (1967), 'The Young Offender', Penguin Books.

West, D.J. (1969), 'Present Conduct and Future Delinquency', Heinemann Educational.

West, D.J. (1973), 'Who Becomes Delinquent?', Heinemann.

West, D.J., Roy, C. and Nichols, F.L. (1978), 'Understanding Sexual Attacks', Heinemann.

Wootton, B. (1959), 'Social Science and Social Pathology', Allen & Unwin.

18   Humanising the deviant: affinity and affiliation theories

John Muncie and *Mike Fitzgerald*

INTRODUCTION

A major focus of sociological theories about crime in the past
forty years has been to explore a wide range of human
behaviour which can be defined within the broad rubric of a
non-conformity to social expectations. As such, a 'grey' area
of *deviancy* lying in the space between criminality and conformity was identified which seemed to defy the easy positivist
explanations of previous criminology. The concept, however,
can suffer from an extreme cultural relativism. Responses from
the public to the question 'Who's deviant?' predictably included
prostitutes, drug-addicts, radicals and criminals, but also
career women, Christians, pacifists, divorcees, know-it-all
professors, perverts and the President of the United States
(Simmons, 1969, p.3).
   More particularly the sociological study of deviancy was
usually associated with analyses of rule violation, victimless
crimes (drug-taking, homosexuality) and anti-social behaviour
which, while being potentially subject to law enforcement, were
not necessarily always seen as 'criminal'. The concept of
deviance helped to widen out the debates about the causes of
crime by questioning the easy distinction between crime and
conformity established by traditional criminology. The studies
of deviance indeed had enormous implications for the analysis
of crime. In particular the potential for criminal behaviour
could no longer be dismissed as a consequence of individual
or social pathology, but was explained in terms of behaviour
that was *learnt* and also quite *natural* given the economic and
political circumstances of a particular individual or group
condition.
   Originating to a large extent from the work of the Chicago

Source: article commissioned for this volume. John Muncie and
Mike Fitzgerald are Lecturers in Social Policy, Faculty of
Social Sciences, the Open University.

School on the 'marginal worlds' of juvenile gangs, hoboes and delinquent boys, the deviancy studies were initially all based in the United States and this must be taken into account when examining their particular formulations. It was in the context of a society believed to be rapidly moving towards affluence and equal and open opportunity that delinquency and deviance could first be examined as absolute categories. It was not until the mid-1960s that British criminology attempted to 'test' the American analyses within the context of its more visibly restrictive and closed class structure, and predictably developed different paradigms in which deviancy could be explained.

During the 1970s British deviancy theory continued the critique of the notion of deviancy being absolutist and tried to account for a wide range of deviant, particularly youthful, behaviour by reference to leisure opportunities, social reaction and class position. In broader terms it proposed that an understanding of social rules, social control and the structure of social order must continually inform any analysis of those identified as rule violators.

Such issues are raised initially at the end of this chapter in the section 'New Directions' and discussed more fully in article no.20, 'Law, Class and Control' by Hall and Scraton.

To introduce both the range and developments within deviancy theory we have categorised such theory under the banners of 'cultural affinity' and 'cultural affiliation'.

Cultural affinity is a key element in standard sociological explanations of becoming deviant. Matza (1969, pp.90-1) has described the term as 'a simple and fairly useful conception. Persons either individually or in aggregate develop predispositions to certain phenomena, say delinquency, as a result of their *circumstances*.'

For affinity theories, the key problem is which particular circumstances can be identified in order to separate those who become delinquent from those who do not. While there has been a wealth of different ways of attempting to do this (by focusing on constitutional, personal, social, economic or cultural circumstances), they all adhere to the central tenet: that certain antecedent conditions predispose people or groups to certain predictable outcomes. In this way they all assume that the actions of individuals are determined by the society of which they are a part. Affinity theories thus draw heavily on the principles established by a school of sociology known as structural functionalism. Its core tells us that societies are systems of interrelated parts with individuals acting in accord with each other because they share common standards and values. Such norms constrain each individual and effectuate regular patterns of behaviour. Parsons argues (1951, pp.205-6) that this equilibrium is maintained by mechanisms of socialisation, whereby individuals incorporate the normative standards of society into their personalities, and social control, whereby correct behaviour patterns are enforced by systems of coercion

and punishment. The deviant personality then is defined as
having lacked or escaped the necessary process of socialisation.
In the second section of this article we examine particular
varieties of affinity theories which share this functionalist
outlook, by focusing on the work of Merton, Cloward and Ohlin
and Albert Cohen.

In sharp contrast, the second set of theories we review are
premised on a voluntaristic theory of human nature and a model
of social order made up of a plurality of distinct and incompatible social groups, rather than a dominant uniformity and
consensus. Affiliation theories attempt not to explain the outcome of given circumstances but to describe the *process* by
which the individual is converted to delinquent behaviour
because of the reactions and sanctions provided by others. In
this way attempts were made to understand deviant behaviour
in its own right, rather than as an aberration from some
perceived common consensus. Individuals, it was argued, are
not simply the product of particular environments or of a
specific constellation of circumstances; rather, they actively
engage in creating the social world. Similarly social control is
no longer simply a reaction to deviant behaviour, but plays a
crucial role in the *creation* and amplification of deviance. In
exploring the premises of affiliation we shall focus on the work
of Sutherland, Lemert and Becker. The latter's work on
marijuana-smokers is indeed regarded by many as the classic
study of how our understanding of deviant behaviour, in being
informed by definitions provided by others, is continually
blind to the essential normality and naturalness of the deviants'
activities.

AFFINITY THEORIES

Durkheim's anomie

The proposition that deviant behaviour is a normal adaptation
to living within societies based on values of competitive individualism, and structured by a high division of labour, was
first formulated by Durkheim in 1893. He argued that a society
without deviance is impossible because it is inconceivable that
humans are so inflexible that none will diverge from the norm
or ideal. Moreover deviance is not only inevitable but also
necessary for the health and progress of society. Without the
introduction of new approaches to problem-solving (and thus
necessarily deviant ideas and behaviour), society would remain
static and unchangeable. Deviance, then, is an expression of
individual freedom and is an inevitable concomitant of social
change (see Heathcote's article no.16, 'Social Disorganisation
Theories').

The causes of individual deviation are thus related to the
degree of integration and cohesiveness by which society is
governed at particular times. Durkheim's major study of deviant

behaviour took the form of an analysis of suicide rates. Noting the regularity of suicide rates in given geographic areas, he argued that suicide must be caused by social rather than by individual variables. He suggested there were three primary forms of suicide that arose from egoism, altruism or anomie. Anomic suicide was considered to arise from a state of 'norm-lessness' or lack of regulation in society that occurs particularly during periods of economic crises involving prosperity or recession. Because society encourages individualism and unlimited aspirations, there may be situations when such aspirations cannot be realistically achieved. Unless society imposes regulations upon aspirations, then a state of anomie will occur, resulting in personal crises and a high tendency for suicide (Durkheim, 1952, p.246): 'No living being can be happy or even exist unless his needs are sufficiently proportioned to his means. In other words if his needs require more than can be granted or even merely something of a different sort, they will be under continual friction and can only function painfully.'

Merton's anomie

In 1938 Robert Merton elaborated on the theme of unobtainable aspirations to apply the concept of anomie beyond suicide to all forms of deviance. While Durkheim believed that aspirations were potentially limitless, Merton argued that they were socially produced and thus regulated to some extent, but they could exceed what is obtainable through available opportunities. Similarly Durkheim claimed that anomie resulted from a social failure to control and regulate individual behaviour, whereas Merton proposed that anomie resulted from *strains* in the social structure that pressurised individuals and encouraged the development of unrealistic aspirations. Anomie was thus dependent on the interaction between cultural goals - the aims that define success and status in society - and institutionalised means - the acceptable methods of achieving such goals.

Despite such divergences, both theories maintained that society was generally integrated by commonly shared values and goals, and that malintegration occurred only when there was a disproportionate emphasis on either goals or means. Both share a functionalist analysis of social structure.

American society under the banner of the American Dream, has however, for Merton, placed an over-emphasis on success as a cultural goal. The ideal that anyone, regardless of class origin, religion or ethnicity, can achieve material wealth does not match the essentially closed opportunity structure by which American society is in reality constrained. Such strains, of course, could occur only against the background of an illusory ideology of egalitarianism within a society that was simultaneously structured in terms of inequality and social disadvantage. This is not to argue, however, that the American Dream was pure ideology and unrelated to changes in the material structure of American society. The ideal that 'the road from the log cabin

to the White House is open to all' gained credence as a result
of a vast expansion of white-collar work in the 1940s which
partially altered the nature of the USA class structure.
Class mobility, and in particular the limited working-class movement from manual to non-manual occupations, played an important part not only in raising status expectations and providing
a seeming congruence of values between classes, but also in
allowing those who did not conform to the same monetary goals
of success (typically the unskilled working classes) to be viewed
automatically as a deviant residue and thus worthy of criminological attention.

Merton continues by analysing how such 'breakdowns in the
cultural structure' are responded to by a series of individual
adaptations. These are depicted not as perverse or destructive
but as the meaningful choices and actions of men accepting
or rejecting cultural goals. The adaptations are similarly not
individually induced but reflect a range of choices available to
people, given the position they occupy within the social structure. Besides conformity, Merton noted four 'deviant' adaptations: innovation, ritualism, retreatism and rebellion.

Innovation is the adaptation most inculcated with the image
of the American Dream. It occurs when the value of attaining
goals is accepted and acted out, irrespective of the impro-
priety, immorality or illegality of the chosen means. Thus
those groups situated in the lower echelons of the social hierarchy
may accept success goals but are especially lacking in opportunity. A combination of poverty, expectation and limited
opportunity predisposes such groups towards higher rates of
robbery, burglary and similar property crimes.

While innovation is seen as a typically working-class adaptation, ritualism is explained as typically lower middle class.
Here aspirations are abandoned in favour of strict adherence
to institutionalised means - 'the perspective of the frightened
employee, the zealously conformist bureaucrat' (Merton, 1957,
p.150). Such modes of 'playing it safe', however, remain deviant
because lack of ambition is out of keeping with the norm of
continual striving for success.

Retreatism similarly involves a non-compliance with the consensus of societal values. Means and goals are both rejected.
Rather than coping with the structural strains of society, the
retreatist opts out of the 'rules of the game' altogether. Such
groups as drug-addicts, vagrants, tramps, alcoholics and
psychotics are viewed as highly individualised outsiders seeking
their own rewards commensurate with their own peculiar life-
styles.

Rebellious adaptations to anomie involve not only a rejection
of goals and means but also the intention of altering the social
structure from which such norms emanate. In this way the non-
conforming rebel challenges the legitimacy of the norms and
acts for wider political rather than solely personal interests.

Thus Merton's theory rests on a relatively explicit critique of society: the questioning of the legitimacy of authority and dominant norms in an imperfect society. But, like Durkheim, his ideal remains the possibility of integrating the value of individualism with the demands of the social order. The dys-functions caused by anomie remain peripheral rather than basic to the social structure. The contradictions he adequately raises are based on questions of value rather than the material con-ditions which have produced the American Dream ideal. He fails to explain the primacy of such ideals as symptomatic of capitalist economic structures. Thus he can rely on such assumptions that persons officially treated as deviant accurately represent those involved in such behaviour and can explain their behaviour by reference to a perceived common code by which the entire American population is subsumed, even if not always conforming.

Subcultural adaptations

Merton's theory attempts not only to locate the specific cause of deviance but also to explain its various forms. The crucial developments following Merton have been less comprehensive, concerned largely to explain adaptations as subcultural rather than individual. The first notable response was provided by Albert Cohen's work on delinquent boys and the subculture of the gang in Chicago (1955). Cohen argued that Mertonian modes of adaptation to structural strain failed to account for non-utilitarian, malicious and negativistic behaviour in working-class delinquent subcultures. Delinquents usually steal items of minor value or are involved in acts of petty vandalism and ritualised violence. How could this be explained within Merton's utilitarian framework whereby all actions were viewed as a rational means to an end? Accordingly Cohen explains delin-quent motivations by reference to problems of adolescent status rather than anomie. He viewed the gang as a subculture operating within a different value system from that by which Merton characterised the whole of American society. Subcultures are distinguishable through specialised vocabulary, shared internal beliefs and special ways of dressing and acting. He argued that working-class children use delinquent subcultures as a way of reacting against and adjusting to a dominant middle-class society that discriminates against them because of their lower-class position. Their *status frustration* becomes visible in negativistic forms of delinquency whereby the middle-class ethics of ambition, tangible achievement, deferred grati-fication, cultivated manners and respect for property are rejected and reversed. By a process of 'reaction formation', middle-class values are inverted to offer a 'collective solution' in which 'the delinquent's conduct is right by the standards of his subculture precisely because it is wrong by the norms of the larger culture' (A. Cohen, 1955, p.28).

Similarly Cloward and Ohlin (1961) explain working-class deviancy as a collective rather than an individual solution,

but mark a return to Mertonian principles of high aspiration
and low opportunity. In this version, though, the problem
for working-class delinquents is to achieve a high status position in terms of lower-class rather than middle-class criteria.
As such, they combine elements of Mertonian anomie and
Sutherland's *differential association* theory by arguing that
criminal behaviour is learnt from association with a social milieu
in which the codes of such behaviour are widely available and
highly esteemed. Working-class males are committed to success
mainly in material terms but as defined by working-class
criteria. Their response does not involve reaction formation
but a turning to illegitimate means which are dependent on
the availability of learning and opportunity. Conventional goals
are internalised but within the realisation that legitimate means
are limited or blocked. Working-class neighbourhoods possess
access to illegitimate means, although these are differentially
available. Cloward and Ohlin go on to provide a typology of
differential responses via a criminal subculture, a conflict-
gang subculture and a retreatist subculture occupied by those
who have failed to take advantage of both legitimate or illegitimate means. They are concerned then with both the origins
and transmission of deviant life-styles. People are envisaged
as being placed in cultures which they have learnt by differential association and as facing particular problems of anomie
which emanate from the degree of either legitimate or illegitimate
opportunities that such an association offers them. Nevertheless the diversity of subcultures within society is overlooked
by Cloward and Ohlin. They inherit the consensual basis of
Merton that there is one all-embracing cultural goal. Now,
however, there are two types of institutionalised means to
achieve such ends: the legitimate and illegitimate. The former
is available primarily in respectable society, the latter in
the organised slum.

In conforming to the methodology of functionalism Cloward
and Ohlin attempted to explain how the origins and development of delinquency were system determined. This perspective
is largely maintained except when analysing the retreatist subculture. Here membership is explained primarily as a matter of
personal choice and individual differences. As they had shifted
anomie theory to explain collective actions, a new way forward
had to be found to analyse the meaning of individual forms
of deviancy.

Anomie theory was also faced with a series of other problems.
In particular Matza and Sykes questioned the degree to which
delinquent boys were determined by their socialisation and
suggested that their commitment to delinquent norms was only
partial (1961). Members of a subculture, if taken individually,
are not then entirely committed to its norms. They proposed
that the so-called delinquent shares many values with the
middle-class citizen. Rather than forming a subculture which
stands in antithesis to the dominant order, they argue that

such 'deviants' adapt such acceptable values as masculinity,
material aspiration and physical courage but translate them
into behaviour 'that the majority are usually too timid to
express' (p.171). Dissociated from the middle-class-dominated
context of school and work, working-class youth look to
leisure as a means of recovering that autonomy that has been
lost elsewhere. Thus working-class youth differ from the rest
of society only to the extent that they make more demands on
and have higher expectations of their leisure times. The basic
values in society remain 'accepted by both the delinquent and
the larger society of which he is a part' (p.719).

The first British application of American subcultural theory
in Downes's study (1966) similarly found little evidence of
Cohen's 'status frustration' among the working-class boys of
East London either in school or work. Rather they dissociate
themselves from any belief in work, except as a necessary form
of income, and deflect their interests, achievements and
aspirations into leisure pursuits. As such, leisure rather than
delinquency provides working-class youth with a collective
solution to their problems. The connection between working-
class leisure and delinquency becomes apparent if leisure
aspirations also remain unfulfilled. The opportunities for leisure
in the 1960s may have increased with an expansive teenage
entertainment industry, but access to its commodities involves
both expense and consumer subjugation. When access is limited
because of the inability to acquire the necessary symbols of
subcultural leisure, or when the expectation of action is met
with 'nothing going on' - then working-class youth may reach
a 'delinquent solution' by 'pushing the legitimate values of
teenage culture to their logical conclusion' (Downes, 1966,
p.134).

A critique of anomie is offered by both Matza and Downes
because the 'basic values of society' are now not viewed as a
unitary system but comprise a plurality of many different
streams capable of including both subterranean and delinquent
traditions. In this way Matza went on to criticise the view
that subcultural values were intrinsically oppositional to those
of the mainstream and suggested that conventional and delinquent values were overlapping and interrelated (1964). Instead
of delinquent acts being conceived of as a direct expression
of delinquent norms and thus system determined, they become
dependent on particular individuals and situations. The line
of enquiry was thus shifted from system determinants to
examinations of the delinquent as a person and the nature of
his interpersonal relations.

Moving to a 'general theory of deviance'
Albert Cohen clearly identified this problem in 1965 and attempted to formulate the preconditions for a 'general theory of
deviancy' by combining anomie theory with interactionism to
account for not only the genesis of deviant behaviour, but also

its cultural transmission via personal interaction. He asserts
that the central flaw of anomie theory is that it does not take
account of individual or social *reactions* to delinquent behaviour
that will affect its subsequent development or negation. Although
he maintains that individual deviancy is a product of anomie,
the concept is now removed from a consensual model of society
to a situation whereby deviance is understood as a continually
shifting *process* in which the aspirations of actors are part
of a plurality of social values intrinsically affected by differential social reactions (A. Cohen, 1965).

AFFILIATION THEORIES

Albert Cohen's refinement of anomie theory to take account of
social reaction to crime and deviance was an attempt to fuse
two separate and irreconcilable theoretical positions. Structural functionalism considers people to be passive and their
actions determined by external power, authority and control
structures. In contrast, interactionism is a voluntaristic
theory, which sees people as actively engaged in constructing
their social world, and thus grants authenticity to their own
accounts of what they are doing and why. In his synthesis,
Albert Cohen was responding to the interactionist challenge
to the dominance of structural functionalism in the 1960s.

The rise of this new approach has been accounted for by
reference to changes in American society during the 1960s.
Finestone, for example, has argued (1976, p.187) that during
this period
> the tempo of social change in American society quickened.
> Movements of social reform - the civil rights movement, the
> women's movement, and the gay movement - cumulatively
> induced a change in the collective self-image of the Ameri-
> can people. Their view of their society as a cohesive organic
> whole, dedicated to the pursuit of common goals, was increas-
> ingly replaced by an image of America as a mosaic of diverse
> groups, each with its own separate goals and its own insis-
> tent demands for justice, equality and freedom. The belief
> that public life was based upon a far-reaching consensus
> was belied by the emergence of many competing perspectives.

It was in response to the impetus provided by these social
changes, and to the internal development and expansion of
sociology, that structural functionalism was challenged by
interactionism and later labelling theory. For Finestone and
others this was 'an attempt to formulate a conception of deviance
that would be compatible with such a pluralistic view of society'
(Finestone, 1976, p.188).

Symbolic interactionism
Symbolic interactionism presents a view of the world which
emphasises the *flexibility* of individual responses to social

situations. As a theory it owes much to the pragmatic philosophy
of 'subjective realism' and indeed echoes the appreciative and
'looking-glass' approach of the Chicago School. Central to it is
the concept of *meaning*, and the variability of meaning in
everyday life. George Herbert Mead (1934), for example,
stressed that 'the self' is a social construct, and that the way
in which individuals act and see themselves is in part a consequence of the way other people see and react to them. This
indeed was seen as the most tangible focus for sociological
enquiry. In symbolic interactionism, the focus shifts from
macro social structures to the micro inter-personal and inter-
group interactions which make up social life. Social life is
thus presented not as fixed and immutable, but as a constant
process of adaptation to changing social situations. It was
Blumer who formulated symbolic interactionism as a general
sociological perspective, applicable to all forms of human
relationships (1969, p.67):

> In making the process of interpretation and definition of
> one another's acts central in human interaction, symbolic
> interaction is able to cover the full range of the genetic
> forms of human association. It embraces equally well such
> relationships as cooperation, conflict, domination, exploita-
> tion, consensus, disagreement, closely knit identification
> and indifferent concern for one another. The participants
> in each of such relations have the same common task of
> constructing their acts by interpreting and defining the
> acts of each other.

Symbolic interactionism, then, was a crucial reference point
for a pluralist theory of deviance which had to take account
of both the political nature of social control and the increasingly
problematic nature of meaning. In a society made up of diverse
and frequently competing groups, as the USA was characterised,
many social situations become both ambiguous in meaning and
also the site of potential conflict (Finestone, 1976, p.190):

> The more complex and differentiated a society, and the more
> sensitive individuals become to their group identifications,
> the more problematic become the social encounters among
> individuals of competing groups. Those who work with
> deviance must ask the questions: Who says a particular act
> is deviant? Who has the power to make this concept of
> deviance stick?

Chicago and beyond
In attempting to answer these questions, grand theorising of
general structures is replaced by empirical studies focusing
on concrete social practices in which theory is implicit rather
than explicit. This emphasis on empirical study renewed interest
in the 'appreciative' wing of the Chicago School which entered
and explored deviant worlds (see Heathcote, 'Social Disorganisation Theories'). This work, however, overemphasised
the separation of the deviant's world from mainstream society.

As Matza observed (1969, p.71):
> to establish that the worlds of hobos and taxi-dancers, for
> instance, had their own rules, regulations and rewards, the
> Chicagoeans and subsequent sociologists tended to minimize
> the importance of the fact that ... most deviant groups
> existed in the context of conventional America, drew sus-
> tenance from the milieu, dispersed services to it, recruited
> persons from it, and frequently delivered repentant devia-
> tors back to it.

The later appreciative studies, particularly Becker's work on
marijuana-smokers, were thus more concerned to examine not
the isolation, but the interrelations of deviant and non-deviant
worlds. In turn this shifted enquiry away from causative
propositions of deviant behaviour towards the process of how
behaviour comes to be defined or labelled as deviant.

Such an approach also owes much to the work of Sutherland
and his development of the work started by the Chicago School.
It was in the work of Sutherland that the concept of affinity
was challenged and the alternative concept of 'affiliation'
suggested. Sutherland's twin concepts of 'differential association' and 'differential social organisation' effectively undermine notions of crime, first, as a personal pathology, and
second, as the outcome of social disorganisation. 'Differential
association' maintains that 'a person becomes delinquent because
of an excess of definitions favorable to violation of law over
definitions unfavorable to violation of law'. Such definitions
are learnt in a normal learning process; i.e. criminal behaviour
is not a product of 'lack' of socialisation, but tends to be
learnt in identical fashion to non-criminal behaviour. This
learning includes both the often complex techniques of committing crime and the specific motives, drives and attitudes
by which such behaviour is rationalised.

Learning occurs because of association with other people
and, particularly, other people in groups. But Sutherland
does not argue that it is simply the association of an individual
with a deviant group which makes that individual criminal.
Rather, the effectiveness of the learning process depends on
the frequency, duration, priority and intensity of differential
association.

In his use of differential social organisation theory, Sutherland overturns the strain theories discussed earlier. Based
on pluralist rather than functionalist theories, differential
social organisation recognises the existence of many different
social worlds, each with its own internal values and objectives,
and using different means to achieve these different goals.
Sutherland thus explicitly rejected the Mertonian idea that
crime and deviance were the outcome of differential access to
the same goals. Differential social organisation, therefore,
recognises the existence of separate and *competing* social
worlds, with their own norms and values, while differential
association seeks to understand how these norms and values

are transmitted.

Sutherland's theory of differential association in a social order characterised by differential social organisation was developed over a number of years. The fullest outline first appeared in Sutherland and Cressey (1947, p.77):

1. *Criminal behavior is learned.* Negatively, this means that criminal behavior is not inherited, as such; also, the person who is not already trained in crime does not invent criminal behavior, just as a person does not make mechanical inventions unless he has had training in mechanics.

2. *Criminal behavior is learned in interaction with other persons in a process of communication.* This communication is verbal in many respects but includes also 'the communication of gestures.'

3. *The principal part of the learning of criminal behavior occurs within intimate personal groups.* Negatively, this means that the impersonal agencies of communication, such as movies and newspapers, play a relatively unimportant part in the genesis of criminal behavior.

4. *When criminal behavior is learned, the learning includes (a) techniques of committing the crime, which are sometimes very complicated, sometimes very simple; (b) the specific direction of motives, drives, rationalizations, and attitudes.*

5. *The specific direction of motives and drives is learned from definitions of the legal codes as favorable or unfavorable.* In some societies an individual is surrounded by persons who invariably define the legal codes as rules to be observed, while in others he is surrounded by persons whose definitions are favorable to the violation of the legal codes. In our American society these definitions are almost always mixed, with the consequence that we have culture conflict in relation to the legal codes.

6. *A person becomes delinquent because of an excess of definitions favorable to violation of law over definitions unfavorable to violation of law.* This is the principle of differential association. It refers to both criminal and anti-criminal associations and has to do with counteracting forces. When persons become criminal, they do so because of contacts with criminal patterns and also because of isolation from anti-criminal patterns. Any person inevitably assimilates the surrounding culture unless other patterns are in conflict; a Southerner does not pronounce 'r' because other Southerners do not pronounce 'r'. Negatively, this proposition of differential association means that associations which are neutral so far as crime is concerned have little or no effect on the genesis of criminal behavior. Much of the experience of a person is neutral in this sense, e.g. learning to brush one's teeth. This behavior has no negative or positive effect

on criminal behavior except as it may be related to associations which are concerned with the legal codes. This neutral behavior is important especially as an occupier of the time of a child so that he is not in contact with criminal behavior during the time he is so engaged in neutral behavior.

7. *Differential associations may vary in frequency, duration, priority, and intensity.* This means that associations with criminal behavior and also associations with anti-criminal behavior vary in those respects. 'Frequency' and 'duration' as modalities of associations are obvious and need no explanation. 'Priority' is assumed to be important in the sense that lawful behavior developed in early childhood may persist throughout life, and also that delinquent behavior developed in early childhood may persist throughout life. This tendency, however, has not been adequately demonstrated, and priority seems to be important principally through its selective influence. 'Intensity' is not precisely defined but it has to do with such things as the prestige of the source of a criminal or anti-criminal pattern and with emotional reactions related to the association. In a precise description of the criminal behavior of a person these modalities would be stated in quantitative form and a mathematical ratio be reached. A formula in this sense has not been developed, and the development of such a formula would be extremely difficult.

8. *The process of learning criminal behavior by association with criminal and anti-criminal patterns involves all of the mechanisms that are involved in any other learning.* Negatively, this means that the learning of criminal behavior is not restricted to the process of imitation. A person who is seduced, for instance, learns criminal behavior by association, but this process would not ordinarily be described as imitation.

9. *While criminal behavior is an expression of general needs and values, it is not explained by those general needs and values since non-criminal behavior is an expression of the same needs and values.* Thieves generally steal in order to secure money, but likewise honest laborers work in order to secure money. The attempts by many scholars to explain criminal behavior by general drives and values, such as the happiness principle, striving for social status, the money motive, or frustration, have been and must continue to be futile since they explain lawful behavior as completely as they explain criminal behavior. They are similar to respiration, which is necessary for any behavior but which does not differentiate criminal from noncriminal behavior.

Sutherland was not concerned with explaining *why* a person has particular associations. He argued simply that in every society characterised by differential social organisation, different people are exposed to a variety of associational ties.

But, as Matza has pointed out (1969, p.107), Sutherland was not always sensitive to the movement of ideas and people between deviant and conventional worlds.

Partly obsessed by the idea of ecology, Sutherland nearly made his subject a captive of the milieu. Like a tree or a fox, the subject was a creature of affiliational circumstances except that what Sutherland's milieu provided was meaning and definition of the situation. Sutherland's subject was a creature, but he was half a man. Had Sutherland appreciated the interpenetration of cultural worlds - the symbolic availability of various ways of life everywhere - and more important, had he appreciated that men, but not trees or foxes, intentionally move in search of meaning as well as nourishment ... if, in other words had he rejected the notion of radical cultural separation along with an ecological theory of migration well suited for insects but not man, his creature would have been wholly human.

Sutherland's theoretical advances were limited because they regarded the actor as a passive recipient of criminal and noncriminal motives and omitted a notion of human purpose and meaning. But Sutherland at least partially transformed the traditional object of criminology into a subject whose actions were far from meaningless. It was left to the labelling theorists to humanise fully deviance by making explicit two basic features of human life in the social world: consciousness and intention.

The labelling perspective

By making explicit the importance of consciousness and intention, and by granting authenticity to deviants' accounts of their activities, labelling theory effectively humanised deviance. It achieved this by radically shifting the object of criminological study away from individual motivation towards analysis of the types of social situations which enable behaviour to be defined as deviant and provoke social reaction and control. Plummer has identified four central problems on which labelling theorists focus (1979, p.88):

(1) What are the *characteristics* of labels, their variations and forms?
(2) What are the *sources* of labels, both societally and personally?
(3) How, and under what *conditions* do labels get applied?
(4) What are the *consequences* of labelling?

The essence of labelling, then, is that it provides a 'useful series of problems designed to reorientate the former mainstream study to the consideration of the *nature, emergence, application* and *consequences* of deviancy labels' (1979, p.88), which seeks to shift attention towards *definitional* questions (why is particular activity deviant or criminal?) and away from motivational questions (why does X engage in a particular activity?). In looking at the work of labelling theorists, we will focus on some of the work of Lemert and Becker, who are identified as central figures in this theoretical approach.

Lemert, for example, begins his study of juvenile delinquency in the USA by showing that 'one of the most striking developments in the picture of child and youth problems has been the great increase in contacts between youth, law enforcement bodies and the juvenile court' (1971, p.1). Between 1957 and 1973, the rate of cases of delinquency disposed of by the juvenile courts per 1,000 child population increased from 19.8 in 1957 to 34.2 in 1973. He traced this rise against the increasing influence of the 'rehabilitative ideal' among agencies of juvenile social control. This ideal positively encourages maximum intervention in the lives of many people in order to alter intimate aspects of their beliefs, values, behaviour and group affiliations. The authority to do this is legal and also based loosely on theories of psychological and sociological positivism (see Sapsford's 'Individual Deviance' and Heathcote's 'Social Disorganisation Theories').

Lemert argues that, under the guise of the rehabilitative ideal, definitions of juvenile delinquency have been expanded to include a variety of behaviour outside the criminal law. He shows how what is known as juvenile delinquency is in fact a social construction of behaviour and actions. It was for this reason, and from the findings of his other research (for example, into the functioning of the grand jury), that Lemert presented a theory of deviance, which argued that social control and not behaviour was the key to understanding deviations. In his view, social control becomes a 'cause' rather than an effect of deviation. For Lemert, then, it is not deviance which leads to social control, but social control which leads to deviance.

In making this argument, he identifies three basic concepts: social reaction, primary deviance and secondary deviance. These concepts are all illustrated in the following examples of classroom behaviour taken from 'Social Pathology', published in 1951:

> For one reason or another, let us say excessive energy, the schoolboy engages in a classroom prank. He is penalized for it by the teacher. Later, due to clumsiness, he creates another disturbance and again he is reprimanded. Then, as sometimes happens, the boy is blamed for something he did not do. When the teacher uses the tag 'bad boy' or 'mischief maker' or other invidious terms, hostility and resentment are excited in the boy, and he may feel he is blocked in playing the role expected of him. Thereafter, there may be a strong temptation to assume his role in the class as defined by the teacher, particularly when he discovers that there are rewards as well as penalties deriving from such a role. There is, of course, no implication here

that such boys go on to become delinquents or criminals,
for the mischief maker role may later become integrated
with or retrospectively rationalized as part of a role more
acceptable to the school authorities. (p.77)

For Lemert, the range of the teacher's responses to the boy
represent the societal reaction: 'The societal reaction is a very
general term summarizing both the expressive reactions of
others (moral indignation) toward deviation and action directed
to its control' (1951, p.64).

By locating deviance in the context in which it takes place,
he was able to distinguish between primary and secondary
deviation, and to recognise the importance of social reaction
in the manufacture of secondary deviance. Primary deviation
was defined by Lemert as an isolated, initial action of rule-
breaking which is not regarded as personally significant by
the rule-breaker. Secondary deviation occurs when the deviant,
in response to social reaction to that initial act, reorganises
her or his identity around the deviant role. In making this
distinction, he emphasises, first, deviance as process, and,
second, that social reaction and social control are not simply
passive and predictable responses to deviant activity, but play
an active and compelling role in the creation and promotion
of deviance: 'social control must be taken as an independent
variable rather than as a constant, or merely reciprocal
societal reaction to deviation. Thus conceived, social control
becomes a "cause" rather than an effect of the magnitude and
variable forms of deviation' (1972, p.49).

Becker, in his early study of marijuana-smokers, provides
a classic example of affiliation theories. Again, his concern is
not with motivational questions about why people smoke
marijuana, but with definitional questions of how, why and
with what consequences marijuana-smoking is characterised
as a deviant activity (1963, p.8):

Social groups create deviance by making the rules whose
infraction constitutes deviance, and by applying those
rules to particular people and labeling them as outsiders.
From this point of view, deviance is not a quality of the
act the person commits, but rather a consequence of the
application by others of rules and sanctions to an 'offender.'
The deviant is one to whom that label has successfully been
applied; deviant behavior is behavior that people so label.

Becker was interested in labelling in so far as it generated
a social object, the deviant, but also in the process of interaction through which labels were successfully applied. He was
particularly concerned to emphasise the interaction between
labeller and labelled in the process of creating deviance, and
insisted that rules are social objects, negotiated by the offender
and others, rather than fixed, immovable, universal laws which
are applied automatically and without discrimination to any
rule-breaker. For Becker (1963, p.84):

deviance is not a simple quality, present in some kind of

behavior and absent in others. Rather it is the product of
a process which involves responses of other people to the
behavior. The same behavior may be an infraction of the
rules at one time and not at another; may be an infraction
when committed by one person, but not when committed by
another; some rules are broken with impunity, others are
not. In short, whether a given act is deviant or not depends
in part on the nature of the act (that is, whether or not it
violates some rule) and in part on what other people do
about it.

Becker's formulation, thus far, is based on a voluntaristic
conception of human nature, and a pluralist model of society,
and relies heavily on an interactionist framework. Like Lemert,
Becker recognises individuals as actively engaged in constructing their social world, rather than being passive objects of
a particular social formation.

But in the middle of his analysis of the 'careers' of marijuana-
smokers and of the processes by which they are labelled
'deviant', Becker shifts his position. Once a person has been
identified and labelled as 'deviant', Becker switches away from
an interactionist approach to a social organisational one,
replacing a voluntaristic conception of human nature with a
determinist one. Marijuana-smokers are no longer playing an
active part in the process of labelling; they are the passive
recipients of a stigmatising label imposed from above which
has specific consequences for the deviant (1963, p.10):

> Being caught and branded as deviant has important con-
> sequences for one's further social participation and self-
> image. The most important consequence is a drastic change
> in the individual's public identity. Committing the improper
> act and being publicly caught at it places him in a new
> status. He has been revealed as a different kind of person
> from the kind he was supposed to be. He is labelled a
> 'fairy,' 'dope fiend,' 'nut,' or 'lunatic' and treated accord-
> ingly.

Finestone has argued that the reason for this shift in theoretical approach can be traced to Becker's difficulties in
accommodating the crucial concept of power in an interactionist
framework. Becker experienced the same difficulty in working
out his concept of 'career', which is located firmly in a social
organisational framework (1963, p.24):

> A useful conception in developing sequential models of
> various kinds of deviant behavior is that of *career*. Origin-
> ally developed in studies of occupations, the concept refers
> to the sequence of movements from one position to another
> in an occupational system made by any individual who works
> in that system. Furthermore, it includes the notion of 'career
> contingency,' those factors on which mobility from one posi-
> tion to another depends. Career contingencies include both
> the objective facts of social structure and changes in the
> perspectives, motivation and desires of the individual.

Similarly, Lemert has argued that the concept of deviant career is irreconcilable with an interactionist framework.

Within the labelling perspective, then, we can already identify a major theoretical disjuncture. Deviance is, on the one hand, negotiated. Individuals construct their social worlds, interacting with other individuals and groups. But once a person has been labelled as deviant, the stigma automatically attaches itself, and a person becomes a passive recipient of systematically determined forces. Interactionism, then, is useful in the process of 'becoming' (a marijuana-smoker, a mental patient, a prostitute, a homosexual), but, once labelled, it is unable to explain the consequences of labelling for the individual deviant. Becker, for example, makes few empirical connections between his two central concepts: labelling and career. His difficulty in making such connections can partly be accounted for by the inconsistencies of the pluralist model of social order on which his interactionist framework is constructed. Pluralist theory is premised upon a differentiated, heterogeneous model of society in which different groups hold different beliefs and values. But Becker insists that the labels imposed on particular forms of behaviour are universally recognised and accepted, suggesting a degree of consensus of beliefs and values inconsistent with a pluralist framework.

Specifically, without a theory of power, interactionism is unable to account for the processes by which labels are made to stick, and the consequences of being labelled are unfolded. Moreover, without an adequate theory of power, Becker is unable to specify the criteria by which particular labels are developed and sustained.

If deviance is simply behaviour that people so label, then so is conformity. Such an assertion provides us with no guidelines for working out which behaviour is regarded as 'deviant' or 'conforming', and why. While it is important to recognise that deviance is not constant, that it changes over time within one society, and varies between societies, we also need to explain how and why such relativism occurs, and acknowledge that, at any particular time, there is some measure of agreement about particular types of behaviour. As Taylor, Walton and Young argue (1973, pp.146-7):

> Our objection ... to one assumption of the social reaction position is this: that we do not act in a world free of social meaning. With the exception of entirely new behaviour, it is clear to most people which actions are deviant and which are not deviant... We would assert that *most deviant behaviour* is a *quality of the act*, since the way in which we distinguish between *behaviour* and *action* is that behaviour is merely physical and action has meaning that is socially given.

Moreover, it has been argued that labelling theorists, while insisting on the relativism of deviant behaviour, reinforce and create new categories of deviance (Plummer, 1979, p.97).

More important, perhaps, is the contradiction inherent in the twin assertions of labelling theorists, first, that there is 'secret' deviance which goes unrecognised, and second, that deviance exists only when behaviour is identified and labelled as deviant. But if deviant behaviour exists only when it is publicly recognised and labelled, how can 'hidden' deviance be as widespread in the society as labelling theorists claim?

Labelling theorists were correct to challenge the one-dimensional, system-determining functionalism we discussed earlier in this article. Lemert, for example, insisted that the notion that such a society [the USA] has a common-value hierarchy, either culturally transmitted or structurally induced, strains credibility (1972, pp.26-61). But labelling theorists, in their anxiety to avoid the pitfalls of functionalism, took no account of the social structures, both formal and informal, that do exist. The complex investment procedures, large-scale service and management functions, and major programmes of social engineering, both at home and abroad, which characterise contemporary capitalism do not exist by chance or without structural form. In their concentration on street-level interactions, labelling theorists were unable to address the general questions about the relationship between crime, law and the state (see Hall and Scraton, 'Law, Class and Control').

NEW DIRECTIONS

During the 1970s a variety of studies attempted to explain delinquent behaviour by reworking and amalgamating versions of anomie, subcultural, interactionist and labelling theories. This work was carried out largely in Britain and has been subsumed under the general umbrella title of a 'new' or 'radical' criminology. Despite their reliance on different and opposing theoretical traditions, they all mark a shift away from asking behavioural questions - What initially causes an individual to commit a deviant act? - to posing definitional and structural questions - Why does an act become to be defined as deviant? Who enforces such definitions and in whose interests?

The new directions continue the tradition of humanising deviance by explaining deviant acts as the rational and logical responses of individuals and subcultures to constraints in their social situation, rather than simply dismissing them as immoral or illegal. Furthermore, the study of deviancy is expanded beyond a restricted analysis of deviant acts. Studying deviancy becomes a central pivot in asking questions concerned with the way in which society is structured and the nature of its power relations.

Moral panics
Chronologically the first major study to tackle such questions was Stan Cohen's (1972) work on 'mods' and 'rockers'. His

approach is based on a transactionalist analysis which examines
how definitions of deviance are constructed and developed
within the interaction (or transactions) between those being
judged and those making moral and legal judgments of others'
behaviour. He utilises Lemert's (1967) concepts of primary and
secondary deviance, arguing that primary deviance is so
diffuse in its causal motivation that it defies unitary explanation. Of more importance is secondary deviation, or deviant
behaviour developed as a means of defence, attack or adaptation
to the problems created by social reaction to primary deviation.
Social reaction launches actors away from intermittent deviancy
(as described by Matza (1964)) towards a firm commitment to
a deviant career. Once publicly labelled as deviant, actors
are cut off from dominant value systems and develop alternative
systems which increase or amplify the visibility of their
deviancy.

Stan Cohen begins by accepting the tenets of the anomie
perspective in subcultural theory, arguing that the structural
strain experienced by British adolescents in the form of status
frustration and blocked leisure opportunities in the mid-1960s
led to two distinct and highly visible subcultural adaptations -
'mods' and 'rockers'. The bulk of his study, though, illustrates
the importance of social (and particularly media) reaction to
such 'folk devils' as vital contributors to the creation and
definition of a more widespread 'moral panic' about youthful
lawlessness which characterised the entire decade. By comparing the actual violence and damage to property incurred
on the east and south coast beaches in 1964 with media report-
age of the events, Cohen concludes that the official reaction
to such subcultures was out of all proportion to the actual
threat offered to societal values. When policy-makers, judiciary,
politicians and editors similarly perceive the 'threat' in stereotypical and overactive terms, then a moral panic may be created
which could have serious and long-term repercussions not only
in changing legal and social policy, but also in affecting the
way in which society conceives itself.

In this way Cohen questions the dominant view that events
happen and the media simply report them. Rather he shows how
the media *select* and present information about crime and
deviancy which tends to isolate such activity and heighten
social reaction. For example, the media latched onto the labels
'mods' and 'rockers', emphasised a particular image of such
groups as violent and unruly, and bolstered the position of
those advocating more control. The core of his argument is that
the media do not simply reflect social reality, but are able to
define it in a particular way. Thus in times of rapid social
change when traditional values are shaken up and disturbed,
the ensuing public disquiet is resolved by the media by identifying certain social groups as scapegoats or folk devils. They
become the visual symbols of what is wrong with society, while
the more intractable and structural problems to do with

restricted opportunities are simultaneously overlooked or passed by. The singling out of deviant groups and social reaction to them may also result in an amplification of their deviance, both in real and perceived terms. Re-using Wilkins's notion of a deviancy amplification spiral (1964), coupled with Lemert's concept of secondary deviation, Cohen argues that the effects of societal reaction and social control may result in the deviant person identifying with the label attached to himself and thus perceiving himself as being more separate and deviant. Thus the positions of definer and defined become polarised and irresolvable. De-amplification then is usually attained only by deterring potential and existing deviants with more punitive - actual or threatened - control measures. The book ends on the following pessimistic note (1972, p.204):

> More moral panics will be generated and other as yet name-less folk devils will be created. This is not because such developments have an inexorable inner logic, but because our society as presently structured will continue to generate problems for some of its members like working-class adolescents - and then condemn whatever solution these groups find.

Hall and his colleagues (1978) re-used the concept by identifying a series of moral panics to do with permissiveness, vandals, scroungers, drug-abusers and so on which characterised the 1960s and early 1970s, culminating in 1972-3 with the moral panic of 'mugging'. Their analysis, however, shifted the terms of debate from particular subcultures and adaptations to anomie, to an analysis of crises of hegemony (how rule/consent of the people is achieved/maintained) within the political spectrum of recurring industrial disputes, high unemployment, inflation and the law and order campaigns of the late 1960s and 1970s. They replaced Stan Cohen's loosely defined notion of 'social control' with a more historically and socially specific analysis of *state control*. The notion of moral panic is now used as one element in the process whereby the state is able to divert public opinion to particular *symptoms* of industrial collapse rather than the *causes* of such collapse.

In the early 1970s the use of the label 'mugging' and the ensuing panic served to disguise industrial unrest and also gave weight to those advocating an increase in law and order campaigns. Within the climate of such a panic, support for strengthening the powers of the police force and providing harsher sentences for offenders was legitimated. The real problems of Britain could then be defined as ones solely of *lawlessness*, rather than social deprivation and class inequality.

The notion of 'moral panic' is central to both studies in explaining how particular social groups (working-class youth/ black youth) are identified as worthy of police and judicial attention. The implications of such identification, however, are not as narrow. A moral panic is the first link in a chain of events leading to the maintenance of rule in a society by a

legitimised coercion and a general exercise of authority. Thus
a cycle of moral panics plays directly into the construction of
a law and order society which has repercussions not only for
convicted offenders but for whole populations.

Subcultures, class and leisure

In contrast to most American research, recent British studies
of youth subcultures are not primarily concerned with explaining delinquency. Rather, they tend to explore the field opened
up by Downes's (1966) analysis that working-class boys respond
to lack of opportunity by dissociation rather than status frustration, and consequently use *leisure* rather than delinquency
to provide a solution to their collective problems. Thus, studies
of deviancy have expanded their field of enquiry to explore
the links between youth groups, leisure styles and class location. This shift is partly the outcome of the failure of post-war
research in Britain to discover the structured and 'differentiated' gangs which informed Albert Cohen's and Cloward and
Ohlin's work. Britain has produced instead a number of
spectacular and deviant (rather than delinquent) predominantly
working-class youth subcultures ranging from 'teddy boys',
'mods' and 'rockers' to 'skinheads' and 'punks'.

It was Phil Cohen's research (1972) on 'mods' and 'skinheads'
in London's East End that first explored in detail the ways
in which youth experiences were both class specific and encoded
in leisure styles. He shows how these two groups emerged as
authentic, but limited, solutions to a range of ideological and
economic contradictions facing a working-class community
experiencing substantial dislocation and social change. In the
late 1950s and early 1960s the East End was a target for
redevelopment and rehousing, resulting in the eventual depopu-
lation of the area, undermining of community solidarity, and
destruction of family businesses and local craft industries.
Accordingly, the prospects of employment diminished, particularly for the 'respectable' skilled working class. These
changes, of course, affected both the youthful and the adult
members of the class, but it was the youth who experienced
these problems most acutely and it was they who attempted to
resolve them through their leisure activities. Such a resolution,
though, is illusory because it operates at the ideological level
and remains 'imaginary' or 'symbolic' because it does not confront the material and economic causes of the class's problems.

Phil Cohen thus analyses subcultures in their cultural context, discusses the influence of material change and contradictions and suggests a form of problem-solving based on
ideological resolutions. These allow sections of working-class
youth to solve problems 'magically' via leisure and subcultural
style which are facing the working class as a whole.

Cohen's work was later refined by Clarke and his colleagues
(1975) who explained the particular content of successive post-
war youth subcultures by reference to their class and cultural

location (whether dominant or subordinate), and their interaction with their respective parent cultures. Each subculture
represents ways of adapting to and reacting against both its
parent/adult culture and also that class/culture which stands
in opposition to it. The concept of subculture is now essentially
related to the dynamics of class relations within capitalist
society. Social class provides the primary mediating role in the
genesis and development of youth subcultures. In contrast
to American subcultural theory, the behaviour of youth can
now be seen as symptomatic of the very instability of a society
in which a dominant class attempts to retain hegemony while a
subordinate class attempts to wrest more control from the
dominant class or otherwise improve its position. Against this
context of class conflict and common class problems, the
generationally-specific responses of subcultures can be
explained. Thus the rise of 'teddy boys', in the mid-1950s was
located within the social context of unskilled youth unemployment and their lack of access to education and leisure, against
a contradictory dominant ideology of growing affluence and
classlessness. The 'teds' resolved such contradictions by reas-
serting working-class values of toughness, masculinity and
territoriality but by adopting styles of dress and music which
simultaneously marked a reaction against the working class's
more complacent and 'grey' elements.

Later in the mid-1960s the 'mods' attempted to take part in
the 'new affluence' by creating their own style of conspicuous
consumption based on smart well-cut clothes, scooters and
R and B music which similarly constituted a parody of the
consumer society in which they were situated.

Clarke and his colleagues also tried to account for the more
diffuse middle-class counterculture of the late 1960s within
the same theoretical framework. Thus they argued that subcultures of dominant culture such as beatniks, hippies, drop-
outs, mystics and radical students represented a crisis of
authority within dominant culture itself. The wide-ranging but
highly individualistic, romantic and utopian attempts of the
counterculture to achieve self-discovery and social change
through the creation of 'alternative' life-styles is explained in
terms of the wider choices and options available to middle-class
youth because of their preferential class position.

In this way post-war deviant youth groups are accounted for
by reference to inter and intra class relations. Each uses the
relative freedom of leisure to 'win space' for its own particular
'focal concerns'. The choices made are neither arbitrary nor meaningless, but represent forms of struggle between and within dominant and subordinate cultures acted out on the streets, in the
schools and on the shop floor. Most significantly the study of
deviant youth now helps to illustrate how class domination in capitalism is not simple and deterministic. Capitalism is never secure
but is the sphere of a constant struggle between ideologies and
cultures. Subcultures are thus symbolic forms of resistance:

symptoms of the capitalist crises, economic upheavals and
political dissents which have characterised the post-war period
in Britain.

Labelling theory reconsidered

At the same time as the work on moral panics and subcultures,
class and style was being developed, attempts were being made
to resolve some of the internal contradictions of labelling,
and answer the increasingly vociferous criticisms levelled
against it. Becker, for example, has insisted that the work of
labelling theorists has been misrepresented. He acknowledged,
for example, that 'the act of labelling, as carried out by
moral entrepreneurs, while important, cannot possibly be conceived as the sole explanation of what alleged deviants do'.
But to focus on social reaction does reveal the ways in which
labelling and stigmatising *do* make it harder for the labelled to
continue the normal routines of everyday life and thus provoke further 'abnormal' actions. Most crucially, Becker maintains that labelling was never intended as a full-blown social
theory, but 'rather a way of looking at a general area of
human activity, a perspective whose value will appear, if at
all, in increased understanding of things formerly obscure'
(1974, pp.42-4).

Plummer has picked up this point in a recent defence of
interactionism. He also starts from the premise that labelling
has been seriously misunderstood. 'Labelling, then, should not
be equated with a theory or a proposition, but should be seen
as a perspective in deviancy research. And because of this
it can harbour several diverse theoretical positions' (1979,
p.90). He acknowledges the strengths of the criticisms levelled
against the labelling perspective, but insists that the criticisms
can be countered. He sees one of the major problems as the
need to reconcile absolutist conceptions of deviance with
relativist ones. He proposes to resolve this by distinguishing
between societal and situational deviance. The former refers
to 'those categories that are either (a) commonly sensed by
most of society's members to *be* deviant, or (b) lodged in
some abstract meanings, such as the law or reified norms which
cannot be wished away by individual members'. Societal deviance
acknowledges general agreement over the *identification* of
deviance, though there remains dissension about the *appropriateness* of such a label and the consequences for the individual
of its imposition.

Situational deviance, on the other hand, refers to 'the actual
manner in which members of society go about the task of creating rules and interpreting rule violations as "deviance"...in
context' (Plummer, 1979, p.98). This conceptualisation acknowledges that people, at an individual, everyday level, have
some capacity to neutralise or reverse societal definitions of
deviance, and to construct for themselves rules and definitions
which are at odds with those commonly held.

This distinction, which would allow for both an absolutist definition of deviance, and a relativist one, might be useful conceptually in the study of crime and deviance, but the connection between the two concepts has yet to be worked out. The re-introduction of interactionism to contemporary debate, particularly in Britain, may have tempered the thrust of class theorists (whose recent work is discussed by Hall and Scraton in 'Law, Class and Control'), but a lasting impact remains yet to be substantiated. It is important not to throw out all the insights of labelling in the rush to class analysis and to acknowledge its role in the regeneration and re-orientation of psychological theorising about crime and deviance.

References
Becker, H. (1963), 'Outsiders: Studies in the Sociology of Deviance', New York, Free Press.
Becker, H. (1974), Labelling Theory Reconsidered, in Rock, P. and McIntosh, M. (eds), 'Deviance and Social Control', Tavistock.
Blumer, H. (1969), 'Symbolic Interactionism', Englewood Cliffs, Prentice-Hall.
Clarke, J. et al. (1975), 'Subcultures, Cultures and Class', Working Papers in Cultural Studies, nos 7-8, University of Birmingham.
Cloward, R. and Ohlin, L. (1961), 'Delinquency and Opportunity: a Theory of Delinquent Gangs', Routledge & Kegan Paul.
Cohen, A. (1955), 'Delinquent Boys: the Culture of the Gang', Chicago, Free Press.
Cohen, A. (1965), The Sociology of the Deviant Act: Anomie Theory and Beyond, 'American Sociological Review', vol.30, no.1, pp.5-14.
Cohen, P. (1972), 'Subcultural Conflict and Working-Class Community', Working Papers in Cultural Studies, no.2, University of Birmingham.
Cohen, S. (1972), 'Folk Devils and Moral Panics', Paladin.
Downes, D. (1966), 'The Delinquent Solution', Routledge & Kegan Paul.
Durkheim, E. (1952), 'Suicide', Routledge & Kegan Paul.
Finestone, H. (1976), 'Victims of Change', Westport, Conn., Greenwood.
Hall, S. et al. (1978), 'Policing the Crisis', Macmillan.
Lemert, E. (1951), 'Social Pathology', New York, McGraw-Hill.
Lemert, E. (1967), 'Human Deviance, Social Problems and Social Control', Englewood Cliffs, Prentice-Hall (2nd ed. published 1972).
Lemert, E. (1971), 'Instead of Court', National Institute of Mental Health, Washington, D.C.
Matza, D. (1964), 'Delinquency and Drift', New York, Wiley.
Matza, D. (1969), 'Becoming Deviant', Englewood Cliffs, Prentice-Hall.

Matza, D. and Sykes, G. (1961), Juvenile Delinquency and Sub-
    terranean Values, 'American Sociological Review', vol.26,
    pp.712-19.
Mead, G.H. (1934), 'Mind, Self and Society', Chicago University
    Press.
Merton, R. (1938), Social Structure and Anomie, 'American
    Sociological Review', vol.3, pp.672-82.
Merton, R. (1957), 'Social Theory and Social Structure', New
    York, Free Press.
Parsons, T. (1951), 'The Social System', Routledge & Kegan
    Paul.
Plummer, K. (1979), Misunderstanding Labelling Perspectives,
    in Downes and Rock (eds), 'Deviant Interpretations', Martin
    Robertson.
Simmons, J.L. (1969), 'Deviants', Berkeley, Cal., Glendessary
    Press.
Sutherland, E. and Cressey, D. (1974), 'Principles of
    Criminology', 8th ed., Philadelphia, Lippincott.
Taylor, Ian, Walton, Paul and Young, Jock (1973), 'The New
    Criminology', Routledge & Kegan Paul, 1973.
Wilkins, L. (1964), 'Social Deviance', Tavistock.

19   The person and group reality

Rudi Dallos and *R. J. Sapsford*

---

1 INTRODUCTION: ON 'BEING A CRIMINAL'

This is an account by John McVicar, who became one of the
most famous criminals in Britain, partly because of his sensational escape from Durham Prison in 1968. The account from
which extracts are given here was written while he was awaiting trial after his recapture and was published in the 'Sunday
Times', 4 November 1973.

I was born, in March 1940, during the London blitz. My
earliest memories are associated with shelters and doodle-
bugs, but I can't ever have been really frightened by the
war as I know it has had no traumatic effect on me. I was
raised in a family which included my parents, myself and
my sister Janice, born two years after myself. My father
was excused from being called up because of bad health and
worked out the war years in the railway yards. He also had
a combined corner house and shop (newsagent and tobac-
conist) in the back streets of West Ham. My father ran the
shop and we all lived at home from about 1942 until I
received my first prison sentence. I have no memories of
my father during the war years, simply a vague impression
of his being about.

The main feature of my father's life was the long and
exhausting hours he worked during every day of it. I know
nothing of his background, except that he was of Scottish
extraction; he never spoke about himself, he was a reserved,
solitary, even a morose man. Yet he married a woman who
was warm, emotional, sociable. It made a bad match, but
they had had two children before they realised it, and they
never separated in spite of the recurrent crises which were
the dominating feature of their relationship. My upbringing,
and my sister's, took place against the background of their

Source: article commissioned for this volume.

constant arguments, rows, and occasionally fights. As parents, my mother was loving and indulgent, my father cold and severe; but he was never patently cruel or arbitrarily violent with either of us.

I entered Infants' School in the autumn of 1945. The most significant thing about my feeling about my father at that time was my indifference, because it had no positive content. I don't think I was as yet aware of his drinking, but certainly his hostility to my mother and his many absences had prevented the process of identification between father and son from developing naturally.

But the absence of a male to model myself on had not interfered with my adjustment to the idea that I was a boy and my adoption of the standards which I saw as being appropriate to a boy.

My upbringing left me with a number of attitudes and traits which, while they did not necessarily make me a criminal, made it possible for me to be one if the opportunity arose. The opportunity did, and I took it, for a number of reasons, of which money was the only one I was aware of, although it was a lot more complex than that.

Perhaps the real strength of the criminal, his incorrigibility, his immunity to the deterrent effects of punishment, or the possibility of punishment, lies not so much in exploiting the opportunity of getting away with it as in the crude philosophy he lives by. Once you accept the virtue of taking risks, and stake your self-esteem on measuring up to them, then the possible consequences are like the chances of getting gored to the bullfighter or of crashing to a racing driver. The professional criminal, who would only rarely transgress if he knew he would get caught, accepts the risk of imprisonment, or whatever other punishment if he should fail to evade detection. Imprisonment is part of the game....

Socially, crime relieved me of all normal responsibilities towards my family. Out of prison, I had enough money to cover my commitments; inside, I couldn't contribute, but I couldn't be reproached for this, for ostensibly at least I had stolen in order to discharge my obligations. My mother instinctively summed it all up in colloquial language one day when I and my pals were in the house: 'You must all like it in there, you always are in there, and when you're not, you're always talking about it.'...

Perhaps freedom is the most precious thing a man possesses, more precious than absence of pain or suffering, and maybe that is why taking it away is the only real means of punishment the bench retains in our civilised times. All the crimes I have committed since I began that eight-year sentence were committed while I was chasing freedom. I don't know if that 'excuses' any more than it 'explains'. The two years in which I was at large were the happiest period of my life, but they were always over-shadowed by fear and

anxiety. If I had had that experience earlier, I know I
would never have amassed a 23-year sentence. But I can't
claim any sweeties. In the end, perhaps, all I can do is to
hope for some luck and ask for some mercy.

2 THE NEW PSYCHOLOGY

All the earlier articles in this section of the Reader have been
to varying extents deterministic - they have looked for 'causes
of crime', factors which determine whether individuals will
offend against the law.[1] The two 'psychology' articles in particular have treated people very much as if they were *machines
for behaving*: the first, by Sapsford, covered a 'hardware'
approach to the machine: crudely put, that people become
criminal because of the way they are built - and the second,
by Dallos, covers 'programming' and the idea that crime is
determined by what the organism learns, especially during the
early and formative years. There are large elements of determinism in the 'sociology' articles as well, with the suggestion
that crime is determined by the 'input' from the physical or
the social environment. Causal explanations of crime are well
established in the 'folk wisdom' of everyday life, and you will
have seen some of them in the autobiographical passage by
John McVicar above. Note, for example, his comments on
identification and modelling, strongly reminiscent of the
Freudian approach, and how his 'upbringing left [him] with a
number of attitudes and traits which ... made it possible for
[him] to be [a criminal] if the opportunity arose.'
    Equally well established in the McVicar account and in folk
wisdom, however, is the notion of man as an *individual*, with
values, goals, intentions and responsibility for his or her own
actions. 'Perhaps the real strength of the criminal ... lies ...
in the crude philosophy he lives by', or again 'All the crimes
I have committed since I began that eight-year sentence were
committed while I was chasing freedom.' What would 'explanations' of crime and deviant behaviour look like if they followed
this second line of approach instead of the first? What kind of
account can we build of criminals and other deviants based on
an assumption that they are rational and goal-seeking decision-
makers rather than machines driven by their nature and their
surroundings?
    An example of the insights which this approach may give
is provided by the work of the American sociologist Erving
Goffman on the life of mental patients as seen from their own
perspective and how this may contrast with the perspective
adopted by the doctors and the institution (1970, pp.220-1,
270):
    In everyday life, legitimate possessions ... are typically
    stored, when not in use, in special places ... These stor-
    age places protect the object from damage ... [and] can

represent an extension of the self and its autonomy ...
... When a patient, whose clothes are taken from him
each night, fills his pockets with bits of string and rolled
up paper, and when he fights to keep these possessions
... he is usually seen as engaging in symptomatic behaviour befitting a very sick patient, not as someone who is
attempting to stand apart from the place accorded him.

In other words, sometimes behaviours which seem bizarre to
others may be rational even in the terms of those others: there
is nothing irrational in using pockets as a substitute for a
non-existent locker. While they may sometimes remain bizarre
to others who have 'better' ways of marking the boundaries
of self, there may still be a rationale for them within the life of
the person doing them. To write them off as mere symptoms
is in some ways to *debar* ourselves from understanding them,
rather than to explain them.

This kind of thinking is well established among sociologists.
George Herbert Mead, in his lectures in Chicago during the
first third of this century, was arguing for a crucial difference
between animal *reaction* and human *conduct*, for the importance
of *self* and *self-consciousness* as factors in human conduct,
and for the individual's capability to be aware of the self both
as subject and as object. The school of Symbolic Interactionists
which developed out of Mead's ideas has never held the dominant
place in sociology but has constituted a significant minority
paradigm since the 1930s and has contributed strongly to the
study of crime and deviance through the work of writers such
as Goffman, Lemert and Becker. Some elements of this approach
are to be seen in the ideas of clinical therapists during the
whole of this century (e.g. Haley, 1973, 1976). In academic
psychology, however, the adoption of an interactionist perspective, stressing the interactive nature of the self and the
negotiation of *meanings* in a cultural context, has been a
radical and rather recent departure from the discipline's
predominantly deterministic history.

The new psychology - to coin a rather trite name for it - is
characterized by a growing distaste for a psychology which
purports to be a science of behaviour and a growing inclination towards *understanding* of what behaviour means in context rather than *explanation* of how it comes about and how it
can be manipulated. This line of thinking stresses the active
nature of man - that we are actors who strive to create a shared
reality which is fulfilling, not organisms merely *reacting* to
environmental pressures or running out our lives as machines
wound up by nature. Equally important is our *interactive*
nature: we learn who we are from the actions of others, and the
world within which we live is a social world made up of *people*,
not just things and pressures. Most fundamental of all is the
tenet that the proper subject-matter of psychology is the
meaning of actions and situations, not the causes of behaviour.
We may live in a physical world, and to some extent our

potential for action may be limited by physiology or environmental conditioning. However, what is seen as more important is the fact that we are thinking, probing and interpreting beings who live in a complex culture and are free, up to a point, to put our own construction on events and act accordingly.

For many who adopt this approach, one consequence is that autobiographical accounts such as the McVicar extract assume a far greater importance than they have since the last century. The predominant trend in psychology since the turn of the century has been away from introspection and towards observables which can be measured 'scientifically' by the 'objective' observer. In this article, however, little of the work cited is quantitative in its approach; most is based on case-studies or the accounts which actors give of their own lives. Researchers of this kind put great stress on understanding events from the point of view of those involved in them rather than imposing their own pre-formed theories on complex events. They see as a weakness of quantitative approaches (experiments and surveys) that they are artificial social interactions, and therefore that any results may be specific to the research situation and not generalizable to life outside it. For their greater ecological validity and their greater sensitivity to the unexpected, however, 'qualitative' researchers pay the price of low internal validity: they do not have the strengths of the quantitative approach at its best, that the conclusions may be seen to follow rigorously from unambiguous evidence and that the research could be repeated by others. The tension between the quantitative and the qualitative is an unresolved dispute in the social sciences, and we would not presume to attempt its resolution here.

It would not be possible, in this limited space, to cover all the diverse lines of thinking, research and 'therapy' we are classing together as 'the new psychology', so we have concentrated on giving a flavour of several different approaches, using particularly those authors who have taken their examples from the field of crime. The study of crime has not in any way been central within this paradigm: unlike the sociological Symbolic Interactionists, whose research has often concentrated quite deliberately on oppressed or stigmatized classes, psychologists in this genre have by and large found *all* behaviour problematic, and the concept of deviance is a trifle foreign to them. Where work has been done on deviants it has mostly been in the field of mental health, as an expression of the growing 'anti-psychiatry' movement (see, for example, Szasz, 1962). However, the work cited here on the determination *of* the self *by* the self and on the constraints on such freedom cannot but be influential in any future psychology of crime.

One name that will crop up very frequently in this paper is that of George Kelly, an American psychologist and counsellor, whose 1955 book 'The Psychology of Personal Constructs' has

had a profound influence on the whole of social psychology.[2]
Kelly puts forward the idea that we see the world not as given
but as constructed: we *make* the perceived world (and particularly the social world) by interpreting the ambiguous evidence
which we receive in the light of our developed theories about
what kind of world it is, and we act in order to test our
theories and thence to modify them in the light of experience.
Kelly's model of man is that we are scientists, seeking to
explain the world in just the same way as the psychologist or
sociologist seeks to explain it. In various sections you will
meet John Shotter's philosophical and psychological analyses
of man's essential freedom to determine his or her own self,
the analysis of behaviour as reflecting value-systems (exemplified here in the work of Nick Heather), and examination of
how 'criminals' actually see themselves and how they may
deliberately shape their worlds. We also discuss constraints
on freedom - Berne's analysis of socially provided 'scripts'
which we may be constrained to follow, the work of Bateson
and Laing on interaction and communication within the family
system, and how the wider structure of society may impose
constraints at the level of the individual. Our intention is to
emphasize how man can be constrained by factors outside
himself and still be a determining factor in his own development, because our actions and the way we construct the social
world themselves have an effect on the nature of that world.

In this article, in other words, we have reviewed the
pressure in recent psychological thought towards an emphasis
on social perception, symbolized meaning and deliberate action
rather than on the kind of research that stems from a deterministic model of man and looks for causes external to the
person. Such thinking itself embodies a model of man, of course,
and an extremely optimistic one: man is self-perfectible, given
a little help. We may be trapped into actions which are in fact
the unmediated product of our circumstances or our upbringing, rather than truly the result of rational decision, but this
is because we are unconscious of the causal factors involved.
Once we become aware, the self itself is able to act as a causal
agent, and we take control of our lives again. In any case,
causation is not a linear process but a circular one where
human action is concerned. We may be determined in part by the
social world, but the social world is itself in part determined
by our actions and decisions.

3 FREEDOM OF ACTION

The 'man' which this kind of psychology sees as its field of
study, then, is a rational actor making rational choices. Freedom of choice and action is much more heavily stressed than
are constraints upon action and 'causes' of behaviour (within
limits which are discussed in sections 4 and 5 below), and

this is the crucial distinction between the new psychology and the more determinist lines of theory we discussed in our earlier articles. The individual is seen not as a passive recipient of experiences and as passively reacting to internal or external 'forces', but as actively making sense of the world and taking action in order to discover it or to change it. Moreover, this 'construction' of the world, which replaces the more passive concept of perception, is seen as an essentially *social* process – the social world is the most important part of our reality, and other people are our main source of information – so that this kind of psychology stresses very heavily the importance of *communication*.

In the recent history of psychology, the notion that we *construct* our reality rather than simply *perceive* it is closely associated with the name of George Kelly, as we said earlier. His philosophical/psychological theory of how the human mind operates has had a profound influence upon both clinicians and academic researchers (the latter perhaps because the book also included a paper-and-pencil test which is still regarded as one of the best ways of describing individual experience systematically). Kelly posits that the man or woman in the street or in the laboratory is no less of a scientist than the observer or the experimenter. Both make tentative propositions about the nature of the world stemming from a more or less integrated body of theory, and test them by taking action and observing the outcome. Our perception is not a process of receiving information but rather one of construing evidence, and we do not interpret in a vacuum but make sense of the world by means of theories about it. Kelly's position is therefore most compatible with a strongly individualist perspective. Each of us perceives the world through his or her own construct-system, which is the most important thing determining our actions, and so individuals are expected to be unique. Looking for 'general laws' of the mechanistically causal variety is seen as a fairly pointless activity. Construct theory does not set out to offer general causal laws or explanations. In fact, Kelly explicitly rejected normative psychology, though there may be considerable similarities between individuals with particular patterns of construing which allow some tentative or superficial generalizations to be made.

Three aspects of this view of man are crucial not just for Kellian psychology but for this whole way of thinking about what it is to be human. The first is that we do not receive facts, but rather interpret evidence to conform with our pictures of the world (or modify the pictures); we *control*, to an extent, how we perceive the world. I may have believed, for example, (i) that sudden and clipped speech is a sign of anger, (ii) that people who show anger are likely to reject me, and (iii) that it is certain aspects of *my* behaviour which underlie this rejection. If I then find that someone whom I thought liked me starts talking to me in this fashion when I have not been

behaving in ways which I know produce anger, something in
my set of linked theories must be wrong, and the wrongness
will have consequences. Perhaps the 'signs' are *not* always
associated with anger, so I had better be careful how I interpret them. Perhaps the person doesn't really like me (so, to
my loss, I have a smaller circle of friends), or anger isn't
always linked to rejection (which would be a relief, but is a
risky proposition to believe), or rejection can be only a
temporary affair (another risky proposition, entailing treating
someone as a friend even though he has temporarily rejected
me). Or perhaps my mere presence can provoke anger, and
I am more of a worm even than I thought I was (a conclusion
that could herald the onset of clinical depression). Whatever
reinterpretation I adopt, I change the world by adopting it;
my world is my construction, not something given and unchang-
ing.

There are considerable similarities between this approach
and the 'cognitive balance' and 'cognitive dissonance' theories
put forward by such writers as Heider (1958) and Festinger
(1962). The shared postulate between the two systems of
thought is that we strive for logical consistency in our view
of the world, so that we have to re-make our attitudes to suit
our experience. Someone hating alcoholics and finding that
an old friend has lapsed into drink must rethink his attitude
to alcohol, or separate the drinking from his judgments about
the person who drinks, or lose a friend. (If he also believed
himself steadfast in his relationships, he must either begin to
doubt this belief - and come to dislike himself - or more likely
re-define the drinker as someone who has changed beyond all
recognition or was 'never a real friend' - i.e. shifting the
blame from himself to the drinker.) Kelly does point out,
though, that some individuals may instead elaborate 'subordinate' constructs - for example, I may define my alcoholic
friend as a special case because of his various childhood problems. A construct system may lack logic to an outsider but
still retain a personal consistency.

The second important point, closely related, is that our
world is shaped as much (or more) by our prior expectations
as by the immediate facts. It has been pointed out by the
sociologist William Runciman (1966) that it is not absolute level
of income or amount of 'trappings of wealth' which determine
whether people consider themselves poor or 'hard done by', but
their perception of how well others whom they regard as comparable are faring. Many writers, including Roth (1962) and
Sapsford (1979), have illustrated how people in institutions
measure their term of service as long or short not just in months
or years but rather in comparison with the group of fellow-
inmates with whom they feel their 'case' has something in common; indeed, finding such a 'comparison-group' is a crucially
important task for them. What we feel we are entitled to expect
shapes not just our actions, but also our perceptions of what

we have received. One graphic example of such a process at work is given by Tittle (1972) in his description of a therapeutic institution, some of whose inmates were voluntary patients while others were committed there by the criminal justice system. He found that perceived deprivation was much more salient in determining mode of socialization than was actual deprivation. Those inmates who saw themselves as 'prisoners' had restriction of liberty as the aspect of the regime which made them take this stance; those who saw themselves as 'patients', on the other hand, gave the large amount of freedom they experienced as the reason. Prior expectation of how much freedom to expect made some see the institution as a prison by comparison with their expectations, while others saw it as a hospital. To some extent the attitude adopted was independent of legal status: there were voluntary patients who saw themselves as prisoners, and prisoners who saw themselves as patients.

A third important point to stress is the extent to which the concept of *communication* is central in this model of man. As we have already seen when considering the Symbolic Inter-actionist approach of writers such as Mead and Goffman, there is much strength in the notion that we learn who we are and what to expect from our interactions with others and thus that the nature of our reality is crucially affected by social inter-action. Kelly argues further that empathy lies at the core of interaction, that we interact effectively with others only when we share in their construing and can understand how they perceive reality. Only thus can we make sense, within our own pictures of the world, of the actions they may choose to take.

For the study of criminal and deviant behaviour, one of the many possible corollaries of this line of thought might be that we should treat 'deviants' as rational actors entirely responsible for their chosen behaviour. For example, John Shotter (1974, 1975) proposes that autonomous self-agency requires a view of the world as *indeterministic*: that is, that not everything in the future is *wholly* determined by what has gone before. In such a world the future has multivalent possibilities. People may or may not choose to follow their social programming, for example, at a particular point in time. Once the choice is made, we have rendered the world determinate, but before the choice it was an indeterminate world. 'We have to form our own principles to shape our own conduct as agents in an intrinsically indeterminate world'. (We are, to quote Sartre (1943), 'condemned to be free'.) This line of thought would require us to treat 'deviant' behaviour as deliberately running counter to the 'socially-approved norm'.

However, the deviant himself may not perceive himself as being in any way deviant. Fransella (1968, 1977) discusses the idea of individuals rejecting the deviant actions from their construct of self: for example, stutterers, or the arsonists who divorced themselves (conceptually) from those who are

likely to commit arson - the incongruent activity becomes
regarded as 'non-self', not typical of oneself, having no
implications for one's general behaviour. One way of rejecting
responsibility might be to cast the blame firmly on external
circumstances.

Julie Holborn (1975), for example, has done an interview
study of prisoners who had persistently committed petty
crimes which revealed that they tended very much to attribute
their crimes to external factors rather than to take responsibility for them, and that they had little faith in their own
ability to reform. When the men to whom she talked were asked
how they came to commit their current offence, about a third
mentioned some sort of problem as a reason. A majority spoke
of practical (generally financial) difficulties, but other 'causes'
were interpersonal (generally matrimonial) problems, sudden
loss of wife or mother, or specifically psychological conditions
such as depression. She notes, however, that 'the prisoners'
problems were seldom confined to one area of life, but were
spread across their entire range of social functioning'. More
than half of her sample said they had committed their crime
with associates, and many blamed their friends or the general
milieu for their offences. Some of the pubs and clubs which
they frequented provided an atmosphere in which crime was
made easy, or even the stimulus for violent offending. Some
said they had become involved with the 'wrong crowd' at work
and gone along with them - particularly during times of personal
or financial stress. Some men followed trades - such as that
of scrap-metal dealer - that afforded opportunities to drift
easily over the borders of the law from time to time. Heavy
drinking was another factor mentioned by half the sample, and
was typically associated with petty and futile offences (see
Banks and Fairhead (1976) for a somewhat similar account).
Only a quarter of her sample 'did not relate their offences to
other aspects of their lives, but emphasised that they offended
by deliberate choice'. The remaining three-quarters were
inclined to shift the blame from their own deliberate choice to
the influence of drink, friends, milieu or situational problems
(Holborn, 1975, p.8; see Matza, 'Delinquency and Drift' for
an extended and well-theorized account of how such feelings
may find their expression in confirmed deviancy):

> The research worker was particularly struck by how easy
> most prisoners felt it was to get into trouble. Indeed, it
> seemed to demand no more effort than getting caught in a
> shower of rain ... They seem to feel that chance operated
> by producing situations which lowered their resistance to
> such an extent that it became inevitable that they would
> drift into trouble ... Some felt that they had more control
> than others in preventing the occurrence of these situations,
> but shared the common lack of faith in their capacity for
> choice when actually overtaken by pressure of events.
> [They have the] feeling that they drifted into trouble

rather than actively sought it.

Another way of coming to act deviantly without classifying oneself as 'a deviant' would be somehow to mislearn the 'rules' of communication and thus to misperceive the social reality in the context of which the act is committed. One such case is reported by Tschudi and Sandsberg (1977) in a paper on Kellian therapy. Their approach is to analyse the construct-system of their client - his or her beliefs about the nature of the world - in order to identify areas in which sets of beliefs about consequences of actions act against each other to trap the client into damaging behaviour.[3] The rapist, for example, may hold views of the world which amount to saying, on the one hand, that approaching a woman as a fellow human being leads inevitably to damaging rejection. If he wants to approach a woman at all, therefore, he *must* do so by force or fraud. But this in turn leads to a 'relationship' which does *not* satisfy his real needs, and no amount of cognitive restructuring of the world as one in which his behaviour is reasonable can over-come its basic lack of satisfactory power even for himself.

> There is ... no reason to imply ... that rapists enjoy their
> conquest and show of power ... The rapist cannot risk
> rejection and turns to exhortation. This bars him from
> intimacy, and he is stuck with the pathetic position that
> 'she really enjoyed it'. (p.345)

The authors also point out that some rapes are able to occur, in part, because they draw on social 'games' that have rules, and the conclusion is already 'scripted' implicitly in the open-ing moves. He draws up next to a woman, for instance, and opens his car door, offering her a lift. She has either to make a scene or to accept - those are the rules. He is then free, however, to use another set of rules and consider that she has already accepted an embryonic sexual advance, and so the rape scene progresses. Each participant in the interchange may thus believe - or at least be able to assert - that it is the other who deviates from the 'accepted rules'.

It is also possible to commit proscribed acts in accordance with values which are shared by *non*-deviants; in other words, the 'deviants' would be those people who act in *statistically* non-deviant ways on values which are shared by everyone, but who happen to get caught and therefore labelled. This process is illustrated in some recent work reported in 1980 by Nick Heather, again drawing on Kellian theory and methods. Heather noted that many studies of the 'values' which underlie our behaviour posit two conflicting value-systems: (i) the conventional values attached to work, family, etc., and (ii) a 'subterranean' value-system which emphasizes the search for adventure and excitement, a disdain of routine work and an acceptance of aggressive toughness as a proof of masculinity. Several sociological theorists (e.g. Albert Cohen, 1955; Sutherland and Cressey, 1966; Cloward and Ohlin, 1961) would claim that delinquents have adopted the second of these value-systems at the expense of the first, but writers such as Matza and Sykes (1961) have argued that delinquents and non-delinquents share *both* systems of values, differing only in the means they adopt to achieve their goals. (These approaches are discussed by Muncie and Fitzgerald in article no.18.) Heather attempted a crucial test of these theories by comparing a group of 'respectable' middle-class school prefects with an age-matched group of working-class offenders in a penal institution, using a variant of Kelly's technique to elicit the values to which they subscribed. Analysis of the results showed two independent value-systems corresponding to the two described above and, in line with Matza and Sykes, both value-systems were elicited from both groups, with the conventional values being dominant for most people in both groups. (A subsidiary study established that the differences were not simply class based.) However, he did find that the 'subterranean' values appeared to be *stronger* for the delinquents than for the prefects – they accounted for a larger percentage of the variance.

Finally, one may self-consciously accept that one is 'a deviant' and change one's world accordingly. Muncie and Fitzgerald discuss Lemert's concept of 'secondary deviation', the process whereby labelled individuals come to see themselves as identified with the group of people bearing the label and as sharing their norms and values rather than the societal ones. (It is fairly easy to see this process as an expression of what Heider and Festinger talk about: the individual changes his natural comparison group to reduce the dissonance between his sense of self-value and society's negative attitude towards him.) That this kind of cognitive restructuring of the world can indeed occur is also illustrated by Heather's work: in a few cases he found that the subterranean value-system *was* actually the dominant one, and these were the boys with the longest delinquency records, so we might reasonably see this as an empirical illustration of the secondary deviation process in action.

So, to summarize, we may see deviant behaviour as rational in three different ways. It may be (a) not only rational but entirely normal, or (b) rational but within a misperceived world, or (c) normal and rational only in the light of a variant system of values. Options (b) and (c) imply some limitation upon our freedom of action or choice, because they beg the question of where the misperception or the variant value-system comes from. Three kinds of answers have been given to this question: (i) socialization in the psychological sense – early learning and upbringing, and particularly the interpersonal impact of the family, (ii) socialization in the sociological sense – the impact of major institutions such as schools and the media (and the family again) in transmitting norms and values, and (iii) the fact that we are born into an already existing culture and set of social structures upon which we can have some formative impact but which we are not free entirely to recreate.

Most of the rest of this article looks at (i) and (iii) - the impact of the family (drawing on writers such as Berne, Laing and Bateson) and the slowly developing corpus of speculation about the impact on the individual of the wider society that has grown out of the writings of Marx and the arguments of women's liberation movements, for example, about the constraints on consciousness implicit in how society is organized.

4 THE DEVELOPMENT OF THE 'SELF'

The primary concern in this section will be to consider how the development of the 'self' occurs in relation to others. In particular the emphasis will be on the function of the family in constructing a reality for its members. However our concern will not be, as it was predominantly in Dallos's article no.17, with causal explanations of the influence of parents on the children, but with a consideration of how realities, including the individual member's sense of self, come out of a process of negotiation or interaction. This is substantially different from Kelly's approach in one important respect: for Kelly, reality is unique to the individual and intra-psychically defined, while the interactionist perspective proposes shared, mutually defined realities arising from a process of negotiation. For example:

'He's a really vicious man!'
'Yes, but he's not as bad as Eric, though.'
'No, I suppose he's not *too* bad, really.'
'On the other hand, I can see your point ...', etc.

The possibility of such an approach was hinted at in Dallos's earlier discussion of Kohlberg's cognitive theory of moral development, where 'progress' is seen as dependent on the interactions between the child and others. For example, parental discipline was not seen in a unilateral way - that is, as the parents' effect on the child - but as a negotiation in that the effect of the discipline was regarded as mediated by the child's interpretation of it.

We want to concentrate on two main approaches to considering the family: the interactionist and the existential-phenomenological. Both of these explain deviance in terms of the interactions within the family. Our concern will be mainly with examining actions within the family context that may be labelled by 'outsiders' as deviant but are not deviant *within* this context.

Social programming

As a prelude, we can consider the work of Berne (1966, 1974, 1977), who brought an essentially psychoanalytic basis to his work but became concerned in the *transactions* that occurred between people in terms of three ego states which we are all seen to possess: 'parent', 'adult' and 'child'. How we employ

these ego states in adulthood was seen to be a result of a
process of 'social programming', primarily in childhood, whereby
in adult life we act out, almost as if robots, various *games*
and *scripts* that significant socializing agents (in particular,
parents) have taught us.

Berne became particularly interested in types of social
interactions which involved a series of such *ulterior transactions*. He called these 'games'. The game 'Cops and Robbers'
is seen to be an adult version of the childhood game of 'hide
and seek' in which the fun lies in being found. If Dad or friends
find the child too quickly then there has not been enough
suspense, and if they take too long, the child becomes impatient
and is likely to give clues such as making a noise. Berne suggests that the adult 'professional' criminal represents a child
who is a 'bad sport' and does not want to get caught. These
criminals come to court rarely in comparison to those who *are*
playing 'Cops and Robbers' properly, for example, the burglar
who leaves 'his calling card in gratuitous acts of violence'
(Berne, 1966). The straight professional takes care to leave
no clues, whereas the 'Cops and Robbers' criminals act as if
they *want to be caught*. (See also the chapter on 'extremes'
in Cohen and Taylor, 1976.)

In Berne's view, most games involve an element of *psychopathology*. The underlying goal is often the resolution, usually
in a maladaptive way, of some psychological conflict stemming
from childhood. Berne trained in psychoanalysis and uses
concepts derived from Freud's work to explain the causes of
games. In the case of 'Cops and Robbers', the psychological
gain is seen to do with 'material indemnification for old wrongs'
and being caught therefore provides a form of reassurance.
Note how similar this is to the Freudian explanations concerned
with atonement for guilt covered in Dallos's article - Moral
Development and the Family. Berne argues that parents teach
their children how to behave, think, feel and perceive (perhaps
intentionally, perhaps unawares). For example, a father says
to his son: 'Don't let me catch you going to that house on
Bourbon Street, where there are women who'll do anything you
want for five dollars.' Since the boy didn't have five dollars,
he stole it out of his mother's purse, intending to go to Bourbon
Street the following afternoon. But mother happened to count
her money that same night and found it where the boy had
hidden it, and he was caught and punished. He learned his
lesson well. 'If I'd gone down right after dinner instead of
putting it off until the next day, everything would've been
all right.' (The account is paraphrased from Berne, 1966.)
Berne's point is that the instructions for the child's life-
script are implicit; father's very prohibitions in a sense define
and elaborate possibilities for the child which he or she may
not have otherwise considered. As in the 'Cops and Robbers'
game, the outcomes for the individual may also be scripted,
such as the inevitability of losing or the need to win. A grim

example is given by Berne (1977) of a man of twenty-three
who shot his fiancée and then turned himself in. At his trial
he stated repeatedly that he had felt from the age of nine
that he would end up in the electric chair. Apparently he had
spent his life, in some sense, heading towards this goal, eventually using his girl-friend as the means for 'setting himself
up'. Liberation from this pre-programming is achieved by a
realization of one's essential autonomy which is fostered in
transactional group therapy by helping the individual to discover his or her particular scripts and games.

Interactionist views

Though offering an interaction approach, Berne's system is
too general in that the three ego states cannot adequately
account for the complexities of the self. Mead (1934) and others
also emphasize how the 'self' develops from a process of social
interaction, but take a 'molecular' as opposed to Berne's
'molar' approach. The 'I' is the response of the organism to the
attitudes of the other; the 'Me' is the organized set of attitudes
of others which are assumed. The attitudes of the others constitutes the organized 'Me', and then 'I' react towards their
perceptions of 'Me'. The 'I' and the 'Me' constitute the two
components of the self. Following John Shotter's views, the
'I' is the source of freedom and agency in individual action
which responds to or considers the interactionally constructed
'Me'. Part of this 'Me' comprises the roles that individuals feel
that they have to play: 'I'm a doctor' is essentially the 'I'
looking at the 'Me' constructed by expectations arising from
others as a result of my interactions with them. Cooley (1912)
elegantly describes this process in terms of 'a looking-glass
self': that is, we see ourselves in terms of the reflections of
ourselves from the people with whom we interact.

Fundamental to the interactionist view, then, is that individuals are never considered in isolation from their interactive
partners (including *imaginary* ones). It proposes that it is not
possible to understand an individual's actions without examining
the influence of others in shaping it. Actions are considered
in terms of patterns of interaction, a 'dance' of the significant
participants. The emphasis on the 'here and now' of interaction
as most essential for explaining an individual's actions, rather
than their previous history, makes intra-psychic approaches
such as trait/type theories of personality redundant. The
approach is to consider patterns of interaction within the
individual's most influential social groups, such as the family,
as crucial, rather than attempting to reify by the use of labels
such as 'delinquent'.

For example, an interactionist account of sexual deviancy
considers the building up of sexual *meanings* from interaction
with others, particularly at the critical stages of adolescence.
These interactions with others provide the mirror by which
individuals see themselves. Further to this, through others,

early experiences may be retrospectively interpreted and ascribed sexual meanings – for example, as a homosexual encounter or wish (Plummer, 1975). The individual's present and past actions (and possibly the future) are given meaning by the persons with whom he or she characteristically interacts. Deviance, then, is seen very much as developing within the context of the individual's most influential socializing groups, such as the family and peers.

Such an interactive approach has interested a number of investigators, one of the most influential being Gregory Bateson. His approach had been to consider this interactive circular process of communication in social groups, such as the family, in terms of a systems theory or cybernetics approach. He refers (1972) to the 'cybernetics of the self': that is, the 'self' is seen in terms of the patterns of interaction and communication that the person engages in with others.

To Bateson, one of the fundamental attributes of 'mind' is a responding to differences in order to self-correct – a process illustrated at a very primitive level by the thermostat in a central heating system. Man is seen to be essentially such a system, albeit a very complex one, responding to differences in the outside world (which includes the social environment). This view suggests that the self's development in terms of autonomy and self-control has been misconceived in terms of a *linear* process of man exerting control over things, whereas it is more appropriate to consider these in terms of a *circle* of interaction between man and his world, each affecting the other.

Within the family the individual is continually interacting with others, and these interactions define the self. The family is seen as developing rules or norms representing the nature of these relationships around which there is variation or negotiation – e.g. 'Don't argue with Dad.' If, however, 'trouble starts to brew', there may be general uneasiness, attempts to change the topic or in some extreme cases someone might start to act or talk 'crazy' or even become 'physically ill'. As a result of these stabilizing manoeuvres the norm or rule holds, until next time.

Bateson (1979) points out that systems theory proposes a 'stochastic' view of the self and the family; that is, a tendency towards change and evolution as a result of a random process (as in evolution and the principle of mutation). Hence, together with a tendency for equilibrium, families also have a tendency to change or evolve to new balance points or rules. Pathological or disturbed families particularly are seen as being 'stuck' or incapable of breaking out of fixed patterns.[4] For example, violence or deviance in or outside the family can lead to change or reappraisal of the rules, but in some families the change mechanism has somehow stuck so that such acts can become part of the pattern. When these acts are particularly destructive eventually someone may become physically or psychologically damaged.

Bateson provides an explanation of how the family can become stuck by a consideration of the communications involved. He suggests that the negotiation of the family rules can be seen in terms of the two basic aspects of communications. Any communication is seen as conveying two messages; the 'literal' part which conveys factual information, and the 'metaphorical' part which conveys a set of instructions as to 'how the message is to be taken'. This metaphorical part contains definitions about the relationship between the communicators; for example, 'you are to see me as dominant in relation to you' (Jackson, 1965).

Various sorts of 'double-binds' may result if the participants do not share a definition of the relationship. For example, they may see each other's behaviour in different ways: 'I was just helping you' - 'No you weren't, you were trying to get in my way.' In some cases one family member typically engages in this and appears to refuse to accept the definition of the other. The following is an example of such a process (Bateson, 1972, p.217):

> A young man who had fairly well recovered from an acute schizophrenic episode was visited in hospital by his mother. He was glad to see her and impulsively put his arm around her shoulders, whereupon she visibly stiffened at this contact and he quickly withdrew his arm. She then asked, 'Don't you love me any more?' He then blushed and she said, 'Dear, you must not be so easily embarrassed and afraid of your feelings.' He was able to stay with her only a few minutes more and following her departure he assaulted an aide and was put in the tubs.[5]

Such double-binds are seen as occurring in all families, but are more frequent or characteristic of highly disturbed ones.

In particular, friction sometimes leading to violence may develop where there is an attempt by one member to change a relationship which has been mutually defined as 'complementary' (as in dominance-submission, sadism-masochism, nurturance-dependence) to one which is 'symmetrical', that is where each partner responds in the same way. Adolescence often represents such a situation with the son negotiating a new man-man (as opposed to child-man) relationship with the father. Other members of the family typically behave so as to counteract the struggles that ensue (typically to do with life-stages such as adolescence, parenthood, retirement), or else serious problems can develop.

A central aspect of family life, certainly in the West, is that of a power hierarchy and the associated conflicts that arise from the need for parents to make the children do certain things, such as toilet-training, hygiene or diet. This of necessity interferes with the child's autonomy as a person, with his or her own feelings and wishes. The child's co-operation can often be solicited, giving the illusion of choice and therefore undamaged self-esteem, but on occasion it seems inevitably that a show of force is resorted to. Punishment, in the form of smacking, for example, constitutes a complementary relationship of the form 'I am bigger than you.' Aside from this, the Newsons suggest that normally the strength of the smack is less important than its significance as defining the boundaries of the above power and status relationship – showing the child how far he or she may go with impunity and thus (paradoxically) defining an area of security and safety (1976).

smacking happens as one element in a *pattern of understanding* between the mother and the child. The mother has a fairly consistent set of principles, roughly corresponding to her authoritarian or democratic attitude, which she hopes in time to communicate to the child by her words and actions, and through which she expects to socialize him into the sort of person she values; and, within this framework of principle, she not only smacks but tries to evaluate for the child the meaning of her smack. It is probably true to say that the precise form of an aggressive act is less important than the fact that it has occurred; and it is certainly true that the objective force of a smack is less significant to the child than the spirit in which it is delivered.

The Newsons argue that excessive use of physical punishment represents a sense of insecurity in the parents, since it undermines their 'credibility as benign charismatic parents who do not need to punish their children in order to gain their co-operation and respect'. How they feel about resorting to violence, though, in turn reflects their own childhood experiences and their basic political attitudes – their views and expectations as to the 'proper' way of managing power relationships.

Addiction

Bateson has provided an example in his writings of how the onset, the escalation and particularly the *maintenance* of addictive conditions such as alcoholism (which can in themselves be classed as criminal acts or contribute to their occurrence) can be explained within the framework of the alcoholics' interaction with real and imaginary others. Though less concerned with the *onset* of drinking, Bateson lends support to the widely held notion that the initial drinking of the potential alcoholic represent an 'escape' from the pressures of life. However, he makes the interesting proposal, similar to Kellian views, that alcoholics are partly trapped by their particular philosophy. Though Kelly views the individual as having a unique set of constructs, it seems obvious, as Bateson points out, that certain constructs are inherent or characteristic of particular societies ('superordinate' constructs). For example, in Western society one such widely held perspective would be a version of dualism couched in a competitive mind-over-matter view of the world which may be reinforced by family and friends.

The drunken state may function to relieve the individual
of the pressures of life, such as feelings of failure or inadequacy, partly by a dulling of their need to control or compete.
Bateson's central concern, though, is with the consequent
changes in the person's social system: relatives and friends
take on *complementary* relationships - forbearance, pity, pro-
tectiveness - which contrast strongly with their previous
competitive or symmetrical relationships (as shown in typical
male social drinking - for example 'Another drink?' - 'Yes,
if you're having one'). The alcoholic's pride may now be hurt,
and so a phase of drinking may be entered into where others
(or *internalized* others) are felt to be challenging them to 'beat
the bottle'. Becoming drunk now provides a relief from the
torment of this challenge. The characteristic outbreaks of self-
destructive or aggressive acts can be seen as evidence of
such torment.

The life of alcoholics is then seen to alternate between periods
of sobriety in which they are involved in a symmetrical (competitive) relationship with real and/or imaginary others and a
drunken condition where they are in a complementary state of
being looked after by others and defeated by the bottle.
Bateson (and Alcoholics Anonymous) suggest that the only
escape from this deadly struggle is for the alcoholic to 'hit
bottom'. In Bateson's view this represents a change of philosophy which allows them to accept a complementary relationship
with 'the bottle', that is, an acceptance that it is stronger
than they are and there is little point in trying to fight it or
'control' themselves. Without this, periods of sobriety may
occur, but alcoholics become 'cocksure' and feel a need to 'show
off' that they have beaten it. Obviously such an acceptance
is supported by a resolve, and support from others, not to
drink again at all, otherwise 'hitting bottom' leads to total
self-destruction. Quite frequently salvation is accompanied by
taking on possibly less destructive complementary relationships
such as with God, in the case of religious conversions.

The initial use of other (illegal) drugs similarly can be seen
as a form of escape, possibly escalated by initially competitive
usage - though in the case of marijuana it has been argued
that competitive usage is more likely to be a feature of the
novice still soaked in competitive philosophies than the more
experienced 'dope head', since the euphoric and sedative effects
are seen as reducing aggressive and competitive tendencies
(Leary, 1970; Masters and Houston, 1966). In addition, since
awareness and other abilities are unimpaired and in some cases
enhanced, the formation of complementary relationships between
users and family, friends, etc., is less likely. The general
liberalization of attitudes towards usage has also reduced the
formation of such relationships, though this is not the case
with so-called 'hard drugs'.

Bateson suggests, then, that individuals' actions should be
regarded in terms of the influential systems such as the family

in which they are involved. In the case of the alcoholic, for
example, the other family members come to need his or her
alcoholism in order that they can play their complementary
roles.[6] That this is the case is further suggested by evidence
of families where another member may take on a particular
deviant role when the initial deviant is removed from the family
or when a 'cured' deviant falls back into the role on returning
to the family (Haley, 1973, 1976).

Existential phenomenology
Earlier in this article the work of Mead was mentioned briefly
in an explanation of the formation of the 'self' as an interactive
process. This was a central consideration of R.D. Laing, who
employed some of Bateson's formulations on communication and
in particular double-bind processes. Laing's particular concern,
however, was with 'experience' and the development of the
'self' in terms of the person's relationships with the others in
the family (though the findings from families apply to any
influential social group in the person's life). Laing considered
that 'all identities require another'. The other, by his actions,
may impose on self an unwanted identity. But the 'self' develops
as a process not only of the person's experience of the actions
of others but also of the person's experience of the other's
experience of them. He termed these perceptions *metaperspec-*
tives (e.g. 'I think she sees me as violent', 'I know you think
I might steal from you', and so on). Hence the individual
develops a sense of self though this range of experience based
on the actions of the others in the family towards him or her,
and also upon an *assumption* of their experience of him or her.
This is then a circular process, since subsequently the person
is likely to act differently. (For example, 'They think I'm
violent. Stuff them!' (scowl, kick, etc.). All of which may
confirm to the others that he or she *is* violent.) It is in such
ways that the individual becomes moulded into a particular
person or way of being in the world. That is, the self is
always relational, in that it involves others. The self formed
in the family is seen as fundamental in explaining the way people
are, how they see themselves and consequently how they act.
For example, they may have come to view themselves in deviant,
pathological or criminal ways, so that is how they will act
inside and outside the family.
   An interesting illustration is provided of how we may *induce*
others to accept our view of them. We persuade a person to
be something or someone (sometimes other members of our past
as opposed to immediate family) (Laing, 1971, pp.121-2):
   Mother (to fourteen year old daughter): You are evil.
   Daughter: No I'm not.
   Mother: Yes, you are.
   Daughter: Uncle Jack doesn't think so.
   Mother: He doesn't love you as I do. Only a mother knows
         the truth about her daughter, and only one who

> loves you as I do will ever tell you the truth about
> yourself no matter what it is. If you don't believe
> me, just look at yourself in the mirror carefully and
> you will see that I'm telling the truth.

Though this dialogue may appear sinister, we can see how
common it is by substituting 'nice' words like 'pretty', 'clever'
or 'good' for 'evil'. In other words, Laing considers that this
kind of value-opposition is normal - i.e. common - behaviour.

The sense of self formed in the family is seen to be extremely
important and enduring into the individual's adult life outside
the family. Laing suggests that we cling to these identities: we
can be a happy person, sad, criminal and so on, but most
importantly we must *be someone*. A destruction or disconfirma-
tion of one's identity can be a terrifying and damaging experience leading to desperately pathological (self-destructive and
violent) acts. Laing provides a case-history of John, the son
of a prostitute and a naval officer, who was disowned by his
father following his (John's) failure to become a naval officer
in his turn. According to Laing, his father had taught him
that he was his son 'not unalterably as is normal', but that
'You are my son if I say you are, and you are *not* my son if I
say you are not.' This inconsistency and conflict subsequently
led John to commit various acts, as a result of which he became
labelled as a psychopathic delinquent (violent and with no
moral awareness). In Laing's view the father had succeeded
in destroying John's identity as his son.

This state is described as an 'ontological insecurity'; that
is, a feeling of not really existing. Being told by his father
that he was not his son any more meant he didn't really exist,
he had no identity. Such a state throws people into confused,
desperate actions. Stealing can be seen in some cases as such
an attempt to gain control, 'If you steal what you want from
the other you are in control; you are not at the mercy of what
is given' (Laing, 1965, p.98).

There is a wider sense in which the individual experiences,
and is experienced in, the family system. Ferreira (1963)
refers to a set of beliefs, the 'family myth', shared by all the
family members, concerning each other and their positions
and relationships in the family. Unlike the 'front' or social
facade it is an inner image - that is, the way the family appears
to its members - to which they contribute and which they strive
to maintain. This myth may be mapped onto the external world,
so that in some cases the sense of hopelessness felt, for
example, about the conflict between East and West may be a projection of childhood feelings of hopelessness about the conflict
between parents (Laing, 1971).

Laing has suggested that in many ways various types of
psychopathology and deviance are a means of living in a crazy
world. The individual transfers his 'family myth' onto society
and others, but the reverse also happens: society is transferred into the family. 'Some families are run more on

organizational or business lines; some are institutions' (Laing, 1971, p.12). Again the process is circular, for example in the sense that the man's business relationships may already be a transference of his family relationships. To speculate briefly, the cliché family of the Mafia boss presents a facade of kindness which contrasts starkly with the murderous business relationship. The true nature of the relationships and expectations, the 'family myth', become apparent in the power struggles which may ensue; for example between father and the 'son and heir'. Laing and Cooper (1964) make a passionate statement of how the family is a microcosm of the nature of the relationships in society. In particular it is seen as a 'carrier' or perpetuating agent of people's alienation, estrangement and abuse of each other. Society and the family affect and mirror each other in an infinite spiral of 'projection' and 'introjection'. Laing and Cooper suggest, therefore, that the family provides a setting in which much human misery and suffering can develop. The 'death of the family' is therefore seen as inevitable in order to build a healthier society. Laing never quite completed this argument or explained how the 'revolution' was to be achieved; nevertheless if you are not convinced by Laing's view of the power of the family in making you the way you are, just look at yourself in the mirror carefully and wonder if he's right!

Having arrived at this point, we seem to be at an impasse. We have argued that individuals are essentially actively constructing their world; that they are free, but that this freedom is constrained by the family in one sense and in another that the very choices a person has are structured by the family. To some extent, then, we are proposing the family as some sort of causal agent, as Dallos did in article no.17. There are fundamentally important differences, though: here it has been argued that the individual ultimately decides, but that the range of choices sensed to be available are limited by the family; as provider of the child's initial picture of the world and as the system within which the adult's action is located, the family may severely constrain not only our freedom of action but even our ability to perceive the world. Some recent work using a Kellian approach suggests that families develop a set of shared constructs, rather like avenues in a town, along which they decide to move òr not (Procter, 1981). Rather like Ferreira's family myth, these are shared by all the members. The important point is that deviant activity may be construed as acceptable by the family, but individuals play different parts in the family, so not all will be deviant. As Ferreira points out, the part an individual plays must be viewed in terms of the individual *and the relationship*; each represents what the Chinese call a 'chien': a fabled bird that had only one eye and one wing. Two such birds must unite for flight to be achieved.

5 SOCIETY AND ALIENATION

In the previous section, reference was made to the role of the wider society in influencing particular views of the world shared by its citizens - the alcoholic's epistemology, for example - and also to the rules, norms and values that govern and maintain family life. The emphasis, though, has been on how the individual's construction of reality and his sense of self are products of interchange with the immediate socializing groups, and in particular the family. However, there have been interesting attempts to relate the individual to broader social realities in terms of the effects of institutions, class structures, religions and the law. Marx (1844) in his early writings, for example, produced an account of the psychological effects of a capitalist economy and philosophy which extended and criticized Hegel's ideas of 'alienation'.

Essentially Marx suggested that the nature of capitalist economy and philosophy is such as to estrange man from his true nature. He regarded man's essential nature as concerned with a need to be free, to pursue the realization of his creative powers and abilities through meaningful work. The products of such work were objects representing man's essential being and harmony with nature. Such products are an essential part of ourselves; in selling them or being forced to give them away we are removing a part of ourselves. An individual's pride, self-esteem and spirit are represented by these products of his work. In capitalist societies, Marx argued, there is a disruption and brutalization of this natural process. The worker is paid to produce for someone else and the relationship is such that his products are never in fact his. He becomes merely a producing unit, and the more he produces the less value each item has. He never or rarely sees his own products again; like a child taken at birth, a relationship is never established.

This estrangement or alienation from one's products, Marx would suggest, leads to an alienation from one's self, one's true nature. Man begins to see his entire existence in terms of being some sort of a production unit. Man's essential difference from animals is his capacity to be conscious of his existence and life-activity and subject it to his will. He engages in labour to satisfy his needs, biological and spiritual. However, for alienated man, virtually his entire existence becomes subjugated to work that barely satisfies his biological needs and ignores his spiritual ones. Such self-alienation has profound effects not just on the individual but also on his relationship with others. In seeing the self as an object under the *power* of others such as his employers or her husband, he or she comes to see others in similar terms. Others, then, are subjects which can possess or be possessed by him. We can all be bought. Yet others have argued that all women in our society are even more profoundly alienated from their selves than are some men, seeing the alienation as inherent in patriarchal rather than specifically capitalist structures.

Reich (1934) developed the theme of alienation particularly
in relation to sexuality, which he considered in a psychoanalytic
framework. In his view, part of the alienation which occurs
in capitalist societies was a denial of sexuality as an essential
part of human nature. By sexuality, he further meant free
loving, fulfilment of one's 'orgiastic potential'. In particular he
pointed out (Millett, 1970, p.164) how the

> mystical idealization of chaste motherhood ... in Nazi
> Germany was ... a particularly efficient means not only of
> utterly equating sexuality with procreation but also of sup-
> pressing and inhibiting female sexuality altogether and con-
> verting it into a state-directed process of human reproduc-
> tion for what were often lethal ends.

This process of alienation leads people to see themselves and
others as objects dispossessed of part of their true nature -
in particular their sexuality. Because of the restrictions in
society on sexuality as confined to marriage, and views of it
as immoral, individuals can experience a frustration of their
sexuality. In Freudian terms the need becomes transformed to
guilt and the individual reverts to earlier stages of psychosexual
development such as the anal-sadistic (see Dallos's article no.17).
Hence sexuality can become brutalized, resulting in rape and
sadistic acts towards such depersonalized objects.

To Reich it seemed that this process was essentially to do
with the individual's view of himself, an alienated view, including a divorce from his true nature. Various feminist writers
have picked up this theme (Greer, 1971; Millett, 1970): the use
of women as sexual *objects* by men in patriarchal societies rather
than an acceptance of them as human with needs and feelings.
(It is not difficult to see how hard it is for men to regard
women other than as objects, when many societies, including
capitalist ones, in fact encourage people to see themselves and
others in alienated ways.) Part of this process is represented,
for example, in legal practice regarding the crime of rape.
A sexually experienced woman may be greatly disadvantaged,
since the issue can turn from a consideration of her feelings
and intentions towards the particular man to a view of her as
'immoral' and therefore an object or 'fair game'.

A number of 'movements' or 'schools of thought' have
developed in recent Western society, such as certain factions
of the women's movement and 'humanistic psychology', which
try to combat what they perceive as a growing tendency in
our culture to treat people as objects and thus ultimately to
regard oneself as an object. Whether their roots be political,
sociological or psychological, and whether or not they accept
marxist perspectives on how to understand society's problems,
they have in common their desire to identify and to combat the
simplified and stereotyped views of ourselves that we hear
so often (and so often uncontested) from the socializing agencies
of society that we come to accept them as self-evident truths.

The other perspectives of crime discussed in this article may also be seen as a part of this attack on depersonalization.

A number of writers have emphasized how such an alienated view of man pervades psychiatric treatment (Laing and Cooper, 1964; Brown, 1974; Heather, 1976; Kennedy, 1980), in the excessive use of 'chemotherapy', for example, to treat so-called illnesses such as depression and forms of deviancy. Particularly women as the professional child-minders have been dealt with in this way rather than being permitted an investigation of the roots of their depressions. Laing and Cooper also point out how the family in fact represents a microcosm of society's values and inculcates them in its members. There may be a *collusion* on the part of the man and wife to accept the 'medical mode', since it is less threatening. That the individual could hope to challenge society itself, including doctors, psychiatrists and criminologists, is too much to expect. As Laing points out, one of the protections a family is seen to offer is from the outside world, which is fantasized to be extraordinarily dangerous. Through such a terror the family perpetrates its own oppression on the children. In fact Cooper's (1971) desperate prescription for improving society involves the short-circuiting of this process of alienation by bringing about the 'death of the family'. However, Phil Brown (1974) criticizes this as a tactic that is more likely to scare members of average families away from any such move. Instead, he suggests that the family's economic role as a massive consumer unit (which, having been seduced to false needs, upholds such materialistic society) must first be changed.

6 CRIME AND THE NEW PSYCHOLOGY

In this article we have considered the extent of human freedom and the constraints upon it. We found considerable evidence that the human being does not so much *see* the world as *construct* it, and that our past expectations and the whole corpus of our theories about the nature of the world are what shape our actions quite as much as the pressures of the environment. The new psychology, as we have called it, takes this discovery and builds on it a picture of a man as perfectible once he has realized and overcome the constraints on his (or her) freedom of action and understanding. (The perfected man or woman would be a social and interactive being, however; as with the image of the one-winged bird we used at the end of section 4, it may take two to fly.)

We have also looked at the nature of the constraints on freedom or understanding. Berne, for example, has shown that many people may 'take the easy way out' and slot into some prescripted life-style that offers immediate gratification but at the expense of any room for development or fulfilment in one's life. Laing and Bateson have shown the perils of faulty communication, the way in which the child's world may be misshaped by it, and how the family unit can shape the child for its own purposes in ways which may leave him unable to act autonomously as an adult. Much of this article has been about faulty socialization and imperfect development of the autonomous self, because we believe that many of our constraints derive from early experience. However, such constraints may perhaps be overcome. Even Freud, of all psychotherapists the most strongly and avowedly determinist in his theories of how we are motivated, believed that imperfect socialization could be corrected once we become aware of the constraints on our thoughts and reactions; to foster this awareness is a central aim of psychoanalytic therapy.

This approach to the 'problem of crime' could lead fairly naturally to three different pictures of what it is.

(a) On the one hand, some people who commit crimes might do so because they are still caught in the constraints, acting rationally on their own terms but within a world which they have fundamentally misconstrued. Examples would be people trapped in one of the 'scripts' that Berne discusses or in the 'rape script' described in section 3 above, or children whose perception has been distorted through socialization, as described by Bateson or Laing. Such criminals' greatest need would be for help to overcome their constraints or to reshape their social milieu, though it might be necessary to put them under restraint, pending such help, for the protection of others.

(b) However, we could distinguish within this broad class a second type whose 'constraints' are that they grew up in a variant subculture - their behaviour is subculturally normal but deviant with respect to the wider culture. (This possibility is discussed by Muncie and Fitzgerald in article no. 18.) Here the ethics of intervention are much less clear cut and must depend on one's view as to the proper use of social power, a topic taken up by Hall and Scraton in the last article.

(c) On the other hand, the ideal self-actualized individual who has overcome the constraints of culture and upbringing might still commit crimes. One could act rationally, and within a world which is correctly construed, but still be deliberately at variance with the generally accepted norms. (One might consider, for example, that those who refused to bear arms, this century, in Germany or Vietnam were deliberately in conflict with the norms of their society, but one could not reasonably call them irrational or constrained.) Here, presumably, they would have quite simply to act as they saw fit and to take the consequences of their action in terms of social sanctions. This is one of the bases of the 'justice' perspective to correction which has grown up during the last twenty years - that there should be 'tariff' penalties for offences and that the whole notion of treatment is invidious.

Thus far, as you will see, the approach of the 'new psychologists' adds nothing very startling to debates on social policy:

only two kinds of approach to policy suggest themselves, and
we are still talking of a mixture of 'treatment' and 'penalty',
though perhaps one based on a more enlightened and empathic
understanding of why offences occur. Nor does it solve the
dilemma about 'responsibility', on which current forensic practice is impaled. The law is often forced to assert that a defendant is at one and the same time a product of his environment
or upbringing and yet responsible for his actions, and the
new psychology nails itself to this self-same cross.

This is one criticism of this perspective, that it has not yet
been applied extensively or successfully to questions of social
policy - except perhaps in the field of psychiatry, where it
has been more fully developed. Two other and more far-reaching
criticisms may also be raised, and both amount to charges of
naivety on the part of psychologists.

One such criticism concerns the *model of man* which underlies
this style of thinking. The new psychologies have far more in
common with the attitudes of, say, Rousseau or John Stuart
Mill than they ever could with those of Hobbes, in that they
have as goal the perfection, emancipation or self-actualization
of the individual, and in that they see the constraints on self-
actualization as emanating from society and from history. The
varied lines of this perspective differ as to whether the individual is perfectible: Laing or Bateson, for example, would
probably doubt that one can ever be free of society's influence
or in control of the pressures which others bring to bear on
one. None the less, if there were such a thing as a perfected
individual freed of the unconscious constraints imposed by
society and the family, he or she would not commit rape or
other such 'caused' offences. This is not a discovery of the
new psychological perspectives, or even a hypothesis; no
evidence whatsoever is needed to establish its truth. Rather it
is an axiom within the humanist approach, true by definition:
if a man commits rape, he is not to be counted as self-actualized.
We should be aware that this value-laden picture of the perfect
man underlies the new psychologies, though at varying depths.
We should also be aware of the opposite, but equally value-
laden, axiom of many determinist psychologies: that man is
inherently selfish and is held in check by society.

A second basic criticism concerns the *model of society* that
many such psychologists hold. Some few, particularly those of
marxian leanings, have tried to come to grips with the nature
of the wider culture and society within which individuals live
and into which they are born - we looked at a little of this work
in the previous section. Somehow implicit in much of humanist
psychology, however, is a picture of society as made up
entirely and only of individuals, and one which has no history.
We speak of 'overcoming the constraints of culture', but some
would argue that they cannot be overcome from within - that
society must change before we can even perceive that we are
constrained - because the power of the existing order shapes

the child irrevocably. More important, we speak of social reality and the social order as negotiated between individuals, but a realistic appraisal must admit that many aspects of the wider social world (e.g. the law and the courts) are not open to individual negotiation.

Yet we do see considerable strengths in this way of thinking about what it is to be human, even after admitting these limitations. To say that the constraints on our freedom may be stronger than this rather simple presentation of the new psychology's approach may have suggested is not to deny the existence of freedom, because social causation is not linear but circular; we ourselves create some of the pressures which impel us and others. 'Men make history, but ... not in circumstances of their own making,' Marx points out in 'The Eighteenth Brumaire'; none the less, as he admits, men do make history.

Notes

1 By 'causes' or 'determinants' here we mean such factors as can be observed and are external to the person. One may also speak of ideas, thoughts or feelings as 'causing' or 'determining' behaviour, but this uses the words in a different sense. It does not imply, for example, that I can necessarily change your behaviour by manipulating something which is external to you.

2 For a shorter and eminently readable account of Kelly's perspective, see Bannister and Fransella (1971).

3 The therapeutic techniques that have been developed out of Kelly's theories typically involve three stages: imagination, acting (or role-playing) and behavioural incorporation. The individual is asked first to imagine different ways of being and behaving which might be more acceptable or desirable to him than his current repertoire. Then he or she is asked to act these out for a while - playing the 'roles' in conjunction with the therapist, or trying them out in some part of his daily life for a few weeks, with a view to becoming able to *predict* how people will respond to him if he changes. Finally, if the response is acceptable to him, he incorporates the change into his behavioural repertoire and becomes different. (For a fuller account see Bannister, 1977.)

4 There is an implicit unclarity in Bateson's writing as to whether he is talking only about families labelled as having a 'pathological' or 'disturbed' member, or whether he thinks it necessarily true that fixity is itself pathological. On the whole he appears to take the latter position: that a potential inability to adapt to changes in circumstance, even without present disturbance, is to be seen as pathological.

5 'The tubs' are the baths used in some psychiatric hospitals as a form of treatment - or rather, control - for distressed and violent patients.

6 Note, however, that Bateson is not necessarily talking

of the family as a *cause* of the behaviour, but rather as
a system which may help to maintain it; the behaviour has
a function to play within the family.

References
Banks, C. and Fairhead, S. (1976), 'The Petty Short-Term
Prisoner', Barry Rose, Chichester.
Bannister, D., ed. (1977), 'New Perspectives in Personal
Construct Theory', Academic Press.
Bannister, D. and Fransella, F. (1971), 'Inquiring Man',
Penguin Books.
Bateson, G. (1972), 'Steps to an Ecology of Mind', Ballantine,
New York.
Bateson, G. (1979), 'Mind and Nature: a Necessary Unity',
Wildwood House.
Becker, H.S. (1963), 'Outsiders: Studies in the Sociology of
Deviance', Free Press, New York.
Berne, F. (1966), 'Games People Play: the Psychology of Human
Relationships', Deutsch.
Berne, F. (1974), 'What Do You Say after You Say Hello?',
Deutsch.
Berne, F. (1977), 'Beyond Games and Scripts', Grove Press,
New York.
Brown, P. (1974), 'Toward a Marxist Psychology', Harper &
Row, New York.
Cloward, R.A. and Ohlin, L.E. (1961), 'Delinquency and
Opportunity: a Theory of Delinquent Gangs', Routledge &
Kegan Paul.
Cohen, A.K. (1955), 'Delinquent Boys: the Culture of the
Gang', Free Press, Chicago.
Cohen, S. and Taylor, L. (1976), 'Escape Attempts: the
Theory and Practice of Resistance to Everyday Life', Allen
Lane.
Cooley, C.H. (1912), 'Human Nature and the Social Order',
Scribner, New York.
Cooper, D. (1971), 'The Death of the Family', Allen Lane.
Ferreira, A. (1963), Family Myths and Homeostasis, 'Archives
of General Psychiatry', vol.9, pp.457-63.
Festinger, L. (1962), 'A Theory of Cognitive Dissonance',
Stanford University Press.
Fransella, F. (1968), Self-Concepts and the Stutterer, 'British
Journal of Psychiatry', vol.114, pp.1531-5.
Fransella, F. (1977), The Self and the Stereotype, in Bannister
(ed.), 'New Perspectives in Personal Construct Theory'.
Goffman, E. (1970), 'Asylums: Essays on the Social Situation
of Mental Patients and other Inmates', Penguin Books
(Doubleday, New York (1961)).
Greer, G. (1971), 'The Female Eunuch', MacGibbon & Kee.
Haley, J. (1973), 'Uncommon Therapy', Norton, New York.
Haley, J. (1976), 'Problem-Solving Therapy', Harper & Row,
New York.

Heather, N. (1976), 'Radical Perspectives in Psychology', Methuen.

Heather, N. (1980), The Attraction of Delinquency, paper presented to scientific meeting of British Psychological Society's Division of Criminological and Legal Psychology, King's College, London, 14 March.

Heider, F. (1958), 'The Psychology of Interpersonal Relationships', Wiley, New York.

Hobbes, T. (1651), 'Leviathan, or the Matter, Forme and Power of a Common-wealth, Ecclesiasticall and Civill', Andrew Crooke, London (recent edition, Penguin Books, 1968).

Holborn, J. (1975), Casework with Short-Term Prisoners, in McWilliams, W.W. (ed.), 'Some Male Offenders' Problems', Home Office Research Study no.28, HMSO.

Jackson, D.J. (1965), The Study of the Family, 'Family Processes', vol.4, pp.1-20.

Kelly, G.A. (1955), 'The Psychology of Personal Constructs', (2 vols), Norton, New York.

Kennedy, I. (1980), Unmasking Medicine (the Reith Lectures, I), 'Listener', 6 November.

Kohlberg, L. (1968), The Child as Moral Philosopher, 'Psychology Today', vol.2, pp.25-30.

Laing, R.D. (1965), 'The Divided Self', Penguin Books.

Laing, R.D. (1971), 'The Politics of the Family, and other essays', Tavistock.

Laing, R.D. and Cooper, D. (1964), 'Reason and Violence', Barnes & Noble, New York.

Laing, R.D. and Esterson, A. (1970), 'Sanity, Madness and the Family: Families of Schizophrenics', Tavistock.

Leary, T.F. (1970), 'The Politics of Ecstasy', MacGibbon & Kee (also Paladin).

Lemert, E.M. (1951), 'Social Pathology: a Systematic Approach to the Theory of Sociopathic Behavior', McGraw-Hill, New York.

Marx, K. (1844), 'Der achtzehnte Brumaire des Louis Bonaparte', Stuttgart (English edition, 'The Eighteenth Brumaire of Louis Bonaparte', Central Books, 1977).

Masters, R.E.L. and Houston, J. (1966), 'The Varieties of Psychedelic Experience', Holt, Rinehart & Winson, New York.

Matza, D. (1964), 'Delinquency and Drift', Wiley, New York.

Matza, D. and Sykes, G. (1961), Juvenile Delinquency and Subterranean Values, 'American Sociological Review', vol.26, pp.712-19.

Mead, G.H. (1934), 'Mind, Self and Society', University of Chicago Press.

Mill, J.S. (1859), 'Essays on Liberty', Parker, London.

Mill, J.S. (1863), 'Utilitarianism', W. Ridgway (recent edition, including 'On Liberty', Dent, 1972).

Millett, K. (1970), 'Sexual Politics', Doubleday, New York, (also Fontana).

Newson, J. and Newson, E. (1976), 'Seven Years Old in the Home Environment', Allen & Unwin.

Plummer, K. (1975), 'Sexual Stigma: an Interactionist Account', Routledge & Kegan Paul.

Procter, H. (1981), Family Construct Psychology: an Approach to Understanding and Treating Families, in Walrond-Skinner, S. (ed.), 'Developments in Family Therapy', Routledge & Kegan Paul, pp.350-66.

Reich, W. (1934), 'Dialektische Materialismus und Psychoanalyse', Copenhagen (English version in 'Selected Sex-Pol Essays 1934-37', Socialist Reproduction, 1973).

Roth, J. (1962), 'Timetables', Bobbs-Merrill, Indianapolis.

Rousseau, J.-J. (1762), 'Du Contrat social: ou, principes du droit politique', Amsterdam (English version, 'The Social Contract', Dent, 1978).

Runciman, W.G. (1966), 'Relative Deprivation and Social Justice: a Study of Attitudes to Social Inequality in Twentieth-Century England', Routledge & Kegan Paul.

Sapsford, R.J. (1979), Learned Helplessness, Reactance and the Life Sentence, unpublished PhD thesis, University of London.

Sartre, J.P. (1943), 'L'Etre et le néant', Paris (English edition, 'Being and Nothingness', Methuen, 1969).

Shotter, J. (1974), What Is It To Be Human? in Armistead, N. (ed.), 'Reconstructing Social Psychology', Penguin Books.

Shotter, J. (1975), 'Images of Man in Psychological Research', Methuen.

Sutherland, E.H. and Cressey, D.R. (1966), 'Principles of Criminology' (6th ed.), Lippincott, Chicago.

Szasz, T.S. (1962), 'The Myth of Mental Illness: Foundations of a Theory of Personal Conduct', Secker & Warburg.

Tittle, C.R. (1972), 'Society of Subordinates', Indiana University Press.

Tschudi, F. and Sandsberg, S. (1977), Loaded and Honest Questions: a Construct Theory View of Symptoms and Therapy, in Bannister (ed.), 'New Perspectives in Personal Construct Theory'.

20 Law, class and control

Stuart Hall and *Phil Scraton*

THE EMERGENCE OF THE 'CRITICAL PARADIGM'

In 'Humanizing the Deviant' (article no.18), Muncie and Fitzgerald chart the emergence of a 'radical' approach to deviancy
theory in terms of the shift from the study of deviant behaviour
to the 'posing of definitional and structural questions'. This
movement away from the liberal-pluralist positions which
characterized 'mainstream' criminology in the 1940s and 1950s
was a gradual process, achieved by a series of internal modifications to the theory rather than by a single sharp break.
Initially, deviancy theory offered only an implicit critique of
'consensus' theories of the social order by focusing on the
plural worlds of the deviant, the relativity of social rules, and
the meaningful rather than the 'pathological' nature of the
deviant act. However, it became clear that social theorists of
deviance would also have to explain the dominant character of
the rules from which the deviant 'deviated'. 'Becoming deviant'
had to include an account of the institutional arrangements
by which deviance was defined, labelled and processed.
　The marking of deviance was thus identified as part of the
way a society defined its 'limits of tolerance'. The social reaction to deviance was therefore an essential part of the process
of maintaining social order. But 'social reaction' was principally
located in those social agencies and institutional practices
which Becker and others had vividly illustrated in their studies.
These agencies did not 'determine' the deviant act, but they
provided a set of organizational consistencies for its processing
and treatment. They had to be included in the analysis. This
constituted a crucial bridge, linking earlier emphases on 'the
self in social interaction', with more institutional arrangements.

Source: article commissioned for this volume. Stuart Hall is
Professor of Sociology and Phil Scraton is Lecturer in Criminology, Faculty of Social Sciences, the Open University.

'Labelling theory' added a further dimension. It posed the
questions which Becker (1967) first framed: 'Who has the
power to label whom?' 'Which definitions of the situation stand
highest in the hierarchy of credibility?' Clearly the agencies',
not the deviant's. How, then, was this definitional power
exercised? By following this lead, deviancy theorists came to
confront the inescapable connections between the defining
agencies, the hierarchy of power, the maintenance of the
dominant social rules and the problem of social order. Deviancy
theory could no longer be restricted to 'appreciating' the exotic
worlds of the outsiders, since this marginalizing of certain
groups was only the reverse side of the process by which a
social order maintained conformity to its rules.

While 'deviancy theory' re-engaged with the substantive
issues concerning the social order and the nature of the state,
its conception of the state remained simple and generalized.
For Becker (1974), it included 'elites, ruling classes, bosses,
adults, men, Caucasians, superordinate groups' - a motley
assemblage. For Matza (1969), it was an all-encompassing
oppressive power - 'Leviathan'. For Lemert (1952, p.55), it was
simply '*the* societal control culture'. This generalized form of
social control was a catch-all conceptualization, embracing a
loosely defined set of programmes, agencies and institutional
interventions. Nevertheless, this shift in the direction of
'social control' questions provided part of the ground from
which the 'critical' paradigm emerged.

The sociological movement in law and crime
Developments within deviancy theory must also be seen in the
context of a longer movement which Hunt has characterized as
'the sociological movement in law' (Hunt, 1976b, 1978). The
early twentieth-century American development of a school of
'sociological jurisprudence' had attempted to examine the
external 'influence of social, economic, psychological and other
non-legal factors ... in the concrete content of legal propositions'. Roscoe Pound, a leading member of this school, characterized these influences in terms of the play of different
interests on the law - an approach not very different from that
of the pluralists. Later, the 'Realist' school attempted to use
the law as an instrument of reform and posed questions about
the 'social consequences' of the law. However, no strong conception of the state emerged from these approaches.

Early sociology also focused on the social foundations of law
and crime, Durkheim (1938, pp.65ff.) identified crime as 'normal',
law as the embodiment of the normative order of society. For
Durkheim, however, legal constraint was a form of general social
control arising, not from the state or the ruling classes, but from
society. Society, in effect, 'policed' itself. By contrast, Weber's
concern with the rationalistic and universalistic form of law
which had evolved in capitalist societies of the West was firmly
linked to market relationships and rational calculation. Weber

acknowledged that the law implicates all the other relations of power in which its functioning is embedded. His conception of the legal function as a form of legitimate domination was underpinned by the fact that the state exercised a 'monopoly of legitimate violence'.

Marx and Engels wrote extensively about law and crime. Yet they did not develop a consistent analysis of either. They inherited a powerful but unsystematic view, common to the labour movement and oppressed social groups, that crime was a product of the competitive and exploitative conditions of capitalism and that the law often constituted an instrument of class domination. Marx analysed the role of law in creating the conditions from which early capitalism emerged; he also analysed the role of law in 'bourgeois ideology'. He often treated law as a part of the political, juridical and ideological 'super-structures' which arose from and corresponded to the economic foundations or 'base' of capitalism. Engels attributed crime to the economic conditions of the poor, and the 'demoralizing' effects of exploitation and competition – a view he shared with other nineteenth-century social investigators (discussed by Frank Heathcote in article no.16). He sometimes argued that crime represented the 'nascent revolt' of the oppressed in the social war against capital. Marx, however, took a pessimistic view of the criminalized classes – the 'lumpen proletariat' – whom he regarded as a parasitic social force.

In the early years, there was no distinctive school of 'marxist criminology'. Karl Renner's (1949) 'functionalist' account stressed how law had facilitated the transition from feudalism to capitalism. Willem Bonger (1969) made the first consistent attempt to provide a marxist framework for the analysis of crime. He sought to establish a causal link between crime and material conditions by looking at the effects of competition and 'egoism' on 'criminal thought'. This focus on 'egoism' produced an analysis more 'Durkheimean' than 'marxist'. The previously unknown work by the Soviet jurist Pashukanis (1978) on the bourgeois form of law has only recently become influential. The marxist concern to establish a link between crime and 'demoralizing' conditions has many parallels with the descriptive environmental analyses discussed by Heathcote (p.358). However, the latter were more concerned with controlling these 'breeding-grounds' of crime than with abolishing them.

Towards a 'radical criminology': wider contexts
The emergent 'critical' paradigm was further influenced by the fracturing of the mainstream paradigms in sociology itself, and the accompanying political ferment in Europe and the USA in the 1960s. This helped to radicalize social science whilst politicizing society itself.

The dominant approach within mainstream sociology in the 1940s and 1950s was that of an empirical science. The dominant theoretical paradigm – structural functionalism – assumed that

society was an integrated, functioning 'whole'. Social order
was maintained through the functional integration of the major
institutions, which formed a 'social system' into which a plurality
of individual social groups and interests was incorporated.
Around this institutional order there clustered a 'central value
system', a focus of value-consensus and of authority, which
maintained a set of common values: 'an approximately consensual pattern' to which the great majority subscribed (Shils,
1961, p.119).

This model was underpinned by a set of 'domain assumptions'.
The most important of these was that advanced industrial
societies were 'pluralist', able to manage competing interests
and achieve an 'ideal' balance between order and diversity.
The main institutions did not constitute a unified 'power structure' because they exercised 'countervailing power' over each
other, this system of 'checks and balances' helping to keep
society open. Thus no structural barriers stood in the way of
the eventual incorporation of the whole of society within 'the
centre'. Class interests, material differentials and ideological
divisions had, it was argued, markedly declined.

Structural-functional and 'pluralist' approaches tended to
converge around the concept of a 'common value system' or
consensus. Parsons and Shils (1951) and Parsons (1951), for
example, stressed the 'integrative' elements within the social
system. Shils (1975) argued that class conflicts had been
'domesticated'. Daniel Bell (1960) foretold the 'end of ideology'.
Lipset (1960) also argued, from a more pluralist perspective,
that the fundamental problems of the industrial revolution had
been solved: the workers had achieved industrial and political
citizenship, the conservatives had accepted the welfare state,
and the democratic Left had abjured the excesses of state
socialism on the grounds of its dangers to individual freedom.
This composite sociological vision took the USA as the prime
'pluralist' case, and its dominance within the social sciences
coincided with the growth of the USA to world power status,
in the early days of the Cold War. Pluralism thus became the
'sociological face' of American global hegemony.

This hegemonic moment was shattered by political events in
the 1960s. In the USA, the growth of a civil rights movement
against racism in the 'Deep South', spreading to the northern
cities, drew attention to the contradictions in the 'consensus'
of pluralist democracies, and the palpable failures to 'incorporate' large sections of the population. The persistent differentials between blue-collar workers and the managers of
the great corporate enterprises undermined the affirmation of
the disappearance of class differentials, and the pluralist
version of the distribution of wealth, power and opportunity.
This was followed by the rise of student protest, the national
agitations against the Vietnam War, the 'radicalization' of many
sectors of American society, the crisis in the cities, the growth
of the 'counter-cultural' movements among young people and

the beginnings of a new feminism. The intimate relationships
between military expenditure, the great corporations and 'big
government', within what President Eisenhower called 'the
military-industrial complex', became the object of political agitation. C. Wright Mills (1956, 1969) argued that these echelons
of power formed a 'power elite', which had become an 'irresponsible history-making institution' in the dangerous conditions
of nuclear stalemate. The policies of this 'power elite' - in
welfare, law-making, foreign investment and military policy,
power relations pursued on a global scale - ceased to be viewed
as naturally benign. America, the paradigm case of 'pluralistic
affluence' in the 1950s, had become, by the end of the 1960s,
a society which some commentators described as verging towards
social disintegration.

These developments challenged and undermined 'pluralist'
and structural-functionalist orthodoxy. A searching critique
of the role of social sciences research in the formation and
implementation of American global policy and strategy was
mounted. Much had been made of the need for social scientists
to be 'value neutral'. But now, it was argued, the sociological
ideas of 'value neutrality', when practised within the parameters
of American corporate and military policies, had become little
more than a convenient cover for the institutional incorporation
of social scientists as a professional 'service sector' to the
military-industrial complex. Pursuing 'modernization' on a world
scale, it was argued, meant viewing programmes of containment
and control at home, and of intervention and subversion abroad
as mere 'technical' exercises. Many similar criticisms of the
sociologist's role as a technician of power were voiced by the
radical student movement in Europe (cf. Cohn-Bendit, 1969).
In the political ferment of the 1960s, the dominant pluralist and
structural-functionalist paradigms disintegrated and the
sociological fraternity abandoned theoretical and methodological
orthodoxy. Social scientists, confronting this disintegration of
their theoretical universe, had finally to face what Alvin Gouldner defined as 'the coming crisis in western sociology'.

Gouldner (1970, 1973) questioned the validity of 'value-
neutrality' in the social sciences and American sociology's
'methodological dualism'. He exposed the underlying 'domain
assumptions' of pluralist doctrine. There had been, he said,
a systematic evasion of the problems of structure and power.
The weight of his critique, however, rested on the role, position
and consciousness of the social investigator. Social scientists
could not abstract themselves from the conditions in which they
worked. His critique bore down especially sharply on criminologists. Helping to operate programmes of social control without questioning their wider objectives, they had made themselves into 'technicians of the welfare state'. Deviancy theorists,
who set out on their voyages of exploration and 'appreciation'
from their safe bases in Academia to discover the exotic
hinterlands of Bohemia, were in danger, he said, of becoming

social voyeurs - the 'zoo-keepers of deviance' (1968). Gouldner's
remedy was a 'reflexive' sociology, based on a synthesis of
marxism and functionalism.

These were the conditions from which a number of critical and
'radical' strands emerged. There was a revival of 'conflict
theory' - directly counterposed to 'consensus theory'. Theorists
such as Quinney (1970, 1974), Turk (1969) and Chambliss
(1969, 1975), applied 'conflict theory' directly to criminology.
Others read the attack on 'value-neutrality' as a clarion call
to a more overt radical political commitment, with sociologists
and criminologists taking up a clear 'partisan' stance. What
mattered, Becker (1967) asked, was 'Whose Side Are We On?'
Thus emerged a more explicit political commitment, directed
against the hidden agenda of 'control' behind the liberal front
of welfare policies. If 'social control' was a mode of defence for
the dominant social order, they argued, then 'deviance' must
be a form of 'proto-rebellion'.

One consequence of this was the growing 'politicization of
deviance'. There evolved a structural critique of the dominant
institutions, at home, of big business and the state, and of
the institutions of imperialism abroad: the 'true' criminals. This
analysis of the political consequences of the 'criminalization'
of deviance led to the growth of alternative academic institutions, like the School of Criminology at Berkeley and the Union
of Radical Criminologists in the USA, and - in Britain - the
work of the National Deviancy Conference (see Stan Cohen's
article no.13, p.220).

These organizations provided the framework for a convergence
of critical theory with radical political practice. They took up
a 'politics of support' for outsider groups - drug-users,
prisoners, gypsies, welfare claimants, homosexuals. The critical
analysis of the control aspects of welfare precipitated a radicalization of some social workers, especially in probation and
psychiatric care. Radical academic lawyers become involved in
tenants' movements, community action groups, neighbourhood
law centres. There was a revitalization of 'radical theory'.
There were, however, real difficulties in forging links between
this defensive politics of 'the outsider' and the more traditional
politics of working-class political and industrial struggle. This
presented problems for both political strategy and analysis.
It led some to question the element of romantic identification
within the politics of 'liberation', and the adequacy of the
theoretical positions on which this politics was based. This,
in turn, helped to deepen the analysis. What was required was
a new 'fully social theory of deviance', which could demonstrate
theoretically the connections between law and the state, legal
and political relations, the economic basis and functions of
crime. On this terrain, the links between a 'radical politics'
of deviance and a 'critical' version of marxist and neo-marxist
theories were finally forged.

Towards a 'new criminology'
One major effort to synthesize these trends and tendencies was
the volume entitled 'The New Criminology', by Taylor, Walton
and Young. It was this work which issued the explicit call for
a 'fully social theory of deviance' and launched a programme
of work. Such a criminology had to be developed, they argued,
in the real world through a commitment to the 'abolition of
inequalities in wealth and power'. Despite this explicitness,
'The New Criminology' owed its broad impact, in fact, to its
attempt to synthesize several different traditions. It retained
roots in the respect for the 'diverse and unique' worlds of
everyday life, which first attracted the social interactionists,
and the preoccupation with meaning and 'authenticity' which
characterized the work of the early deviancy theorists. It
appropriated the dimensions of power and social control through
its absorption of social reaction theory. It combined these with
a firmer location of 'the power to criminalize' in the social
relations, state structures and political economy of advanced
capitalism. The study of crime was to be grounded in material
conditions, the capitalist division of labour, and the structural
inequalities of wealth and power which the law helped to preserve. These previously hidden connections had to be restored:

> A full-blown theory [they argued] would be concerned to
> develop explanations of the ways in which particular his-
> torical periods, characterized by particular sets of social
> relationships and means of production, give rise to attempts
> by the economically and politically powerful to order society
> in particular ways.

In emphasizing the links between crime and a general social
theory, they adopted a broadly 'marxist' theory of the social
formation which, they proposed, would locate 'social control'
within a specific structure of power and exploitation. Thus the
'new criminology' attempted to forge a synthesis between neo-
Meadean interactionist theories, with their concern for 'meaning',
and a neo-marxist political economy, with its concern for
historical process and structure.

A social theory of 'criminality' was at the heart of this enterprise. 'Criminality' did not arise from biological inheritance,
flawed human nature, personality disorder or evil intent, but
was 'politically, economically and socially induced'. It arose
from 'material necessity' and 'material incentive'. Criminalization
was thus one of the principal means of containing the effects
of these conditions. Its function, ultimately, was to contain
resistance, to preserve a particular social order and to underpin a particular division of labour. A criminology not committed
to 'the abolition of inequalities of wealth and power' was bound
to be correctional, taking the generative structures of crime
for granted. Its objective was the most efficient and effective
means of containing the consequences of crime. The 'new
criminology' opposed traditional, correctional criminology as
the 'empirical emasculation of theories' and the 'depoliticization

of criminological issues'. The study of crime could not be hived off and compartmentalized from the analysis of crime within the context of the social totality. These arguments were made explicit in the programme for a 'new criminology' which was to consider (Taylor, Walton and Young, 1973, pp.270-6, summarized):

1 the wider origins of deviance in terms of the cultural, structural and socio-psychological conflicts within wider society;
2 the situated background of specific deviant action;
3 a grasp of the actual act in terms of wider origins and the situated background;
4 the immediate origins of social reaction;
5 the structural, wider contexts of social reaction;
6 the reception and effect of social reaction by and on the deviant;
7 the subsequent persistence and change in action.

In this scheme, such terms as 'wider context' and 'situated' are constantly repeated. The programme proposed to retain the focus on the immediate interactions between the deviant and the agencies of control, but to situate, contextualize and locate them in a broader, historical and structural framework. This was a bold and ambitious programme which, however, proved difficult to defend in its own terms.

This programme was developed further in a subsequent volume of essays entitled 'Critical Criminology' edited by Taylor, Walton and Young. The earlier volume (1973) had been based on an internal critique of conventional criminological theory: classical, positivist and structural-functional positions (see article no.14 by Jock Young). The authors now laid down a more politicized grid. Following the American exposure of the 'control' features behind the benign face of 'corporate liberalism', they elaborated their own exposé of the reformist limitations of the British variants within social democratic criminology. 'Reformist' criminology aimed to control crime by a rigorous application of law, while working politically to 'improve conditions' in the longer term. It regarded the state as an empty vessel, which could be used either as an instrument of correction or of reform. The new criminologists, however, identified the hidden element of 'control' within the reformist programmes promulgated by the Labour governments of the mid-1960s and 1970s.

More explicit was the authors' adoption, in 'Critical Criminology', of a marxist, materialist analysis. 'Laws', they quoted Marx as saying, 'perpetuate a particular mode of production' (1975, p.52). By this Marx meant that bourgeois law was predicated on the 'legality' of contract and the defence of property rights. Furthermore, law not only regulated the capitalist form of waged labour but, in its criminal and 'preservation of the peace' aspects, punished the property offences of the poor while maintaining stable and peaceful conditions for the 'regular' exploitation of labour. However, they also quoted Marx's further observation that 'the influence exercised by laws on the

preservation of existing conditions ... had to be examined
separately' (their italics: Marx 1971). This stressed the
complex, indirect and uneven correspondences between legal
relations and economic processes. The 'project' they proposed
was, therefore, neither simple nor straightforward, and called
for a major development in theoretical sophistication. How this
was to be done without falling back into reductionist arguments (i.e. regarding the law as simply the 'legal expression'
of the economy) was left largely unanswered by their programme.

The arguments advanced in 'Critical Criminology' remained
inconclusive. Yet the case was not fanciful or far fetched. Law
is not everywhere and anywhere the same. It is adapted in
form and function to the social relations which it regulates.
Capital accumulation and capitalist economic relations are based
on a system of law with a developed concept of property, contractual obligation and the rights of private possession as
three of its principal conditions of existence. The criminal law,
in its preoccupation with property crimes, maintains and
defends a particular division of the social product. The pursuit
of 'legal equality' in a society based on the unequal division
of wealth, property and power has meant that the law legitimates
and legalizes precisely those inequalities. These considerations
had led Marx to argue that laws 'help to perpetuate a particular
mode of production'. Yet there remained the dangers of
reducing the law to its economic functions, ignoring its specificity and the contradictory relation of different classes to it.
Did 'the rule of law' really function exclusively in the interests
of the dominant class? Critical criminology fell short of the
answers to these questions.

Marxist theory and Left idealism
At this juncture there emerged a number of critical debates
which have proliferated and expanded, leading to research and
analysis which have critically developed propositions which the
new criminologists first synthesized. They had invoked the
authority of Marx; but the warrant for a variety of positions,
many of them internally contradictory, existed within the
marxist tradition. Hirst (1975), for example, argued forcibly
against the whole project of developing a 'marxist criminology'.
He viewed crime as marginal to marxism, which was principally
concerned with the laws and tendencies of capitalism. 'Crime
and deviance are no more a scientific field for marxism than
education, the family or sport.' Marx, Hirst contended, was
concerned with how the working class could become an
organized political force, capable of overthrowing capitalist
relations. Criminals, who lived off class exploitation, often
exploiting - through crime - the exploited classes themselves,
were largely parasitic on capitalist relations. Hirst therefore
considered the identification of radical deviancy theorists with
the 'lumpen classes' to be a form of petty-bourgeois romanticism.

These were timely warnings against the temptation to read all crime and deviance as nascent forms of class struggle. Hirst questionably characterized the 'new criminology' as still imprisoned within a 'pre-given field of sociology' a charge which did less than justice to the break which had been made with correctional criminology perspectives. But he rightly questioned the mixed parentage and the theoretical eclecticism which characterized the 'new criminology's' early synthesis.

Jock Young confronted some of these complexities in - Working-Class Criminology - a contribution to 'Critical Criminology'. He addressed the problem of 'romanticism' inherent in radical writings, which tended to identify all crime and deviancy as forms of quasi-rebellion. These writings promised not simply an end to correctionalism, but also a utopian-libertarian suspension of *all* forms of law and the total 'decriminalization' of society. This implied that the 'rule of law' was unimportant to the oppressed. It ignored the threats to the working class itself under state socialism where there was no effective legal barrier to the exercise of arbitrary state power. It suggested that crime was only a ruling-class conspiracy, an ideological process, which had no material reality. Young has correctly criticized this position as 'idealist' (1979). He appropriated Gouldner's critique of the 'zoo-keepers of deviance' and associated with it the critique of 'exposé criminology', devoted merely to unmasking the wickedness of the system and the legalized illegalities of the powerful. The substitution of one villain for another, Young argued, did not change the terms of the explanation. It neglected the contradictory material of the reality of crime, and replaced analysis with simple moral outrage.

Against this 'romanticism', Young argued for a *new realism*. In a society predicated on private property and possession, the law's pursuit of property crime was not, as the romantics suggested, a moral outrage, but normal and predictable. The 'rule of law' was not simply a 'bourgeois myth' since it had a material basis in the interests which the poor have in ensuring that their scarce property is defended against illegal appropriation. If, Young argued, the working classes were not only the object of intensive crime control but also suffered the consequences of crime, then their 'stake' in social justice was not simply a reformist illusion, but contained a real and rational core, which no 'radical critique' could abolish. New theories could not be generated simply by turning old ones on their heads.

The critique of social control
Another warning shot fired across the bows of a 'radical criminology' was an influential paper by a historian, Stedman Jones (1977), which exposed two weaknesses in the idea of 'social control'. First, it could be used to designate a generalized 'pressure to conform' arising from society (the sort of

usage found in Durkheim). Some marxist approaches, however, attributed social control to the ruling classes, as a defence of their privileged social and economic positions. Within early radical criminology, use of the term 'social control' tended to fluctuate wildly between these two, incompatible meanings. Second, Stedman Jones criticized the functionalist nature of the concept. This suggested that society was 'normally' a smooth-running, well-integrated, functional unity in which the excessive exercise of 'control' was an aberration. This failed to take account both of the inevitable conflicts between capital and labour and the rooting of control, not simply in the normative order, but in the social relations of production. 'Social control', uncritically adopted from pluralist and conflict theories, had been substituted for 'consensus' at the centre of critical theory. Otherwise, both theories operated as 'mirror-images' of one another. Both advanced a simplified explanation of social order and legitimacy in complex industrial societies.

This stark opposition between 'control' and 'consent' was thus theoretically deficient. A 'consensual' view of society omitted the disciplining and regulatory functions of law. The 'social' control' perspective, however, adopted a purely coercive view of the law. In the first view, law, naturally, served the interests of all. In the second view, there was a permanent opposition between an all-coercive state, serving the interests of the ruling powers, and a permanently disciplined and powerless class of the dispossessed. Moreover, 'social control' explained the exercise of power almost exclusively in terms of the play of naked force and coercion. But 'power' also implies authority, the deference of the powerless to the 'right' of the powerful to rule, and the legitimation of power through the democratic process. The complex combination, in modern class democracies, of force and authority, of regulation and liberties, of coercive habit and legitimate consent, was barely recognizable in the picture offered by either of these alternative models. Specifically, the view of policemen, social workers, teachers, philanthropists and reformers as wholly disinterested beneficiaries of society was just as unconvincing as the 'social control' caricature of them as simply and solely the unconscious agents of state repression.

The evident inadequacies of the 'social control' concept, on which the first moves towards a 'critical criminology' were grounded, provided a powerful stimulus to new explorations in theory and research, and a deepening of the critical paradigm. The same impetus to overcome weaknesses of reductionist explanations of law and crime led also to research in other areas: for example, a marxist analysis of the state and the relations between economic, political and ideological processes, which has proved highly influential within 'critical criminology'. These developments in theory also produced the first attempts to develop a feminist criminology (Smart, 1976). Some of this recent work on crime and law is selectively reviewed in the second part of this article.

CURRENT DEBATES IN THE 'CRITICAL THEORY' OF LAW AND CRIME

The most difficult set of problems confronting 'critical criminology' in the wake of the publication and reception of 'The New Criminology' was how to conceptualize the relations between the law, crime and other processes in society. This problem arose from the principal 'domain assumption' of critical theory: the study of law and crime cannot be separated from the political, social and economic structures and relationships of society. This proposition was implicit in the call for a 'fully social theory of deviance'. In the rest of this article, we examine some of the many different attempts, explored by critical theorists, to settle this issue. We focus this review through a series of debates, concerning (a) the role of law in capitalist societies and the relation between law and the state; (b) the relationship between crime, law and class; (c) the debate concerning the notion of 'the rule of law'. We draw, without distinction, on the work of 'critical criminologists', on recent contributions to social theory and on historical research into crime and the law.

The role of law in capitalist societies

The most troublesome of the connections to explain is that between the law and economic processes and relationships. The difficulties arise from the fact that most attempts to show how the law relates to economic processes conclude by reducing the specificity of the functioning of the law to its underlying economic class content. This is clearly inadequate. In recent 'critical theory', we can distinguish two broad approaches to the question of the law and capitalism. There are those which tend to deduce the law directly from an analysis of capitalist economic relations; and those which deal with this connection via an analysis of the functioning of the state. We begin with the second set of debates.

Why approach law via 'the state'?

The state plays a central role in both 'liberal' and 'critical' theories, though the former does not often make a theory of the state an explicit part of its general understanding of law. In critical theory, questions of 'the state' have only recently begun to command extensive consideration. (In this respect, 'critical theory' has replicated a weakness in classical marxism, where the theory of 'the state' remained, until recently, largely undeveloped.) Liberal-democratic theory does clearly predicate its explanation of the impartiality of the law on a particular theory of the state. It argues that, in modern capitalist societies, the legal and political systems have been separated

off from the direct influence of economic interests. The power
to legislate and rule has been delegated to government and
state, which superimpose the 'general will' or interest of all
groups and classes over the many particular and competing
interests which inevitably arise. The legitimacy of the state
and the law thus depends on their universal and 'representative'
character, rooted ultimately in the 'consent of the people'. It
is the fact that governments legislate and the law adjudicates
'in the name of society as a whole', which renders their extraordinary powers legitimate. Where society is cross-cut by
competitive interests, only the state and the law can claim to
speak in the name of the 'general interest'.

If the state is rooted in popular consent, and represents
the 'general will', the law, which derives directly from laws
legislated in parliament, will also be universal and therefore
an impartial force for justice. While, by definition, law operates 'coercively', in that it prescribes what can and cannot be
'legally' done, it exercises such coercion in democratic societies
'legitimately', because it expresses 'the popular will'.

This 'consensus' view of law and the state assumes an absolute
separation between economic process and the field of action of
law and the state. This is expressed in the classic doctrine of
'the separation of powers'. This means that those who own and
manage the economic system cannot, simply by virtue of that
position, govern or exert a preponderant influence on the state,
or expect anything but 'impartial justice' from the law. They
have been 'separated' from direct political power (a) by the
introduction of universal suffrage - one person, one vote -
which distributes political power 'equally' amongst all citizens;
this forecloses the attempt by any single class interest to
'colonize' the state. This is reinforced by (b) the 'rule of law'
which compels the law to treat all 'legal individuals' equally and
impartially, to apply the law universally, without fear or favour.
Thus, rich and poor alike are 'equal in its sight'. These two
factors, it is argued, have broken the tendency for economic
power to be directly translated into systematic political and
juridical 'bias'. Indeed, whereas competitive economic relations
are based on inequality (e.g. the unequal relation between
those who possess the means of production and those who have
to sell their labour power for a wage), and produce a hierarchy o
social inequalities (the typical class structure of modern
capitalist societies), the state and the law are the sources of
a positive, countervailing, equalizing power. They compensate,
at the political and juridical level, for the unequal distribution
of economic power and wealth.

Liberal-democratic theorists acknowledge that this is a rather
'idealized' picture, and they have been obliged to develop a
number of substantial modifications to make it fit a reality
where wealth and power remain highly concentrated. Critical
theorists, on the other hand, have to explain not only these
continuities of wealth and power but the proposition that,

under capitalism, the state and law, which represent themselves
as the guardians of 'equality', actually function to maintain
and perpetuate structural inequalities. One way of demonstrating this 'illusory' nature of the bourgeois state and law is to
ask, not what the state *is* but what the state *does*.

The state ultimately depends on the capacity of the economy –
the basis of its productive wealth – to 'deliver the goods'. Goods
are produced and wealth amassed, in our type of economy, by
a set of economic relations which are 'capitalist' in character,
including the private ownership and management of the means
of production; the process of private capital accumulation; the
maximization of profit; the expropriation of surpluses, etc.
A situation where the state itself actively undermines its own
economic basis is hard to imagine. It must, therefore, be compelled to maintain the general viability of the economic system
and, if possible, create conditions in which efficient production
and profitability can expand. It must, therefore, also actively
maintain all those relations on which this type of economic
system necessarily depends. The state and (especially) the law
are also charged with maintaining public order and social
stability. In effect, this means maintaining the existing social
order by, for example, setting legal limits to the freedom of
action of those who might wish to challenge or transform it
radically, especially by 'violent' means. The 'defence of the
social order' logically and objectively entails maintaining that
form of order favourable to the existing disposition of social
and economic forces; and we can derive this without positing
any conscious 'conspiracy' on the part of judges, rulers,
politicians or administrators. Further, as the spheres of operation and intervention of the modern state have rapidly expanded,
so the state – in this view – has increasingly to intervene
directly in the economy, thus breaking down the classic separation. But it is also increasingly implicated in maintaining *all*
those institutions outside the economy on which the viability and
success of a capitalist society depends. For example, through
taxation, the state provides funds for a universal system of
education. The education system, amongst its many other functions, distributes and qualifies different sections of the population with those skills and attitudes which a modern economy
needs to run efficiently. The list of the 'reproductive' functions
of the modern state could be expanded infinitely; but the essential point is clear. The state and the law are implicated, directly
and indirectly, in maintaining a viable capitalist economy. They
must also maintain that type of rule, authority and order which,
in the long run, supports and reproduces the existing division
of labour, and secures the social and legal foundations of an
economic system on which the viability of the whole nation
depends. We are no longer dealing with the liberal state in a
period of 'laissez-faire' when it was said to play a largely 'night-
watchman' role. We are analysing an interventionist state,
constantly intervening in economic and social life, and this

exposes the fragile basis on which the separation of economics from politics is supposed to depend.

It is interesting that, when the case is put in this form, liberal-democratic theorists do not dissent from it, even though they do not necessarily take the full consequences of what they have conceded. Thus Partridge (1971) has written, in response to Miliband's book 'The State in Capitalist Society':

> in the nature of the case, is the state not an institution one of whose functions is the maintenance of social order ...? One would expect it always to be a central concern of the state to act when necessary and as it can to preserve social stability ... its manner of protecting stability and continuity of working will almost inevitably be to protect those basic or central institutions on which the existing order depends ...

The problem for critical theorists, then, must be to demonstrate how this growing structural 'convergence of objective interests' between the state, the law and the dominant, economic interests and class relationships in society is squared with their claims to impartiality and universality. They have to explain this apparent contradiction. A number of different solutions to this problem have been proposed within critical theory.

Variants of 'state and law' theory
The first variant is the 'instrumentalist' one. This regards the state as the direct instrument of class rule, and the law as a tool of class oppression. Some approaches have taken this 'instrumental' view quite literally. Thus, conflict theorists like Quinney have asserted that

> Contrary to the dominant view, the state is created by the class that has the power to enforce its will on the rest of society. The state is thus a political organization created out of force and coercion. The state is established by those who desire to protect their material basis and who have the power to maintain the state. The law in capitalist society gives political recognition to powerful private interests. Moreover, the legal system is an apparatus created to secure the interests of the dominant class. Contrary to conventional belief, the law is the tool of the ruling class.
>
> Quinney, *Critique of Legal Order*, 1974, p.52).

This is a contentious argument; and its cogency is not advanced by its simplicity. It affirms where it ought to explain and demonstrate. Glaringly, it fails to explain why a system so manifestly biased and coercive appears to so many as fair and just. It explains neither the 'legitimacy' of law nor the 'consensual' nature of the state in democratic societies. It is a highly reductionist position. Not surprisingly, Quinney has been obliged to modify and sophisticate his argument in subsequent contributions (cf. the more recent 'Class, State and Crime').

A second variant recognizes the distinction between those who 'dominate' at the economic level of society and those who 'rule'. How, then, is the correspondence of interests between

them secured? Miliband, in 'The State in Capitalist Society'
explains it in terms of the similarity of class background,
interests and outlook between those who run the economy and
the personnel of the state and legal institutions. He focuses on
the common class background, close educational ties, family
and personal connections, and the shared ideological acclimatiza-
tion to explain why institutions staffed by such people will
naturally incline to favour dominant social and economic interests.
    This view usefully contests the worst excesses of 'consensus'
and 'impartiality' arguments. It is supported by many studies
of the class composition and social background of those who
hold high judicial office (e.g. Zander, 1968; Neal-Tate, 1975;
Goldstein-Jackson, 1970; Griffith, 1977). The differential
application of justice to different social classes has also been
widely noted in the literature. The state and the law, for
example, are noticeably lax when pursuing annual tax fraud
(largely attributable to tax evasion by the wealthy large corporations, and currently estimated at £3,000m annually), while
those who 'scrounge' off social security (currently estimated
at £300m) are vigorously pursued and punished. Judicial policy
varies significantly as between 'white-collar' and other 'crimes
of the powerful, and the crimes of the poorer classes' (cf. Carson
and Wiles, 1971). In Miliband's terms, these differential attitudes and policies can be attributed to the class composition
of the judiciary, and the inclination to look less favourably on
the 'fiddles' of the poor than on the 'illegalities' of the well-
off. As Westergaard and Resler (1975) remark, 'What matters ...
is just the simple fact of the abyss that separates the world of
the bench, bar and law from the world of ordinary workers'.
    Miliband's argument thus usefully alerts us to one source of
'judicial bias'. It pitches its explanation, however, almost
exclusively in terms of the personnel who staff the state and
legal apparatuses. It is a highly 'individualistic' argument.
Moreover, like Quinney, Miliband tends to assume a homogeneity
of 'ruling-class interests', with a straight, unproblematic transmission belt from economic-class interests to the instrumentaliza-
tion of the law and the state. These are highly disputable
assumptions. They assume no structural functions or tendencies
of the state, apart from those implanted in it by the biases of
its personnel. But, as Westergaard and Resler argue, this is
an insufficient cause, since 'the test of power', they argue,
'is not *who* decides; but what is decided - and what not' (1975,
p.246).
    The third position, accordingly, takes a different line. It
argues that the 'correspondences' between state, law and
economy cannot be explained by looking simply at individuals,
since these spheres are linked by a more structural connection.
In this view, the state and law, under capitalism, have an objective relationship to classes and the economy, which cannot be
adequately expressed in terms of the social background of
the individuals recruited to serve in their ranks. This is a

position adopted by many recent structuralist writers, and the
work of Poulantzas can be taken as representative of this
approach.

For Poulantzas (1973), the state is neither an instrument nor
a tool. It must be understood, not as a unified 'thing', but as
a relation. By this, he means that, through the state, different
relations in society - above all, relationships between the fundamental classes - are organized into a definite system of power.
The state is the place where the power co-ordinates of society
converge. The state links people to government, individuals
to the nation, economic interests to policy and legislation. For
Poulantzas, the state has two functions. It imposes a certain
kind of cohesion on society, drawing diverse relationships into
a unity. It is also the place where popular consent for particular
policies is organized: above all, the consent of the dominated
classes to the continuity and legitimacy of the dominant. But
why, we may ask, don't dominant economic-class interests rule
directly? Why do they require the 'mediation' of the state?

These questions have been answered in different ways in
classical marxist theory. Engels (1942) argued that the state
arose out of the division of society into classes. An institution
was required which would be vested with legal and constitutional
authority; which could secure the foundations of the capitalist
division of labour and diffuse its requirements throughout
society. Above all, it should be an apparently 'independent
power', mediating social conflicts so that the struggle between
the contending classes should not degenerate into total social
war. In a well-known passage (1942, p.97), he argued the
need for

> an institution which set the seal of general social recognition
> on each new mode of acquiring property and thus amassing
> wealth ... which perpetuated, not only this growing cleav-
> age into classes, but also the right of the possessing class
> to exploit the non-possessing, and the rule of the former
> over the latter ... The state was invented.

The critical point is contained in Engels's phrase, 'set the
seal of general social recognition'. The argument is that a
society where the dominant economic class ruled directly, legis-
lating purely in its own interests, would lack popular legitimacy
and be simply an economic dictatorship. Somehow, the consent
of the people has to be secured, and a 'general interest' established, whilst the continuity of class domination is maintained.
The state is pre-eminently capable of mediating class relationships in this particular way because of its double character.
Its claims to legitimacy derive from its basis in universal suffrage. It can therefore claim to represent all classes, and the
'general interest'. Yet it tends to exclude policies which favour
the collective interests of labour. It translates popular consent
into support for policies directed towards the long-term interests
of capital and those classes which most profit from the system -
bestowing on those particular class-interests the gloss and

sanction of a general popular legitimacy. Thus Marx and Engels argued, in 'The German Ideology', that the state was the means by which class interests are represented as 'the general interest' and 'the general interest as ruling'. Marx also argued that 'In civil law, the existing property relationships (which favour the capitalist class) are declared to be the result of the general will.' (Marx and Engels, 1970, p.81).

The mediation of the state, then, generalizes class interests which, apparently, lose their true class character. Poulantzas examined at length how this 'trick' of representation was accomplished. It was based, he argued, on the apparent independence or autonomy of the state, law and politics from the economy. Capitalist economic relations are rooted in the conflict between classes. While the modern state does arbitrate between corporate bodies (e.g. the unions, employers, federations, etc.), it does not formally recognize classes as such. It subsumes class interests into the 'national interest', which only a state - which is 'above all particular interests' - is able to represent. For example, throughout the 1960s and 1970s, the state actively intervened to limit wages and prevent them outpacing profits. This was done in the name of the 'national interest' - though it may well be thought to have favoured the interests of employers over those of wage-earners. Also, the law deals with the legal individual rather than classes, which have no legal status. As the law is structured more clearly around individual rights (as opposed, say, to trade union rights), its processes inevitably fragment classes, breaking them down into legal individuals. Only the state can combine these competing individuals into a 'whole'. This 'whole', however, is not the antagonistic ensemble formed by the relations between the classes, but the non-antagonistic whole - 'the nation', 'the people', 'the general will' - into which, as individuals, they have been incorporated. For Poulantzas, then, the state and the law are gigantic machineries of representation, which reach down into a society composed of antagonistic class relations, fragments classes into individuals, and recomposes them as citizens with equal political and legal rights.

This process, by which the state and law appear 'autonomous' of class interests, and classes are 'atomized' into individuals (Poulantzas called it the 'isolation effect') has a number of significant effects. It disorganizes the dominated classes and mystifies their real conditions of exploitation. Thus, they cannot recognize their real class interests, or fight as a united class against their exploitation. It obliges them to 'live' their relation to their real conditions of exploitation in an atomized way. These individual relationships are then fixed by being elaborated through the concepts and practices of the legal and political process, which is filled out with such popular, common-sense notions as 'the citizen', 'individual rights and liberties', 'the rule of law' and 'juridical equality'. These are the key concepts of bourgeois political-juridical ideology, and

of common-sense understandings of how law and the state
function, and why they are legitimate.

The displacement of the class basis of the state also enables
different factions of the ruling class to operate through the
state to construct a social unity around policies and strategies
which, in fact, favour their long-term interest. Bourgeois
political-juridical ideology binds sectors of the dominated classes
to those long-term strategies by diffusing the 'requirements'
of the system as a set of universal goals and thus coordinating
society under their direction, thereby securing 'hegemony'.

Poulantzas and the structuralists deploy these arguments with
great theoretical skill. As an explanation, a structural approach
has many advantages over a purely instrumental or individualistic argument. Their critics argue, however, that they reduce
the state and law to a structural necessity, operating exclusively
to the permanent advantage of capital. It is difficult to see how
their spell could ever be broken. Advantages won from the
state by the struggle of the dominated classes (e.g. welfare
rights) are hard to explain on this basis. The notion that struggle and resistance might achieve some results seems foreign to
it - although Poulantzas constantly makes reference to the
limiting effects of 'the class struggle' on state action. Structuralist theories, then, tend towards a high level of abstraction
and sometimes overstate the functional relationship of the state
to capital.

A fourth, a similar, approach, is that advanced by Holloway
and Picciotto (1978), and Fine (1979). Here, the ideological
character of law and the state is grounded not in the separation
of politics and the law from the economy, but as the direct product of the economic relations of capitalism and their 'logic'.
This approach also derives from Marx's analysis of the economic
process in 'Capital'. Marx (1961) argued that, under capitalism,
wage-labour produced a surplus which is not returned to the
worker in the form of wages but expropriated by capital. Production relations are therefore founded on class exploitation.
In the market, however, where goods and labour are exchanged
for a price and profits realized, capitalist and labourer meet,
not as exploiter and exploited but as 'buyer' and 'seller'. They
are equal parties to an apparently 'free' contractual exchange.
Thus relations of market exchange (based on equivalence between
the contracting parties) overlay, disguise and displace production relations (which are relations of non-equivalence). The
state, however, guarantees this 'fiction' of exchange equivalence and the law gives it legality in the form of legal equality
and fairness. Thus the law codifies exploitation by giving it
a legal form. It therefore mystifies exploitation. Workers
experience the exploitative relations of capitalism ideologically,
and 'live' their relation to it exclusively in terms of its fairness
and equality: thus wages are fought over only in terms of 'a
fair day's wage for a fair day's work'. Law masks the real content of economic relations. Turning this proposition around,

these authors argue that the law is therefore only a 'fetishized expression' of the economic relations which underpin it, but which are concealed in its form, practice and language.

Whereas Poulantzas tries to account for what is specific to the functioning of the state and law under conditions of bourgeois democracy, Holloway and Picciotto tend to explain them directly in terms of their 'hidden' economic content. They attempt to overcome the tendency to reductionism by showing how law and the state, once established, go through their own specific phases of historical development (for example, Picciotto, 1979). But, although they cannot be accused of reducing everything to the economic level, they do ultimately derive everything from economic relationships. This reflects their desire to overcome the traditional division of society into economic 'base' and legal-political 'superstructure', and to ground the study of law (superstructure) directly in the social relations of production and 'the material conditions of life (Picciotto (1979, p.167)). But this approach tends, ultimately, to rob the law of any specificity or effectivity of its own, since it is only a form of 'mystification' – an empty legal form with a 'hidden' economic content. Its truth, therefore, always lies elsewhere.

The fifth variant is that which derives from the influence of the Italian theorist Antonio Gramsci (1971, 1977), whose work greatly influenced Poulantzas. Unlike Poulantzas, however, Gramsci places the notion of 'struggle' at the very centre of his conception of the state. The function of the state is to master a field of struggle in the attempt to bring society into line with the structural tendencies set by the economy. The economy, however, cannot fully dictate these aims. Nor can it be conceived as functioning on its own outside the particular political and ideological conditions. In addition to its role of regulating the economy, the state is also required to organize society, civil, moral and intellectual life around a series of 'fundamental historical tasks'. The state is the site and agency through which popular consent for these is won or lost. Gramsci did not believe this organizational task to be either easy or necessarily successful. Hegemony is a form of 'mastery' achieved only through constant struggle and its success ultimately depends on the balance between the contending forces in any area in which the state seeks to intervene. The functional character of the state could not, for Gramsci, be derived from some general theory of the state's function and practice. It could be established only by analysing the 'state of play' in a particular historical conjuncture. Italy was just such an example of a country where capitalist relations prevailed, but where the state had never succeeded in enlarging the social and cultural basis of its rule.

Gramsci distinguished a situation where the different classes remained 'corporate' (i.e. enclosed within their own limited class interests), and rule depended on the exercise of direct domination; and one where a particular sector of capital had

succeeded, through the state, in generalizing its interests
across society, drawing sectors of the dominated classes into
an alliance, forming - within the state and society - a 'historical
bloc'. Such a 'bloc' is then able, for a time, to exercise an
enlarged social authority over national life, ruling, not by
'domination' so much as by 'leadership'. In such hegemonic
moments, the state mobilizes sufficient popular legitimacy and
support to enable it to undertake a reconstruction of social
life, propagating the requirements of the system as a series
of national historical tasks. In this way it brings about 'not
only a unison of economic and political aims, but also intellectual
and moral unity, not on a corporate but a "universal" plane,
and thus (creating) the hegemony of a fundamental social
group over a series of subordinate groups' (1971, p.58).

Where many other theorists emphasized the coercive nature
of state rule, Gramsci placed centrally an 'ethical and educative'
conception of the state and of law. Hegemony could not be
reduced to economic domination alone, but required the re-
shaping of civil, political, intellectual and ethical life in line
with the general tendencies and direction of the whole social
formation. This made the role of the state in 'winning consent'
to this enlarged social leadership a pivotal issue. This shift
in emphasis gave Gramsci a greater purchase on the functioning
of modern class democracies than many rival theories, which
neglected the element of consent. His conception of law was
essential to this enlarged conception of 'hegemony'. For him,
the law was an instrument of education, part of the organizational function of the state, and a means whereby society
was tutored and shaped. On the one hand, it sanctioned conduct which threatened the establishment of hegemony: on the
other, it rewarded conduct which favoured it. The 'repressive
and negative aspect' of the law only made sense when seen as
intrinsic to the 'positive, civilizing activity undertaken by the
state' (1971, pp.246-7).

Much of Gramsci's writings were left in an unfinished and
unsystematized form, and they are open to more than one
interpretation. Some have argued that he does not altogether
escape from a complex kind of 'class reductionism'. Nevertheless,
his work does undercut a priori arguments, forcing the theorist
to leave the general, abstract level and attend to particular
historical conjunctures. It gives a specificity and effectivity
to what classical theorists would call 'the superstructures' in
ways which undercut many common forms of reductionism or
economism, although it does not present a systematic theory of
the state and law. Many recent studies of crime and the law
have used Gramsci's approach, including studies of the eighteenth century by Thompson (1975), Hay et al. (1975), and
the analysis of the relation between the growth of 'law-and-
order' campaigns and the crisis of hegemony in the 1970s by
Hall et al. (1978).

LAW, CRIME AND CLASS

We turn now to studies concerned with the relationship between the law, crime and class. Here, we examine the argument that crime is best explained as the product of class conditions. We do so by looking at three themes: (a) the relation of crime to 'surplus' and 'marginal' populations; (b) social crime and the 'politicization' of deviance; (c) 'criminalization' as a mode of control.

The vast proportion of those who are processed in the criminal justice system are drawn from the working class. The research of J.W. Douglas on a national sample of children indicates that 15 to 20 per cent of boys from manual workers' homes had been convicted of at least one offence by the age of seventeen, compared with only 10 per cent from 'white-collar' homes, and 5 per cent from professional and salaried families (Douglas, in Carson and Wiles, 1971). These figures are derived from recorded court convictions, and do not tell us the real class distribution of crime. They underestimate the extent of 'white-collar' crime, much of which may not be perceived as 'crime'. Police stereotypes of 'the criminal' are also predominantly working class (Chapman, 1968; Young, 1971; Armstrong and Wilson, 1973; Cain, 1973; Cohen, 1972). The connection between crime and the working class is now a standard hypothesis in criminology, supported by more than a century of research into the social conditions of the labouring classes and the poor. Studies of poverty and poor communities have established the natural and organic link between crime and the 'normal' social life of those who live in what has become known as conditions of 'multiple deprivation'. Marx and Engels discussed crime in the context of the social conditions of the early factory pro-letariat, and Engels gave a vivid description of these connec-tions in 'The Condition of the Working Class in England'.

The problem is that most of these studies are descriptive, observing but not explaining the connection between crime and poverty. Indeed, a number of different and contradictory explanations have been derived from these observations. Crime may arise in these conditions, it is argued, because the poor are 'demoralized'; or both poverty and the high incidence of crime may be causally imputed to the lack of character and conscience of the poor; or poverty and material deprivation may 'drive' the poor to crime, as a 'solution' to deprivation. These may be useful hypotheses, but they are clearly insuf-ficient as an explanation of crime. If crime is a 'solution' to poverty, why is it only a minority of the poor who adopt it? If poverty drives the poor to crime, what drives the rich, well-off or professional classes?

The 'demoralization' hypothesis only provides the beginnings of a explanation: and it is noticeable that it has been adopted by both radical and conservative theorists. The theory was widespread - almost a common-sense observation - in the nineteenth century. The answer seemed to lie in the 'moralization' of the poor - a task which the evangelical, proselytizing and philanthropic classes undertook with considerable dedication. Engels, however, also noted that the 'conditions of labour ... spawned by industrial capitalism lead to the brutalization and degradation of life', of which crime was a direct index (in Cain and Hunt, 1979, p.149). His solution was not to 'moralize' the poor but to abolish poverty. Engels, to some extent, and Bonger (1969) later, attributed 'demoralization' not just to physical degradation but to the competitiveness and 'egoism' fostered by the capitalist way of life. This was a view they shared with non-marxist social theorists, like Durkheim. 'Egoism', however, even if it were an adequate explanation, could not be limited to the labouring poor. Such theorists do not make enough of a distinction between the 'competitive struggle for existence', and the 'competition for profitable advantage'. These distinctions tend to disappear into the catch-all category of 'egoism'.

Crime and the 'surplus populations'
A more developed theoretical argument, which attempts to explain (rather than simply describe) how the degrading social conditions which may precipitate crime arise, is to be found in the theory of 'relative surplus population', defined by Marx, in 'Capital' (I, p.632), as 'the reserve army of labour'. Capitalism is subject to periodic fluctuations and cannot always maintain the total labour force in permanent employment. This is not only because production and trade are cyclical, and capitalism is an unplanned system; but also because, as capital develops its productive capacity through technical improvements, sections of the work-force are 'deskilled' (as a result of the decline in the demand for traditional skills) or thrown into temporary or permanent unemployment. Marx argued that this process, with its immeasurable human costs, had positive value for capitalism: it facilitated technological development, allowed capital to restructure, forced labour to move to other jobs or to acquire new tasks and skills. Also, the constant threat of redundancy and the competition for jobs served to moderate wage demands. This process tended to divide the working-class as between the 'employed' and the 'unemployed'. It put pressure on the employed to work for lower rates of pay, under threat of being thrown on 'the scrap-heap of history'. The constant movement of workers between trades, the disappearance of artisan and early productive skills, and the ever-present reality of unemployment were constant features of early industrial capitalist development, and continue to be central to the functioning of capitalist economies today.

During periods of recession, the 'surplus population' sinks into destitution, as living standards decline. Marx observed that this was likely to be the fate of most workers at some time of their lives. He divided the surplus population into three

categories. First, the 'floating' surplus, consisting of those
displaced or 'deskilled' by the introduction of new machinery.
Second, the 'latent' surplus, consisting of the unemployed
in the countryside, who only become evident as agricultural
employment declines and new opportunities open up in the
factories and cities. Third, the 'stagnant' surplus are those
in more or less permanent irregular employment, who provide
'an inexhaustible reservoir of labour power'. Further, Marx
identified those who dwelled in 'pauperism', the 'demoralized
and ragged'. Pauperism, he said, 'is the hospital of the
active labour army ...' (1961, I, p.644). These constituted
the 'dangerous' classes, the term increasingly adopted for them
in the nineteenth century, because their conditions were seen
as a breeding ground of dissension and a potential threat to
civil order.

It is noticeable that Marx excludes from the 'victims of industry' those whom he labels 'vagabonds, criminals, prostitutes'
(ibid, p.643). Though he had great sympathy for those thrust
by capitalism into pauperism, he showed little for the 'criminal
classes' – the 'lumpenproletariat', a parasitic stratum, living
off their own class, lacking the solidarity which develops under
conditions of organized labour, and prone to recruitment into
reactionary causes as the 'hired mobs' of populist demagogues.

The link – unemployment, destitution, crime – has provided
an important starting point for research which has developed
the 'surplus population' thesis. Stedman Jones (1971), for
example, discusses crime as one outcome of the casual labour
market which prevailed in London's East End (especially in
the docks, where labour has traditionally been 'casualized'),
particularly in the 1880s and 1890s, when changes in patterns
of unemployment drove a new wedge between the employed and
what were called the 'residuum' – the outcasts. Some studies
have interpreted the Luddite movement in the early nineteenth
century, which involved extensive destruction of machinery
in the textile industry, as arising directly from the displacement of older artisan skills by new inventions (Darvall, 1934;
Thompson, 1968). Recent studies of crime in the Third World
have highlighted the way in which movements of world trade
and foreign investment have tended to improve the conditions
of that small sector of local labour linked to exports and
metropolitan capital, while 'marginalizing' large sectors of the
indigenous population, especially the rural and urban poor.
The high incidence of crime in the shanty-towns of large
capital cities in developing societies can thus be related to the
same processes of economic dependency which structure the
local labour markets (Allan, 1970; Worsley, 1972; Obregon,
1974).

An extension of the 'surplus population' argument can be
found in the growing literature on 'marginalization'. This notes
the high crime-rates among groups which are not only vulnerable to cyclical unemployment, but which are driven to the

margins of society for other reasons. Such 'outcast groups' are forced to survive outside regular employment in the illegal economies of the cities, often by crime, petty theft, illegal dealing and hustling. Some writers have analysed the patterns of crime amongst such stigmatized groups as black youth, gypsies, the Irish, and – in America – the Chinese, black, Chicano and Spanish populations and other sectors of the under-class of the very poor. These sectors are clearly 'pauperized': whether, as a twentieth-century phenomenon, they fit Marx's characterization of the 'lumpenproletariat' is more open to question. Marx's 'lumpen' was a relatively small group; but many have noted, under modern capitalist conditions, the growth of a new kind of 'underclass', which includes not only the permanently unemployed and the marginalized but also the physically and mentally handicapped, the aged poor and other groups of the 'multiply deprived' who live below the poverty line and are heavily dependent on welfare state benefits. This may be a new, post-welfare state phenomenon, though in cities like Naples in southern Italy, where no extensive welfare support system exists, substantial sectors of the population can survive only through a more or less permanent dependence on the black market and illegal economy (Macciocci, 1973). This core underclass of the unemployed does not always play the reactionary political role which Marx envisaged for the 'lumpen'. But their interests are clearly different from, and can be opposed to, those of the majority who are desperately holding onto jobs.

Two recent studies of street crime illustrate well the com-plexities of relating crime to what Spitzer (1975) terms 'pro-blem populations'. In the study of the 'mugging' epidemic, identified especially with black youth in Britain in the 1970s, Hall et al. (1978) pointed to the chronic conditions of high unemployment as one of its precipitating conditions. The analysis was supplemented by consideration of the growth of white racism and the 'scapegoating' of black youth, with the consequent development of a quasi-political consciousness, based on a positive revaluation of their black identity and resistance to the tough policing measures adopted. In this example, it is clear that marginal employment alone could not constitute an adequate explanation of 'mugging' without taking other cultural, political and ideological factors into account. Platt and Takagi (1978), in their study of American street crime, relate the incidence of crime among marginal groups to the 'relative surplus population' thesis. 'Monopoly capitalism emiser-ates increasingly large portions of the working class and pro-letarianizes the lower strata of the petty-bourgeoisie, degrades workers' skills and competency in the quest for higher pro-ductivity, and organizes family and community life on the basis of its most efficient exploitability'. Significantly, they also employ a version of the 'demoralization' thesis: 'it con-sequently makes antagonism rather than reciprocity the norm of social relationships. Under monopoly capitalism, family and peer relations become even more brutal and attenuated'. They also touch the 'underclass' thesis: blacks, Chicanos and Puerto Ricans are, they argue, disproportionately over-represented in police records because they are 'disproportionately concentrated in the super-exploited sectors of the working class'. However, they go on to show that street crime is largely an 'intra-class and intra-racial phenomenon' - the poor taking advantage of the poor. Street crime thus divides the working class against itself, deepens the divisions between employed and unemployed, sharpens racial antagonism, confirms ethnic stereotypes, and depreciates the quality of life in working-class neighbourhoods. It helps to recruit 'respectable' residents into campaigns for tougher 'law and order' measures. Even if crime can be said to be precipitated by conditions of poverty, marginalization and 'super-exploitation', it provides no solution to these problems.

In general, the 'relative surplus population' thesis does not provide a sufficient explanation of crime. It can only establish some of the possible precipitating conditions out of which certain crimes arise amongst some sectors of the poor. It surpasses more descriptive accounts by showing that poverty is not a 'natural' condition, but is related to the rhythms of capital accumulation, producing 'accumulation of wealth at one pole ... accumulation of misery, agony of toil, slavery, ignorance, brutality and mental degradation at the opposite pole' (Marx, 'Capital', III, p.645). But this, in itself, does not *explain crime*. Further hypotheses would have to be added to explain why some of the immiserated adopt the 'solution' of crime, while others do not. Moreover, the theory does not distinguish between what we might call 'survival' and 'professional' crime. Nor can it explain the vast range of crimes which occur outside of the marginalized. These would include 'career-based' professional crime (McIntosh, 1975), the 'crimes of the powerful' (Pearce, 1976), and crime at work (working class, professional and white collar). These considerations remind us that crime is not a unitary phenomenon; hence it may be fruitless to try to find a single causal factor to explain its many complex varieties.

Examples of this diversity can be found in the growing literature on crime at work (Mars, 1974; Ditton, 1977, 1979; Henry, 1978; Henry and Mars, 1978). These writers tend to reject a class analysis because crime at work is identified as a 'hidden' or 'informal' economy, 'to the side' of the mainstream economy. The argument is that the separate system of part-time crime exhibits its own structure of social relations, with its own momentum and consequently provides its own explanation of crime. Again, the general category - 'crime at work' - is used here to lump together such very different activities as petty fiddling and large-scale computer fraud. It fails to explain the different histories and motivations which underpin these very diverse forms. Further, it fails to show that the diverse forms of crime at work reflect a differential structure of opportunity to commit such crime which, in turn, reflects the wider class and occupational system. The 'fiddles' in which some workers engage differ, in definition, character, access and control from similar activities when performed by white collar employees and managers; and both are very different from large-scale industrial or corporate crime (Pearce, 1976). 'Fiddling' is often a means of supplementing low pay and, in some occupations, has traditionally been regarded as part of the 'perks' of the job. Large stores and supermarkets regularly 'write off' a much larger proportion of their turnover to internal fiddling than they do to shoplifting. By contrast, a good deal of 'white-collar crime' is not perceived as crime at all, but an extension of the privileges of white-collar status. Both differ from the opportunities open to some managers and accountants to use company funds for private deals or to manipulate the books. Syndicate illegality by big business – through, for example, tax fraud – far from being a crime, is often regarded as the skilful exploitation of existing 'loopholes' in the law, stimulated by a sharp sense of business advantage.

These substantive differences in the apparently homogeneous category, 'crime at work', clearly reflect differences in opportunity, stemming from the hierarchical ordering of occupations and the labour force. An explanation of 'crime at work' would, therefore, have to recognize that the differing patterns of crime exist within, and are structured by, the social relations of capitalist industry and business, and reflect the inequalities of status and work conditions between the different occupational classes. Thus, contrary to the argument of some 'hidden economy' and 'part-time crime' theorists, 'crime at work' can be usefully related to questions of class and class structure (Scraton and South, 1981). On the other hand, the kind of class analysis which is relevant to 'crime at work' is very different from that which is deployed in debates concerning unemployment, the surplus population thesis and crime. While both kinds of crime may be illuminated by taking their point of departure from the structural relations and processes of advanced capitalism, quite different aspects of the theory would be required to explain each. Once again, the claims to have discovered, in class theory, a single and adequate general theory of crime seem untenable.

The 'politicization' of crime

The recognition that crime is not a long-term solution to the problems of poverty or low wages, and that most working-class crime is practised against the working class itself, has undercut the tendency in 'radical criminology' to romanticize the deviant and the criminal as a social rebel and to redefine crime as a form of social protest. This tendency was based on a false syllogism: crime arises from poverty, which is created by capitalism; therefore, since crime is an 'illegal' solution to immiseration, it must be a disguised protest against the capital- ist system. The temptation to follow this 'anti-capitalist reason- ing' has been strengthened by the relatively non-revolutionary character of working-class politics in the advanced capitalist countries. This has encouraged radical theorists to substitute the traditional agent of social change - the industrial working class - by the deviant and the super-exploited. Engels occa- sionally spoke of crime as a form of 'primitive rebellion', a stage of nascent revolt in the social war between oppressors and oppressed. However, he also called crime 'the earliest, crudest and least fruitful form of rebellion'. It was a purely individual response, working on, rather than attempting to change, the conditions which created it. It did not redistribute wealth between rich and poor, but only transferred it from the pockets of some of the poor to others of the same class. Thus it 'never becomes the universal expression of public opinion of the working-man [sic], however much they might approve of it in silence' (Engels, in Marx and Engels, 1975, p.502).

The problem with the interpretation of crime as 'primitive rebellion' is that it once again fails to draw the necessary distinctions. Historians have been concerned to identify those crimes which contain a strong element of social protest and political activities which society has labelled as 'criminal'. But they have been careful to distinguish these from the broad category of 'normal' crime, and especially from professionalized crime, which contain little or no 'social protest' element (cf. Hobsbawm, 1972b). The distinctions between 'social' and 'normal' crime are difficult to make precisely, but they remain important. Hobsbawm has studied the extent of what he calls 'social banditry' in pre-capitalist and agrarian societies (Hobsbawm, 1959, 1972a). Bandits, though outlawed by the state, remained within their communities, were regarded locally as 'heroes' of the common people, and led the struggles for justice and the redistribution of wealth and property. Their crimes could be regarded as a form of class struggle and banditry was often accompanied by peasant uprisings. Never- theless, Hobsbawm carefully dissociates 'social banditry' from professional criminals and 'common robbers' who victimized local communities for the sake of individual gain. He argues strongly that this form of 'primitive rebellion' diminished as industrial capitalism developed. The same distinctions can be derived from studies of other 'illegal social movements' (e.g. Thompson, 1968; Hobsbawm and Rudé, 1969; Rudé, 1952, 1962, 1964).

Radical criminologists have sometimes tended to confuse all types of crime with 'social crime'. Social conditions may well provide one of the precipitating conditions for some forms of crime. And some criminal groups have, sometimes, been singled out by the media and treated repressively for social or political reasons. Though it is their crimes which appear to attract

attention, they may in fact be the victims of wider attitudes of
social hostility, which find a conveniently displaced expression
through the focusing on the criminal aspect. Hall et al. (1978)
argued that the massive publicity and tough policing directed
at the street crime of black youth in the 1970s may have arisen
because of the growth of racist attitudes among the white
population towards black immigrants. (It is interesting that,
by the 1970s, black youth had become labelled as a sector of
the population 'prone to crime', whereas in the 1950s both the
West Indian and Asian immigrants were said to be unusually
'law-abiding'. Attitudes had clearly changed.) A social element
can, therefore, sometimes be identified in both the circumstances
producing a growing involvement in crime by such groups, and
in the way their crimes are dealt with. Resistance to the target-
ing of such vulnerable populations by 'tough policing' (as
is the case in some of the black communities in the 1980s) may
then precipitate a quasi-political resistance among marginal
groups which are singled out in this way.

However, this does not make crime itself 'social' in any
meaningful way. Street crime is not, in any obvious sense,
'progressive', either for the group itself, or for the working
class as a whole. Nor is it likely to stimulate a long-term solution through progressive social change. Indeed, despite their
growing 'politicization', such crimes continue to have all the
negative consequences outlined by Platt and Takagi (1978).
They divide the class, nourish racism, popularize 'law-and-
order' campaigns, victimize the poor and make poor communities
less safe and amenable places in which to live. Thus, far from
providing a solution to social conditions, crime exacerbates
the problems and sharpens the contradictions. We should be
aware that poverty and long-term unemployment will increase
the propensity of the poor to commit 'survival' crime. But
elevating such offenders into 'social rebels' romanticizes and
simplifies a complex social problem. Young (1975, 1979) correctly
identified it as an example of 'Left idealism'.

Criminalization as control
One argument which makes the distinction between 'social' and
'normal' crime even more difficult to draw, and which has
strengthened the 'social rebel' thesis, is the proposition that
criminalization is part of the armoury of class control. An act
is not a 'crime' until it has been legally defined as such.
Criminalization - the application of the criminal label to a particular social category - is a process, and depends both on how
certain acts are labelled and on who is doing the labelling. The
criminal label is applied to many actions which the majority of
the population would regard as 'illegal'. But it can sometimes
be applied to activities which the authorities oppose, not
because they are 'criminal' but because they are politically
threatening. In such circumstances, 'criminalization' can provide
the justification for political containment. 'Criminalization' is

a particularly powerful weapon, when used in this way, because it mobilizes considerable popular approval and legitimacy behind the state. People are more likely to support state action against a 'criminal' act than they would the use of the law to repress a 'political' cause.

It may sometimes be advantageous to the authorities, then, to try to contain a political or social movement by stigmatizing it exclusively in terms of its criminal element. For all the complexities in the Northern Ireland case, it may be argued that although people may have had sympathy with the plight of the Catholic minority, few questioned the application of the law, or the extraordinary legal powers of the Prevention of Terrorism legislation, when action in support of their political case assumed the form of bombing campaigns against civilian populations. The problem with such examples is that, since 'illegal acts' have, clearly, been committed, criminalization has a real content, and cannot be dismissed as a convenient ideological construction by the state. Nevertheless, even when no deliberate intention is involved, the process of criminalization may have, as one of its unintended effects, the diversion of attention from the social or political content of a movement, at the expense of highlighting its criminal form. If black youth are thought of exclusively as 'muggers', people will be less willing to consider the fact that they constitute the social group with the highest relative rate of unemployment.

There are many historical examples where some variant of this 'criminalization' thesis has been argued. E.P. Thompson (1975), in his study of the appearance of mounted foresters, disguised with 'blacked' faces in the Royal Forests in the early eighteenth century, has argued that this was part of a prolonged social struggle to preserve ancient common rights against the encroachment of new property relationships. The Walpole government, however, found it easier to deal with this social struggle by describing 'the Blacks' as part of a seditious mob, and helping to spread rumours of a Jacobite conspiracy to overthrow the Protestant succession. At the end of the eighteenth century, those who led the radical agitations for the right to form unions, for the improvement of wages and conditions and a reform of the franchise were frequently charged in the courts for 'seditious treason', although the conspiracy to commit violence was rarely proven. (In the most famous of these cases, the leaders of the London Corresponding Society were cleared of their charges by a disbelieving jury.) More recently, it has been argued that fostering the image of Robert Mugabe as a 'violent terrorist' helped to justify the military campaigns of the Rhodesian government against the nationalists, diverting attention from both its own illegal status and the political nature of the demand for black majority rule. (The public image of Mugabe had to be rapidly modified during the course of his democratic succession to power in Zimbabwe.) Some have argued that the concentration on the activities of

the IRA 'bombers and gunmen' in the mid-1970s helped to
divert public attention from the plight of the Catholic minority
in Ulster. The recent reintroduction of the law into industrial
relations, a feature of government policy in the 1970s and
1980s, has been interpreted by some as an attempt to control
the wage militancy of workers by 'criminalizing' certain traditional trade-union activities (e.g. picketing).

At the base of these interpretations is the thesis that
'criminalization' not only emphasizes, but exaggerates, the
degree of violence involved, at the expense of political motives.
Thus, in industrial relations, it is the violence of the pickets
which is pinpointed, rather than the importance, for the success of the strike, of preventing supplies getting through to a
factory. Focusing on the violence, it is said, makes it easier
to mobilize popular support for measures of containment. There
is a revulsion against violence, especially when portrayed as
'mindless'. People know that, taken to its limits, violence
threatens the very foundations of the state and undermines the
'rule of law'. Hence they will rally against a political cause,
once the violent label has been made to stick.

In many of these examples, 'criminalization' is defined as a
process which can be employed to underpin the repressive
or control functions of the state. This further compounds the
difficult distinction between 'normal' and 'social' crime, since
criminalization may help to fuse the two. The problem remains
that, even when violence is used only tactically, it is always
double-edged. It will be widely thought to break the agreement
to pursue conflicts by other than openly violent means – the
basis of the social contract and the legitimacy of the state.
The state is then certain to react, by fair means or foul. This
makes it difficult to disentangle those instances where criminalization is part of the maintenance of social order, and where
it is not. However, the concept does usefully highlight one
possible function of the law in the ideological containment of
class conflict.

THE 'RULE OF LAW' AS AN ARENA OF STRUGGLE

We turn, finally, to a set of debates which puts the ideological
role of law in a new context, and which summarizes many of the
arguments reviewed earlier. This is the debate about the 'rule
of law'. In many ways, the 'rule of law' is the paradigm 'test
case' for critical theory, since it is the cornerstone of the
liberal-democratic theory of law. It has also become the site of
an intense debate within critical work.

By the 'rule of law', liberal theorists mean that conflicts
and disputes must be settled within the framework of legal
procedure. They regard the 'rule of law', which is supposed
to apply universally to all classes and to the state itself
(formally, at least, not 'above the law'), as a guarantee of the

rights and liberties of the citizen. It stands as a legal barrier against the exercise of arbitrary state power. It entails 'due process', a body of formal protocols which must be observed in the administration of justice and the adjudication of civil disputes. It includes the keystones of bourgeois law; the right to 'trial by jury', and the law by habeas corpus (i.e. the law cannot deprive citizens of their liberty without speedily preferring a specific charge, and bringing 'the body or person' of the accused before the court for trial). The widespread application of, and respect for, the 'rule of law' is what is said to make British society a stable, legal and just social order.

We saw earlier that some critical theorists argue that the law imposes an illusory form of 'legal equality and fairness' on an economic and social system founded on inequality and exploitation, a process which is the principal source of legal mystification. Picciotto (1979), for example, argues that 'the rule of law' belongs to the 'liberal moment' of the bourgeois state when the conditions of free exchange were regulated principally by the economic relations of capitalism, and the law was required only to secure the subordination of labour to capital by giving this relation a *universal* legal expression. This moment is now passing, as the state is required increasingly to intervene directly to create the conditions for successful capital accumulation. In these circumstances, it is argued, to uphold the liberal 'rule of law' is to uphold a set of 'increasingly hollow myths'. To reform it, however, by giving its abstract claims to equality a fuller content, would be equally contradictory. The 'rule of law' should not be 'upheld' but 'transcended' (1979, pp.176-7).

The alternative view is best exemplified by the arguments advanced by the historian, E.P. Thompson, in his writings on eighteenth-century law and crime (1975), and in his recent contributions to debates about the jury system and the expansion of police powers (1980). He argues, with respect to the eighteenth century, that this is a clear case in which the law was powerfully and extensively 'colonized' by the dominant classes – the aristocracy and landed gentry. The exercise of legal authority was the principal means by which a precarious social order was maintained. Also it was often used to advance and protect their expanding property rights and social authority. The 'class content' of the rule of law, under these conditions, is now not in dispute amongst social historians (cf. Brewer and Styles, 1980). Further, Thompson has shown how the law served as the principal means by which a society was 'educated' out of a reliance on paternalism and custom and into a formal legal respect for the rights of property and private possession. The law intervened directly in the new economic relations of an increasingly market and commercial society, as well as providing the language in which these new relationships were articulated, and the ultimate means by which they were enforced. In this sense, the law played a critical role in the formation, not just of agrarian capitalism, but of bourgeois social order. Its function cannot therefore be confined to any one sphere. The law played a role at all levels of society - the political, the economic, the ideological (Thompson, 1978). It was an instrument of social hegemony. Nevertheless, Thompson argues, the practice of 'putting oneself on the law' was not limited to the powerful classes only, but embraced all sections of society, though not equally (Brewer and Styles, 1980). It was a means of redress against grievances, a defence against arbitrary power which the poorer classes could try to win over to their cause. Popular disturbances and riotous tumult were aimed explicitly at bringing the law into play on the side of 'popular justice' (Thompson, 1968; Rudé, 1952, 1964). Moreover, even the most sustained and violent social upheavals were ultimately constrained to struggle within the framework of a society based on 'law'.

Thompson's argument, therefore, is that the law is never monolithic. It cannot be unproblematically assigned to one social class or interest in society. Its function differs, depending on the relative strength of the social forces which struggle around and within it, and on the balance between these forces. The law is not a thing, but a relation. Its formal rules can be given a different social and economic content in different historical moments and at different periods of struggle. Thus, in the eighteenth century, the common people - as well as the powerful classes - had a contradictory interest in maintaining the 'rule of law' and this remains the case today. Thompson shows how the legal 'rights of free-born Englishmen', which the bourgeoisie had earlier advanced as a barrier to monarchical power, were subsequently appropriated into more radical and popular traditions, and used as a lever to extend and defend the 'rights and liberties' of the common people. The undoubted role of the law in maintaining a particular set of economic relations, in establishing class hegemony and legitimating a system of power, does not adequately account for the real, historical complexity of its functioning. The 'rule of law' is a contradictory social relation, an arena of struggle. It is something which the poor and the oppressed have struggled *against*, struggled *within*, and sometimes struggled *for*.

Since so much of 'critical theory' draws its inspirations from Marx, it is worth remembering that both Picciotto's (1979) and Thompson's (1975, 1978, 1980) positions can find their warrant in Marx's writings. This indicates how little the qualifying adjective, 'marxist', tells us about the complexities of theoretical positions. This is not simply the result of internal inconsistencies in Marx's works, but related to the different levels of abstraction at which his theory works. Holloway and Picciotto's (1978) propositions derive from those parts of Marx's writings in 'Capital' which discuss the 'laws of motion' of a capitalist economy at a very high and abstract level. They generalize these laws across societies and historical epochs in order to expose capitalism's 'fundamental movements'. They tend to

abstract, specifically, the economic relationships characteristic
of this mode. Thompson's work derives from the more historical
parts of 'Capital' and Marx's other writings, in which he deals
with very specific historical societies and periods, and takes
account of the whole social formation, including its political,
legal and ideological aspects. When Marx is working at the first
level of abstraction, he assigns law a more fixed, determined
and 'functional' role within capitalism. Law is the arena of legal
mystification, a 'veritable Garden of Eden of the bourgeois
rights of man' (Marx, 1961, I, p.176). But when, for example, he
discussed the results of the Factory Acts in the mid-nineteenth
century, he treats law more problematically. Here, the workers,
in alliance with some sections of the middle class, did win a
'legal victory'. They used the law to set limits on the capitalist's
right to extend the working day and to exploit child and women's
labour. Some entrepreneurs attempted to circumvent these
limits by flouting the law. Thus it was in the workers' interest
to enforce the law - a difficult task, since the factory owners
were often judges in their own courts. On a larger canvas, the
legal restrictions on the length of the working day could be
said to have favoured the development of capitalism, forcing
manufacturers to compensate for the loss of working hours by
expanding the scale of production and introducing technical
innovations. In the long term, the law could be said to have
been 'functional' to capitalist expansion as a whole. Equally
clearly, it did not favour the short-term interests of many
individual capitalists and was strongly resisted by them. Moreover, there was no united 'ruling class' view at the time, since
some favoured legislation while others did not.

These latter arguments break with any notion of an immediate,
'functional fit' between the law and the economic 'interests of
capital'. They break with the idea of capital always expanding
on its own terms, driven by some inevitable law or 'logic', and
the notion of a homogeneous ruling-class strategy. Instead,
a contradictory picture emerges. Long-term benefit to capital
as a whole has to be rescued or recuperated out of short-term
necessities inimical to particular capitalists. There is no
historical guarantee that capital must prevail, and no certainty
that it can prevail on its own terms, outside of the limits imposed
by contestation and struggle. The outcomes of particular struggles, sometimes waged within and about the law, sometimes
against it, will have real and pertinent effects on how particular
historical struggles develop. Law, in this sense, is constitutive
of (i.e. it creates) the very conditions of historical development and struggle, and does not merely reflect them. The
results of legal struggles matter because they have real effects.
This 'marxism without final guarantees' now represents a set
of developed positions within critical theory, strongly con-
testing more determinist versions. Both variants continue to
struggle to command the theoretical space in which critical
debates about the historical and sociological explanations of

law and crime currently revolve.

Thompson (1978, 1980) sometimes goes so far as to speak of the 'rule of law' as an 'unqualified good' which should be defended at all costs. This is clearly a polemical formulation, and is at variance with his more qualified historical arguments. In general, the great contribution which historical research has made to the critical theory of law and crime is to insist that neither crime nor law can be adequately treated as abstract, homogeneous entities, whose functions can be generalized in an a priori fashion across different periods and circumstances. It has broken down the tendency to see 'law' as exclusively a weapon of class control, and 'crime' as always an authentic form of class struggle. It has therefore forced critical criminology to unpack its own speculative generalizations. Crime and law must be examined in their particular historical functioning, in different periods and under different historical circumstances. Their function will almost always be contradictory, rather than simple. Weight must be given to their diverse forms and changing contents. It is only by paying due attention to the play of different forces and interests on the law that we can begin to set the struggles conducted in and around crime and the law in their proper explanatory framework.

References

Allan, C. (1970), Lumpenproletariat and Revolution, Political Theory and Ideology, in African Society seminar, Centre for African Studies, University of Edinburgh.

Anderson, P. (1980), 'Arguments within English Marxism', New Left Books.

Armstrong, G. and Wilson, M. (1973), City Politics and Deviancy Amplification, in Taylor, I. and Taylor, L. (eds), 'Politics and Deviance', Penguin Books.

Becker, H. (1963), 'Outsiders: Studies in the Sociology of Deviance', Free Press, New York.

Becker, H. (1967), Whose Side Are We On?, 'Social Problems', 14, 3, pp.239-47.

Becker, H. (1974), Labelling Theory Reconsidered, in Rock, P. and McIntosh, M. (eds), 'Deviance and Social Control'.

Bell, D. (1960), 'The End of Ideology', Free Press, New York.

Bonger, W. (1969), 'Criminality and Economic Conditions', Indiana University Press.

Brewer, J. and Styles, J. (1980), 'An Ungovernable People', Hutchinson.

Cain, M.E. (1973), 'Society and the Policeman's Role', Role'. RKP.

Cain, M.E. and Hunt, A. (1979), 'Marx and Engels on Law', Academic Press.

Carlen, P., ed. (1976), 'The Sociology of Law', Sociological Review Monograph no.23.

Carlen, P. and Collison, M., eds (1980), 'Radical Issues in Criminology', Martin Robertson.

Carson, W.A. and Wiles, P. (1971), 'Crime and Delinquency in Britain', Martin Robertson.

Chambliss, W.J. (1969), 'Crime and the Legal Process', McGraw-
Hill, New York.
Chambliss, W.J. (1975), The Political Economy of Crime: a
Comparative Study of Nigeria and the USA, in Taylor I.,
Walton, P. and Young, J. (eds) (1975), pp.167-80.
Chapman, D. (1968), 'Sociology and the Stereotype of the
Criminal', Tavistock.
Cohen, P. (1972), 'Subcultural Conflict and Working-Class
Community', Working Papers in Cultural Studies, no.2,
University of Birmingham.
Cohn-Bendit, D. (1969), 'Obsolete Communism', Penguin Books.
Darvall, F. (1934), 'Popular Disturbances and Public Order
in Regency England', Oxford University Press.
Ditton, J. (1977), 'Part-Time Crime: an Ethnography of Fiddling
and Pilferage', Macmillan.
Ditton, J. (1979), 'Controlology: Beyond the New Criminology',
Macmillan.
Durkheim, E. (1938), 'The Rules of Sociological Method', Free
Press, New York.
Engels, F. (1942), 'The Origin of the Family, Private Property
and the State', Progress Press, Moscow.
Engels, F. (1969), 'The Condition of the Working Class in
England', Panther.
Fine, B. (1979), Law and Class, in National Deviancy Con-
ference, 'Capitalism and the Rule of Law'.
Goldstein-Jackson, K. (1970), Social Background of the
Judiciary, 'New Society', 14 May.
Gouldner A.W. (1968), The Sociologist as Partisan, 'American
Sociologist', 3, pp.103-16.
Gouldner, A.W. (1970), 'The Coming Crisis of Western Socio-
logy', Basic Books, New York.
Gouldner, A.W. (1973), 'For Sociology: Review and Critique in
Sociology Today', Penguin Books.
Gramsci, A. (1971), 'Selection from the Prison Notebooks',
Lawrence & Wishart.
Gramsci, A. (1977), 'Selections from Political Writings 1910-
1920', Lawrence & Wishart.
Griffith, J. (1977), 'The Politics of the Judiciary', Fontana.
Hall, S. et al. (1978), 'Policing the Crisis: Mugging, the State
and Law and Order', Macmillan.
Hall, S. (1980), In Defence of Theory, in Samuel, R. (ed.),
'People's History and Socialist Theory', RKP.
Hay, D. et al. (1975), 'Albion's Fatal Tree: Crime and Society
in Eighteenth-Century England', Allen Lane.
Henry, S. (1978), 'The Hidden Economy', Martin Robertson.
Henry, S. and Mars, E. (1978), Crime at Work, 'Sociology',
vol.12.
Hirst, P.Q. (1975), Marx and Engels on Law, Crime and
Morality (revised) in Taylor I. et al. (1975).
Hobsbawm, E.J. (1959), 'Primitive Rebels', Manchester U.P.
Hobsbawm, E.J. (1972a), 'Bandits', Penguin Books.

Hobsbawm, E.J. (1972b), Social Crime, 'Bulletin of the Society for the Study of Labour History', University of Warwick.

Hobsbawm, E.J. and Rudé, G. (1969), 'Captain Swing', Weidenfeld & Nicolson.

Holloway, J. and Picciotto, S. (1978), 'State and Capital: a Marxist Debate', Edward Arnold.

Hunt, A. (1976a), Law, State and Class Struggle, in 'Marxism Today', June.

Hunt, A. (1976b), Perspectives in the Sociology of Law, in Carlen, P. (ed.), (1976).

Hunt, A. (1978), 'The Sociological Movement in Law', Macmillan.

Jones, G. Stedman (1971), 'Outcast London', Penguin Books.

Jones, G. Stedman (1975), Class Expression v. Social Control? A Critique of Recent Trends in the Social History of 'Leisure', 'History Workshop Journal', no.4, August, pp.162-70.

Lemert, E.M. (1952), 'Social Pathology', McGraw-Hill, New York.

Lipset, S. (1960), 'Political Man', Doubleday, New York.

Macciocci, M. (1973), 'Letters to Louis Althusser', NLB, London.

McIntosh, M. (1975), 'The Organization of Crime', Macmillan.

Mars, G. (1974), Dock Pilferage, in Rock and McIntosh (1974).

Marx, K. (1961), 'Capital', vols I-III, Lawrence & Wishart.

Marx, K. (1971), 'Critique of Hegel's "Philosophy of Right"', Cambridge University Press.

Marx, K. (1973), 'The Grundrisse', Penguin Books.

Marx, K. and Engels, F. (1970), 'The German Ideology', Lawrence & Wishart.

Marx K. and Engels, F. (1975), 'Collected Works', vol. 4, Lawrence & Wishart.

Matza, D. (1969), 'Becoming Deviant', Prentice-Hall, Englewood Cliffs.

Miliband, R. (1969), 'The State in Capitalist Society', Weidenfeld & Nicolson.

National Deviancy Conference/CSE (1979), 'Capitalism and the Rule of Law: from Deviancy Theory to Marxism', Hutchinson.

Neal-Tate, C. (1975), Paths to the Bench in Britain, 'Western Political Quarterly', no.28.

Obregon, A.Q. (1974), The Marginal Role of the Economy and the Marginalized Labour Force, 'Economy and Society', 3(4).

Parsons, T. (1951), 'The Social System', Routledge & Kegan Paul.

Parsons, T. and Shils, E.A. eds (1951), 'Toward a General Theory of Action', Harvard University Press.

Partridge, P. (1971), 'Consent and Consensus', Macmillan.

Pashukanis, E.B. (1978), 'Law and Marxism: a General Theory', Inklinks.

Pearce, F. (1976), 'Crimes of the Powerful', Pluto.

Picciotto, S. (1979) The Theory of the State, Class Struggle and the Rule of Law, in National Deviancy Conference, 'Capitalism and the Rule of Law'.

Platt, T. (1978), Street Crime: a View from the Left, 'Crime and Social Justice', vol.19, spring-summer.

Platt, T. and Takagi, P. (1978), Behind the Gilded Ghetto, 'Crime and Social Justice', vol.19, spring-summer.

Poulantzas, N. (1973), 'Political Power and Social Classes', NLB.
Quinney, R. (1970), 'The Social Reality of Crime', Little, Brown.
Quinney, R. (1974), 'Critique of Legal Order', Little, Brown.
Quinney, R. (1980), 'Class, State and Crime', 2nd ed., Longman, New York.
Renner, K. (1949), 'The Institutions of Private Law and their Social Functions', Routledge & Kegan Paul.
Rock, P. and McIntosh, M., eds (1974), 'Deviance and Social Control', Tavistock.
Rudé, G. (1952), 'Paris and London in the Eighteenth Century', Fontana.
Rudé, G. (1962), 'Wilkes and Liberty', Oxford University Press.
Rudé, G. (1964), 'The Crowd in History', Wiley, New York.
Scraton, P. and South, N. (1981), 'Capitalist Discipline, Private Justice and the Hidden Economy', Occasional Papers in Crime and Deviance, Middlesex Polytechnic.
Shils, E. (1961), Center and Periphery, in 'The Logic of Personal Knowledge', Routledge & Kegan Paul.
Smart, C. (1976), 'Women, Crime and Criminology', RKP. & Kegan Paul.
Spitzer, S. (1975), Towards a Marxian Theory of Deviance, 'Social Problems', vol.22, no.5, June, pp.638-51.
Taylor, I., Walton, P. and Young, J. (1973), 'The New Criminology: For a Social Theory of Deviance', RKP.
Taylor, I., Walton, P. and Young, J. (1975), 'Critical Criminology', Routledge & Kegan Paul.
Thompson, E.P. (1968), 'The Making of the English Working Class', Penguin Books.
Thompson, E.P. (1975), 'Whigs and Hunters', Allen Lane.
Thompson, E.P. (1978), 'The Poverty of Theory', Merlin Press.
Thompson, E.P. (1980), 'Writing by Candlelight', Merlin Press.
Turk, A. (1969), 'Criminality and Legal Order', Rand-McNally, Chicago.
Westergaard, J. and Resler, H. (1975), 'Class in a Capitalist Society', Heinemann.
Worsley, P. (1972), Frantz Fanon and the Lumpenproletariat in Miliband, R. and Savile, J. (eds), 'The Socialist Register, 1972', Merlin Press.
Wright Mills, C. (1956), 'The Power Elite', Oxford University Press.
Wright Mills, C. (1969), 'The Sociological Imagination', Penguin.
Young, J. (1971), The Role of Police as Amplifiers of Deviancy, in Cohen, S. (ed.), 'Images of Deviance', Penguin Books.
Young, J. (1975), Working-Class Criminology, in Taylor, I., Walton, P. and Young, J. (eds), 'Critical Criminology'.
Young, J. (1979), Left Idealism, Reformation and Beyond: From New Criminology to Marxism, in National Deviancy Conference, 'Capitalism and the Rule of Law'.
Zander, M. (1968), 'Lawyers and the Public Interest', Weidenfeld & Nicolson.

Index